A Histor
12(

a Marina,
alla memoria di Antonio,
e ai loro figli,
carissimi tutti

A History of Florence
1200–1575

JOHN M. NAJEMY

This edition first published in paperback 2008
Originally published in hardback 2006
© 2006, 2008 John M. Najemy

Blackwell Publishing was acquired by John Wiley & Sons in February 2007. Blackwell's publishing program has been merged with Wiley's global Scientific, Technical, and Medical business to form Wiley-Blackwell.

Registered Office
John Wiley & Sons Ltd, The Atrium, Southern Gate, Chichester, West Sussex, PO19 8SQ, United Kingdom

Editorial Offices
350 Main Street, Malden, MA 02148-5020, USA
9600 Garsington Road, Oxford, OX4 2DQ, UK
The Atrium, Southern Gate, Chichester, West Sussex, PO19 8SQ, UK

For details of our global editorial offices, for customer services, and for information about how to apply for permission to reuse the copyright material in this book please see our website at www.wiley.com/wiley-blackwell.

The right of John M. Najemy to be identified as the author of this work has been asserted in accordance with the Copyright, Designs and Patents Act 1988.

Wiley also publishes its books in a variety of electronic formats. Some content that appears in print may not be available in electronic books.

Designations used by companies to distinguish their products are often claimed as trademarks. All brand names and product names used in this book are trade names, service marks, trademarks or registered trademarks of their respective owners. The publisher is not associated with any product or vendor mentioned in this book. This publication is designed to provide accurate and authoritative information in regard to the subject matter covered. It is sold on the understanding that the publisher is not engaged in rendering professional services. If professional advice or other expert assistance is required, the services of a competent professional should be sought.

Library of Congress Cataloging-in-Publication Data

Najemy, John M., 1943–
  A history of Florence 1200–1575 / John M. Najemy.
    p. cm.
  Includes bibliographical references and index.
  ISBN: 978-1-4051-8242-3 (paperback : alk. paper)
  1. Florence (Italy)—History—1421–1737. 2. Florence
(Italy)—History—To 1421. I. Title.
  DG737.4.N35 2006
  945′.51—dc22

                                   2005037147

A catalogue record for this book is available from the British Library.

Set in 10/12pt Sabon by Graphicraft Limited, Hong Kong
Printed in Singapore by C.O.S. Printers Pte Ltd

07   2013

Contents

Illustrations

Maps

Acknowledgments

I t is a pleasure to acknowledge those who made this project possible and sustained it in a variety of ways. My sincerest appreciation and warmest thanks go to Christopher Wheeler, who invited me to write a history of Florence and whose support never wavered even as it took longer to complete than either of us expected. To the National Endowment for the Humanities, which provided the means, and to Walter Kaiser, who extended the welcome, I am grateful for a year spent as visiting professor at Villa I Tatti, where, in that most lovely of places and with the many kindnesses of the library staff, I drafted the early chapters. At Blackwell I thank Angela Cohen for her unfailing patience and expert editorial guidance, Tessa Harvey for graciously accepting a somewhat longer book than we had anticipated, and Louise Spencely for perceptive and judicious copy-editing. Special thanks to Greg Tremblay for again generously sharing his expertise in computer technology in connection with the maps, and to Humberto DeLuigi of Art Resource for help in selecting the illustrations. To the team of scholars who created the "Online Tratte" – the amazingly complete computerized database of Florentine officeholders – I am grateful for a remarkable resource that facilitated aspects of research that once required laborious compilations of lists in the archives. But so much remains available only in Florence's rich archival and manuscript collections, and I thank the staffs of the Archivio di Stato and Biblioteca Nazionale Centrale for efficient and friendly assistance in the many years of research on which this book depends.

It would be literally impossible to acknowledge every colleague and friend who has helped with an idea, source, citation, correction, and most of all encouragement. But a few must be mentioned. I extend my sincere appreciation to Robert Black for his valuable assessment of several chapters, to Carol Lansing and Christine Shaw, who read the manuscript for Blackwell and gave helpful advice about trimming it, and to Robert Fredona for generously reading drafts of all the chapters and making insightful suggestions for improvement. They all saved me from mistakes and oversights. To Amy Bloch I owe more than I can say here, even as I offer my deepest thanks for the exquisite care and critical judgment with which she read the entire manuscript, for indispensable help particularly with chapter 11 and with the illustrations and maps, for wise advice about nearly every issue and problem, and for the steadiness of her sustaining support.

I dedicate this book with gratitude and affection to the family that welcomed me to Italy long ago and has indeed been family to me all these years, and especially to Marina whose extraordinary generosity that first year, amid many other cares, made all the difference.

JN
Florence
November 2005

A Note on Italian Terms, Abbreviations, and Translations

For reasons of typographic clarity, frequently used words in Italian have been left in roman type. Most of these are the names of institutions.

The following abbreviations are used in the text:

ASI = *Archivio storico italiano*
ASF = Archivio di Stato di Firenze

Translations of Dante's *Divine Comedy* are from Dante Alighieri, *The Divine Comedy*, translated with a commentary by Charles S. Singleton, 3 vols. (Princeton, 1980).

Introduction

Florence might be thought, of all cities, not to need an introduction, for its legend always precedes it: the "birthplace" of the Renaissance and the "cradle" of modern Western Civilization. I hope that many readers will be drawn to this book out of affection for that Florence, an affection I share whenever I take off my historian's hat and recall the experience of being captivated, more than forty years ago, like so many others before and since, by Florence's palaces, churches, sculptures, pictures, books, poetry, speech, and people. What needs introducing here is not of course that seductive Florence, whose power cannot be denied, but rather the following chapters in which I offer an interpretation of nearly four centuries of Florentine history, *not* from the perspective of the legend that makes of this city an inexplicable miracle, an enchanted land of geniuses whose achievements evoke admiration and astonishment, but essentially without history or context. Whenever I reflect that, until Brunelleschi built the great dome atop the cathedral, no one knew how it could be done, or that, before Dante wrote the *Commedia*, nothing like it had even been attempted in European literature, I feel a sense of awe at such marvels. But praise is one thing, and history another, and specialists in the history of architecture, sculpture, painting, and literature have long since integrated the cultural achievements of Florence and the Renaissance into appropriate historical contexts.

A more troublesome effect on historical understanding (and more difficult to eradicate) is the legend's persistent idealization of the bearers of Florentine wealth and power as enlightened patrons, promoters of culture, and exemplars of civility. Renaissance princes and self-styled patricians were sometimes these things, and we are not wrong to admire their role in producing the splendid culture of the age. But seen only or chiefly in this light, they become indistinguishable from the elegant figures in the paintings they commissioned, decorously presiding over a utopian world of order, proportion, and moderation, without conflict or unwelcome noises. In fact, Florence's history was replete with conflicts, both within the elite class and between this class and other classes: the "popolo" that created the guild republic and challenged the elite to justify its power within a normative framework of law and political ethics; and the artisan and laboring classes, whose exertions and skills produced the material culture that ranged from prized textiles to the stones of rich men's homes, and who in turn challenged the popolo to allow the guild republic to embrace its full implications. In the course of their tense interactions, all three classes underwent major transformations, but none more than the elite of great families which experienced several metamorphoses in four centuries. Florence's history and culture evolved through these conflicts and class antagonisms, through what Machiavelli called (in the preface to his *Florentine Histories*) the "divisioni" that he believed common to all republics but that he saw as especially complex in Florence.

From this perspective, Florence was not unique: other Italian city-republics from Padua and Bologna to Siena, Perugia, and even Rome experienced similar divisions and conflicts. Florence thus shared with the rest of communal Italy a development that had no precedent in European history. In the thirteenth-century cities of northern and central Italy, the popolo, organized in guilds and neighborhood military associations and imbued with notions of citizenship and the common good absorbed from ancient Rome, launched the first politically effective and ideologically sustained challenge to an elite class, a challenge that succeeded, not in displacing the elite, but in transforming it. In Florence this challenge lasted longer and had deeper effects than elsewhere. Indeed, for the first time, a European "nobility" radically revised its politics, culture, and social attitudes in response to constant pressure from another class. Their dialogue of power shaped Florence's republican experience, engendering a rich variety of reflections and reactions from chroniclers, writers of family memoirs, humanists, poets, and political theorists of both classes. I have tried, wherever and as far as possible, to let them speak, and because they wrote endlessly about politics, competitions for power, and the shape of government, there is much political history in this book. But their approach to politics was typically through the lens of the social, and in at least two senses: through an understanding of collective interests and antagonisms involving economic and fiscal issues, public order, and law; and also and equally through an intense awareness of family solidarities, factional loyalties, ties of clientage and patronage (in the social sense), and marriage alliances. All these aspects of their social, economic, and cultural existence informed Florentine politics and discourses of politics. The interpretation offered here thus combines thematic treatments of society, economy, and culture, set in precise political contexts, with a political narrative that depends on and regularly refers to society and culture.

I have chosen chronological parameters that embrace a "long history" of republican Florence, from the medieval commune dominated by feudal families, to the emergence of the autonomous republic with its internal political conflicts and growing territorial dominion, to the wars and crises of the early sixteenth century which imposed a principate under imperial tutelage that in turn refashioned Florentine society and culture. I begin in the early thirteenth century when the great families dominated the city center as a warrior class with their towers and fortified enclaves, and the popolo was already constructing the associations that produced the guild republic in the century's last two decades. By the fourteenth century Florence was a theater of triangular struggles among an elite that had discovered a new identity as international merchants and bankers, the guild-based popolo, and the working classes, mainly in the huge textile industry, whose brief conquest of a share of power in 1378–82 proved to be a transforming moment that frightened the popolo into relinquishing its historic challenge and cooperating in regimes led by an elite that now styled itself as a civic and patriarchal aristocracy. For the next century, elite regimes, including the unofficial rule of the Medici family, dominated Florentine politics and culture. Because they increasingly represented the potential for the kind of princely order that had ended communal government in other Italian cities (and thus embodied the danger of "tyranny"), the Medici eventually alienated much of the very elite from which they emerged and were exiled and replaced by a broadly based republic in 1494. For the next forty tumultuous years, Florence was again the scene of a triangular conflict, this time among popular republicans, elite families with their own brand of aristocratic republicanism, and the Medici. The last and most radically popular of all Florentine republics, that of 1527–30, frightened the elite (much as the participation of the working classes in government had frightened the popolo 150 years earlier) into abandoning the republic and accepting, however reluctantly, the Medici principate they had resisted for decades.

It has been more than thirty-five years since Gene Brucker, teacher to us all, published the most recent English-language general introduction to Renaissance Florence.[1] It would be presumptuous folly to think of "replacing" that wonderful and still vibrant book. Thus the intended justification of the present work is that it adopts a different approach in covering a longer period and analyzing politics, society, and culture within a diachronic framework. Indeed, there has been no attempt in English at a narrative history of Florence since Ferdinand Schevill's treatment seventy years ago of an even longer

---

[1]   G. A. Brucker, *Renaissance Florence* (New York, 1969; reprint edn. Berkeley, 1983).

period of the city's history.[2] Mountains of new scholarship have appeared in the last two generations, and one more justification for a book of this kind (whether or not this one meets it) is the need for a synthesis of what has become an entire mountain range of specialized scholarship on Florence. However, in order not to make this book longer than it already is, I have not cited everything that might deserve to be mentioned. Besides those works from which I borrow specific data or whose analyses I summarize, I have restricted bibliographical citations to particularly significant items, mentioning wherever possible works in English together with what I consider the most important contributions of our European colleagues.

That there has been and continues to be so much attention to Florence is not, as some suspect, a function of the old myths and legends. Historians are drawn to Florence because of the unparalleled riches (and this is no myth) of the archival and manuscript sources that permit in-depth inquiries into more and more varied questions than is possible anywhere else. All this scholarship, which has grown beyond the realistic possibility of both mastering the work of the past and keeping up with what emerges every month, sometimes feels more like an avalanche in which one can easily be buried. Trying to stay on top of all the new work as I wrote these chapters has been a humbling and ultimately futile experience. Even as I decide to close the shop and not further test the patience of a very patient publisher, the latest new books are on my desk, demanding revision of this or that argument. I can only ask their forgiveness; they will have to wait for the next history of Florence.

---

[2]   F. Schevill, *History of Florence from the Founding of the City through the Renaissance* (New York, 1936), reprinted as *Medieval and Renaissance Florence*, 2 vols. (New York, 1963).

1

The Elite Families

From at least the early thirteenth century Florence's history was dominated by a competition, more intense and longer-lasting than similar confrontations elsewhere in Italy, between two distinct but overlapping political cultures and classes: an elite of powerful, wealthy families of international bankers, traders, and landowners organized as agnatic lineages; and a larger community of economically more modest local merchants, artisans, and professional groups organized in guilds and called the popolo. Although both classes originated in the economic expansion and political fragmentation of Italy in the eleventh and twelfth centuries, only after about 1200 do their social physiognomies emerge with clarity. It is not easy, or perhaps necessary, to say which of them took shape first. The early commune was an association of self-selected citizens from mostly elite families that did not embrace the entire population, and the early growth of the popolo took place outside the commune's formal structures. When, in the early and mid-thirteenth century, the popolo began to challenge the elite and recast the commune in its own image, its political culture and institutions displayed strength and sophistication suggesting an already long development. This chapter offers a portrait of the early elite (its family structures, modes of behavior, self-image, and culture), as the next chapter will do for the popolo. They are thus presented separately for purposes of analysis, but elite and popolo in fact emerged and developed in constant dialogue and conflict.

Florentines typically called these powerful families the "grandi," whose literal translation as the "great" is clumsy and potentially misleading. Since "grandi" were not a legally defined order with titles, "nobility" would be even more misleading, and "aristocracy," apart from implying judgments that may be unwarranted, suggests long-term hegemony that cannot account for the mobility and conflict within Florence's volatile class structure. Thus I use "elite" as the best, but not perfect, English equivalent.

Lineages

In canto 16 of *Paradiso* Dante has his ancestor Cacciaguida look back with nostalgia to the great families of the smaller and allegedly more virtuous Florence of the mid-twelfth century. Dante wrote at the height of Florentine economic power and demographic expansion in the early fourteenth century, and in the aftermath of one of the greatest explosions of violence perpetrated by elite factions. His purpose in fashioning the myth of an earlier, simpler, more tranquil Florence was to highlight the corruption and devastation that great wealth and political rivalries had inflicted on the city.[1] By contrast, Cacciaguida describes an elite still uncontaminated by either wealth or power. While this picture of early civic and moral purity is largely invented, the families mentioned in *Paradiso* 16 are not at all fictional. But to a Florentine of Dante's generation most of them would have seemed echoes of a very distant past. Some were extinct and others, so Cacciaguida himself points out, were shadows of what they once were. Except for a few (Donati, Della Bella, Visdomini, Tosinghi, Lamberti, and Adimari) still politically active at the end of the thirteenth century, Cacciaguida's families were no longer the elite of Dante's day, most having fallen into decline by at least the middle of the thirteenth century. The list of once great families highlights the fact that, in little more than a century, economic growth and political turbulence had consigned much of the old elite to oblivion and generated a new one.

The new elite, formed in the middle of the thirteenth century, made Florence the economic giant of Europe and dominated the life of the republic for the next two centuries and more. The thirteenth century was thus a crucial time of consolidation for these emerging families and for the institutions and practices that made them resilient and durable, above all the agnatic lineages, or patrilineal descent groups, that allowed wealthy families to preserve and share material resources and thus encouraged cooperation among kin. Agnatic lineages were communities of kinsmen descended from a common paternal ancestor.[2] In practice they were also limited to the males of the patriline: the sons, nephews, grandsons, great-grandsons and so on of an ancestor recognized as having established the family's wealth and status. Members of a lineage

---

[1]   C. T. Davis, "Il Buon Tempo Antico," in *Florentine Studies: Politics and Society in Renaissance Florence*, ed. N. Rubinstein (Evanston, 1968), pp. 45–69.

[2]   C. Lansing, *The Florentine Magnates: Lineage and Faction in a Medieval Commune* (Princeton, 1991), pp. 29–105.

did not live together, although they might live near one another, sometimes in contiguous houses. Nor were lineages associations with legal standing or a formal constitution. The most direct manifestation of the concept of family represented by the agnatic lineage was inheritance, normally limited to male heirs in the male line. Cognatic kin (blood relatives on one's mother's side) and affinal kin (relatives through marriage) were excluded from inheritance. Women were considered members of their fathers' lineages and were not legally barred from inheriting; indeed, there are examples of men without sons who bequeathed property to daughters. But most elite Florentines feared that property left to daughters would eventually find its way into the patrimonies of the families into which these daughters married, most obviously through their sons who belonged to their fathers' lineages. In lieu of a share of inheritance, daughters were instead provided with often quite substantial dowries that were essential to negotiating a prestigious marriage. Although entrusted to a woman's husband for the lifetime of the marriage, the dowry remained her property and could be reclaimed when her husband died.

A second feature of elite inheritance practices was partible inheritance. Primogeniture was not practiced in Florence, and fathers divided their estates in equal shares among all sons (except those who became professional religious). In the case of the large urban residences (palazzi) and towers that every elite family possessed, and which were crucial to its prestige and political presence (see Map 1), the equally inherited shares also remained undivided joint property, which meant that no one was allowed to alienate his share without a collective decision of the co-owners. These customs reveal the central purpose of the agnatic lineage: to accumulate resources, manage them jointly, and prevent the fragmentation and dispersal of property. Not all inherited wealth was necessarily constituted by fractions of jointly owned property, but for palaces and towers it was a common arrangement meant to enhance the status of kinsmen who otherwise would each have had less power than they all enjoyed as members of the lineage.

Pooling such resources within the lineage made upper-class families more visible to friends, neighbors, and rivals and more conscious of themselves as collectivities of interests, ambitions, and memories, even if not always in perfect harmony. Elite families began to use surnames as a sign of status. Some evolved from the given name of the lineage's "founder," others from the localities in the surrounding countryside (the contado) from which families typically emerged. The Abati took their name from an ancestor called Abbas (in Latin) in the late twelfth century, and the Nerli derived theirs from the notary ser Nerlo, also of the twelfth century.[3] The family of the Visdomini, who managed the estates of the Florentine bishopric during vacancies, took their surname from the title attached to their role as "vice-lords" (*vicedomini*)

---

[3]   Ibid., pp. 40–72.

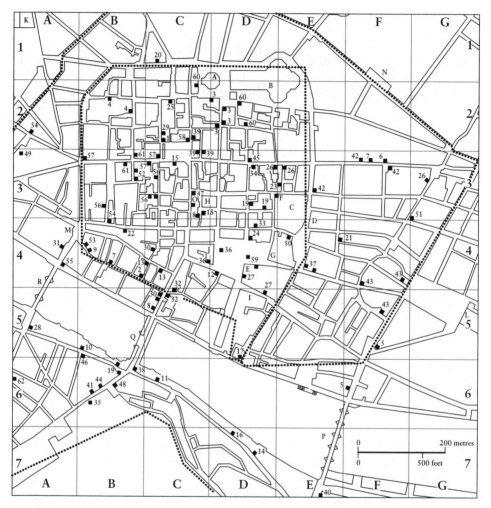

Map 1 Location of towers and/or palaces of prominent Florentine families in the thirteenth and fourteenth centuries (some families had more than one tower or palace), and major civic and ecclesiastical buildings (based on the maps in G. Fanelli, *Firenze* [Rome and Bari, 1980, seventh edn. 2002]). The inner dotted perimeter is the approximate location of the eleventh-century walls (the "ancient circle" mentioned by Dante's Cacciaguida in *Paradiso* 15 [see below, p. 61]); the outer perimeter (which reaches beyond this map) marks the walls of the 1170s.

Key to map 1

Location	Families	Location	Families	Location	Families	Location	Buildings
2C	1. Abati	4B	22. Davanzati	4–5F	43. Peruzzi	1–2CD	A. Baptistery
4B	2. Acciaiuoli	3DE	23. Della Bella	6B	44. Pitti	1–2DE	B. Cathedral
2CD	3. Adimari	4D	24. Dell'Antella	3D	45. Ricci	3E	C. Badia
2B	4. Agli	2C	25. Della Tosa	5–6B	46. Ridolfi	3–4E	D. Palazzo del Primo
5–6F	5. Alberti	3DE, 3G	26. Donati	3C	47. Rondinelli		Popolo (Bargello)
3F	6. Albizzi	4–5D	27. Foraboschi	6B	48. Rossi	4D	E. Palazzo dei Priori
3F, 4B	7. Altoviti	5A	28. Frescobaldi	3A	49. Rucellai		(Palazzo Vecchio)
5C	8. Amidei	2C	29. Galligai	4E	50. Sacchetti	3DE	F. Torre della Castagna
4B	9. Ardinghelli	4–5C	30. Giandonati	3G	51. Salviati	4D	G. Mercanzia
5B	10. Barbadori	4A	31. Gianfigliazzi	3B	52. Sassetti	3CD	H. Orsanmichele
6C	11. Bardi	4–5C	32. Girolami	4B	53. Scali	5D	I. San Pier Scheraggio
4D	12. Baroncelli	4D	33. Giugni	2A, 4B	54. Soldanieri	4C	J. Santa Cecilia
4BC	13. Buondelmonti	3D	34. Gondi	4A	55. Spini	1A	K. Santa Maria Novella
7D	14. Canigiani	6B	35. Guicciardini	3BC	56. Strozzi	5G	L. Santa Croce
3C	15. Caponsacchi	4CD	36. Infangati	3BC	57. Tornaquinci	4A	M. Santa Trinita
7D	16. Capponi	4E	37. Magalotti	2C	58. Tosinghi	1F	N. Santa Maria Nuova
5D	17. Castellani	6B	38. Mannelli	4D	59. Uberti	3C	O. Arte della Lana
3C	18. Cavalcanti	2–3C	39. Medici	2D	60. Visdomini	6–7E	P. Ponte Rubaconte
6B, 3D	19. Cerchi	7E	40. Mozzi	3B	61. Vecchietti	5BC	Q. Ponte Vecchio
1C	20. Cerretani	6B	41. Nerli	6A	62. Velluti	4–5A	R. Ponte Santa Trinita
4E	21. Covoni	3E, 3F	42. Pazzi				

of episcopal property.[4] But the surnames of most elite families were either patronymics denoting a purported lineage founder (e.g., Strozzi, Alberti) or toponyms indicating place of origin (Dell'Antella, Quaratesi). Some lineages became so large after a few generations that their many branches were no longer closely related and the original strategy of accumulating joint property became impracticable across the entire lineage. There were at least 116 adult males sharing the Bardi name in 1342, but the banking company of that name was owned and controlled by a much smaller group of Bardi. Occasionally, branches established new lineages and their own names, but kinsmen sharing a common surname (*consorterie*) usually maintained a kind of loose and theoretical solidarity for generations and even centuries. While large *consorterie* sometimes attempted to act in concert, or were feared for the potential power of their numbers, it was clearly impossible for all their members to participate in joint property or business arrangements.

But even when lineages ceased to function principally as consortia for the joint ownership of property, the social and emotional dimension of belonging to such a family was of enormous importance to elite Florentines, who took great pride in having names like Uberti, Donati, Adimari, Bardi, and several dozen others. Because of the prestige they conferred, surnames spread quickly among wealthy elite families, and from there to the popolo, but they were never as common outside the elite as within. Among slightly over 2,000 citizens listed as government creditors in 1345 in the quarter of Santo Spirito south of the Arno, only 258 (13%) had family names. The list contains fifty-

---

[4] Ibid., pp. 65–6; G. Dameron, *Episcopal Power and Florentine Society, 1000–1320* (Cambridge, Mass., 1991), pp. 64–6 and passim.

two different surnames, but just four (Bardi, Frescobaldi, Nerli, and Rossi) account for 60% of the 258. In 1427, by contrast, 37% of all household heads in the tax rolls had surnames, and in 1480 almost half. By the fifteenth century there were some 1,200 family names in Florence.[5] In the thirteenth and fourteenth centuries, surnames were among the signs distinguishing elite from non-elite. Pride in the name and the need to preserve an exact record of ancestors generated the idea that families had histories; genealogical reconstructions produced narratives linking the generations. An early example of the genre is the *Cronichetta* of Neri Strinati, written in 1312, and based, so he says, in large part on the memory of family events recounted to him over many years by various elders, especially Madonna Ciaberonta, who, having died in 1267 at the astonishing age of 115, was presumably able to provide details going back to the last third of the twelfth century. For every male in the family, Neri was interested in recording, above all, sons and property.[6] The genre of the family chronicle evolved quickly in the fourteenth century, eventually producing in large numbers the *ricordi* and *ricordanze* that became perhaps the most characteristic expression of the elite's sense of social place.[7]

An illuminating example of the elite's concern for family origins and history is the chronicle of Donato Velluti.[8] Born in 1313 and writing in the late 1360s, Velluti reveals both the typical upper-class thirst for information about origins and ancestors and the acute consciousness of how little even solidly established families of the time actually knew about themselves before the mid-thirteenth century. "Because men desire to know of their birth [*di sua nazione*] and ancestors, and how marriage alliances with other families have occurred, and how wealth has been acquired," Velluti begins, "I have thought to make a record and memorial [*ricordanza e memoria*] of what I have heard about such things from my father and from family members older than myself, and of what I have seen in legal documents, account books, or other writings, few as they may be, and of what I myself have seen or experienced." Because the written sources were few and mostly recent, Velluti, like Neri Strinati, relied in great part on the memory of family elders. He could not confirm the family legend that the Velluti had migrated to Florence from Semifonte in the Valdelsa. The earliest documents he found concerned business dealings of his great-grandfather Bonaccorso and his three brothers in 1244. Of Bonaccorso's

[5]   A. Molho, "Names, Memory, Public Identity in Late Medieval Florence," in *Art, Memory, and Family in Renaissance Florence*, ed. G. Ciappelli and P. L. Rubin (Cambridge, 2000), pp. 237–52 (239–42).
[6]   Lansing, *Magnates*, pp. 46–8.
[7]   An overview: P. J. Jones, "Florentine Families and Florentine Diaries in the Fourteenth Century," *Papers of the British School at Rome* 24 (1956): 183–205.
[8]   Ch. M. de la Roncière, "Une famille florentine au XIVe siècle: Les Velluti," in *Famille et parenté dans l'occident médiéval*, ed. G. Duby and J. Le Goff (Rome, 1977).

father Piero and grandfather Berto he knew only their names. But about Bonaccorso and his brothers Velluti knew that they lived together in the Oltrarno, that they had a small tower whose location he specified, and that they were engaged in business with a shop in Borgo San Jacopo. Three of the brothers had children, and Donato reports their names and those of all their descendants. Although Velluti could not find the name of his great-grandfather's wife, he did not ignore either the Velluti women or those who married into the family, regularly naming the daughters and mothers of Velluti men. It was thus not for lack of interest or effort that he was unable to name his paternal great-grandmother, which presumably means that Donato's father could not name his grandmother. Family memory was precious, no doubt all the more because it was fleeting. Part of the problem was that, despite the desire to appear old and established, many lineages, the Velluti included, were of fairly recent origin. Another problem for the preservation of memory was the length of generations in the male line. Velluti's father Lamberto, born in 1268, was forty-five years old when Donato was born. Donato never knew his paternal grandfather Filippo and was unsure of the year of his death. And the portrait he gives of his great-grandfather Bonaccorso has about it an aura of inflated legend: that he lived to the age of 120, was a bold and strong warrior who fought heretics and whose body was all "stitched together" from the many wounds he suffered in battles and skirmishes, and who, after losing his sight at the age of one hundred, kept himself vigorous by walking three to four miles every day on his balcony for another twenty years.[9] All of this could have been true, but it could also have emerged from the need for a heroic and virile founder of the family's fortunes.

Knighthood and Feuds

Velluti's comments on his great-grandfather's physical strength and prowess in combat reflect the prominence of martial valor in the elite's early self-image: "Very sure of himself in matters of arms, he was a great *combattitore*." By the time Velluti was writing, the great families were no longer a warrior aristocracy, and their pride in military deeds became entirely a matter of nostalgia. Even Dante in the early fourteenth century knew that he was invoking a lost past when he fashioned his distant ancestor Cacciaguida as a crusading knight. But thirteenth-century elite families, both the newer lineages and the older ones that traced their prominence back to the twelfth century, actively cultivated the practice and culture of war, and most elite families counted in their ranks many knights. Knighthood was a formal title, originally bestowed by imperial

[9] *La cronica domestica di messer Donato Velluti*, ed. I. Del Lungo and G. Volpi (Florence, 1914), pp. 3–7, 72–3.

authority (Cacciaguida says that the emperor Conrad "girt me with his knighthood"), although city-state governments also created knights and expected military service from them. Trained in mounted combat and providing their own horses and armor, knights formed the cavalry of the communal army.[10] In the thirteenth century, knights performed this service themselves instead of hiring replacements, as would happen in the fourteenth century. Because of the considerable cost, most knights came from elite families, and, to judge from their numbers, the military and cultural ethos of knighthood was universal throughout the elite. The chronicler Giovanni Villani estimated that there were 250 knights in Florence in the 1280s. But by the 1330s he could count no more than 65.[11]

The Florentine elite were never a professional warrior class; they were not full-time fighters and they typically combined the ceremonial and cultural trappings of knighthood, and occasional participation in actual warfare, with more prosaic business careers as merchants or bankers. Even the bellicose Bonaccorso Velluti, according to his great-grandson, "was an expert in business," in his case the business of importing cloth and having it dyed in Florence. In keeping with Donato's ideal portrait of him, he is of course described as a pillar of uncompromising rectitude in mercantile dealings. But the part-time quality of the elite's military activities in no way lessened their dedication to it as the most visible symbol of their status, and as one of the ways in which they made themselves a distinct class and advertised their consciousness of the fact by putting cultural and ritual distance between themselves and the popolo. Elite and popolo were both primarily merchants and in many cases members of the same guilds; thus economic activities alone did not suffice to mark the distinction between the classes. The culture of knighthood served this purpose well, because it carried with it the courtly ethos that linked the elite to the social world of the upper classes in both the Lombard principalities to the north and the Neapolitan kingdom to the south. It is a striking feature of the Florentine elite's response to the emerging republican polity in their own midst that they turned with greater insistence and ostentation to the emulation of a courtly culture that was imported from elsewhere.

Villani describes a two-month party, or "corte" (8.89), held in 1283 by the elite family of the Rossi and their neighbors in the parish of Santa Felicita in the Oltrarno. The Rossi were a leading elite family and were later included among the politically disenfranchised magnates by the popular government, whose unfavorable view of them may have stemmed from the conviction in

---

[10]   As was true all over communal Italy: J.-C. Maire Vigueur, *Cavaliers et citoyens: guerre, conflits, et société dans l'Italie communale, XIIe–XIIIe siècles* (Paris, 2003).

[11]   Giovanni Villani, *Nuova Cronica*, ed. G. Porta, 3 vols. (Parma, 1990–1), vol. 3, 12.94, pp. 197–8; hereafter cited by book and chapter (according to Porta's division of the work into 13 rather than 12 chapters).

1284 of one of the family's young men for armed assault against an Oltrarno neighbor from the Ubriachi family, also subsequently relegated to magnate status. The lavish "corte" of the previous year may have been just as offensive to the republican popolo that generally detested such elite ostentation. The festivities opened in June for the celebration of Florence's patron saint John the Baptist and lasted throughout the summer. Villani says that a "thousand or more men" took part, all dressed in white robes and forming a "company" or "brigade" led by a "lord of Love." The estimate may be excessive, but even half that number would have been an astonishing gathering spilling out from family palaces and courtyards into the narrow streets and still small public spaces of the thirteenth-century city. Many women also took part, as the brigade engaged in games and amusements and "dances of ladies and knights," who paraded through the city playing musical instruments and going from one banquet to another. Villani calls it the "most noble and renowned court ever held in Florence or Tuscany," adding that many noble courtiers and court entertainers from Lombardy and all Italy came to participate. In such festivities the Florentine elite families loudly advertised their emulation of foreign cultural styles, the patronal and proprietary domination they exercised within their parishes and neighborhoods, and the central place of knighthood in their image of themselves as bearers of idealized notions of both love and war.

The popolo viewed the elite's fondness for knighthood and courtly rituals with suspicion and hostility. One indication of this is the role assigned to these cultural factors in the famous story of the murder in 1216 of Buondelmonte de' Buondelmonti, the event that allegedly divided the elite into warring factions and plunged the city into the chaos of civil war. The earliest extant version of the story is contained in an anonymous chronicle written toward the end of the century.[12] If the author was not an actual partisan of the popolo, his account of the already legendary event was certainly heavily influenced by its critique of the elite's social style. No reader of the chronicle would have failed to notice that all the major protagonists in the story belonged to families that were made magnates. Whatever the actual facts of the episode, this writer embellished them with an anti-aristocratic twist in which the elite's propensity for violence emerges from its very predilection for the courtly rituals surrounding knighthood. The account functions in a sense as a parable of the original sin that required the popolo's punishment of the elite.

The setting is a celebration, six miles from Florence in the village of Campi, of the knighthood of Mazzingo Tegrimi dei Mazzinghi, to which "all the best people of Florence" – the city's knightly aristocracy, all identified by the honorific "messer" accorded to knights – "were invited." The author calls it a

---

[12] *Cronica fiorentina compilata nel secolo XIII*, in *Testi fiorentini del Dugento e dei primi del Trecento*, ed. A. Schiaffini (Florence, 1954), pp. 82–150 (117–19).

"corte," complete with the required buffoon or jester, who, no doubt doing what he thought was expected of him (or what someone told him to do), approached the tables where the knights were seated and snatched up the plate of messer Uberto degli Infangati, who became intensely angry. Seeing this, messer Oddo Arrighi dei Fifanti berated Infangati, who called Arrighi a liar. The latter picked up a plate of food and shoved it in Infangati's face. The chronicler underscores the gap between the pretensions of this self-styled aristocracy and its actual behavior: although introduced as "valorous," Oddo Arrighi is described as berating Infangati "villanamente" – rudely, roughly, with overtones of boorish rusticity, and thus the opposite of the courtly valor and refinement expected of the "best people" – and escalating the confrontation from words to actions. The entire "corte" was now in an uproar: in the ensuing fight, with tables cleared away and weapons introduced, Buondelmonte de' Buondelmonti, who had had no part in the original altercation, wounded Oddo Arrighi in the arm with a knife. The chronicler says that he too did this "villanamente," thus extending his negative judgment to both sides of the conflict and suggesting that they were all a failed would-be courtly aristocracy whose behavior more nearly resembled that of loutish peasants than that of a true court. The wounding of Oddo Arrighi escalated and politicized the conflict. Arrighi "held a meeting of his friends and relatives," including the Counts of Gangalandi, and the Uberti, Lamberti, and Amidei families. In moments of confrontation and conflict, the account reminds us, elite families appealed to their allies, including families with which they had established marriage alliances. And marriage was also their preferred solution to the conflict at hand. The assembly decided that peace could be ensured through the marriage to Buondelmonte of Arrighi's niece, the daughter of a sister who had married into the Amidei. The plan was destined to fail, and the anonymous writer mocks the elite's methods of conflict resolution by using explicitly political language for their attempt at peacemaking: the assembly convened by Arrighi is described as a "council," and the marriage alliance as a "treaty." The implication is clearly that great families were as inept at politics as they were at courtly self-discipline.

Until the recommendation for peace through marriage, the story has exclusively male protagonists, even as the marriage "treaty" implies the ready cooperation of the women whose lives it affected. Elite honor depended on docile women willing to be married off for political reasons. Here too the chronicler points to the gap between the elite's pretensions and the chaotic reality of its behavior. As soon as the marriage was agreed to, Madonna Gualdrada, wife of messer Forese Donati, secretly sent for Buondelmonte and talked him out of the engagement. Once again the conflict escalates with the introduction of another great family name. The Donati would have been familiar to contemporary readers as a leading family in the factional wars around 1300, one whose only apparent connection to the other families of the story is an implied familiarity with the Buondelmonti. In fact, it is not actually the Donati who enter the story – no Donati men play any role – but rather one of their wives. Families that counted upon the passivity of women, so the episode implies, in fact put women in precarious and liminal situations in which their loyalties and ambitions might be neither predictable nor controllable. The intervention of Madonna Gualdrada destabilized the dubious peace constructed by the men. Her seduction by proxy of Buondelmonte played on his sense of insecurity as a proud young man being pushed around by his elders. Addressing him as a "shamed knight," she underscores both his claim to honor as a knight and the denial to him of the full measure of that honor by the overriding needs and interests of the family as defined by its collective fathers. Yet again the author points to an inherent contradiction in elite family structure. Lineages presupposed a convergence of interests and outlooks among men, especially between fathers and sons. Yet they constantly produced cohorts of young men who had to wait too long for their share of family honor and who were as much under the thumb of patriarchy as were the women. It is no accident that the author invents, or dramatizes, a secret entente between a married woman and a young unmarried man as the cause of the unraveling of the plan worked out by the male elders. Madonna Gualdrada taunts Buondelmonte by telling him he has brought shame on himself in agreeing to marry Arrighi's niece out of fear of the Fifanti and the Uberti, and she urges him to renounce the agreement and marry instead one of the Donati women, perhaps her own daughter. If he does so, she assures him, "you will always be a knight of honor." Buondelmonte quickly agreed, the narrator says, "without any counsel," and without having taken the matter, as he ought to have, to his elders. He thus broke the cardinal rule of elite lineages by acting on his own, as a free agent, without getting advice and support from his family's leaders and allies.

By breaking this rule Buondelmonte sealed his own fate. The next day, with crowds gathered from both groups of families for the wedding, he failed to appear and went instead to pledge his engagement to the Donati woman. The insult to the Amidei and their allies might as well have been a declaration of war. An incensed Oddo Arrighi called another "council," this time "of *all* his friends and relatives," who met in a church, presumably because of their increased numbers. He lamented the dishonor done to him by Buondelmonte, and from the assembled elders came a variety of recommendations: some said that Buondelmonte should be beaten and others that he should be wounded in the face. But Mosca dei Lamberti warned that anyone resorting to such half measures would be inviting even worse retaliation and that, this being a case in which "a thing done cannot be undone," Buondelmonte would have to be killed. This advice, made famous by Dante in *Inferno* 28 (in which he placed Mosca), assumed that, whereas humiliation or injury would surely entail further acts of revenge, murder would not. The most likely explanation for such an apparently odd argument is that Buondelmonte had angered and alienated his own family by acting unilaterally. If he remained alive, his family could not have avoided the obligation to avenge him; but once he was killed, so Mosca seems to have reasoned, his exasperated friends and relatives would not have retaliated. A month and a half later on Easter morning, at the very spot where the planned engagement was to have taken place in front of the Amidei palace, the "vendetta" was carried out. Buondelmonte, accompanied by his new Donati bride on his wedding day, was knocked from his horse by messer Schiatta degli Uberti (the first action in the story by anyone from this powerful family) and killed by Oddo Arrighi himself.

According to this and other accounts, the Buondelmonti murder was the spark that ignited the war of Guelfs and Ghibellines, the great conflict that dominated Florentine and Italian history for most of the thirteenth century. The explanations for the rivalries and antagonisms that divided Florentine elite families over many decades are certainly more complex than this tradition allows. But the story's importance lies in what it reveals of the family structures, social conventions, and collective self-image of the elite, and also of the popolo's critique of the elite. If the account is in part parody and exaggeration, it parodies and exaggerates attitudes and institutions central to the life of these families: the expectation of family solidarity and the leadership of the elders; the networks of "friends and relatives" mobilized in times of crisis; the marginal position of women between their natal and marital families; the control of neighborhoods and churches by families or clusters of families; coalitions of family groups in political factions with their "councils"; the role of marriage in consolidating factions; knighthood and the emulation of the courts; and the easy and frequent recourse to violence and vendetta. The point of the story is surely the close and even causal connection between these structural features of elite family life and the constant episodes of violence and revenge that they inflicted on the city. At every stage of the story, the elite's preferred methods of containing violence and resolving conflicts only led to more and more violent conflicts. The story portrays the elite, with its pretensions to being a ruling class, as a disastrous failure that could not even control its women and young men. Such implications were no doubt polemical and tendentious, but not entirely unfounded. The elite's propensity for violence and vendetta was always the popolo's first article of indictment in its list of grievances against these overmighty families. Most of the thirteenth-century descriptions of this behavior come from chroniclers sympathetic to the popolo or from legislation passed by popular governments seeking to curb it, but fourteenth-century court records and elite memoirs confirm the picture of the elite families as a generally unruly lot, given to frequent acts of aggression against their fellow citizens. Most contemporaries accepted as axiomatic that the greatest threat to public order came, not from the poor or the working classes, but from the powerful and prestigious families that dominated the center of the city with their fortress-like palaces and towers. The story of the Buondelmonti murder encapsulates that conviction. Dante's Cacciaguida likewise laments the violence of the great families when he refers to the Amidei as the "house of which was born [Florence's] weeping, by reason of its just resentment which has slain you and put an end to your glad living." He also damns the victim of that resentment: "O Buondelmonte, how ill for you that you did fly from its nuptials at the promptings of another. Many would be happy who now are sad if God had committed you to the [river] Ema the first time you came to the city."

Elite vendettas were usually directed at families or factions of the same class. Vendetta may be thought of as codified private justice: a system for handling and sometimes resolving disputes without the intervention of law or courts. The thirteenth-century elite's preference for private justice has generally been explained in terms of codes of honor and structurally ingrained patterns of behavior that demanded retribution for insults or injuries. One theory, which focuses on the ritual dimension of feuding, hypothesizes that feuds were a way of containing conflict within certain limits and rules that made them a mechanism for limiting chaos, for channeling hostilities into actions and reactions that contemporaries recognized as governed by custom and therefore manageable.[13] But it is important to distinguish the intra-class violence perpetrated by elite families against each other from the inter-class violence that particularly provoked the anger of the popolo. Violence against persons outside the elite emerged from class rather than purely factional tensions. Behind much elite violence was the growing antagonism between the elite, which wanted above all to remain master of its own house, and the popolo, which had already begun creating laws, institutions, and forms of public coercion whose first purpose was to rein in the turbulent elite. Although popular governments applied tough sanctions against elite violence in the late thirteenth century, elite vendettas were at least as common at this time as in any previous generation. Much elite violence, whatever the specific origin in this or that quarrel, can thus be seen as collective acts of defiance against the constraints imposed by the popolo: loud statements that the elite wanted no meddling from self-declared governments of guildsmen in what it considered its own internal affairs. From this perspective, the pursuit of vendetta was a politically motivated rejection of the popolo's emerging norms of the supremacy of law and the internalized discipline of the good citizen.

---

[13]   See A. Zorzi, "Politica e giustizia a Firenze al tempo degli Ordinamenti antimagnatizi," in *Ordinamenti di Giustizia fiorentini: studi in occasione del VII centenario,* ed. V. Arrighi (Florence, 1995), pp. 105–47; and G. Dameron, "Revisiting the Italian Magnates," *Viator* 23 (1992): 167–87.

In fact, even thirteenth-century vendettas did not occur without some intervention of law and government. The most revealing description from the elite itself of an early vendetta is Velluti's reconstruction of his family's feud with the Ghibelline Mannelli family. It began in 1267, the year the Guelf faction regained control of the city and settled old scores against the Ghibellines, when Ghino Velluti, the son of a brother of Velluti's great-grandfather, was killed by the Mannelli, who were angry over Ghino's part in securing the cancellation of a decree of banishment against an enemy of theirs. A late thirteenth-century chronicler reports that the first hostile action against the Ghibellines by the returning Guelfs was an assault on Mannello Mannelli's father by a member of the Rossi family.[14] If this was the event that sparked the retaliation, Mannello presumably killed Ghino to avenge the insult to his father's honor in the exoneration of the latter's assailant. Mannello was exiled by the Guelf regime, but this did not satisfy the Velluti, who waited twenty-eight years to exact their revenge. When they finally did so, it was in another politically charged moment, the feast day of the Baptist (June 24, which was both a civic and religious holiday) in 1295, a year in which the elite was trying to weaken the popular movement that had inflicted magnate status on so many of them. Two brothers of the murdered Ghino, together with Donato's father Lamberto, attacked and killed Lippo di Simone de' Mannelli during the celebrations. That they carried out the vendetta on a civic holiday of a year in which the elite was trying to bring down the popular government suggests that it was also an open challenge to the popolo's efforts to tame elite violence.

The Mannelli immediately accused not only the four attackers, but also Donato's grandfather Filippo of having ordered the murder. Filippo appeared in court to confront his accusers, who produced no fewer than twenty-four witnesses, men and women, to testify against him. "May God be praised," comments Donato, the witnesses proved nothing and he was acquitted. The silence of the witnesses (he adds that one of them "in effect said little or nothing") may have been the result of either fear or complicity in the cover-up. In either case, such cooperation was the very stuff of elite power. The actual perpetrators did not appear before the court, presumably because their participation in the murder could not be denied. The court found them guilty in absentia and assessed heavy fines that were paid on their behalf by the same Velluti banking and trading company that had been founded by Bonaccorso Velluti and his brother's sons, including Ghino, who was murdered in 1267, and the two brothers who carried out the vendetta in 1295. Donato matter-of-factly refers his family readers to the relevant page of the company ledger for the payment of the fines and court costs in what was treated in effect as a business expense. The obligations of vendetta and honor here overlapped with

---

[14] *Cronica di Paolino Pieri fiorentino delle cose d'Italia dall'anno 1080 fino all'anno 1305* (Rome, 1755), p. 33.

family business partnerships. Donato remarks that "thus we carried out the vendetta of our relatives [*consorti*] and we paid our share." However, because the company was beginning to experience difficulties as a result of loans extended to "the lords and barons of France and England," they had to borrow the money from neighbors and allies. Moreover, the commune agreed to reduce the fines by almost half if the Velluti and their friends cancelled credits in the communal debt by the same amount. In effect, the Velluti avoided much of the penalty assessed against them by getting a group of friends to forgive the commune sizeable shares in the public debt. Donato openly admits that this agreement was made possible by the influence the Velluti enjoyed in the government at the time. The vendetta was thus absorbed into broader forms of fiscal and political cooperation among the elite families whose objective was to thwart the strict application of the laws against upper-class violence. Circumventing the courts and the criminal justice system must have been at least as satisfying, and as central to the preservation of elite honor, as the vendetta itself against the Mannelli.

The commune also intervened to mediate and ratify formal acts of peace between warring families. Although the Mannelli signed a peace with the Velluti through a legal representative, they still treated them with rancor and hostility. The commune forced them to declare another peace on July 17, 1295, in the presence of communal officials. Three Mannelli, acting on behalf of over twenty other men of the family, and seven Velluti, acting on behalf of three of their relatives, met to swear promises of peace and exchange the traditional kiss on the mouth. The Velluti represented at this peacemaking came from all three of the extant patrilines descended from Donato's great-grandfather. Both families were required to provide guarantors (*mallevadori*, or *fideiussores* in legal Latin), who put up a sum of money to be forfeited to the commune if any of the parties violated the peace. Both the Velluti and the Mannelli recruited *mallevadori* from both magnate families (four for each side, with one represented on both sides) and non-magnate elite houses. Among the Velluti's magnate guarantors were two Frescobaldi, an Abati, a Pulci, and two Rossi; their non-magnate guarantors included members of the Guicciardini, Soderini, Del Bene, Machiavelli, and a larger number of less well known names. The Mannelli's magnate guarantors were two Gherardini, two Rossi, two Bardi, and a Mozzi, with a smaller number of non-magnates.[15]

Rituals of peacemaking thus involved not only the commune but also the wider community of the elite. To the extent that such rituals legitimated and reinforced the very family and class solidarities that undergirded codes of honor and the vendettas that sustained those codes, formal reconciliations also legitimated the vendetta itself. The entire process, from murder to punishment to peacemaking, provided the elite families with occasions to affirm their

---

[15] Velluti, *Cronica domestica*, pp. 10–18.

independence from, and contempt for, the popolo's attempts to rein them in and make their behavior conform to standards of civil moderation. The elite insisted on being a law unto itself even when it needed to do so through the institutions of communal government.

Political Alignments and Factions

The elite families transferred much of this same attitude to their political behavior and style. From as early as the twelfth century, elite politics turned on factional conflict, on fierce rivalries between groups of families who did not hesitate to appeal to outside powers for help in their struggles against domestic rivals. The chroniclers represent an early eruption of conflict in 1177–80 as an uprising by the pro-imperial Uberti in protest against their exclusion from the early commune's chief magistracy, the consulate. According to the anonymous late thirteenth-century account, it was a veritable "war" that lasted over two years because "the Uberti obeyed neither the consuls nor any other authority."[16] Villani describes the Uberti as the "most powerful and greatest citizens of Florence" (6.9) and says that, with their followers among "both the nobles and the *popolo*, they made war on the consuls" because the government was not to their liking. The parties "fought from neighborhood to neighborhood" and "armed their towers, which were numerous and from 100 to 120 *braccia* high. Indeed, because of this war many new towers were built at that time by the communities of the *contrade*, with money raised from the neighborhoods, and they were called the towers of the companies." Evidently the factions were organized through neighborhood associations that even had the power to collect funds and build towers for defense. The civil war resulted in many deaths and several great fires that destroyed entire sections of the city. Apparently the Uberti made their point: from 1180, they and their allies appeared regularly in the consulate.

   It is difficult to say if these events were the origin of the great division that dominated the history of the Florentine elite for the next century. Each conflict built on earlier antagonisms, and the search for a precise moment of origin is necessarily futile. But the split certainly became deeper and increasingly irreconcilable in the first half of the thirteenth century. Our sources for these early factional conflicts are the chroniclers of the late thirteenth and early fourteenth centuries, and they tended to superimpose the later history and structure of upper-class factionalism onto earlier episodes like the Uberti uprising and the Buondelmonti murder. The Uberti may indeed have been a pro-imperial family even in the late twelfth century, but whether the fighting of 1177–80 "gave birth," as Villani puts it, "to the accursed parties" is more

[16]   *Cronica fiorentina*, ed. Schiaffini, p. 104.

problematic. The "parties" to which Villani alludes here are the Guelfs and Ghibellines (which he later claims arose in the aftermath of the Buondelmonti murder of 1216). But the names Guelf and Ghibelline, denoting respectively the papal and imperial parties, did not come into common use until the 1240s. Villani provides a guide to the early divisions within the elite in his survey of thirty-eight Guelf and thirty-one Ghibelline families that he claims constituted the core of the parties after 1216. Many of these families belonged to the old ruling group of the consular commune, and fifteen of the Guelf and thirteen of the Ghibelline families are present in Cacciaguida's roll-call in *Paradiso* 16. It is unclear whether Villani borrowed from Dante or the other way around. But it is also possible that they both drew on earlier and now lost sources, or that the collective memory of family participation in the early feuds was still quite precise around 1300. Almost all the families in Villani's list went on to play leading roles in the great mid-century civil war between Guelfs and Ghibellines: twenty of the Guelf and twenty-one of the Ghibelline families are among those he lists as combatants in the 1240s, and fifteen of the Ghibelline families and no fewer than thirty-three of the Guelf families will appear in his lists of exiles in, respectively, 1258 and 1260. The overwhelming majority of these families (thirty-three Guelf and twenty-seven Ghibelline) were subjected to magnate status by popular governments in the 1280s and 1290s and deprived of the right to hold communal offices, and they account for sixty of the seventy-three city lineages designated as magnates. Although a few of these sixty magnate families, in particular the Bardi, Frescobaldi, Scali, and Cerchi, remained powerful despite magnate status, most of the others disappeared from the ranks of the ruling class by 1300. The names continued to evoke a memorable past, but little more, and by the time Villani compiled his 1216 list of families they were a nearly vanished elite. The history of the thirteenth-century elite is thus the story of the decline, and in part the self-destruction, of the ruling families of the first half of the century, and their replacement by new families whose power was more solidly anchored in trade and banking.

The internecine strife that erupted in the 1240s between the factions led to repeated banishments and confiscations over the next two decades: Ghibellines exiled and confiscated the property of Guelfs in 1248 and 1260; and Guelfs exiled Ghibellines in 1258 and banished and plundered many more in 1267–8. In the process, the entirety of the old elite was weakened politically and economically. After 1267 the victorious Guelfs compiled a register of families and individuals of their party whose property had been confiscated or damaged by the Ghibellines in 1260–6,[17] as well as a roster of the Ghibellines that they in turn sent into exile.[18] From these compilations a reasonably complete

---

[17] The *Liber extimationum*, ed. O. Brattö (Göteborg, 1956).
[18] *Il Libro del Chiodo*, ed. F. Klein with S. Sartini (Florence, 2004).

picture of the composition of the elite factions emerges. Eligible for compensation for damages were 626 households from some sixty Guelf lineages, representing perhaps 2,500 individuals, from both city (about 1,500) and contado
(1,000). About a third of these sixty families came from the old elite that until
the 1270s provided the leadership of the Guelf party, but whose wealth was
mostly in land, not in commerce or banking: the Buondelmonti, Donati, Rossi,
Cavalcanti, Gherardini, Sacchetti, Giandonati, Vecchietti, Arrigucci, Tosinghi,
Della Bella, Adimari, and others. The remaining two-thirds were families with
greater involvement in trade or banking, and they included some older houses
(Bardi, Mozzi, Scali) and a larger number of families that had more recently
entered the economic elite (Canigiani, Alberti del Giudice, Magalotti, Mancini,
Acciaiuoli, Altoviti, Spini, and others).[19] Remarkably, the number of Ghibelline
families exiled in 1267 (62, with a total of perhaps 1,400 individuals) was
almost exactly that of the Guelf families seeking compensation for damages.
Those with the largest number of exiles, and presumably therefore the largest
and most powerful families of their faction, were the Ubriachi (35), Uberti
(28), Scolari (27), Tedaldini (18), Amidei (16), and Lamberti (16). But of the
leading Ghibelline families only the Ubriachi, Mannelli, Brunelleschi, Strinati,
and Abati were moderately prominent in banking and commerce. Other smaller
and less powerful Ghibelline families had more of an economic role (Bonizzi,
Macci, Dell'Antella, Pulci, Portinari, Strozzi, and Saltarelli), and they largely
survived the change of regime and eventually merged with the prosperous
Guelf elite of the last third of the century. Their Ghibellinism may have been
more a matter of pragmatic accommodation than deep conviction. The preference for the Guelf cause (under some pressure from the papacy in the 1260s)
of most of the rising commercial and banking families sealed the fate of
Florentine Ghibellinism. Within a year, the core of the old Ghibelline elite was
in exile and never returned to the city.[20]

Shorn of its Ghibelline component, the Florentine elite after 1267 consisted
of a combination of the triumphant Guelf wing of the old upper class and
the newer merchant families. Until about 1280, the older families maintained
their leadership role. The politically most influential lineages were all from
the old elite (Adimari, Cavalcanti, Della Tosa, Rossi, Tornaquinci, Bardi,
Buondelmonti, and Pazzi), as were eleven of the sixteen families with the
largest claims for damages. Some older Guelf families began to establish themselves in the expanding commercial and banking sector. The Bardi and Mozzi
had already formed major companies; the Bostichi, Pazzi, and one branch of
the Rossi engaged in moneylending; and the Gherardini and Sacchetti had

[19]   Analysis by Brattö in *Liber extimationum*, and S. Raveggi, in S. Raveggi, M. Tarassi,
D. Medici, and P. Parenti, *Ghibellini, Guelfi e popolo grasso: i detentori del potere
politico a Firenze nella seconda metà del Dugento* (Florence, 1978), pp. 13–21.
[20]   Raveggi, in *Ghibellini, Guelfi*, pp. 23–72.

members in the Calimala guild. But with the exception of the Bardi and the Mozzi, the leading families of the 1270s were enjoying their last generation of real power and prestige, and nearly all of them (including the Bardi and the Mozzi) were declared magnates by popular governments. Just behind them in political influence in the 1270s was a large and expanding group of merchant families, mostly of recent prominence, who constituted the emerging plutocracy that became the new Florentine elite of the next seventy or so years. Slightly older families in this group were the Cerchi, Frescobaldi, and Scali, who built some of the biggest banking enterprises of the late thirteenth century. Newer ones included the Spini, who collaborated with the Mozzi as bankers in England; the Canigiani and Ridolfi, who engaged in money-lending; the Acciaiuoli, who formed a major merchant company of the next generation; and others like the Altoviti, Mancini, Magalotti, Medici, and Velluti, who all gained a foothold in the elite in these years. They were joined in the 1280s by the Cerretani, Girolami, Pitti, Albizzi, and the Peruzzi (who founded a banking firm second in size and importance only to the Bardi), by some formerly Ghibelline merchant houses that quietly and successfully merged with the dominant Guelf faction (Ardinghelli, Dell'Antella, Portinari, and Strozzi), and by still others that emerged over the next two decades (Baroncelli, Biliotti, Bonciani, Bordoni, Capponi, Castellani, Corsini, Covoni, Davanzati, Guadagni, Guasconi, Ricci, Rondinelli, and Rucellai).[21]

The emergence of this new plutocracy made Florentines acutely conscious of the difference within the elite between older families with limited connection to commerce and newer ones whose wealth exceeded anything previously seen and whose mercantile activities were radically transforming Florentine society and the city's relationship to the outside world. Dante's Cacciaguida points to this awareness in *Paradiso* 15 and 16. The chronicler Dino Compagni's account of the origins of the feud between the Cerchi and Donati in the late 1290s is grounded in the perception of this same distinction. Although the Cerchi had been prominent from early in the century, they were not as old as the Donati. Compagni calls the Cerchi "men of low estate, but good merchants and very rich; they dressed well, [and] kept many servants." In 1280 some Cerchi bought the palazzo of the old Ghibelline family of the Counts Guidi, which was "near to the houses of the Pazzi and Donati, who were of more ancient lineage [*più antichi di sangue*] but not as rich. The Donati, seeing the Cerchi rising – they had walled the palace and increased its height, and lived in high style – began to nurse a great hatred of them."[22] The Cerchi, Donati, and Pazzi were all old Guelfs from the same area of the city,

[21] Tarassi, in *Ghibellini, Guelfi*, pp. 91–164.
[22] Dino Compagni, *Cronica*, ed. G. Luzzatto (Turin, 1968), 1.20, p. 45; this and other translations of Compagni are from D. Bornstein, *Dino Compagni's Chronicle of Florence* (Philadephia, 1986), with book and chapter numbers given in the text.

and the Cerchi's purchase of a Ghibelline family's palazzo was in no obvious way a slight to their neighbors. The resentment of the Donati, who were not a mercantile family, focused on the conspicuous display of wealth by a family of more recent and greater prosperity. Moreover, the Cerchi, unlike older families generally rooted in one neighborhood, owned property all over the city and had begun to act (so their enemies believed) as though the city itself were somehow theirs. For a number of years around 1290 the communal priors resided in a house rented from the Cerchi in the area north of the Bargello, then the palace of the communal military and judicial official known as the podestà. Older but less wealthy families like the Donati resented this combination of wealth and the influence it could buy. Rivalries spawned or inflamed by the flaunting of disproportionate wealth, influence, and power by one family within the elite were a recurrent source of factional division.

But the factions do not neatly conform to the distinction between older and newer families, or between those more or less involved in big business, and the precise causes of the fierce antagonisms between the factions remain obscure. Curiously, the protagonists themselves did not leave accounts or justifications of these conflicts. The descriptions we have come from the chroniclers of the popolo, whose motivation was to highlight the irrationality and irresponsibility of elite factionalism. They thus make little effort to explain how and why the feuds made any coherent sense even to those who participated in them. It is difficult to see class or socio-economic factors behind the eruption of these feuds. Relatively older and newer families, and families with greater and lesser involvement in trade and banking, can be found on both sides of the factional divides. The long view of thirteenth-century elite factionalism does of course show that the victorious Guelfs of the last third of the century consisted predominantly of newer and mostly mercantile families, although in the decade after the Guelf restoration of 1267 the party's leaders still came mainly from older families with less involvement in trade or banking. Florence's economic expansion does indeed explain why an elite of merchant families emerged as a dominant and even ruling class by the early fourteenth century. But it does not explain why certain families or groups of families fell on one side or the other of either the Guelf–Ghibelline conflict of the mid-thirteenth century or the split among the Guelfs around 1300.

We must not underestimate the wider pan-Italian ideological dimension of the Guelf–Ghibelline split and the attempts of emperors from Frederick Barbarossa in the twelfth century to Henry VII in the early fourteenth century to bring the Italian cities under imperial overlordship. No doubt many Ghibellines supported the imperial cause with the same passionate intensity with which Guelfs opposed it. Less clear is why certain families supported the Ghibellines and others joined the opposition. Only in the 1260s does an economic rationale emerge: the alliance among the Guelf commercial elite, the papacy, and the house of Anjou (who united to defeat the Ghibellines) opened broad avenues for economic profits in the south of Italy conquered by the Angevins. But party antagonisms long predated this development, and the general impression is that until then Guelf–Ghibelline alignments were influenced more by local issues than by international politics or ideologies. And what can explain the violent divisions around 1300 between two groups of families that were all nominally Guelf? How did such local antagonisms become so entrenched and fierce?

If elite feuding and violence are placed in the context of relations between elite and popolo, elite conflicts appear above all as competitions for followers and clients from the non-elite classes. A powerful family was by definition one with a large number of men from the middling ranks of society willing to support their patrons in neighborhood or city councils, to walk with (or behind) them on ritual and festive occasions, and to gather in the streets in front of the family's palazzo and tower in times of tension or conflict. We know much more about the modalities of patron–client relations in later periods of Florentine history than we do for the thirteenth century, but the underlying motivation on the part of the elite patrons was no doubt similar: rivalries between upper-class families were fundamentally contests for the support and allegiance of the lesser families and individuals of their quarters or neighborhoods. What made a family great and powerful in the eyes of Florentines was not only its wealth, antiquity, and political offices, but also the perception that it commanded the loyalty and support of a greater number of allies, clients, and "lesser" neighbors than did its rivals. Compagni illuminates the search for allies by powerful families in times of danger in his account of the growing animosity between the Donati and the Cerchi around 1300 (1.20). As "the hatred grew day by day," the Cerchi began to stay away from meetings of the Guelf Party and to "align themselves with the *popolani*." "They drew with them many citizens . . . and other powerful clans," and "the *popolo minuto* loved [the Cerchi] because they disapproved of the conspiracy against [the popular leader] Giano della Bella." Of Corso Donati Compagni says that he had many armed men in his service and a "great entourage" (2.20). He was called "the Baron" because of his haughty demeanor, and when he rode through the city "many cried 'long live the Baron,' and the city seemed to belong to him." A visibly large armed following and recognition from the streets of such strength were the measure and manifestation of a family's or factional leader's power.

Compagni's description of the riot that nearly occurred at the funeral of a Frescobaldi woman (1.20) assumes that factional flare-ups, typically occurring in public settings and before an audience, were meant to make the greatest possible impression on ordinary Florentines. The funeral took place in the piazza that still carries the family name on the Oltrarno side of the Santa

Trinita bridge in front of the Frescobaldi palace. Temporary seating was provided for citizens and neighbors, with knights, doctors, and jurists sitting higher up and others lower down. The Donati and Cerchi sat as distinct groups directly facing one another across a small open space. This obviously planned seating arrangement clearly spelled trouble, which soon arrived. When someone on one side rose to his feet (Compagni does not even trouble to say which side), "either to straighten his clothes or for some other reason," the other side, thinking this might be a prearranged signal for action, also stood up and put their hands on their swords. The others responded likewise and the fight was on. On this particular occasion, says the chronicler, wiser heads prevented a mêlée, but not before a large number of Cerchi supporters ran to the family's palaces to receive orders to attack the Donati. The confrontation thus generated a public display of Cerchi strength that served as a warning to the Donati and a demonstration to the city at large of the speed with which loyal Cerchi followers could gather in support of their leaders. The event seems almost choreographed, a ritual confrontation in which everyone knew the parts they were expected to play.

Another example, also from Compagni (1.22), is the fight that occurred during the Mayday festivities of 1300 when open hostilities again erupted between the Donati and Cerchi. Each year elite families celebrated the advent of spring on the first of May with dinners and dances in the semi-enclosed "courts" of their inner-city enclaves. Bands, or *brigate*, of young men, organized by faction, went from court to court to dance, and separate *brigate* of women danced within their neighborhoods. According to Compagni, the Donati *brigata*, which included members of the Bardi and Spini families and "other companions and followers," actually went looking for a confrontation with the Cerchi *brigata*, and in the ensuing fight a Cerchi had his nose sliced off. The accusations and recriminations divided the entire city: "the great, middling, and little men and even the clergy could not help but give themselves wholeheartedly to these factions, this man to one and that man to the other." Here too the confrontation served to clarify loyalties, to strengthen the sense of obligation among "companions and followers," and thus to sharpen the boundaries between the factions. In the ensuing consolidation of factional loyalties, the polarizing momentum made it difficult for anyone not to line up on one side or the other. Compagni's analysis of the Cerchi faction highlights their elite allies, but also underscores their non-elite following: with them were "all the Ghibellines," because they thought they had less to fear from them; the former supporters of the popular leader Giano della Bella, because it seemed to them that the Cerchi had mourned his expulsion; Guido Cavalcanti (the poet and friend of Dante) who hated Corso Donati; Naldo Gherardini, because he was an enemy of the Manieri, who were related by marriage to Corso Donati; messer Manetto Scali and his kinsmen, because they were related by marriage to the Cerchi; messer Lapo Saltarelli, also related to the

Cerchi by marriage; messer Berto Frescobaldi, because he had received loans from the Cerchi; messer Goccia Adimari, because he quarreled with his own kinsmen (who supported the Donati); Bernardo di messer Manfredi Adimari, because he was a partner in the Cerchi trading company; three members of the Della Tosa family, because they were angry with their kinsman, messer Rosso, who had deprived them of honors and privileges; the Mozzi; the major branch of the Cavalcanti; and many non-magnate families and members of the popolo. Compagni's analysis of the Donati faction is less detailed: "long familiarity and friendship" motivated the loyalty of their leading allies, the Della Tosa and Adimari, and, presumably, that of the other major families he lists (Pazzi, Rossi, Bardi, Bordoni, and Cerretani). But the Donati too had followers in the ranks of the popolo.

One purpose of elite efforts to enlist clients and followers was to control the popolo. Paradoxically, fighting amongst themselves helped elite families neutralize the popolo politically by recruiting as many of them as possible into their factions. Great families thus competed for followers, and the competition frequently led to hostilities that provided ideal occasions for displaying the strength and solidarity of a family's following. A brawl, even the threat of one, would get out the "troops" and allow a family's street power to be seen and measured. Quarrels between factions were thus a necessary part of the process by which great families demonstrated their greatness. Success in this competition meant greater prestige and security, more influence in the councils of government, and greater physical control of neighborhoods and the inner city. But the essence of such conflicts was the competition for loyalties and support among the middle and non-elite classes. Factions began as alliances of elite families whose strength was increased by the combination of their formerly separate contingents of non-elite clients. When these alliances and the competitions between them spilled out of their neighborhoods to other parts of the city, the potential for urban civil war became very real. And when, finally, external conflicts demanded that powerful families declare for one side or the other, these divisions coalesced into two large groupings. This happened in the 1230s and 1240s when the Guelf and Ghibelline parties took shape, and it happened again, with the split in the Guelf party, around 1300. Whatever the precise circumstances of such divisions, the history of elite factionalism in Florence is inseparable from the still larger and deeper conflict between elite and popolo.

Culture and Religion

In the first half of the thirteenth century, Florence's place on the European cultural and literary map was minor. It had nothing to compare with Bologna's faculty of law, the schools of philosophy and theology at Paris and Oxford, or the innovative poetry of Provence and Sicily. Florentine cultural ascendancy was established suddenly and even dramatically in the second half of the century. Brunetto Latini revived the study of classical rhetoric and wrote a learned encyclopedia. Although Florence still lacked a university, the schools at Santa Croce and Santa Maria Novella became the most important centers of the intellectual impact in Italy of the Franciscans and Dominicans. With the poetry of Guido Cavalcanti and then Dante, the Florentine (or Tuscan) language emerged as Italy's leading literary vernacular. In the early fourteenth century Giovanni Villani and Dino Compagni brought the writing of history to new sophistication, and Giotto and Arnolfo di Cambio made Florence a major center of artistic and architectural innovation.[23]

This suddenly flourishing culture certainly reflected the city's burgeoning wealth and its increased contacts with the major centers of European learning and culture. But its literary culture moved along two distinct tracks, reflecting the preferences of elite and popolo. The popolo, as we shall see, grounded its culture in history, the notarial arts, and the civic and rhetorical traditions of classical Rome, whereas the elite generally remained distant from, even disdainful of, such interests. The two literary genres preferred by the elite, as both producers and consumers of literature, owed much to foreign and courtly influences: the aristocratic love poetry that borrowed much from Provence and Sicily; and the emerging genre of the novella that took as its characteristic setting the courtly societies, particularly of Naples and France. Both genres exclusively favored the emerging Tuscan vernacular. By contrast, the culture of the popolo was increasingly bilingual: the growing attachment to the rhetoric, literature, and history of ancient Rome generated both a revival of classical Latin and a robust vernacular historiography built on Roman models and pointed the way to the Latinizing humanism of the Renaissance. But most Florentine vernacular poets of the last decades of the thirteenth century came from elite families: Neri de' Visdomini, Migliore degli Abati, Pacino di Filippo Angiolieri, and Chiaro Davanzati. There was a woman in this group, Compiuta Donzella, to whom a number of poems are attributed and others addressed. The elite also dominated the group of poets that Dante famously baptized in *Purgatorio* 24 as the practitioners of the "dolce stil novo." The Frescobaldi, a powerful family of Calimala merchants and bankers who were declared magnates, produced three generations of poets: Lambertuccio, his son Dino (who is counted among the important *stilnovisti*), and grandson Matteo. The *stilnovisti* also included Gianni Alfani, from another Calimala family of bankers that did business with both popes and emperors, and the well-known jurist Cino da Pistoia, who belonged to one of

---

[23] An overview: G. Holmes, *Florence, Rome and the Origins of the Renaissance* (Oxford, 1986).

that city's great magnate clans. Apart from Dante, only one of these poets, the notary Lapo Gianni, came from the popolo.[24]

The most famous of the *stilnovisti* (again leaving aside Dante) was Guido Cavalcanti, whose fame as a brilliant and learned poet was accompanied by a reputation for aristocratic "disdain" and political behavior that aroused the popolo's mistrust. It is in Dante's encounter with Guido's father in *Inferno* 10 that Guido is said to have "disdain" for either Virgil or Beatrice, but it can usefully stand for Cavalcanti's general reputation. The Cavalcanti were old Guelf elite and magnates. In 1267, in an effort to pacify factional hatreds with marriages across the Guelf–Ghibelline divide, the young Guido was betrothed to the daughter of the legendary Ghibelline captain Farinata degli Uberti, whom Dante also meets in canto 10 among heretics whose sin is Epicureanism. Ghibellines were often (and wrongly) accused by their enemies of heresy, especially denial of Christian belief in the soul. The Cavalcanti were not Ghibellines, but Guido's difficult poetry on the phenomenology of love (especially the canzone "Donna me prega") is filled with allusions to philosophical and possibly unorthodox notions about the soul that have been variously interpreted as Averroistic or Aristotelian. The very difficulty of his poems gave rise to the suspicion that he belonged to some secret and heterodox cult.[25] While they recognized his genius, to the writers of the popolo Cavalcanti's interest in esoteric doctrines made him suspect. Compagni called him "courtly and bold, but disdainful and solitary and fixed on his studies" (1.10), with the evident implication that there was something unhealthy about one who devoted himself so assiduously to love poetry and philosophy. Villani similarly commented that he was "like a philosopher, and talented in many things, except that he was too irritable and quick to anger" (9.42). Cavalcanti's reputation as an irascible and contemptuous freethinker even reached Boccaccio who, fifty years later, included in the *Decameron* a story about how Guido, with his propensity for philosophical speculation, Epicureanism, and even atheism, arrogantly and insultingly refused to join a band of pleasure-seeking friends who sought his company (6.9). But the other reason for their critical view of him was Cavalcanti's politics, for he and his family were major protagonists in elite vendettas and factionalism. According to Villani (9.1), the Cavalcanti had a "great war" with the Buondelmonti, who were allies of the Donati. Compagni reports that Guido, as a leading partisan of the Cerchi and enemy of Corso Donati, many times looked for occasions to insult Corso, who in turn tried to assassinate him, to which Cavalcanti responded by inciting a band of young Cerchi followers to join him in assaulting Corso.

---

[24] *Poeti del Duecento*, ed. G. Contini, 2 vols. (Milan and Naples, 1960).
[25] L. Nelson, Jr., ed. and trans., *The Poetry of Guido Cavalcanti* (New York, 1986); Guido Cavalcanti, *The Complete Poems*, trans. M. Cirigliano (New York, 1992).

The incident started a larger fight that, in Compagni's words, "increased the hatred" between the parties. Cavalcanti's role was apparently so prominent that in the summer of 1300 the government exiled him, together with other leading members of both parties. Although his poetry rarely touches on political themes, one sonnet urges a kinsman named Nerone to pursue the vendetta against the Buondelmonti. The combination of his violent and impulsive behavior on the streets, so typical of his class, the lack of any concern (at least in his poetry) for the havoc that such actions rained on the city, and a style of philosophical poetry that raised doubts about his orthodoxy, must all have fed the perception of Cavalcanti and perhaps other poets of his group as intellectuals fundamentally alien to the civic culture of the popolo.

Two telling pieces of contemporary testimony confirm the class tensions surrounding Cavalcanti's reputation and the kind of poetry he wrote. In his commentary on "Donna me prega" the Florentine doctor Dino del Garbo observed that the "passion of love is most found among gentlemen [*hominibus nobilibus*], great and powerful either because of their progeny or because of much wealth or virtue of soul. Other men from the *popolo* [*homines alii populares*] are more given to thoughts of civic works which are necessary in life. Noble and powerful men, because they are not concerned with such labours, are more likely to be involved in thoughts centring on this passion" of love.[26] Compagni addressed a fascinating sonnet to Cavalcanti in which he reminded his "friend" of the many times he had praised him for his wisdom, physical prowess, military skill, and his sophisticated and refined learning, which all display Cavalcanti's "nobeltate ed arte" in equal measure. Compagni was here ironically juxtaposing the cult of "nobility," typical of elite families, and "arte," whose meanings included work, skill, industriousness and the discipline associated with guildsmen (whose guilds were known as *arti* in the vernacular). "But you," Compagni continues, "have no need of great nobility, nor of an armed following, for he who has *cortesia* keeps only a small *corte*. You are indeed a man with a great following. Ah! What an excellent merchant you would have been!" Compagni thus distinguishes genuine *cortesia*, the sum of qualities that make for elegance and good character, from *corte*, here used in the sense of retinue or following. To reinforce the point, he finishes the poem by saying that "If God led everyone to a just destiny by setting right all that is distorted, He would give *cortesia* to those who need it [a line that can also mean "to those who have professions"], and would make you a worker [*ovrere*: one with a skill or profession, and thus a guildsman], so that you may earn your living and I may exhibit the generosity [that comes with *cortesia*]." Underscoring the social gulf separating himself from Cavalcanti, he simultaneously wants Cavalcanti and his class to give up their pretensions to "nobility,"

[26]   Holmes, *Florence, Rome*, p. 91.

their factions, and clients, and embrace instead the social values of merchants and guildsmen.

The *Novellino* is the oldest collection of vernacular stories in Italian literature.[27] Its author is unknown, but its language shows he was Florentine, and references to contemporary figures place its composition between 1280 and 1300. From the themes and settings of the stories it is also possible to reconstruct the work's social ambience and audience, particularly from its idealized representation of the Florentine elite. Unlike many of Boccaccio's and Sacchetti's stories, the *Novellino*'s tales largely ignore the city's civic and mercantile environment. Its stories have either foreign or imaginary settings (or both): the courts of France, Provence, England, and Sicily; the magical world of generous and wise kings, knights and ladies, astrologers and necromancers. Its major sources, direct or indirect, were French and other foreign literary traditions of the twelfth and thirteenth centuries: the Arthurian tales of Lancelot, Guinevere, and the Round Table, the tales of Tristan and Isolde, and a variety of other French and Provençal texts, which nourished the courtly pretensions of Florentine elite families.[28] The *Novellino* was written in precisely the decades in which the popolo's attempt to control elite behavior relegated many elite families to magnate status. The elite responded by turning to these foreign and courtly codes of conduct to confirm a collective identity that ignored the restrictive civic framework and tense competition between the two political cultures. It was in a sense the elite's literature of dreams: the expression of a perhaps imprecise but deeply felt yearning for nobility and "cortesia" that served as a counter-argument to the popolo's emerging civic ethos.

Some of its stories make a direct connection between this dream-world of courtly elegance and the aspirations of the elite. In story 99, a young man intensely loves a "gentile pulzella," who, however, loves another. When she arranges for her lover (assisted by the usual group of companions) to take her away on horseback, a mix-up occurs as her would-be lover happens to ride by at the moment she rushes from her house. Only miles out of the city does she realize she is not with her betrothed. But her tears turn to love when she sees the comfort her suitor offers and the "honor" he pays her. Meanwhile, the lover who was expecting to meet her at her family's home sets out with his companions in pursuit of the fleeing couple. Finding them asleep in each other's arms, they decide to wait until they awaken, "and then we'll do what we have to do." But they too fall asleep, and when the new lovers awaken to

[27]   *Novellino e Conti del Duecento*, ed. S. Lo Nigro (Turin, 1964; reprint edn. 1983); *The Novellino, or one hundred ancient tales*, ed. and trans. J. P. Consoli (New York, 1996).
[28]   S. Battaglia, *Capitoli per una storia della novellistica italiana dalle origini al Cinquecento* (Naples, 1993), pp. 103–52.

the sight of their pursuers in deep sleep, the young man says, "They have shown us such great *cortesia* that it will not please God if we harm them." So they take one of the horses of the sleeping brigade, release the others, and ride off. In this imaginary world, which negates the violent reality of upper class vendetta, *cortesia* turns the competition for a woman's love, and even her abduction, into a playful game of hide-and-seek on horseback. Other stories show Florentines as expert in the ways of the courts. Story 80 displays the courtly savoir-faire of the poet, Migliore degli Abati, member of an elite Ghibelline family, who actually did travel to the Sicilian court of Charles of Anjou in 1270 to request that the king spare the Abati in the general destruction of Ghibelline property after the Guelf victory. The story presents Migliore as a "well-mannered" knight who "could sing well and spoke Provençal exceedingly well." With his courtly graces evidently outweighing his Ghibelline past, "the noble knights of Sicily gave a banquet in his honor" and then took him to the rooms of the court ladies. Here the violence of the Guelf–Ghibelline wars is quietly forgotten in a celebration of the common courtly culture in which Migliore is described as being fully at home. In fact, so comfortable is he with the knights and ladies of the court that he criticizes their use of aloe and amber to perfume the women's quarters, telling them that such things cause ladies to lose the "good natural odor" provided by nature. The delighted knights applaud the Florentine's wise advice and clever speech. The heroes of the *Novellino* are knights, kings, and the (usually young) "men of the courts" who embody *cortesia* and, as models of elegant conduct, know how to handle difficult situations, not with violence or harshness, but with quick wit and natural grace. The few stories about merchants in the *Novellino* present them either as usurious moneylenders, forced by their wives' appetite for ever more expensive clothes to charge exorbitant rates of interest (26), or as dishonest traders willing to cheat their customers by diluting wine with water (97). In this way too the stories reveal their undercurrent of class tensions.

The two cultures did not easily coexist. While Cavalcanti and the *stilnovisti* ignored history and politics, the popolo shied away from love poetry and the *Novellino*'s world of courtly elegance. The only bridge between them was Dante, not in the sense that he reconciled them, but in that he began as a practitioner of *stilnovismo*, moved for a time closer to the civic culture of the popolo, and then went on to things all his own. His early poetry, culminating in the *Vita nuova*, emerges from the cult of idealized love and shows influence (and eventual divergence) from Cavalcanti. In parts of the *Divine Comedy* he subsequently embraced the popolo's critique of elite misrule, but the philosophical, theological, and prophetic poetry of the great poem ultimately transcended the conflicts of Florentine life.

Religion too exhibits divergences between elite and popolo, at least in the early thirteenth century. Before the coming of the mendicants, says Villani, "the city was evilly corrupted by heresies, among others the sect of the Epicureans through their vices of sensuality and gluttony" (5.30). Since there was no known "sect of Epicureans" in medieval Florence, Villani was probably expressing the widespread suspicion that within the elite, especially its Ghibelline wing, a cult of sensuality and worldly skepticism had supplanted true Christian faith. Noting the condemnation of Emperor Frederick II, leader of the Ghibellines, by the Council of Lyons in 1245, Villani commented that the emperor was "convicted on several counts of heresy" (7.24), adding his opinion that Frederick "certainly was not a Catholic Christian, since he always lived more for his own pleasure and enjoyment than by reason or just laws." Dante too condemned Frederick, together with Farinata degli Uberti, for denying the immortality of the soul. This certainly exaggerated perception of an Epicureanism that rejected fundamental articles of Christian faith was one of the ways in which the popolo took its distance from the elite. But heretical, or at least heterodox, religious ideas were not entirely absent among the elite. Catharism had established itself in twelfth-century Florence, with its doctrine of radical dualism and rejection of all things material, including the body, and with its own ecclesiastical structures and even bishops. By the early fourteenth century, when Villani was writing, the perception that Epicureanism and Catharism had both found adherents among the elite resulted in a conflation of these two starkly different philosophies into what the popolo saw as contempt for the Christian faith. Villani attributed the rapid growth and popularity of the mendicants in the early thirteenth century to their successful campaign against a heresy that he first describes as Epicurean but among whose examples he cites the Patarines, or Cathars.[29]

Catharism attracted considerable support from elite families. Inquisition records reveal that members of the Macci, Pulci, Nerli, Baroni, Cavalcanti, and Sizi accepted the Cathar "consolation," attended sermons by Cathar "perfects," and protected co-religionists from the inquisitors.[30] The Dominican Inquisition of the 1240s either suppressed Florentine Catharism or drove it underground, since most of the evidence for its flourishing presence in Florence is from the first half of the century. But the association between Ghibellinism and Catharism remained strong. In 1283 the Franciscan Inquisition condemned Farinata degli Uberti, nineteen years after his death, for having accepted the consolation.[31] A notable feature of Florentine Catharism was its appeal to a significant number of (mostly elite) women. Women dissatisfied with the

---

[29] J. N. Stephens, "Heresy in Medieval and Renaissance Florence," *Past and Present* 54 (1972): 25–62.

[30] C. Lansing, *Power and Purity: Cathar Heresy in Medieval Italy* (Oxford, 1998), pp. 71–6.

[31] N. Ottokar, "La condanna postuma di Farinata degli Uberti," in Ottokar, *Studi comunali e fiorentini* (Florence, 1948), pp. 115 23.

restrictive roles imposed on them by the marriage practices of their class may have found appealing a religion that, in rejecting the body as part of the corrupt material world, also considered marriage as a sinful state and refused procreation, at least among the perfect. Even when unhappiness with the constraints of the marital state did not drive women as far as Catharism, it could still cause them to embrace more conventional religious forms as avenues of escape. The best known example is the story of Umiliana de' Cerchi, who rejected both her marriage and the conspicuous wealth of her banker husband, sold her worldly goods to give money to the poor, and, to the great dismay of her natal family, refused to remarry after her husband's death although she was still a young woman. Umiliana eventually became a Franciscan tertiary and lived a life of prayer and mystical contemplation in which she shunned her kinsmen and even her children.[32] Umiliana's story suggests that the Franciscan third order provided a haven for upper-class widows who refused the demands of their families; indeed, it may have been a likely refuge for men and women of all social classes who felt alienated from elite social, economic, and family structures.

There is less evidence that the Dominican order, created above all to combat dissidents and heretics, especially the Cathars, functioned in any comparable way as a magnet for the disaffected. Florentine Dominicans attracted a somewhat greater proportion of their membership from elite families, while the Franciscans had greater appeal for the middle ranks of the popolo and for non-elite immigrants from the contado. Only 14% of Florentine Franciscans at Santa Croce around 1300 came from city families with surnames (some but not all from the elite), and two-thirds of them were identified by their families' places of origin in the contado. By contrast, 43% of the Dominicans at Santa Maria Novella came from city families and included many old elite names (Adimari, Bardi, Cavalcanti, Donati, Mannelli, Soldanieri, Spini, Tornaquinci, Uberti, and Visdomini), and other more recent merchant but still elite families (Acciaiuoli, Macci, Medici, and Strozzi).[33] The Franciscan emphasis on poverty as a superior spiritual state, combined with the critique of wealth to which it gave rise, probably found more sympathetic adherents among the less wealthy, whereas the austere philosophical traditions of the Dominicans may have appealed somewhat more to the upper classes. But the great mendicant preachers, in particular the Dominicans Remigio de' Girolami and Giordano da Pisa, addressed political and economic questions that concerned all classes, and they did so with considerable independence.

[32] A. Benvenuti Papi, "Umiliana de' Cerchi. Nascita di un culto nella Firenze del Dugento," *Studi francescani* 77 (1980): 87–117; Lansing, *Magnates*, pp. 109–24.

[33] D. Lesnick, *Preaching in Medieval Florence: The Social World of Franciscan and Dominican Spirituality* (Athens, Ga., 1989), pp. 40–85 (table on p. 47).

2

The Popolo

Definitions

Side-by-side with the elite was the class that sometimes cooperated with it, sometimes challenged it, and which, in Florence as elsewhere, was called the "popolo." The word was (and is) used in different senses that require clarification. It sometimes meant all Florentines, or all those eligible to participate in political life. But it more often referred to non-elite citizens, sometimes including the laboring classes of artisans and salaried workers (usually called the "popolo minuto"), but most often signifying the non-elite middle classes, thus evoking the "populus" of the ancient Roman republic. When Florentines spoke of the popolo in specifically political contexts, they usually understood it as synonymous with the large majority of guildsmen who did not belong to elite families. The guild community was in continuous evolution during the thirteenth and fourteenth centuries, and thus even in this more specific usage the meaning of "popolo" depended on the number of guilds and the professions and economic categories they embraced at any given moment.

What separated elite and popolo was never a straightforward distinction between "major" and "minor" guilds. Even the categories of major and minor guilds were fluid. Minor guildsmen were indeed an important component of the popolo, but the center of the popolo's political strength was among the non-elite members of the same major guilds in which merchants and bankers from elite families were enrolled. The distinction between elite and popolo cut through the memberships of the major guilds, making the internal politics of these guilds a key ground of conflict between the classes. Only in the oldest and most aristocratic of the guilds, the international merchants, bankers, and large-scale commodity traders of the Calimala, was the elite always the majority. In the guild of the Giudici e Notai the jurists were a small minority and came mostly from elite families, whereas the many notaries were socially of the popolo. The guild of bankers and moneychangers (Cambio) included powerful international merchant companies of the elite (like the Peruzzi) but also many non-elite moneychangers closer to the social status of the popolo. Among the manufacturers of woolen cloth (Lana), the split between elite and popolo was anchored to the difference between the mostly elite producers of high-quality cloths for the foreign luxury market and the non-elite producers of coarser and cheaper cloths for local and regional markets. The Lana was the most contentious site of conflict between elite and popolo in the major guilds. By contrast, in the guild of Por Santa Maria, which combined the manufacturers of silk cloth and retail cloth merchants, and which eventually included goldsmiths, shirtmakers, and a host of artisan groups, the popolo was the large majority, as it was also in the complex composite guild that combined the doctors and the importers of specialty goods and spices, and later admitted as an equal third subdivision the shopkeepers who sold a wide variety of household goods and items of personal apparel (Medici, Speziali, e Merciai). The same was true of the guild of the manufacturers of furs and fur-lined coats (Vaiai e Pellicciai), which, although officially a major guild, was closer in social composition and political influence to the minor guilds. In these last three major guilds the names of elite families were scarce compared to those known only by patronymics.

Thousands of regional and local merchants, moneychangers, small-scale textile manufacturers, retail cloth traders, and shopkeepers rubbed elbows with the elite in the same guilds and engaged in a two-century struggle with them for control, not only of these guilds, but of the guild community and, through it, the commune. Among the chief causes of the turbulence of Florentine political life until about 1400 was the fluctuating and ambivalent position of these non-elite major guildsmen, who sometimes, generally in periods of economic prosperity, accepted the political leadership of the elite and shared power with it in regimes from which the rest of the guild community was excluded, thus producing periods of what is usually thought of as oligarchic government but which always depended on the cooperation of the non-elite major guildsmen. At other times, under the impact of economic and/or military and fiscal crises, the non-elite major guildsmen broke with the elite and looked to the minor guilds for allies in attempts to diminish elite power. Alliances between these two major components of the popolo gave birth to a series of popular governments that challenged elite hegemony over a century and a half, changing the character of the elite and the shape and structure of communal government. The most politically charged meaning of "popolo" referred to the popular governments produced by these alliances of non-elite major guildsmen and minor guildsmen – for example, when Giovanni Villani wrote about a 1289 agreement between the seven major guilds and five minor guilds that it was "almost the beginning of a *popolo* [*quasi uno cominciamento di popolo*] from which the *popolo* that began in 1292 took shape" (8.132).

Besides the seven guilds ultimately known as the major guilds, scores of other guilds came into being throughout the thirteenth century with no limit or control. Not until 1293 did the Ordinances of Justice give formal political recognition to twenty-one guilds, including the seven and fourteen others later known as the minor guilds. Before 1293, the existence of dozens of smaller and autonomously constituted guilds represented the potential for a guild-based popolo extending far down the social and economic hierarchy. This was no doubt one of the chief reasons why even the popular government of the mid-1290s decided to limit the number of politically recognized guilds. In fact, the middle-class popolo never sought the inclusion in the guild federation, and thus in government, of the myriad categories of artisans that were all forming their own guilds. Popular government was thus beset by a fundamental contradiction from the outset. Even as it aimed to expand the role of guilds and the power of the guild community in government and needed the support of the most prominent minor guilds to do so, it simultaneously sought to limit this expansion and prevent many categories of artisans and all laborers from organizing into guilds, thus denying them the very right of association that was the basis of the popolo's own claim to control of government.

The fourteen other guilds given official standing by the popular government included the largest and most important of the city's artisan trades (they are listed in the next section). Most of the other guilds not included in the federation of 1293 either merged with one or another of the recognized guilds or disappeared within a generation. But the potential they once represented was not forgotten. At two points in the fourteenth century, in the 1340s and again in the 1370s, Florence's hitherto unincorporated artisans and workers demanded guilds of their own and admission into the guild federation, thus expanding the popolo. Here was the second major source of political turbulence in the early Florentine republic: the pressure to extend the right of guild association to the masses of politically aware but disenfranchised workers and artisans. The social complexity of Florentine politics emerged from this triangular struggle: the guild-based popolo, itself crisscrossed by divergent interests and social identities, saw on one side an elite whose arrogance and power it sought to curtail and on the other an array of artisans and workers it was determined to keep at bay. Only in the aftermath of 1378, when the most radical of the popular governments created three new guilds of textile workers and artisans, did the frightened non-elite major guildsmen abandon any further attempts to create popular governments in alliance with the minor guildsmen, thus definitively aligning themselves with the elite.

Two further sources of potential confusion concerning the popolo need to be addressed. The first is that not all elite families were declared magnates, and those that escaped (like the Peruzzi, Alberti, Rucellai, Medici and Strozzi, to name only a few) were, and are, often referred to as *popolani*. Magnates were a large and visible part of the elite class, not a class by themselves. But this should not be confused with the social distinction between elite and popolo: the only sense in which non-magnate elite families were *popolani* is that they were not magnates and could hold office. The conflict at the center of Florentine politics in the thirteenth century was not between magnates and the upper-class non-magnate *popolano* families; it was rather between the entire elite (magnate and non-magnate) and the popolo. A second source of confusion derives from the fact that the distinction between elite and popolo was never defined in law and was often a grey area. Florence had no legally designated nobility: no institutional boundary between elite and popolo, no noble titles to distinguish the former from the latter. The popolo included major guildsmen who were close to the elite in many respects and often formed business part-nerships with members of elite families. The line between elite and non-elite was a matter of perception, which sometimes made it difficult (and still does) to say whether certain individuals or families belonged to the elite or the popolo. During periods of cooperation between elite and popolo, many middle-rank families sought acceptance into the elite ranks through marriage alli-ances, business partnerships, and patronage relationships. Families regularly rose, in the perception of their fellow Florentines, from popolo to elite. The chief differences between elite and non-elite families, at least in the eyes of the elite (differences that even great wealth could not obliterate), were family size, a lineage's antiquity, and, in the thirteenth century, the cultural trappings of knighthood. Everyone recognized that the Bardi (magnates) and the Alberti (non-magnates) were both great elite families, and no one thought that Dino Compagni, even though he was a wealthy merchant, belonged to that class. But at any given moment there were families that hovered on the invisible boundary between the classes. The Girolami are a good example: a politically successful but relatively small family of woolen cloth manufacturers that first appeared in the late 1270s and early 1280s and sided with the popolo over the next two decades but went on to achieve a place among the second tier of Florence's notable families. Were they part of the lesser elite or the upper ranks of the popolo?

Because of the steady movement of families from the periphery of the elite into the circle of established families, some historians conclude that the popolo was not a class or even a movement representing the interests of definable segments of Florentine society. Some have gone so far as to see in the popolo only factions or splinter groups of the elite itself and thus to assert that politics in a city-state like Florence was limited to infighting for positions of supremacy within a defined circle of more or less established families. This is the view first systematically advanced by Nicola Ottokar in 1926 in an influential prosopographical study of the composition of the ruling class at the end of the thirteenth century, in which he criticized the class-conflict explanation of these same years advanced by Gaetano Salvemini in 1899, who had seen "magnates" and "popolani" as distinct classes with divergent economic interests: the magnates as a feudal class whose wealth was predominantly in land and the "popolani" as a commercial bourgeoisie.[1] But both historians used "popolani" to refer to upper-class non-magnate families. By this definition Ottokar was correct in arguing that the magnates were not a class and that their economic activities and interests were in many cases identical to those of leading "popolani." He and the many historians who followed his approach went on from there to deny any and all class conflicts, a view that reduces Florentine politics to mere quarrels within the upper class. Between an aristocratic ruling class on the one hand and the occasional eruption of the masses in the form of raw street power on the other, this approach to Florentine history sees nothing in between. What such approaches miss is precisely the popolo and the entire alternative political culture that it represented and promoted. At the center of this popular political culture were the ideas and assumptions associated with guild association and the kind of political community to which they gave rise.

Guilds

Thirteenth-century Italy witnessed an explosion of self-constituted associations: the spontaneous formation of societies and organizations for purposes that ranged from religious devotion (confraternities) to security (armed neighborhood companies) to resistance against the economic pressure of grasping bishops (rural communes)[2] to the protection of collective interests by practitioners of the same trade or business (guilds). These were not the exclusive property of the popolo, as elites also joined confraternities and guilds. But armed neighborhood companies, rural communes, and the great majority of

---

[1] N. Ottokar, *Il comune di Firenze alla fine del Dugento* (Florence, 1926; reprint edn. Turin, 1962); G. Salvemini, *Magnati e popolani in Firenze dal 1280 al 1295* (Florence, 1899; reprint edn. Milan, 1966); J.-C. Maire Vigueur, "Il problema storiografico: Firenze come modello (e mito) di regime popolare," in *Magnati e popolani nell'Italia comunale* (Pistoia, 1997), pp. 1–16.
[2] Dameron, *Episcopal Power*, pp. 93–140.

guilds emerged from the need to find collective strength in such associations by those who lacked powerful families. Throughout communal Italy the popolo depended chiefly on armed companies and guilds to advance its interests. Both forms of association appeared in Florence no later than the early thirteenth century and provided channels of political representation that brought the popolo into government. In the first popular government of 1250–60 the armed companies were the preferred avenue to power, but by the second half of the century, for reasons to be explored in the next chapter, the guilds became the popolo's central institutions.

In their guilds, merchants, manufacturers, shopkeepers, artisans, and notaries who did not come from powerful lineages found security, political strength, and cultural identity, much as elite Florentines looked for the same things in their families. In thirteenth-century Florence guilds proliferated, as scores of professional, merchant, trading, and artisan groups formed themselves into legal corporations, each with its own internal governance.[3] The creation of guilds did not depend on, and was neither encouraged nor obstructed by, the commune: they emerged from the assumed right of any professional collectivity to give itself legal organization on the basis of the voluntary oaths of its members. In the 1230s each Calimala merchant periodically renewed his promises, sworn on the gospels, to "acknowledge, observe, and implement everything that the consuls of the merchants of Calimala shall require of me within the terms of their office," never to defraud creditors, to observe and conduct themselves in accordance with the guild's statutes, and to advise the consuls "as best I know how" whenever requested.[4] The first rubric of the oldest surviving complete redaction of statutes of a Florentine guild, the 1296 constitution of the used-cloth dealers (Rigattieri), preserves their oath: "I who am or will be of this guild swear on the holy gospels to hear, give heed to, and observe any and all just and honorable commands and decrees" of the consuls and not to defraud creditors.[5]

Underlying the foundation of so many guilds was the increasing specialization of economic activities in Florence's burgeoning economy, a process that led, for example, to separate guilds for different branches of the textile industry, as manufacturers of woolen, silk, and linen cloth, retail cloth dealers, and used-cloth dealers all had their own guilds. The building trades also divided into

[3]   The classic work: A. Doren, *Das Florentiner Zunftwesen vom 14. bis zum 16. Jahrhundert* (1908, reprint edn. Aalen, 1969), trans. G. B. Klein, *Le arti fiorentine*, 2 vols. (Florence, 1940).
[4]   ASF, Manoscritti 542, n.p. Published in G. Gandi, *Le arti maggiori e minori in Firenze* (1929; reprint edn. Rome, 1971), p. 49, n. 1.
[5]   *Statuti dell'Arte dei Rigattieri e Linaioli di Firenze (1296–1340)*, ed. F. Sartini (Florence, 1940), p. 3.

different guilds, one for builders in wood and stone, a second for woodworkers and carpenters. The chance survival of documents does not permit a chronology of guild creation, only the dates at which their existence is first attested. The elite merchants of Calimala went back to at least the twelfth century; by 1202 the bankers and moneychangers had created a guild, and by 1212 the jurists and notaries and the manufacturers of woolen cloth had done so. By 1300, there is evidence of as many as seventy or eighty such associations in the city, and more beyond the walls. Even the handful of millstone makers in the little village of Montici just outside the city established a guild, complete with the two features that denoted a professional corporation's legal status: elected consuls and written statutes.[6] Economic expansion and specialization explain why so many trades were ready and able to form guilds. But their motivation in doing so was that guilds provided an answer to the dilemma of how trust could be established between parties to commercial transactions in a society that had grown too large to generate it through personal ties alone. Buyers of goods or services, investors, depositors, or parties to any contractual agreement needed guarantees concerning their purchases or the companies or banks in which they invested money. They needed recourse in the event that the person or company at the other end of the sale or deposit or contract produced shoddy goods, acted in bad faith, or failed to honor the terms of the agreement. This was especially necessary when economic transactions occurred across distances that made it impossible for the parties to know each other. In the absence of legal recourse (and sometimes concurrently with it, as a form of added pressure), foreign creditors pressing claims against a Florentine company often asked their own governments to declare reprisals against all Florentine merchants in their territory as a way of forcing either Florence's government or other Florentine merchants to render justice and compel the offending company to satisfy creditors. Reprisals meant confiscation of goods and possibly arrest, causing serious interruptions of trade and business even for merchants who had nothing to do with the dispute for which they had been declared, and their resolution could drag on in the courts for years.[7] To avoid reprisals, merchants and artisans created guilds and voluntarily submitted to their jurisdiction, giving them authority to hear and adjudicate claims from outside parties bringing civil actions against fraudulent or bankrupt members of the guild.

Guilds institutionalized the guarantee that merchants plying the same trade had the will and the means to establish standards for the exercise of

---

[6]   R. Davidsohn, *Forschungen zur Geschichte von Florenz*, 4 vols. (Berlin, 1896–1908) vol. 3, p. 232.
[7]   A. Del Vecchio and E. Casanova, *Le rappresaglie nei comuni medievali e specialmente in Firenze* (Bologna, 1894).

their profession, to oversee and regulate their members' activities, and to punish members who violated those standards or defrauded clients, customers, or depositors. The four, six, or eight elected consuls, sometimes assisted by a committee or council, functioned as a tribunal in civil and commercial cases. The consuls of the moneychangers' guild swore an oath "to govern [*regere*] the guild and all the moneychangers of the city and its territory who are bound to us by oath, for the common utility of the whole guild, in good faith and without fraud" or favoritisms. They also promised "to gather to render justice [*ad ius reddendum*] every Monday and Friday and any other days they wish."[8] The guild council, consisting of from a dozen to as many as several dozen members depending on the size of the guild, functioned as a legislative body that wrote the rules governing jurisdiction, the norms regulating the exercise of the profession, and the procedures for the election of consuls and other officers. Each guild had in effect a small-scale republican structure in which the authority exercised by consuls and councils was authorized by the guild's own membership. Such a self-governing structure was, in the language of medieval jurists, an *universitas*, a legally recognized association brought into being by the mutual promises and oaths of its members. The commune itself had long been recognized as an *universitas*, based on similar assumptions and principles. In the 1270s the term began to be used in connection with the guilds, including artisan guilds. As an *universitas*, a guild was a "fictive person" endowed with legal standing that could, like actual persons, assume obligations, bring and be subject to actions in court, own property, and be represented by one or more persons of its own designation. Just as private persons appointed procurators (or representatives) to act in their name, so an *universitas* could empower its consuls or any member to act on its behalf and assume obligations that were binding on all the members. Such designated representatives could act on the guild's behalf without the necessity of securing the approval of the members on each separate matter. Guilds thus embodied an early form of legal representation: the theory and practice by which one or more persons could legitimately act in the name of a larger group that had given those few the authority to do so. Each guild exercised judicial, punitive, executive, and legislative powers over its members and could do so because its consuls and councils were held to represent the will of those who voluntarily created the association. The theoretical and structural similarity of communes and guilds nourished the idea that guilds had a central role to play in communal government.

The normative values of guild association combined a broadly social dimension with more specifically political aspects. In both areas guilds represented

---

[8]   *Statuti dell'Arte del Cambio di Firenze (1299–1316)*, ed. G. C. Marri (Florence, 1955), pp. 3, 10.

answers to problems of social organization, discipline, civility, and later political and constitutional issues: answers that differed starkly in both principle and practice from those promoted by the elite. In the Tuscan vernacular guilds were "arti," and the word itself denoted norms and standards of professional discipline. "Arte" meant a skill that could be taught and learned, a collective discipline, enshrined in both custom and written rules, governing professional ethics. Guild statutes underscored the sanctity of contract and what were held to be the ancient "customs," or "usages of merchants," the *consuetudo* or *usus mercatorum*, which included resolution of disputes through law and impartial adjudication of rights. Guilds were not of course a paradise of mutuality and brotherhood; fissures and antagonisms, both personal and collective, were frequent. But in guilds the means employed for the resolution of conflicts were strikingly different from those used by the elite where the collective discipline of a lineage or faction depended on the patriarchal authority of strong and charismatic leaders and on hierarchical ties of patronage and obligation. A guild's authority to discipline was subscribed by the members themselves, codified in written statutes, and administered by the members as many of them took turns in the consular office. The political dimension of guild culture began with the elective and shared nature of executive-judicial authority that rotated among the members. Guildsmen elected their consuls and councils for terms of usually four or six months and were accustomed to the notion that positions of power were held briefly and that officeholders were accountable for their conduct. Consuls were obligated to the observance of statutes that could only be modified with the consent of the guild's legislative council. Thus their powers were delegated to them by the membership. Consent, representation, delegation, accountability, and the supremacy of written statutes were the fundamental political assumptions embedded in guilds. They made of the guild community a very different kind of political culture from that of the elite families.

The twenty-one officially recognized guilds included in the 1293 federation had a combined membership of about 8,000 members, or 28–30% of the city's adult males in an estimated population of 100,000. The seven major guilds had some 3,200 members (40% of the membership of the twenty-one guilds), several hundred of whom belonged to elite families. The large majority of major guildsmen and the approximately 4,800 artisans and shopkeepers of the other fourteen guilds constituted the popolo. In this period Florentines distinguished the five so-called "middle guilds" (butchers, shoemakers, smiths, builders and wallers, and used-cloth dealers), with a total membership of perhaps 3,000, from the nine "minor" guilds (retail sellers of wine; innkeepers; sellers of salt, oil and cheese; tanners and leather craftsmen; armorers; locksmiths, makers of iron tools, and coppersmiths; harness-makers; woodworkers and lumber merchants; and bakers) with a combined membership of about 1,800. This uneven distribution of population among the three sub-divisions of the guild federation reveals the relative weakness of the nine minor guilds. The popolo's chief strength rested with the non-elite members of the major guilds together with the large middle guilds. Indeed, the popular movement of the 1280s was initially limited to these twelve guilds (often called the "twelve major guilds"), to which the other nine guilds were added in a secondary role in 1293. Although the popolo within the top twelve guilds needed the support of the nine minor guilds, it was the former who led. From the beginning of its political ascendancy, the popolo was beset by a split between its upper ranks of merchants and textile manufacturers and the weaker constituency of artisans and shopkeepers. And beyond these were the various categories of workers, skilled and unskilled, who sought, mostly in vain, either membership in the established guilds or guilds of their own.

Many guilds were themselves alliances or federations of two or more distinct professional groups. This happened because the popolo decided to limit the number of guilds admitted to a political role to twelve in the 1280s and twenty-one in 1293. Excluded trades and professional groups looked for alliances with the established guilds. Some groups, like the shopkeepers (*merciai*) who sought entrance into the guild (Medici, Speziali, e Merciai) that had belonged to the doctors and importers of spices and specialty goods, or the silk merchants who allied with the retail cloth dealers in Por Santa Maria, achieved equal status with their guilds' other components. In other cases, they could achieve no more than subordinate status, subject to the guild's jurisdiction, but without equal access to the consulate or council. The circumstances of these subordinate categories varied from that of the painters in the guild of the Medici, Speziali, e Merciai, who had their own statutes and thus a position of modest independence under the umbrella of the guild's jurisdiction, to that of the dyers in the woolen cloth industry who gradually lost whatever collective rights they had as a recognized subdivision within the guild and became subject to its harsh regulatory and police powers without any representation in its political structure. Throughout the guild community these "minor branches," as they were called, existed in a great variety of political and legal relationships to the guilds' dominant professional groups, and such issues were regularly foci of contention and dispute. The Florentine guilds must not be seen through the lens of any romanticized view of medieval guilds as associations that blunted competition and conflict in peaceful brotherhood and affective mutuality. Conflicts of interest and power occurred within guilds, just as struggles among groups of guilds took place within both the federation and the commune. When challenging the elite in times of crisis, the guild community used the rhetoric and ideals of solidarity and equality, but within the guilds divisions and disputes regularly occurred among categories with divergent interests.

Culture and Education: Notaries

The prominence of the popolo depended in large part on its remarkable educational achievement. Here, as in many other north and central Italian cities, a veritable revolution in the history of education occurred. For the first time in European history, literacy spread significantly beyond the clerical establishment and elite classes to include more modest merchants, shopkeepers, artisans, and even some laborers. Literacy obviously means different things at each of these levels, but by 1300 the large majority of Florentine men and a sizable minority of women could read and write, at least in the vernacular, at basic levels of competence needed for keeping account books, religious devotions, and participation in their guilds and confraternities. A smaller number had formal training in Latin, first in the language and then in the study of classical authors, and some went on to careers as jurists or churchmen when they did not join the family business. The real revolution was that thousands of families below the level of the elite educated their children. At the primary level, education was not the task of public schools. Communal governments in some smaller cities hired teachers, but in Florence parents themselves engaged the services of private tutors or sent their children to large classes organized by the more enterprising of these teachers. Since teachers had no guild and were not employed by the government, no systematic records of their employment, names, or numbers survive. But the names and contracts that have come to light reveal that many teachers were notaries, others clerics, and still others men and women with no other known profession.

Giovanni Villani gives extraordinary figures on the number of students at each level of schooling in Florence in the 1330s (12.94). In a population that he estimated at 90,000, he says that boys and girls between the ages of six and eleven learning basic literacy skills numbered between 8,000 and 10,000. If children between these ages were approximately the same 14.75% of the total population as in 1480,[9] 9,000 pupils would mean that 68% of boys and girls attended school (and 10,000 pupils would have been 75%). That Villani's figures are at least plausible is confirmed by the fact that a century later 80% of household heads submitted fiscal declarations written in their own hands.[10] The ability to read and write in the vernacular was universal in the guild community and extended to large numbers of non-guild artisans, women, and workers. Among the possessions of a dyer in 1420 were "a book of Dante,

[9]   A. Molho, *Marriage Alliance in Late Medieval Florence* (Cambridge, Mass. 1994), pp. 411–15, appendix 4.
[10]   R. Black, "Education and the Emergence of a Literate Society," in *Italy in the Age of the Renaissance, 1300–1550*, ed. J. M. Najemy (Oxford, 2004), pp. 18–36.

a book of Cecco d'Ascoli, and a book of the Epistles of Ovid," all in the vernacular.[11] Students who completed this primary schooling were able to read vernacular texts and had the rudiments for the serious study of Latin. Secondary education came in two forms, both seemingly limited to boys. Parents chose between abacus school, which taught commercial arithmetic and provided training in skills essential to merchants and shopkeepers, and "grammar" school, which taught Latin and classical authors. According to Villani, between 1,000 and 1,200 boys were enrolled in six abacus schools, and another 550–600 studied Latin and logic in four "large schools."[12] The expansion of education and literacy had practical causes and purposes in a society in which middle- and even lower-class laypersons kept account books, wrote letters, read guild statutes, signed and needed to understand contracts, and read their prayers. A 1313 contract between a teacher and a parent specified that the tutor should teach his student "in such a way that he can read and write all letters and accounts and be well trained to take his place in the shops of guildsmen."[13] Expanding literacy was an expression of the size and vitality of the guild community and thus also of the needs of a burgeoning urban economy and of the thousands of Florentines who either ran their own businesses and shops or worked under contract with a textile manufacturer and needed literacy to manage their financial affairs.

Particularly important is the prominence of notaries among Florentine teachers (at the secondary more than the primary level), for it was through them that Roman politics, history, law, rhetoric, and moral philosophy became the bedrock of the education and culture of the popolo.[14] The culture of the popolo is rightly thought of as mercantile, but it was no less a culture of notaries and of their characteristic skills, habits of mind, and intellectual points of reference. Their influence came partly from their numbers. In 1280 the guild they shared with the jurists included 65 of the latter, 374 notaries in the city, and another 204 in the contado. By 1338 the number of jurists had not changed (66), but the notaries (no longer distinguished between city and contado) had increased to 880. They were also a powerful force for cultural integration between city and countryside, since many were either immigrants

---

[11]   F. Franceschi, *Oltre il "Tumulto": i lavoratori fiorentini dell'Arte della Lana fra Tre e Quattrocento* (Florence, 1993), p. 289n.

[12]   P. Grendler, *Schooling in Renaissance Italy: Literacy and Learning, 1300–1600* (Baltimore, 1989); C. Davis, "Education in Dante's Florence," in Davis, *Dante's Italy and Other Essays* (Philadelphia, 1984), pp. 137–65.

[13]   R. G. Witt, "What Did Giovannino Read and Write? Literacy in Early Renaissance Florence," *I Tatti Studies* 6 (1995): 83–114 (104), my translation.

[14]   P. Gehl, *A Moral Art: Grammar, Society, and Culture in Trecento Florence* (Ithaca, N.Y., 1993), pp. 204–11.

from the contado or had recent family origins there. A famous example is Petrarch's father ser Petracco, a notary from Incisa in the upper Valdarno. Notaries were professional writers of contracts, wills, and a wide variety of legal documents. Some set up private practices in which they drafted documents for sales of land, business partnerships, marriage and dowry agreements, and testaments for a variety of clients in their neighborhoods or towns. Others worked full-time for an institution: hospitals, guilds, confraternities, and ecclesiastical entities. And still others were employed by communal governments as official letter-writers (and as such were the precursors of the humanist chancellors of the fifteenth century), as redactors of the final form of legislation passed by the communal councils, or as keepers of official records in any number of government offices and committees. And many supplemented their income as teachers. Their training in Roman law provided the solid command of Latin and a basic expertise in law that enabled them to write official documents with the proper formulas and language. In order to ensure the quality of their work, the guild tested notaries in "gramatica [Latin], scriptura et contractibus."

In the decades around 1300, many notaries translated into Tuscan both ancient Latin and contemporary French texts.[15] Andrea Lancia (c.1280–1356), best known as the author of an important commentary on Dante's *Comedy*, translated Ovid's *Ars amandi* and *Remedia amoris*, Seneca's letters, and Virgil's *Aeneid*. Bono Giamboni rendered Orosius and the military theorist Vegetius into Tuscan. Filippo Ceffi translated Ovid's *Heroides* (and also compiled the influential *Dicerie da imparare a dire a huomini giovani e rozzi*, a handbook on how to teach young rustics to speak properly). Domenico di Bandino, born in Arezzo but resident in Florence for many years, wrote an encyclopedia based on wide reading in Roman historians and moralists. Alberto della Piagentina translated Boethius's *Consolation of Philosophy* into Tuscan. Zucchero Bencivenni translated medical treatises from French. About some we know only that they owned important, often ancient, literary works. Giorgio di Bastiano owned a copy of Domenico Cavalca's Tuscan translation of Pope Gregory the Great's *Dialogues*. A manuscript of the minor works of Seneca containing marginal notations by the notary Giovanni Cambini tells us that, in addition to owning it, he also read it with some care. The vogue of translation of Roman historical works extended beyond notaries: Bartolomeo da San Concordio, a Pisan Dominican who lived in Florence translated Sallust's *Conspiracy of Catiline* and his *Jugurthine War*; and an unknown writer (some think it might have been the young Boccaccio) translated Livy's *History of Rome*.

[15]   R. G. Witt, *In the Footsteps of the Ancients: The Origins of Humanism from Lovato to Bruni* (Boston, 2003), chap. 5 ("Florence and Vernacular Learning"), pp. 174–229.

Notaries also composed original works that reflected their wide culture.[16] Francesco da Barberino (1264–1348), also a jurist, wrote several didactic poems, including the *Documenti d'amore* and the *Reggimenti e costumi di donne* on the proper upbringing of girls and norms of conduct for women at different stages of life. His poetry displays a broad familiarity with the works of pagan and Christian antiquity and is grounded in the educability of citizens around Aristotelian notions of moderation. Other notaries were drawn to writing history. Giovanni di Lemmo da Comugnori wrote a chronicle of Florentine history from 1299 to 1320, as did the better known ser Naddo di ser Nepo da Montecatini later in the century. And then there is the very early example of ser Garzo dell'Incisa (d. 1280), who composed *laude* (devotional songs sung in confraternities) and assembled the oldest extant collection of vernacular proverbs. Ser Garzo evidently transmitted his literary interests, humble as they were, to his son Parenzo, and the latter in turn to his son Petracco, who is known to have possessed manuscripts of works of Virgil and Cicero, as we know from Petracco's son Francesco, who modified his patronymic to the more elegant sounding Petrarca. The three generations of notaries interested in literature and antiquity in Petrarch's family background tell us much about the importance of the culture of notaries in the emergence of humanism.

With Roman law as the foundation of their professional expertise, some notaries developed a deep interest in classical antiquity, literature, and history. Certainly the most important of these is Brunetto Latini, chancellor of the first popular government of 1250–60, a political exile for the next half-dozen Ghibelline years, and thereafter one of the central figures of Florentine culture until his death in 1295. Latini focused on the rhetorical and political dimension of Roman culture, especially Cicero's notion of rhetoric as a civilizing force and as central to a virtuous political life. He perceived Cicero less as the contemplative philosopher he had seemed to earlier readers, and more as a citizen-statesman who employed eloquence to protect the liberty of his republic from would-be tyrants. His translations included a portion of Cicero's rhetorical treatise *De inventione* and several of the orations. The encyclopedic *Tresor*[17] that Latini wrote in French during the exile (and which was soon translated into Tuscan, perhaps by Latini himself) is built on the twin pillars of Aristotelian political ethics (mostly from the *Ethics*, not the *Politics*, which was just then receiving its first Latin translation) and Ciceronian ideas of

---

[16] See *Il notaio nella civiltà fiorentina, secoli XIII–XVI* (Florence, 1984), pp. 107–50.
[17] *Li livres dou Tresor*, ed. F. J. Carmody (Berkeley, 1948); trans. P. Barrette and S. Baldwin, *The Book of the Treasure* (New York, 1993).

citizenship and social duty.[18] From Aristotle and Cicero he drew, and constantly promoted, the ethical values of citizenship, the superiority (for the Italian cities at least) of government by citizens themselves, the notion that virtue was enhanced by civic duty, and a view of education as the training of citizens not only for their occasional office in government but also for the sake of a peaceful society grounded in justice. Latini adopted the Aristotelian ideal of moderation as the goal of the virtuous citizen who faithfully plies his trade or profession, lives without excess, and seeks justice and fairness in his business dealings. With unmistakable allusions to the popolo's organization in its "arti," Latini wrote in the *Tresor* that "politics includes, and teaches us, all the arts [*ars*] necessary to the community of men." Citizens should follow the nature of their trades and strive to maintain the middle ground in their "art" and live according to "justice," which is "halfway between gaining and losing and cannot exist without giving and taking and exchanging." For Latini, justice, the central concept in the popolo's political language, thus emerges from just business dealings among artisans and merchants; ideal citizens are those formed by their trades. Latini's ethico-political views applied his reading of Aristotle and Cicero to the experience of the popolo in its guilds.[19]

No one more than Brunetto Latini was responsible for making Roman history and rhetoric central to the popolo's culture. Although Dante condemned him to Hell in his great poem for a sin that is still disputed (the traditional interpretation focuses on sodomy, but intriguing arguments have been made for religious heterodoxy and for his republican rejection of imperial over-lordship[20]), he nonetheless paid tribute to Latini in canto 15 of *Inferno* as the teacher who taught him "how man makes himself eternal," an ambiguous phrase that may refer to the secular and political nature of the studies promoted by Latini and thus the effort, seen by the mature Dante as misguided, to affirm universal values in the earthly city. Villani similarly paid honor to Latini when he reported his death and called him "a great philosopher and excellent teacher of rhetoric" who "expounded the *Rhetoric* of Cicero and wrote the good and useful book called the *Tresor* and many other books on philosophy and on the vices and the virtues" (9.10). Villani summed

---

[18] Witt, *Footsteps*, pp. 182–5, 201–10; Holmes, *Florence, Rome*, pp. 71–88; Davis, "Brunetto Latini and Dante," in Davis, *Dante's Italy*, pp. 166–97; Q. Skinner, "Ambrogio Lorenzetti: The Artist as Political Philosopher," *Proceedings of the British Academy* 72 (1986): 1–56 (15–17).

[19] J. M. Najemy, "Brunetto Latini's Politica," *Dante Studies* 112 (1994): 33–51.

[20] P. Armour, "Dante's Brunetto: the Paternal Paterine," *Italian Studies* 38 (1983): 1–38; R. Kay, *Dante's Swift and Strong: Essays on "Inferno" XV* (Lawrence, Kans., 1978).

up his appreciation of Latini by saying that he was "the one who began to teach the Florentines to be less coarse, to make them capable of speaking well and knowing how to guide and rule our republic according to the art of politics [*secondo la politica*]." These were the foundations of the popolo's culture: moral philosophy, especially that of the Romans; rhetoric as the foundation of ethics and society; and the union of public speech, civic duty, and a politics of justice. The kind of poetry accepted into this vision of education tended to be mostly didactic. In the Tuscan poem he called the *Tesoretto*,[21] Latini imagines a courtly encounter between a knight and four ladies representing the virtues as a lesson on good conduct that underscores the necessity of a general re-education of the elite according to the popolo's values of moderation and civility. The personified virtues teach the knight to moderate his behavior, to avoid erotic excesses and gambling, to take part in the political life of his commune, to shun vendettas whenever possible and instead to resolve his disputes through law and lawyers. Latini was the chief voice of the thirteenth-century popolo's vision of urban society as a community grounded in law and justice, and of its determination to bring the city's unruly elite to an acceptance of such ideas.

Religion

The culture of the popolo was deeply influenced by the turbulent religious currents of the thirteenth century: heresies, the rise of the mendicant orders, and the emergence of the laity as a creative agent in religious life.[22] Defense of orthodoxy and the church became characteristic of the popolo's religion, and rhetoric against heresy a part of its critique of elite politics. For example, in October 1300, just a few months after the government, still under the influence of the popolo, banished leading members of the Black and White factions in an attempt to contain their spreading violence, the councils passed a law reaffirming the commune's determination to give the papal inquisition full support in its fight against heresy. Responding to the wishes of the cardinal legate Matthew of Acquasparta, who had come to Florence to mediate between the factions and urge a tougher policy against heresy, the government declared that the "city, commune, and *popolo* of Florence, and especially those persons by whom the Florentine *popolo* and commune are at present being governed, have always and consistently been devoted with pure hearts to the Guelf party

---

[21]   *Il Tesoretto*, ed. M. Ciccuto (Milan, 1985); trans. J. B. Holloway, *Il Tesoretto (The Little Treasure)* (New York, 1981).
[22]   An up-to-date overview: G. Dameron, *Florence and Its Church in the Age of Dante* (Philadelphia, 2005), pp. 164–216.

and to Holy Church, and have not only protected but indeed increased and amplified the liberties of the church whenever necessary, especially for the preservation of the faith and the suppression and extirpation of its enemies, the Patarine heretics and their supporters."[23] In fact, only small segments of the upper class had ever been touched by heretical ideas, but the memory of this threat to Catholic orthodoxy left a sense of urgency about the defense of the faith that the popolo made its own and added to its arsenal of political weapons against the elite.

Fundamental to the religious culture of the popolo was its symbiotic relationship to the mendicants and the creation of confraternal associations whose earliest examples were inspired by the mendicant defense of orthodoxy. By the 1220s the Franciscans and Dominicans were established at opposite ends of the city, respectively at Santa Croce and Santa Maria Novella, where they later constructed the enormous basilicas that still dominate their neighborhoods. Other mendicant orders became established in the 1250s and 1260s: the Augustinians at Santo Spirito, Servites at Santissima Annunziata, Umiliati at Ognissanti, Friars of the Sack at Sant'Egidio, and Carmelites at Santa Maria del Carmine. Mendicant churches were all located either outside the walls of the 1170s or in the Oltrarno section, the neighborhoods in which immigrants from the contado were settling in large numbers. The friars were popular among immigrants in need of the community and social services that the new orders provided or supported: care for the sick, alms for the poor, lodging for travelers, honorable burials, but also preaching and organized devotion. Some Florentines joined the orders, but many more from all over the city imitated the forms and aims of mendicant piety in lay society: social commitment, expressed through practical attention to the needs and problems of urban society, pastoral work in the world, the sanctification of everyday life, renunciation of ostentatious wealth, and, in all these respects, the imitation of Christ.

Because Florentine families at this time were reluctant to see their daughters renounce marriage, the number of women who joined the second Franciscan order of Clarisses, named for its founder and Francis's collaborator Clare, was limited. More popular was the non-clerical Order of Penitents, consisting of laypersons, many from the middle orders of society, who wore a religious habit but continued to live at home with their families and to practice their professions. In a sense, the Penitents were the mendicants' representatives in lay society. They typically accepted the ownership of property forbidden to the friars and administered hospices for travelers and hospitals for the sick and poor, including the Hospital of San Paolo near Santa Maria Novella, which became one of the city's largest. At the end of the thirteenth century they divided over the question of how much autonomy their association should

[23] ASF, Provvisioni, Registri, 10, f. 280.

have from ecclesiastical authorities, and some moved into the third orders of lay brothers and sisters who were more closely supervised by their respective orders. Tertiaries wore a religious habit and observed an austere mode of life governed by a formal rule but were not required to renounce marriage or lay society. Never particularly numerous in Florence, tertiaries usually came from socially elevated families and often left bequests to support hospitals and hospices for the poor.[24]

It was above all in confraternities that Florentines, especially of middle social standing, expressed their enthusiasm for religious association modeled on the mendicants.[25] Confraternities were formal voluntary associations of lay-persons governed by statutes and elected officers, and in this respect they were like guilds. But in Florence, unlike Venice, there was always a clear distinction between guilds, which exercised jurisdiction over professional groups, and confraternities, which did not and in most cases were not organized by profession. Confraternity members met regularly for prayer, penitence, philanthropy, or the singing of vernacular religious songs. From perhaps no more than a handful in the mid-thirteenth century, they multiplied rapidly: at least eighteen were founded before 1300, forty-three by 1348, and sixty-eight by 1400. Many confraternities were located near or in mendicant churches in neighborhoods where contado immigrants concentrated and were founded by, or in some connection with, these new arrivals from the countryside, who seem to have brought with them a vital aspect of the religious culture of the contado, where an astounding 180 confraternities have been counted before 1400.[26]

Earliest among Florentine confraternities were the laudesi companies whose chief purpose was the singing of hymns to the Virgin. The centrality of Marian devotions in their activities signals their link to the campaign conducted by the Dominicans, and slightly later by the Franciscans as well, against the Cathars, who denied that Mary had given birth to a divine being. Among the confraternities founded in the 1240s during the high tide of mendicant anti-Catharism were those of the Vergine Maria delle Laude at Santa Croce and San Pier Martire e Laude della Vergine Maria at Santa Maria Novella; they were followed by laudesi confraternities at the Carmine in 1249, San

---

[24]   A. Benvenuti Papi, "Fonti e problemi per la storia dei penitenti a Firenze nel secolo XIII," in *L'ordine della penitenza di San Francesco d'Assisi nel secolo XIII* (Rome, 1973), pp. 279–301.

[25]   For what follows: J. Henderson, *Piety and Charity in Late Medieval Florence* (Oxford, 1994); and M. D. Papi, "Confraternite ed ordini mendicanti a Firenze: aspetti di una ricerca quantitativa," *Mélanges de l'École française de Rome* 89 (1977): 597–608.

[26]   C. M. de la Roncière, *Religion paysanne et religion urbaine en Toscane (c.1250–c.1450)* (Hampshire, 1994).

Marco in 1250, Santissima Annunziata in 1263, San Felice in Piazza in 1277, Sant'Egidio in 1278, the cathedral of Santa Reparata in 1281, Santa Trinita in 1300, and Ognissanti in 1336. So important was hymn-singing that at least two of them established schools for lay singers. Over several generations hundreds, perhaps thousands, of Florentines must have received at least a rudimentary education in the fundamentals of vocal music. Something of the social significance of these confraternities emerges from the memorable character Boccaccio created in *Decameron* 7.1, Gianni Lotteringhi, a member of a laudesi company with ties so close to the Dominicans that he was "appointed frequently to the post of captain of the *laudesi* of Santa Maria Novella, with the task of supervising the school [of lay singers] and performing other little duties" in the confraternity. Gianni is easily duped by his wife because devotion to his confraternal duties caused him to stay away from home and not pay enough attention to her. Boccaccio was satirizing the conventional religiosity of ordinary Florentines, but it is precisely in its conventionality that the portrait rings true. Gianni is a fictional representation of the new men who made some money but came from undistinguished families: he was a *stamaiuolo*, an independent agent in the textile industry who bought combed wool and hired women spinners to whom he paid low piece-rates for turning the wool into yarn that he then sold to the producers of woolen cloths. He was wealthy enough to buy a summerhouse in the country, where his wife regularly met her lover, while he was occupied in town with his business and his confraternity in which his role "made him feel much more important." In return for frequent donations and gifts, the friars "taught him a few good prayers," and "other bits of silliness, which he held dear and stored away most diligently for the salvation of his soul." In Boccaccio's character we see the combination of social and spiritual motives that led Florentines to join confraternities in large numbers, especially those elements of the popolo in search of communities that could give them a sense of self-esteem and a social prominence they otherwise lacked.

Confraternities provided community, solidarity, and social services for artisans and women. The dyers of the quarter of Santa Croce founded a confraternity in 1280, Sant'Onofrio dei Tintori, which began building a hospital in 1339. Another religious company of artisans, San Giovanni Decollato dei Portatori di Norcia, was founded in 1297 and ran a hospice for travelers, and perhaps immigrants, near the northern gate of the city in via San Gallo. The fact that the two earliest known artisan confraternities (and it is likely that there were more) both administered social services suggests that such associations typically attended to the practical needs of both members and non-members as they cemented their own sense of social solidarity through common prayer and worship. The Wool guild always feared the possibility that confraternities of artisans within the industry might result in organized challenges to the domination of the merchant-entrepreneurs, and in 1317 it excluded artisans from one such confraternity at San Marco. Less threatening was the Compagnia di San Luca formed by the painters in 1339. The existence of a religious company of women at San Lorenzo in 1303 and another founded in 1365 at Santa Maria Novella suggests that there may have been others that provided women with religious and social community. Flagellant confraternities, which emphasized penitence and the imitation of the suffering Christ, did not become popular in Florence until the mid-fourteenth century. Only three have been discovered before the 1330s, when three more were founded in quick succession. Following the great plague of 1348, and perhaps in part because of its terrors, flagellant confraternities became more numerous: eight more by 1390, and in 1399 alone, the year of the outbreak of religious enthusiasm associated with processions of penitents dressed in white and hence called the Bianchi, no fewer than seven flagellant companies were founded in Florence.

Still other confraternities specialized in charitable activities; some assisted their members with occasional financial help and burials, while others distributed alms to the poor, supported and administered hospitals and schools, and provided assistance to widows, foundlings, and prostitutes. Among the most prominent of the early charitable confraternities were the Bigallo, founded no later than the 1240s, which ran a number of small hospitals in the contado; the Misericordia, which administered bequests to the poor; and Orsanmichele, founded in 1291 as a laudesi company and soon a magnet for pious bequests owing to the popularity of the cult that grew up around an allegedly miracle-working image of the Virgin on an internal pillar of the loggia of the communal grain market. At first the grain merchants and purchasers supported the cult, but it became so popular that the confraternity was soon making a great deal of money from the sale of candles to worshippers, and, as the membership grew (estimated at between two and three thousand), from their dues and contributions as well. Orsanmichele attracted the devotions of Florentines of all classes and the charitable inclinations of both elite and popolo (Dino Compagni was a member). Its expanding wealth made Orsanmichele the principal vehicle in the fourteenth century for the distribution of alms to Florence's poor. By the 1330s the company's annual income was in excess of 10,000 lire, and in 1329 the commune entrusted Orsanmichele with the distribution of the 2,000 lire that the government gave each year to the poor. Orsanmichele eventually became in effect an agency of government, especially after the huge bequests that came to it in the aftermath of the 1348 plague, but originally it was one of many private associations created largely by the popolo for a combination of social and religious purposes.

From the combined philanthropy of religious orders and confraternities and the charitable initiatives of private individuals, early fourteenth-century Florence could boast an extensive network of social services. Villani counted no fewer than thirty hospitals and hospices with a total of a thousand beds for "the poor and the infirm," including Santa Maria Nuova, founded in 1288 by Folco Portinari, father of Dante's Beatrice. But most hospitals emerged from the collective efforts and donations of thousands of Florentines who joined confraternities or para-ecclesiastical groups like the Order of Penitents. The religion of the popolo had its doctrinal side in the fight against heresy, and its devotional side in the singing of *laude* and in cults like that of the Orsanmichele Madonna. But for the popolo these purposes flowed naturally and obviously into the provision of social services and aid to the poor. It was here that the popolo's religious life most revealed the impact of the mendicants who promoted the notion that holiness and religious merit could be acquired by laypersons, married or not, in all walks of life, and in any professional status, through actions that responded to the earthly needs of one's fellows citizens and thus through the virtue of "caritas." One did not need to be a monk removed from society or shrouded in contemplation in order to obtain God's favor.

In their preaching as in their religious associations and social services, the mendicants displayed the same symbiotic relationship with the popolo.[27] Franciscans and Dominicans attracted large crowds from all social levels to their public sermons. Preachers from both orders regularly addressed the concerns and dilemmas of an urban laity wrestling with the moral implications of rapidly and unevenly accumulating wealth, of changing economic practices and attitudes, and of social mobility and political tensions. But it would be one-sided to imagine this only as the influence of preachers on the laity. In many respects, above all in the choice of themes, preachers felt the influence of the laity, who, like most audiences, voted with their feet. Had they not found the real and pressing issues of their lives addressed in these sermons, they would not have attended in such numbers. And in this sense the mendicants (in Florence and elsewhere) received the imprint of the popolo as much as the popolo did that of the orders. This can be seen especially in the writings and sermons of Remigio de' Girolami, whose two treatises on civic peace, *De bono communi* and *De bono pacis*, probably emerged from sermons he gave to the Florentines on the evils of factionalism and the necessity of suppressing individual ambition in favor of the common good. Remigio constantly urged the Florentines to compose their differences and embrace peace. Despite his intellectual training in the Aristotelianism that dominated Dominican education at Paris, Remigio pointed to the heroes of ancient Rome as models of virtuous and selfless citizenship, quoting and praising Cicero as a patriotic citizen who exemplified the true nobility that is attained through virtue, not

---

[27] Dameron, *Florence and Its Church*, pp. 207–11.

by birth. In one of his sermons he told the Florentines that God had given them seven special gifts: "abundance of money, a noble coinage, abundance of population, a civilized way of life, the wool industry, skill in the production of armaments, and a vigorous building activity in the contado."[28] This perception of Florentine achievements is entirely from the discourse of the popolo: the production, rather than the conspicuous consumption, of wealth; the gold florin, first minted in 1252 by the first popular government; population growth, mainly through immigration from the countryside; and the productivity of the woolen cloth industry in which the popolo was much involved. But nowhere more than in his praise for the "civilized way of life" (*civilitas vivendi*) does Remigio reflect the ideology of the popolo and its attempts to domesticate the elite and make it conform to civic and civilized norms of collective existence. He also underscores the dangers of misuse or abuse of these gifts, suggesting that the proper exercise of worldly and secular activities, including the production and accumulation of wealth, will meet with God's favor. It amounted in effect to a benediction of urban society as defined by the popolo.[29]

No Franciscan sermons have survived from this time, but from the writings of those who taught at Santa Croce it is clear that the Franciscan impact on the Florentine popolo was inseparable from the great dispute within the order over the literal observance of the prohibition against owning property. The Spirituals insisted on strict poverty and rejected the legal arrangements by which the so-called Conventuals used property without owning it. Two of the most influential intellectual leaders of the Spirituals, Pierre Jean Olivi and Ubertino da Casale, were lectors at Santa Croce in the 1280s, and their teaching (and possibly preaching) on the question of poverty conveyed to many Florentines, perhaps Dante among them,[30] their sustained and harsh critique of the church's wealth and worldliness and of the openly political ambitions of its popes. Whether or not directly influenced by the Spirituals, the Florentine popolo maintained a consistent opposition to papal interference in the affairs of the city, as the anti-ecclesiastical legislation of later popular governments makes clear. In the meantime, the Spirituals found much sympathy in Florence and Tuscany. Even after being declared heretics by Pope John XXII in the 1320s and driven underground by the Inquisition, they survived and re-emerged in the years of the papal–Florentine war of 1375–8.

---

[28]   C. Davis, "An Early Florentine Political Theorist: Fra Remigio de' Girolami," in Davis, *Dante's Italy*, pp. 198–223 (206).

[29]   Remigio's treatises and selections from the sermons in M. C. De Matteis, *La "teologia politica comunale" di Remigio de' Girolami* (Bologna, 1977); see also T. Rupp, "Damnation, Individual, and Community in Remigio dei Girolami's *De Bono Communi*," *History of Political Thought* 21 (2000): 217–36.

[30]   C. Davis, "Poverty and Eschatology in the Commedia," in Davis, *Dante's Italy*, pp. 42–70.

Critique of Elite Misrule

Nearly all thirteenth- and fourteenth-century Florentine writers on politics and history came from the popolo. Latini, the anonymous chronicler sometimes called pseudo-Brunetto, Compagni, Dante, Giovanni Villani, and later his brother Matteo, and Marchionne di Coppo Stefani were all major guildsmen, but from the non-elite ranks. Several had close ties of marriage or business with the elite. Compagni's mother was a daughter of Manetto Scali. Giovanni Villani was a business partner of, successively, the Peruzzi, Buonaccorsi, and Bardi. Dante's mother was from the Ghibelline family of the Abati, and he himself married Gemma Donati, a distant cousin of Corso. As we know from his imaginary encounter with Cacciaguida, Dante liked to think he descended from a family of knights and noble crusaders, but in fact his father was a moneylender with no significant part in political life. Some Alighieri held office in the popular government of 1250–60, but thereafter they make only sporadic appearances in the councils until 1300 when Dante became the first and only member of his family to sit on the priorate. Despite his denunciation of the popolo for excessive political ambition (*Purgatorio* 6) and his contempt for new wealth (the "subiti guadagni" of *Inferno* 16) and contado immigrants (*Paradiso* 16), Dante expressed many of the same criticisms of the elite that we find in other writers, who all excoriated the elite for its factionalism and overweening ambition.

In addition to implying, in the *Tesoretto*, that Florence's knightly upper class sorely needed lessons in civility and moderation, in the *Tresor* (2.114) Brunetto Latini rejected the elite's claim to nobility and political hegemony. Denying that nobility was dependent on birth, antiquity of lineage, or wealth, he argued that "those who delight in a noble lineage and boast of lofty ancestors, unless they themselves perform virtuous deeds, do not realize that they are disgraced rather than honored by the fame of their forebears. For when Catiline conspired secretly at Rome, he did nothing but evil, and when he spoke before the senators of the uprightness of his father and the nobility of his line and the good it had brought to the city of Rome, he certainly spoke more to his shame than to his honor. . . . But concerning true nobility, Horace says that it is virtue alone." Elsewhere (2.54) he exhorted would-be "nobles" to "perform always, therefore, acts of virtue." "A man is called noble on account of his noble and virtuous deeds . . . , not because of his ancestors." Dante adopted this critique of the elite's pretensions to nobility when he wrote in the *Convivio* (4.29) of "those who, because they are of famous and ancient lineage and are descended from excellent fathers, believe that they are noble, but have no nobility in themselves."[31]

---

[31] Davis, *Dante's Italy*, pp. 180–6.

The condemnation of factionalism was universal among these writers. Remigio denounced the factions from his pulpit at Santa Maria Novella and in his political tracts. The conflict between Black and White Guelfs seemed to him by far the worst division the city had ever known: "there was never so much disjunction or clash of wills between Ghibellines and Guelfs or between people and nobles as is now seen to exist between Blacks and Whites."[32] He criticized both factions for moral deficiencies and failure to embrace justice and the common good, a concept he identified with the "good of the commune," thus affirming the priority of the commune's welfare over that of any individual, family, or group. In the *Cronica fiorentina* once attributed to Brunetto Latini, the legendary episode that culminates in the Buondelmonti murder functions as a kind of fall from grace that forever dooms the elite families to fratricidal madness. The later violence between the Donati and Cerchi generated "much evil to the shame of the city and its citizens; for all the *grandi* and *popolari* of the city took sides, thus reviving the ancient hatreds of the Uberti and the Buondelmonti, whence all Italy has shed blood."[33]

Giovanni Villani had a more ambivalent view of the elite families that reflected the shifting political tendencies of the popolo. In times of peace and prosperity, he praised the wisdom of the elite leaders, including his business partners. But when elite factions threw everything into turmoil, he did not hesitate to condemn their failings. In describing the outbreak of the fighting between Black and White Guelfs in 1300, he noted that Florence had never been in a happier or more prosperous state, owing both to the "nobility of its fair knights," and its "brave *popolo*" (9.39). But "the sin of ingratitude, aided by the enemy of humankind [the devil], engendered arrogant corruption from such prosperity, on account of which the good and happy times ended for the Florentines." Against the background of this overarching drama of moral failure, Villani recounts the hatred that developed between Donati and Cerchi because of "envy" and "boorish ingratitude." Despite their power, wealth, and excellent marriage connections, the Cerchi "were uncivilized and ungrateful, as are those who rise in a short time to prestige and power." The Donati "were gentlemen and warriors, not especially rich, but were called Malefami": people of ill repute. When the Guelf party tried to put a stop to the brewing hatred and asked Pope Boniface VIII to persuade Vieri de' Cerchi to make peace with Corso Donati, Villani reports that Cerchi, "who in other matters was a wise knight, in this one was not very wise and too stubborn and hot tempered," and that he rejected the pope's mediation," thus making another enemy in the pope. The subsequent eruption of violence between armed bands of the two factions was the spark that lit the fuse: "And this was the beginning

---

[32]   Ibid., p. 207.
[33]   *Cronica fiorentina*, ed. A. Schiaffini, in *Testi fiorentini*, p. 148.

of the scandal and division of our city of Florence and the Guelf party, whence many evils and dangers soon followed. . . . And just as the death of messer Buondelmonte was the beginning of the Guelf and Ghibelline parties, so this was the beginning of the great ruin of the Guelf party and of our city." Villani saw the failures of the elite families as ones of character and judgment, moral lapses produced either by enervating prosperity, by a too recent and too sudden rise to power and wealth that could not wipe away boorishness and irascibility, or as the work of the ever-present "enemy of humankind." He was too close to the elite to see its violence as structural and systemic.

The great voice of the early fourteenth-century popolo, more embattled and more bitterly critical of the elite, was Dino Compagni. A merchant and member of the guild of Por Santa Maria, Compagni was for twenty years a leader of the popular movement. His political life came to an end with the victory of the Black Guelfs in 1301–2, and he watched in disgust as even the triumphant Blacks split into new factions and kept the city in a state of semi-permanent violence for another decade. In his dramatic account of the rise and fall of the popular government of the 1290s and the subsequent eruption of the elite's factional wars, Compagni organized the narrative with a precise selection of details to highlight his conviction that popular government was the only viable obstacle to the violence of the elite, against whose arrogance and abuse of power the chronicle conducts a fierce and sustained polemic. Compagni's knowledge of history and the rhetorical arts is visible in the work's literary sophistication, clearly influenced by classical models, particularly Sallust. He addresses his protagonists and introduces speeches in direct discourse, including his own, to dramatic effect. In Compagni we see especially well exemplified the political and cultural elements typical of the popolo: the intensity of his commitment to the popular cause; the devastating critique of the elite; and the assumption that effective political action is grounded in persuasive speech and thus in the rhetorical arts whose best models were found in Roman oratory and history.[34]

Unlike Villani's exclusive emphasis on the elite's moral failings, Compagni adds the perspective of how elite family structures conditioned their political behavior. He too juxtaposes the Buondelmonti murder and the war between Blacks and Whites, but he does so to support a more complex argument. After summarizing the Buondelmonti episode (1.2), Compagni jumps to the 1280s and the movement that produced the popular government whose fall was the beginning of the disastrous slide back toward elite factionalism and violence. A key moment of this regression includes a broken marriage alliance, whose

---

[34]   G. Pirodda, "Per una lettura della *Cronica* di Dino Compagni," *Filologia e letteratura* 52 (1967): 337–93; D. Moro, *Fonti e autonomia di stile nella Cronica del Compagni* (Galatina, 1971).

inclusion in the narrative is clearly intended to evoke for the reader the analogous moment in the Buondelmonti story. Compagni reports (1.20) that Corso Donati decided, after the death of his first wife, to remarry and selected a young woman of the Da Gaville family who was her deceased father's only heir. His attention is on the lineage and inheritance structures of the elite families: "Her relatives did not approve" of the marriage because they "expected this inheritance," which, if she married Corso and made her Donati children her heirs, would have passed out of the Da Gaville lineage, something that no elite family contemplated with equanimity. It happened that the Cerchi were related to the Da Gaville and supported their effort to block the marriage. But "the girl's mother, seeing that [Corso Donati] was a very handsome man, agreed to the marriage against the will of the rest of the family." The Cerchi became angry and tried to prevent the inheritance from falling into Corso's hands, "but he took it by force." The intervention of the mother exactly parallels the action of the Donati wife who lured Buondelmonte away from the marriage to which he was pledged in violation of the agreements previously worked out among the feuding families. In fact, Compagni notably embellishes the woman's role in his version of the Buondelmonti episode, and his point emerges clearly from the parallel: the very structures of marriage, inheritance, and lineage solidarity that defined the elite and made its families powerful were also the fatal weaknesses that led it again and again, in endless repetition of the "original" fall, into quarrels and violence that took the whole city down with them. In such episodes Compagni provides a subtle critique of the "private" origins of the elite's ultimately very public feuds. The critique is not limited to denunciations of their violence, arrogance, and contempt for law and civility, although such denunciations are of course not lacking. His point is that the damage elite families regularly did to themselves and the city sprang from the very institutions of their family life. Even when they were behaving according to the best standards of their class and protecting the interests and honor of their lineages, they were inexorably sowing the seeds of disputes and divisions. Compagni was implicitly challenging the legitimacy of the elite as a governing class on the grounds that even its well-meaning members were inevitably complicit in the structural flaws of their collective existence. Hence the need, central to the popular movement (and his own role in it), for mechanisms of conflict resolution and forms of public power and authority capable of overriding and controlling the elite's natural instincts.

By the time he wrote the *Divine Comedy* Dante was no friend of the popolo. But he was no friend of anything about Florentine politics, and he pulled no punches in excoriating the elite families for their misdeeds. The encounter with Farinata degli Uberti (*Inferno* 10) begins in relative civility when the Ghibelline captain hears the pilgrim's Tuscan speech and inquires about his visitor. But when he asks the deceptively simple, but in fact dangerous, question,

"Who were your ancestors?" and Dante reveals his Guelf origins, they immediately trade taunts about which party threw the other out more often and more effectively. Apparently forgetting the "noble fatherland" for which he had expressed concern upon first seeing Dante, Farinata encapsulates his own loyalties as entirely focused on family and faction when he snarls that his Guelf enemies were "fiercely adverse to me, my ancestors, and my party." And when he asks the pilgrim why the Florentine "popolo" had become so hostile to him and his kindred and needs to be reminded that it was the result of the slaughter inflicted on the Florentines at the battle of Montaperti by the Ghibelline army in 1260, Dante underscores the blindness of elite families that regularly lost sight of the horrors they inflicted on the city through partisan conflicts. In fact, Dante's Hell contains many of the legendary leaders of both the Guelf and Ghibelline parties in the mid-thirteenth century.

In *Paradiso* 15–17, every virtue of Cacciaguida's twelfth-century city points to some flaw in the bloated metropolis of 1300. In those days, Florence "within her ancient circle . . . abode in peace, sober and chaste," still free of the massive immigration from the contado in the next century that, according to Dante, changed its character: the "intermingling" of people from the countryside only brought troubles and corruption. But the examples Cacciaguida gives of the kind of people that would have been kept away if the old boundary between city and contado had been respected are not those of peasants or artisans, but the great families at the center of the elite's violent history. The Cerchi "would [still] be in the parish of Acone," and the Buondelmonti still in their ancestral home in the Valdigreve. Thus, the imaginary Florence of Dante's good old time kept the unruliest elements of the elite in a state of rural isolation. Moreover, Cacciaguida claims, the elite families already in the city were very different from those of Dante's day, still uncontaminated by conspicuous displays of wealth, lacking the necklaces, coronals, and embroidered gowns that now are "more to be looked at than the person," and the excessive dowries that now "cause fear to the father of every girl." In those days, men went "girt with leather and bone" and did not desert their women "for France," because they were not yet international merchants and bankers. "With unpainted faces," virtuous women then worked at home at their spinning wheels and watched over their children, telling them the legends of Florence's origins, the tales of "the Trojans, and Fiesole, and Rome." Cacciaguida's city was a community of loyal citizenry "pure down to the humblest artisan." Dante's language directly echoes the popolo here: the old Florence of his imagination was a city of artisans, or guildsmen, exercising their *arti*. The eminent families whose names Cacciaguida intones were not yet "undone by their pride" or ruinous factionalism and were still committed to an ethic of good citizenship and civic duty: "With these families, and with others with them, I saw Florence in such repose that she had no cause for wailing. With these families I saw her people so glorious and so just, that the lily was never set reversed upon the staff, nor made vermilion by division" – an allusion to the changing flags of factions alternating in power. Dante's ideal city is a utopia defined by the ideals of the popolo and its polemic against elite misrule. He himself suffered exile when the Blacks achieved their violent victory and expelled both their upper-class enemies and the last remnants of the popular government. With good reason to be angry at the factions, his denunciation of them emerges from many of the same perceptions that animated the popolo's critique of elite misrule.[35]

A generation later Boccaccio included in the *Decameron* a story (6.6) that gives a glimpse of how average Florentines, in taverns and streets, may have joked about the pretensions and arrogance of elite families. The story is about an entertaining storyteller named Michele Scalza, who finds himself in an argument "about which Florentine family is the most ancient and noble." His friends suggest the Uberti and Lamberti, both very old lineages, but Scalza disagrees and declares the Baronci to be the oldest and most noble family. But the Baronci were a relatively new family, and Scalza's friends challenge his choice. Undeterred, he explains: "As you know, the more ancient a family is, the nobler it is." His proof that the Baronci were the most ancient is as follows: "the Good Lord made the Baronci when He was [still] learning to paint, but made everyone else after He had learned. . . . All the others, as you must have noticed, have well made, suitably proportioned features, but take a look at the Baronci faces: some have long thin ones, others have impossibly fat ones; some have long noses, others stubby ones; some have chins that jut out to meet their noses, some have jaws the size of donkey jaws; you'll find some with one eye bigger than the other, just like the faces children make when they're first learning to draw. Therefore, as I say, it's obvious that the Good Lord made them when He was learning to paint, which makes them more ancient than any other, and consequently more noble."[36] His listeners so liked Scalza's explanation that they applauded his judgment: the ugly Baronci were indeed Florence's, and the world's, noblest family.

[35] J. M. Najemy, "Dante and Florence," in *The Cambridge Companion to Dante*, ed. R. Jacoff (Cambridge, 1993), pp. 80–99.
[36] Giovanni Boccaccio, *The Decameron* trans. G. Waldman (Oxford, 1993), pp. 395–7.

3

Early Conflicts of Elite and Popolo

Four times in 130 years the Florentine popolo instituted governments that briefly reined in the elite but had lasting effects on its political strategies and collective identity. The fifteenth-century elite, although perhaps more firmly in control than preceding elite regimes, was profoundly transformed. Popular challenges forced the elite to redefine the legitimacy of its claim to power and pressured it into gradually accepting, albeit in modified form, much of the popolo's vision of government. The four principal popular governments were the "primo popolo" of 1250–60, which removed elite Guelfs and Ghibellines from government and limited their ability to dominate politics and the inner city; the "second" popolo (as Villani called it), which promulgated the 1293 Ordinances of Justice, subjected a large group of elite families to magnate status, and barred them from major political offices; and the governments of 1343–8 and 1378–82, whose radical fiscal and economic policies will be considered in due course. Popular governments came to power in times of crisis in elite governance (factional violence, costly wars, bankruptcies, or huge government indebtedness) that caused the non-elite major guildsmen to abandon cooperation with the elite and form alliances with the minor guildsmen, with whom they implemented controversial reforms that punished the elite and reduced its power. Popular governments became progressively more radical, partly because fiscal and foreign policy crises became more acute, but also because each of these governments expanded the social base of the popolo, either by bringing more of the guild federation to a share of real power or by acceding to the demands of artisans, and ultimately workers, for guilds of their own and a place in communal politics. Although the elite adjusted to each threat and always managed to regain control, it emerged on each occasion significantly transformed in its political methods and style and even its collective identity.

Before 1250

Executive authority in the early commune was vested in a committee of (generally twelve, sometimes fewer) consuls, first documented in 1138. Elected annually, and mainly from elite families, the consuls were advised by representatives, also called consuls, of two elite associations: the merchants of Calimala and the association of knights, the *societas militum*. Two councils, the General Council of 300 and Special Council of 90, were also sometimes consulted. The earliest appearance of the one-man chief executive known as the podestà occurred in 1192–3 when the imperial party was in power.[1] The earliest podestà were citizens (the first was from the elite Caponsacchi family), but in the early thirteenth century they were increasingly recruited from other Italian cities and gradually supplanted the consular office. Even so, the pre-1250 commune was dominated by elite families who were still primarily a landowning class with ties to their ancestral homes in the contado and a warrior class whose knights constituted the cavalry of the communal army.[2]

Yet the ground was already being prepared for the challenges to come. On the one hand, economic expansion and specialization resulted in new guilds unwilling to accept the Calimala's early monopoly of representation of upper-class business and economic categories. As merchants in a particular sector increased and became conscious of their distinct collective interests, they broke away from the Calimala and formed their own guilds, while professional and artisan groups not represented by the Calimala also formed associations. In addition to the new major guilds, a federation formed in 1193 by an unknown number of artisan associations suggests an even earlier history of "minor" guilds. Neighborhood associations coalesced into organized districts that soon demanded, as did the new guilds, representation in the communal councils. In 1224 an unusual session of the General Council of the commune was convened to consider fiscal reform and accusations against the ruling elite concerning mismanagement of communal finances. Two embryonic forms of political representation, territorial and professional, were here juxtaposed:

---

[1] E. Faini, "Firenze al tempo di Semifonte," in *Semifonte in Val d'Elsa e i centri di nuova fondazione dell'Italia medievale*, ed. P. Pirillo (Florence, 2004), pp. 131–44.
[2] D. De Rosa, *Alle origini della repubblica fiorentina: dai consoli al "primo popolo" (1172–1260)* (Florence, 1995), pp. 9–31; P. Santini, *Studi sull'antica costituzione del comune di Firenze* (1903; reprint edn. Rome, 1972).

in addition to the Calimala consuls, the General Council included the consuls of the bankers' and woolen-cloth manufacturers' guilds, representatives of a confederation of minor guilds, and twenty citizens from each of the six administrative subdivisions (the sesti). A committee with representatives from each sesto was elected to review the work of all fiscal and treasury officials over the previous twenty years.[3]

Elite factionalism opened the way to greater influence for these newly organized popular associations. While upper-class factional rivalries in the Italian cities went back at least to the twelfth century and everywhere had local origins, these divisions became enmeshed, inevitably if obscurely, in the efforts of successive Holy Roman Emperors to bring under their control the wealthy city-states that lay within the old boundaries of the empire. When one faction aligned with the emperor, its opponents took the anti-imperial side, and when pro- and anti-imperial parties from different cities formed alliances, the dimensions of what may have begun as purely indigenous feuds became much greater. Emperors also found natural allies in the powerful feudatories of the countryside who resisted the growing power of the communes and sought confirmation of their privileges and titles from their formal overlord. At stake for the commune was its campaign to weaken the great rural families and control the surrounding territory.[4] Emperor Frederick I (r.1152–90), called Barbarossa and from the Hohenstaufen family of Swabia, waged a thirty-year war from the 1150s to the 1180s against the communes. In 1155 he invaded Tuscany with the support of the counts Guidi and Alberti but could not subdue Florence. After being defeated by the Lombard communes in 1176 at Legnano near Milan, he accepted a treaty (1183) in which the cities of the Lombard League acknowledged imperial sovereignty while securing de facto autonomy. Barbarossa's son Henry VI (r.1190–7) likewise sought with the support of the feudatories, and with greater albeit brief success, to bring Florence under imperial power. But when he died the Tuscan cities formed a league and swore resistance to further incursions of imperial power.[5] When Otto IV (1198–1218) of the Welf family demanded oaths of fidelity from all the communes, Florence was the only one to refuse.[6] The second Frederick Hohenstaufen, Otto's former rival for the imperial throne and the son of Henry VI and the last Norman princess of Sicily, became

---

[3] De Rosa, *Alle origini*, pp. 100–1.
[4] Dameron, *Episcopal Power*, pp. 69–77.
[5] A. Zorzi, "La Toscana politica nell'età di Semifonte," in *Semifonte in Val d'Elsa*, pp. 103–29.
[6] R. Davidsohn, *Storia di Firenze*, 8 vols. (Florence, 1972): Frederick I, vol. 1, pp. 673–871; Henry VI, vol. 1, pp. 873–912; Otto IV, vol. 2, pp. 9–83; Frederick II, vol. 2, pp. 87–151, 207–527.

emperor in 1220 and in the 1230s launched his own war to subdue northern and central Italy.[7]

It was at this point that the Florentine factions sifted into parties known as Guelf (from the name Welf and signifying Frederick's enemies) and Ghibelline (an Italianization of Waiblingen, a Hohenstaufen stronghold in Swabia). In the mid 1240s, when the elite was in a state of civil war, the Dominican campaign against Cathar heresy intensified and a new office of "Captain of the People" appeared in 1244, indicating some reaction from the popolo in the face of growing elite violence. Although there was probably no connection between the two events, both were aimed at the Ghibellines. Frederick responded by sending his son, Frederick of Antioch, to preside over the city as podestà and imperial vicar. Fighting between Guelfs and Ghibellines led to particularly intense clashes in 1248 from which the city's non-elite population kept its distance; according to Villani, "the *popolo* and commune of Florence kept itself united for the welfare, honor, and good condition of the republic" (7.3). Help from the emperor tipped the balance toward the Ghibellines, and the leading Guelf families left the city and took refuge in their countryside strongholds. The triumphant Ghibellines sowed the seeds of revenge by destroying many Guelf towers and palazzi. Among the non-elite, sentiment was building for a different kind of political order that might weaken the parties and diminish their ability to engulf the city in war. Nor did the imperial administration enjoy much favor with the majority of Florentines who paid heavy taxes to support a war in which they had little interest. The opportunity for action came in September 1250 when a contingent of Guelf exiles defeated a Ghibelline force at Figline in the upper Arno valley. When the news reached Florence, crowds gathered in the streets calling for government by the popolo.

Primo Popolo

A committee of "good men," as Villani calls them, looking for a safe place to meet in the face of hostility from both the imperial administration and the Ghibellines, particularly the Uberti who hounded them from one location to another until they were welcomed into the fortified houses of the Anchioni family in San Lorenzo, discussed political reform for several weeks. On October 20, 1250, they announced the new face of Florentine government. The first and most basic of their innovations was the reorganization of urban space. They instituted twenty armed neighborhood companies, each led by a standardbearer and four rectors elected within the company for a year.

---

[7]   The standard biography: D. Abulafia, *Frederick II, A Medieval Emperor* (Oxford, 1988).

The companies enrolled all males between the ages of fifteen and seventy, excluding knights. Each company had a distinctive standard (gonfalone) that served as a symbol of neighborhood identity and solidarity, some featuring dragons and lions rampant. So powerful was the symbolic value of the standards (Villani describes all twenty) that the administrative zones they represented came to be known, metonymically, as gonfaloni. The Capitano del popolo, a non-Florentine appointed for one year with the responsibility of sounding the bell and summoning the neighborhood militias whenever necessary, replaced the podestà as the commune's chief military and judicial official. Even more impressive in some respects was the organization of the contado, where ninety-six parishes each became the home of a militia company, also with standardbearers and rectors, and organized into regional leagues. The main function of the militias was to ensure peace and security against elite factions that had often barricaded and besieged entire neighborhoods.

The new chief magistracy was the office of twelve Anziani, or Elders, two from each sesto, elected twice a year, probably by leaders of the military companies and the guilds. The Anziani ran day-to-day affairs of government and had broad judicial, financial, and administrative powers and the exclusive right to initiate legislation (as did the later priors). To become law their proposals had to gain the approval of the legislative councils, both the older ones and the new Credentia, with six representatives from each sesto, and the Council of the Capitano del popolo, whose twenty-four regular members were frequently joined by the 100 standardbearers and rectors of the militia companies and the consuls of the guilds.[8]

How "popular" was the primo popolo? Its most popular feature was the wide base of support indicated by the participation of the militia representatives and the guild consuls, all elected within their associations, in the Council of the Capitano, and their consultation by the Anziani on matters including war and taxes. Names of more than one hundred Anziani from 1250 to 1260 reveal the exclusion of knights and the presence of only six from families of the old consular ruling group and another dozen from other pre-1250 families. The primo popolo clearly attempted to remove the families associated with the elite parties and to replace the old governing class with new men. On the other hand, most of the Anziani came from families associated with the major guilds and were involved in banking, trade, and the legal profession. Among those whose professions have been identified were many Calimala merchants, some bankers or moneylenders, a dozen from Por Santa Maria, twenty jurists or notaries, and five from the Wool guild. No representatives of the minor, or artisan, guilds have been identified among these officeholders.[9]

---

[8] Davidsohn, *Storia*, vol. 2, pp. 509–18; De Rosa, *Alle origini*, pp. 140–5.
[9] De Rosa, *Alle origini*, p. 171.

The situation in the legislative councils shows the same effort to limit the participation of the old ruling group. Knights were excluded from the new councils of the popolo, and, although they still sat in the two older councils, of 661 members of the various councils in 1255–6, only fourteen were knights.[10] Here too the overwhelming majority came from the major guilds, but the presence of a few minor guildsmen suggests that the primo popolo felt it necessary to make some gesture toward them. Indeed, on one occasion in 1251, among twenty-eight council members whose professions can be identified were five minor guildsmen or artisans, nine lawyers, twelve notaries, and two doctors. A council of 1256 included a tailor and two shoemakers in addition to five lawyers, eight notaries, and two doctors.[11] Although minor guildsmen were clearly a small minority, the numerous notaries, although major guildsmen, came from decidedly non-elite (and in many cases contado) families, adding significantly to the popular presence in the councils.

Yet the chief sense in which the government of 1250–60 was "popular" rests in the exclusion of much of the ruling class of the preceding period and the limited role of known Guelfs and Ghibellines. Less than a quarter of the Anziani and only 17 percent of council members were affiliated with either party and were vastly outnumbered by persons with no known connection to the parties. Moreover, the numbers of Guelfs and Ghibellines were roughly equal: slightly more Guelfs than Ghibellines among the Anziani, the reverse in the councils. The significance of this obviously carefully monitored policy is clear: the popolo tried to steer a middle course between the parties and to present itself as a dominant third force capable of limiting their influence. At the beginning of the decade, the primo popolo was essentially neutral between Guelfs and Ghibellines. It recalled the exiled Guelfs of 1248, but banished no Ghibellines and tried to avoid antagonizing either party. Outside pressures ultimately forced the primo popolo to become embroiled in the very party struggles it tried to suppress and caused it to draw closer to the Guelfs and alienate the Ghibellines. Until then, however, the policy of neutrality between the parties was a major achievement of this first attempt at an alternative to elite dominance. The primo popolo was not a social revolution; it emerged from a split within the elite, between those committed to the factions and those who saw such alliances as damaging to the economic interests of their class and city. Although knights may have been barred from the Anziani, there is no evidence of families designated as magnates or of punitive legislation against them. The largely successful effort to remove the parties from the center of the political stage was made possible in part by the support of the guilds and the military companies in exchange for some representation in

[10]   Salvemini, *Magnati e popolani*, p. 9.
[11]   De Rosa, *Alle origini*, p. 177.

government. The primo popolo thus foreshadows the analogous policies of later popular governments that reached even farther from the elite for support to mount more radical challenges.

To reduce the elite's ability to conduct urban warfare, the primo popolo significantly reconfigured the physical city. Its most dramatic policy was the systematic reduction of the towers that elite families used as defensive strongholds and impregnable bastions from which to rain down rocks and missiles against their enemies. Before 1250 Florence was a veritable forest of family towers (see Map 1), some as high as 120 *braccia* (70 meters, 230 feet) and thus more than two-thirds the height of Brunelleschi's fifteenth-century dome atop the cathedral. The primo popolo ordered them all reduced to a maximum of 50 *braccia* (29 meters, 96 feet), insisting that no private tower rise higher than that of the new palazzo del popolo (the Bargello) built in this decade. Cutting down family towers symbolically asserted public over private power and simultaneously limited the towers' effectiveness in street warfare. The government used the stones from the destroyed upper portions to expand the city walls on the south side of the river. Another dimension of the popolo's urban policy was the construction of wide, straight streets that led into the center and facilitated the quick movement of security forces. The best example is via Maggio (originally Maggiore) in the Oltrarno district and the connecting Santa Trinita bridge, which afforded quick access from the southern gate into the inner city where the elite had its enclaves.[12]

With Frederick II's death in December 1250, the Ghibellines were in disarray throughout Italy, and Florence under the primo popolo asserted its power in Tuscany as never before. After bringing the contado under control, the government eliminated any potential support for the Hohenstaufen in Tuscany. When Frederick's son Conrad readied an expedition to southern Italy, the primo popolo, worried that the Ghibelline city of Pistoia might become a rallying point for his Tuscan supporters, sent an army in 1251 to overturn the Pistoian regime. Although successful, this action compromised the popolo's declared neutrality between Guelfs and Ghibellines. Florentine Ghibellines began to fear that the new government was inevitably more a friend of the Guelfs than of theirs, and some decided to leave the city and join their allies elsewhere in Tuscany. Even more ominous was the formation of an anti-Florentine league of Ghibelline cities, including Pisa and Siena. But for the next several years, the primo popolo met all challenges, defeated Siena, took Pistoia a second time, pushed back a Pisan attack on their ally Lucca, cleaned the Ghibellines out of Figline and the Sienese out of Montalcino, occupied Poggibonsi and Volterra, imposing on the latter a constitution modeled on their own, and frightened the Pisans into conceding to Florentine merchants privileges and

---

[12]   F. Sznura, *L'espansione urbana di Firenze nel Dugento* (Florence, 1975), pp. 122–3.

exemptions from taxes and customs duties. The Florentines, Villani wrote (7.58), called 1254 the "victorious year," as the primo popolo became the undisputed power in Tuscany. An inscription placed in the west wall of the new palazzo del popolo exalted the city's wealth, victories, fortune, and power, claiming for Florence the right to rule the sea, the land, and the entire world, and predicting eternal triumph, in the manner of Rome, over subjects to be ruled with justice and law. Exaggerated as they are, these boasts reflect the growing appeal of ancient Rome to the popolo, and it has been plausibly argued that Brunetto Latini, chancellor and notary of the Anziani, may have composed these famous lines.[13] A second way in which the primo popolo advertised, and increased, Florentine power was the minting of the gold florin, with the lily on one face and the image of the city's patron saint, John the Baptist, on the other. Since Carolingian times no state in the West had minted gold coins until Frederick II imitated the coins of the ancient Roman emperors, but no city had ever done so until Genoa and Florence minted florins almost simultaneously in 1252. It was a proclamation of sovereignty, another politically charged imitation of ancient Rome, and a symbol of Florence's expanding wealth.

The revival of party antagonisms eventually drew the primo popolo into a major war that destroyed it. Villani gives a good example (7.61) of the danger the popolo faced, not only from Ghibellines, but also from elite Guelfs. In 1255 the government sent 500 knights, under the command of the Guelf captain Guido Guerra of the Counts Guidi, to help an ally against its Ghibelline enemies. When the count reached Arezzo, then at peace with Florence, he stormed in and, "against the wishes and without any mandate from the commune of Florence," expelled the Aretine Ghibellines. The popolo was "furious with the count" and sent an army to take Arezzo and readmit the Ghibellines. Here was a case of an overmighty Guelf, from a noble family accustomed to exercising jurisdiction in territories under its control, making his own foreign policy and pursuing objectives defined more by loyalty to the Guelf party than by the government whose cavalry he commanded. By 1258 tensions between Guelfs and Ghibellines were increasing, as Frederick II's son Manfred, now king of Sicily, began a military campaign to revive Hohenstaufen hegemony throughout Italy. The Tuscan Ghibellines saw in Manfred their chance for revenge against the Guelfs and for the destruction of the primo popolo. In July 1258 the government uncovered a plot, led by the Uberti and supported by Manfred, to overthrow the popolo. When the Uberti ignored a summons, a crowd attacked their palaces and killed one of them and several of their followers. Two others confessed and were executed. The Uberti left Florence

[13] R. MacCracken, *The Dedication Inscription of the Palazzo del podestà in Florence* (Florence, 2001); Davidsohn, *Storia*, vol. 2, pp. 614–16.

and went to Ghibelline Siena, and with them went all or part of seventeen other Ghibelline families, including the Fifanti, Guidi, Amidei, Lamberti, Abati, and Soldanieri. Over the next year Manfred won one victory after another and seemed unstoppable. To the dismay of the Florentine Ghibellines, however, he tried to win the Florentine popolo to his side, but negotiations broke down when the Florentines refused to receive a royal governor who intended to reform their statutes. By 1260 it was clear that the Ghibelline–Hohenstaufen–Sienese were preparing for war, and the Florentine popolo had no choice but to close ranks with the Guelfs.

The communal army, distinct from the militias set up in 1250 for internal security, consisted of six units corresponding to the sesti, each a combination of infantry and cavalry. Cavalry service was provided by men from wealthy families or substitutes hired by them. The infantry was divided by categories of service under separate commanders. Partly recruited from the city and partly from the contado districts that were an extension of the sesti, the total force of the Florentine army in the war of 1260 was approximately 16,000: 1,400 city cavalrymen; 8,000 contado infantry; 4,000 city infantry; 2,000 crossbowmen and archers; 300 shield-men from the city; and only 200 foreign mercenaries, all cavalrymen.[14] Villani (7.78) says that even this huge Florentine contingent was only part of the Guelf army whose infantry he estimated at 30,000. Although smaller, the Ghibelline–Sienese army routed the Florentines at Montaperti on September 4, 1260, a day forever remembered with grief by the Guelfs and the popolo, and commemorated by Dante, as his pilgrim reminds Farinata degli Uberti, as the battle "that made the river Arbia run red with blood" (*Inferno* 10) and later prompted the harsh laws against Ghibellines. Farinata justifies his part in the war saying that he was not alone, or without cause, but that he was indeed the only one who prevented Florence from being utterly destroyed. Here Dante alludes to the legend according to which Manfred ordered the city razed to the ground and its population resettled elsewhere, an order that the other Ghibelline captains were prepared to execute, except Farinata who announced that he had not fought all these years to see his city obliterated, but to return and live there.

Montaperti was the end of the primo popolo and the beginning of six years of exile for leading Guelfs, who left the city within days of the catastrophe. The Ghibellines, recalling the punishments inflicted on them in 1258, destroyed, according to the *Book of Damages*, 103 palaces, 580 smaller houses, 85 towers, and a large number of shops and warehouses. The property itself

---

[14]   D. Waley, "The Army of the Florentine Republic from the Twelfth to the Fourteenth Century," in *Florentine Studies*, ed. N. Rubinstein, pp. 70–108 (77). The government detailed its military units in the *Libro di Montaperti*, ed. C. Paoli (Florence, 1889).

was not sold but rented, which made its recovery possible some years later. Also punished were the leaders of the primo popolo. About a third of the exiled families, and half the merchant families among them, had had one or more members among either the Anziani or the councils of the primo popolo,[15] some of whose non-elite leaders were also exiled, most notably Brunetto Latini. The Ghibellines dispatched the entire constitutional structure created in 1250 and installed a government essentially of the Ghibelline party under the podestà Guido Novello of the Counts Guidi (ironically a cousin of the Guelf Guido Guerra) who governed in the name of Manfred Hohenstaufen.

Angevin Alliance

Ghibellines ruled Florence for six years, with the lordly Uberti behind the scenes and a group of mostly old Ghibelline elite dominating the councils (Abati, Amidei, Caponsacchi, Lamberti, Mannelli, and Soldanieri). Merchant families were not lacking in the second tier of politically prominent families of these years, which indicates that the Ghibelline regime was not hostile to the merchant and banking class. On the other hand, the participation of non-elite guildsmen was negligible, even if a few dozen artisans were among those punished by the Guelfs after 1267.[16] The fatal weakness of the Ghibelline regime was its inability to control the influence of Florentine merchant capital in and outside the city. The commercial and banking companies whose leading partners were exiled in 1260, such as the Bardi, Mozzi, Rossi, and Scali, temporarily lost their Florentine property but not their far-flung investments and assets, which were beyond the reach of the Ghibellines. Even companies that continued to direct operations from Florence were difficult to control. No one realized the potential significance of this more than the pope elected in August 1261, the Frenchman Urban IV, who turned his pontificate into a crusade to destroy the Hohenstaufen and put an end to their repeated attempts to control the peninsula and encircle and dominate the papacy. Urban needed someone capable of challenging Manfred on the battlefield, and his French connections led him to Charles of Anjou, count of Provence and brother of King Louis IX. Despite grandiose ambitions, Charles had little money and no army. Large sums had to be raised quickly, and the obvious source was Florentine bankers, whom Urban pressured to join the war against the Hohenstaufen by threatening to release their debtors from their obligations, interrupt the importation of Flemish cloth to Florence, and subject them to confiscation of goods and even imprisonment. In secret negotiations papal

---

[15]   Raveggi, in *Ghibellini, Guelfi*, pp. 13–21.
[16]   Ibid., pp. 23–52.

representatives offered to exempt from these punitive measures merchants willing to enter into formal pacts and to pledge financial support for the Angevin military campaign. Remarkably, over two years these negotiations continued without the Ghibelline governors of Florence knowing of them or at least without being able to stop them. The regime's financial and economic underpinning was being pulled out, piece by piece, from beneath its feet. At least 181 Florentine bankers and merchants from twenty-one major companies solemnly pledged loyalty to the papacy and the Guelf cause and committed themselves to the destruction of Ghibelline rule in Florence and Hohenstaufen power throughout Italy.[17] They included (just to name the most important) the companies of the Scali, Mozzi, Spini, Pulci-Rimbertini, Bardi, Cerchi, Frescobaldi, and Rossi. These pacts were the foundation of a momentous rearrangement of power in Italy, as the already great and still growing wealth of Florentine merchant-bankers turned decisively against the Ghibellines and Manfred, allied with the papacy and Charles of Anjou, and made Florence the financial core of a Guelf entente that linked the city to France and to what was about to become the Angevin south of Italy. The German–Hohenstaufen–imperial orbit in which the commune had emerged and developed was now replaced by a papal–French–Angevin orbit that offered new and greater opportunities for Florentine commercial expansion.

The expanding opportunities for Florentine bankers began with their role in financing Charles's army. They provided him with interest-bearing loans whose repayment came from ecclesiastical taxes that they collected on behalf of the papacy throughout Europe, and especially in France. The pope declared Manfred a Muslim and a heretic, which officially made the war a crusade and permitted the collection of crusading taxes. In many cases, prelates and ecclesiastical institutions, unable to pay their assessments in cash, borrowed the money from the same Florentine bankers at substantial rates of interest. Florentine firms thus secured a double profit from loans both to Charles and to those asked to repay his debts. But the bankers gained in yet another way that in the long run was the most lucrative of all. To secure continued access to Florentine cash, Charles granted ample commercial, trading, and banking privileges to his creditors in the southern Italian territories that he was about to conquer. Southern Italy was opened to Florentine investment and lending, to the marketing of luxury cloths from the Florentine textile industry, and in general to commercial activities unencumbered by taxes or duties. For the next eighty years, the Angevin South became perhaps the major source of Florentine wealth. While still negotiating his loans, Charles sailed from Marseilles to the Ligurian coast in May 1265; by year's end his army was

---

[17]   Davidsohn counted 146 individuals; *Storia*, vol. 2, p. 765; Raveggi raises the number to 181; *Ghibellini, Guelfi*, p. 60.

ready, and on January 6, 1266, he had himself crowned king of Sicily, in effect a declaration of war against Manfred, whose forces he engaged and defeated on February 26 at Benevento, northeast of Naples. Manfred was wounded and soon died, and, with Hohenstaufen ambitions finally quelled, Ghibellines everywhere were weakened. Charles of Anjou was ruler of the South and the greatest power in Italy.

In Florence the repercussions were slow to unfold. The restoration of exiled Guelfs did not occur until over a year later, in April 1267, when Angevin troops finally arrived in Tuscany. In the intervening year the popolo re-emerged, displaced the Ghibellines, and then attempted to prevent the imposition of a Guelf regime. In the aftermath of Benevento, the suddenly precarious Ghibelline regime opened negotiations with Pope Urban's successor, Clement IV, who demanded that Florence's Ghibellines offer reconciliation to the Guelfs. As the frightened Ghibellines temporized, Clement pressured them to appoint two Bolognese noblemen, a Guelf and a Ghibelline, as joint holders of the office of podestà. They instituted a committee of thirty-six Guelfs and Ghibellines, both *"popolani* and *grandi"* (writes Villani, 8.13). The thirty-six assumed the reins of government from their meeting place in the guildhall of the Calimala, and among their "many good decisions" was to recognize the federation and military organization of the seven "major" guilds, which were permitted to arm themselves, hire military captains, and assemble their members in designated meeting places, so that (says Villani) "if anyone attempted an uprising by force of arms, the guilds would come to the defense of the *popolo* and the commune under their banners." From this alliance of the seven guilds also came a committee of their representatives, called the "priorate of the guilds," in the second half of 1266. For the first time, the security and political aspirations of the popolo were entrusted to the guilds, establishing a precedent for the more successful role they assumed in 1282 and 1293.

Realizing that the Ghibellines were losing control of the situation, Guido Novello called for cavalry contingents from the Ghibelline cities of Tuscany and assembled a force of 1,500 knights. When, in November, the thirty-six refused to approve a tax to pay for these troops, Ghibelline families, led by the Lamberti, rioted and assaulted the thirty-six at the Calimala guildhall, crying "Where are these thirty-six thieves? We'll cut them to pieces" (Villani, 8.14). Rival contingents of popolo and Ghibellines squared off for battle, but on November 11 Guido Novello made the incomprehensible mistake of taking his formidable force out of the city, intending to return and engage the popolo from a safer direction. When his knights reassembled the next day, they found the gates closed and a defiant popolo determined to keep them out. The Ghibelline government promptly collapsed; only six years after its great triumph, Ghibellinism was finished in Florence.

In a gesture meant to revive the primo popolo's policy of neutrality between Guelfs and Ghibellines, the thirty-six readmitted some exiled Guelfs and arranged marriage alliances between the parties. But most Guelfs wanted revenge for the years of exile and the confiscations and destruction of property. As the thirty-six apparently split over whether to readmit the intransigent Guelfs, who included the party leaders, the offices of the Anziani and the Capitano del popolo suddenly reappeared and declared the commune's neutrality between the parties. But all the other players in this drama, including the bankers who had financed the war, the pope, and of course Charles of Anjou, wanted the elimination of the Ghibellines from Florence's government. Clement invited Charles to send troops into Tuscany, and the popolo prudently submitted to papal authority even before the Angevin army arrived in April 1267. The Guelfs got their revenge, exiling Ghibellines and confiscating their property, which was sold and divided among the Guelf party, the commune, and households that had suffered damages at the hands of the Ghibellines.[18] With the exile and economic dismemberment of the Ghibelline lineages, the thirty-year war between the elite parties finally ended.

Charles of Anjou was made podestà and given rule over the city for ten years, during which he was represented by a series of lieutenants. He imposed a government dominated by the Guelf party, which, no more kindly disposed to popular institutions than the Ghibellines, abolished the Anziani, the Capitano del popolo, and the priorate of the guilds, but not the guilds themselves. Surprisingly, it was not the merchant-bankers allied with the papacy and the Angevins that assumed power.[19] Of the families whose companies made big loans to Charles (chiefly the Frescobaldi, Bardi, Scali, and Cerchi, nine of whom received knighthoods from him in 1267[20]), only the Bardi were regularly present in the Guelf councils of 1267–80. Despite their decisive role in the Guelf victory, it may have been the very fact of excessively close ties to Charles that kept these families from power, as many began to fear Angevin domination of Tuscany. But economic realities worked inexorably to redefine the ruling class. The old Guelf elite, although victorious in 1267, began to lose ground as many families slipped into political oblivion in this last generation of their glory and the merchant and trading giants became the core of a newly configured elite. This was by no means the triumph of a "bourgeoisie" over an "aristocracy." It was rather a process of evolution within the elite itself, a replacement at the center of power of elite families that did not adapt to the age's booming capitalism by equally elite, if somewhat more recent, families

---

[18] Holmes, *Florence, Rome*, p. 17; Tarassi, "Il regime guelfo," in *Ghibellini, Guelfi*, p. 95; the *Liber extimationum*, ed. O. Brattö.
[19] Tarassi, in *Ghibellini, Guelfi*, pp. 97–164.
[20] Holmes, *Florence, Rome*, p. 14; Tarassi, in *Ghibellini, Guelfi*, pp. 141–2.

that did. However, simultaneously and as a consequence of economic expansion at the local level, in particular the boom in the textile trades, the non-elite popolo of the guilds also gained strength and prepared to challenge the entire elite, both its old and new components. These two developments are sometimes confused and even conflated. Although they overlapped, they were distinct: on the one hand, a transformation of the elite from a predominantly (but never exclusively) warrior class characterized by its knighthoods, city enclaves, and countryside strongholds into a class increasingly (although still not entirely) defined by far-flung mercantile activities across Europe and the Mediterranean; and, on the other hand, the rise to unprecedented political strength through their guilds of a coalition of local merchants, manufacturers, shopkeepers, artisans, and notaries. Both processes come into full view around 1280.

Priorate of the Guilds

In 1277 Charles's ten-year lordship in Florence ended, but he had no intention of relinquishing power. The papacy now saw Angevin ambitions as not so different from those of the Hohenstaufen; by controlling Florence, Charles had similarly surrounded the papal state. Because ongoing tensions between Guelfs and Ghibellines were the surest justification for a prolonged Angevin presence in Tuscany, Pope Gregory X attempted a general reconciliation of Florentine Guelfs and Ghibellines. He was unsuccessful, but when in 1278 Pope Nicholas III announced a similar project in several central Italian cities, the idea was received warmly as both the Guelf government and the Ghibelline party in exile sent requests to the pope for the appointment of a "paciarus," or peacemaker. Nicholas appointed his nephew, Cardinal Latino Malabranca, whose father had served as podestà in Florence in 1238.[21] Because he was temporarily occupied elsewhere, the cardinal appointed as his representative Andrea de' Mozzi, a Florentine prelate, later the city's bishop, whose brother Tommaso was among the heads of the powerful Mozzi-Spini banking firm that had financed the Angevin–Guelf victory. When Cardinal Latino arrived in Florence in October 1279 he took up residence in the Mozzi palace on the Oltrarno side of the Rubaconte bridge. Mozzi support for the pope's policy suggests that other families of new wealth also supported it.

Cardinal Latino negotiated reconciliations between Guelfs and Ghibellines (including the Buondelmonti and Uberti), and between feuding Guelfs, reconciling, for example, the Adimari with the Donati and Della Tosa. In January 1280 he announced the "general peace" and mutual reconciliation of the

---

[21] M. Sanfilippo, "Guelfi e ghibellini a Firenze: la 'pace' del Cardinal Latino (1280)," *Nuova rivista storica* 64 (1980): 1–24.

parties and instituted a new executive magistracy, the Fourteen, with eight Guelfs and six Ghibellines. Many Ghibellines were allowed to return and recover their property, although fifty-five of their most powerful leaders were kept in exile, including the sons of Farinata degli Uberti. On the delicate question of the distribution of seats in communal magistracies, the Peace authorized a committee, equally divided between Guelfs and Ghibellines, to conduct an inquiry into the party affiliations of all citizens between the ages of twenty-one and seventy and prepare three lists of self-declared Guelfs, Ghibellines, and neutrals. Political offices were to be divided according to the results.[22] This is a fascinating detail about which we can only wish we knew more, above all whether the survey was actually carried out. Particularly striking is the assumption that each citizen had the right to express a political affiliation and that the distribution of offices should reflect the relative weight of the three groups. It was obviously a sign of the reviving popular movement that citizens would have been free not to declare themselves Guelfs or Ghibellines, but rather as "communes sive indifferentes," neutral and unaffiliated, and that neutrals would also have their proportional share of seats in government. Even the intention to carry out such a referendum reveals that, a generation after the primo popolo, many Florentines saw themselves as a third force independent of both Guelfs and Ghibellines. Since there is no evidence that the projected political census was actually conducted, it seems likely that, once Cardinal Latino left the city, the elite found a way to scuttle this novel idea that would have reduced its power.

One aspect of the cardinal's Peace that pointed to the future was the role of the guilds as its guarantors. In February 1280 the Peace was ratified by the Guelf and Ghibelline parties whose differences it sought to compose, and in March eight guilds obligated themselves with formal promises to the observance of the agreement. The eight guilds included five major guilds (Jurists and Notaries, Wool, Por Santa Maria, Doctors and Specialty Importers, and Furriers) and three of the guilds that would soon be classified as middle guilds (Butchers, Smiths, and Shoemakers). Since the Furriers were a major guild in name only, and because the Jurists and Notaries, Por Santa Maria, and the Doctors and Specialty Importers all contained many more non-elite than elite members, this group of guilds was heavily weighted toward the non-elite popolo. For the first time, the power of legally recognized and self-constituted guilds to generate binding collective obligations on behalf of their members was used to buttress a Florentine government. The eight guilds separately appointed representatives ("syndics and procurators") who appeared before the cardinal "on their own behalf and in the name and on behalf of the aforementioned associations and corporations and their members" and

[22] Salvemini, *Magnati e popolani* (1899), pp. 320–33 (325).

promised "to follow and obey the cardinal in all things pertaining to the observance of his Peace and the implementation of the recently promulgated judgment against any association or person acting against the Peace." In addition, "they conceded to the cardinal full and free power to punish at his discretion" the guilds and their members "if they neglected to carry out" the terms of the agreement to which they had pledged themselves. And to this end, they obligated themselves, the guilds they represented, and the assets of the corporations and their members.[23] This arrangement is testimony to the quiet success achieved by the guilds during the preceding decades in becoming repositories of legitimacy that derived from the voluntary, and hence secure, nature of the promises that guilds, as *universitates*, were able to make. Their role in supporting the Peace and its reforms thus appropriated the solution they themselves embodied to the problem of how to create legitimate authority. The link was still indirect, because these guarantees were offered to the cardinal as mediator and peacemaker, not directly to the magistracy of the Fourteen that he created. But the legitimacy of this government rested, albeit at one remove, on the coercive power voluntarily conceded to the cardinal by the guilds. Within the short space of two years representatives of the most powerful guilds replaced the Fourteen as the commune's chief executive committee.

In March 1282, Sicily exploded in rebellion against its Angevin rulers, causing Charles to abandon Tuscany and defend his suddenly endangered southern kingdom. For the first time in half a century, neither Guelfs nor Ghibellines had powerful foreign supporters, and the division of seats in the Fourteen became meaningless, as power quickly shifted away from both parties. From at least 1281 the Fourteen had regularly consulted the consuls of the seven major guilds, and in 1282 the five middle guilds were formally recognized and given the right to send representatives to the councils. Even the elections of the Fourteen were increasingly carried out by the consuls of the seven, and on one occasion the twelve, guilds. And in June of 1282, the transfer of power to the guilds culminated with the institution of the "priorate of the guilds." Compagni (1.4) recalls that he was one of a group of six "*popolani* citizens" who, worried about Guelf infringements of the Peace of 1280 and the possibility of renewed partisan fighting, "went about persuading the citizens" and succeeded in winning support for the election of three "priors of the guilds, to aid the merchants and guildsmen whenever necessary." He describes the mood surrounding the establishment of the new office: "The *popolani* became so emboldened when they saw that these three met with no opposition, and [the priors] were so aroused by the candid words of the citizens who spoke of their liberty and the injuries they had suffered, that they dared to make ordinances and laws which would have been hard to evade. They did not accomplish

[23]   ASF, Capitoli, 29, ff. 345–6; Ottokar, *Il comune*, pp. 10–11.

much else, but considering their weak beginning this was a great deal. . . . They were called the Priors of the Guilds; and they stayed secluded in the tower of the Castagna near the Badia so that they did not have to fear the threats of the powerful." Within a year the priorate displaced the Fourteen.

As Compagni reveals, at its inception the priorate was the voice (and ears) of those who saw themselves as victims of the "powerful." During those heady months of the reviving popular movement, the idea that the guilds and their representatives could and should protect the interests and security of "merchants and guildsmen" against the "threats of the powerful," and that "the small and weak should not be oppressed by the great and powerful," acquired much emotional force. The first priorate had three members, and, while they were not elected as representatives of their guilds, they did in fact come one each from the Calimala (Bartolo di messer Jacopo de' Bardi), Cambio (Rosso Bacherelli), and Lana (Salvi di Chiaro Girolami). The succeeding priorate expanded to six members, one for each sesto. But, as Villani explains, this also meant an expansion of the number of guilds from which the priors were elected: "to these three greater guilds they added the guild of the Medici e Speziali, the guild of Por Santa Maria, and that of the Vaiai e Pellicciai. And gradually there came to be added all the others up to the twelve guilds" (8.79). Somewhere in these months, as we have seen, the five middle guilds were admitted to the ranks of the guilds with political standing, and Villani reports that the consuls of all twelve guilds participated in the bi-monthly election of new priors. Looming behind the early expansion of the number of guilds represented in the priorate was the question of how many guilds would ultimately have or demand access to the new office, a question of potentially enormous consequence given the existence of dozens of guilds. An early indication of the dilemma came in August 1282, when in deliberations concerning the election of the Fourteen (who still held office side-by-side with the newly created priorate), one speaker proposed that they be elected by the consuls of "thirty-two guilds." Which guilds he had in mind is impossible to say, but the very notion that so many guilds might participate in the election of communal magistrates no doubt reflected the pressure coming from many artisan guilds for a political role.

Over the next decade, the elite managed to control the elections and produce priorates cumulatively dominated by members of five major guilds. From 1282 to 1292, Calimala and Cambio jointly had 46% of the posts, Giudici e Notai 19%, Lana and Por Santa Maria each 10%. The rest were scattered among the other guilds or held by persons whose guild affiliation is unknown.[24] Fourteen of the 156 families appearing in the priorate in these years had five or more seats, cumulatively holding ninety-eight (26%) of the posts, and fifteen

[24] Ottokar, *Il comune*, pp. 18–19.

families had four priors each. These twenty-nine families accounted for 41% of the priors in the decade. But they were not the ruling Guelf elite of 1267–80. With some exceptions, the politically successful families were now from the banking and commercial class. The Girolami, a family that supported the popolo, led with twelve appearances and were followed by the Altoviti (10), Bardi (10), Acciaiuoli (9), Becchenugi (7), Canigiani (7), Cerretani (6), Falconieri (6), and Ristori (6). Not one was an old Guelf family from the early part of the century. Among families appearing four or more times, only the Tornaquinci and Visdomini belonged to the old elite: a meager representation of the traditional Guelf aristocracy that dominated communal politics as late as the 1270s. The institution of the priorate thus promoted the rise to leadership within the elite of merchant-banking families and the gradual slide into obscurity of older families.

But the expectations that the priorate would produce a non-partisan government protective of the "small and the weak" were disappointed, and the popolo had to wait until the 1290s to try again. Compagni acknowledges (1.5) that the early priorate failed to reduce elite power and arrogance. Although they had been appointed to "watch over the wealth of the commune," to "deal justly with all," and to ensure "that the small and weak should not be oppressed by the great and powerful," he wrote, "things soon changed, since the citizens who held that office dedicated themselves not to keeping the laws, but rather to corrupting them." They protected friends who ran afoul of the law, plundered the communal treasury, and instead of protecting the weak let them be "attacked by the *grandi* [magnates] and by the rich *popolani* who held office and were related by marriage to the *grandi*. . . . For these reasons the good *popolani* citizens were unhappy, and they blamed the office of the Priors, because the *grandi Guelfi* had become lords." In this revealing passage, Compagni laments the control of the new institution by "grandi" who were just as objectionable in his eyes as the old elite: a lordly and haughty ruling group that he saw as a combination of magnates and wealthy non-magnates linked to them by marriage. In his eyes the class that had to be reined in was not limited to the magnates; it was the entire elite, magnate and non-magnate, against which his "good *popolani*" of the non-elite guild community needed to marshal their forces.

In the late 1280s the ruling elite took the city into a war against Ghibelline Pisa and Arezzo. Despite a notable victory at Campaldino in 1289 (in which Dante is said to have fought), the war dragged on inconclusively for several years. Both Villani and Compagni emphasize that many knights from magnate families played a leading role at Campaldino, in particular Corso Donati and Vieri de' Cerchi, who emerged a decade later as leaders, respectively, of the Black and White Guelfs. Villani reports that the "*popolani* became suspicious that the *grandi* out of pride in their victory might oppress them even more than usual; and for this reason the seven major guilds banded together with the next five guilds, and they made arrangements for arms and shields and banners" (8.132). It was about this alliance that he remarked that it was "almost the beginning of a popular government." Since a political alliance between the seven and the five guilds had already occurred in 1282, the "banding together" of 1289 may have extended it to military cooperation. Somewhere in these years, most likely in either 1287 or 1289, nine more guilds received formal recognition and the right to carry arms and assemble their members under official banners. These were the nine "minor" guilds, several of which were combinations of related professions that until then probably had their own guilds. For the moment, these guilds had no political role and were not invited to send their consuls to the communal councils. But the recognition of their right to bear arms could only have occurred with the approval and support of the twelve established guilds, which evidently felt the need to augment the guild community's street strength in the event of hostilities. These nine guilds would subsequently be included in the guild federation of 1293.

Second Popolo and the Ordinances of Justice

On November 24, 1292, an unusually long debate on the election of the next priorate occurred in a special session of the council of the consulates of the twelve major guilds, in which at least nineteen persons, including many who were not consuls of their guilds, expressed a variety of opinions about the election. Among the speakers were members of elite families (Cerchi, Acciaiuoli, Strozzi), jurists, a notary, a woolen cloth manufacturer who was the nephew of Remigio de' Girolami, a poet, a member of the butchers' guild, and Dino Compagni. The chief issue was how much electoral influence the guild consuls should have: proposals for giving an equal say in the nomination and/or final approval of candidates to the independently elected consuls of the twelve guilds would bring more new men, recruited more evenly from the twelve guilds, into the priorate; conversely, bypassing the guilds and entrusting the election to a body selected by the outgoing priors would limit access to the priorate to the same elite that dominated the office during the previous decade. Opinions were about evenly divided between these two approaches. The most radical suggestion came from a representative of the butchers' guild, Dino Pecora, who favored a priorate of twelve members, one from each guild to be selected by the other eleven guilds. This would have given the non-elite guilds (the five middle guilds together with the Vaiai e Pellicciai, and usually also Por Santa Maria and the Medici e Speziali) a majority of votes in selecting priors from the all guilds, including those in which the elite was more heavily

represented. Although it was not accepted, this proposal reflected the preference of middle and minor guildsmen that all twelve guilds share equally in
the priorate and its election. Equal representation and equal influence in the
voting would have relegated the few heavily elite guilds to permanent minority
status. Other speakers in the November debate who agreed in principle on a
wider distribution of offices within the guild community formulated more
moderate versions of the same approach. Compagni recommended that the
consuls of each of the twelve guilds nominate six candidates from their own
guild, one from each sesto, who would then be voted on, one by one, by all
the assembled consuls. The candidate with the highest number of votes in each
sesto would be its prior. This allowed each of the twelve guilds to nominate
its own candidates and gave the non-elite elements of the guild community
the heaviest influence in the voting. But, although he wanted no guild to have
more than one prior in any given priorate, Compagni did not insist that the
guilds have equal numbers of priors over the long term. Compagni's proposal
was approved with some modifications, but it faced opposition from the lawyers and members of elite families who also argued against all similar plans.
The debate was a breakthrough for the popolo and the guild community in
establishing the autonomy and equality of each guild in nominating candidates and the equality of all twelve guilds in the final voting.[25] For the next
century, the autonomy and the equality of the guilds, applied to a variety of
changing circumstances, became the hallmarks of guild republicanism. But
the movement's Achilles' heel was its inability to resolve the question of how
many guilds would be allowed to participate in elections or governments based
on these principles.

The six priors elected in December 1292 (from six different guilds) sat
down with three jurists and wrote the most important political document in
Florentine history, the Ordinances of Justice, first promulgated on January 18,
1293.[26] Borrowing heavily from the similar legislation of Bologna's popular
government, which had much earlier harnessed the power of both guilds and
armed neighborhood societies, the Florentine Ordinances did two overwhelmingly important things: they 1) created a formal federation among the guilds
and placed the executive branch of Florentine government in its hands, and
2) codified and expanded existing anti-magnate legislation, subjecting ultimately

[25]   J. M. Najemy, *Corporatism and Consensus in Florentine Electoral Politics, 1280–
1400* (Chapel Hill, N.C., 1982), pp. 32–42.
[26]   1293 edition in F. Bonaini, *ASI*, n.s., 1 (1855): 37–71; reprinted in *Ordinamenti di
Giustizia, 1293–1993*, ed. F. Cardini (Florence, 1993). Revised 1295 redaction in
Salvemini, *Magnati e popolani* (1899), pp. 384–423. On the Ordinances, see, in addition to Salvemini and Ottokar, Zorzi, "Politica e giustizia," in *Ordinamenti di giustizia
fiorentini.*

140 lineages of the city and contado to tougher applications of the obligation to provide surety and harsher penalties for crimes against non-magnates. In revisions of April 1293, they also barred the seventy-two families of city magnates from the priorate and guild consulates. Appropriating the concept of justice to legitimate both its constitutional reforms and its policy toward the magnates, the Ordinances borrowed the Roman law definition of justice as the "constant and perpetual desire to ensure to each his right [*ius*]" and declared it the foundation on which the Ordinances themselves "are deservedly called 'of justice'" and promulgated for the "welfare of the *res publica*." The first rubric created the formal federation of twenty-one guilds, claiming that "that is judged most perfect which consists of all its parts and is approved by the judgment of them all." The second part of this sentence is a loud paraphrase of a famous maxim of Roman law, *quod omnes tangit debet ab omnibus approbari* (that which touches all must be approved by all), which, although not applied to government in its original context, was frequently used by medieval jurists to assert that legitimate rule depended on consent. In this version, the "parts" are the guilds, and the whole that they constitute is in one sense their federation and in a larger sense the "res publica" whose welfare the Ordinances promote. The Ordinances thus affirmed that the legitimacy of Florentine government depended on the consent of the guilds. Each of the twenty-one guilds was required to appoint a legal representative empowered to swear an oath on behalf of his guild to "construct and preserve the good, pure, and loyal society and company of these same guilds," to honor and defend the communal magistrates, priors, guilds, and the whole Florentine "populus," and to obey and give aid and counsel to the magistrates, if necessary with arms. They also swore mutual defense among all the guilds and their members to "preserve and defend the justice and right [*iustitia* and *ius*] of the guildsmen, so that they are not oppressed or unduly burdened by any person or persons." If any magnate oppresses or molests a guildsman, the consuls of that guild, and of all the guilds if necessary, must go to the podestà, the Capitano, and the lord priors to expose the offense and ask them to take all necessary measures to terminate it and protect the injured guildsman "in his right and his liberty [*in suo iure et libertate servetur*]." Thus the Ordinances link the preservation of *ius* (and hence *iustitia*) to both the provisions for punishing magnate violence against non-magnates and to the guild federation ("this present society and company, sacrament and universal union among all the guilds").

Although the political provisions of the Ordinances bound the commune more closely to the guild federation, there was still no agreement on how to elect the priors. The relevant rubric specified no procedures, requiring instead that at the end of each two-month term the consuls of the twelve guilds and others appointed by the outgoing priors should debate and decide the matter anew. It did however establish that candidates for the priorate had to be members of one of the twenty-one guilds and also regularly active in the trade or profession of their guilds. The requirement of regular exercise of a profession threatened the eligibility of some members of elite families who, although enrolled in guilds, were not necessarily continuously active in their family firms. But the chief threat to the elite's political standing was the exclusion of knights, which was the first step toward the ineligibility of all magnates. The Ordinances also created a new office from which magnates were likewise barred: the Standardbearer of Justice, added to the priorate as the seventh member of the executive magistracy and elected by the consuls of the twelve guilds. Although a participant with equal voting rights in the deliberations of the priors, the Standardbearer's original function was to lead the popolo's internal security force of 1,000 men selected "from the *popolo* and the guildsmen" and to destroy the homes and property of magnates who killed or seriously injured non-magnates. To prevent magnate uprisings when the Standardbearer and his troops marched on the home of a guilty magnate, the guildsmen were required to be armed under their banners and ready to obey "viriliter et potenter" the orders of the Capitano. Such displays of force must have been great public spectacles of the vengeance and justice of the popolo. Dino Compagni, the third Standardbearer of Justice in June–August 1293, reports (1.12) that he led the troops to destroy the property of a magnate family whose kinsman had killed a Florentine in France. Something of the mood of this remarkable year emerges from his comment that these early destructions of magnates' homes "led to a bad practice of the other Standardbearers, because when according to the laws they were supposed to destroy something, the *popolo* called them cowards if they did not destroy it utterly. And many distorted justice for fear of the *popolo*."

The anti-magnate provisions of the Ordinances built on earlier legislation. The first anti-magnate laws followed Cardinal Latino's Peace. In March 1281 a law required certain members of powerful families to post a monetary bond for good behavior, and in July another strengthened the podestà's authority to regulate feuds and punish acts of violence, referring to "magnates and powerful men [*magnates et potentes*] from both parties" as frequent instigators of crimes and public disorders that threatened "to subvert the good and peaceful state" of the city.[27] This measure gave the podestà and Capitano of the popolo authority to investigate and punish perpetrators with incarceration, banishment, or the obligation to post bond. But it was an ad hoc procedure, without any fixed list of magnates subject to these penalties. In 1286 another law required all adult males of certain families to provide surety; made household heads responsible for the good behavior of brothers or sons who failed to

[27]   Salvemini, *Magnati e popolani* (1899), pp. 334–48 (340–1).

provide surety and threatened the latter with destruction of their property; bound all members of these families to the observance of communal laws; prohibited the carrying of arms by their servants; and, for the first time, instituted a list of specified families all of whose members fell under these regulations as "magnates." The incumbent priors were authorized to compile the list and include it in the communal statutes. Two criteria, one specific, the other nebulous, determined the selection of magnate families: the presence in a family for at least twenty years of a knight, and a family's public reputation.[28] Collective responsibility of families for the crimes of their members and the designation of entire families as magnates opened the way for the harsher laws of 1293.

In addition to requiring the destruction of property for murder or crippling injury inflicted on non-magnates, the Ordinances imposed much higher than usual monetary penalties for assaults, lesser injuries, and seizure of property. Proof of guilt could be established by witnesses, and exceptions to the obligation to provide surety were eliminated. The Ordinances did not attempt to outlaw vendettas and feuds among magnates themselves; it was violence, intimidation, or oppression against non-magnates and the commune that the Ordinances sought to punish and deter. Yet the real aim may have been to modify the behavior of magnates by weakening and breaking the influence of elite factions over non-elite citizens. An intriguing rubric of the Ordinances prohibited non-magnates from assembling at the home of any magnate during riots, or when the Standardbearer of Justice moved through the streets with his armed force, thus attempting to cut the vertical links of patronage and clientage that drew non-elite into elite factions. Fights between factions that included non-elite followers naturally produced casualties among the latter; thus, prohibitively harsh penalties for the death or injury of non-magnates no doubt deterred magnates from relying on such followers. The aim was to isolate magnates in their own social world, to sever their ties to non-magnates and thus diminish the ability of vertically integrated elite factions to spread violence throughout the city. In the long run the policy was successful, but in the shorter run of the next two decades it was, as we shall see, a spectacular failure.

In January 1293, thirty-eight elite city families were declared magnates. But the next priorate of February–April, which included Giano della Bella, identified by all the sources as the leader and inspiration of the popular government, nearly doubled the city magnates to seventy-two families, further toughened the penalties for magnate crimes, enlarged the security force to 2,000 men, and barred magnates from the guild consulates and most of the communal

---

[28] Zorzi, "Politica e giustizia," pp. 122–7; Ottokar, *Il comune*, pp. 103–9; Salvemini, *Magnati e popolani* (1899), pp. 360–77.

councils. About two-thirds of the seventy-two families belonged to the old elite: the legendary leaders of both the defunct Ghibelline cause (Uberti, Lamberti, Amidei, Soldanieri) and the victorious Guelfs (Donati, Buondelmonti, Adimari, Cavalcanti). Almost certainly by design, the roster contains about as many Guelf as (former) Ghibelline families. Some older magnate families were still politically prominent (Della Tosa, Cavalcanti, Donati) or active in commerce (Abati, Rossi), but most were already in decline, and it cost the popular government little to affirm the magnate status of no longer powerful families that had probably been declared magnates in 1286. Much more significant, and the real challenge to the elite, was the inclusion of more than two dozen families from the merchant elite, new and old, including some from each sesto: Rossi, Frescobaldi, Mannelli, Bardi and Mozzi in Oltrarno; Cosi and Manieri in San Pancrazio; Scali and Spini in Borgo; Abati, Cerchi, and Pazzi in Porta San Piero; Cavalcanti, Pulci, Bagnesi, and Franzesi in San Pier Scheraggio; Agli, and Amieri in Porta Duomo.[29] If one purpose behind the expansion of the magnate rolls was to deter and discourage factions, it was crucial to do so in all neighborhoods.

The presence among the magnates of so much of the economic elite makes it impossible to argue, as many have, that the Ordinances mark the rise to power of the capitalist elite that had been pushing older "feudal" families from the centers of power. Behind the popular government of 1293–5 were the non-elite guildsmen who viewed with suspicion the entire elite (old and new, Guelf and Ghibelline, bankers and landowners). To have attempted to relegate the entire elite to magnate status would of course have provoked an upper-class revolt. What the popolo did instead (and this had to have been planned) was to split the elite between magnates and non-magnates. Punishing certain families served as a warning to others and probably earned the popular government a degree of grudging cooperation from those not made magnates. An interesting example is that of the Peruzzi, bankers nearly as rich and powerful but not as old as the Bardi. Why were they not made magnates? Perhaps because their first appearance in political life came after the creation of the priorate, but also because Pacino Peruzzi, a leading investor in the family company, regularly argued in the debates on electoral procedures throughout 1293 in favor of giving the consuls of the twelve guilds greater influence in electing the priors, as he did, for example, on February 14. Can it be a coincidence that his kinsman Giotto Peruzzi, the head of the company, was elected on that day and thus sat on the same priorate of February–April 1293 with Giano della Bella that expanded the list of magnate families? The Peruzzi may have been spared because they cooperated with the popolo.

[29] Complete lists in Lansing, *Florentine Magnates*, pp. 239–40, based on Salvemini, *Magnati e popolani* (1899), pp. 375–7.

That the government established in 1293 did not represent the interests of the merchant-banking elite emerges clearly from the composition of the twelve priorates over the next two years. Of eighty-four priors and Standardbearers of Justice, thirty-seven (44%) were their families' first priors.[30] Most elite families, obviously the magnates but also many non-magnates, were shut out: the Acciaiuoli, for example, who had nine priors in the previous decade, had none in these two years; also without priors were the Canigiani, Pitti, Capponi, Baroncelli, Corsini, Medici, Salviati, Ricci, Guicciardini, Rucellai, Covoni, and many others. The Altoviti, Peruzzi, Becchenugi, Guadagni, and Girolami (if they rank as elite) all had two priors, and another fifteen to twenty elite families each had one. But the great majority were from the middling ranks of the major guilds, and many reached the office for the first time. In the five years from 1293 through 1297 (during which the guild consuls had a major role in elections), seventy-three families had their first prior, whereas in the preceding five years forty-six did so (despite the fact that the priorate had only been created in 1282).

Just as the primo popolo gave monumental architectural expression to its challenge to the elite families by lopping off their towers and building a fortress-like seat of government for itself (today's Bargello), the second popolo likewise began planning a new palace of the priors (now Palazzo Vecchio) in 1294 at the peak of its power (see Plate 1). But building got underway only in 1298, when, according to Villani (9.26), increasing tensions "between the *popolo* and the *grandi*" over elections of the priorate and the recrudescence of elite factions made it "no longer safe" for the priors to meet, as they had, in houses rented from the Cerchi. Construction was far enough advanced in just a few years for the priors to take up residence. Originally designed to face north and thus to overlook the area where the houses and neighborhood enclave of the proud Ghibelline Uberti once stood, its builders changed course and had the imposing structure face west. Even so, the new palace and its piazza, which was systematically and carefully enlarged over many decades, symbolically buried the greatest of Florence's elite families. With its fortress-like rustication, echoes of Roman architecture, and huge tower, the palace of the popolo loudly announced resolute defiance of the elite.[31]

---

[30] P. Parenti, "Dagli Ordinamenti di Giustizia alle lotte tra Bianchi e Neri," in *Ghibellini, Guelfi*, p. 252ff., pp. 324–6.

[31] N. Rubinstein, *The Palazzo Vecchio, 1298–1532: Government, Architecture, and Imagery in the Civic Palace of the Florentine Republic* (Oxford, 1995); M. Trachtenberg, *Dominion of the Eye: Urbanism, Art, and Power in Early Modern Florence* (Cambridge, 1997); M. Trachtenberg, "Founding the Palazzo Vecchio in 1299: The Corso Donati Paradox," *Renaissance Quarterly* 52 (1999): 966–93.

Plate 1   Palace of the priors (Palazzo Vecchio), begun c.1298 as the political center of the "second popolo," possibly designed by Arnolfo di Cambio (Scala/Art Resource, NY)

Elite Resurgence: Black and White Guelfs

Led by the magnates, the elite did all it could to bring down Giano della Bella and the popolo. Dino Compagni, Giano's loyal supporter and close adviser who shared his hostility to the "grandi," recounts their campaign to under-mine the popular government as the prelude to the ghastly spectacle of open civil war between the reconstituted elite factions in the first decade of the fourteenth century. According to Compagni, the lawyers began to subvert the spirit and intent of the Ordinances. The magnates accused Giano of leading the movement not for justice but to destroy his enemies. They planted rumors about the machinations of this and that group against him, provoking Giano to support punitive measures that only generated real hostility from these groups. They thought about assassination. They brought into Tuscany a French knight, Jean de Châlons, to use intimidation and force to "crush the *popolo*"; Compagni makes a point of mentioning that Vieri de' Cerchi, future leader of the White Guelfs, agreed to the plan. A group of elite *popolani* organized a conspiracy against Giano, as Compagni himself discovered during the meetings of a commission appointed to revise the communal statutes. Giano, "more brave than prudent," responded with more of his characteristic inflexibility and indignation. Magnates held a meeting in which a Frescobaldi complained that these "dogs of the *popolo*" had deprived them of honor and offices; he urged that they take up arms and kill Giano and as many of the popolo as they could. But Baldo Della Tosa countered with a plan to "conquer them with cunning" by spreading rumors that the popolo planned to let Ghibellines back into government. Such rumors, he argued, "would sow discord among the *popolo*, and defame Giano, and detach from his side all the powerful among the *popolo*" (1.12–15).

The campaign to discredit Giano succeeded in early 1295, when, in another of his endless feuds, Corso Donati sent armed retainers to wound a kinsman and a man was killed. The case came before the podestà's court, as required by the Ordinances, but a corrupt judge returned an acquittal against all the evidence. Although the podestà had been deceived by his judge, the citizens blamed the podestà and attacked him in his palace. Giano, who was at that moment "with the priors" (a detail that reveals his ongoing influence in government even when not in office), jumped on his horse and rode into the crowd to persuade them not to harm the podestà. But the crowd turned against Giano, pushed him aside, and pursued their assault against the fleeing podestà. Giano's disgrace was the moment his enemies had been waiting for. They blamed him for the disorders, and some of his supporters advised him to leave the city until things calmed down. Once gone, he was officially banished, on March 5, 1295, and his house ransacked and destroyed. According to Compagni (1.16–17), Giano's exile seriously weakened the popular government whose policies and reforms now began to be ignored as the elite gradually regained the upper hand against a leaderless popolo. The Ordinances remained in place but were not always enforced, and the guild consuls lost control over the election of the priors. Elite factionalism resurfaced and hostilities soon erupted between the so-called Black and White Guelfs.

The popular party did not disappear in these years and remained strong enough to maintain the exclusion of magnates from the priorate. But the factions began to attract supporters from both the non-magnate elite families that had supported the popolo and from the popolo itself. Compagni denounced with particular anger those of the popolo who sided with a faction. As the elite succeeded in rebuilding vertical ties of patronage with clients from the popolo, the emboldened factions were soon at each other's throats. Understanding why families joined one or the other of these factions is as difficult as identifying the reasons behind the split between Guelfs and Ghibellines two generations earlier. Indeed, Guelfs and former Ghibellines are found among both Blacks and Whites, and both factions included merchants and bankers. Competition between rival banking families may have played a role, since the Whites were led by prominent bankers, the Cerchi, and among the Blacks the Spini were Pope Boniface VIII's most important creditors.[32] But it is difficult to imagine why the banking families among the Blacks, chiefly Bardi and Spini, would have let a non-mercantile family, the Donati, assume leadership of their faction. And if economic rivalries were really behind the split, it is especially difficult to understand why they would have let hostilities unfold to the extremes of civil war and massive destruction, as in fact happened. Moreover, many families, including some banking families, were divided in their loyalties (Adimari, Della Tosa, and at least ten others, including the Bardi and Frescobaldi). Such internal splits seem incompatible with the notion of economic rivalries between families.

Compagni's analysis of what he saw as the sometimes personal, sometimes accidental, but never principled motives behind factional loyalties suggests the need for a cultural approach. Essential to the prestige of elite families was competition with other families, not only for economic advantage, but for power and favor among the people, for clients and followers, for control of neighborhoods and churches, for allies in other cities and the support of powerful foreign lords, for reputation, dignity, preeminence, and glory. It was not yet part of the culture and collective imaginary of such families, especially in the aftermath of the popolo's challenges, to accept non-competitive, peaceful coexistence for their collective benefit. It would take another generation and the chastening experience of ferocious civil war for (some members of) this unruly elite to come to such an understanding of their class interests. By 1300 the elite was thoroughly factionalized. The Cerchi-led Whites counted among their magnate allies the Adimari, Cavalcanti, Gherardini, Frescobaldi, Scali, Mozzi, Nerli, Abati, and some of the Della Tosa, and, among their non-magnate allies, the Dell'Antella, Canigiani, Falconieri, Girolami, and Rinucci. The Blacks' magnate contingent included the faction's undisputed leader Corso Donati and his family, and the Spini, Pazzi, Visdomini, Bardi, Rossi, Brunelleschi, Tornaquinci, Buondelmonti, Franzesi, and the other branch of the Della Tosa. Among the leading Black non-magnate lineages were the Acciaiuoli, Alberti del Giudice, Albizzi, Altoviti, Ardinghelli, Becchenugi, Bordoni, Cerretani, Guadagni, Magalotti, Mancini, Medici, Peruzzi, Strozzi, and Velluti. Whites and Blacks had roughly equal numbers of magnates, but the Blacks had the advantage of much greater strength among non-magnate elite families.

---

[32] Holmes, *Florence, Rome*, pp. 168–70. G. Masi, "I banchieri fiorentini nella vita politica della città sulla fine del Dugento," *Archivio giuridico* 9 (1931): 57–89; Masi, "La struttura sociale delle fazioni fiorentine politiche ai tempi di Dante," *Giornale dantesco* 31 (1928): 1–28.

The violence escalated in 1300 between the factions and between elite and popolo. That year's Mayday celebrations produced a public confrontation between the factions, and in June magnates attacked a procession of the guilds and their consuls shouting, "We are the ones who were responsible for the victory at Campaldino [in 1289], yet you have taken from us the offices and honors of our city" (Compagni, 1.21). To prevent further violence, the priorate sent into exile magnate leaders from both factions: for the Blacks, Corso Donati, Rosso della Tosa, Pazzino de' Pazzi, and Geri Spini, and, from the Whites, three of the Cerchi (but not their leader Vieri), the poet Guido Cavalcanti, Baschiera della Tosa, and Baldinaccio Adimari. But the attempt at evenhandedness broke down when the Cerchi exiles were allowed to return later that summer. Nor could the government control the efforts of the factions to secure external allies. Corso Donati and the Spini appealed to Pope Boniface, while the Whites sought support within Tuscany, particularly in Pistoia, Arezzo, and Pisa, which earned them the opprobrium of being friends of Ghibellines. As the elite yielded again to its old habit of bringing in foreign powers to defeat internal enemies, the intervention of outsiders made the conflict less amenable to resolution from within.

Boniface requested the intervention on behalf of the Blacks of Charles of Valois, brother of the French King Philip IV, with whom, ironically, Boniface had been locked for years in a struggle for control of the French church. Officially dubbed a "peacemaker" by the pope, Charles approached and entered Tuscany with a force of 500 knights in the summer of 1301. Yet it was no secret that he intended to repatriate the Black exiles and put their faction in power. Fearful of what his army might do, all parties agreed to elect, for the term October–December 1301, a non-partisan priorate, which included Dino Compagni, to deal with the crisis. Increasingly apprehensive, Florentines said of this priorate that it was, as Compagni himself put it, "the last hope," even as in retrospect it was clear that "we should have been sharpening our swords." Charles sent envoys demanding that he be welcomed to the city, and Compagni's priorate responded that, the matter being of such great moment, "they did not want to do anything without the agreement [*consentimento*] of their citizens." What happened next shows how deeply engrained the political ideas of the guild republic were in Compagni's political reflexes. The priors "called a general council of the Guelf party and of the seventy-two guilds, all of which had consuls, and they asked each one to submit a written statement on whether the guild wanted messer Charles of Valois to come to Florence as a peacemaker." For Compagni and his fellow priors, the "consentimento" of citizens was to be obtained by asking each guild for its autonomous and freely given opinion based on consultations among the members. As to why they requested opinions from seventy-two, rather than twenty-one, guilds, we can only speculate that they appealed either to the many guilds still outside the 1293 federation or to the subdivisions of the twenty-one guilds as if they were autonomous guilds, or both. The intent was evidently to increase the number of guilds whose members, so they hoped, were more likely to be neutral between the factions and critical of their feuds, and thus to augment the chances of a vote against Charles's entry into the city. In these hopes, the priors of the "final remedy" must have been deeply disappointed, for the guilds "all replied, in speech and in writing, that he should be allowed to come and should be honored like a lord of noble blood – all except the bakers, who said that he should be neither received nor honored, for he was coming to destroy the city" (2.5–7). Compagni lets the bakers' lonely voice stand as a prophetic warning of what lay ahead.

From the moment of Charles's arrival in early November 1301, Compagni's account has about it an air of ineluctable tragedy. Accompanying Charles were Corso Donati and the Blacks, who insisted on the immediate removal and replacement of the priors (against which Compagni protested with the by now touchingly naive argument that this would violate the Ordinances of Justice). On November 8 the Blacks installed priors of their own choosing. Despite promises to respect the safety of citizens and property, six days of chaotic violence ensued during which old scores were settled, enemies eliminated, property confiscated and destroyed. Some months later, decrees of exile were handed down against the Cerchi, Della Tosa, Adimari, Mozzi, Scali, and many other Whites: 559 men were exiled and 108 assessed fines.[33] Among them was Dante, then communal envoy at the papal court, who stood accused of fraud, extortion, and obstructing the peacemaking efforts of Charles and Boniface. Cited to appear before the podestà's court, Dante did not return, was declared a rebel in March 1302, and spent the rest of his life in exile.[34] Also exiled was the notary ser Petracco, who went to live in Arezzo, where Francesco was born. Although his conviction was rescinded six years later, he preferred to accept a post at the papal court of Clement V in Avignon. Exiled Whites eventually joined forces with old Florentine Ghibelline exiles and other Tuscan Ghibellines and spent years planning a revenge and a return that never happened.

Florence was now in the hands of Corso Donati and his chief magnate lieutenants, Rosso della Tosa, Pazzino de' Pazzi, Geri Spini, and Betto Brunelleschi, with the support of the magnate and non-magnate houses of his faction. Compagni bitterly remarked that "none of them can deny that he was a destroyer of the city. Nor can they say that any need constrained them, other than pride and competition for offices" (2.26). Although an oversimplification

---

[33] Holmes, *Florence, Rome*, p. 179.
[34] R. Starn, *Contrary Commonwealth: The Theme of Exile in Medieval and Renaissance Italy* (Berkeley, 1982), pp. 60–85.

of what was at stake in 1300–2, it describes well enough the actions of the Black leaders over the next decade, as they turned on one another and indulged yet again in the elite's historic weakness of factional splintering. New rivalries and ruptures now pitted Corso Donati against Rosso della Tosa, and each took with him a contingent of Blacks. Donati played on the resentments of magnates and persuaded thirty-two of them, mostly from older families but including the Bardi, to swear an oath to overturn their continued exclusion from political offices. Rosso della Tosa had more of the magnate merchants on his side (Pazzi, Frescobaldi, and Spini) and many non-magnate elite. In 1304, with the danger of a new civil war looming, Pope Benedict XI sent Cardinal Nicholas of Prato to negotiate a reconciliation of the rival factions of Black Guelfs and an agreement with the White exiles. In April the cardinal organized a public ritual of reconciliation in piazza Santa Maria Novella. Another result of his mediation was the re-establishment of the neighborhood military companies first created by the primo popolo in 1250. Evidently, the popolo was still strong enough to demand something for itself. Peace among elite factions may still have depended, as it did in 1280, on the popolo's support. The standardbearers of the military companies also received a new role as advisers to the priors, thus becoming the first of the priorate's two advisory colleges. Nicholas then turned his attention to the exiles and invited fourteen of them, including an Uberti and a Cerchi, to come to the city for negotiations. Compagni noted the warm welcome they received from "many old Ghibelline men and women [who] kissed the Uberti arms." Even the fiercely antagonistic branches of the Della Tosa made peace, and "the popolo took great hope from this" (3.7).

But the promising events of early 1304 ended in disaster. Compagni believed the Blacks had no real wish for peace with the exiles, whose representatives began to sense both the futility and danger of their presence in the city. They left on June 8, and the cardinal followed them out of town the next day. Violence immediately exploded, according to Villani (9.71), between the supporters of Cardinal Nicholas's mediation and the Black Guelf leadership. Compagni reports that it was the Medici and Della Tosa who started the street fighting on June 10 that led to the great disaster. The Cavalcanti seemed on the verge of bringing the city center under their control when a fire, set by Black leaders to dislodge the Cavalcanti, spread quickly and, with the help of a strong wind, destroyed the center of Florence. Villani says that 1,700 palaces, towers, and houses were consumed; Compagni thought it closer to 1,900 (3.9). The people, he says, were "stunned" by the devastation but did not dare complain about those responsible for it, because they "ruled the city tyrannically." Villani enumerated the destroyed areas: the loggia of Orsanmichele; the palaces and houses of the Abati, Macci, Amieri, Toschi, Cipriani, Lamberti, Cavalcanti, Gherardini, Pulci, and Amidei; the whole of via Calimala with its many shops;

everything around the Mercato Nuovo and the church of Santa Cecilia; via Por Santa Maria all the way to the Ponte Vecchio, into via Vaccherreccia (toward the new palace of the popolo), behind the church of San Pier Scheraggio, and all the adjacent neighborhoods down to the Arno. He summed it up by saying that on that day the "marrow and core" of the city went up in flames. The great fire of 1304 was the lowest point to which the elite families had ever brought their city.

In 1308 Corso Donati tried one last time to rid himself of inconvenient allies and assert uncontested leadership. It is possible that Donati, aware of the emergence at the conclusion of protracted factional struggles of single ruling families in many northern Italian communes (such as the Visconti in Milan and Este in Ferrara), may have aspired to a similar position in Florence for himself and his family. If, as Compagni reports, Rosso della Tosa harbored the ambition "to exercise lordship in the manner of the lords of Lombardy" (3.2), it is easy to imagine that Donati did as well. Perhaps provoked by the reinforcement of the Ordinances of Justice in 1306 and the institution of the Executor of the Ordinances, Donati assembled another faction of disgruntled magnates (Compagni calls it a conspiracy) that included the Bardi, Rossi, Frescobaldi, Tornaquinci, Buondelmonti, and the non-magnate Medici and Bordoni and planned an armed assault on the palace to demand a new government. The attempted coup may have been the closest medieval Florence came to getting its own version of one of those "lords of Lombardy." But rivals from within his now splintered faction thwarted whatever ambition Donati harbored. Rosso della Tosa and other leading Blacks got wind of his plans and had Corso and his associates accused and sentenced. Donati barricaded himself in the family enclave near San Pier Maggiore, and, as the newly restored military companies of the popolo, led by the podestà, Capitano, and Executor, attacked the stronghold, he waited for help from friends, who, however, seeing the forces arrayed against him, prudently deserted him. Although Corso escaped and took refuge in a monastery outside the walls, he was hunted down and killed.

Compagni considered Corso Donati the greatest of the popolo's enemies and yet wrote with a kind of awe about the unforgettable "barone." In addition to his famous comparison (2.20) to "Catiline the Roman, but more cruel," in which Compagni mixes praise for Corso's physical presence, speech, good breeding, and intellect with the devastatingly straightforward judgment that "his mind was always set on evildoing," he said of Donati's "bad death" (3.21) that he "lived dangerously and died reprehensibly. He was a knight of great spirit and renown, noble in blood and behavior, and very handsome in appearance even in his old age, of fine form with delicate features and white skin. He was a charming, wise, and elegant speaker, and always undertook great things. He was accustomed to dealing familiarly with great lords and noble men, and had many friends, and was famous throughout all Italy. He was the enemy of the *popolo* and of *popolani*, and was loved by his soldiers; he was full of malicious thoughts, cruel and astute. . . . Everyone commonly said that the ones who ordered his death were messer Rosso della Tosa and messer Pazzino de' Pazzi; and some people blessed them, while others did the opposite."

Although it was difficult to discern at the moment, Corso Donati's death heralded the end of an era. Within four years, Rosso della Tosa, Betto Brunelleschi, and Pazzino de' Pazzi were all dead, the last two murdered in acts of revenge by the Donati and Cavalcanti. Occasionally serious conflicts and conspiracies within the ruling group continued, but never again would the city be engulfed in open civil war pitting private elite armies against one another. Nor, for the next century, would any Florentine dominate the political stage as thoroughly as did Corso Donati: not until Cosimo de' Medici did so with very different means in a transformed political world. The disappearance of violent fissures within the elite and of larger-than-life figures like Corso Donati and Farinata degli Uberti, whose fame, power, and charisma were the product of the dramatic divisions of their class, reflect deep structural transformations at work within the elite and its relationship to the popolo. The circumstances of Corso Donati's downfall likewise signal these changes. His enemies, even among the magnates, appealed to the government to have him condemned, and the assault on his stronghold was carried out by the popolo's military companies, led by three communal officials, two of whom had been instituted by the popolo. The popolo was not yet ready to launch another political challenge (which came only several decades later), but the manner in which Donati was brought down with the cooperation of members of his own class and faction means that the elite, even some magnates, were now, at least sometimes, willing to work through the popolo's institutions to deal with what everyone recognized as the embarrassing spectacle of an over-mighty citizen who refused to adapt. Through the violence of the century's first decade and all the angry attempts to "break the *popolo*," the Ordinances were not abrogated, the priorate of the guilds remained the chief communal magistracy, magnates were still barred from sitting on it, and Florence did not succumb to a "lord." However reluctantly, the elite was gradually acquiescing in an order of things it had long resisted.

4

Domestic Economy and Merchant Empires to 1340

A lthough the elite families of Cacciaguida's twelfth-century city were not as unconcerned with wealth and commerce as Dante wants us to believe, their economic activities focused mainly on the acquisition of land in the contado and the importation of Flemish cloth to be finished and dyed in Florence. These were important foundations for subsequent commercial and industrial expansion, but in the twelfth and early thirteenth centuries Florence lagged behind Venice, Genoa, and Pisa in international trade, behind Siena and Lucca in banking, and behind the Flemish and several Italian cities in textile manufactures. The takeoff of the economy occurred relatively quickly in the second half of the thirteenth century, when Florentines became increasingly prominent as international commodity traders, merchants, bankers, and textile manufacturers.[1] By 1300 they were European leaders in all these areas. But the elite's part in this boom needs to be understood within a larger picture of economic structures involving both the guild community and the working classes in the textile, building, and provisioning trades, where growing employment attracted immigrants from the contado and nourished the city's huge population increase.

Population: City and Contado

Beyond the city lay the contado, the surrounding hinterland that originally embraced the dioceses of Florence and Fiesole and then expanded as Florence brought more territory under its control. By 1300 it extended roughly twenty-

---

[1] E. Fiumi, *Fioritura e decadenza dell'economia fiorentina*, ASI 115 (1957): 385–439; 116 (1958): 443–510; 117 (1959): 427–502; reprint edn. (Florence, 1977).

five miles north (to Barberino and Borgo San Lorenzo in the Mugello valley and beyond to Scarperia), a similar distance northeast (to Dicomano), fifteen miles east (beyond Pontassieve to the northern end of the Casentino), thirty miles southeast (including the upper Arno valley to Montevarchi), twenty-five miles southwest (to Castelfiorentino, Certaldo, and Poggibonsi in the Valdelsa), twenty miles down the lower Arno valley (to Empoli), but only some ten miles west by northwest (just beyond Signa and Campi). In the 1320s Florence pushed farther in this direction and took control of the Monte Albano, but not until 1350 was even nearby Prato incorporated into the dominion. Later, when larger cities like Arezzo and Pisa came under Florentine rule, they were referred to as the district[2] (see Map 3, page 472).

Because of low urban birth rates and high infant mortality, Florence, like most pre-modern cities, did not generate its own population growth, which depended on immigration from the heavily populated contado. Estimates for the pre-plague contado derive from Villani's figures of 70,000 men able to bear arms in 1300 and 80,000 in 1338 (an increase due to the expanding area under Florentine control), which indicate an overall contado population between 280,000 and 320,000. This dense rural population had been increasing steadily for two centuries and by the late thirteenth century was growing beyond the contado's ability to supply sufficient work. Hence, large numbers of rural families left their overpopulated towns and villages and migrated to the metropolis. By 1300 the combined population of city and contado was over 400,000, but rural population was already stagnating and in some areas declining, owing partly to emigration and partly to a decreasing birth rate. The great epidemics that began in the 1340s, especially the devastating Black Death of 1348, reduced contado population by one-half to two-thirds, and recurrences of the epidemic kept it low for a long time: between 100,000 and 140,000 in the second half of the fourteenth century, 125,000 in 1427, and 110,000 in 1470. Not until the sixteenth century did the contado begin to recover, reaching 220,000 by mid-century. It approached its medieval peak only in the eighteenth century, with 282,000 in 1745, which underscores just how densely populated the contado was in the century before the Black Death.

Late twelfth- and thirteenth-century Florence was protected by walls built in the 1170s. In the thirteenth century's rapid growth, new neighborhoods spilled over and surrounded these walls. Between 1200 and 1300 the city's population tripled, or even quadrupled, to an estimated 120,000, a huge metropolis by medieval standards. The arrival of wave after wave of immigrants from the countryside throughout the thirteenth and early fourteenth centuries deeply

---

[2]   Ch.-M. de la Roncière, *Prix et salaires à Florence au XIVe siècle (1280–1380)* (Rome, 1982), pp. ix–x; P. Pirillo, *Costruzione di un contado: i fiorentini e il loro territorio nel basso medioevo* (Florence, 2001).

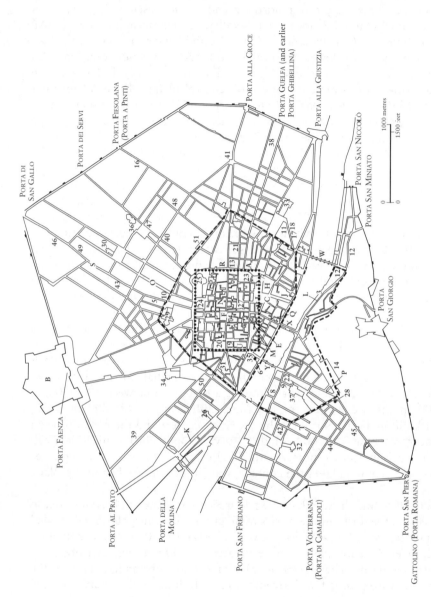

Map 2 Florence's three circuits of walls with major churches, hospitals, and civic buildings, and family palaces built in the fifteenth century (based on the maps in G. Fanelli, *Firenze* [Rome and Bari, 1980; seventh edn. 2002])

Key to map 2

Family palaces	Churches	Convents (continued)	Streets
1. Boni (Antinori)	23. Badia	44. Sant'Elisabetta delle	K Borgo Ognissanti
2. Corsi-Alberti (Horne)	24. Baptistery (San Giovanni)	Convertite	L Via de' Bardi
3. Da Uzzano	25. Cathedral (Duomo,	45. San Vincenzo d'Annalena	M Via Calimala
4. Del Pugliese	Santa Maria del Fiore)		N Via Calzaiuoli
5. Dietisalvi-Neroni	26. Ognissanti	Hospitals	O Via Larga
6. Gianfigliazzi	27. Orsanmichele	46. Bonifazio	P Via Maggio
7. Gondi	28. San Felice in Piazza	47. Innocenti	Q Via Por Santa Maria
8. Lanfredini	29. San Lorenzo	48. Orbatello	R Via del Proconsolo
9. Machiavelli	30. San Marco	49. San Giovanni Decollato	S Via San Gallo
10. Medici	31. San Pancrazio	50. San Paolo	T Via de' Serragli
11. Morelli	32. Santa Maria del Carmine	51. Santa Maria Nuova	U Via Tornabuoni
12. Nasi (2) (one is now	33. Santa Croce		V Via Vacchereccia
Torrigiani)	34. Santa Maria Novella	Civic buildings and spaces	
13. Pazzi	35. Santa Trinita	A Bargello	Bridges
14. Pitti	36. Santissima Annunziata	B Fortezza da Basso	W Ponte Rubaconte
15. Rucellai	37. Santo Spirito	C Loggia dei Lanzi	X Ponte Vecchio
16. Scala		D Mercanzia	Y Ponte Santa Trinita
17. Serristori	Convents	E Mercato Nuovo	Z Ponte alla Carraia
18. Spinelli	38. Le Murate	F Mercato Vecchio	
19. Strozzi	39. San Jacopo di Ripoli	G Palace of the Parte Guelfa	City walls
20. Tornabuoni	40. Santa Maria degli Angeli	H Palace of the Priors	Roman walls •••••••
21. Valori	41. Sant' Ambrogio	(Palazzo Vecchio)	Walls of 1170s ━━━━
22. Vettori	42. Santa Monaca	I Piazza Signoria	Walls of 1284–1333 ━━▪━
	43. Sant'Apollonia	J Uffizi	

affected the character of the city, physically and culturally. Immigrants flooded into new neighborhoods in the Oltrarno, necessitating the construction of three new bridges between 1220 and 1252 and an extension of the walls in 1258. In the last quarter of the century, immigration peaked and new settlements extended ever farther from the old walls in every direction. In 1284 the government began constructing a much larger set of walls, completed only in 1334, which enclosed an area almost eight times that of the earlier walls and included the neighborhoods in which the mendicant orders were building their great basilicas of Santa Maria Novella and Santa Croce and where they and their lay followers built the hospitals that served the needs of immigrants newly arrived from their ancestral villages (see Map 2). The social and cultural imprint of a century and more of constant immigration from the contado provides the background to the complaint voiced by Dante's Cacciaguida in *Paradiso* 16 when he says that the "mixing of people [*la confusion delle persone*]" was the origin of the troubles of a city that would have done better to keep its boundaries "at Trespiano and Galluzzo," just a few miles, respectively, to the north and south. It was the lament of a social conservative who would have traded the economic growth that was both cause and effect of immigration for the imagined ideal of a smaller, self-contained community without the cultural and political upheavals that Dante associated with the newcomers. That so many people came to the city is evidence not only of an overpopulated contado but also of the capacity of an urban economy in a long phase of steady expansion to absorb an ever larger labor force. Thousands of notaries and skilled artisans brought with them professional skills, and still more former agricultural workers came in search of employment in either the textile or building trades.

According to Matteo Villani, who continued his brother Giovanni's chronicle after his death in 1348, the city lost 60 percent of its people in that one awful summer. Tax rolls from 1352 record 9,955 households in the city, which indicates a population between 40,000 and 45,000. Some recovery occurred over the next generation. A 1380 tax census lists 13,074 households and an exactly counted population of 54,747 (4.19 persons per household). But the plagues kept returning: in 1400 (when 12,000 people died) and again in 1417 and 1424. By 1427, according to the Catasto, Florence had 37,245 inhabitants distributed in 9,780 households (only 3.80 persons per household). For the city, too, recovery came only with the general increase of the European population in the sixteenth century. A 1552 census counted 59,000 inhabitants, but in only 9,527 households (6.21 per hearth), which means that the birth rate was finally, and significantly, increasing. But, in the city as in the contado, only in the eighteenth century did the population equal and exceed its medieval high. Florence and its contado in 1300 were more densely populated than they would be for the next four centuries, a fact of crucial importance for understanding the city's economy before the Black Death.[3]

Textiles, Building, and Provisioning

The roster of Florence's guilds reveals the enormous importance of the textile and clothing trades.[4] In the early fourteenth century, the Wool guild alone counted between 600 and 700 investor-entrepreneurs in 200–300 firms, and the industry employed at least 10,000 artisans and workers in the various phases of production. A significant percentage of the Calimala's 200 members invested in the 20 firms that each year, according to Villani, imported 10,000 bolts of cloth, worth 300,000 florins, to be dyed and resold. Many, perhaps a majority, of the 500–600 members of Por Santa Maria were local cloth retailers, and a smaller number produced silk cloth. The 200 members of the Rigattieri bought and sold used cloth. Measured by the number of entrepreneurs and laborers, the manufacture and sale of textiles constituted Florence's largest complex of economic activities. The non-textile sector of the clothing trades included the guilds of the furriers, whose 200 members produced and sold fur

---

[3]   D. Herlihy and C. Klapisch-Zuber, *Tuscans and their Families: A Study of the Florentine Catasto of 1427* (New Haven, 1985; original French edn. Paris, 1978), pp. 60–95.
[4]   On the clothing trades: C. C. Frick, *Dressing Renaissance Florence: Families, Fortunes, and Fine Clothing* (Baltimore, 2002).

coats and linings; approximately seventy-five tanners who manufactured leather clothing among other products; and the shoemakers whose 1,550 members in the city (and another 1,300 in the contado) made and repaired footwear. Before the Black Death, over 3,000 of the city's estimated 8,000 guildsmen were involved in one or another of these trades, whose combined workforce was approximately 15,000.

The manufacture of woolen cloth was the heart of the domestic economy. According to Villani (12.94), in 1300 some 300 firms annually produced over 100,000 bolts of cloth. By the 1330s, the number of firms had declined to 200, and annual production to between 70,000 and 80,000 bolts. But the average value of cloths doubled with respect to a generation earlier, because the industry now produced higher quality cloths from superior English wool. He estimated the total annual value of production in the 1330s at 1,200,000 florins, not including profits, and calculated that one third or more of this sum was paid out in wages that supported 30,000 persons. For 200 firms to produce 70,000 bolts of cloth, average annual production per firm would have had to be 350 bolts. Although evidence from after the Black Death points to considerably lower production levels (from 1355 to 1374 firms produced an average of between 122 and 140 bolts per year),[5] in these same decades some firms produced 250 and more bolts and would have produced still more if the Wool guild, for reasons to be explored in due course, had not set a production ceiling of 220 bolts per firm. Buonaccorso Pitti, a member of one of the guild's leading families, says that the woolen cloth operation of his father Neri (1306–74) produced 1,100 bolts each year.[6] But it is unclear whether the measure of a bolt remained the same over this period. In Florence the *panno* or *pezza* was usually about 36 yards long, but throughout Europe and Italy it varied from 30 to 50 yards, and it is possible that the length changed over time even in one place.

There is another point of entry into the reliability of Villani's figures, and that is his estimate of annual labor costs of 400,000 florins and his assertion that 30,000 persons (workers and their dependents) lived on this sum. These figures yield hypothetical annual per capita living costs among workers of 13$\frac{1}{3}$ florins. In Florence, the value of luxury goods, property, and major commercial transactions was measured in gold florins, while workers' wages were paid and goods bought and sold locally in silver soldi and denari: twelve denari made one soldo, and twenty soldi made one lira, which was a money of account, not an actual coin. There was no fixed exchange rate between florins and lire, and market fluctuations determined their relative value. When the

[5] F. Franceschi, *Oltre il "Tumulto." I lavoratori fiorentini dell'Arte della Lana fra Tre e Quattrocento* (Florence, 1993), p. 8.
[6] Buonaccorso Pitti, *Ricordi*, in *Mercanti Scrittori*, ed. V. Branca (Milan, 1986), p. 355.

florin was first coined in 1252, it was introduced as equivalent in value to the lira and thus worth 20 soldi. But silver money steadily lost value against the florin, which was worth 34 soldi by 1280, 47 in 1300, 65 by 1320, held steady between 60 and 70 until the mid-1370s, and was worth between 70 and 80 from then until 1410.[7] In the years to which Villani's data refer, with the florin at 62 soldi, annual per capita living costs of 13⅓ florins were equivalent to 825 soldi, or 2.26 soldi per day. A comparison is possible with the 1380s, when actual daily living costs for unmarried workers were 3 soldi, or 1,095 per year, and 10 soldi for a family of five, or 2 soldi per day per person.[8] Villani's implied estimate for the 1330s, based on aggregate wages, is thus quite close to living costs fifty years later, which makes his assumptions concerning total labor costs and the number of persons supported by this sum certainly plausible. With 30,000 persons dependent on the wages paid by the industry, even just one worker per household of four yields 7,500 workers. But much of the spinning and weaving was done by women who worked to supplement their families' incomes, and many households had two persons employed in one or another of the various stages of production. Adding the women spinners and weavers to the 7,500 household heads who worked in the industry, we easily arrive at a total workforce of 10,000 in an overall population of 120,000. To doubt Villani's figures on production and employment requires an alternative explanation for this large population and for how all those people earned their living. The guild's merchant-entrepreneurs found bigger profits in producing a smaller number of cloths of higher quality and value,[9] thus presumably employing fewer workers by the 1330s than they had in 1300. But even with this possible decline in the number of workers, Florence remained heavily dependent on the woolen cloth industry. Assuming that at least half the population was of working age (in 1427, 55% was between the ages of 15 and 64[10]), 10,000 textile workers in a population of 120,000 means that about one of every six men and women of working age was employed in the manufacture of woolen cloth. And if we add the merchant owners, their bookkeepers, and agents, the proportion is still greater. The industry's general prosperity in the fourteenth century helps to account for the growing population before the plague and its respectable recovery in the second half of the century. But when the industry shrank after 1400, Florence's population sank to the lowest level in its entire history.

[7]   R. A. Goldthwaite and G. Mandich, *Studi sulla moneta fiorentina (secoli XIII–XVI)* (Florence, 1994), pp. 87–92.
[8]   Franceschi, *Oltre il "Tumulto,"* pp. 261–6.
[9]   H. Hoshino, *L'Arte della Lana in Firenze nel basso medioevo: il commercio della lana e il mercato dei panni fiorentini nei secoli XIII–XV* (Florence, 1980).
[10]   Herlihy and Klapisch-Zuber, *Tuscans,* p. 187.

The entrepreneurs of the guild bought, imported, and kept ownership of both the wool and the cloth made from it throughout the complex production process, which alternated between workplaces owned by the entrepreneurs and the shops and homes of independent artisans. The initial stages of cleaning, sorting, beating, and combing the wool were performed in the owners' workplaces by large crews of mostly unskilled wage-workers, later called Ciompi. Of the stages of this initial preparation of the wool, only the washing process took place in the shops of independent artisans. The wool was then distributed to spinners, including many women, most of whom worked at home. Agents representing the owners made regular rounds through working-class neighborhoods, delivered the wool and set rates of pay and completion schedules, and returned to collect the yarn and pay the spinners. The yarn in turn was distributed by agents to weavers, who worked either at home or in modest shops, and always for piece-rates. From the weavers the agents collected the bolts of cloth that were still in need of a whole series of finishing processes. The burling, washing, fulling, and stretching of the cloth occurred in large workplaces, some owned by the guild and some by individual entrepreneurs, whereas the dyeing, mending, napping, and pressing of the finished product were performed by artisans in their shops. Skilled artisans, especially dyers, often employed workers in shops of their own that required substantial investment. Among textile artisans the dyers were the wealthiest and potentially most independent. The industry was thus a complex mix of centralized workplaces, independent and occasionally well-to-do artisans like the dyers, poorer but still independent artisans like spinners and weavers who worked at home, and a mass of unskilled wage laborers in the shops of both owners and artisans. Tensions ran high in this most important of Florence's industries, in part because the guild of owners denied to all these categories the right to form associations while at the same time claiming and exercising tight regulatory control and often punitive jurisdiction over them all.[11]

The construction industry was a major employer of labor and source of domestic wealth. In 1358 the guild of Maestri di pietra e legname (master masons, wallers, and carpenters) registered over 400 members in the city and 272 in the contado, a total of almost 700 a decade after the plague. A 1391 list records a total of 915, without distinguishing between city and contado. The Legnaiuoli, woodworkers and cabinetmakers, numbered 200 in 1391. An industry that counted between 900 and 1,100 enrolled guildsmen after the plague may very well have had twice that number before it and an equal number of unskilled laborers and apprentices. The largest among the many early fourteenth-century building projects were the city walls and the new

[11]   A. Doren, *Die Florentiner Wollentuchindustrie vom 14. bis zum 16. Jahrhundert* (Stuttgart, 1901).

cathedral. Begun in the mid-1290s, the construction of the cathedral was entrusted in 1331 to the Wool guild, as was the Campanile, or bell tower, in 1334. Designated percentages of treasury payments and receipts of indirect taxes were assigned to fund construction. A communal audit of 1359 revealed that in the preceding twenty-six years the cathedral project's total income amounted to over 300,000 lire (almost 95,000 florins).[12] From 1333 to 1348, the 127,500 lire spent at the cathedral works would have paid a year's living costs for over 3,000 people. By the 1370s and 1380s government subsidies to the cathedral reached 3 to 3⅓ percent of ordinary revenues.[13] The workforce varied with the seasons and stages of construction: between 1375 and 1378 (and this was during a war) the total of skilled and unskilled workers at the project each month ranged from 80 to 225 (and more often than not was over 200, but some part-time), including between 40 and 140 masons.[14] Whereas the Campanile was built fairly quickly between 1334 and 1357,[15] the construction of the cathedral continued, with many and sometimes long interruptions, until the 1420s when, with the church otherwise complete, there remained the great task of building the dome (see Plate 2).

The first four gates of the new circuit of walls were erected in 1284–5, but work was interrupted until 1299 and again in 1304. Construction resumed in 1310 and continued until the walls were completed in 1334. Between 1313 and 1329 at least 170 masons and master wallers were employed, and no doubt hundreds of workers who hauled the massive amounts of stone needed for the more than five-mile circuit of walls with their seventy-three towers spaced every 380 feet, many of them more than 130 feet tall, as well as the wood for fifteen huge gates (see Plates 3 and 4). Construction was financed initially by the requirement that every will include a bequest for the walls, and then by periodic subsidies from the commune, assignments from tax revenues, and forced contributions from the clergy. In one particularly intense six-month period of work in 1323, the treasurers of the Officials of the Walls recorded spending 14,000 lire.[16] During these same decades major construction sites existed all over the city. Additions to the former palace of the primo popolo (the Bargello) continued into the 1320s, even as the palazzo of the second

[12] D. F. Zervas, "Un nuovo documento per la storia del Duomo e del Campanile di Firenze, 1333–1359," *Rivista d'arte* 39 (1987): 3–53.
[13] M. Haines, "Firenze e il finanziamento della Cattedrale e del Campanile," in *Alla riscoperta di piazza del Duomo in Firenze, 3: Il Campanile di Giotto*, ed. T. Verdon (Florence, 1994), pp. 71–83.
[14] La Roncière, *Prix et salaires*, pp. 290, 330.
[15] M. Trachtenberg, *The Campanile of Florence Cathedral: "Giotto's Tower"* (New York, 1971).
[16] R. Manetti and M. C. Pozzana, *Firenze: le porte dell'ultima cerchia di mura* (Florence, 1979), pp. 44, 65, 77–8, 82, 208, 225–36.

Plate 2 The Cathedral–Baptistery complex. Left to right: Baptistery of San Giovanni (begun in eleventh century); Bell Tower ("Campanile," 1334–57, original design by Giotto); Cathedral of Santa Maria del Fiore (known as the "Duomo," begun in mid-1290s, original plan by Arnolfo di Cambio, and dome by Filippo Brunelleschi, 1420–36) (Alinari/Art Resource, NY)

popolo was under construction. The hospital of Santa Maria Nuova was begun in 1286. The Dominican basilica of Santa Maria Novella was built between 1280 and 1360, and the Franciscans built Santa Croce from 1295 until well into the fifteenth century. The granary-oratory of Orsanmichele was rebuilt in the late 1330s. And the middle and later part of the century saw the construction of the loggia of the confraternity of the Bigallo in 1352–8, the loggia of the priors (later called the Loggia dei Lanzi) in 1374–81, and the palace of the Mercanzia, begun in 1359.

Public and ecclesiastical projects were only one part of the building boom of the early fourteenth century. The great fire of 1304 necessitated a general rebuilding that lasted many years. Until then, much of Florence had been built in wood (not the palaces and towers of the elite families, but the humbler homes and shops of artisans and workers). After the fire the city was rebuilt

Plate 3 Florence c.1480: The "Catena map," woodcut, showing the city enclosed by the third circuit of walls completed in 1334, with gates and towers (Scala/Art Resource, NY)

Plate 4   Porta Romana, the southernmost gate of the third set of walls (Alinari/Art Resource, NY)

largely in stone, which took longer and cost more. There is no way of knowing how many masons worked on such projects, nor how many laborers they employed. In the fifteenth century, master wallers typically organized and supervised small crews that included an assistant and one or two wage-earning laborers.[17] Some indication of the ratio of skilled wallers to unskilled laborers emerges from the building records of Santa Maria Nuova, where approximately 130 laborers were employed between 1350 and 1380, and 108 master masons between 1358 and 1380.[18] If we conservatively estimate 1,500 masons, wallers, and carpenters before the plague and at least an equivalent number of non-skilled workers and apprentices, the total work force in the building industry could easily have exceeded 3,000.

Another look at the list of guilds reveals the prominence of the cluster of trades that provided food and drink to the city's population. Four guilds were

[17]   R. A. Goldthwaite, *The Building of Renaissance Florence* (Baltimore, 1980), p. 126.
[18]   La Roncière, *Prix et salaires*, pp. 273, 321.

involved in provisioning: the butchers; sellers of cured meats and fish, oil, and cheese; wine retailers; and bakers. Before the plague, these guilds had a total of approximately 1,000 members in the city, many with assistants, apprentices, or hired workers. In 1330 the butchers had 330 members in the city and another 189 registered in the contado. Villani's statistics on the annual consumption of meat in the city help to account for the size and stature of this guild, which alone among the provisioning trades ranked among the top twelve guilds. Each year, he says, the city consumed 4,000 cattle and calves, 60,000 sheep, 20,000 goats, and 30,000 hogs, a total of 114,000 animals, which probably yielded some 7,000,000 pounds of edible meat, or 64 pounds per person for the population over the age of three (110,000), and in reality more than that since some religious ate no meat. Moreover, the number of days in which the consumption of meat was prohibited for the laity as well (Fridays, Saturdays, and all of Lent, altogether about 140 days) means that on days when meat was eaten the average daily per capita ration was more than a quarter of a pound. The wealthy no doubt ate more than the poor, but meat of one sort or another (and Villani says nothing of chicken or fish) was part of the daily diet of the vast majority of Florentines, laborers and the working poor included.[19] After the plague, the number of butchers declined in rough proportion to the population: 156 in the city and 45 in the contado in 1352, but by the century's end contado membership climbed back to 179.

The guild of retail wine sellers counted 92 members in 1336. Curiously, it slightly increased in size after the Black Death, with 105 members in 1353. Villani says that in the mid-1330s between 55,000 and 65,000 *cogna* of wine were sold each year in the city. Taking 60,000 as the average for these years, this yields a total consumption of between 24 and 27 million liters (opinions differ about the size of a *cogno*),[20] or somewhere between 200 and 225 liters per person. If we assume that children drank less than adults (and infants not at all), the annual per capita consumption among adults was perhaps close to 300 liters. The retail sale of wine was clearly a big business, especially since this huge amount was sold by only 100 dealers, who on average must each have handled 250,000 liters per year. Because the price of wine varied considerably, it is difficult to estimate the total value of sales. In the 1330s the price per *cogno* varied between 8 and 12 lire; if 10 lire was the average price, the annual value would have been 600,000 lire (at the time, 185,000 florins). In the second half of the century, the price of wine was 2½ times higher, which means that, if per capita consumption remained steady in a population smaller by half, the total value of sales actually increased to 750,000 lire.

---

[19]   Ibid., pp. 387–8; also E. Fiumi, "Economia e vita privata dei fiorentini nelle rilevazioni statistiche di Giovanni Villani," *ASI* 111 (1953): 207–41. My thanks to Allen Grieco for generous help with patterns of consumption of food and drink.
[20]   La Roncière, *Prix et salaires*, pp. 31–2, 129.

In the early fourteenth century the guild of Pizzicagnoli e Oliandoli, who, in addition to oil, cheese, and cured meats, sold fruit, nuts and a long list of other foods, increased its city membership from 200 to over 400, including many women. The only datum Villani gives for consumption in this sector is the 400 wagonloads of melons that he says entered the city each day every July. Even if each wagonload contained only 125 melons and deliveries were made on only 20 days of the month, the resulting 8,000 deliveries would have supplied a million fresh melons to the city every July.

Bread was of course the heart of the pre-modern diet. The guild of bakers had 174 members in 1337 and 243 in 1347, including 40 women. Villani, who counted 146 bakers in the mid-1330s, says that the city consumed 140 *moggia* of grain every day, compared to 800 per week, hence 114 per day, in 1280: a 23% increase that matches the population growth. A *moggio* was equivalent to 420 kilograms, or 924 pounds. This yields total daily consumption in the 1330s of almost 59,000 kg, or 130,000 pounds, equivalent to over a pound of bread per person per day. Assessing the economic significance of grain transactions is complicated by the wildly fluctuating prices caused by uneven harvests and the government's policy in times of scarcity of buying grain and selling it below cost. Despite the productivity of the contado, which in good years produced 80% of the 150,000 *moggia* needed to feed itself and the city, and the ample supplies imported from southern Italy, it was impossible to prevent periods of short-term scarcity and skyrocketing prices. Between 1320 and 1335, the average price per *staio* (one twenty-fourth of a *moggio*) ranged from a low of $7^1/_2$ soldi in 1321 to a high of 30 in the year of greatest scarcity, 1329, when the government purchased grain below the market price and distributed it at no cost to charitable organizations.[21] The total value of grain sales could thus be very different from one year to the next. In the "normal" years of the early and mid-1320s, the average cost was $12^1/_2$ soldi per *staio*, which means that the roughly 1,225,000 *staia* of grain (140 × 365 × 24) sold each year cost Florentine consumers approximately 765,000 lire, or 235,000 florins. After the crisis years of 1328–30, prices returned to a high normal of 16 soldi in 1331–5, and, assuming consumption at normal levels, total grain sales would have been worth 980,000 lire, or 300,000 florins in each of these years.

Merchant Companies and the Mercanzia

In 1308, the year of Corso Donati's death, the Florentine merchant elite created an association destined for a long and significant role in the city's

---

[21] For grain production and prices and communal policies: G. Pinto, *Il libro del biadaiolo: carestie e annona a Firenze dalla metà del '200 al 1348* (Florence, 1978), pp. 50–1, 63–70, 77–8, 107–30.

economic and political life. For the protection of their collective interests the international import–export merchants and bankers of the five major commercial guilds (Calimala, Cambio, Lana, Por Santa Maria, and Medici, Speziali, Merciai) formed the *universitas mercatorum*, or Mercanzia. At least eight leading merchant companies ended in bankruptcy between 1300 and 1310, including the Nerli, Davanzi, Mozzi, Abati-Bacherelli, Ardinghelli, and Franzesi. Bankruptcies meant panicky creditors, especially foreigners who often turned to their governments and petitioned for reprisals. Guild courts, created in the previous century to deal with creditors' claims against insolvent Florentine merchants, were not equipped to extend their influence and enforce their judgments beyond Tuscany and Italy, and in any case each guild's jurisdiction was limited to its members. Florence's international merchants thus needed a stronger and swifter judicial apparatus through which to satisfy foreign creditors and protect Florentine interests abroad. In March 1308 the five major commercial guilds instituted the "office of the *universitas* of the Mercanzia" with an executive committee of Five Councilors, one from each guild, who in these early years were elected by the same guilds' consuls. Later that year the commune's legislative councils accepted a petition submitted "on behalf of the merchants of Florence" for the institution of a foreign judicial official within the Mercanzia. In August 1309 the priors formally recognized this official's jurisdiction in civil actions by foreigners against Florentine debtors and his power to enforce existing laws against Florentines who defrauded creditors. The Mercanzia's chief purpose was to prevent reprisals and enhance the security of Florentines "throughout the world" by forcing Florentine merchants to honor their agreements and satisfy creditors. It thus functioned as a civil court, not unlike the guilds, but with the important difference that its jurisdiction extended to any and all Florentines, including residents of the contado and district, "whether or not they are members of guilds," thus cutting through the complex and contested limitations on the jurisdiction of individual guilds. At a creditor's request, the official of the Mercanzia could compel Florentine companies to submit account books for investigation.[22]

The Mercanzia emerged from a prehistory of de facto cooperation and consultation among the consuls of the major commercial guilds on such issues, and the statutes of at least two guilds refer to such collaboration among the responsibilities of their consuls. Indeed, the initiative for the formalization of this cooperation came from the merchant elite itself, and the commune did little more than extend its recognition to an authority created by the interna-

[22] A. Astorri, *La Mercanzia a Firenze nella prima metà del Trecento* (Florence, 1998), pp. 11–50; G. Bonolis, *La giurisdizione della Mercanzia in Firenze nel secolo XIV* (Florence, 1901).

tional merchants of the five guilds. The new official was hired and monitored by the Mercanzia, not the commune. But the Mercanzia was more than a tribunal. As an *universitas*, or corporate association, it represented the interests of Florence's merchant community to the commune and foreign governments and protected those interests by legislating in matters of commercial law. Indeed, from at least 1312 it had its own statutes. The Mercanzia had no formal membership: any merchant of the five guilds who engaged in trade or banking outside the Florentine dominion could be elected to the Five or sit on any of the association's ad hoc committees that dealt with particular problems. The larger significance of the Mercanzia is that, for the first time, the elite was defining itself with reference to economic interests and responsibilities, representing itself as a community of merchants rather than as a warrior class or as partisans of church or empire. As a product of (a portion of) the guild community, the Mercanzia also signified the elite's implicit acceptance of the guilds and the customs and procedures by which merchants and guildsmen typically resolved disputes, settled bankruptcies, and managed relations amongst themselves and with the outside world. Participating in the Mercanzia were all the city's great merchant and banking families, except for the politically significant, but numerically small, contingent of magnate merchant houses (Bardi, Scali, Spini, Mozzi, Frescobaldi, and a few others), but even they were regularly represented on the Mercanzia's committees by non-magnate business partners. Former Guelfs and Ghibellines, former Blacks and Whites cooperated in the association's judicial, administrative, electoral, and diplomatic functions. Venerable non-merchant families like the Donati, Cavalcanti, Della Tosa, and Adimari largely disappeared from center stage at this point, not because a new class of merchants suddenly arose, but because an already powerful economic elite finally realized that the worst possible response their class could make to the popolo's challenge was a continuation of party conflicts. They decided in effect that those older non-mercantile elite families had provided singularly ineffective leadership for their class, especially in the preceding decade, and that they now needed a new collective representation of themselves grounded in the institutionalization of their economic interests and responsibilities. The Mercanzia represented not a new elite but rather a new image of a changing elite.

Eligibility for the Mercanzia's committees was restricted to members of the five guilds who "from Florence export goods beyond the city and its district or who import goods to the city of Florence from any part of the world beyond the city and district, or who engage or invest in money-changing and lending in any part of the world." This criterion cut through the memberships of the major guilds. Retailers, providers of services, producers, artisans and lenders whose activities were confined within the Florentine dominion had no part in the Mercanzia. This was as close as the economic elite could come to an institutionalized distinction between themselves and the rest of the guild community. By this definition, the Mercanzia's constituency included some guildsmen who bought and sold within Tuscany and central Italy and did not engage in truly international trade, but the great companies found it much easier to assert their leadership within this group than they did in the more heterogeneous full membership of the five guilds, let alone the broader community of twenty-one guilds. Merchants who traded beyond the borders of the Florentine dominion, whether internationally or regionally, had significant interests in common: from the security of trade routes and negotiated reductions of customs duties to protection against reprisals. Regional traders did not lack incentives for cooperation with international merchant-bankers, and from such shared interests and frequent contacts the elite was able to forge a degree of consensus within the Mercanzia that was unattainable in their separate guilds. The Mercanzia thus embraced those merchants, who, even if not from great families, depended on the success of the economic elite for their prosperity. Most importantly, the Mercanzia could ignore the popular pressures to which individual guilds and the full guild federation were subject.

The size of the Mercanzia's constituency (what I will call the Mercanzia elite) varied according to economic trends and investment patterns. Only when it needed to raise funds did the association compile comprehensive lists of all the companies that fell under its criterion of international trade or banking. The earliest such list, from 1322, names 264 companies, sometimes with investing partners identified but often without their names or precise number.[23] Thirty-four of them (with a total of between forty-five and fifty investing partners) came from the other sixteen guilds (the Mercanzia felt no need to restrict fiscal assessments to only the five guilds). The remaining 230 companies had approximately 500–600 investing partners, and it was from this group, whose size and composition fluctuated from year to year, that the Mercanzia recruited its governing cadres. Most of the merchant companies of elite families are in this list, which is organized by sesti: in Oltrarno, the Bardi, Capponi, Amadori, Antinori, Del Bene, Corsini, Pitti, Biliotti, Da Panzano, Guadagni and Ridolfi; in Borgo, the Acciaiuoli, Altoviti, Davanzati, and Gianfigliazzi; in San Pancrazio, the Rucellai, Da Sommaia, and Minerbetti; in Porta Duomo, the Aldobrandini, Rondinelli, and Medici; in San Pier Maggiore, the Albizzi, Portinari, Rittafede, Covoni, Ricci, and Falconieri; and in San Piero Scheraggio, the Scali, Dell'Antella, Sacchetti, Soldani, Peruzzi, Alberti, Ammanati, Orlandini, Macci, and Pulci. The 500–600 investing partners of all 230 major guild firms were Florence's early fourteenth-century economic oligarchy, and these family companies were its inner core.

In the century of their greatest prosperity, roughly 1250–1340, Florence's international trading and banking companies created an economic empire

---

[23]   ASF, Mercanzia 136, September 24 and October 13, 1322, n.p.

unprecedented in its nature and scope, with business and branches extending from London to the Levant. By accumulating and investing capital on a scale never previously attempted, they marshaled and controlled financial resources far in excess of those of their investing families and partners and beyond the local and regional economy. The crucial factor was their ability to attract deposits from a wide variety of investors in Florence, Italy, and throughout Europe and the Mediterranean. Companies were never the common property of families or lineages, and nothing like a majority of a lineage's members invested in a company. But they were nonetheless identified by the name of the family whose members owned a controlling portion of the shares. The frequency with which members of the same lineage contributed capital to the formation of companies suggests that such cooperation must have been viewed as a natural extension of the pooling of resources for other purposes that characterized elite lineages. Each company was a partnership, or *societas*, formed by two or more investing partners, and, in the case of large companies, by ten, twelve, fifteen, or more, each of whom supplied a portion of the firm's capital, or *corpo*. The family partners typically sought to increase the company's working capital by accepting partners from outside the family. Companies remained in existence until the partners decided to terminate their legal relationship, close the books, and distribute profits (or losses) proportionally according to their shares. More or less the same group of partners, with occasional substitutions, additions, or deletions, would soon thereafter sign a new contract bringing into existence a new partnership even as the firm's financial and commercial operations continued without interruption.[24] All partners shared in the unlimited liability that was a hallmark of these early companies: in the event of bankruptcy, creditors could demand satisfaction from any and all assets of all the partners.

The best known of the early companies is that of the Peruzzi,[25] whose account books survive for seven consecutive partnerships from 1300 to the company's demise in 1343 and provide the amounts of the partners' invested capital through 1335. The 1300–8 company had seventeen investing partners: seven Peruzzi, with a total of 74,000 lire a fiorino of capital and ten non-family members contributing 49,000 lire a fiorino. (The lira a fiorino, henceforth l.f., was a money of account worth $^{20}/_{29}$ths of a florin. Thus, 74,000 l.f.

---

[24] R. de Roover, "The Story of the Alberti Company of Florence, 1302–1348, as Revealed in its Account Books," *Business History Review* 32 (1958): 14–59; reprinted in R. de Roover, *Business, Banking, and Economic Thought in Late Medieval and Early Modern Europe*, ed. J. Kirshner (Chicago, 1974), pp. 39–84.

[25] For what follows: E. S. Hunt, *The Medieval Super-Companies: A Study of the Peruzzi Company of Florence* (Cambridge, 1994); A. Sapori, "Storia interna della compagnia mercantile dei Peruzzi," in *Studi di storia economica medievale* (Florence, 1940), pp. 243–84.

were worth about 51,000 gold florins.) The seven Peruzzi included the firm's head, Filippo di Amideo; his son Geri; Filippo's three nephews, Giotto, Tommaso, and Arnoldo, the sons of his deceased brother Arnoldo; and two sons, Filippo and Rinieri, of a fourth son, Pacino, of the deceased Arnoldo. The ten non-Peruzzi partners included three from elite families (two Baroncelli brothers and a member of the magnate Infangati) and seven from families in the grey area between elite and popolo, including the young Giovanni Villani. Evidently the elder Filippo died in 1308, because in the reorganized partnership of 1308–10, which was otherwise composed of more or less the same partners and a similar balance among their investments, he is replaced by his sons Guido and Amideo. From 1300 to 1343, twenty-two Peruzzi contributed capital to the formation of one or more of the firm's successive partnerships; all twenty-two were lineal descendants of Amideo: Filippo, three of his sons, and four of his grandsons; and Arnoldo's three sons, nine grandsons, and two great-grandsons. Clearly, a strong sense of lineage cohesion dictated the company's family component.

Total Peruzzi capital climbed from 124,000 l.f. in 1300–8 to 149,000 l.f. in 1310–12, then declined to 118,000 in 1312–24 and 60,000 in 1324–31, and rebounded to 90,000 in 1331–5. Between 1300 and 1331, family members consistently held between 54 and 60 percent of the capital shares, and it was only with the partnership of 1331–5 that non-family shareholders owned more than half. But here too there was notable continuity in the roster of families and individuals who went into business with the Peruzzi. Some, like the brothers Gherardo and Tano Baroncelli (the latter replaced in the last partnership by his two sons) stayed with the Peruzzi over the lifetime of the company. Filippo Villani, who replaced his brother Giovanni among the shareholders in the reorganization of 1308, was still a partner in 1335–43. Catellino Infangati remained a partner from 1300 to 1335; Giovanni di Ricco Raugi from 1300 to 1331; Gherardo di Gentile Bonaccorsi from 1310 to 1335; and Stefano di Uguccione Bencivenni from 1310 to 1343. In fact, the ranks of the non-family partners were so steady that, after the acceptance of two new partners in 1308 and two more in 1310, not a single new partner was included until the reorganization of 1331, when six new partners (including three brothers from the Soderini family) joined the company. Ties between the Peruzzi and their investing partners were indeed durable.

What distinguished Florentine companies from the long-distance merchants of the maritime republics of Venice and Genoa was the magnitude of their assets, which far exceeded even these already impressive outlays of capital. At the closing of the books in 1335, Peruzzi assets amounted to 742,247 l.f., and in 1318 the Bardi company estimated its assets at 1,266,756 l.f.[26] Such

---

[26]   Hunt, *Peruzzi Company*, p. 121.

immense assets and business volume were made possible by the deposits the companies accepted from investors who, unlike the partners, were guaranteed a fixed annual rate of return: in the case of the Peruzzi, initially 8%, and 7% after 1325. Most depositors had no family or marriage connection to the firm; they included nobles, ecclesiastics, merchants, and landowners from all over Europe, including Florentines, who invested their money with the companies expecting, and usually receiving, handsome returns. Deposits accounted for the lion's share of the companies' liabilities (debts owed to creditors). In 1335 the Peruzzi company's far-flung branches reported eighty-eight depositors in the Naples branch, for a total of 120,960 l.f.; eighty-one in Avignon (where the papacy was located after 1309) for a total of 59,568 l.f.; twenty-two in Paris (46,290 l.f.); thirty-nine in Sicily (43,083 l.f.); twenty-four in Barletta (32,997 l.f.); twenty-eight in Pisa (20,768 l.f.); fifty-one in Rhodes (18,802 l.f.); eleven in Venice (11,481 l.f.); and twenty-one in Tunis for a more modest total of 6,039 l.f. Altogether (and data for some branches are missing or incomplete), 370 depositors had 382,421 l.f. on deposit with the company. Even if the number of depositors does not seem high (but missing, of course, are the local Florentine depositors), the amounts invested were enormous. The combination of capital investments and large-scale deposits allowed the companies to engage so massively in the trading and lending that brought them (and their investors) such great wealth.

Cumulatively, foreign depositors in the scores of international companies numbered in the thousands, and their willingness to entrust such large sums to Florentine merchant-bankers bespeaks a remarkable confidence in the companies' ability to safeguard their investments and generate substantial profits, especially in an age in which governments did not insure or protect deposits. Their confidence was generated by the companies' record of success: throughout these decades the Peruzzi regularly paid depositors the promised return while also distributing profits to the investing partners that varied from 11 to 18 percent. But trust also required guarantees, or collateral: the demonstration that, in the event of disaster or bankruptcy, the companies possessed assets convertible to cash with which to repay creditors. The collateral that sustained the companies' good faith was (and could be nothing but) land. In an economic system built on credit and long-distance transactions vulnerable to a variety of risks including bad debts, loss of political favor, bad harvests, piracy, and royal insolvency, land was the only unassailably secure collateral that the companies, or the families behind them, could offer. In the case of the Peruzzi, this is surely the real significance of the formation in 1283 of a separate partnership among the sons of Arnoldo and Filippo for the acquisition of property in the Florentine contado. Of all the motives for the accumulation of land by elite Florentine families, that of providing security for deposits invested in their companies must have been among the most urgent. It has sometimes been supposed that heavy investment in land meant a retreat from the riskier forms of business. While this is perhaps sometimes true, the two forms of investment were not only compatible, but functionally linked. Land was an essential precondition for the companies' expansion and success, and when, in the crisis of the 1340s, panicked depositors demanded repayment, these accumulations of land were at the center of the ensuing contentious legal and political battles. Simultaneous investment in land, commerce, and banking was always characteristic of the Florentine companies.

The companies' investments fell into three categories: trade, lending, and manufacturing. For any single firm, the first two were the most significant, although their combined investment in textile manufactures constituted a major portion of the industry. Trading embraced the legendary "spice" trade, which included actual spices, like pepper, sugar, saffron, and cinnamon, and a huge range of luxury and specialty items imported from the eastern Mediterranean, the Black Sea, or points farther east, such as cotton, alum, dyes, perfumes, silks, and even jewelry, purchased for resale throughout Italy and Europe. But bigger profits came from imports of wool from England, Spain, parts of France, and North Africa, cloth from Flemish and French cities, and grain purchased in Sicily and Puglia and resold in northern and central Italy and throughout the European Mediterranean. The grain trade was especially lucrative for the Florentine companies, who enjoyed a virtual monopoly of exports from the South. Profits in commodity trading depended on volume, and the magnitude of grain exports by Florentine companies, although usually on ships leased from Venetians or Genoese, is staggering. Between 1300 and 1309, 70% of grain exports from Sicily went to Tuscany. In one extraordinary year, 1311, the Florentines exported 107,000 *moggia* of grain from Puglia, twice Florence's annual consumption, and between 1327 and 1331 the companies exported an annual average of 29,000 *moggia*.[27]

To secure the monopolies, privileges, and exemptions from duties in exporting grain from southern Italy and wool from England, the Florentine companies became bankers to the rulers of these kingdoms and extended them long lines of credit. Florentines had long been in the business of lending to governments, at least from the time of the financing of Charles of Anjou's war against Manfred when the Angevin treasury borrowed huge amounts in return for trading privileges in the South and the right to collect church revenues. By the early fourteenth century, with the papacy under heavy French influence, collecting ecclesiastical revenues in France was no longer as profitable as it

[27]   D. Abulafia, "Southern Italy and the Florentine Economy, 1265–1370," *Economic History Review*, ser. 2, 34 (1981): 377–88; D. Abulafia, "Sul commercio del grano siciliano nel tardo Duecento," in *La società mediterranea all'epoca del Vespro* (Palermo, 1983), vol. 2, pp. 5–22; both reprinted in Abulafia, *Italy, Sicily, and the Mediterranean, 1100–1400* (London, 1987). See also Hunt, *Peruzzi Company*, pp. 130, 48.

had been, and by the 1320s Florentine business shifted to England, as the woolen cloth industry at home began producing more high quality cloths from English wool. Where once the companies bought English wool to sell in Flemish cities, they were now sending huge amounts to Florence itself where it was re-sold to scores of manufacturers in the Wool guild. Special privileges in wool exports inevitably required generous loans to the English crown. The Frescobaldi were the first Florentine company to engage in large-scale lending in England,[28] but it was the Bardi and Peruzzi who made the combination of lending and wool exports a huge enterprise whose profits were almost as great as the risks. War erupted between England and France in the late 1330s, increasing Edward III's thirst for cash, and the already established privileges of the Florentine companies became ever more dependent on their provision of loans to a king who could at any moment have removed the Bardi and the Peruzzi from the lucrative export trade.

It is a mark of the profitability of English wool exports that the Florentine companies continued to provide Edward with the ever larger loans he needed to fight the French. Both in the Angevin South and in England, lending was not a separate business from which the companies necessarily or always expected repayment with interest. Together with the cash receipts they generated, loans were the means by which the companies secured privileges for exports. For three quarters of a century, from the 1260s when they first entered into such agreements with the Angevins until about 1340, the Florentines made steady profits of such magnitude that they were able to funnel constant amounts of cash into the treasuries of these kingdoms. But when the English loans ballooned and began to outrun the profits generated from wool exports, the companies collapsed. Villani, who withdrew his deposit in the Peruzzi company in 1339, estimated (13.55) that the English crown owed a total of a million and a half florins to the Bardi and Peruzzi, five times the annual ordinary income of the Florentine commune. If it sometimes seems that Florence had two different economies – an international economy of traders, bankers, and merchants who were more often than not in London, Avignon, Naples, or the Levant, and a local economy of cloth manufacturers, artisans, shopkeepers, and laborers – they were nonetheless intimately linked. Many Florentines had deposits with the companies and depended on their prosperity. And the domestic textile industry depended on imported wool that would have been far more costly or even unavailable without the companies' special relationship to the English monarchy and control of the export trade. Without the textile industry Florence would have been a much smaller and economically less potent city.

---

[28]   R. W. Kaeuper, "The Frescobaldi of Florence and the English Crown," *Studies in Medieval and Renaissance History* 10 (1973): 41–95.

Taxation and Public Finances

Florence's economy was affected in important ways by the government's fiscal policies. In the thirteenth century communal expenditures were limited, except in times of war when a direct tax based on assessments ("estimo") of the worth of each citizen's property was occasionally collected, as, for example, during the war against Arezzo and Pisa in the late 1280s. Direct taxes were always unpopular among the wealthy and were resorted to only sporadically when unusual expenses exceeded regular communal revenues. In 1315 the estimo was abolished for city residents (but maintained in the contado), as the elite-dominated government decided to base its finances on a combination of indirect (or consumption) taxes and borrowing.[29] This was a political decision, made by, and in the interests of, the class of wealthy merchants and property owners. The priorate that presented the proposal for the abolition of the estimo to the legislative councils included members of the merchant-banking families of the Alberti, Altoviti, Rucellai, and Ricci, and they had been elected by their predecessors who included members of the Soderini, Peruzzi, Acciaiuoli, and Medici families. The elite evidently assumed that economic growth would generate sufficient revenues through indirect taxes to pay the interest on the loans the government regularly needed. But receipts from indirect taxes, impressive as they were in good times, had their limits, and attempts to squeeze more revenue from such taxes with higher rates restricted consumption, thus undermining the prosperity of the economy and ultimately reducing revenues. At the same time, government borrowing could only be successful if loans were repaid promptly with the promised interest. In fiscal emergencies the commune borrowed more, often at higher rates of interest, only to find itself saddled with a growing debt and ever larger interest obligations, which necessitated more borrowing and put more pressure on indirect taxes. The elite's rejection of direct taxation, which would have limited the need to borrow and resulted in a smaller debt, meant that the commune's solvency required a flourishing economy and avoidance of too many years of higher than normal expenditures. But the emerging competition for hegemony in Tuscany made it difficult to avoid war, and it was indeed military expenses that proved the undoing of a fiscal system based on loans and indirect taxes.

By the end of the thirteenth century, indirect taxes (gabelles) were already the commune's major ordinary source of revenue. No estimates of "normal" government spending or income survive from this early period. For the mid-

---

[29]   B. Barbadoro, *Le finanze della repubblica fiorentina: imposta diretta e debito pubblico fino all'istituzione del Monte* (Florence, 1929), pp. 124–31; M. Ginatempo, *Prima del debito: finanziamento della spesa pubblica e gestione del deficit nelle grandi città toscane (1200–1350 ca.)* (Florence, 2000).

1330s, Villani (12.92) estimated regular annual income (excluding loans) at about 300,000 florins, half of which came from the two most lucrative gabelles: 90,000 florins from goods entering the city (the gate gabelle) and 59,000 florins from the tax on wine sold at retail. Other indirect taxes included the gabelle on the slaughter of animals (15,000); required purchases of salt (15,000); contracts and notarized documents (11,000); the grinding of grain into flour (4,250); the slaughter of animals in the contado (4,400); pawnbrokers' licenses (3,000); and taxes on renters of communal property (4,150) and on citizens accepting high-ranking offices in other cities (3,500). Other major sources of revenue were the estimo on the contado (30,000 florins) and fines collected through the courts (20,000).

In reviewing communal finances, Villani included among ordinary expenditures (12.93) only the "stable and necessary" costs of 40,000 florins associated with a long list of judicial and administrative offices. He omitted other, far greater, expenditures because they fluctuated so much from year to year, above all military expenses and the cost of "the walls, bridges, and [the cathedral of] Santa Reparata." Nor did he mention among these ordinary expenses interest payments on loans. But just a few pages earlier (12.90) he reported that in two and a half years of war against the Della Scala of Verona in the late 1330s the commune spent more than 600,000 florins and still owed 450,000 florins, which, assuming conservatively an average of 10% interest, meant annual interest payments of 45,000 florins. He added (without specifying which ones) that gabelle receipts for the next six years were assigned to the repayment of this debt. In these war years, the combination of military costs, interest payments, and ordinary administrative expenses already exceeded regular annual income, and this did not include the walls, bridges, cathedral, or grain purchases. This was (and long remained) the dilemma of Florentine public finance: any period of protracted and costly military expenditures instantly created deficits that could only be covered by borrowing at high interest rates, which in turn made it necessary to increase the rates at which the gabelles were collected. And when people had to pay more for the necessities of daily life, they bought less, if not of these necessities then of something else, or fell into debt themselves, and the economy weakened.

Gabelles are an inherently regressive form of taxation, whose burden falls more heavily on the poor and working classes. Moreover, the rates were increased, in some cases dramatically, from the late thirteenth through the fourteenth century.[30] The only exception is the gate gabelle on grain, which decreased in the early fourteenth century and otherwise remained steady at

[30]   Ch.-M. de la Roncière, "Indirect Taxes or 'Gabelles' at Florence in the Fourteenth Century: The Evolution of Tariffs and Problems of Collection," in *Florentine Studies*, ed. Rubinstein, pp. 140–92.

12 denari per *staio*. The gate gabelle on oil went from 3 soldi per *orcio* (an 85-pound barrel) in the 1320s to 15 in the second half of the century. The tariff on hogs brought into the city increased from 6 to 60 soldi per head between the 1330s and the 1350s and settled at 40 in the 1370s. And the gate tax on wine (separate from the tax on its retail sale) went from 10 soldi per *cogno* in 1320 to 60 in the 1350s, and thereafter settled at 50. The tax on wine sold retail went from 6% of the sale price in 1299 to 33% in 1342, and 40–50% after the 1348 plague. As a consequence of the two taxes on wine, its retail price reached levels nine and ten times higher in the 1350s than at the beginning of the century. The commune required each household to buy prescribed quantities of salt and raised both mandated quantities and the per-unit tax, with the result that its price increased from 6–12 soldi per *staio* in the 1290s to 20–40 in the 1330s, and 80–120 after 1350. In most cases the biggest percentage increases occurred before the plague and put growing pressure on the working classes for whom the added cost of items of daily consumption represented a significant percentage of household budgets at a time when wages were stagnant. According to Villani (10.324), in 1325, during a major war against Lucca, a combination of new taxes and higher rates increased gabelle revenues from 180,000 to 250,000 florins in one year. In the early fourteenth century, the commune generally sold gabelle receipts in advance of their collection, either to individuals or, in the case of the retail sale of wine, to the guild of the Vinattieri, for an agreed-upon price, and the expected profit for the purchaser further increased the burden on consumers. By mid-century the government abandoned this practice and collected gabelles directly through its own officials.

Elite-led governments financed military expenses through loans repaid with interest. Loans could be general or restricted, required or voluntary. General compulsory loans (prestanze) were assessed on all households. Citizens paying their full assessments on schedule became creditors of the commune with the right of repayment with interest. Some (but not all) forced loans were repaid, but repayment often required another loan. The government paid interest when it could but often suspended interest payments when funds were more urgently needed elsewhere. Citizens paying less than their full assessments lost the right to interest, and for these less affluent households the loans thus became direct taxes. Restricted loans were assessed on select groups of wealthy merchants, or their companies, and their repayment, with annualized rates of interest of 10 or 15 percent, was guaranteed in advance by the assignment of specified communal revenues, usually gabelles (as in the case noted by Villani). Such loans were sometimes voluntary, in which case interest rates were even higher. Before about 1340, for as long as the commune was able to repay restricted loans on schedule, they were a secure and lucrative form of investment for the wealthy. Moreover, the commune often delegated responsibility for their collection and repayment to special committees on which major creditors themselves served and were thus able to arrange terms of repayment and interest for their own loans.

The assessment of prestanze was an endlessly contentious issue. To impose a forced loan, the priors sought authority from the councils to assess an overall amount to be divided among the city's districts. Separate committees of assessors were appointed in the sesti (and, after the reorganization of 1343, in the sixteen gonfaloni). In the 1320s, these committees consisted of forty members in each of the two most populous sesti (Oltrarno and San Piero Scheraggio) and thirty in each of the other four, each being divided into five smaller ones, all of which went to work separately and in secret to determine each household's share of the total amount to be raised in their district. Five sub-committees each produced an estimate for every household: the highest and lowest were rejected and the average of the middle three was the amount assessed. The multiplicity of committees was designed to diminish the corruption and favoritisms to which any assessment of fiscal burdens of neighbors by neighbors was vulnerable and made it difficult to blame, and therefore seek revenge against, a specific individual for one's assessment. But this did not of course eliminate complaints about unfair treatment.

After the abolition of direct taxation in the city in 1315, government borrowing and the public debt grew steadily. In the mid-1320s, war against Lucca and its ruler, Castruccio Castracani, created the first of many fiscal crises. For several years the two cities dueled for control of Tuscany, and in 1324–5 the war went badly for Florence as Castruccio's armies rampaged through Florentine territory, sometimes very close to the city, whose new walls were not yet completed. In September 1325 Florence suffered a devastating defeat at Altopascio (east of Lucca), and that November the government imposed the new indirect taxes that increased gabelle receipts by almost 40%. Short-term restricted loans of 28,000 and 20,000 florins, assessed in June–July 1325, were to be repaid with interest of 8 percent from the salt and contract gabelles. Prestanze were also levied to finance both military expenditures and the short-term loans from wealthy families and companies: a 41,000-florin prestanza in June 1325, and another for 50,000 florins in February 1326, which was to be used, among other things, to pay off a short-term 15,000-florin loan advanced by a select group of companies including the Bardi, Peruzzi, Scali, Acciaiuoli, and Alberti. No one with estimated wealth of less than 1,000 lire (approximately 320 florins) was meant to be obligated to this prestanza. The register for San Piero Scheraggio shows that 390 of the sesto's 561 assessed households paid between 4 and 10 florins, 41 paid less than 4, and the remaining 130 between 10 and 123 florins. With 561 households contributing in this one district, as many as 3,000 must have been assessed throughout the city, which means that, if this prestanza did not reach the working classes or poorest artisans, it certainly went beyond the elite. Lucrative short-term loans extended by members of elite families were being repaid with handsome interest from the receipts of both regressive indirect taxes, whose burden fell most heavily on the working class, and forced loans largely collected from the popolo and the guild community.

In 1325 military and financial crises induced the elite to seek help from its traditional ally in the South, the Angevin kingdom of Naples. King Robert sent his son Charles, duke of Calabria, to assume emergency powers in Florence. In July 1326 Charles and his wife were given a lavish formal entry, together with more than twenty princes, counts, and lords (all named by Villani, who was evidently very impressed by this show of royal, noble, and feudal ritual), Charles's 1,500 knights and 400 more in the service of his vicar, Walter of Brienne. The Florentines made Charles lord, or *signore*, of Florence for ten years, with the conditions that he respect the city's laws and elected officeholders and not "impose any forced loans or direct taxes except in conditions of urgent necessity," and even then only "with the advice, agreement, and decision of the priors and the councils." Charles did exactly what they feared. He began with a new prestanza of 60,000 florins in August 1326, which was, however, distributed according to new criteria that required the wealthy to pay more than they had in previous prestanze. Then in October he reinstituted the estimo by a ducal decree for which he did not seek the approval of the councils. Lamenting the "iniquities" and "inequalities" of a fiscal system in which "the poor and powerless are unjustly compelled to sustain the burdens of the powerful and wealthy,"[31] Charles appointed a committee of foreign judges to assess the wealth, including property, capital investments, and credits, of every citizen in the city, contado, and district. Most remarkably, graduated tax rates were applied to various categories of wealth: 0.83% on houses; 1.25% on other landed property; 1.66% on investments and credits; and a progressive scale of rates for business profits that went from 1.66% to more than 5% for profits over the modest sum of 100 lire. And these taxes were collected as frequently as was deemed necessary: a first collection in March 1327, which Villani (11.17) says brought in 80,000 florins; a second six months later; and a third in 1328. These were direct taxes, not forced loans, and hence without either repayment or interest. Charles and his advisers evidently believed that the only solution to Florence's fiscal dilemma was direct taxation of capital and profits as well as real property. The reform's explicit intention was to relieve the burden of gabelles and forced loans on the working classes, artisans, and the poor.

The warmth with which Charles had been welcomed in 1326 quickly turned to hostility among the elite families who detested his fiscal reforms. Open

[31]   Barbadoro, *Finanze*, pp. 161–2.

conflict was averted by Charles's sudden death in November 1328, and within three months a new elite government once again abolished the estimo. Resentment against Charles also focused on his own apparently limitless spending. Villani estimated that, in the nineteen months between mid-1326 and January 1328, the Florentines paid a grand total of 900,000 florins to cover Charles's military and other expenses (which still did not bring victory over Castruccio, who, however, fortunately for Florence, also died in the autumn of 1328), a sum so huge that Villani felt it necessary to confirm its validity by telling his readers that "I can in truth testify to it, because I was among the communal auditors." A comparison is possible here. A treasury audit for 1325 (the year of the military disaster at Altopascio and before Charles assumed power) concluded that expenditures amounted to 1,104,276 lire, roughly 340,000 florins, of which almost 79% went for military expenses. If Villani is right, the Florentines paid Charles 67% more than that on an annualized basis (568,000 florins) over those nineteen months. In January 1328, shortly after Charles left Florence for what was meant to be a temporary absence, the priors wrote a letter to the community of Florentine merchants in Naples, perhaps hoping that its contents would reach the court. They lamented the condition of the republic's finances: "You know that the gabelles are assigned to the duke's officials to pay the 200,000 florins [that they agreed to provide him each year, before other subsidies]. Since the duke came here, besides the gabelles, there was a forced loan of 60,000 florins; then the estimo was instituted and 120,000 florins came from two collections. And every old communal tax and source of income has been squeezed as much as possible." The priors bemoaned their inability to find the 10,000 florins needed to keep the construction of the walls going, or even enough money with which to pay the salaries of the podestà, Capitano, and other officials. "Think about it," they added: "We used to be able to keep a thousand cavalry for slightly more than 100,000 florins. Now [under the duke's rule] a thousand cavalry cost us 200,000 florins. And think of this: what ever would we do if something unexpected happened that caused our gabelles not to yield the usual amounts?"[32] Although their successors might have asked the same question with even greater urgency after the estimo was again abolished in early 1329, for the next decade a prosperous economy kept gabelle receipts high. But by 1340 the Florentines did indeed have to face the dreaded contingency pondered by the priors of January 1328.

[32]   Ibid., pp. 563–4.

5

The Fourteenth-Century Dialogue of Power

Elite Dominance, 1310–40

From the end of the factional wars around 1310–12 until the crises of the 1340s, Florence's elite enjoyed its first long period of political dominance without catastrophic internal divisions. This was the golden age of the merchant-banking elite, the generation in which the great companies made huge fortunes and controlled both domestic politics and foreign policy without much apparent opposition from the popolo. In fiscal and economic issues, electoral politics, the administration of justice and commercial law, the elite made government serve its interests. Coming after fifty years of challenges culminating in the guild federation of 1293, the Ordinances of Justice, and the anti-magnate laws, the popolo's acquiescence in elite hegemony requires explanation. Part of the answer is that, while suppressing its old addiction to violent forms of factionalism, for the first time the elite assumed responsibilities of governance within the institutional framework established by the popolo (although naturally in pursuit of its own interests) and thus created conditions in which the popolo could choose cooperation over confrontation. A second factor was the elite's gradual adoption of a collective identity defined by its commercial activities and an ethos of prudence, calculation, and profit. The galloping prosperity of the merchant companies in these decades also removed the incentive to challenge an economic leadership that benefited both classes.

Except for one last quixotic attempt in 1343, by the 1320s it was clear that the elite was not inclined to turn the clock back to the 1260s–70s, when first one, then the other, of its factions ruled unencumbered by the popolo and the guilds. Between 1310 and 1340, the popolo's constitution remained in place even as real power concentrated in the hands of several dozen elite families. The decision not to dismantle popular institutions was critical, for it would certainly have brought guildsmen into the streets, as happened in 1343. But as it gradually became more disposed to work within a framework it had previously rejected, the elite also introduced new institutions (like the Mercanzia) in its own interests, sought to control the guilds from within, and revised electoral procedures for both the priorate and guild consulates.

Strategies for controlling the guilds varied in approach and degree of success from guild to guild and were perhaps most successful in the bankers' and moneychangers' guild. Until 1329 all the guilds governed themselves and conducted their elections autonomously, and their internal politics thus varied considerably. Contests for power in the major guilds between elites (who wanted smaller memberships, restricted leadership, ample authority for the consuls, and a weaker guild council) and non-elite members (who favored more inclusive membership, more representative procedures in consular elections, a wider distribution of offices, and greater balance between consuls and council) took a different form in each case and, except in the Cambio, yielded no decisive victory for either side until the elite began using the Mercanzia to dominate the guilds in the major reform of communal and guild elections in 1328–9.

In 1300 the Arte del Cambio had 355 members in 138 companies, all with a "tavola" or "banco" in the city (the criterion that distinguished the Cambio's membership from the Calimala, whose merchant-bankers did not have a local operation). The Cambio included large elite banking firms like the magnate Pazzi with 17 investing partners, the Peruzzi with 15, the Canigiani (12), the magnate Abati (at least 11), the Macci (11), Sassetti (10), Bonciani (8), Dell'Antella (7) and magnate Visdomini (7), and many smaller non-elite firms: 95 of 138 companies belonged to two partners or a single investor. New members paid a fee to join, unless they had a close relative already in the guild. In 1300 a modest entry fee of one hundred soldi (then about two florins) facilitated access to the guild for many non-elite moneychangers without fathers, sons, or brothers among the members. Consular elections involved a significant portion of the membership in a two-stage process: the outgoing consuls selected forty-eight members, but no more than one per firm, which made it difficult for large elite companies to dominate elections. The forty-eight each nominated six guild members, for a total of 288 nominations, and the six receiving the most votes became the electors of the new consuls.[1] Between a third and a half of the guild's firms had some part in each election.

---

[1] *Statuti dell'Arte del Cambio di Firenze (1299–1316)*, ed. G. Camerani Marri (Florence, 1955), p. 4 and pp. 86, 144, 254 for what follows.

Over the next two decades, the membership shrank and elections concentrated in fewer hands. In 1301 there were 321 members (10% fewer than in 1300), and the loss came entirely from the ranks of one- and two-man firms, which declined from 95 to 62, perhaps as a consequence of a five-fold increase in the matriculation fee. The fee increased again in 1313 and 1317, when it temporarily reached twenty florins, and settled back to ten florins thereafter. In 1313 the guild acknowledged that many persons wishing to join the guild refused to do so "on account of the great sum of money they must pay" and temporarily lowered the fee. But the membership continued to shrink. By 1314 there were only 110 members in 52 companies, and, after recovering to 154 in 84 companies in 1320, it sank in 1324 to 114 members in 61 companies and only 89 in 57 companies in 1329.[2] Consular elections were now controlled by a more restricted group. The 48 were reduced to 24, then to 16, and in December 1313 the outgoing consuls appointed the 16 who then chose the six electors of the new consuls. Five of the six came from the committee of 16 and included a Strozzi, a Dell'Antella, and a Guicciardini who was a partner in the Macci firm. The new consuls chosen by them included a Strozzi (the son of the elector), an Unganelli, and a Da Panzano, who was also on the committee of 16. The names alone indicate the preponderant influence secured by the guild's elite in these more tightly controlled elections. But a year later the consuls reported to the guild council that many were complaining that their election had violated the guild's statutes, that the election records and oaths were nowhere to be found, and consequently that they could not legally exercise their office or adjudicate civil cases. The consuls asked the council's advice, but also made a proposal of their own: "because there are many things that need to be done in and on behalf of the guild that the consuls cannot do except with the advice of the men of the guild, and because it is tedious and laborious to assemble all the members on account of the small number of them regularly present at their banks," they requested that "by authority of this council they be allowed to deliberate, decide, and act on any pressing matters during their term of office and do whatever they deem useful and beneficial for the guild, on their own, with or without a meeting of the council, as they shall see fit." Lapo Strozzi, a member of the council in session, rose to say that he believed the consuls did indeed have the full and legitimate authority of their office and that their appointment of other guild officials should be considered valid "as if [the consuls] had been elected according to the regulations contained in the statutes." He also favored entrusting the consuls with full powers to "legislate, command, decree, carry out, and delegate in the aforementioned

---

[2]   ASF, Arte del Cambio 6 (1300), 7 (1301), 10 (1320 and 1324), 12 (1329); Manoscritti 542 (1314).

matters."[3] The council accepted Strozzi's recommendation, confirmed the consuls in their office, and agreed to the requested expansion of their powers – all in the wake of what had begun as a challenge to their legitimacy, and without any denial of the charge that their election had violated the statutes. By 1319 Cambio consuls were practically naming their own successors, as the council's powers gradually yielded to their expanding authority.

Eligibility criteria for the consular office also divided elite and non-elite in the Cambio, especially the requirement, first imposed by the Ordinances of Justice for the priorate, that officeholders be actively engaged in their businesses at the time of their election. The guild's revised statutes of 1313 declared that only two of each contingent of four consuls would have to be regularly present at their banks, a modification that preserved the political eligibility of investing partners not directly involved in the daily operation of their firms and perhaps even of matriculated members temporarily unaffiliated with a firm. Thus, just when many active moneychangers were being excluded from the guild because of high matriculation fees, guildsmen who were not active participants in a firm had their access to the consulate preserved. Temporary ineligibility for former consuls (the *divieto*) was reduced from two years to one, a clear sign that a restricted group was dominating the consulate. But in 1318, when the one-year *divieto* was confirmed, it was justified by a renewal of the ban against electing members who were not "resident" at their firms. Such rapid changes in eligibility requirements are symptomatic of persistent disagreement between the guild's elite, which sought to limit the membership and control the consulate, and the non-elite members who preferred a larger membership and wider distribution of offices. Over two decades the elite succeeded in transforming the guild from a large association with wide participation in elections to a much smaller body more tightly controlled by an inner circle. Yet, as it excluded many moneychangers and local lenders from membership, the guild claimed the right to regulate their activities and exercise jurisdiction over the growing numbers who now practiced their trade without the benefit of guild membership.

Similar developments occurred in the Wool guild. Villani reports (10.30) that in 1311 the guild broke into "great discord and factions" over the consulate, and that "the city was nearly in an uproar because of it." This had been preceded by clashes in 1310 resulting in punishments that were described seven years later, when the consuls were authorized to review and increase them, as having "often given rise to protests that have not yet ceased and from which many scandals might still ensue." In the earliest surviving statutes (1317), dyers, finishers, folders, and menders were, like the merchant-entrepreneurs (*lanaiuoli*), eligible to hold guild offices, and the guild's council of forty-eight

---

[3] ASF, Arte del Cambio 54, n.p.

had to include finishers and dyers as well as merchant-entrepreneurs.[4] But by 1333, artisans were being listed in a separate register and were prohibited from manufacturing cloth and holding guild offices, now reserved for the *lanaiuoli*. Although the Lana remained a very large guild throughout the four-teenth century, here too there was a notable reduction of the membership that may reflect growing elite influence. In 1332 the guild counted over 600 *lanaiuoli*, and unspecified numbers of brothers and sons among the partners suggest a membership closer to 700. Many came from elite families: Albizzi (twenty-one members in many different partnerships), Corsini, Ridolfi, Pitti, Peruzzi, Capponi, Alberti, Covoni, Valori, Orlandini, Rondinelli, Davanzati, Tolosini, Biliotti, and Ricci. But the majority of *lanaiuoli* were non-elite, many identi-fied only by patronymics. By 1353, despite substantial annual additions of new members from the mid-1340s, Lana membership declined to just over 400. This is of course in large part attributable to the Black Death, but in the district of San Martino that specialized in the production of higher quality cloths from English wool, the numbers actually increased and included a particularly heavy representation of elite families who generally dominated the industry's luxury-cloth sector.[5]

In elections of the communal priors, the elite gradually deprived the guilds of the influence they won in the 1290s. After 1310, elections were mostly conducted by the outgoing priors with grants of special, temporary authority, called *balìa*, to appoint successors, sometimes for several future terms. On one occasion in 1323, the priors selected successors for twenty-one bimonthly terms. Such elections regularly produced elite-dominated priorates, but their weakness was that everyone knew who was responsible for electoral deci-sions, and thus who was in and out of favor with the ruling group of the moment. Resentments among excluded families or factions had easy targets, and complaints of favoritism and abuse of power led to the creation in 1321 of a second advisory college, the Twelve, which joined the priors in executive deliberations. Charles of Calabria and his vicar Walter of Brienne simply appointed the priors during their rule, but when Charles died in late 1328 the elite seized the opportunity to carry out far-reaching reforms of three central aspects of the Florentine political world: the elections of priors and guild consuls, and the configuration of the legislative councils.

The authors of the electoral reform were the incumbent priors of October–December 1328 and six citizens they appointed to assist them: thirteen men among whom the representatives of elite families dominated (Jacopo Alberti, Gentile Altoviti, Tinoro Guasconi, and Maso Valori among the priors; Donato

---

[4]   *Statuto dell'Arte della Lana di Firenze (1317–1319)*, ed. A. M. E. Agnoletti (Florence, 1940), pp. 19, 84.
[5]   ASF, Arte della Lana 19 (1332) and 20 (1353).

Acciaiuoli, Tommaso Corsini, Giotto d'Arnoldo Peruzzi, and Taldo Valori among the six). They invented the system of nominations, general scrutinies, and sortition (extraction by lot) that, in its essential features, remained in place until the late fifteenth century. Its purposes were to consolidate elite control of the priorate, reduce disputes over elections, and enhance their legitimacy through complexity, impersonality, and secrecy, thus making it impossible to attribute the results to particular persons, committees, or factions. Unlike all earlier Florentine elections, the procedures devised in 1328 did not select priors for specific future terms; instead, they declared the eligibility of a much larger group of citizens, all of whom would sooner or later, depending on the chance extraction of name-tickets, take their turns in office. The names of approved citizens remained secret until they were gradually revealed in the bimonthly extractions of the tickets.

In this earliest version of the procedure, candidates were nominated by three committees: the incumbent priors, the six Guelf Party captains, and the Five of Mercanzia, who here made their first appearance in communal electoral politics. Particularly striking is the absence of the guild consuls, a sure sign of the elite's desire to reduce guild influence in these elections. Equally remarkable is that only eighteen men were responsible for making nominations. Although there were no numerical limits, control of nominations by so few probably did not result in the many thousands nominated some decades later. The second step was the scrutiny: nominees were put to a vote, one by one, by a scrutiny council that included the incumbent priors, the nineteen district standardbearers, the Five of Mercanzia, two consuls from each of the twelve major guilds, and thirty additional members selected by the priors. Thus, only twenty-four guild representatives, from only the twelve guilds, were included among the eighty-five voting members. The names of nominees receiving two-thirds of the votes were written on tickets that were placed in pouches and drawn by lot every two months. New nominations and scrutinies were to be held every two years, and for all subsequent scrutinies nominations were also requested from the priorate's advisory colleges of Twelve and Nineteen. A crucial feature of the 1328 reform, which remained in place only until 1339, was that the name-tickets of those placed in office were not eliminated from the pouches (as they subsequently would be), but were transferred to the same pouch into which the names of those approved in the next scrutiny were also placed, and from which extractions continued when no names remained in the first pouch. Thus, citizens approved in the first scrutiny who served terms in office were automatically placed in subsequent pouches and made indefinitely eligible for the priorate, even if they were not approved in later scrutinies. Restricting nominations for the first scrutiny to the small elite committees of priors, Guelf Party captains, and Five of Mercanzia established the elite core of the office-holding class for the next generation.

A few weeks later, in January 1329, a version of the same plan was adopted for the election of guild consuls. For each of the twelve major guilds, nominations were requested from the priors, each guild's consuls and twelve other members, and the Five of Mercanzia with six of each guild's members. Nominees of the seven major guilds were put to a vote in a single scrutiny council of eighty members consisting mostly of the priors, their colleges, and members of these guilds selected by them. For the five middle guilds, the same procedures yielded a scrutiny committee of sixty-eight. Guild elections were thus dominated by the priors and colleges, whose own election had just been brought under the control of the elite. A separate law for the nine minor guilds gave full control over the election of their consuls to the Five of Mercanzia. Nominations came both from the consuls and their advisers within each guild and from the Five and their handpicked advisers in each guild. The scrutiny council consisted of the Five and two members from each of all twenty-one guilds, all selected by the Five, which made the representatives of the minor guilds a minority in their own scrutiny. For all guilds, as for the priorate, those approved in the first scrutiny of 1329 were made permanently eligible by having their name-tickets recycled into subsequent pouches (a practice discontinued in this case in 1337). This was a watershed moment in the history of the guilds, which here lost the autonomy they had enjoyed for a century and more in electing their own consuls.

Reshaping the legislative branch of communal government followed on the heels of the electoral reforms. By the 1320s there were no fewer than five councils, all of which had to consent to initiatives from the priors and often rejected them (particularly concerning forced loans and expenditures). When, in February 1329, the priors proposed abolishing the estimo (and burning its records, thus removing written evidence of direct taxation!), the councils, whose popular majorities obviously considered the estimo a more equitable form of taxation, defeated it. A week later, the next priorate presented a bill for restructuring the councils themselves. The law of February 20, 1329, reduced the cumbersome cluster of legislative councils to just two, the Council of the Popolo and the Council of the Commune. To the former's 140 regular members, the law added as ex officio participants the priors, colleges, and consuls of the twelve guilds, the latter now chosen in tightly controlled elections. Nine days later, on February 29, the Signoria re-presented to the newly configured councils the proposal for abolition of the estimo, and this time it passed (although still with notable opposition: 128–47 and 178–62).[6] Further fine tuning of the councils came a few months later when another law authorized the priors to make up to twenty-five substitutions in the Council of the

---

[6] Barbadoro, *Finanze*, pp. 190–4.

Popolo and forty in that of the Commune, which gave the ruling elite a way of neutralizing or at least reducing popular opposition whenever it surfaced.

The reforms of 1328–9 consolidated elite power without discarding the popolo's institutions and produced a decade of stable oligarchic government and a restricted office-holding class recruited from (or allied with) the elite. Between 1329 and 1342, 302 citizens from 207 families shared the 584 available positions on the priorate. Almost three-fifths of them held office more than once: 89 twice, 75 three times, 13 four times, and 1 five times. Although non-elite citizens were among those most frequently elected, the elite families cumulatively dominated. Seven families had between nine and fifteen priors (14% of the seats): Strozzi (15), Ricci, Albizzi, and Rucellai (12 each), Altoviti and Baroncelli-Bandini (10 each); and Acciaiuoli (9). These and another six families (including the Ardinghelli, Bordoni, and Peruzzi) held a fifth of the posts. In these fourteen years, only thirty-eight families reached the priorate for the first time, compared to 104 new families between 1312 and 1325.[7] At least 70% of the priors were from the Calimala, Cambio, or Lana,[8] and the priors from the minor guilds were no more than a handful.

Within the major guilds the results of the new system of consular elections were mixed. Small elites dominated the Cambio and Calimala. Only forty-six individuals (two-thirds of them Mercanzia merchants and bankers) held 156 available posts in the Cambio between 1329 and 1341; twenty-four held the office four or more times and collectively held 74% of the posts. Taddeo di Donato dell'Antella was a Cambio consul seven times in thirteen years. In the Calimala, sixty-six individuals held the 143 posts whose occupants have been identified; at least 70% were Mercanzia merchants. Although the magnate Bardi were ineligible for the consulate, their partner Taldo Valori was the Calimala's most frequent consul with five appearances. But in the Wool guild 141 members shared 311 available posts, partly because of the eight-man consulate, partly also because of the Lana's non-elite majority: only 36% of Lana consuls were Mercanzia merchants. In Por Santa Maria eighty-five members shared 143 posts, although more than half were Mercanzia merchants. In the Medici, Speziali, e Merciai, 207 seats were held by ninety-nine members, of whom only a quarter were Mercanzia merchants. Although the electoral controls imposed on the guilds contributed to the general quiescence of the popolo, the potential for a popular resurgence clearly existed in these three large guilds.

For the first time, Florentine electoral procedures widened upper-class consensus by promising the whole of the elite (minus the magnates), and much of the upper ranks of the popolo as well, a steady collective monopoly of

[7] Najemy, *Corporatism*, pp. 99–125.
[8] M. B. Becker, *Florence in Transition*, vol. 1 (Baltimore, 1967), p. 17.

power in which at least some members of most of the important families would see their names come up sooner or later in the electoral lottery. The results overwhelmingly favored the elite and did so while muffling its internal divisions and helping it become (or appear to become) a unified ruling class whose power was legitimated by the apparent impersonality of electoral institutions.

Crisis of the 1340s and the Third Popular Government

The unraveling of elite dominance began with a combination of costly war and economic contraction. After Castruccio Castracani died, Lucca came into the hands of Mastino della Scala, lord of Verona and of an expanding territorial state in northern Italy. Apprehensive about the intrusion of an external power in Tuscany and fearing that Mastino had ambitions beyond Lucca, Florence allied with Venice, which also felt threatened by the Della Scala state to its west. The two republics fought Mastino for three years (1336–8) in an expensive war in which Florence's government had to borrow heavily and increase indirect taxes. According to Villani (12.50) it also enlisted the cooperation of leading banking companies to bolster communal credit weakened by prior debts. A committee of ten from major companies was empowered to raise money and given control of 250,000 florins of gabelle revenues to guarantee repayment of loans; it assessed loans totaling 100,000 florins, a third of which came from their own companies, and the remainder from other citizens who could choose one of three options. Those willing to lend directly to the commune were promised 15% annual interest. Citizens preferring not to risk lending to the commune were invited to extend loans to one of the companies represented in the committee and receive 8%, while the companies transferred their loans to the commune and received 5%. Those unable to make the loans in either manner could cede their obligations to the companies, which made loans on their behalf and collected interest from both the commune and the citizens whose debts they assumed.[9]

For perhaps the first time, the companies here became an integral part of the commune's fiscal apparatus, not only by making their own loans and guaranteeing repayment from gabelle revenues, but also by providing the security that some lenders needed and by assuming the debts of others. Through these channels, the companies helped raise revenue for the commune and began investing more and more of their own assets in government credits from which they earned substantial interest. They were functioning in effect as banks for

[9]   Barbadoro, *Finanze*, pp. 571–83.

the commune; through the committee of ten they also controlled the commune's fiscal policies. While the government increasingly depended on the companies for both direct loans and revenues made possible by securing or assuming other citizens' loans, the companies likewise became dependent on the government's ability to pay the interest that they in effect had promised themselves. And that in turn depended on the health of the economy and continued high receipts from the gabelles. But within a few years gabelle receipts began to decline. The gate gabelle, which produced 90,000 florins in 1337–8, yielded only 65,000 in 1342 and 1343. Taxes on wine sold retail went from 60,000 florins in 1337–8 to 36,000 in 1343.[10] Because of dwindling yields, gabelle purchasers and collectors became more difficult to find.[11] The situation worsened when Florence settled with Mastino in 1341 by buying Lucca for 250,000 florins, which provoked Pisa into war against Florence and triggered another wave of heavy borrowing, higher debt, and more pressure on the gabelles in a weakening economy. By the summer of 1341 a major crisis loomed.

The full dimension of the crisis emerges only when the commune's fiscal difficulties are seen in the context of the companies' growing problems, which stemmed partly from declining profits in the southern Italian grain trade, and also from the risky decision of the Bardi and Peruzzi to concentrate so much of their assets in England at precisely the moment when war between England and France cut the companies off from the traditionally profitable relationship with France. In return for loans to the crown, the companies sought a monopoly of wool exports from England. In 1337 the Peruzzi alone lent Edward nearly 175,000 florins. In 1338, having consolidated a joint venture in order to pool their assets, the Bardi and Peruzzi promised Edward even more extensive loans, 60% from the Bardi and 40% from the Peruzzi, in return for expanded control of wool exports and the right to collect royal taxes in England. Between 1338 and 1340, their loans amounted to 126,000 pounds sterling, or 840,000 florins. When the 1337 Peruzzi loans are added, the total for the three years (and this does not include whatever loans the Bardi may have made on their own in 1337) exceeds a million florins. Villani's estimate (12.88) of the sums lent to Edward is higher: 1,365,000 florins ("worth a kingdom," he added), 57% (780,000 florins) owed to the Bardi and 43% (585,000 florins) to the Peruzzi. But it is close enough to what the surviving documents tell us to make it believable. From the royal treasury the companies received cash payments of 104,000 pounds sterling, just under 700,000 florins, and were no doubt expecting more. During these same two years they exported to Italy 7,365 sacks of English wool, enough to produce 53,000 bolts of cloth. Profitable wool exports, together with tax concessions and other privileges might have

[10] La Roncière, "Indirect Taxes," tables inserted facing pages 160 and 176.
[11] Becker, *Florence*, 1:127–8.

made up the 300,000 florin deficit between cash advances and payments received. But it was enormously risky and depended, fatally, as it turned out, on two things: the king's continued good will toward the companies and ability to repay them in one way or another, and the confidence of the companies' depositors.[12]

What is often referred to as Edward's 1339 "default" specifically excluded the Bardi and Peruzzi from the suspension of payments and was not the cause of their bankruptcies.[13] They continued making loans through 1340–1, albeit on a smaller scale. But Edward's mounting problems were not a good sign and must have frightened depositors. In fact, matters were already disintegrating. In November 1340 a large number of Bardi, but including only one company shareholder, joined the Frescobaldi, Rossi, and some magnate clans of the contado in an uprising, motivated, according to Villani (12.118), by their harsh treatment at the hands of an overly zealous judicial official. The conspiracy may have had nothing to do with the precarious condition of the Bardi company, but among the priors in office at that moment was their influential partner Taldo Valori, who, Villani says, tried to prevent the other priors from sounding the alarm. Whatever the origin of this curious episode, which resulted in the banishment of several conspirators and a quick reaction by the popolo (manifested by a procession of "all the guilds" on November 26, subsequently an annual event observed on All Saints' day), it cannot have helped those Bardi who were trying to keep the company afloat. In July 1341 the worsening fiscal and military situation prompted the priorate to ask the councils to entrust emergency powers to a committee of Twenty largely composed of representatives of the banking companies, including Pacino Peruzzi, who had taken over the leadership of his firm, and his partner Salvestro Baroncelli; Jacopo di Donato Acciaiuoli and his investing partner Vanni Bandini; and members, associates, or partners of the families and/or companies of the Buonaccorsi, Strozzi, Corsini, Ricci, Albizzi, Medici, Alberti, and Dell'Antella. Of the two members of the Twenty with connections to the Bardi we again find Taldo Valori.[14] These were the elite of the elite: the same banking and trading companies that had been borrowing on the commune's behalf were now given full control of government to salvage the commune's finances and their own. The Twenty imposed one forced loan after another and, according to Villani (13.3), left the commune a debt of 400,000 florins, not counting the 250,000 florins still owed to Mastino della Scala. In October the Florentines were badly defeated on the battlefield by the Pisans, and ten days later Pope Benedict XII suddenly removed the Florentine companies, including

[12]   Hunt, *Peruzzi Company*, pp. 184–211.
[13]   Ibid., p. 207.
[14]   Becker, *Florence*, 1:145–7.

the Bardi and Peruzzi and excepting only the Acciaiuoli, as collectors and transmitters of papal revenues. Like the pope, depositors all around Europe were beginning to doubt the viability of the overextended companies. At the end of 1341 some smaller firms went into default. In June 1342 the Buonaccorsi (one of whose partners was Giovanni Villani) closed its operations in both Naples and Avignon. Depositors began demanding their money, and the chain reaction collapse became an avalanche as depositors of other, still solvent, companies also claimed their investments. The crisis was underway, and the Florentine elite needed quick and drastic help to save its economic empire.

Once again they opted for extensive powers in the hands of a prestigious foreigner and chose Walter of Brienne, Charles of Calabria's former vicar in 1326–8. Brienne was a known quantity and was well connected in both Naples and Avignon, where the threatened companies faced many angry creditors. The bankers who invited him to assume military and political leadership hoped he would enact the inevitably unpopular policies needed to save their companies. In early 1342 they also gave him command of the communal armies fighting Pisa. But Brienne had ambitions of his own and in September had himself declared *signore* of Florence for life. As it happened, he remained in office for a mere ten months before being driven out by the same elite families that had brought him in. After his expulsion on July 26, 1343 (which also became a civic holiday), and the gruesome murder of his most hated officials, the Florentines created the legend of the brutal and corrupt despot who tried to deprive them of their liberty. Brienne did enforce communal laws with particular severity, inflicted huge fines and capital punishment on transgressors, and contemptuously disregarded the republic's officials and councils. But the other side of the story is his serious and substantially successful effort to put the commune's fiscal affairs in order with reforms that threatened elite interests. Having alienated the elite, he sought to broaden his political support among both minor guildsmen and the textile artisans with measures that further enraged the elite. His brief *signoria* reawakened latent social tensions that led, after his ouster, to the formation of a new popular government.[15]

Brienne tried to stop the growing debt from consuming the city's wealth through indirect taxes. To reduce government spending, he ended the war against Pisa and suspended the assignment of gabelle revenues to debt repayment and interest. He instituted a stricter system for assessing wealth and collecting taxes in the contado and, most important of all, reinstituted the estimo and direct taxation in the city: the same policy attempted by Charles of Calabria and quickly annulled by the elite-dominated government that succeeded him. Both aspects of this new fiscal regime damaged elite interests. Whereas the companies, needing cash to pay worried creditors, expected regular

[15]   Ibid., 1:148–72.

interest payments on their large investment in the debt, they faced instead a suspension of payments and the simultaneous imposition of direct taxes. Brienne was not trying to ruin the companies. In fact, he approved a three-year immunity for the Dell'Antella company against civil actions by creditors, which, subsequently extended to other firms, gave the companies time to build their cash holdings, pressure their debtors, and protect landed property from the bankruptcy commissions through fictitious sales or alienations.[16] But, while willing to help them in this way, Brienne's fiscal reforms could not have come at a worse time for the companies.

So Brienne turned elsewhere to build a political constituency. He released the guild of the Vinattieri from its debts to the commune for the suddenly declining gabelle on the retail sale of wine and reduced the similar obligations of the provisioning guilds. Already precarious social relations were further destabilized by his approval of a petition in November 1342 from the dyers of the textile industry asking for release from subordination to the Wool guild and permission to form their own guild. Lamenting the Lana's arrogance ("grandigia") and the "many unjust ordinances" that had nearly reduced them to "poverty," the dyers outlined with notable precision the circumstances of their mistreatment. They accused the *lanaiuoli* of deliberately delaying the balancing of their account books and waiting four and five years before paying even a fraction of what they owed them. The dyers had no legal recourse except to the guild's own consuls, who also unilaterally decreed the piece-rates for their work and imposed a tax on it. The "wickedness and arrogance" of the Wool guild had reached the point where the dyers, "deprived of all rights and honor," might have to abandon their shops and profession: a not so veiled threat of a strike. They thus begged the duke to liberate "them from the yoke" of the Wool guild and permit them a guild with their own consuls. Brienne accepted the petition and declared the dyers and related categories of artisans to be "one and the same body and *universitas*" subject to the jurisdiction and regulatory power of no other guild.[17] The dyers' guild lasted only as long as Brienne's short period of rule, but it signaled the awakening of the political aspirations of Florence's laboring classes.

Brienne went further. He protected and raised the status of salaried workers in the woolen cloth industry by appointing officials to oversee the various categories of workers and to monitor the jurisdiction and regulatory power traditionally exercised by the Lana. And in a series of holidays in the first half of 1343, culminating in the celebrations on June 24 of the feast day of the Baptist, he made two dramatic changes in the organization of the processions.

---

[16]   A. Sapori, "Il quaderno dei creditori di Taddeo dell'Antella e Compagni," *Rivista delle biblioteche e degli archivi*, n.s., 3 (1925): 159–80.
[17]   C. Paoli, *Della signoria di Gualtieri duca d'Atene* (Florence, 1862), pp. 82–3.

He permitted workers to march in brigades of their own, with banners and uniforms that established their status, for the first time, as collective participants in the commune's ritual life. And he revived an older tradition of organizing processions by guild (abandoned during the period of elite dominance in favor of organization by gonfalone) and allowed the members of each guild to march under its banner in a grand visual and performative display of the republic as the federation of its guilds. The processions of guilds and workers in their separate formations may have occurred peacefully enough on that Baptist's day of 1343, but the tension was just beneath the surface (and, for the Wool guild, no doubt very much in the open). Brienne's approval of the dyers' guild, the first expansion of the guild federation since 1293, and simultaneous organization of workers into associations which, while not guilds, pointed toward that revolutionary possibility, were dramatic signs of expanding social conflicts that would later be played out within the framework of the guild republic.

Brienne may have been a hero to workers, but he had become a lethal danger to the elite and to the Wool guild. Elite families, including magnates, led the conspiracies against him and tried to take political control after his departure. In the vacuum left by Brienne's expulsion the magnates reached for the political rights they had lost in 1293. Bishop Agnolo Acciaiuoli assembled a committee of fourteen, all from prominent elite families and including magnates, who proceeded to abolish the Ordinances of Justice and the office of Standardbearer of Justice. In electoral reforms that lasted only six weeks, the committee gave the magnates a third of the seats in a twelve-man priorate and half the seats in the advisory colleges and held a general scrutiny in which magnates constituted a third of the nominating and scrutiny committees. (The only action of the six-week "magnate" regime that survived its demise was the administrative reorganization of the city into quarters and of each quarter into four gonfaloni.) Magnate and non-magnate elite families were closing ranks, no doubt in view of what they saw as dangerous stirrings within the guild community. But the guildsmen viewed this magnate resurgence with alarm, as this was the one moment after 1293 when the elite tried to jettison the popolo's constitution. Political grievances and aspirations were now erupting from all sides. On September 22 guildsmen surrounded the palace and forced the removal of the magnate priors (from the Mannelli, Foraboschi, Spini, and Adimari families). The next day, Andrea Strozzi (quickly repudiated by his family) led an aroused mob of poor workers through the streets denouncing the gabelles and the "popolo grasso." Magnates, furious over their expulsion from the priorate, barricaded their neighborhoods, and on September 25 fighting broke out between magnates and self-mustered contingents of the popolo. With civil war looming, some non-magnate elite families prudently abandoned their magnate confreres and joined the popolo. A force of 1,000 men from San

Lorenzo led by the Medici and Rondinelli (says Villani, 13.21) quickly overran the enclave of the Cavicciuli (a branch of the Adimari). But the powerful magnate clans of the Oltrarno (Frescobaldi, Rossi, Nerli, Mannelli, and above all the Bardi) put up fierce resistance that was overcome only when the troops of the popolo advanced first over the Ponte alla Carraia to attack Frescobaldi strongholds and then went up the hill of San Giorgio to assail the still defiant Bardi from behind. According to Villani, the "enraged" popolo attacked and destroyed twenty-two Bardi palaces and houses, inflicting damages of over 60,000 florins.

The twenty-one guilds (the dyers' guild evidently already abolished) quickly seized the initiative, establishing a new popular government that reissued the Ordinances and again deprived magnates of political eligibility. Although the new government agreed to remove certain families from the magnate ranks (Spini, Scali, Brunelleschi, and some of the Adimari, Rossi, Mannelli, Nerli, and Della Tosa), it turned in the other direction for political allies and gave the minor guilds an unprecedented share of power. Villani says that the government's first decisions were carried out "with the advice of the consuls of the twenty-one guilds" (13.19) and that "the *popolo* rose in influence, audacity, and power, especially the middle and lower guildsmen, for at that time the government of the city fell to the consuls of the twenty-one guilds" (13.22). Both Villani's account and the official documents of the popular government over the next five years repeatedly highlight the influence and authority, not of the twelve guilds that dominated the federation of 1293, but of all twenty-one guilds and their consuls.

In October 1343 the popular government threw out all the electoral pouches and held a new scrutiny that produced an office-holding class radically different from that of the 1330s. Guilds made their own independent nominations, and 3,446 citizens were nominated. The scrutiny council was expanded to 206 members, including representatives of all the guilds, and only 110 votes were needed for approval. For the first and only time in Florentine elections, the names of approved citizens were not written on individual name-tickets, but organized into groups of eight, two from each quarter and all eight on a single ticket, by election officials known as "accoppiatori" (from their function of joining names into groups). The tickets were placed in a pouch, and the eight citizens on the ticket drawn by lot every other month became the priors. In pre-determining the composition of the priorates, the accoppiatori were required to include three minor guildsmen in each priorate, the first time that the fourteen guilds were guaranteed a minimum share of seats. If not enough minor guildsmen had been approved in the scrutiny to meet the quota, the accoppiatori could add the names of persons who had come closest to the 110-vote level. And if, when a ticket was drawn, any of the eight was unable to assume the office, replacements were chosen from those who had received between 90 and 110 votes. Thus, although Villani (13.22) says that only 10% of the nominees were approved in the scrutiny, these provisions resulted in the election of a significant number who had not received 110 votes. Altogether, the various categories of eligible citizens came to about 800. During the almost five years in which the priorates pre-selected in 1343 were drawn and placed in office, exactly one-third of the priors (88 of 265) were minor guildsmen, and the great majority of the two-thirds from the major guilds were non-elite, with only a few priors from elite families. No fewer than 136 families had their first priors in these years, more than three and a half times the number of new families in the fourteen years between 1329 and 1342. It was the combination of the guaranteed minimum three seats for minor guildsmen and the inclusion of so many non-elite major guildsmen that made this popular government the most popular thus far.[18] Villani (13.43) unleashed invective against Florence's new rulers, calling them "artisans, manual laborers, and simpletons," and complaining that "the majority of the guild consuls, by whom the commune was then being ruled, were lowly guildsmen just arrived from the countryside, or foreigners, to whom the republic mattered little and who were even less capable of governing it. Willingly do they pass laws with much haste, but with no foundation in reason." Villani's bitterness spoke here, perhaps because he had been a partner of both the Peruzzi and the Buonaccorsi. In fact, the new government, far from being incompetent, met the still unresolved dilemmas of the public debt and the looming bankruptcies with innovative policies that succeeded in bringing down the economic powerhouses of the preceding two generations.

Funded Public Debt and Bankruptcies

The new popular government first addressed the debt. On December 29, 1343, it consolidated the commune's outstanding debts into one "mountain," or Monte, of indebtedness that approached 800,000 florins and suspended interest payments, intending to repay the principal to creditors. In 1344 shares were made negotiable; creditors unwilling to wait for repayment could now sell their credits for whatever price they might bring on the market. By early 1345, according to Villani (13.36), the debt was reduced to 570,000 florins, but it had become clear that full amortization was unlikely or impossible. In February a priorate that included a used-cloth dealer, a butcher, a dyer, a notary, the father (Coppo) of the chronicler Marchionne Stefani, and only one member (a Machiavelli) who would qualify for the second rank of elite families, presented to the councils a proposal that radically transformed the

[18]   Najemy, *Corporatism*, pp. 126–65.

administration and nature of the debt by terminating (actually prohibiting) repayment of principal and commencing 5% annual interest payments in perpetuity. Since the law required the assignment of 2,074 florins each month from the gate gabelle to pay interest, which amounts to just under 25,000 florins for the year, total indebtedness was evidently 500,000 florins at the moment the Monte was funded. To the bankers and merchants then negotiating with creditors and desperately in need of liquidity, the law of February 1345 was a calamity. Someone with 1,000 florins in the Monte from loans made at, say, 15% expected 1,150 florins if the loan was repaid after one year, and 1,300 (or slightly more with compounding) if repaid after two years. With the suspension of interest payments at the end of 1343, he still expected the principal of 1,000 florins. But he was now told that he would receive just 50 florins a year without return of principal. Creditors would have to wait twenty years merely to recover the equivalent of the principal. And for those seeking to sell their shares, the reduction of interest to 5% caused a precipitous drop in their market value estimated at 70–75%: those 1,000 florins in credits were now worth only 250–300 florins. The collapsing banks thus saw huge amounts of wealth disappear just when they most needed either to sell or redeem their shares.

But in August 1345, six months after funding the debt and terminating the repayment of principal, another law invited voluntary investment in the Monte and reinstituted return of principal under certain conditions. To raise 50,000 florins, the government allowed Monte creditors to make additional loans and receive in return, not only the principal of the new loan, but also repayment of existing credits in the same amount. Speculators began buying credits in order to participate in this new investment opportunity. Credits of, say, 100 florins, purchased on the open market at 30% of nominal value, would have allowed an investor to make a new loan of 100 florins and to receive, after two years, 200 florins: a 70-florin profit on a 130-florin investment (27% annual return). Over the next decade, many citizens made such voluntary loans, making handsome profits and allowing the government to reduce total indebtedness from 500,000 florins to 360,000 in 1350, and just 270,000 in 1358.[19] The negotiability and devaluation of Monte credits allowed anyone with cash to enter the market, buy shares for a fraction of their nominal value, and receive the full value in return for another loan, also repaid, of equal amount. Speculators who bought credits and made these lucrative loans to the commune came chiefly from the ranks of the "new men" who came to power in 1343. A major transfer of wealth occurred in Florence in these years as the "new men" managed communal finances to their own benefit and to the detriment of the

[19]   R. Barducci, "Politica e speculazione finanziaria a Firenze dopo la crisi del primo Trecento (1343–1358)," *ASI* 137 (1979): 177–219.

weakened elite. Over the next few years the social composition of the commune's creditor class underwent significant change. In 1347, 2,900 creditors were registered in the quarter of Santo Spirito, among whom those with family names, and mostly from the elite, had the largest average shares. But by 1351, Santo Spirito's creditors were reduced to slightly over 1,700, no doubt partly due to the plague, but partly also to the ongoing amortization of the debt. Now the largest average shares belonged to persons without family names and identified by their fathers' and grandfathers' given names – non-elite new men of the popolo.[20]

The second major dilemma was the banking crisis. In October 1343 the Peruzzi declared insolvency. Following the usual procedure in bankruptcy cases, their creditors petitioned the priors and legislative councils for the appointment of syndics, legal representatives who took control of the company's books and prepared a summary of assets and debts to reach an agreement for the distribution among creditors of a certain percentage (expressed in soldi per lira) of outstanding credits from proceeds of the sale of assets. Creditors could also take claims to the podestà's court, which had the authority to seize the property and persons of fraudulent bankrupts who fled the city to avoid courts and creditors. Finally, the Mercanzia had jurisdiction over cases in which reprisals were threatened or declared; it could mediate between the sometimes conflicting claims of the creditors' syndics and the podestà's court, hear petitions from either creditors or bankrupt merchants, and review and overturn settlements already reached between companies and syndics. As soon as a company announced a state of insolvency, events moved forward on all three fronts. On October 27 the councils approved the appointment of syndics requested by the Peruzzi creditors. Two weeks later, the company's legal representatives, or procurators, appeared before the Mercanzia to argue that it had no authority to confiscate Peruzzi assets; on the same day a Genoese creditor filed a claim with the Mercanzia for credits worth 4,250 florins, suing immediately for 60 and reserving the right to claim the remainder as the company's assets were gathered and sold. On several occasions procurators for the Peruzzi went back to the Mercanzia to argue that, in view of agreements between them and the creditors' syndics allowing Peruzzi partners to return to the city without fear of arrest or seizure of their goods in order to assist in the search for the company's assets, the podestà and his judges had no authority to order such arrests or seizures.[21] Evidently some creditors had

---

[20]   A. Molho, "Créanciers de Florence en 1347: un aperçu statistique du quartier de Santo Spirito," in *La Toscane et les Toscans autour de la Renaissance, cadres de vie, société, croyances. Mélanges offerts à Charles-M. de la Roncière* (Aix-en-Provence, 1999), pp. 77–93.

[21]   ASF, Mercanzia 1081, ff. 31–2, 32v–34, 56–57v; Mercanzia 1084, ff. 3v–4v.

indeed filed suits in the podestà's court. Similar claims and legal actions were being filed in the Mercanzia against, and on behalf of, the Dell'Antella, Da Uzzano, Buonaccorsi, and Acciaiuoli companies, and later the Bardi.

Companies needed time to collect from their own debtors and hide or transfer assets beyond the reach of the syndics and courts. The crucial asset to be protected was of course the land that served as the indispensable collateral for large-scale deposit banking. Here indeed was the kind of credit crisis in which land was meant to be the guarantee or insurance for creditors. But its sale would make any recovery impossible, and the companies tried to hide as much of it as they could. Allegations of fraudulently alienated assets were one aspect of the court battles. A second issue was the question of the priority of claims from foreign and local creditors. It is likely that the collapsing companies had asked Walter of Brienne, with his Neapolitan connections, to assume power in order to reassure important depositors in the South that their credits would receive preferential treatment. But the popular government announced that the claims of foreign creditors would be honored only when the assets that companies had in the cities or territories of those foreign creditors were recovered and added to the total assets to be distributed among creditors. Foreign creditors thus had first to ask their own governments to initiate proceedings against persons in their territories who owed money to the bankrupt companies. This was clearly an attempt to delay repayments to foreign creditors. In 1345, trying to hold off ecclesiastical creditors, the Florentine government also blocked church courts from claiming jurisdiction in bankruptcy (or other) cases, except when permitted by the priors and guild consuls.

In the competition between foreign and local creditors, the popular government made clear its intention to promote the interests of the latter. Into the confusion of claims, counterclaims, and overlapping jurisdictions, it introduced legislation in April 1344 that gave the Mercanzia overriding authority to prosecute all Florentine merchants who had declared bankruptcy within the previous ten years, or who might do so in the future, and to enforce existing agreements between companies and creditors "provided that such agreements are made with the consent of two-thirds of the creditors from the city and contado of Florence." In July two more laws entrusted these powers to a joint committee of twelve and the Five of Mercanzia, which had full authority over all bankruptcy cases, including the power to arrest fraudulent bankrupts, seize assets, dismiss negligent or fraudulent syndics, review, modify, or overturn any and all settlements between syndics and bankrupt merchants, and decide who the "real" creditors and debtors were and in what amounts. Their broad power to revoke existing settlements was also subject to the approval of two-thirds of a company's local Florentine creditors, all counted equally and not proportionally to the amounts of their credits. But the most important aspect of the committee of twelve (soon expanded to sixteen) was its election, not by the five guilds that traditionally controlled the Mercanzia, but by the consuls of all twenty-one guilds, at least two-thirds of whom had to be present for a valid election. This was another instance of the popular government's constitutional grounding in the full guild community, but never before had the elite Mercanzia been placed under the political influence of all twenty-one guilds. Predictably, the result was the near exclusion of the elite and the heavy predominance of non-elite major guildsmen and minor guildsmen on the bankruptcy committees. To guildsmen like the retail cloth dealer Simone di Bertino, the harness maker Maffeo di Giovanni, the shoemaker Salvi di Martino and dozens of other artisans and shopkeepers, the popular government entrusted final authority to oversee the bankruptcies of the greatest and most powerful Florentine companies.[22]

A preliminary agreement between the Peruzzi and their syndics was reached in September 1344 for restitution to creditors of four soldi per lira (20%). The syndics then petitioned for the appointment of an official to sell assets and distribute the proceeds as quickly as possible. But delays ensued throughout the next year until the Mercanzia's committee of sixteen finally took control of the Peruzzi bankruptcy and in December 1345 ordered four members of the family to hand over to the syndic-in-chief 3,000 florins worth of "land and farms" that had evidently not been part of the original settlement. A few weeks later the committee declared two other family members fraudulent bankrupts for refusal to obey its decisions.[23] The Sixteen were clearly pressuring Peruzzi partners to yield more assets, and in June 1347 a second and final settlement was reached that nearly doubled the reimbursement to creditors, with an additional three soldi, three denari per lira, to $36\frac{1}{4}$%.[24]

The Bardi were the biggest of the bankrupt companies. Early in 1346, the government asked the bankers' guild to provide an opinion concerning the assets of insolvent merchants. Why exactly the priors thought advice was needed is unclear, unless of course they only wanted legal cover for what they intended in any case to do. The Cambio met on January 27 and advised that syndics be required to compile complete lists of landed holdings of bankrupt companies and that these lands, farms, and buildings remain unused and uninhabited until creditors were repaid from their sale. In April the communal legislative councils approved precisely this policy, albeit by very close votes.[25]

---

[22]   ASF, Mercanzia 149, f. 19v; 150, ff. 11v–12; 152, 22v–23v; and 153, no pagination, November 23, 1346.

[23]   ASF, Mercanzia 4180, ff. 10v, 17–17v.

[24]   A. Sapori, *La crisi delle compagnie mercantili dei Bardi e dei Peruzzi* (Florence, 1926), pp. 160–8.

[25]   ASF, Arte del Cambio 57, f. 5–5v; Provvisioni, Registri 34, ff. 34v–36v; Sapori, *La crisi*, pp. 175–81.

Forbidding the use of properties and putting them all up for sale together promptly drove down their value. Not by coincidence, at that very moment the Bardi were handing over their books to creditors. Syndics were appointed in April, and by August a settlement was reached for a payout of nine soldi, three denari per lira ($46\frac{1}{4}$%), which, however, specifically excluded the company's English and Neapolitan creditors, presumably because assets had not been recovered from those kingdoms. Included in the settlement were proceeds from the sale of a huge amount of land: Ridolfo de' Bardi alone possessed 30,000 florins of landed property. With the artificial devaluation of the land and the exclusion of so many foreign creditors from the settlement, a huge fortune in landed property was transferred at bargain prices to local buyers. In the case of one such purchaser of Bardi property, the steps of his involvement are revealing. Jacopo di Renzo was a moneychanger in the Arte del Cambio who participated in the guild's deliberation on the property of insolvent companies. Evidently also a depositor in the Bardi bank, he was appointed chief-syndic in April to oversee their bankruptcy. And when the property of Ridolfo de' Bardi was sold, Jacopo di Renzo himself bought two farms, whose value was estimated at 1,220 florins, for only 600 florins. The sale of Bardi land was deliberately contrived to recover only a portion of its actual worth, as bargains were picked up by the new men of the popular government while many foreign creditors protested in vain. Lamenting the fate of the "unfortunate [foreign] creditors [who] were abandoned and impoverished," Villani (13.55) called the fall of the Bardi and the other companies the "greatest ruin and disaster that the commune had ever known," even as he angrily noted that "some guildsmen and lenders" (was he thinking of men like Jacopo di Renzo?) profited from events that "deprived our lost and desolate republic of its strength." For Villani, there was blame all around. He pointed both to the greed of companies that imprudently "put their own money and that of others into the hands of foreign lords" and to the "evil leveling effects of the laws and ordinances of our commune and corrupt government," an allusion to the popular government's policies that forced the companies to sell so much land at reduced prices and thus consigned them to oblivion.

Elite Recovery and Popular Reaction

In the mid-to-late 1340s, the popular government faced mounting hostility from both workers burdened by higher indirect taxes and elite families that found a new locus of unity in a revived Guelf Party and launched a campaign to discredit the new men by accusing them of being "foreign" immigrants and Ghibellines. In 1346 the Parte Guelfa promoted a law requiring the guilds to identify among their members recent contado immigrants unable to prove that they, their fathers, and grandfathers had been born in the city: 426 persons were deprived of office-holding rights, including sixty notaries, thirty members of Por Santa Maria, forty in the Medici, Speziali, e Merciai, and most of the rest from the minor guilds.[26] The law's prologue gives a glimpse of the nascent political rhetoric that would soon take hold within the elite: offices, it insisted, should be entrusted only to persons "in whom is borne, implanted from birth, the devotion of true sons to the city, people, and commune of Florence as to their true mother." Here the civic community is imagined as a family in which loyalty could only come from the affective bonds of blood and filial love. In accusing new men of Ghibelline sympathies, the elite similarly wrapped itself in emotional appeals to civic loyalty. In 1347 the Parte supported a law prohibiting Ghibellines convicted as rebels against the commune, or any of their descendants, from holding office. Ghibellinism was a dead issue by the middle of the fourteenth century, but the term carried powerful if inevitably vague overtones of generic disloyalty to commune and church that could tarnish reputations. Here too the elite embraced a rhetoric of blood and family: persons of dubious loyalty were endeavoring "to separate devoted and faithful children from their venerated mother, the Holy Roman Church, mother of her Guelf children."[27]

The catastrophe of the Black Death in 1348 gave the elite the opportunity to undo the results of the 1343 scrutiny and intensify its political attack on the guilds. All government activity came to a halt in April as the plague devastated the city and killed half or more of the population in a few months. When the horror subsided in August, it was evident that the huge mortality made the electoral lists unusable. An ad hoc committee, or balìa, dominated by members of elite families removed the names of the deceased and of "foreigners" and held a new scrutiny whose results were added to the pouches, but with each name on its own ticket. It also cut the minor guilds' share in the priorate to two seats, but its boldest decision was to combine different minor guilds and reduce their number from fourteen to seven. The traditional number of twenty-one guilds was restored two years later, but the balìa's action certainly reflected elite anger over the policies of the guild-dominated popular government. The traditional numerical superiority of the minor guilds made any government based on the participation of all twenty-one guilds inimical to elite interests.

For the next two decades a tense compromise prevailed in which neither elite nor popolo had things exactly to its liking. An electoral reform of 1352 reflected the compromise. Nominations now came from the guilds as well as

[26] Najemy, *Corporatism*, pp. 153–7.
[27] G. Brucker, *The Society of Renaissance Florence: A Documentary Study* (1971; reprint edn. Toronto, 1998), pp. 86–7.

the Parte Guelfa and the college of the Sixteen, but guild representation on the scrutiny council was limited and controlled by the priors and colleges, who appointed 70% of the council. Scrutinies were scheduled at three-year intervals, with separate sets of pouches resulting from each. Sortition always began from the oldest set of pouches still containing any tickets and proceeded chronologically through the others until a priorate was constituted; indeed, a scrutiny's pouches might not come into use until years after that scrutiny. Any given priorate typically included members drawn from the pouches of from two to five scrutinies, making it impossible to attribute a particular priorate's composition to any one scrutiny and thus enhancing the stability and legitimacy of the procedures. Compromise was also reflected in the results. There was a steady arrival of new men, mostly non-elite major guildsmen: between 1352 and 1377, 48% of the seats went to members of 313 families whose first prior came after 1343, including 222 with a first prior after 1352. But many fewer new families reached the priorate than during the popular government of the 1340s: an annual average of 8.5 in 1352–77 as against 28 per year in 1343–8. On the other hand, older families regained a significant share of the electoral spoils: 181 pre-1343 families had 52% of the seats in these 26 years. Of 45 families with 7 or more priors, only 6 had their first prior after 1343; the other 39 were mostly from the elite, led by the Strozzi (with 14 priors), and including the Medici, Rucellai, Altoviti, Rondinelli, Alberti, Salviati, Covoni, Ridolfi, Peruzzi, Capponi, Baroncelli, and the two leading political families of this generation, the Ricci and Albizzi.[28]

New factions emerged around these two families and originated in a competition for control of the San Giovanni quarter where both lived.[29] The Ricci were bankers and had allies among the Alberti, Medici, Rondinelli, Ridolfi, Covoni, and within the popolo. The Albizzi, producers of woolen cloth who counted supporters among the Strozzi, Corsini, Altoviti, Soderini, Rucellai, and Baroncelli, gravitated toward the Guelf Party and espoused its anti-Ghibelline, pro-papal, and elite views. For example, the Albizzi favored relaxation of the *divieti* that prohibited members of the same lineage from succeeding one another in office except after designated intervals, and which thus reduced the presence of large elite families in the priorate; they even argued for the admission of magnates to certain offices. Although equally dominated by elite families, the Ricci faction was more sympathetic to the new men and generally supported the guild community in opposing these ideas. Dividing the factions above all were the Parte Guelfa's attempts to purge the office-holding class of so-called Ghibellines. In 1358 the Parte revived the

---

[28]   Najemy, *Corporatism*, pp. 166–216.
[29]   For what follows: G. Brucker, *Florentine Politics and Society, 1343–1378* (Princeton, 1962), pp. 148–296.

issue by promoting a controversial law that reconfirmed the bans against Ghibellines in office, permitted secret accusations of suspected Ghibellines, and gave the Parte itself a freer hand in investigating and prosecuting suspects. Some twenty persons were tried and convicted in the first few months. A simpler method of discrediting its enemies was a "warning" (*ammonizione*) not to accept political office or face prosecution. These warnings intimidated political opponents and generated much fear, as well as anger and resentment, over the next two decades. Viewing such tactics as a cynical attempt to drive new men from office, the Ricci and the guild community tried to curtail the "anti-Ghibelline" campaign. Although the Parte issued fewer warnings in the early 1360s (about thirty in five years), it occasionally outraged public opinion by targeting respected citizens with spotlessly Guelf family backgrounds, provoking storms of protest and calls for reining in the Parte. In 1362 it even accused and put on trial the chronicler Matteo Villani, brother of Giovanni, possibly in retaliation for his criticism of the Parte in the chronicle, especially his view that the 1358 law was "iniquitous" and "evil."[30] By the early 1370s the Parte's intensifying campaign against its enemies unleashed a backlash that was the origin of another popular government.

Although sometimes bitter and deep, factional divisions in the 1350s and 1360s never approached the chaos of earlier times. As always, elite patronage networks sought to attract clients from the popolo and thus weaken horizontal ties of class solidarity with vertical links of patronage, but they no longer gave birth to private armies. Elite political action increasingly entered the civic spaces created by the popolo, in particular at this time the consultative assemblies (called pratiche), convened by the priors to hear the views of influential citizens. Unlike the legislative councils, in which only voting and little or no debate occurred,[31] a pratica was a forum for the expression of opinions but not for voting. These advisory sessions, in which, beginning in the late 1340s, groups of citizens were periodically invited to offer advice to the priors on important matters, became and remained a central feature of Florentine political culture until the end of the republic. Some citizens were invited because of their personal prestige or that of their families, while others represented bodies like the Parte Guelfa, the Mercanzia, the Twelve, the Sixteen, and occasionally the guild consuls. Pratiche made no decisions, and the priors were not bound to follow the views expressed in them. Their purpose was rather to air opinions

---

[30] G. Brucker, "The Ghibelline Trial of Matteo Villani (1362)," *Medievalia et Humanistica* 13 (1960): 48–55; reprinted in Brucker, *Renaissance Florence: Society, Culture, and Religion* (Goldbach, 1994), pp. 29–36.

[31] As can be seen in *I Consigli della Repubblica fiorentina. Libri fabarum, XVII (1338–1340)*, ed. F. Klein (Rome, 1995); and *I Consigli della Repubblica fiorentina. Libri fabarum XIII e XIV (1326–1331)*, ed. L. De Angelis (Rome, 2000).

and forge consensus around government policy. Florentines paid close attention to who was invited to these sessions, who spoke, and in agreement with whom (or not), and with what effect on policy. Predictably, the elite preferred small gatherings recruited from their class, while guildsmen wanted larger, more representative meetings. The emergence of the pratica as a stage for political debate and for demonstrations of the influence of powerful citizens was another important step in the civilizing of the Florentine elite.

Between 1350 and 1370 the popolo made no attempt to resurrect the popular constitution of the 1340s, while the elite accepted, sometimes grudgingly, the presence of new men in office and the limits placed by *divieti* on office-holding by large families. That neither faction was able to dominate the other also reassured the popolo. But after 1370 two developments destabilized this compromise and prepared the way for the next popular government: intensifying conflicts between elite and non-elite major guildsmen, especially in the Wool guild; and a sudden rapprochement between the factions that galvanized the popolo into action. Controversies in the Wool guild were the first sign of the breakdown of consensus.[32] In the 1350s and 1360s the guild was governed by small committees (balìe), appointed by the consuls and composed largely of members from elite families, which were not obligated to seek approval of their actions from the guild council or, apparently, even to report to it. For example, in November 1369 a consulate including members of the Albizzi, Rucellai, Rondinelli, Capponi, and Ridolfi selected a balìa committee of eight with members from the Albizzi, Rucellai, Rondinelli, Del Palagio, and Salviati. Not only were three of the guild's elite families represented on both the consulate and the balìa; the Lana's leading families also came from both sides of the Albizzi–Ricci factional divide. But a movement of opposition to this concentration of power in a few elite families surfaced in January 1370, when the guild council suddenly prohibited the consuls from tampering with the established schedule for guild elections (as they had in the past), insisted that elections of the guild's notary be restored to the council (on the grounds that "that which touches all must be approved by all"), and established tighter control by the council over the appointment of balìe. Four years later, the guild council strengthened its role, requiring that henceforth petitions and proposals before the council be read aloud separately and in the vernacular rather than Latin, "so that they may be more clearly and openly understood by the council members," and mandating council meetings at least twice in each consular term of four months, "whether or not there is pressing business," because "when the assembled members of the guild regularly consult

[32]   For what follows: J. M. Najemy, "*Audiant omnes artes*: Corporate Origins of the Ciompi Revolution," in *Il Tumulto dei Ciompi: un momento di storia fiorentina ed europea* (Florence, 1981), pp. 59–93.

and talk with one another in such meetings, many issues are raised and brought to the attention of the consuls that redound to the honor, utility, and benefit of the guild and its members." Reasserting the council's prerogatives and opening guild government to broader participation were the responses of the non-elite majority to the elite's earlier monopoly of power.

Behind these political struggles lay economic issues and disputes over production levels and labor costs. In the late 1360s, the industry underwent significant expansion, mostly in the high-quality export sector controlled by elite families like the Albizzi, Pitti, and Del Bene. Increased production also drove up wages, in both the luxury-cloth sector and the manufacture of cloths for the local and regional markets. Rising labor costs were a threat to the viability of the smaller firms of non-elite producers of cheaper cloths. This is the picture of their difficulties presented in two enactments of the guild council in 1372, which complained that some producers were luring workers away from other firms with promises of higher wages and loans to pay off debts incurred to former employers. Their remedy was a more rigorous enforcement of existing limits on the number of cloths each firm was allowed to produce in a year. Production quotas began in 1349, just after the plague, probably in an effort to support the price of cloth in the face of plummeting demand. No member of the guild was allowed to produce more than 220 bolts per year, and no more than 50 in the first year. In the expansion of the 1360s, many members petitioned the guild for exemptions from the 220-bolt limit, while others circumvented the regulation by having separate quotas approved for two or more partners that cumulatively exceeded the limit. Those seeking to halt this expansion and contain rising wages persuaded the guild council to restore production ceilings for all firms, however many partners they had, and to require workers who had borrowed from employers during periods of unemployment to remain bound to those employers until they paid off their debts, thus depressing wages to subsistence levels and limiting the freedom of workers to seek higher wages elsewhere. Conflicts of economic interest pitted elite producers of high quality cloths, who needed laborers and were willing to pay them more, against producers of cheaper cloths, who reacted to their predicament by seizing political control of the guild and using this power to impose the restrictions on production and workers' mobility that they hoped would solve the problem of rising wages. By one measure at least they were successful: after 1372 no producer was allowed a quota in excess of 220 bolts. But their success came directly at the expense of the industry's workers, who were now threatened by both shrinking employment and stagnant or declining wages. For the guild's non-elite majority these temporary victories were a reaffirmation of traditional principles of guild government. Similar challenges occurred in other major guilds. In Por Santa Maria the practice (first instituted in 1346) of giving each of its three major subdivisions (*membra*) an equal number of seats in the consulate and council was restored in 1371 and the role of the council subsequently expanded. And in the Medici, Speziali, e Merciai a similar effort revived the prerogatives of the council and guaranteed the guild's *membra* equal and autonomous roles in electing council members.

In 1371, perhaps reflecting the conflicts within the major guilds and in part generating them, came the popolo's furious reaction to the reconciliation between Uguccione de' Ricci and Piero degli Albizzi and Ricci's apparent conversion to the Parte's anti-Ghibelline campaign. The event alarmed the guildsmen, who saw the protection afforded until then by Ricci opposition to the Parte suddenly evaporate. Amid protests and accusations against the specter of a united elite centered in the Parte, in April 1372 the priors convened an unusually large pratica, in which Filippo Bastari, a respected citizen independent of the factions, and from a family on the border between elite and popolo, spoke at length of the dangers of factionalism, calling for unity and attacking the usurpation of public authority by powerful private individuals: "whoever wants something from the commune should not have recourse to private citizens but to the priors and colleges. In order to curtail ambition, lest anyone show himself to be above the commune, the priors should favor those citizens who want the commune to be above all citizens. The lord priors and their colleges should be the heads of this city, and not certain private citizens."[33] Bastari's protest against the illegitimate power of "privati cives" through their patronage networks was echoed in the subsequent creation of a balìa with a mandate "to remove sects and divisions and repress and restrain the power and audacity" of overmighty citizens. The balìa entrusted military and foreign policy to a new council that included two representatives from each guild and ninety-six citizens drawn by lot, six from each gonfalone; it created the office of the Ten of Liberty to investigate factions; suspended the office-holding rights of three Albizzi (including their leader Piero) and three Ricci (including Uguccione); gave the consuls of the twenty-one guilds, together with the priors and colleges, authority to review petitions requesting that members of elite families accused of certain crimes be declared magnates; and expanded the governing committee of the Mercanzia to seven with two representatives of the minor guilds. Restoring the guild consuls to crucial functions in government, including the enforcement of new punitive measures against elite misbehavior, signaled the revival of the popolo. In the next few years members of the Ridolfi, Albizzi, Strozzi, Brancacci, and Benelli families were made magnates with the votes of the guild consuls, and in 1373 the legislative

---

[33] Brucker, *Florentine Politics*, pp. 244–65 (252–3). Bastari's speech is summarized by Marchionne di Coppo Stefani, *Cronaca fiorentina*, ed. N. Rodolico (Città di Castello, 1903–55), rubr. 731. Stefani will henceforth be cited in the text by rubric.

councils extended the exclusion of the Albizzi and the Ricci from communal offices to ten years. The balìa of 1372 initiated the last resurrection of guild republicanism.

War against the Church

What really destabilized the relative calm of the preceding decades was the war against the papacy, which, together with the political revolution it precipitated, was a veritable watershed in Florence's history.[34] For more than a century, since the Guelf alliance of the 1260s, the republic had maintained close ties with the papacy. Florentines had almost always been the most important among the popes' bankers (as they would again be after this crisis), and Florence had fought, either with or in sympathy with the papacy, against Ghibellines from the Hohenstaufen to Henry VII to the lords of Pisa (Uguccione della Faggiuola), Lucca (Castruccio Castracani), and Verona (Mastino della Scala). Guelfism and loyalty to the church were at the center of Florence's self-image; hence the dramatic significance of the decision to go to war against the church and the traumatic internal divisions it generated.

During the early years in Avignon, the papacy lost control of its territories in central Italy, which wrapped around the Florentine dominion from Rome to Umbria and north to the Romagna and Bologna. They even lost control of Rome itself, sometimes to the always turbulent Roman nobility, other times to popular governments. In 1353 Innocent VI appointed the Spanish cardinal Egidio Albornoz as legate to undertake the reconstitution of papal authority in central Italy. Albornoz's patient work over the next decade in bringing many cities back under papal rule inevitably produced border disputes and controversies with Florence. By 1370 some Florentines began to see the papacy's reviving presence as a threat to Florentine security and hegemony in Tuscany itself, as rumors abounded that the church sought to subvert Florence's rule over its own subject cities. In the spring of 1375 Pope Gregory XI ended a war against Visconti Milan, and many feared that his chief military commander, the English mercenary John Hawkwood, would bring his army into Tuscany and against Florence. To prevent this, Florence bought off Hawkwood, paying him the immense sum of 130,000 florins, and then appointed a committee of eight, later dubbed the "Eight Saints," to pay for Hawkwood's bribe with a forced loan on the local clergy: the bishop, abbots, monasteries, and all

---

[34] Brucker, *Florentine Politics*, 297–335; D. Peterson, "The War of the Eight Saints in Florentine Memory and Oblivion," in *Society and Individual in Renaissance Florence*, ed. W. J. Connell (Berkeley, 2002), pp. 173–214; and A. W. Lewin, *Negotiating Survival: Florence and the Great Schism, 1378–1417* (Madison, N.J., 2003), pp. 339–56.

the landed wealth controlled by ecclesiastical institutions. At the end of July the government crossed its Rubicon by allying with (traditionally Ghibelline) Milan, a decision widely seen as being aimed at the pope. War commenced, and its prosecution was entrusted to another committee of eight with extensive powers to conduct military policy and raise and spend monies as they saw fit. Stefani said of them that "they did the greatest things ever done until then" (752). The Otto di balìa who ran the war included four from elite families (Alessandro de' Bardi, Giovanni Magalotti, Andrea Salviati, and Tommaso Strozzi), two non-elite major guildsmen (the spice dealer Giovanni Dini and the woolen-cloth manufacturer Guccio Gucci), and two minor guildsmen (the wine retailer Marco di Federigo Soldi and the grain dealer Tommaso di Mone).

First among the "great things" they did was to systematically undermine Albornoz's two decades of work by dispatching Florentine agents to foment rebellion in forty cities of the papal states, including Bologna, Perugia, Orvieto, and Viterbo. They also used ideology as a weapon, asking their recently appointed humanist chancellor Coluccio Salutati to write eloquent public letters urging the papal cities to throw off the "tyranny" of a corrupt papacy in favor of the "liberty" of free cities. In letters to the people of Bologna and Perugia, Salutati linked the liberty that Florence enjoyed, and that he encouraged them to embrace, to the republicanism of ancient Rome. Without mincing words, he denied the legitimacy of papal rule because monarchy could never reflect the will of the people and could only be imposed on those deprived of liberty. Salutati also grounded Florentine liberty in the historic traditions of the popolo. He proclaimed the good fortune of cities ruled by "merchants and guildsmen, who naturally love liberty and are more gravely oppressed by the pain of subjection," who "desire peace in which to practice their *artes*, love equality among citizens, and do not glory in the nobility of family or blood."[35] He thus tied the cause of independence from external tyrants (like the pope) to the ideology of the guild republic.

Gregory's military response produced few results in Tuscany. Hawkwood honored his agreement not to make war on Florence, confined his activity to the papal territories, and in 1377 abandoned Gregory and joined the anti-papal league. Gregory's other captains ironically limited their depredations to the papal Romagna, including a horrendous sack of Cesena in February 1377. Most effective among the pope's responses to Florentine subversion of papal rule was the imposition, on March 31, 1376, of an interdict prohibiting all religious services in Florence and its territory and declaring Florentines subject to arrest and confiscation of their goods throughout Europe. Suspension of the Mass (except on specified holy days), denial of communion to the laity,

[35]   R. G. Witt, "The 'De Tyranno' and Coluccio Salutati's View of Politics and Roman History," *Nuova rivista storica* 53 (1969): 434–74 (454–5).

the absence of processions, public prayers, extreme unction, burial services, and a host of other rites fundamental to the cultural and devotional identity of Christian society confronted Florentines of all social ranks with dilemmas of conscience and loyalty that were not easily resolved, even in the midst of strong anti-clerical and anti-papal sentiment. Debates raged in the pratiche over whether to observe the interdict, and, while some counseled defiance, the Eight of War decided to obey it. Without priestly services and sacraments, Florentines created their own forms of devotion and prayer in processions and confraternities. Stefani says that a "compunction seemed to seize the citizens" (757), as men and women filled all the churches every evening singing lauds and spending large sums on candles and books. Processions of the "whole people" with relics and music were held daily; more than 5,000 flagellants, including children, beat themselves as 20,000 people followed in procession; young men from elite families dedicated themselves to prayer, fasting, begging, and the conversion of prostitutes. While Stefani may have exaggerated the numbers, the city clearly responded to the interdict with heightened levels of religious enthusiasm and emotion, almost as if to show that they could be better and more devout Christians than the pope who had imposed this unjust sentence. Another chronicler commented that citizens, deprived of the sight of the host, believed that "we see it in our hearts, and God well knows that we are neither Saracens nor pagans; on the contrary, we are and will remain true Christians, chosen by God."[36]

Religious enthusiasm spilled over into heterodoxy and even heresy. Remnants of the dissident Spiritual branch of the Franciscans, the Fraticelli, whose insistence on the literal observance of the vow of poverty and critique of the church's material wealth had led to their attempted secession from the order in the late thirteenth century and subsequent condemnation by Pope John XXII, emerged from hiding in these years and found protectors and followers in a city angry with the pope and hungry for religion. Their denunciation of the papacy and church hierarchy for their corrupting wealth and power found sympathetic audiences in a city at war with a "tyrant" pope. Even the prophetic streak of Joachite origin that had nourished the Spirituals' sense of historical destiny reappeared in force: the conviction that their persecution at the hands of a false church was the necessary prelude to a millenarian transformation of church and society. The spread of improvised devotions, heterodox ideas, and prophetic fantasies, in the absence of the clerical discipline that normally guided the religious impulses of the laity, produced violations of the interdict. Influential citizens urged the resumption of religious services, and in October 1377 the government reversed itself and decided to defy the interdict by ordering

---

[36] *Diario d'anonimo fiorentino dall'anno 1358 al 1389*, in *Cronache dei secoli XIII e XIV*, ed. A. Gherardi (Florence, 1876), p. 308.

the clergy to begin saying Mass again. Forced resumption of religious services split both the laity, uncertain about defying a papal order, and the local clergy. Parish priests were for the most part willing to obey the government, but the upper echelons, more beholden to papal authority, sought ways to avoid the dilemma. When, under papal pressure, the bishops of Florence (Angelo Ricasoli) and Fiesole (Neri Corsini) left Florentine territory, the commune responded by requiring prelates to remain at their posts under penalty of heavy fines and confiscations. For the most part the local clergy, with whatever qualms of conscience, stayed put.[37]

Gregory's interdict also launched an economic war by ordering governments throughout Europe not to do business with Florentine merchants and bankers, threatening to prosecute them, and urging other rulers to do likewise. Florentine business interests were damaged, but not broken. Hundreds of Florentine merchants left Avignon, and bankers, chiefly the Alberti, obviously lost their lucrative positions there. Elsewhere there were occasional expulsions and confiscations, but most governments ignored the papal order, notably the king of France, who actually protected Florentines. The merchant diaspora found ways to protect its assets and wait out the storm, and recovery, even in Avignon, quickly followed the end of the war.[38] In the meantime, Florentines had economic cards of their own to play. At the end of 1376 the government began confiscating and selling local church property to finance what was becoming a costly war. Ironically, the most outspoken proponent of seizing church property and using it to fight the papacy was a Medici, from a different branch of the family whose later economic and political fortunes were so closely tied to the papacy. In September 1376, Salvestro de' Medici advised the government in a pratica that "the bishops of Florence and Fiesole and all prelates of the city of Florence, should be sent to the pope to procure his withdrawal from the war and induce him to make peace. If he does not, then let all ecclesiastical property come into the commune, and let the war be fought at the clergy's expense."[39] A committee was appointed to compile a census of ecclesiastical property and commence selling it, even as some were reluctant to purchase property that they feared might have to be returned to the church in an eventual settlement. It was the largest and most systematic disendowment of any territorial church before the Reformation.

In the spring of 1377 papal mercenaries recaptured Bologna and deprived Florence of a crucial ally. Later that year talks broke down when Gregory announced that his price for peace would be an indemnity of 1,000,000 florins,

---

[37]   R. C. Trexler, *The Spiritual Power: Republican Florence Under Interdict* (Leiden, 1974), pp. 109–66.

[38]   Ibid., pp. 44–108.

[39]   Brucker, *Florentine Politics*, p. 317.

an astronomical sum that was more a provocation than serious negotiation. He also tried to split the war leaders from the people by declaring them heretics; the commune responded with another huge tax on the local church and more confiscations of church property. As the stalemate dragged on, the pro-papal and anti-war Parte Guelfa stepped up its campaign to discredit the government with more "warnings" against war leaders and supporters who were chiefly from the popolo. Gregory's death in March 1378 rescued Florence from a war whose repercussions in the economic sphere and on the consciences and divided loyalties of its citizens were far more serious than any military threat. Under his successor Urban VI peace negotiations resumed, a truce was declared in May, and a final settlement in July. The commune agreed to an indemnity of 250,000 florins and to the eventual restitution of the massive amounts of confiscated church property. In the meantime it agreed to pay 5% annual interest on the value of the property, which in effect turned local churchmen into communal creditors. The large indemnity and property settlement might suggest that the papacy won the war. But exactly how much of the indemnity was ever paid is unclear. Thirty years later the papacy claimed that 88% was still unpaid, and the restitution of clerical property went on for decades and was probably never completed. Moreover, Urban's election split the cardinals, a faction of whom elected a second pope and thus inaugurated an almost 40-year schism with two competing lines of popes in Rome and Avignon. With both papacies offering concessions to secular governments in return for recognition and support, Florence was able to have some of the debts cancelled and to tighten control over the local church, its courts, and finances. Through much of the fifteenth century, the commune controlled its ecclesiastical establishment more closely than ever before, and from this perspective it may have been the Florentines who won the war of the Eight Saints. None of this was apparent in the short term, however, as the tensions generated by the war between the Guelf elite and the guild community immediately erupted into revolution.

6

Revolution and Realignment

The end of the papal war was the beginning of the series of revolutions that made 1378 the most memorable year in Florentine history, though not one usually remembered with fondness. It began, in June, with a determined response to the Parte Guelfa's excesses from the full guild community, which was quickly overtaken, in July, by a revolutionary movement of workers and artisans who created first one and then three new guilds that joined the guild federation and claimed their share of offices. In August, unskilled textile workers, the Ciompi, created a revolutionary authority of their own, which was immediately crushed by the rest of the expanded guild federation. After dismantling the guild of the Ciompi, the remaining twenty-three guilds established the last and most radical of Florence's guild governments, which ruled from September 1378 to January 1382 until its overthrow by the elite and the beginning of a gradual realignment of class relations that transformed Florentine political culture. Although the convulsions of 1378 and the radicalism of the guild republic of 1378–82 had roots in the long conflict between elite and popolo, the revolutions of artisans and workers frightened both elite and popolo into resolving their historically unstable relationship. After the revolutionary years, the elite realized it needed to anchor its power in a different political style and ideology, while the chastened non-elite major guildsmen definitively abandoned the temptations of guild republicanism and permanently linked their fortunes to the elite. As the catalyst for this metamorphosis of Florentine society and politics, the brief but traumatic insurrection of workers stands as the central event in the republic's history, the continental divide between two different political universes.

Workers' Economic Conditions

Economic grievances drew artisans and wage laborers into politics from at least the mid-fourteenth century, when the working classes began to exhibit an impressive awareness of the factors determining their employment and living conditions and a consistent political agenda centered on the right of association. When the dyers petitioned Walter of Brienne for a guild in 1342, they may have been seeking to recover rights they once had in the Wool guild. Shortly thereafter, unskilled laborers who had never had such rights attempted to organize, although we know of their efforts in the 1340s only from the prohibitions and punishments they provoked. To put the dyers' guild beyond legality and forestall other workers' associations, the 1344 revisers of the communal statutes prohibited any "corpus" or "collegium" of workers involved in manufacturing woolen cloth, specifically mentioning the dyers. That same year the established guilds, which had long denied "their" workers the right of association and even simple gatherings, petitioned the government for legislation that subjected to their authority all persons, even if not guild members, who bought or sold items "pertaining" to these guilds. But in reissuing the Ordinances of Justice the popular government of 1343 anchored its own legitimacy in the right of association; thus, without intending to do so, they may have encouraged workers to pursue the same right for themselves. Ironically, a government controlled by guilds forcefully denied workers and artisans rights of association and strengthened guild prerogatives over them.

Workers took to the streets frequently in 1343–5, beginning with the crowd led by Andrea Strozzi in September 1343. In March 1344 three men were fined for leading a band against the Rucellai family (exactly why is not clear), crying "Long live the guilds and the *popolo* and death to the Rucellai and the *popolani grassi*!" A serious attempt to organize workers was thwarted in 1345 when the Capitano del popolo's police arrested the worker Ciuto Brandini and accused him of forming a large association of carders, combers, and other workers in the textile industry that met regularly and even collected dues. To modern eyes it seems a primitive trade union, but in fourteenth-century terms they created a guild, complete with consuls. A government presenting itself as an emanation of the city's guilds ("the Florentine republic," according to several legislative acts of these years, being "ruled and governed by the guilds and guildsmen of this city and their consuls") could not simply convict Ciuto of forming a guild. So the Capitano ruled that, "led by a diabolical spirit," he had "seduced" as many workers as possible into a "wicked association [*iniqua societate*]" in order to provoke "noxious disorders, to the harm, opprobrium, danger, and destruction of the citizens of Florence, their persons and property, and the stable government of the city." From their "illegal plots," the court intoned, "tumult, sedition, and disorder would have arisen."[1] Appeals from Ciuto's associates to the priorate for his release, and threats of a strike and an uprising ("motivated," says an anonymous chronicler, by the desire "to be better paid"), were to no avail, and he was quickly convicted and executed.[2]

Unrest among workers in the 1340s reflected their deteriorating economic circumstances: a combination of low wages and increases in gabelle rates that made it their worst decade of the century. After the 1348 plague, while indirect taxes continued to rise, the population catastrophe drove wages suddenly higher. For masons, builders, and their apprentices, daily wages tripled after the plague and stayed at the same high level for the next two decades; in other industries they at least doubled. Prices also rose, but not as much as wages, and conditions were never better for fourteenth-century workers than in the decades 1350–70. Prosperity within individual households depended of course on the balance of incomes and mouths to feed and on whether employment was regular or sporadic. Unmarried masons with no dependents who found steady work generally earned twice what they needed for basic living costs even before the plague, and three and four times their living costs over the next twenty years. Before the 1340s, masons' households consisting of two adults and two children with a single income managed to make ends meet. In the 1340s they earned only 70% of living costs, but 150–180% in the succeeding decades. Unskilled laborers in the building industry earned about half as much as skilled masons, but unmarried ones still earned more than the cost of basic necessities before the plague and much more after it. But families with two adults and two children and only the single income of an unskilled apprentice or journeyman never earned enough to cover costs, either before or after the plague, despite the doubling of wages. Sporadic employment only made matters worse. Unskilled wage laborers were the most vulnerable workers, and for them survival depended on charity or reducing costs, for example, by sharing living quarters with relatives.[3]

Two factors in particular made workers' economic status precarious even in good times: debt and taxes. Workers' indebtedness was widespread. Data are lacking for before 1378, but each year in the 1380s an estimated 300 workers received court orders to repay creditors (hence possibly 3,000 over the decade),

---

[1] N. Rodolico, *Il popolo minuto. Note di storia fiorentina (1343–1378)* (Florence, 1968), pp. 99–104; partly trans. in Brucker, *Society*, pp. 235–6.

[2] V. Rutenburg, *Popolo e movimenti popolari nell'Italia del '300 e '400*, trans. from Russian by G. Borghini (Bologna, 1971), pp. 105–14; Brucker, *Florentine Politics*, pp. 110–11.

[3] Ch.-M. de la Roncière, "La condition des salariés à Florence au XIVᵉ siècle," in *Tumulto*, pp. 13–40; and his *Prix et salaires*.

and each year eighty had their goods confiscated for failure to do so. In 1427, 81% of 357 households of textile workers in the Santo Spirito quarter reported debts in their Catasto declarations, on average equivalent to 55% of assets,[4] and debts exceeded assets in 30% of the city's households.[5] It is difficult to imagine that the situation was much different in the 1370s. Wool guild records are filled with reports of confiscations for unpaid debts, requested by creditors and carried out by guild officials who carted off furniture, beds, mattresses, tools, and equipment, including the looms of poor weavers, making it impossible for them to work.[6] Some spent months in debtors' prison. Creditors could be shopkeepers, pawnbrokers, or landlords, but mostly employers. *Lanaiuoli* frequently extended loans to their workers either for the purchase of looms or other tools or to cover living costs during times of unemployment. Debts carried interest, which reduced real income, as did indirect taxes, which increased dramatically between 1340 and 1360, creating real misery in the 1340s and cutting deeply into the higher wages of the 1350s–1360s.[7]

Although nominal wages in the 1370s remained much higher than before the plague, they declined somewhat from the preceding decades, as did real incomes (adjusted for prices and taxes). Workers were still better off than they had been before 1348, as evidenced by their increasing (but still limited) presence among households with sufficient assets to be assessed forced loans, although having enough wealth to pay prestanze eventually hurt the minority of well-off workers when assessments rose and collections became more frequent. During the papal war, only 20% of residents assessed in the quarter of Santa Maria Novella paid the full amount and collected interest; 80% of all households and 90% of textile artisans either paid one-third of their assessments or paid others (again, often their employers) as much as a fifth to assume their obligations, losing the interest in either case. In 1375–7, paying their own prestanza assessments cost workers 9–10% of income,[8] whereas paying employers to pay their taxes took an estimated 6%.[9] Prestanze became more onerous during the papal war, and it was on these taxes, not the gabelles, that the revolutionaries focused in 1378. But indignation over heavy taxes and

[4]   Franceschi, *Oltre il "Tumulto,"* pp. 280–5; also Ch.-M. de la Roncière, "Pauvres et pauvreté à Florence au 14ᵉ siècle," in *Études sur l'histoire de la pauvreté (Moyen Age–16ᵉ siècle)*, ed. M. Mollat (Paris, 1974), pp. 661–765.
[5]   Herlihy and Klapisch-Zuber, *Tuscans*, p. 104.
[6]   Examples in Brucker, *Society*, pp. 214–15.
[7]   La Roncière, "Indirect Taxes," in *Florentine Studies*, ed. Rubinstein.
[8]   La Roncière, "La condition des salariés," p. 30.
[9]   R. Barducci, "Le riforme finanziarie nel Tumulto dei Ciompi," in *Tumulto*, pp. 98–100; G. Brucker, "Un documento fiorentino sulla guerra, sulla finanza, e sull'amministrazione pubblica," *ASI* 115 (1957): 165–76.

their effects on the working poor is already apparent in the emotional appeal submitted to the priors in 1369 predicting an "uprising if these forced loans and special levies are not reduced, for there is great privation here. People are living in misery since they earn little and prices have been so high for thirteen months and more. Just think about those who have three or four or five children, and who are assessed two or three florins, and who have to live from the labor of their hands and those of their wives. How can they stay here and live?"[10] Although fully employed skilled workers (especially those with small households) did well between the plague and 1378, debt, taxes, irregular employment, and large families kept many in poverty.

Workers never lived in large numbers in the city center, dominated early on by elite families,[11] and working-class neighborhoods were mainly beyond the perimeter of the twelfth-century walls. Significant social and economic differences distinguished the two main clusters of workers. Unskilled wage laborers in the textile industries predominated in the western and southern sections of the Oltrarno, including the gonfalone Drago Verde (particularly the parish of San Frediano between the Carmine and the river, and the neighborhood called Camaldoli just to the south) and gonfalone Ferza (especially the parish of San Piero Gattolino). These were politically the most radical workers and the chief promoters of the August revolt of the Ciompi. The largest working-class neighborhood north of the river, called Belletri, was centered in the outer reaches of the sprawling gonfalone Lion d'oro north of San Lorenzo and the modern Mercato Centrale. Here lived a more heterogeneous assemblage of wage laborers, skilled artisans, and minor guildsmen that was the principal force behind the July revolution. Two other working-class neighborhoods were in the parishes of Santa Lucia Ognissanti in Santa Maria Novella and Sant'Ambrogio in gonfalone Chiavi in San Giovanni. But the poor (many of them widows and elderly) were present in large numbers everywhere: in 1355, in all sixteen gonfaloni, "miserabiles" (defined as having no property, possessions worth less than 100 lire, and no trade or profession) accounted for at least 22% of households; between 30 and 40% in three gonfaloni; 40–50% in four; and over 50% in two (Lion d'oro in San Giovanni, and Unicorno in Santa Maria Novella, which included Santa Lucia Ognissanti).[12]

---

[10]   Brucker, *Society*, pp. 233–4.
[11]   On class geography: S. K. Cohn, Jr., *The Laboring Classes in Renaissance Florence* (New York, 1980); R. C. Trexler, "Neighbors and Comrades: The Revolutionaries of Florence, 1378," *Social Analysis* 14 (1983): 53–106, reprinted in Trexler, *The Workers of Renaissance Florence* (Binghamton, N.Y., 1993), pp. 61–126; A. Stella, *La Révolte des Ciompi. Les hommes, les lieux, le travail* (Paris, 1993).
[12]   Stella, *Révolte*, p. 192.

The Ciompi Revolution

In 1377 the Parte Guelfa intensified its assault on the government, the new men, and the war party. Led by the pro-papal elite (Piero degli Albizzi, Niccolò Soderini, Carlo Strozzi, Lapo da Castiglionchio, Piero Canigiani, Stoldo Altoviti) and supported by some old magnate houses (Bardi, Rossi, Pazzi, Adimari), the core of the Albizzi faction (Ridolfi, Castellani, Strozzi, Rucellai, Guasconi) and at least one important member of the Medici family, the banker Vieri di Cambio who thus positioned himself at the opposite end of the political spectrum from his cousin Salvestro, the Parte leadership "warned" over ninety citizens between September 1377 and the spring of 1378, driving some from office and depriving others of eligibility. Most were new men who held key positions during the war (like Giovanni Dini). Scores, perhaps hundreds, of secret denunciations of alleged Ghibellines, probably originating from the Parte itself, kept the captains busy deciding the fate of citizens that winter. Accusations typically alleged the actions of a distant ancestor, angry words spoken against the Parte, or a generic intention to harm the Guelf cause. Florence now seethed with partisan and class antagonisms, as Parte extremists persisted even in the face of mounting public outrage. Their opponents became convinced that the Parte was trying to provoke a crisis in order to seize power, reshape the government, and expel the new men.

By the chance of the draw, the priorate of May–June 1378 included as Standardbearer of Justice Salvestro de' Medici, who began his week as presiding chairman on June 18 and presented a proposal for the re-promulgation of the Ordinances of Justice "on behalf of the *popolani*, merchants, and guildsmen of Florence, and the poor and weak who desire to live in peace from their labor and possessions."[13] After eighty-five years, the Ordinances still carried emotional and symbolic weight; this was the guild community's "warning" to the Parte to refrain from further provocations. But when the measure encountered opposition in the advisory college of the Twelve, Salvestro went in person to the legislative councils to announce his resignation in the face of this rebuff. An uproar in the councils persuaded the Twelve to reverse their position. On the 21st, members of the twenty-one guilds assembled in protest against the Parte, and the next day crowds of guildsmen and workers burned the houses of Parte leaders (including those of Lapo da Castiglionchio, Carlo Strozzi, Niccolò Soderini, the Albizzi, Canigiani, Pazzi, Cavicciuli, and Guadagni). According to Stefani (792), some thought it a spontaneous action, others that the order had come "from the palace." On the same day the councils approved a balìa, led by Salvestro and including one consul from each of the twenty-one guilds, which declared Piero degli Albizzi, Carlo Strozzi, and other

[13] *Diario d'anonimo*, ed. Gherardi, p. 504; Brucker, *Florentine Politics*, pp. 364–5.

Parte leaders magnates, relegated some who were already magnates to a new category of "supermagnates" with even tougher penalties, and restored office-holding rights to scores of warned "Ghibellines."

In early July, pratiche made repeated references to meetings, agitations, and disputes within the guilds. Some speakers urged the priors to warn the guilds to desist from excessive demands or precipitous actions, while others advised that they "listen to all the guilds" and act on their requests. "Regarding the agitations," said one speaker, "the priors should convene the consuls, syndics [representatives], and up to four of the best members of each guild separately and make appropriate appeals for peace to each guild separately. They should tell the guilds that when they want something they should confer with the lord priors, who will see to the matter." Resurfacing here were the basic assumptions of the guild republic: equality and autonomy among the guilds and the right of each to an independent voice. Even the Wool guild, caught between the desire of its non-elite majority to punish the Guelf Party and its fear that reviving notions of guild autonomy might push artisans and workers to demand their own guilds, decided to join the movement. Noting, on July 7, that "many of the twenty-one guilds, for the unity, defense, and preservation of all the guilds and guildsmen and for the welfare and liberty of the *popolo* and commune of Florence, have already appointed syndics and procurators for the defense of their guilds and their members, and not wishing to be in disagreement with the other guilds, but rather to come together as one with all the other guilds," the Lana too selected syndics "for the defense and protection of the Wool guild and its liberty and rights."[14] On July 9–10 the legislative councils approved a petition drafted by representatives of all the guilds in the palace of the Mercanzia "for the liberty, security, and tranquility of the twenty-one guilds." It transferred the powers of the June balìa to a council composed of the priorate of July–August, the Seven of Mercanzia, and all the consuls and syndics of the twenty-one guilds; restored the consuls of all twenty-one guilds to key roles in communal and guild elections; terminated the Parte's campaign of intimidation by giving the priorate and colleges a veto over accusations and warnings; annulled all elections within the Parte and gave the guild consuls a role in electing its captains; removed the Mercanzia's authority to nominate candidates for guild offices; limited eligibility for the priorate to guildsmen actively involved in their professions or trades; and entrusted the certification of such active involvement to each guild's consuls.[15] This was in effect a reassertion of the guild republic of 1293 and 1343.

---

[14] ASF, Consulte e pratiche 16, ff. 2–3v, 7; *Diario d'anonimo*, ed. Gherardi, pp. 511–14; Najemy, *"Audiant omnes artes,"* in *Tumulto*, pp. 62–4.
[15] Published in C. [Falletti] Fossati, *Il Tumulto dei Ciompi* (Florence, 1875), pp. 219–23; Brucker, *Florentine Politics*, pp. 376–7; Najemy, *Corporatism*, pp. 222–8.

In mid-July the workers and artisans emerged. Meetings and associations of workers were still illegal, and the balìa, like the government of the mid-1340s, was caught in the contradiction of denying workers the same right of guild association on which it based its own claim to authority. Word reached the government of at least two secret meetings, one in the Oltrarno district, the other north of the river, in which workers exchanged ritual oaths and kisses sealing their intention, according to one chronicler, "to stay together to the death and defend themselves against anyone wishing to harm them."[16] The workers' association that eventually resulted in three new guilds was born in this fraternal bonding and oath-taking. On July 20 workers and minor guildsmen, mostly from Belletri, filled the piazza in front of the palace of the priors demanding that the government, barricaded inside, release those who had been arrested and possibly tortured for information about the workers' meetings. On the same day, thirty-two "syndics of the *popolo minuto*" (of whom at least a fourth were minor guildsmen), drafted and presented two petitions to the priors. Still on the 20th, however, huge crowds began roaming the city, as on June 22, burning the homes of some twenty Parte leaders, including that of the Standardbearer of Justice, Luigi Guicciardini. Under the cloud of this violence, on the 21st the priors received the petitions, the first of which demanded a guild for "the men of the *popolo minuto*" whose consuls would enjoy the same jurisdiction, authority, and power vested in the consuls of the twenty-one guilds, and whose thirty-two syndics would join those of the other guilds on the balìa. The new guild was to have a fourth of the seats in the priorate and colleges, and a scrutiny was planned (in which their own syndics would have had the decisive voice) to determine eligibility among the "minuti."

Together with these political demands came economic, fiscal, and legal ones, including the abolition of the Wool guild's hated foreign official, who had long exercised police powers over workers and artisans; a six-month moratorium on forced loans; the cessation of interest payments on the communal debt; the debt's amortization over a period of twelve years; and reinstitution of the estimo and direct taxation within six months. Amortization of the debt revived the initial aim of the popular government of 1343, but substitution of direct taxation for interest-bearing forced loans was a far more radical demand, intended to end transfers of wealth from workers and artisans to the already wealthy who profited from loans to the commune and to halt the diminution of workers' wages from payments to employers who assumed their prestanza assessments. Although the petition says nothing about indirect taxes, implicit in the call for direct taxation was some relief in this area.

[16] *Cronaca di Alamanno Acciaioli*, in *Cronache e memorie sul Tumulto dei Ciompi*, ed. G. Scaramella (Città di Castello, 1917–34), p. 19.

Chronic indebtedness among workers was addressed in the demand for a two-year moratorium for debts under fifty florins and the commutation of sentences threatening the loss of a limb to monetary fines.[17]

As the councils quickly approved the popolo minuto's petitions, events were unfolding in the streets. Rebuffed in their demand for three seats in the priorate (as they had had in 1343–8), the minor guilds allied with the new workers' guild. On the 21st a crowd of 7,000 workers and guildsmen from all guilds except the Wool guild, which was either unwelcome or refused to join, marched to the palace of the podestà (the Bargello). As many broke in to destroy the records of investigations and convictions of workers, a small band ascended the tower to unfurl the flag of the blacksmiths' guild, on which was depicted a set of tongs. No source tells us why the revolutionaries selected this flag as their symbol, but tongs traditionally signified the application of force to achieve purposes against determined opposition. From the windows beneath they hung the flags of all the guilds, except the Wool guild, together with the Standard of Justice – the flag of the popolo of 1293 and official symbol of government, with its red cross on a white field – that had been seized by the crowd. As the flags announced, the revolution was the work of the entire guild community, minus the hated Wool guild, but with thousands of workers and artisans who now, for the first time, marched with the others under the banner of their own guild. As one chronicler described it, "They settled in for the rest of that day and night, to the honor of God. And there were many of them, rich and poor, each guarding the banner of his guild."[18] It was the high tide of the guild republic, now expanded to include workers and artisans. Sometime that summer an advisory committee recommended that the priors seek the advice of the guild consuls before implementing its proposals, so that "if some or all of them become law, let it be done with the agreement [*concordia*] and consent [or pleasure: *contentamento*] of the guild consuls; and their consent can truly be said to be that of the whole city."[19] Thus the revolution legitimated itself in the right of guilds to represent and express the consent of their members and in the idea that "the whole city" was equivalent to the community of its guilds.

The next day, July 22, the huge crowd moved from the podestà's palace to the priors' palace and demanded the incumbent priorate's resignation. One of the syndics of the popolo minuto, Michele di Lando, a former corporal in the communal army and variously described as a comber, carder, and supervisor of textile workers, entered the palace with the Standard of Justice and declared himself, obviously by prior agreement with the syndics of the guilds, Standardbearer of Justice. "Some young men went up the tower and rang the

---

[17] [Falletti] Fossati, *Tumulto*, pp. 224–33.
[18] *Cronaca prima d'anonimo*, in *Cronache e memorie*, ed. Scaramella, p. 75.
[19] Najemy, "*Audiant omnes artes*," in *Tumulto*, p. 93.

bells for their victory in taking the palace, to the honor of God." Michele and the guild syndics appointed new priors and colleges (only five of the total of thirty-seven belonged to families previously represented in these offices,[20] most being *minuti* or minor guildsmen); replaced the two legislative councils with one consisting of the consuls of all the guilds; and cancelled the proscriptions of alleged Ghibellines since 1357. As a chronicler sympathetic to the revolution put it, "This was done to give a share of offices to more people, so that everyone would be satisfied, and the citizens united, and poor men would have their share, because they have always borne the cost, and no one but the rich has ever profited." Somewhere in these days, the revolutionary government divided the new workers' guild into three guilds: one for dyers, washers, carders, and other skilled artisans of the woolen cloth industry; a second for shirtmakers, tailors, stocking makers, and other artisans in the clothing trades (including many who had previously belonged to the subordinate *membra* of Por Santa Maria); and a third for unskilled textile workers, including sorters, shearers, and beaters, and poor artisans like weavers – those whom contemporaries called the Ciompi. Although there certainly had not been time to compile membership lists, one chronicler estimated that the third guild represented 9,000 workers and all three a total of 13,000.[21] This was probably a rough guess, but even 10,000 new guildsmen, added to 4,000–5,000 members of the twenty-one guilds, meant that just about every male of working age (in a population of 55,000) was a guildsman in the remarkable summer of 1378.

On July 31 the revolutionary government destroyed the old electoral pouches and on August 4 announced regulations for a scrutiny, based on the drastically altered political realities, which reinterpreted the principle of equality among the guilds along class lines. With two-thirds of all guildsmen in only three guilds, the revolutionaries divided the federation into three groups of seven, fourteen, and three guilds and gave each group an equal share of the priorate and colleges. Moreover, the requirement that seven votes among the priors would henceforth be needed to approve any measure ensured that the three *minuti* priors could not be outvoted by the established guilds. Each group of guilds was to have exactly the same number of approved candidates. Of nearly 6,000 nominations (by far the most in any scrutiny to this point, and 70% more than in the much larger population of 1343), approximately 2,800 were major guildsmen, 1,400 minor guildsmen, and at least 1,700 *minuti*. A large scrutiny council of 220, two-thirds of whom were either consuls or syndics of the twenty-four guilds, approved approximately 1,000 citizens and placed their names into separate pouches for the three groups of guilds. When the scrutiny was completed on August 21, bells were rung, Te deums sung,

[20]   G. Brucker, "The Ciompi Revolution," in *Florentine Studies*, ed. Rubinstein, p. 330.
[21]   *Cronaca prima*, in *Cronache e memorie*, pp. 76–7.

and a festive dessert and drink enjoyed by the scrutiny council, one of whose members, the chronicler recently identified as a notary,[22] called it "the good scrutiny, which satisfied the many people who had never held any office but who had always been burdened by taxes."[23]

At the end of August, the unskilled textile workers, mostly from the Oltrarno, broke ranks with the rest of the guild community and elected a committee of Eight, two from each quarter, claiming city-wide authority from their meeting place in Santa Maria Novella. In demanding that name-tickets drawn from the pouches be subject to final approval by the consuls of all the guilds, they mistakenly assumed that the rest of the guild community shared their view that the August scrutiny had not gone far enough in depriving the enemies of the revolution of eligibility. Although this was never put into effect, on the 29th, when the priorate for September–October was drawn, a large crowd of Ciompi insisted that each name be read aloud and rejected several of them. This interference from the piazza in the sortition process and the demand that the government ratify the Eight's decrees destabilized the precarious coalition of old and new guilds. The challenge was met and defeated in the streets. When, on August 30, two Ciompi went to the palace demanding veto power for the Eight over all communal legislation, Michele di Lando had them arrested. The next day he rode out of the palace with the Standard of Justice, cleared the piazza of a militia from the three new guilds, and allowed the older guilds to occupy it. The workers' militia returned, followed by the Oltrarno Ciompi carrying their own flag of the angel. When they refused to surrender it, a battle broke out for control of the piazza: the Ciompi under the flag of the angel against the militias of the other guilds under the Standard of Justice. It may seem ironic that, even as the government called upon the twenty-three guilds to assist in suppressing the Ciompi and driving them from the piazza, the Ciompi met the assault with cries of "long live the *popolo* and the guilds" (Stefani 804). But that irony was built into the origins of the confrontation, with each side grounding the legitimacy of its cause in the century-old guild republic.

The Last Guild Government

The Ciompi were crushed, a half dozen killed, twenty wounded, and many chased into hiding and exile. On September 1 a throng of citizens (a "parlamento") assembled in the piazza and approved the dissolution of the Ciompi

[22]   R. C. Trexler, "Herald of the Ciompi: The Authorship of an Anonymous Florentine Chronicle," in Trexler, *Workers*, pp. 6–29.
[23]   *Cronaca prima*, in *Cronache e memorie*, p. 78.

guild and the removal of Ciompi from the priorate and the electoral pouches. The guild federation was reorganized into two subdivisions of seven major and sixteen minor guilds, with the priorate and all government offices evenly divided between the two groups. The Mercanzia's governing committee was expanded from seven to nine, five major and four minor guildsmen. Otherwise the results of the August scrutiny remained in place, and for the next three and a half years the priorate continued to be dominated by minor guildsmen and non-elite major guildsmen, among them hatmakers, stockingmakers, retail cloth dealers, furriers, goldsmiths, glassmakers, and the like. From September 1378 to January 1382, 189 posts on the priorate were held by 189 individuals, 94 major guildsmen and 95 minor guildsmen, from 186 families, 100 of which had their first prior during these years. Only some 15 priors came from the elite, among them allies of the popular movement like Giorgio Scali and Jacopo di Tommaso Strozzi.

Except for the removal of the Ciompi and their guild, the popular government installed in September 1378 was the direct heir of the revolution of July–August, similarly grounding its legitimacy in the regular consultation of the guilds on policy matters. A good example is the controversy that followed the revelation in December 1379 of a conspiracy against the government that led to the execution of several members of powerful elite families. Fearing retribution if relatives or friends of the executed conspirators were drawn at the next bi-monthly extraction for the priorate, the government debated whether to suspend sortition and handpick the priors. To resolve the issue, it was decided to consult the representatives of all twenty-three guilds, many of whom averred that they could not offer opinions without consulting their members. Discussions took place within the guilds and then among their representatives at the Mercanzia palace, and each guild submitted an opinion: seventeen counseled against abandoning sortition, six suggested other solutions, and the measure was defeated (Stefani, 840). This was a model instance of guild republicanism in practice, with the guilds functioning as equal and autonomous channels for the representation of their constituencies.

Citizens and government alike wrapped themselves in the language of guild fraternalism and solidarity. In July 1378 the woolen cloth manufacturers Alessandro and Bartolomeo degli Alessandri (a branch of the Albizzi, but now a separate lineage) were among prominent members of the Parte Guelfa relegated to magnate status. In February 1379 they petitioned the government for the removal of this stigma and the recovery of office-holding rights, describing themselves as "peaceful merchants and guildsmen" who had always been "brothers and friends of the guildsmen" and had provided work and sustenance to many persons, especially the poor and needy. Another Parte leader, Francesco di Uberto degli Albizzi, declared a magnate in 1372, argued in a similar petition that "all his life he has been a peaceful merchant and guildsman, has humbly associated with men of the *popolo* and guildsmen, and loves and has always loved the good state and government of the *popolo* and the guildsmen."[24] These petitioners knew what sort of language the legislative councils wanted to hear. But the most eloquent expression of the popular government's guild ideology came from the chancellor Coluccio Salutati, who had the difficult task of explaining to foreign governments, above all the papacy, why the popular rulers of Florence had executed Piero degli Albizzi and other champions of the papal party. Salutati enumerated the terrible crimes planned by the conspirators, including murder, torture, and arson, underscoring in particular their nefarious intention to "destroy the honorable corporations of the guilds of our city, through which, by the grace of God, we are what we are, and without which, should they ever be suppressed, the very name of the Florentines would without doubt be erased from the face of the earth."[25] That the chancellor, entrusted with fashioning the republic's image, could have placed the guilds so firmly at the center of what this government believed it was defending demonstrates just how powerful the idea of the guild republic had become.

The government's economic policies constituted the most concerted effort in Florence's history to restructure the institutions and practices that had for so long resulted in transfers of wealth from the working classes to the wealthy. On October 29, 1378, the estimo demanded in July was voted into law (over considerable opposition in the councils and the pratiche); its prologue asserted that "the fair distribution of fiscal burdens, which is consonant with justice, has always pleased right-thinking persons and preserved cities and their citizens in fraternal love." Landed property, investments, government credits, and other forms of moveable wealth were all included in the estimation of taxable assets. A committee of sixty-four, four from each gonfalone, with equal numbers from the seven major and sixteen minor guilds, completed the assessment of city households by the summer of 1379, even as debates continued over the advisability of a direct tax and whether minor guildsmen should be taxed at a lower rate. Voices in the pratiche called for the rich to pay more, for suspension of some gabelles, and for selling property confiscated from exiled Parte leaders. In this atmosphere of acrimonious debate, the estimo came into being, and every other month for the next two and a half years the popular government collected direct taxes based on the calculations of household wealth. Representatives of the elite continued to insist that payments be converted into interest-bearing loans, but the legislative councils, consisting largely of

---

[24]   ASF, Provvisioni Registri, 67, ff. 153v–154; Provvisioni Registri, 68, ff. 53–53v.
[25]   ASF, Signori, Carteggi, Missive, prima cancelleria, 18, f. 108v; quoted in my "Guild Republicanism in Trecento Florence: The Successes and Ultimate Failure of Corporate Politics," *American Historical Review* 84 (1979): 67.

minor guildsmen, routinely rejected the idea. Not until the end of 1381 did upper-class opponents of direct taxation finally succeed, again over considerable opposition in the councils, in abolishing the estimo and retroactively mandating interest payments.[26]

Controversies over the public debt were just as intense. In the 1350s and 1360s, the commune attracted voluntary investment with offers of 10 and 15% interest by assigning credits two or three times greater than the actual loans (the so-called two-for-one and three-for-one monti), thus keeping interest officially at 5% as decreed in 1345. After the papal war the commune had a nominal indebtedness of 2,360,000 florins (including the fictitious doubling and tripling of many loans) and real indebtedness (the amount required to repay principal) of about 1,180,000 florins.[27] Annual interest payments cost about 120,000 florins (5% of nominal indebtedness), more than half the commune's gabelle income in normal years. Although the July 1378 law calling for the suspension of interest and the debt's amortization within twelve years was annulled in September, the popular government immediately began debating the issue again and even sought the opinions of jurists on the legality of suspending interest payments promised and guaranteed by earlier legislation. Debates continued in the pratiche for two years until December 1380, when a priorate consisting of a wine-dealer, retail cloth dealer, baker, spice-dealer, linen manufacturer, moneychanger, dyer, and only one member from the elite (a Buonaccorsi) approved and sent to the councils a proposal "supported by the advice they received from the consuls of the guilds" for the retroactive abolition of the two-for-one and three-for-one monti, the reduction of all interest payments to 5% of real, not nominal, indebtedness, and the gradual return of principal.[28] Stefani, who estimated that 5,000 men and women owned Monte credits, said that "no law so important had been passed in more than a hundred years" (883), claiming that it saved the commune 60,000 florins a year. But "there was much grumbling about it, because many had sold farms and property and left their businesses [to invest in] those 15 and 10 percent loans," while others "had bought credits to make 25 percent [on their investments]" and were now faced with only 5% return. One investor in the debt, naming in his memoirs the priors who authored the law, called the Standard-bearer of Justice, Recco di Guido Guazza, the "Standardbearer of Injustice."[29] Guazza was banished when the popular government fell in 1382.

[26]   N. Rodolico, *La democrazia fiorentina nel suo tramonto (1378–1382)* (Bologna, 1905; reprint edn. Rome, 1970), pp. 295–307; G. Brucker, *The Civic World of Early Renaissance Florence* (Princeton, 1977), pp. 54–5.

[27]   A. Molho, *Florentine Public Finances in the Early Renaissance, 1400–1433* (Cambridge, Mass., 1971), pp. 65–6n.

[28]   Rodolico, *Democrazia*, pp. 458–75; ASF, Provvisioni, Registri, 69, ff. 187–192v.

[29]   Rodolico, *Democrazia*, p. 283.

Direct taxation and reduced interest on the debt might have been enough to push both elite and affluent popolo to opposition and counterrevolution. But there was more. With the creation of the two workers' guilds, the Wool guild lost control over dyers and other skilled artisans. In late 1378, scores of *lanaiuoli* diminished or terminated production, attempting to put dyers and other artisans out of work and break their solidarity.[30] Early in 1379 the commune authorized the Wool guild to reappoint its foreign official but explicitly excluded from his jurisdiction the members of the other twenty-two guilds, including artisans previously subject to the Lana's authority but now independent guildsmen.[31] In March the dyers' guild filed a complaint with the government against two partnerships created in 1377 between the Wool guild and certain dyers in order to control the cost of dyeing cloth. Because, the dyers' guild argued, any partnership involving dyers had to be subject to the jurisdiction of their guild, which the Wool guild obviously was not, the partnerships were illegal. The priors agreed to hear arguments from both sides, instructing the Wool guild to appoint representatives to make its case. Even as it complied, the Lana's council lamented the good old days when, with all the dyers "under itself" and subject to its regulatory authority, it made sure that their services were available in abundance and at the lowest possible cost.[32] The outcome of the dispute is unknown, but the Lana's inability to fix the cost of dyeing cloth continued to plague the once powerful guild. An attempt to negotiate lower prices failed in the summer of 1380, and in November, claiming that it needed to restrict production because of a "shortage of workers," which generally meant high labor costs, the Lana retaliated, in another attempt to deprive dyers of work and drive down piece-rates, by setting low production quotas and freezing them for two years: 279 firms were authorized to produce only 19,500 bolts, an average of 70 per firm.[33] In December the Lana and the dyers agreed to ask the government to mediate their dispute, and, according to Stefani (887), once again the Wool guild was disappointed. By the end of 1381, tensions reached a peak as the Lana bitterly complained of how the dyers impeded the free exercise of the wool trade and even of alleged "threats and intimidation" by dyers against anyone defending the Wool guild in the courts. It appointed yet another committee to find some remedy, excepting of course compromise with the dyers.[34]

[30] ASF, Arte della Lana, 76.
[31] Rodolico, *Democrazia*, p. 457.
[32] ASF, Arte della Lana, 46, ff. 88–9.
[33] A. Doren, *Die Florentiner Wollentuchindustrie*, pp. 526–7.
[34] ASF, Arte della Lana, 46, ff. 109, 112–117v, 128v–131v.

The Wool guild's archive preserves a summary of a conversation, dated November 4, 1381, concerning the ongoing dispute with the dyers, between the cloth producer Giannozzo Alberti, later made famous by his distant cousin Leon Battista as the main character of the third book of the *Libri della famiglia*, and the dyer Francesco di Ricco. Alberti reported to the guild that on the previous day he had met Francesco and "asked him whether the dyers were working." Francesco responded that they were not working and "would not work until Christmas, whether or not there was an agreement." The dyers were evidently on strike. Francesco then asked Giannozzo if he had been present at the meeting of the Wool guild's council on October 30. Giannozzo said he had not attended, but Francesco responded: "I can tell you what happened: they took a vote, and 154 of 157 members voted against any increase in the rates paid to the dyers." Francesco added that "he wasn't worried for himself because he had plenty of work for the time being; the Lana consuls had asked the dyers to work, saying it would be good for them if they did so. So Francesco, together with Andrea di Giuntino, took the initiative to get work started. And they think they'll suffer the consequences."[35] Francesco and Andrea were evidently scabs willing to do the bidding of the Wool guild, hence in close contact with a member of one of its leading families and well informed (better even than Giannozzo himself) about what had occurred in the Lana's council. Although risking the anger of other dyers, Francesco was no doubt counting on protection from the Wool guild if and when plans to break the strike and dismantle the two guilds succeeded. In fact, the Lana's uprising against the popular government was only weeks away.

Counterrevolution

Like its predecessor of 1343–8, the guild government of 1378–82 saw enemies from both directions: on one side the laborers of the disbanded 24th guild, on the other an elite excluded from power and hurt by fiscal reforms. The rupture between the government and the elite families was beyond repair after December 1379 when Piero degli Albizzi, Donato Barbadori, and five other conspirators were executed, fifty more sentenced to death in absentia and confiscation of property, twenty made magnates, and forty deprived of office-holding rights.[36] To these enemies were now added the many *lanaiuoli*, elite and non-elite, who saw no other solution to their war with the dyers than to overthrow the government that allowed them a guild and thus the ability to negotiate collectively. When the *lanaiuoli* revolted in January 1382,

---

[35] Rodolico, *Democrazia*, p. 416.
[36] Brucker, *Civic World*, p. 56.

they took the always ambivalent heart out of the guild coalition. The ensuing counterrevolution gave the elite rather less than it wanted, but it certainly met the demands of the angry manufacturers of woolen cloth.

Fears of plots and conspiracies filled the city with accusations and counter-accusations. When a cloth-shearer with standing in the government was accused of conspiracy, the government's two chief elite allies, Giorgio Scali and Tommaso Strozzi, went to the palace with 400 men and rescued him from execution by the Capitano. An anonymous eyewitness account, reflecting the mood of the popular government's enemies on the eve of its overthrow,[37] reports without a hint of skepticism the rumor that the convicted cloth-shearer was part of a plot to "kill all the Guelfs and deliver the city to messer Bernabò Visconti, lord of Milan" and that his rescuers were "Ghibellines." Threatening to resign in protest over the undermining of his authority in order to force the government to allow Scali and Strozzi to be prosecuted, the Capitano got Scali to "confess" that he too was conspiring to surrender Florence to Milan and was "going to ravage the city and rob and kill all of the Guelfs." Scali was executed "for treason" on January 17, and two more executions on the 20th brought emotions to the boiling point. The "Guelfs" armed themselves and ran through the streets with the banners of the Parte, and "the entire populace marched in processions – the worthy citizens, the soldiers, the people – in an atmosphere of joy and celebration." The notion that the "whole community" was rising in righteous anger against a few traitors in league with a foreign tyrant foreshadows the political myths of the next two generations: the celebration of civic unity, the consensus of all "worthy" men, and the reduction of political opposition to "treason." On January 20 the disintegrating government, under pressure from enraged wool merchants, appointed a balìa composed largely of existing governmental bodies still evenly divided between the two groups of guilds. But the accent was on unity: the balìa insisted that "the needed reforms cannot be lawfully carried out without the full, free, total, and absolute power and authority of the whole Florentine people" and that "this authority cannot be lawfully given except through a *parlamento* and convocation of the whole Florentine people in a general assembly."[38] Such assemblies of the "whole people" were not in fact common in Florence, and certainly not characteristic of the guild movement with its emphasis on representation and each guild's right to its own voice. The fiction that the "whole Florentine people" could give its consent or express a single will, especially through a plebiscitary parlamento, was another element of the emerging ideology of the post-1382 years.

---

[37]   *Alle bocche della piazza: diario di anonimo fiorentino (1382–1401)*, ed. A. Molho and F. Sznura (Florence, 1986); Brucker, *Society*, pp. 78–81.
[38]   Najemy, *Corporatism*, p. 268.

That the counterrevolutionaries intended this to be a decisive and even historic turning point emerges from the stated expectation that the balìa should bring about nothing less than "a new order of things and a new government [*novus status novumque regimen*]" and repeal or revise "the badly conceived" innovations of the past. Pressure from the streets dictated the first of the reforms. According to the anonymous chronicler, on the 21st members of the Wool guild, "together with the prominent citizens," went armed to the Mercato Nuovo and "demanded that the two new guilds be disbanded," which the balìa proceeded to do that same day. Armed bands of *lanaiuoli* ransacked the guildhalls and destroyed the records of the workers' guilds, whose members were returned to the jurisdiction of the Lana and Por Santa Maria. The next day frightened members of the fourteen minor guilds marched on the government palace and (so says the chronicler) reported rumors that the "magnates" were planning to ransack the city. As the elite persuaded itself that the popular government was merely a front for traitorous Ghibellines, the minor guildsmen similarly saw everything through the lens of their ancient fear of elite violence. Unable to believe that the minor guildsmen were sincere in such fears, the chronicler surmised that their real motive was "to disguise the fact that they wished to restore the two disbanded guilds, for they feared that they too would be barred from office." Seeing minor guildsmen descend on the palace in such numbers, the *lanaiuoli* again took up arms and "marched to the piazza where they attacked the butchers" and killed two of them. The demise of the guild republic was symbolically announced when the priors confiscated the flags of the guilds. On the 23rd, members of the seven major guilds and "the rich and prominent citizens" occupied the Mercato Nuovo and demanded that the minor guilds' share of offices be reduced. The next day they demanded the cancellation of the scrutiny of August 1378, which the chronicler identifies as the one "the Ciompi conducted." By Saturday the 25th, the "Guelfs," confident of their control of the streets, "marched through the city with torches and lanterns, and no one uttered a word in protest."

The balìa promptly annulled the "Ciompi scrutiny" and held a new one based on lists compiled by the standardbearers of the gonfaloni, who cast their net widely nominating approximately 5,350 citizens, 50% more than were nominated in the 1350s and only 10–15% fewer than in 1378. But over 70% of the nominees (approximately 3,800) were major guildsmen, nearly the entire population of the seven guilds and an early sign that the new regime intended to promote upper-class consensus and overcome the historic split between elite and non-elite major guildsmen. The balìa decided it would itself serve as the scrutiny committee, together with fifty-four citizens it selected, including powerful figures who became the core of the elite's leadership over the next few decades: Maso degli Albizzi, Niccolò da Uzzano, Filippo Corsini, Piero Baroncelli, and Vieri de' Medici. Two weeks of voting resulted in the approval of about 575 of 3,800 major guildsmen and 300 of approximately 1,550 minor guildsmen. Although the results were, as always, an official secret, it was predictable, given their representation in the scrutiny council, that minor guildsmen would constitute a substantial percentage of approved citizens (one-third, in fact). This prompted a group of elite leaders to attempt either to circumvent the balìa or hijack it to their own purposes. Stefani (913) says that the "families" and the "grandi" met on February 15, four days after the scrutiny's conclusion, and designated forty-three spokesmen to present their demands to the government: that the forty-three be added to the balìa, which should also be purged of anyone who had been "warned" by the Parte in the 1370s; that those exiled by the popular government be readmitted and compensated for confiscated or destroyed property; that the minor guilds' share of seats in the priorate be reduced to three; that sixty magnates be restored to *popolano* status and not required to wait the customary twenty years to regain office-holding rights; and that no one be prosecuted for assaults or murders committed between January 13 and midnight on February 15, a demand Stefani called "diabolical" since it meant that they openly intended to settle scores with violence before the day was out. Two further demands support Stefani's contention that these Guelf leaders had formed the most improbable of political alliances – with the Ciompi: a five-month extension for the payment of forced loans, and reduced assessments for anyone taxed two florins or less. In fact, the forty-three included nine or ten persons either without family names or with indications of artisan or working-class status, but only one, a cloth stretcher, can be identified as a ciompo. The rest were overwhelmingly from elite families, magnate (Bardi, Rossi, Buondelmonti, Cavalcanti, Gherardini, and others), and non-magnate (including Tommaso Soderini, Filippo Corsini, Piero Pitti, Tommaso Brancacci, Carlo Strozzi, Cristofano degli Spini, Vieri de' Medici, Biagio Guasconi, Francesco da Filicaia, Andrea degli Albizzi, and members of the Canigiani, Peruzzi, and Rucellai).

Both Stefani and the anonymous chronicler describe the actions of the forty-three as an illegal attempt to force acceptance of their demands without approval from the priors, councils, or balìa. They marched toward the palace under the banner of the Parte, carried by Vanni di Michele Castellani, occupied and closed off the piazza, and demanded that the priors sound the bell for a parlamento. According to the anonymous chronicler, Chancellor Salutati came out onto the platform and "read and ratified" the document, which gave the forty-three balìa powers to carry out whatever reforms they liked. But the Wool guild and consuls of the other guilds sent a delegation to demand the expulsion of the forty-three, who first answered that "they had no intention of leaving the palace because the people had put them there, and that they would leave only when the people wanted them to."

Cooler heads among the forty-three prevailed, as Francesco da Filicaia advised the others on behalf of the Wool guild (of which he was a member) that all the guilds agreed that the forty-three should resign and go home. The next day the twenty-one guilds swore an oath to remain united, "unto death," against anyone attempting to "overthrow the *stato* of the guilds and the Parte Guelfa."[39] Stefani (914) tells a slightly different story in which the leaders of the gang of forty-three pressured Salutati and the notary of the legislative councils to draft documents that would have turned their demands into law, but that both men refused on the grounds that this had not been approved by the priors. The next day the "good men and the merchants and guildsmen immediately agreed, and the [other] guilds appealed to the Wool guild, whose members went openly into the palace and announced that the 43 should get out immediately and that the [existing] *balìa* was sufficient to do what needed to be done." Thwarted on this occasion, a month later dissatisfied elite leaders were back again, and a similar scenario unfolded, with another list of demands. This time they succeeded in removing seven of the sixteen standardbearers of the gonfaloni, among them Stefani,[40] who says only that "the flags [of the gonfaloni] were taken away from some good men." (919). But the legislative councils resisted most of the elite demands, and for the rest of the year a tense standoff prevailed between the Guelf leaders and the rest of the major guildsmen.

A good example of this tension, but also of changing political winds, came in August when, as Stefani reports (935), the pouches yielded a priorate of "common men," except for its Standardbearer of Justice, Cipriano degli Alberti whose family had been sympathetic to the popular government. Guelf hardliners wanted to use force to prevent them from taking office, but Cipriano went to the palace with an armed escort insisting that he and the priors-elect be allowed to assume their rightful posts. Stefani speculated that if Cipriano "had followed the wishes of the guildsmen, he could have turned the city in whatever direction he wanted." The guilds demanded punishment for those who tried to reject the incoming priorate, and the question was submitted to a pratica in which the advisory colleges made it clear that the practice of consulting the guilds and hearing their views would no longer be welcomed. A spokesman for the Sixteen went so far as to advise that "the guilds should not be allowed to assemble for the purpose of presenting their opinions" to the government. The Twelve, although they thought "no guild should be prevented from addressing" the government, "doubted that any good can come from it." Delegitimizing the guilds and removing them from constitutional functions became prime objectives of the post-1382 regime. Government

[39] *Alle bocche della piazza*, pp. 27–30.
[40] Ibid., p. 35.

gradually came more firmly under the control of elite leaders determined to sever the historic link between republic and guilds and convinced that their counterrevolution should not be limited to undoing the policies and institutions of 1378–82, but indeed that the time had come for a new kind of elite regime, grounded in a rhetoric of unity and consensus, in which hierarchical social relations and paternalistic leadership would seem the natural order of things. But first guild government had to be discredited, and this was done by associating guilds with subversion and working-class rebellion. In relegating the guilds to political oblivion, the elite now had the acquiescence of non-elite major guildsmen whose fear of working-class insurrection finally overcame their old mistrust of the elite. Without their support, guild republicanism steadily receded from the arena of acceptable political discourse.

Fear of the Working Classes

Workers and exiled Ciompi, sometimes with minor guildsmen, were repeatedly accused of attempting to overthrow the regime and restore popular government, and of advancing their cause in the name of the guilds. Former members of the disbanded guilds no doubt continued to agitate for their restoration. In 1383 working-class exiles planned a revolt for July 21, the anniversary of the revolution that brought the Ciompi into government in 1378. Crowds ran through the streets with the flags of their old guilds, crying "Long live the *popolo* and the guilds." In October 1393 a minor guildsman was accused of planning an uprising and saying: "It's necessary to overthrow the present regime, and that can be done by starting a riot, and then we'll become strong with the guildsmen of this city. To achieve this end, we'll cry: 'Long live the guilds! Long live the *popolo* and the guilds!' And guildsmen will all come together and we will fight against the rulers of this regime." For would-be revolutionaries, the connection between guilds and working-class aspirations was rooted in history; for the elite, it was the chief pretext for delegitimating the guilds and removing them from politics. To this end, the ruling group was more than willing to keep alive the perception that linked guilds to working-class conspiracy and rebellion. In 1411 exiled Alberti were accused of fomenting an uprising in which the cry "Long live the *popolo* and the guilds" would win the support of the lower classes.[41] Whether the Alberti actually wrote the old slogan into the script is not clear, but the government was only too happy to accuse them of having done so. By the early fifteenth century, official political discourse made it nearly treasonous to support "the guilds" in any kind of protest against the regime, especially in alliance with workers.

---

[41]   Brucker, *Civic World*, pp. 93, 326.

The notion that workers and the poor constituted a permanent danger became commonplace in the generation after 1382 and sustained deep hostility toward the lower classes. In 1390 a new bishop was installed in Florence, according to the anonymous chronicler, "with little good will from the *popolo minuto*, because it was said that he told those in power: 'If you want to rule and keep control, keep the *popolo* hungry for bread.' And for this reason they hated him."[42] Giovanni Morelli warned against revealing the true extent of one's possessions: grain should be stored at the farm and not brought to one's city house, not only to hide it from tax assessors, but because "if a poor man sees that you have grain to sell and that you're holding on to it to increase its price, he will damn and curse and rob you and burn your house, if he has the power to do so, and he'll make you hated by the entire lower class, which is a most dangerous thing. May God preserve our city from their rule."[43] Here traditional contempt for the envious poor has become class hatred linked to the memory of 1378. In a 1414 pratica, Gino Capponi expressed a similar horror of being ruled by the Ciompi when, in order to say how unthinkable submission to foreign tyranny would be, he declared that it would be "better to live under the government of the Ciompi than under the tyranny of a king."[44] And fifty years after the popular government of 1378–82 the historian Giovanni Cavalcanti reported an angry diatribe, allegedly delivered by Rinaldo degli Albizzi in 1426 to a meeting of the regime's leaders, against "guildsmen and citizens of low condition" who resisted the leadership's policies: the descendants, he said, of those who "for forty accursed months [from July 1378 to January 1382] held this people in servitude," sent to their deaths so many victims from great families and left as many grieving widows and orphans. Even if Cavalcanti invented or embellished this speech, its inclusion in his chronicle dramatizes the emotional excess of upper-class fears, not only of workers, but now also of "guildsmen," described as the descendants of "serfs" from the contado and incapable of civil life because of their bestial nature. He has Rinaldo ask if anyone could ever really doubt that people with names like Bardi, Rossi, and Frescobaldi (all magnate families, like the Cavalcanti, deprived of office-holding rights) had a greater right to offices than did people known only by patronymics or by their humble professions.[45] Upper-class prejudice against manual laborers and shopkeepers was not new, but it received powerful reinforcement from the consciously manipulated memory of those "forty accursed months."

---

42 *Alle bocche della piazza*, p. 90.
43 Giovanni di Pagolo Morelli, *Ricordi*, ed. V. Branca (Florence, 1969), p. 256.
44 *Commissioni di Rinaldo degli Albizzi*, 3 vols., ed. C. Guasti, (Florence, 1867–73), 1:136–7; Brucker, *Civic World*, p. 388.
45 Giovanni Cavalcanti, *Istorie fiorentine*, 2 vols., ed. F. Polidori (Florence, 1838), 1:82; Brucker, *Civic World*, p. 473.

Workers and artisans were also associated with heresy. In December 1382 the government banned the Fraticelli from Florentine territory, claiming that for several years members of the outlawed sect had gone about infecting "simple and ignorant laypersons" with heretical ideas. Franciscan inquisitors resumed their activity, despite some resistance. When the Inquisition arrested a layman on suspicion of heresy in 1383, his son and neighbors rescued him by stoning its officials.[46] In 1384, the inquisitor condemned an alleged heretic and handed him over to the podestà to be burned. According to the anonymous chronicler, "there was a great deal of talk about this all over the city, because it had been a long time since any inquisitor had done this sort of thing in Florence." Even the bishop, the local clergy, and many experts in canon law were against this execution.[47] In both episodes the accused were middle- or lower-class laypersons. The most famous condemnation for heresy in this generation was the 1389 burning of a fraticello, Fra Michele di Berto from Calci in the territory of Pisa (not yet part of the Florentine dominion), who was accused of preaching his heretical opinions to "many men and women" in Florence. An eyewitness account of his sentencing and procession to the place of execution before a huge throng following him at every stage shows that public opinion was divided: "the majority said he was wrong and that no one should speak such evil of the priests. And some said, 'He is a martyr,' and others said, 'He is a saint,' and still others denied it. And there was a greater tumult and disturbance in Florence than there had ever been."[48] These awed expressions of admiration for Brother Michele no doubt confirmed the perception that he and the Fraticelli were indeed dangerous and that heresy had somehow fed the political turmoil of the 1370s. Even if Franciscan heresies were not behind the political activism of the working classes, the repression of alleged heterodoxy in the 1380s certainly reinforced in retrospect the notion that religious and political dissent went hand in hand within the working classes.

Criminal prosecution in the communal courts also contributed to the perception of danger from the lower classes. Ever less interested in crimes committed among and against workers, the courts of the podestà and Capitano concentrated instead on working-class crime against the upper class.[49] Punishments decreed by the Wool guild's court for workers convicted of theft of cloth or tools often included ritual humiliation, with the guilty being paraded through the industry's neighborhoods wearing either a "crown of perpetual shame" or the stolen objects around their necks.[50] Both the communal courts

---

[46] Brucker, *Society*, pp. 250–3.
[47] *Alle bocche della piazza*, p. 53.
[48] Brucker, *Society*, pp. 253–7.
[49] Cohn, *Laboring Classes*, pp. 179–203.
[50] F. Franceschi, "Criminalità e mondo del lavoro: il tribunale dell'Arte della Lana a Firenze nei secoli XIV e XV," *Ricerche storiche* 18 (1988): 573.

and those of the Florentine governors of the outlying territories undertook more systematic prosecution of moral and sexual transgressions, including private and consensual acts of adultery and seduction, whose alleged perpetrators were disproportionately from the working classes and rural village communities.[51] Such strategies of social discipline and criminal prosecution nourished the perception of workers and the poor as particularly predisposed to both violent crime against the upper classes and violations of moral and sexual norms of which the upper class now made itself the stern guardian. Similarly reinforcing such ideas were petitions approved by the priors and legislative councils from persons convicted of sexual crimes and seeking pardons or reductions of their penalties. Read aloud to hundreds of council members, they reproduced the texts of the original convictions in often quite salacious detail, thus advertising the excesses of lower-class behavior. In a sampling of some thirty such petitions, only one involved someone with a surname.[52] In all these ways, government and courts fashioned images of the working classes and the poor, men and women alike, as by nature given to anti-social behavior that regularly turned violent and thus had to be contained.

Fear of the lower classes became politically potent because it lodged deep in the psyches of non-elite major guildsmen as well as in the elite. Particularly revealing in this regard are Stefani's denunciations of workers and the guild regime in which he himself served. Far from being some reactionary elite Guelf, Stefani came from a modest non-elite family. His father Coppo had been an occasional consul of Por Santa Maria. Stefani's social status and guild affiliation were identical to those of Dino Compagni, and his political career, like Compagni's, was largely defined by the popular movement. He held his first major office in 1372 on the newly created Ten of Liberty, served as the commune's envoy to Bologna during the war against the papacy, and held his other offices in 1378–82.[53] In his one term as prior, in November–December 1379, he and his colleagues made the momentous decision to execute Piero degli Albizzi and Donato Barbadori for treason, an action about which he expressed doubts, but not criticism, in the chronicle. His removal from the Sixteen in 1382 shows that he was no friend of the Guelf elite; indeed he was often severely critical of what he called their arrogance and overbearing ambition. Yet, in his account (written under the impact of the events of 1378–82)

---

[51] S. K. Cohn Jr., *Women in the Streets: Essays on Sex and Power in Renaissance Italy* (Baltimore, 1996), pp. 98–136 (126–7).
[52] My unpublished research.
[53] A. De Vincentiis, "Scrittura e politica cittadina: la cronaca fiorentina di Marchionne di Coppo Stefani," *Rivista storica italiana* 108 (1996): 230–97 (276–7); L. Green, *Chronicle into History: An Essay on the Interpretation of History in Florentine Fourteenth-Century Chronicles* (Cambridge, 1972), pp. 91–105.

of Walter of Brienne's *signoria*, Stefani denounced the woolworkers in a vitriolic passage (567) as the latter-day equivalent of Christ-killers: "it was rumored that the duke wished to ally himself with the *popolo* and that he often referred to them saying 'our good people.' He forgot that it was they who crucified Christ, crying 'Die! Die!' And well he should have remembered that they would treat him no better than they had treated Christ, who was a just lord" (as Brienne evidently was not, in Stefani's view). He regarded the lower classes as incapable of rational political action, for they live "*con niun ordine* [without any organization or order] and, being too numerous to assemble or to reach understanding of things," are easily seduced by demagogues (553).

Stefani's anger was not limited to the workers he called the "popolazzo." It was also directed at the guilds and their government for having created the political framework in which workers and dyers could defend their interests: "So great was the power of the guildsmen that in every matter under deliberation they achieved their aims in the councils. . . . Thus whoever has more power gets what he wants, with little concern however for whether it is good or useful for the city; everyone seeks his own advantage as best he thinks he can: neither laws nor statutes count for much in such matters" (877). His reaction to the independent guild of dyers negotiating piece-rates with their former masters in the Wool guild was especially irate. He denounced the "domineering attitude [*soperchio homore*] that predominated among guildsmen" and the "insolence" and "arrogance" of the dyers who "had no concern for who they were" or for the fact that they "used to be governed by and subject to the cloth manufacturers from whom they had their laws and to whose statutes they were subject." Their requests were "so alien to the cloth manufacturers and so abominable to the citizens that it was beyond all measure" (887).[54] He used similar language to condemn Walter of Brienne's organization of the 1343 San Giovanni processions by guilds instead of gonfaloni: "with each guild separate and independent from the rest," he wrote, the "citizens, seeing the exaltation of the *gente minuta*, became highly indignant, because this was beyond all human and divine reason" (575). These outbursts are especially significant because they come from a non-elite guildsman and thus from the class that had risen to power and challenged the elite through its guilds. The old ambivalence of his class, caught between enemies "above" and "below" and alternately fearing one more than the other, here finds resolution: Stefani's is the first clear voice among non-elite major guildsmen to reject, explicitly and loudly, guild republicanism. As we shall see, he was also the first from the popolo to contribute to the refashioning of the image of the elite (despite his often harsh criticism of it).

[54]   Brucker, *Civic World*, p. 52.

Elite prejudice against the lower classes was no less deeply engrained. Whereas for two centuries the calls for order and discipline came from the popolo as it sought to contain the violence of the great families and their private armies, now, remarkably in the space of a single generation, roles were reversed as the elite appropriated the popolo's discourse of civic discipline and turned it against the lower classes. The reversal is neatly encapsulated in Francesco di Tommaso Giovanni's account of the intervention in 1458 of the police magistracy of the Otto di Guardia (of which he was then a member), which captured and executed a convicted thief who had escaped from their custody in the midst of a riot started by friends and neighbors who tried to rescue him: "we disabused the people of their bad habits," he said about the man's decapitation in front of a huge crowd.[55] For him this action was more than merely deserved punishment for a crime; the public display of the state's severity was required to repress that built-in predisposition toward crime that had become central to upper-class perceptions of workers and the poor.

In his *Histories of the Florentine People*, begun around 1415, the humanist Leonardo Bruni demonstrated just how crucial the memory of the Ciompi and the fear of social revolution had become to the political assumptions of the ruling class. His account of the events of 1378 contains a memorable passage that evokes the vivid fear of workers while denying legitimacy to their political aims: "Every day new movements were born, because some people were eager to plunder the possessions of the rich, others to gain revenge against their enemies, and still others to make themselves powerful. This may stand as a lesson for all time [*perpetuum documentum*] to the distinguished men of the city: never to let political initiative or arms into the hands of the multitude, for once they have had a bite, they cannot be restrained and they think they can do as they please because there are so many of them." Well-meaning but misguided attempts at reform had resulted in "making poor guildsmen and men of base condition the rulers of the city" and put "noble and distinguished" families at the mercy of the "stupidity of the aroused multitude. For there was no end or order to the unleashed appetites of the poor and criminals, who, once armed, lusted after the possessions of rich and honorable men and thought of nothing except robbing, killing, and exiling citizens."[56] In this most authoritative of the city's histories, given official status and a government-sponsored translation into Tuscan, "poor" and "criminals" became two ways of referring to a single social category.

[55]   A. Molho, "Cosimo de' Medici: *Pater Patriae* or *Padrino?*" *Stanford Italian Review* 1 (1979): 13–14.
[56]   Leonardo Bruni Aretino, *Historiarum florentini populi libri XII*, ed. E. Santini (Città di Castello, 1914–26), p. 224 (my translation).

Consensus Politics

A new set of political attitudes gradually took hold as an ideology of consensus and paternalistic leadership replaced the republicanism of separate interests. "Consensus" (not to be confused with consent) here stands for a cluster of assumptions about unity, absence of social conflict, the inadmissibility of dissent, and the dutiful acquiescence of good citizens in the natural and benevolent leadership of the elite. For the first time the elite's claim to lead rested on the assent of non-elite major guildsmen in return for a wide sharing of offices. The two aspects of this transformation have sometimes seemed paradoxical, and an exclusive focus on one or the other obscures their functional relationship: on the one hand, the emergence of an inner core of elite families as a largely uncontested ruling class; on the other, the expansion of the ranks of officeholders, but without a share of actual power. Motivated by their fear of the working classes, non-elite major guildsmen accepted their inclusion among eligible officeholders, and an occasional office, as the reward for cooperation with the elite and a mark of recognition of their worth as good citizens. Expanding the political class widened the elite's base of support and enhanced its power and legitimacy.

Electoral policies were thus central to the new political configuration.[57] In 1385 the nomination of candidates for the priorate was freed of all restrictions deriving from proscriptions of alleged Ghibellines; in 1387 the old requirement of active exercise of a trade was similarly abrogated; and even guild membership was no longer a test of eligibility. The result was a notable increase in nominations: from approximately 5,350 in 1382 to 6,310 for the scrutiny of 1391, including 4,584 major guildsmen. They declined in the next scrutiny (of 1411) for which complete lists have survived to 5,265 (3,910 major guildsmen and 1,355 minor guildsmen), perhaps because of the sharp decline in population following several outbreaks of plague. But in 1433, nominations climbed back to 6,354. To put this in perspective: in a population less than half that before the 1348 plague, nominations doubled by comparison with even the popular scrutiny of 1343. Whereas in 1343 one in seven adult males was nominated, by 1391 one in two was nominated, and in 1433 (with a total population of no more than 40,000), two of every three. Although of course a minority of nominees was approved, the secret of the scrutiny allowed many to nurture the hope that they had been successful and to wait patiently for years to find out. Approved candidates initially declined, from roughly 875 in 1382, to 677 in 1391, and 619 in 1393. But by 1411 they jumped to 1,069 and in 1433 to the remarkable total of 2,084. Most of the

[57]   For what follows, see my *Corporatism*, pp. 263–300.

approved candidates were major guildsmen, 884 in 1411 and 1,757 in 1433. Expanding numbers of both nominations and successful candidates contributed to the perception that political participation had never been broader. But the social base from which the political class was recruited was narrowing. Minor guild representation in the priorate was reduced from four to three to two seats, and the composition of the scrutiny committees conformed to the same ratios. An expanding political class was increasingly limited to major guildsmen.

Precisely because so many major guildsmen were being approved and admitted to high office, the elite needed to ensure that real power remained in its hands. The solution, first implemented in 1387, was to allow the officials in charge of placing name-tickets in the pouches (who were still called accoppiatori) to select from candidates successful in the scrutinies a small preferential pool for whom a certain number of seats on the priorate was reserved. At first two, and by 1393 three, of the eight seats were reserved for this handpicked elite whose names went into the so-called small pouch, or borsellino. And because the Standardbearers of Justice were also selected by the accoppiatori, four of the nine seats were henceforth filled from the borsellino, while the hundreds and eventually thousands of other approved citizens competed against much greater odds for the remaining five seats. A contemporary chronicler described the reaction among non-elite citizens: those selected by "the powerful" for the borsellino, he claimed, "were very loyal to their regime [*molto confidenti allo stato loro*]." Everyone was eager to know which priors came from which pouches: "And when the new priors were drawn, citizens said: Which priors are the ones from the *borsellino*? And it was much criticized by the good citizens, because it did not seem a good thing to them to make such a distinction among citizens."[58] Even as the identities of those selected for the borsellino were never officially revealed, it institutionalized (and consolidated the popular perception of) the distinction between an inner circle of real power and the rest of the officeholders.

Even tighter electoral controls were instituted by the inner elite in October 1393, when Maso degli Albizzi, nephew of the Piero executed in 1379, was Standardbearer of Justice. After announcing that it had foiled a conspiracy involving the rival Alberti, thus creating a perception of emergency, the government asked a parlamento to authorize a balìa the majority of whose members consisted of the incumbent priors and colleges and one hundred citizens appointed by them and was a veritable who's who of the ruling group of the next few decades. The families represented, in addition to the Albizzi, included the Da Uzzano, Soderini, Ridolfi, Vettori, Capponi, Pitti, Corsini, and

[58] *Cronica volgare di anonimo fiorentino*, ed. E. Bellondi (Città di Castello, 1915–18), p. 35.

Guicciardini from Santo Spirito; Magalotti, Salviati, Baroncelli, Mancini, Dell'Antella, and Castellani from Santa Croce; Acciaiuoli, Strozzi, Spini, Rucellai, Ardinghelli, Altoviti, Davanzati, and Minerbetti from Santa Maria Novella; and the Medici (both Vieri di Cambio and Giovanni di Bicci, father of Cosimo), Ricci, Alessandri, and Valori from San Giovanni. Once the Alberti "conspirators" had been dispatched, the balìa turned its attention to electoral reforms: it annulled the pouches of a 1385 scrutiny for the priorate and all existing pouches for dominion offices, the Mercanzia, and guild consulates; it scheduled new scrutinies and in the meantime handpicked the guild consuls, Mercanzia councilors, and even the next priorate, thus ensuring the presence in office of trusted allies during the scrutinies (five of the eight handpicked priors for November–December 1393 came from the balìa itself and included Niccolò da Uzzano as Standardbearer of Justice); and it increased to three the seats on the priorate to be filled from the borsellino. But its most audacious action was the appointment of nine accoppiatori to revise the existing borsellini by adding or deleting names as they saw fit, including those of citizens approved in the new scrutiny, thus making them eligible for extraction much sooner. The power given the accoppiatori of 1393 was unprecedented: with complete control over the borsellini, they revised at will the ranks of eligible citizens for nearly half the seats on the priorate and determined the composition of this privileged inner circle for years to come. Appointed by, and from within the ranks of, the balìa, the accoppiatori included Maso degli Albizzi, the most powerful leader of his faction and subsequently Standardbearer of Justice two more times; Andrea Vettori, a Calimala merchant who became Standardbearer in 1395; Giovanni Bucelli, a three-time Standardbearer whose son Francesco was among the next generation's inner circle; Davanzato Davanzati, a banker elected twice as prior and twice as Standardbearer; Bartolomeo Valori, a woolen-cloth manufacturer, three times Standardbearer and one of the most frequent speakers in the pratiche, whose son Niccolò also subsequently belonged to the inner elite; Andrea Minerbetti, a cloth manufacturer, twice Standardbearer, and the father of yet another member of the next generation's ruling group; and three others, including, as required, two minor guildsmen. These nine men determined the shape and size of the Florentine office-holding class for the next generation.

It did not take long for the effects of their work to emerge. After 1393 the number of families reaching the priorate for the first time quickly declined. Whereas each year between 1382 and 1393 from thirteen to twenty-two families had their first prior (and many more than that during the popular government), new families were fewer in the next decade and between 1403 and 1433 averaged under three per year. Families with several priors were mainly older ones: thirty-four of forty-three families with four or more priors between 1382 and 1399 had their first prior before 1343, twenty-four of them before

1300. By comparison with the twenty years before the mid-1390s, the Florentine office-holding class gradually closed the door to newcomers after 1393. This Florentine "serrata" (or closing) was never as tight as that of Venice. Some new families (Morelli, Serristori, and Pucci) went on to hold office with impressive frequency, but they were exceptions whose political success depended on the favor of those at the pinnacle of power. Paradoxically, while it became more difficult for new families to rise into the political class, offices were more widely distributed than ever before. In 1382–99, 977 available seats on the priorate were held by 898 citizens. In 1410–19, 480 posts (excluding the Standardbearers of Justice) were shared by 433 individuals.[59] Between 1382 and 1407, only twenty citizens reached the priorate three or more times (compared to 134 in the twenty-five years before 1378).[60] Nonetheless, the inner elite carefully controlled the limited pool of those who had access to half the seats.

Consensus was also a prevailing myth within the elite. Despite its collective predominance, no one family or group of families clearly led the rest in appearances in the priorate. The families with the most priors in 1382–99 were the Altoviti (9), Salviati (8), Acciaiuoli, Albizzi, Biliotti, Rucellai, and Strozzi (7 each). Until 1434, the inner leadership consisted of some fifty or sixty men who held key offices frequently but whose families did not monopolize them, who sat on electoral committees and balìe, dominated the Mercanzia (and through it the guilds), served as ambassadors and ran foreign policy, and spoke regularly in the pratiche. Attempts to identify the inner elite in the first third of the fifteenth century have focused on frequency of participation in the pratiche as the mark of real influence. Because the regime relied on these advisory sessions to generate consensus around its policies, the frequent participants were those particularly authoritative, influential, and respected citizens who had the best chance of carrying others toward their views. Between 1403 and 1414, fifty-seven men, the overwhelming majority from elite families, spoke in at least twenty pratiche: five spoke more than one hundred times (Filippo Corsini, Piero Baroncelli, Cristofano Spini, Maso degli Albizzi, and Rinaldo Gianfigliazzi), and another fourteen more than fifty times (including Gino Capponi, Lorenzo Ridolfi, and Niccolò da Uzzano).[61] If power was now increasingly a function of the ability to persuade and build consensus, this generation witnessed yet another transformation in the character of the Florentine elite: its emergence as a civic aristocracy skilled in the rhetorical techniques of eloquence and public argument.

---

[59]   A. Molho, "Politics and the Ruling Class in Early Renaissance Florence," *Nuova rivista storica* 52 (1968): 401–20.
[60]   R. G. Witt, "Florentine Politics and the Ruling Class, 1382–1407," *Journal of Medieval and Renaissance Studies* 6 (1976): 243–67.
[61]   Brucker, *Civic World*, pp. 264–5.

Patronage and money remained, however, the foundations of power. Every great family needed wealth with which to build and keep its network of neighbors, friends, and relatives who provided indispensable support in difficult situations. But it was a basic principle of the regime's stability that no family should exceed the others in office-holding or in the reach of its patronage network. Even the Albizzi, despite the prestige of Maso and Rinaldo, did not have the wealth or patronage resources with which to dominate the rest of the elite. Behind the two major political conflicts within the elite at either end of the half-century between 1382 and 1434 – the exile of the Alberti and the struggle with the Medici – lay an unwritten rule that no family of the inner circle should exercise obviously greater power than the others. At the end of the fourteenth century, the Alberti, who acquired vast wealth from papal banking, were the one family capable of upsetting the consensus. Benedetto Alberti had courted the favor of the popular government, was knighted by the Ciompi in July 1378 and appointed one of four civilian chiefs of the armed security force in 1379 (Stefani 795, 830). And Cipriano Alberti defended the guilds in 1382. The enemies they made took advantage of two political mistakes by the Alberti a few years later to destroy the family as a force in Florentine politics. In civic celebrations of 1386, the Alberti dressed their brigade of knights, all in white and gold and "adorned with every ornament," in the family's own coat of arms, instead of the communal insignia, and were forced out of the festivities for excessively glorifying the family. In April 1387, when his son-in-law was drawn as Standardbearer of Justice but was discovered not to be of the required age, Benedetto engaged in what the anonymous chronicler describes as heavy-handed pressure to have him seated in office: "people didn't like Benedetto's tactics, because it seemed to them that he wanted to be *signore* of Florence."[62] Immediately following this episode, the government created the balìa of May 1387, which (in addition to instituting the borsellino) banished Benedetto and Cipriano for two years. In 1393 five Alberti, including Cipriano, were exiled and others barred from office. Accusations of conspiracy and treason continued to rain down on the family and exile was inflicted on more and more of them until, by the early fifteenth century, all Alberti men were banished.

What made the Alberti dangerous to the regime was the combination of great wealth and popular appeal. If any family at this time had the means and will to rise above the others and make one of its own "signore" of Florence (as had happened in most cities in northern Italy), it was the Alberti. In the dialogues *On the Family* written in the 1430s after the exile was rescinded, Benedetto's illegitimate grandson Leon Battista has one of the speakers recall that "in those times" (before the exile) the Alberti contributed no less than

---

[62]   *Alle bocche della piazza*, pp. 62, 65.

one of every thirty-two florins spent by the government.[63] There is no way of verifying the accuracy of this astonishing claim, but a list of voluntary lenders to the commune in 1395 reveals that, of 501 households that made loans, just 52 were assessed 49% of the total and that the fiscal household of the four sons of Niccolaio Alberti lent 130,000 florins, equivalent to 23% of the total contributed by these wealthiest 52 households and 11% of the overall sum. No other household was even close: the next highest assessment was less than a fifth of that of the Alberti brothers. This was the kind of wealth that could threaten the carefully constructed equilibrium among elite families, and it may have been the deeper reason why the ruling group felt it necessary to manufacture pretexts to banish the Alberti. When, a generation later, the enormous wealth of the Medici presented the oligarchy with a similar threat, the ruling group once again tried to banish the giant in its midst. This time they failed, for reasons to be considered later and which once again changed the course of Florentine history. But before that happened, a confident ruling elite utterly transformed not only government and politics, but also political attitudes, foreign policy, Florentine territorial dominion in Tuscany, and the relationship of government to families and citizens.

[63] Leon Battista Alberti, *I libri della famiglia*, ed. R. Romano and A. Tenenti (Turin, 1972), p. 172; trans. R. N. Watkins, *The Family in Renaissance Florence* (Columbia, S.C., 1969), pp. 142–3.

7

War, Territorial Expansion, and the Transformation of Political Discourse

The half-century from the 1380s to the 1430s is the watershed of Florence's republican history. Realignments among the classes transformed politics, intellectual life, social attitudes, and institutions. More changed in these decades than in the previous hundred years. As guild republicanism gradually gave way to consensus regimes under elite leadership, Florence expanded its dominion in Tuscany and began playing a more decisive role as a territorial and military power. Whereas its fourteenth-century wars were relatively brief, the longest being the three-year conflicts with Mastino Della Scala and the papacy, Florence was nearly constantly at war between 1390 and 1454, except in the decade 1414–23. War and the myths needed to sustain it assumed unprecedented importance and generated a patriotic ideology combining a celebration of Florence's domination of Tuscany with its self-assigned duty to defend republican liberty. Within Florence, government authority to police and control, discipline and punish, provide charity and assistance, and enforce norms of behavior and morality significantly expanded. Homosexuality, prostitution, religious behavior, conspicuous consumption, dowries, and marriage all became objects of government regulation and surveillance. Pressures toward social conformity emerged from the ideological needs of consensus politics in a time of near permanent war. And in this same half-century, humanism and the cult of antiquity occupied center stage in cultural life, as citizens and humanists alike appropriated the ancient wisdom of the "studies of humanity" to refashion ideals of citizenship and republican liberty and virtue.

First Visconti Wars

After 1378 the schism that divided the church between rival papacies in Rome and Avignon weakened papal authority in central Italy and left Florence as the undisputed power between Rome and the Po valley. In 1384 Florence purchased control of Arezzo from its French occupiers for 40,000 florins. Over the next two years the Florentines acquired bits of papal territory and flexed their military muscle to the north toward Bologna and east toward Urbino, even warning Pope Urban VI not to meddle in the politics of the two chief cities of the papal states, Bologna and Perugia.[1] Meanwhile, they were instigating a change of regime in Montepulciano (a town south of Siena and Arezzo under Sienese control) at just the moment in the late 1380s when Giangaleazzo Visconti, the ruler of Milan who had already extended his power into the eastern Po valley to Padua, turned his gaze south and began courting the smaller cities of Tuscany that were fearful of Florentine expansion. At the end of 1389 Siena entered into a ten-year alliance with Giangaleazzo, and in 1390 war began between Florence and Milan. Although officially the first of three separate wars, it was really the beginning of a twelve-year struggle that ended only with the Milanese ruler's death in 1402 and consequent disintegration of the Visconti dominions. And even this set of wars was the prelude to a still longer conflict between the two powers that lasted until the 1440s.

The Milanese wars affected Florentine politics and public finances in ways that are apparent from the first years of the conflict. This was a more dangerous war for the Florentines than the struggle against the papacy, not only because their new antagonist was militarily stronger, but chiefly because he had the support of Tuscan cities that wanted above all to avoid being swallowed up by Florence. Support for the war came from elite leaders like Filippo Corsini, Rinaldo Gianfigliazzi and the Albizzi (although Maso himself seems not to have played a major role at this moment, as he would later). Opposition came from the guild community and non-elite merchants, and already by the summer of 1391 the regime was attempting to suppress dissent. After a defeat that provoked criticism of the government, a police official was instituted "with authority over any person and the power to hang or behead anyone as he sees fit, especially those who speak against the *stato* [regime, or government]. The archguelfs arranged this so that others would not speak against them."[2] Perhaps not coincidentally, the councils simultaneously suppressed two religious confraternities "in order to remove divisions among citizens that they say have been limited thus far to words and to

[1]   Lewin, *Negotiating Survival*, pp. 77–96.
[2]   *Alle bocche della piazza*, p. 107; Brucker, *Civic World*, p. 137.

prevent anything worse from erupting."[3] Fear of criticism and too much talk went hand in hand with attempts to manipulate public opinion with processions, public masses, bonfires, and dramatic announcements, all intended to sustain a sense of urgency and preserve support for the regime's war policy. In September, the government organized public celebrations for a major victory by Florentine troops under Hawkwood. But there was also concern about damage to the economy. With some exaggeration, but revealing skepticism about the necessity of the war, the anonymous chronicler complained that "our hired soldiers" (Hawkwood's troops) did more damage stealing whatever they wanted in the contado than the enemy ever did. But he also noted that, with the Milanese blocking shipments from Pisa, "there was much worry throughout the city, because if wool doesn't get here, there's no work in Florence and the city is practically under siege, and the poor will die of hunger, since the price of food soars, no one earns anything, and taxes are heavy for everyone."[4]

Military expenses and fiscal needs in this and subsequent wars against Milan were indeed enormous. Between 1390 and 1392 the communal treasury paid out 2,158,000 florins in war-related expenses alone and collected 1,473,000 florins in forced loans.[5] Although total military expenses for this war were possibly no higher than for the papal war, the sums collected in forced loans were much greater than the 580,000 florins assessed in the earlier conflict, when much of the cost was covered by confiscation of church property. Indirect taxes and levies on the contado were consumed by non-military expenditures, and thus even receipts of nearly a half million florins in forced loans each year were not sufficient. To cover the deficits, the commune had recourse to short-term, redeemable loans from wealthy citizens, sums of unprecedented magnitude that were repaid with substantially higher interest than the Monte paid on credits from forced loans. On one occasion in 1390 it contracted loans from eighty-two households for a total of 834,060 florins, the largest coming from Gucciozzo de' Ricci and his sons (40,000 florins), and ser Ristoro da Figline (30,000), a wealthy notary from the contado and founder of the Serristori lineage (whose first prior, probably not coincidentally, was in 1392). Lenders included both wealthy popolo, like the *speziale* Lorenzo di Vanni (8,000), and the cloth manufacturer Andrea di Maso (6,000), and members of the elite, led by Maso and Ugo Alessandri (20,000), Ardingo di Corso de' Ricci (16,000), Giovanni Castellani (15,000), and Donato Acciaiuoli (14,000).[6]

[3]   ASF, Provvisioni, Registri, 80, f. 69.
[4]   *Alle bocche della piazza*, pp. li–liii, 110, 112–13, 123.
[5]   Molho, *Public Finances*, p. 10.
[6]   Biblioteca Nazionale di Firenze, Fondo Panciatichi, 120, ff. 135–137v; Brucker, *Civic World*, pp. 143–4.

This was the beginning of the commune's dependence on its wealthiest citizens. In July 1395, during the second Visconti war, the government listed loans amounting to the astonishing sum of 1,169,819 florins from 501 lenders: an average of 2,335 florins per household, but with nearly half the total (574,600) coming from just fifty-two households that made loans of at least 5,000 florins and averaged 11,050. After the four Alberti brothers who outdistanced all others with 130,000 florins, came the Spinelli brothers from Castelfiorentino (25,000) and a mix of non-elite and elite lenders, including, among the latter, Forese Salviati (14,000), Vanni Castellani (13,000), Alessandro Alessandri (12,000), Filippo di Lionardo Strozzi (10,000), and Francesco di Palla Strozzi (9,500), and several (in some cases by now former) magnates. The Medici did not yet stand out among communal creditors: only one in 1395, Antonio di Funghello (6,000), and two in 1390, Michele, and Alamanno di Salvestro (respectively, 6,000 and 8,000). But it was no doubt a sign of things to come that in 1401 the commune turned to Giovanni di Bicci de' Medici, founder of the bank that created the family's immense fortune, for ready cash in the amount of 200,000 florins (reimbursed, of course) promised to the emperor-elect Rupert of Bavaria for help in the third war against Milan. The availability in Medici hands of such resources would later propel them to power.

Some Florentines were already fearful of the political consequences of prolonged war and its expense. One was Franco Sacchetti (1335–1400), the leading Florentine writer in the vernacular in the generation after Boccaccio and author of a collection of stories, the *Trecentonovelle*, that comment critically on contemporary politics. Sacchetti came from an old elite family, but during the papal war his cousin Antonio di Forese was one of the eight officials who administered the confiscation and sale of ecclesiastical property.[7] Franco himself served as envoy to one of Florence's mercenary captains in that war, Ridolfo Varano da Camerino, who figures in several of his stories (e.g., 38, 40, and 182) and is portrayed as clever with words but reluctant to lead his troops into battle. In another story (181), he has John Hawkwood contemptuously upbraid two friars for their greeting of "God grant you peace," accusing them of wishing away his livelihood: "Do you want God to let me die of hunger? Don't you know that I live by war and that peace would be my undoing?" Sacchetti denounces Hawkwood, who "well knew how to make sure there was little peace in Italy in his time," and mercenaries in general who do more damage to their employers than to each other and are the chief reason why "so many cities in Italy that were once free are now subject to lords. . . . Therefore let those few [cities] that live free, for they are few indeed,

[7] Brucker, *Civic World*, pp. 279–82; R. C. Trexler, "Who Were the Eight Saints?" *Renaissance News* 16 (1963): 89–94, reprinted in Trexler, *Dependence in Context in Renaissance Florence* (Binghamton, N.Y., 1994), pp. 35–40.

not succumb to the deceits of these professional soldiers. Let them remain at peace and suffer two and three provocations before deciding to go to war." Sacchetti wrote these stinging words in the 1390s when Hawkwood had already become legendary among Florentines: his death in 1394 was commemorated with an elaborate state funeral, attended by the entire political leadership and religious establishment, and the almost unheard-of honor of burial in the cathedral in the choir at the foot of the main altar.[8] But the polemic was not ad hominem. It was the entire professional cadre of career soldiers who "lived on war" that Sacchetti saw as dangerous and caused him to oppose any unnecessary war. In fact, in the summer of 1391, as the war was going badly, Sacchetti addressed a letter to the Standardbearer of Justice Donato Acciaiuoli, urging him to use all his influence to bring the conflict to a quick conclusion. Should he do so, Sacchetti says, he "would win the same glory bestowed on Brutus [the founder of the republic] who was called the second Romulus, because Romulus founded the city of Rome and Brutus preserved its liberty, [which] has no greater enemy than war with its expense. This is what has undone communes and popular governments, and our fatherland has twice experienced it. By God, may it escape the third time."[9] Sacchetti was perhaps alluding to the *signorie* of Charles of Calabria and Walter of Brienne, but in any event his fear that the real danger of war lay in fiscal demands that could undermine liberty was prophetic.

Forty years later, after the consequences feared by Sacchetti had become all too real, Alberti had his character Lionardo in *The Books of the Family* spell out the logic of Sacchetti's worries, underscoring how indispensable fiscal contributions from the wealthy were for Florentine power and expansion: "Those who with arms and blood defend the liberty and dignity of the fatherland cannot always be supported by funds from the public treasury alone. Nor, however, can republics extend their authority and empire without enormous expense. . . . According to what our Benedetto degli Alberti used to say, a public treasury will be most abundantly filled not by numerous sums of those owing money to the state or a large number of tax-paying households; a well-stocked public treasury is one that can claim the affection of all those citizens of at least moderate means, and to which all rich persons will be faithful and generous."[10] Benedetto's dictum about well-stocked public treasuries depending, especially during war, on the loyalty and generosity of the

---

[8]   *Alle bocche della piazza*, pp. 168–9.
[9]   A. Lanza, *Firenze contro Milano: gli intellettuali fiorentini nelle guerre con i Visconti (1390–1440)* (Rome, 1991), pp. 45–50, 163–4; Lanza, "La genesi etico-politica del 'Trecentonovelle'," in *Primi secoli: saggi di letteratura italiana antica* (Rome, 1991), pp. 139–66.
[10]   Alberti, *Della famiglia*, ed. Romano and Tenenti, pp. 171–2.

rich reflects what had begun to happen in Florence as early as the 1390s, when the Alberti themselves were the richest of the Florentine rich. Fiscal necessity was already beginning to narrow the inner circle of power: behind the broad office-holding class required by the politics of consensus, military expenses were concentrating power in the hands of those wealthy enough to underwrite them.

The first Milanese war ended in January 1392 but resolved nothing. Prospects for another war increased when Florence turned the tables on Milan by organizing Padua, Mantua, Ferrara, and Bologna into an anti-Visconti league. In October the Milanese responded by promoting a coup d'état in Pisa that removed a ruler friendly to Florence. Although further hostilities were avoided until 1397, in the intervening years the Florentines sought French help while Giangaleazzo looked to the emperor. Maso degli Albizzi and Rinaldo Gianfigliazzi used their influence to turn opinion within the ruling group toward a hard-line policy against Milan and had the major voices of restraint, Filippo Bastari and Donato Acciaiuoli, sent into exile, respectively, in 1394 and 1396, in both cases with accusations of being too close to the Alberti. In March 1397 war resumed and, with Giangaleazzo's troops devastating the Florentine contado and military expenses once again skyrocketing, it quickly became unpopular as the Council of the Popolo rejected one proposal after another for increased forced loans. In February 1398 the wealthy and largely apolitical merchant from Prato, Francesco Datini, wrote to his partners: "Truly, if we do not have peace, the merchants and guildsmen will be ruined by taxes. Note that we have to pay four or five forced loans each month. May it please God to give us peace quickly so that these levies will cease."[11] Datini claimed he was a citizen of Prato, but the officials of the gonfalone in which he resided in Florence declared that he was indeed a Florentine citizen and therefore subject to forced loans. Over a thirteen-year period he paid 19,500 florins, received approximately 5,750 in interest and returned principal, with net payments amounting to 13,750 florins.[12]

Despite another million florins spent in the second war, Maso degli Albizzi and the inner circle signed a peace agreement in May 1398 that once again left the struggle unresolved. Over the next two years Florentine control of Tuscany and Umbria collapsed as Pisa, Siena, Grosseto, Perugia, Cortona, Chiusi, Spoleto, and Assisi all submitted to Giangaleazzo. At the end of 1400, Lucca withdrew from the anti-Visconti league, leaving Bologna as the only major city in the region still allied with Florence. To make matters worse, in

---

[11]   Brucker, *Civic World*, pp. 144–65.
[12]   Molho, *Public Finances*, pp. 93–7; G. Ciappelli, "Il cittadino fiorentino e il fisco alla fine del Trecento e nel corso del Quattrocento: uno studio di due casi," *Società e storia* 12 (1989): 823–72 (842–3).

November 1400 the regime announced that it had uncovered a conspiracy involving both exiles and internal opponents. Two Ricci were implicated as leaders of a plot to eliminate the regime's inner circle and open the gates to the exiles and the Milanese, and others confessed that the plan had wide support among elite Florentines, including a Medici and the usual contingent of Alberti.[13] In these already inauspicious circumstances the Florentines were again disappointed when the hopes and money invested in the emperor-elect Rupert resulted, in the fall of 1401, in his defeat by the Milanese, who then turned their attention to Bologna. On June 26, 1402, Florentine forces were routed at Casalecchio, near Bologna, which was taken on the 30th. Bereft of allies, the Florentines prepared for an invasion of their territory and a possible siege of the city. For the rest of the summer they waited, making military preparations and seeking an alliance with Venice, until the news arrived on September 12 that nine days earlier Giangaleazzo Visconti had died of plague. Although the threat of invasion dissipated, the state of war continued and the hardliners within the regime now made plans to carry the war into Lombardy. Only in the next year did it become clear that, without its leader, the Visconti empire was breaking up and that the war was in effect over.[14]

Territorial Dominion: The Conquest of Pisa

Seeing one Tuscan city after another side with Giangaleazzo to escape Florentine domination convinced the ruling group that more coordinated control of the region was necessary to prevent a repetition of that experience, especially because territorial expansion had now become a prime objective of all major Italian states. Florence's territorial acquisitions before the 1380s had pushed sporadically beyond the old contado, mostly to the west, including Pistoia and the Monte Albano (1328–31), Pescia (1339), Prato and again Pistoia (1350–1), San Gimignano (1353), Volterra (1361), San Miniato al Tedesco (1370), and several smaller towns, all within a traditional Florentine sphere of influence. After the acquisition of Arezzo in 1384, a broader expansion of Florence's power brought Montepulciano (in 1390 and definitively in 1404), Pisa (1406), Cortona (1411), and Livorno (1421) under the rule of the republic, which thus became the capital of a regional empire.[15] The turning point in the development of the territorial state, the moment when hegemony in

---

[13] *Alle bocche della piazza*, pp. 218–21.

[14] Brucker, *Civic World*, pp. 165–99; Lanza, *Firenze contro Milano*, pp. 13–37.

[15] A. Zorzi, "The 'Material Constitution' of the Florentine Dominion," in *Florentine Tuscany: Structures and Practices of Power*, ed. W. J. Connell and A. Zorzi (Cambridge, 2000), pp. 6–31.

Tuscany emerged as a central objective of foreign policy, was the conquest of Pisa in 1406.

Partly because traditionally Ghibelline Pisa controlled the access to the sea that Florentine merchants coveted, these ancient rivals had fought a series of wars stretching back to the thirteenth century (1280s, 1315–16, 1340–2, and 1362–4). Seeking protection from Florence in the 1390s, Pisa too had allied with Giangaleazzo and was still in Visconti hands after 1402 when Gabriele Maria Visconti assumed rule.[16] At first, Florence avoided confrontation over Pisa and took the offensive against Visconti positions elsewhere in alliance with the Roman papacy. But when Pope Boniface IX's legate Baldassare Cossa recovered Bologna for the papacy and made a separate peace with Milan, the purpose of continuing the war in Lombardy evaporated. Now the Florentines turned to Pisa and made several unsuccessful offers to buy it. A first attempt to take the city by force in January 1404 also failed. Public opinion turned against the prospect of another war, and in June the councils terminated the semi-permanent war balìa of eighty-one created in 1393. Gabriele Maria accepted a French protectorate over Pisa administered by Marshall Boucicaut, governor of Genoa, who, however, willingly listened to offers of a deal that would have ceded Pisa to Florence for 200,000 florins. But when in July 1405 the Pisans learned of a meeting between Maso degli Albizzi and Gabriele Maria, correctly interpreting it as evidence that they were about to be betrayed into the hands of their ancient enemies, they took up arms with cries of "Viva il popolo e libertà," chased Visconti into the citadel (although he was quickly released), and proclaimed their independence. Although taking Pisa was now going to be much more difficult than they had anticipated, the regime's elite leaders, Rinaldo Gianfigliazzi, Filippo Corsini, and, after some hesitation, Maso degli Albizzi, favored going ahead with the purchase, and in August Pisa and its contado were sold to Florence for 206,000 florins (80,000 for Gabriele Maria and 126,000 for Boucicaut), but as a fief under French sovereignty. In the meantime Florence began hiring troops, despite opposition in the councils where nearly a third was opposed to rearming. An emergency council of 120 appointed a war balìa, which included Lorenzo Ridolfi, Niccolò da Uzzano, Filippo Magalotti, Rinaldo Gianfigliazzi, Cristofano Spini, and Bartolomeo Valori. Boucicaut handed over the citadel at Pisa on August 30, but on September 6 the Pisans attacked, overran the Florentine garrison, and occupied the citadel. A resolution by force was now inevitable; public opinion demanded an aggressive response and the angry priors ordered an investigation to determine culpability. In January 1406 a new balìa took office: Bartolomeo Corbinelli, Gino Capponi, Lotto Castellani, Lapo Niccolini, Niccolaio

---

[16] For what follows: Brucker, *Civic World*, pp. 187–208.

Davanzati, Bernardo Cavalcanti, and Maso degli Albizzi were the high command that conducted the war.[17]

Under the command of a Genoese captain, Florentine forces destroyed the Pisan countryside, blockaded and laid siege to the city, cut off supplies, and waited for surrender. Starvation was the main weapon, and the Florentines used it without mercy. A Florentine chronicler dwelt on "the many things done by the [war balìa], very cruel things, in order to have the city of Pisa." He recounted the painful details of women and children forced out of the city by the Pisans as "not useful persons," only to be driven back toward the walls by Florentine troops, refused re-entry by the Pisans, and forced to remain in the scorched area between the walls and the Florentine camp "eating grass like animals and dying of starvation." The Florentines executed anyone trying to bring grain into the city. Cruelties were committed inside the walls as well, as factions took contrasting views on whether to yield or fight to the death.[18] It took thirteen months for the Pisans to surrender. On October 9, 1406, Gino Capponi and Bartolomeo Corbinelli, representing the Dieci, rode into the city, took command, and distributed bread to the famished survivors. Although it consolidated Florentine domination of Tuscany, the conquest came at the cost of human suffering that the Pisans never forgot or forgave, as they made clear in 1494 when they again declared independence and defended it for fifteen years.

Florentine reactions to the conquest of Pisa were ambivalent. Obligatory celebrations, jousting, and processions with the sacred image of the Madonna of Impruneta, brought to the city only on the most solemn occasions, marked the victory. But behind the triumphalism some were aghast at the cruelty and gave signs of troubled conscience over what the republic had done. Acknowledging that hundreds died of starvation and that in a few more days they would all have been dead, Giovanni Morelli commented that Pisa could easily have been taken in an assault, with many lives spared, and expressed doubt about whether it was all worth it: "we didn't know and didn't want to know what honor or profit came of it."[19] Gregorio Dati wrote in his *History of Florence* (8.17.5–6) that the Florentines did what they did "because they were in the right according to the laws of the world and wanted what belonged to them, which they had bought from its lawful owner [Gabriele Maria]." But he also admired the Pisans for the obstinacy with which they defended their freedom: "Never was there a city in the world that held out until death in order not to be overcome as much as the Pisans did, or that knew how to

---

[17] *Cronica volgare di anonimo fiorentino*, ed. Bellondi, pp. 331, 333–4, 335–6, 342.

[18] Ibid., p. 351.

[19] Morelli, *Ricordi*, pp. 463–4; *Mercanti Scrittori*, ed. V. Branca (Milan, 1986), p. 297.

resist with so much determination and intelligence as they did." While believing that "might accompanied by right must always win," Dati did not ignore the sufferings endured by the Pisans: once the bread was gone, "they ate grass, cooked leaves, ground straw, and finally every terrible thing, including dogs, cats, other animals, and the excrement of horses. Nor were they spared the ultimate misery of eating human flesh, even worse than what happened in Jerusalem at the time of the emperors Titus and Vespasian. Adults and children fell dead from hunger every day, and the entire city was filled with grief. Speaking of it fills my heart with horror, because never from [the time of the Roman assault against Jerusalem] has there been such a siege" (8.8–9). The clear echoes here of Josephus' account of the siege of Jerusalem point to the uglier side of the Roman model. "Out of love for the Florentines," Dati added (8.22.9), "I pray God that He will give them the ability to know how to restrain themselves, and not spend money or engage in undertakings against others that would displease God."[20] His warning was about more than foolish spending: it was an admonition that, even with right and might, it was possible to go too far.

The last two big pieces of the territorial mosaic also came as purchases, but without the horrors inflicted on Pisa. In 1411, Cortona was bought for 60,000 florins in the midst of a war (1409–14) with King Ladislaus of Naples.[21] And because Pisa alone was not sufficient for access to the sea, in May 1421 nearby Livorno and Porto Pisano were bought from Genoa for 100,000 florins.[22] If the conquest of Pisa entailed a major reconfiguration of territorial power in Tuscany, the acquisition of Livorno had equally significant consequences of a different sort, as Florence now became a maritime power. Within the year, the government instituted the office of the Sea Consuls to oversee the construction and voyages of a merchant galley fleet, owned by the government and available to merchants who paid to have their goods transported. The first galleys sailed in the summer of 1422 for Alexandria, and within a few years the fleet grew to eleven great galleys and fifteen long galleys that made regular voyages to Italy's Tyrrhenian ports, the Levant, the Aegean, North Africa, southern France, Catalonia, and through the straits of Gibraltar to Southampton and Flanders.[23]

To justify this expanding regional hegemony, the same writers who extolled Florentine liberty also promoted an image of the republic as the bearer of

[20]   Goro Dati, *Istoria di Firenze*, in Lanza, *Firenze contro Milano*, pp. 271–6.
[21]   C. Perol, *Cortona: pouvoirs et sociétés aux confins de la Toscane, XVᵉ–XVIᵉ siècle* (Rome, 2004).
[22]   Brucker, *Civic World*, pp. 427–30.
[23]   M. E. Mallett, *The Florentine Galleys in the Fifteenth Century* (Oxford, 1967), pp. 11, 21–3, 26, 34, 153–76 (lists of voyages, types of vessel, ports of call, and officers).

imperial destiny,[24] a combination that might seem contradictory if it weren't so characteristic of expansionist republics, ancient and modern. Rome was the model, admired by humanists both as a free republic and as the greatest of imperial powers. For many Florentines of this generation, humanists and others, liberty and territorial dominion were linked as cause and effect: because liberty can only survive in a compatible environment, they reasoned, freedom-loving peoples who fight for their own liberty must also protect that of their neighbors. In 1377, during the papal war, Salutati had asserted that it was the ancient Roman republic's "desire for liberty alone that brought forth the empire, the glory, and all the dignity of the Roman people."[25] In 1400, responding to the accusation of the Milanese humanist Antonio Loschi that Florence's systematic suppression of its neighbors' liberties made its rhetoric of liberty hypocritical, Salutati argued that Florence was actually defending them from Milanese tyranny: "so that they would not be throttled by tyranny or despoiled of their ancient dignity, our city has snatched or rescued them from the hands of tyrants and constituted and established them subjects of the Florentines. Thus these peoples have either been born with us in liberty or brought by us to the sweetness of freedom from the bitter constraints of slavery. . . . You believe that the part of the Florentine citizenry which resides in the towns and fields outside the walls of the city, who enjoy freedoms you could never imagine, desires, instead of being subjects of our city, lives of slavery under your master. Such an attitude now is and, I hope, will always be considered the height of folly and madness for those whose greatest glory is to be called Florentines – because they are our people by birth, by right, and by the gift of fate."[26] Leonardo Bruni, in the *Panegyric to the City of Florence*, proclaimed that "to you, men of Florence, belongs by hereditary right dominion over the entire world and possession of your parental legacy. From this it follows that all wars waged by the Florentine people are most just," not only because, given its inheritance of world-wide dominion, Florence "necessarily wages war for the defense or recovery of its own territory," but also because the Florentines had committed themselves to a "struggle against tyranny" that

---

[24]   M. Hörnqvist, "The Two Myths of Civic Humanism," in *Renaissance Civic Humanism*, ed. J. Hankins (Cambridge, 2000), pp. 105–42; Hörnqvist, *Machiavelli and Empire* (Cambridge, 2004), pp. 38–75; and A. Brown, "The Language of Empire," in *Florentine Tuscany*, ed. Connell and Zorzi, pp. 32–47.

[25]   R. G. Witt, "The 'De Tyranno' and Coluccio Salutati's View of Politics and Roman History," p. 452; Witt, "The Rebirth of the Concept of Republican Liberty in Italy," in *Renaissance Studies in Honor of Hans Baron*, ed. A. Molho and J. A. Tedeschi (Florence, 1971), pp. 173–99 (196).

[26]   Coluccio Salutati, "Invectiva in Antonium Luschum Vicentinum," in *Prosatori latini del Quattrocento*, ed. E. Garin (Milan, 1952), pp. 30–3; trans. B. G. Kohl, in *Major Problems in the History of the Italian Renaissance*, ed. B. G. Kohl and A. A. Smith (Lexington, Mass., 1995), p. 275.

began "a long time ago when certain evil men undertook the worst crime of all – the destruction of the liberty, honor, and dignity of the Roman people. At that time, fired by a desire for freedom, the Florentines adopted their penchant for fighting and their zeal for the republican side."[27] Hence their wars were of necessity fought for the defense of liberty.

A much later but telling example of the effect on political discourse of the imperial dimension of fifteenth-century Florence's self-image was the decision of a Medici balìa in January 1459 to make a symbolic change in the name of the priorate, until then still the "priors of the guilds." The change was necessary because "it does not seem appropriate to the dignity, power, and prestige of the city of Florence and the *status* of its government and *regimen*" for its chief executive body to have "the title 'priors of the guilds', implying that they preside over humble and abject persons and base matters. When Florentine ambassadors and citizens are in the company of princes and lords, [this name] causes them to be held in lower esteem and to be less honored." According to the balìa, the old title had been instituted "when the city was small and had little or no territorial dominion [*imperium*] and the wealth of the citizens was meager." But "now that everything has changed and grown in such great measure, the title should be modified and elevated to the dignity and nobility of the office." Thus, "since the city of Florence has been established in a state of true and perfect liberty and is inferior to no other city or republic in its zeal, care, diligence, and passion for the cultivation, protection, and preservation of this liberty, as earlier times have clearly shown in so many and such great wars waged with such fortitude against those who have endeavored to oppress it, it would be not unworthy, indeed entirely consonant with reason, [for the priors] to take their name from that liberty," and henceforth be known as the "priors of liberty."[28] Although the city now had only a third of the population of the commune that created the "priors of the guilds," its territorial dominion was indeed much greater. Here again is the combination of "liberty" and "imperium" and the argument that Florentine devotion to liberty is proved by the "many and great wars waged with such fortitude" against its enemies. With the memory of the Pisan disaster dimmed by time (for the Florentines), the notion that empire served liberty could be invoked without guilt to bolster Florentine sovereignty. And, although the term had been used earlier, fifteenth-century Florentines now increasingly referred to the office of the priors

[27] Leonardo Bruni, *Laudatio florentinae urbis*, in H. Baron, *From Petrarch to Leonardo Bruni* (Chicago, 1968), pp. 232–63 (243–4); trans. B. G. Kohl, in *The Earthly Republic: Italian Humanists on Government and Society*, ed. Kohl and R. G. Witt (Philadelphia, 1978), pp. 135–75 (150–1).

[28] ASF, Carte strozziane, first series, 12, ff. 45–6; Balìe, 29, ff. 118v–119; R. Fubini, "Diplomazia e governo in Firenze all'avvento dei reggimenti oligarchici," in Fubini, *Quattrocento fiorentino: politica, diplomazia, cultura* (Pisa, 1996), pp. 11–98 (87–8).

and Standardbearer as the "Signoria," meaning lordship, and to the priors as "Signori," or lords.

Civic Humanism

Florence's victory over (or escape from) Visconti designs in Tuscany, its conquest of Pisa, successful expansion, and emergence as a maritime power imbued the republic with heady optimism and a heightened sense of destiny. Echoes of this buoyant mood resound throughout the period's political, patriotic, and historical writings, which have received much attention in modern scholarship. In what quickly became, after its publication in 1955, the most influential book of Renaissance and Florentine historiography in the twentieth century, Hans Baron linked the climax of the confrontation with Milan in 1402 to what he saw as a decisive turning point in Renaissance intellectual history. The "crisis," as he termed it, galvanized Florentine political attitudes into a civic ethos of participatory republicanism and converted many humanists from apolitical classicism to a patriotic defense of republican liberty. Baron argued that, whereas Salutati had been unable to sustain a commitment to the republican ideals to which he occasionally gave expression, after the 1402 crisis Bruni, first as a private scholar and then as chancellor, interpreted the wars against Milan as a conflict of republicanism against monarchical tyranny, in which the Florentines seized the historical and moral imperatives incumbent upon them as heirs of republican Rome. Baron called this cluster of political, historical, and ethical ideas "civic humanism" and located its various manifestations particularly in the two humanist chancellors (Bruni and Poggio Bracciolini), two citizen humanists (Cino Rinuccini and Matteo Palmieri), and the merchant and historian Gregorio Dati, who, although no humanist, shared their view of the Florentine defense of liberty. In addition to a spirited defense of republicanism and participatory citizenship, civic humanists promoted the theory of Florence's foundation by, and historical links to, the ancient Roman republic, a re-evaluation of Roman history that condemned Caesar and the emperors as "plagues and destroyers" of republican liberty, and the twin convictions that political liberty was indispensable to cultural and literary vitality and that citizens' active participation in civic life was essential to their moral development. In this generation, Baron believed, Florence's traditional commitment to civic life merged with humanism's appeal to the ethical exemplarity of antiquity to proclaim republicanism as a moral ideal.[29]

---

[29]   H. Baron, *The Crisis of the Early Italian Renaissance: Civic Humanism and Republican Liberty in an Age of Classicism and Tyranny*, 2 vols. (Princeton, 1955); revised one-volume edn. (Princeton, 1966).

Central to Baron's interpretation of the crisis of 1402 was his reconstruction of Bruni's literary production to show the full emergence of civic attitudes in texts written after the crisis and their absence from those that preceded it. Much of his analysis and the ensuing debates focused on the *Panegyric to the City of Florence*, whose florid praise of Florence's liberty and republican constitution Baron saw as reflecting the post-1402 confidence, and on the two *Dialogues to Pier Paolo Vergerio*, the first of which, he concluded, was written before 1402, the second after, and in a very different mood. In the first, Bruni describes (or invents) a debate between the elderly Salutati, who argues that the modern age rivals antiquity in literary and philosophical accomplishments, and a group of younger classical purists, among whom Bruni includes himself, who, assuming the superiority of antiquity, believe that modern scholars cannot debate philosophical issues until they have reassembled with painstaking exactitude the corpus of classical texts. Expressing this militant classicism in the dialogue is Niccolò Niccoli, a scholar who wrote little and whose dedication to the revival of pure Latinity leads him to contemptuously reject the great fourteenth-century writers, Dante, Petrarch, and Boccaccio, for their non-classical Latin and historical inaccuracies. Niccoli also offers a political criticism of Dante for condemning Caesar's assassin, Brutus, instead of praising him for attempting to save the Roman republic's liberty. According to Baron, the disdain in which Niccoli held Florence's already legendary fourteenth-century poets reflects the attitudes of classical humanists before the 1402 crisis. In the second dialogue, however, Niccoli partially reverses his arguments and admits that the fourteenth-century poets were indeed excellent writers, whose apparent inaccuracies stem from their allegorical appropriation of historical figures. Baron saw this reversal as evidence of at least Bruni's (if not the historical Niccoli's) conversion to the civic patriotism that dominated his writings for the next four decades. Debate has swirled around the dating of the texts; many believe that the *Dialogues* were not composed separately, that Niccoli's "recantation" is far less complete and less "civic" than it seemed to Baron, and that Bruni's purposes were to dramatize the tensions between his generation and Salutati, and also within the circle of young humanists, and in any case not to document his or Niccoli's conversion to a philosophy of civic liberty and the active life.[30] On the other

[30]   Leonardo Bruni, *Dialogi ad Petrum Paulum Histrum*, ed. S. U. Baldassarri (Florence, 1994); N. Gilbert, "The Early Italian Humanists and Disputation," in *Renaissance Studies in Honor of Hans Baron*, ed. Molho and Tedeschi, pp. 201–26; D. Marsh, *The Quattrocento Dialogue* (Cambridge, Mass., 1980), pp. 24–37; D. Quint, "Humanism and Modernity: A Reconsideration of Bruni's *Dialogues*," *Renaissance Quarterly* 38 (1985): 423–45; and R. Fubini, "All'uscita dalla scolastica medievale: Salutati, Bruni, e i 'Dialogi ad Petrum Histrum'," *ASI* 150 (1992): 1065–1103.

hand, the civic, republican, and anti-monarchical sentiments of the *Panegyric* and of other later Bruni texts, however much bathed in the excesses of imitated classical rhetoric, and the similar if more muted sentiments of the *Histories of the Florentine People*, can hardly be doubted. Bruni and the texts of the years surrounding 1402 were at the origin of civic humanism's emergence in modern historiography, but the larger historical problem must be approached from the vantage point of the development of Florentine political discourse, both in other writers, like Palmieri, Dati, and Morelli, and in the daily lexicon of Florentine political life.

One point beyond doubt is that the Florentines indeed saw Giangaleazzo Visconti as a mortal threat and the events of 1402 as a crisis in which the republic's "liberty" was at stake. Buonaccorso Pitti, certainly no humanist and disinclined to see things in ideological terms, was an elite insider and key negotiator in Florence's search for military help from both France and the emperor. Pitti wrote that the decision in March 1402 to stop funding the emperor "would have cost us our liberty had death not overtaken the Duke of Milan so shortly after his capture of Bologna. . . . Had he but beaten us, he would certainly have become the lord of Italy in a short time. He was on the verge of conquering us, since he was already master of Pisa, Siena, Perugia, Chiusi, and all their fortified towns." While the danger had been grave, according to Pitti, there is no triumphalism in his explanation of Florence's survival: "Thus it is his death that has saved us and made us grow in power until the present, as one can see, more by luck or the grace of God than by the virtue or wisdom of those who have governed us." For Pitti, the real danger lay in divisions among Florentines: "It seems to me that we have become puffed up with excessive pride and fallen into such great disorder that if the emperor or some other powerful lord should attack us in this disorder in which we exist (since the leaders of our ruling group are still in such discord as they seem to me to be, neglecting the common good and the honor of our commune for their factional interests and private feuds, and being at fault for admitting into the ruling group two kinds of citizens, new men and the young, who have become bold on account of the divisions they see among the leaders) I think little time would pass before this regime [*stato*] would be overthrown, unless God sees to it that our leaders make sincere peace among themselves, pull together for the common good, and stop impeding justice for their separate interests as they now do."[31]

Giovanni Morelli similarly emphasized the gravity of the military situation in 1402. When news of the Florentine defeat at Casalecchio and the occupation of Bologna by Visconti troops reached Florence, he wrote, "we seemed to be lost beyond hope, because we had no army left, in Florence food supplies

[31]   Buonaccorso Pitti, *Ricordi*, in *Mercanti scrittori*, ed. Branca, pp. 428–9.

would not have lasted two months, and the grain harvest was still stacked on the threshing-floors." Noting the eruption of factional divisions in Pistoia and the uprisings of feudal lords in the Mugello and of "Ghibelline exiles" in Arezzo, Prato, and Volterra, Morelli concluded that "if the duke had attacked us, as he could have, he could certainly have deprived us of the harvest and the whole of the *contado*; and the city would soon have been his, I believe." As a non-elite parvenu, Morelli was less inclined than Pitti to criticize the ruling group, but he too attributed the weakness of the Florentine position to internal divisions: "there was much discord within the city because of heavy taxes and recent events among the citizens. . . . The *contado* was more exhausted and impoverished than the city, and there was no peasant in the *contado* who would not have come gladly to burn down Florence." Morelli, as we know, had an exaggerated fear of peasants, but he may not have been wrong in suggesting that the overtaxed *contadini* would have welcomed the Visconti as liberators quite as much as the subject cities did. A few pages earlier he had recounted the alleged plot that led to the banishment of Donato Acciaiuoli in 1396, the Ricci conspiracy of 1400, and still another conspiracy in which members of the Ricci, Medici, and, of course, Alberti were accused of attempting to assassinate Maso degli Albizzi. Morelli twice says that the instigators of this uprising attempted to get the people behind them with cries of "long live the *popolo* and the guilds."[32]

Pitti and Morelli emphasized the danger of internal divisions accompanying the war (and sometimes generating protests against it) almost as much as they did the menace of Giangaleazzo's armies. Perhaps for this reason neither turned the Visconti wars into an ideological crusade for the liberty of Italy. By contrast, those who did, chiefly Bruni and Dati, ignored internal political difficulties and represented the Florentines as a community united in defense of liberty against foreign peril. Dati's *History of Florence* recounts "the long and great war that occurred in Italy in our time between the tyrant of Lombardy, the Duke of Milan, and the magnificent Commune of Florence."[33] Only occasionally does he hint at the cultural gulf between the ruling class and the rest of the population. For example, in reporting the effect of a hermit's prophecy that Giangaleazzo would die in 1402, he comments that "although the leading citizens [*maggiori cittadini*] gave it little credence, the *popolo*, which gives its

[32] Morelli, *Ricordi*, pp. 395–7, 372–3.
[33] Baron, *Crisis* (1966), pp. 167–88; Green, *Chronicle into History*, pp. 112–44; A. P. McCormick, "Toward a Reinterpretation of Goro Dati's *Storia di Firenze*," *Journal of Medieval and Renaissance Studies* 13 (1983): 227–50; C. Varese, "Una 'Laudatio Florentinae Urbis': La 'Istoria di Firenze' di Goro Dati," in Varese, *Storia e politica nella prosa del Quattrocento* (Turin, 1961), pp. 65–91; Lanza, *Firenze contro Milano*, pp. 86–96.

ear to such things, found some comfort in it" (5.5.12). Significant here is the changed meaning of "popolo," which Dati clearly uses to refer to the unsophisticated and uneducated, having evidently lost contact with its traditional usage to refer to his own class, the non-elite guildsmen. But in his account of the war it is "the Florentines" who "become aware of the insatiable appetite of the tyrant," "the Florentines" who "spread their wings over the whole world and get news and information from every corner" (3.1.1–2), in whose "hands alone the liberty of Italy rested," and whose spirit is so alien and averse to being defeated or subjected to others that they never had any doubt, and always believed they had many courses of action, like a brave and secure heart that never lacks a way or a remedy. And they always found comfort in the hope, which seemed to put the sense of certainty in their own hands, that the Commune cannot die and that the duke was only one mortal man whose state would die with him" (5.5.10–11). Dati explains the outbreak of the war solely in terms of Giangaleazzo's ambition to become "lord and king of Italy," an ambition thwarted by "the Florentines" who "became the hedge that never let him move any farther forward" (5.5.8). They succeeded in blocking him, he says, not because of greater military strength, but because of their superior ability to calculate the duke's overextension of his resources, which made them certain that his empire would fall apart as soon as the money began to run out and his hired soldiers deserted him. Time and again Dati stresses Florentine "ragione," which means reason, but also that particular kind of reasoning that has to do with accounts and finances. Here too it was "the Florentines," with no distinction of class or power, who employed this skill to save the city and the "liberty of Italy."

The desire to see "the Florentines" as a harmonious whole, a community united in political ideals and generously providing the wherewithal to pay for their defense, was no doubt a romanticized recollection at some years' distance from the war. But it may also have emerged from the conviction that only by suppressing the memory of internal conflicts would the republic be able to avoid them in the future: if the Florentines believed they had defeated Giangaleazzo because of their unity and dedication to the republic, they might actually develop such unity in facing future threats. Hortatory, as well as the purely celebratory, purposes also inform Bruni's humanist version of the same themes in the *Panegyric*. Like Dati, Bruni claims that "all Italy would have fallen under the power of the Duke of Lombardy had not this one city resisted his power with its troops and sound strategy." He represents the Florentines as a single collective will: "the stout Florentine heart could never know fear, nor could it ever consider surrendering any part of its honor." Because they knew "that it was a Roman tradition to defend the liberty of Italy against its enemies," the Florentines were prepared to protect the reputation bequeathed them by their ancestors. "It was with these things in mind that the Florentine people set out for war in great and high spirits." Bruni displaces the protests over the crushing burden of forced loans into a mythical willingness on the part of the Florentines to spend every soldo to defeat their hated enemy: "They could never place concern for their wealth before their own self-esteem. Indeed they were prepared to lose money and life itself to maintain their freedom. . . . Wealth and money and such things are the rewards of the victors. But those who think that in war they should conserve their wealth, thinking that they make themselves more secure with it, are in fact serving the interests of the enemy more than their own. With such high morale was this city endowed." Bruni acknowledges that no city, including Florence, "has ever been so well governed and established that it was completely without evil men," an oblique reference, it seems, to the conspiracies of the late 1390s and 1400. But he insists that the "perversity and evil of a few ought not to deprive an entire nation of being praised for its virtuous deeds." He thus marginalizes and criminalizes dissent, while insisting that in Florence, if not always elsewhere, there was no conflict between the views of the majority and those of the "best" citizens: "While in other cities the majority often overturns the better part, in Florence it has always happened that the majority view has been identical with [that of] the best citizens."[34] The assumptions that the republic had a better part ("melior pars") whose ideas found docile agreement within the majority, and that opposition was "perverse and evil," were deeply embedded in a vision of politics built around consensus; they emerged from the need to find unity in a society that had experienced deep social conflicts and fought a major war with these social and political antagonisms still very much apparent. Asserting the fundamental unity of all Florentines was wishful thinking, but of the kind that can powerfully affect political behavior.

Giovanni Morelli's reaction to domestic turmoil in the midst of war provides a glimpse of how the politics of consensus, from which civic humanism's assumptions about political participation sprang, functioned among non-elite guildsmen who were relinquishing their historic role as antagonists to the elite. Morelli came from a non-elite family of woolen cloth merchants whose first prior was his cousin Bernardo in 1387. Giovanni and his brother followed their father Paolo into the Wool guild in 1396.[35] Like other non-elites climbing the social ladder, Giovanni married into an elite family with a handicap: in

---

[34] *Panegyric to the City of Florence*, trans. B. G. Kohl, in *The Earthly Republic*, pp. 135–75 (166–7, 158); Latin text in Baron, *From Petrarch to Leonardo Bruni*, pp. 232–63; also Leonardo Bruni, *Laudatio Florentine Urbis*, ed. S. U. Baldassarri (Florence, 2000), pp. 21–2, 28–9.

[35] ASF, Arte della Lana, 99, f. 6v.

this case no less than the Alberti.[36] But he underestimated the risks of marrying Caterina Alberti in 1395, especially since the 1393 balìa had already exiled Caterina's great-uncle Cipriano. Morelli later lamented "that this marriage alliance deprived me of much honor I might have had from my commune." Aware of their lack of success in the scrutinies, in 1404 he and his brother moved to a different gonfalone to improve their chances and openly sought the favor of influential citizens. Without knowing whether these efforts had helped him, and before obtaining his first office (on the Sixteen) in 1409, he anxiously noted that the 1404 scrutiny displeased some elements of the ruling group "because of suspicions they had of many *popolani* whom they did not consider their friends."[37] Morelli's was the dilemma of the non-elite major guildsman trying to navigate among elite factions, insecure without a political base of his own, and dependent on favors for a small place in the political sun. His problematic marriage and slow-starting political career no doubt reinforced already cautious instincts to stay in the good graces of all. He noted that after each of the recent conspiracies the "stato" (the ruling group) consolidated itself by eliminating those suspect to it and increasing police forces to guard the "*stato* and the good citizens." "I have recalled these conspiracies for several reasons, and especially so that our [Morelli] descendants may take these as instructive examples and never work in any way against any *istato* or *reggimento*, being content to follow and support the wishes of the Signoria, and especially to place themselves in the hands of great men from old Guelf families; for you see the harm and shame that come to those who try to oppose them." He underscores the necessity of winning the good graces of the "better citizens," whether through marriage alliances or friendship, and of "leaning on someone in the ruling group, some powerful Guelf who is well thought of and free of suspicion. . . . Make him your friend by speaking well of him, helping him wherever you can, by going up to meet him and offering your services." One should cultivate such powerful men by asking their advice and inviting them to one's home. "Beyond this, always stand by those who hold and possess the palace and the rule of our city, and obey and follow their wishes and commands. Keep yourself from denouncing or speaking evil of their undertakings and actions, even if they are harmful. Stay silent, and depart from your silence only to praise them." Even listening to anything spoken

---

[36] On Alberti marriages: S. K. Foster [Baxendale], *The Ties That Bind: Kinship Association and Marriage in the Alberti Family, 1378–1428*, Ph.D. thesis, Cornell University, 1985; Foster Baxendale, "Exile in Practice: The Alberti Family In and Out of Florence, 1401–1428," *Renaissance Quarterly* 44 (1991): 720–56.
[37] Morelli, *Ricordi*, pp. 341, 430, 532; R. Ninci, "Lo 'Squittino del Mangione': il consolidamento legale di un regime (1404)," *Bullettino dell'Istituto Storico Italiano per il Medio Evo e Archivio Muratoriano* 94 (1988): 155–250.

"against those who rule" is imprudent; it is best to avoid the company of "malcontents," but one must report to the authorities immediately, and without second thoughts, anything one hears spoken against them.

Loyal support for the leadership of the "buoni uomini antichi" was accompanied in Morelli by a frank dislike of "parvenus, guildsmen, and people of modest stature" to whom he wished "prosperity, peace, and happy concord," but whose "reggimento" he did not like (an allusion to the popular government of 1378–82), "although having them to a certain degree mixed in is good for restraining excessively ambitious spirits." He lamented the pointlessness of the doubts the inner elite had about the scrutiny of 1404, because the only reason for disliking those who rule is if one is excluded: "I don't mean one who takes the office for his own evil purposes, but one who has conducted and continues to conduct himself well. Such a person should not be held in contempt or deprived of his honor. [But] if you do these things to him, he will have every reason to hate you." Morelli was making the case for the passively dutiful citizen who merits a share, if only a small one, of offices and "honors." To gain political honors, he needed to seek the favors of "those who rule" by showing them deference and "conducting himself well," to be a virtuous citizen in a political system in which virtue meant conduct acceptable to "those who rule." Morelli was reluctant to see his exclusion from office before 1409 as a function of broader political or social divisions. He could not imagine himself as representing interests or ideas opposed to those of the oligarchy and saw his misfortune as personal, as the result of a marriage that deprived him of what he considered his due in light of the virtuous conduct that in the end finally proved his worth and rewarded him with offices. The conclusion he drew from this experience was not about the social abyss that separated him from the regime's power brokers. It was rather about the importance of being a team player and the small victories that the acceptance of such a role made possible. He wanted to see only the harmonious whole; his "good conduct," political quiescence, and willingness to pay honor to the very oligarchs who had kept him on the sidelines proved to him that virtue would in the end merit honor. "I have recalled this in order to inform you of the methods one should employ to acquire the honor that the commune accords its citizens: doing good, obeying the laws, paying honor to the officials of the commune, to particularly respected citizens, to men of ancient families, and to persons of worth."[38]

---

[38]   Morelli, *Ricordi*, pp. 377, 274–6, 196, 430–1. On Morelli: C. Varese, "I 'Ricordi' di Giovanni Morelli," I and II, in Varese, *Storia e politica*, pp. 37–64; C. Bec, *Les marchands écrivains a Florence, 1375–1434* (Paris, 1967), pp. 53–75; and R. C. Trexler, *Public Life in Renaissance Florence* (New York, 1980), pp. 159–86.

Gregorio (or Goro) Dati was a silk merchant active in international trade and a non-elite member of Por Santa Maria in which, like his father Stagio, he served frequently as consul. Stagio was never selected for the priorate, despite a business partnership with the elite Castellani and several terms as his guild's representative on the Mercanzia's governing committee. Goro's uncle Manetto, a retail wine-seller and minor guildsman, made the family's first appearance in the priorate in 1380. When, in 1412 at age fifty, Goro gained his first major office (the Sixteen), he commented in his diary that until then he did not know whether he was among those approved for the highest offices. Recalling that his father's name had been drawn only after his death in 1374, Dati suggested in effect that the wait had lasted almost two lifetimes. He recognized and accepted his subordinate position in political life: now that he knew he was eligible for major offices, he felt he had "received a great favor" and would have been willing to trade the possibility of additional offices for the opportunity to sit just once on a major executive committee. It was, in other words, more important to him to know that he was considered worthy of office by those who made such decisions than to have an active role with real influence in government. Ironically, he manifests his worthiness by relinquishing all desire for such a role: "In order not to appear ungrateful, and not wishing to stimulate an insatiable ambition which, whatever it achieves, only wants still more, I have decided and resolved that from now on I must never implore favors from anyone" in order to be approved in the scrutinies, "and will instead leave such matters to those who oversee them and let happen to me whatever may please God. Henceforth, whenever my name is drawn for any communal or guild office, I promise to obey and not to refuse the burden and to do as well as I can and know how. In this way I will ward off the vice of ambition and presumption and will live as a free man and not as a slave for favors." Despite this firm resolve to steer clear of the temptation to seek patrons and favors, Dati revealingly specifies the penalties he will impose on himself "in the event I should do otherwise," as presumably he did, since he was subsequently elected prior in 1425 and Standardbearer of Justice in 1429.[39]

Dati understood the citizen's duty and the honor of office in remarkably passive and deferential terms. Contrary to the homogeneity of "the Florentines" in the *Istoria*, in his private diary he explicitly accepts the gulf in politics between "those who oversee" things and make the decisions, and from whom favors are sought and received, and those, like himself, who only had to decide whether to play the game of political mendicancy by imploring favors and patiently waiting for an occasional office. He exhibits the paradox of

---

[39] Gregorio Dati, *Il libro segreto*, ed. C. Gargiolli (Bologna, 1869), pp. 71–3; *Two Memoirs of Renaissance Florence: The Diaries of Buonaccorso Pitti and Gregorio Dati*, ed. G. Brucker, trans. J. Martines, (New York, 1967), pp. 125–6.

the non-elite "good citizen" who embraces the ethic of the active political life while recognizing that it turns him into a "servant" of upper-class political bosses. The historian who sang the heroic deeds of the Florentines in the Visconti wars and lauded his city's defense of liberty represented his own political career as essentially devoid of any purposes or ideas. About his term on the Ten of Liberty in 1405, for example, he said that "I pleased everyone and acted as rightly as I was able." His term on the Twelve in 1421 elicited the comment that "no greater unanimity could be found than that which reigned amongst us." He accepted to serve as podestà of two towns in the dominion in 1424 in order to leave the city during a recurrence of plague and remembered the experience as one in which, "by God's grace, none of us got sick" and during which "I acquired little wealth . . . but was highly esteemed by the inhabitants." And about his term as Standardbearer of Justice in 1429, he commented that "we worked harmoniously together and accomplished a number of good things," of which he mentions only the decision to move a column from the Mercato Vecchio to Piazza San Felice. The only office for which he even hints at a policy he supported was his appointment to the Five Defenders of the contado and the district in 1422: "an onerous office, in which . . . we did a great deal to improve the lot of the unfortunate peasants."[40] Dati's overriding concern was for harmony and cooperation on the committees on which he served, to "please everyone," and to be seen as having "acted rightly." He advocated no policies, represented no interests, expressed no grievances, and proposed no reforms. The *vita activa civilis* of civic humanism was supported by hundreds of men like Goro Dati who saw their role in politics in these passive terms.

Loyalty, deference, personal worthiness, acquiescence in the leadership of those born to it: these are likewise the civic virtues heralded by Bruni. In 1428, shortly after becoming chancellor, he wrote a funeral oration for Nanni Strozzi, a professional soldier from the Ferrara branch of the Strozzi who was killed leading Ferrarese troops in alliance with Florence against Milan. Here too Bruni lauded Florence's constitution, describing it as "popular" because it secured "liberty and equality" for all citizens (a liberty "limited only by the laws and free of fear") and because "the hope of attaining office and raising oneself up is the same for all." Expanded numbers of eligible citizens and officeholders may have given this claim a degree of verisimilitude, but the "hope of attaining office" was not of course the same for all, even for all those approved in the scrutinies. Bruni omits any mention of the borsellino and the two-tiered system of eligibility it institutionalized. Yet the examples of Morelli and Dati show that the hope they nourished for so long of someday obtaining an important office strongly conditioned their political behavior and attitudes.

---

[40]   *Two Memoirs*, ed. Brucker, pp. 128, 133, 136–7.

Bruni may have been echoing an illusion, but it was an illusion that mattered. He understood that the hope to which he pointed engendered a commitment to dutiful citizenship grounded in personal worth: it demanded that citizens "show diligence, skill, and a serious and morally acceptable way of life, for our city requires in its citizens virtue and uprightness of character. Anyone who has these things is considered of sufficient birth to govern the republic."[41] This is the same link that Morelli and Dati made between personal and civic virtue. And the sign of that virtue was cooperation with and deference to the leadership. That Bruni was arguing for the superiority of republicanism and the active life is only one (and perhaps not the most original) of his contributions to Florentine political discourse. He was also legitimating a new oligarchic republicanism in which good citizens (of the popolo) respected their "betters" (within the elite).

Bruni's most celebrated model of virtuous citizenship is the largely fictional Dante of the little "biography" written in 1436, circulated in many manuscripts, and later widely printed. Choosing Dante to illustrate the humanist ideal of citizenship was tricky, because the historical Dante was an angry exile who hurled one invective after another at the city that banished him and derided Florentine claims to political sovereignty. For Dante, republican autonomy constituted criminal rejection by an arrogant city in rebellion against divinely instituted imperial authority. But Dante was also the author of the greatest poem in the Florentine language, a work that did as much as the republican tradition to fashion the city's cultural identity.[42] Humanists who accepted the legitimacy of imperial authority, like Salutati in the *De Tyranno*, had no difficulty praising Dante for both his political views and his poetry. But what was a republican civic humanist like Bruni to make of the tensions of Dante's legacy? Bruni turns Dante's life into a cautionary tale in the deceptively simple biography. Rejecting Boccaccio's representation of Dante's life and poetry as the products of turbulent emotions of love, Bruni depicts Dante – before the exile – as a virtuous citizen who fought in the commune's army and held political offices, and as a family man who married and raised children. Civic duties and family responsibilities reinforce each other in this idealized portrait, because, as Bruni paraphrases Aristotle's notion of the city as a family writ large, "man is a social animal," and "his first joining, from the multiplication of which is born the city, is husband and wife, and nothing can be perfect where this is lacking."

---

[41] Baron, *Crisis* (1966), pp. 556–7, translation mine. Cf. *The Humanism of Leonardo Bruni: Selected Texts*, ed. G. Griffiths, J. Hankins, and D. Thompson (Binghamton, N.Y., 1987), pp. 121–7.

[42] S. Gilson, *Dante and Renaissance Florence* (Cambridge, 2005); on Bruni's *Vita*, pp. 112–24.

Bruni acknowledges that Dante's banishment was imposed by "a perverse and iniquitous law." But he portrays Dante in exile as abandoning the restraint inculcated by citizenship and marriage: at first "he tried with good works and good behavior to regain the favor that would allow him to return to Florence" (an echo of Morelli's advice about winning the favor of the powerful), but he fatally lost patience when Emperor Henry VII came to Italy. Dante "could not maintain his resolve to wait for favor, but rose up in his proud spirit and began to speak ill of those who were ruling the land, calling them villainous and evil and menacing them with their due punishment through the power of the emperor." When Henry died, "Dante entirely lost all hope, since he himself had closed the way of a change of favor by having spoken and written against the citizens who were governing the republic," thus making himself responsible for turning an unjust sentence into a justly permanent exile. For Bruni, even innocent exiles owed obedience, respect, and deference to the republic and to those who "ruled the land." Dante's failure to honor this obligation left the city's rulers with no choice but to banish him for life. Good citizens controlled the passions and exercised self-discipline. Domestication of the passions was also central to the kind of poet Bruni wanted to believe Dante was. "One may become a poet," he says, in two ways: either through "incitement and motion of personal genius by some inner and hidden force, which is called 'furor' and having one's mind possessed," or "through knowledge and study, through learning and art and prudence." Even as he admitted that the first is the way to "the highest and most perfect kind of poetry," Bruni concluded that Dante was a poet of "the second sort," for "he acquired the knowledge which he was to adorn and exemplify in his verses through attentive and laborious study of philosophy, theology, astrology, arithmetic, through the reading of history and through the turning over of many different books."[43] What might seem an odd judgment of Dante as a poet was in fact integral to Bruni's purposes. In both politics and poetry he wanted citizens whose attitudes and behavior were shaped by the consensus, sociability, and discipline of a civic world that sought to banish dissent with a new politics of personal virtue.

The Civic Family

A generation and more younger than Dati, Morelli, and Bruni, Matteo Palmieri is in many ways the most instructive example of the wider influence of civic

[43] H. Baron, *Leonardo Bruni Aretino: Humanistisch-Philosophische Schriften* (Leipzig, 1928), pp. 50–63; trans. A. F. Nagel in *The Three Crowns of Florence: Humanist Assessments of Dante, Petrarca, and Boccaccio*, ed. A. F. Nagel and D. Thompson (New York, 1972), pp. 57–73, reprinted in *The Humanism of Leonardo Bruni*, ed. Griffiths et al., pp. 85–95.

humanism. Neither professional humanist nor chancellor, yet thoroughly versed in the ancient texts that constituted the "studies of humanity," Palmieri came from a non-elite family and grew up in a Florence confident of its newly won preeminence in Tuscany and conquest of Pisa (of which he wrote an account in the rhetorical Latin characteristic of humanist historiography[44]), and increasingly drawn to the history and literature of ancient Rome in its educational and cultural life and political discourse. His vernacular dialogues *On Civic Life*, written in the 1430s, begin with a paean to republican virtue: in an unstable world, "the most nearly perfect life seemed to me to be one of some fine republic where men hold to such a degree of virtue that they can live with dignity in their daily lives without error or danger." For instruction in the "arts and disciplines" essential to such an existence, Palmieri considered the great fourteenth-century writers inappropriate: Dante's works are too obscure, Petrarch's too difficult for beginners, and Boccaccio's unfortunately filled with "lascivious and dissolute examples of love." It was in the Latin and Greek authors that he found an abundance of "precepts appropriate to teaching the best civic life." However, given the inaccessibility of the original texts to those without Latin and Greek and the poor state of the translations, Palmieri decided to write his own book of civic instruction and guidance in the vernacular "to show the tested way of virtuous citizens with whom one has lived and could live on earth." He selected Agnolo Pandolfini, "an old and well-instructed citizen," as the spokesman for this civic wisdom, and two young men from the elite families of the Sacchetti and Guicciardini, "two of the best youths of our city," as Pandolfini's eager listeners and questioners.[45] The choice of interlocutors is itself reflective of the roles played by elite and popolo in humanism's impact on Florentine society. Although Pandolfini achieved a position of respect in the ruling group and was a frequent speaker in the pratiche, his was not an elite family: they immigrated from the contado in the fourteenth century, Agnolo's grandfather was a notary, his father a silk merchant, and the family had its first prior at the end of the popular government in January 1382. The selection of the older "new man," learned in the classical texts and imbued with civic ideals, as the teacher of two young members of more ancient and prestigious families subtly underscores the popolo's historically deeper attachment to both humanism and the civic ethos, and the elite's still incomplete refashioning through these cultural and political discourses.

It was in this generation that elite Florentines first began routinely to be educated in the *studia humanitatis*.[46] Roman historians, moralists, playwrights,

---

[44]   Matteo Palmieri, *La presa di Pisa*, ed. A. Mita Ferraro (Bologna, 1995).

[45]   Matteo Palmieri, *Vita civile*, ed. G. Belloni (Florence, 1982), pp. 3–10.

[46]   R. Black, *Humanism and Education in Medieval and Renaissance Italy* (Cambridge, 2001), and P. F. Grendler, *Schooling in Renaissance Italy: Literacy and Learning, 1300–1600* (Baltimore, 1989).

and rhetoricians became central to the elite's educational curriculum as never before. Humanists made more texts available (e.g., Cicero's *Letters to His Friends*, Plautus' lost plays, and the full text of Quintilian's *Education of the Orator*), and demand for such works (and for better Latin translations of Plutarch's popular *Lives*) increased within the Florentine political class. Members of the elite became amateur humanists of considerable distinction. Palla di Nofri Strozzi joined Bruni and other young humanists to study Greek with the Byzantine scholar Manuel Chrysoloras in 1397 and later translated Greek and Latin works and built a major manuscript collection. Antonio Corbinelli also studied Greek, was a friend and "companion of study" of the famed humanist educator Guarino Guarini and assembled one of the great collections of manuscripts of classical works, including many in Greek. Nicola di Vieri de' Medici, son of the family's politically most prominent member in the 1390s and Cosimo's fourth cousin, likewise collected manuscripts and befriended humanists, including Bruni (who dedicated a translation of Demosthenes to him) and Alberti (who included him as an interlocutor in the *Profugiorum ab aerumna libri*). Cosimo de' Medici himself studied with the humanist Roberto de' Rossi, put together the greatest of all libraries of classical works, took part in discussions led by the Camaldolese humanist Ambrogio Traversari, and became the age's most famous patron of humanist learning. And Alessandro Alessandri, another of Rossi's students, was the dedicatee of Palmieri's *On Civic Life*.[47] Many more could be mentioned, as the cultural and social history of the Florentine elite became inseparable from the influence of humanism. Professional humanists, who did the serious classical scholarship, wrote the important books, and served as chancellors, were for the most part not from the elite; they came either from humble origins in the dominion (Salutati from Buggiano near Pescia, Bruni, Marsuppini, and Accolti all from Arezzo, and Poggio from Terranuova Bracciolini in the upper Valdarno) or from non-elite families in the city: Niccolò Niccoli's family were cloth manufacturers but enjoyed neither wealth nor political standing after 1400; and Giannozzo Manetti, although he became quite wealthy, came from a family of money-changers who were among the mid-fourteenth-century "new men." The relatively few humanists with elite origins were either magnates (e.g., Roberto de' Rossi) or exiles (chiefly Alberti, who was also illegitimate and whose humanist education was entirely non-Florentine). By Palmieri's time, humanism

---

[47] L. Martines, *The Social World of the Florentine Humanists, 1390–1460* (Princeton, 1963), profiles of 45 "men connected with Florentine humanism," pp. 303–50 (316–18, 319–20, 323–4, 326–7, 329–30); J. Hankins, "Cosimo de' Medici as a Patron of Humanistic Literature," in *Cosimo "il Vecchio" de' Medici 1389–1464*, ed. F. Ames-Lewis (Oxford, 1992), pp. 69–94; D. V. Kent, *Cosimo de' Medici and the Florentine Renaissance* (New Haven and London, 2000), pp. 21–7, 33–8.

had a growing elite readership that eagerly accepted his popularization of ancient wisdom concerning the virtues and proper conduct of good citizens in a republic.

Borrowing heavily from Cicero's *On Duties* and Quintilian's *Education of the Orator*, Palmieri's *Vita civile* elucidates the ideal citizen's moral formation and obligations to the republic in both private life and politics. Central to Pandolfini's instruction is that the citizen officeholder must "not think of himself as a private person, but as representing the juridical [or corporate] person of the whole city [*rapresentare l'universale persona di tutta la città*] and as having been transformed into a living republic. He should know that the public dignity has been entrusted to him, and the common good left to his good faith." To "represent the *universale persona*" of the whole city echoes the old language and theory of corporate association and representation, of the commune as an *universitas* endowed with a fictive, legal personality. But the notion had become detached from its original context and now served to anchor moral exhortations to unity and consensus. Officeholders, says Pandolfini, must remember two principal ideas taught by Plato and conveyed by Cicero: to keep the utility of the citizens foremost in all they do; and to "preserve the body of the republic." Thus, "the foundation of every republic rests on civic unity [*unione civile*]," and he who does not observe these precepts and "promotes the welfare of some against others sows the seeds of scandal and the most serious animosities, from which erupt internal wars and divisions" ending in exiles, rebellions, slavery, and tyranny. As the Greek cities succumbed to internal dissension and lost their liberty to Philip of Macedon, so Florence similarly has allowed internal conflicts (Pandolfini mentions Guelfs and Ghibellines and Black and White Guelfs) to bring it perilously close to the permanent loss of liberty to Charles of Valois, Robert of Naples, Charles of Calabria, and Walter of Brienne: "civil conflicts are what have always undone and will always undo republics."

Underlying such conflicts, according to Palmieri's spokesman, is "unjust government." Indeed, the first task of justice is to "equitably confer political offices ... according to each man's dignity." Pandolfini acknowledges that elite and popolo had always had different ideas about how this "dignity" ought to be defined. "The nobles and the powerful say that dignity resides in great wealth and in old and magnanimous families," whereas the "popolari" say that it consists in the "*humanità* and benevolent sociability of a free and peaceful social existence." Even in these studied generalities, Palmieri accurately captures the disagreement between the classes, and, because their divergent views led to so many "civil conflicts," he opts for neither opinion. Instead, he has Pandolfini prefer the definition of dignity offered by "wise men" who say that it resides in "active virtue [*operativa virtù*]." "Let those whose responsibility it will be to distribute offices in the city follow the most approved advice and award the offices to the most virtuous. For nothing is more worthy among men than the virtue of those who work for the public good." Citizens who base their claim to offices on the deeds of their ancestors deprive themselves of any right to honor: "Let him who merits honor give proof of himself, not of his family members." This might seem like an argument against the elite, but Palmieri is quick to have his speaker add that where "the claims of virtue are equal, nobility is always to be preferred." Although he insists that "no one should disdain being governed by virtuous men from humble beginnings and unknown family origins," his examples from Roman history make it clear that such men were and always would be exceptions.[48] Implicit in Palmieri's discussion is the assumption that virtue is the only path of entry into civic life for "popolari," who gain offices exclusively through the recognition of personal merit by social betters. In the republic of virtue, which supplanted the republic of interests, "virtue" meant demonstrating personal worth to those with the power to reward it. It was a useful political discourse for a ruling elite that needed to accept the Datis and Morellis into office, thus maintaining the fiction of "popular" rule, but without admitting them to a share of power, and civic humanists buttressed it with the authority of antiquity and the examples of virtuous Romans. It appealed to both elite and popolo for different reasons. For the popolo, it provided consolation for the loss of power by redefining its new passivity as virtue and good citizenship and ennobling its acceptance of elite hegemony. For the elite, it reinforced its self-image as a natural aristocracy of citizen fathers by underscoring the affinities it wanted to see (and wanted others to see) between itself and the idealized virtues of Roman civic and moral life: patriarchy, patriotism, and *pietas*.

This transformation of political discourse gradually accustomed Florentines to thinking of their republican polity as a family writ large and of its elite governors as the collective fathers of the civic family: a revolution in language that shaped political assumptions for the rest of the century, culminating in the posthumous designation of Cosimo de' Medici as "pater patriae" (father of the fatherland). It also affected the ways Florentines thought about their families, fathers, and paternal authority. Family and republic began to be thought of as species within the same genus, as governed by the same, or similar, obligations of deference and obedience, and by the same norms of benevolent power wielded by the possessors of such authority. For two hundred years the popolo had sustained a political discourse of the republic as a guild writ large, as a fraternal association of equals, and thus antithetical to notions of "natural" hierarchy. As guild republicanism was delegitimated, the popolo gradually absorbed into its political language an idealization of elite lineages as exemplary communities of rational decision-making and naturally

---

[48]   Palmieri, *Vita civile*, pp. 131–8.

benign leadership. It began with Stefani in the 1380s, who not only insisted that artisans and laborers were incapable of rational political action but also praised the "wisdom, gentility, and order" of the "grandi," among whom he believed it was easy to achieve agreement "because they revere the wisest person of their line, or, at most, the wisest few." Precisely because there are "fewer of them to be convened and consulted," they can discuss their affairs and bring their wishes and desires into harmony (553). Even in their private behavior, or some romanticized perception of it, elite families began to function as models of republican government in which the experienced few should always rule with the deference and passive agreement, or consensus, of those who willingly recognize them as benevolent fathers. The family, or rather that particular image of it based on uncontested but beneficent paternal authority, was the perfect metaphor for an oligarchic republicanism in which a relatively small group of elite families and leaders legitimated their power, not through processes of active consent or representation of divergent interests, but with the acquiescence of thousands of individuals willing to see the elite's authority as an extension of the kind of paternal power that they too, or so they were told, should exercise within their own households.

Civic humanists took up the metaphor and made the analogy more explicit. In the *Panegyric* Bruni lauded the Florentine constitution by claiming that "under these magistracies this city has been governed with such diligence and competence that no household [*domus*] was ever organized with greater discipline [*disciplina*] by a solicitous father." "Disciplina" here signifies the learning or knowledge that fathers bring to their duties, the instruction they impart to those over whom they exercise responsibility, the obedience owed by the latter, and the regulation and surveillance to which they are subject, with the hint of punishment for failure to acquiesce. Bruni's "disciplina" is simultaneously culture, education, power, and conformity to authority. A republic so conceived serves the interests of its ruling class, not only by likening its power to the unquestioned natural authority of fathers, but also by entrusting to government the responsibility of socializing its citizen/children in civic norms. Bruni also applied the metaphor of paternal authority to the Florentines' relationship to their Roman "parents": "If the glory, nobility, virtue, grandeur, and magnificence of the parents can also make the sons outstanding, no people in the entire world can be as worthy of dignity as are the Florentines, for they are born from parents who surpass by a long way all mortals in every sort of glory." And in arguing that Florence could legitimately pursue territorial ambitions as a "possession of [this] paternal legacy,"[49] Bruni suggested that even the subject territories had their place in the metaphor of the state as a patriarchal family.

---

[49]   *Laudatio*, ed. Baldassarri, pp. 33, 15; trans. Kohl, *Earthly Republic*, pp. 150, 173.

In the first book of the *Vita civile* Palmieri outlines the duties of fathers in educating their children. At its conclusion, Luigi Guicciardini asks a question that brings to the surface the assumptions, but also the anxieties, surrounding the expanding notions of paternal authority: "Must good sons always obey their fathers, or, [if not] in what things?" Pandolfini thinks the question a useful one because he "understands that any law of human obedience resembles obedience to fathers." Paternal authority, in other words, is the model for all forms of political power. He tells a story about a conversation he had as a young student with two others, one of whom insisted that obedience to a father's commands admits of no exceptions, because we must always obey him to whom we are most obligated. His other companion asserted the seemingly perverse opinion that a father should never be obeyed, because, if a father commands honorable things, we do them, not because he so commands, but because to do so is "virtuous and just"; if he orders us to do evil things, we must not do them at all. And in neither case must a father be obeyed. They took the dilemma to their teacher, who resolved it by rejecting both arguments and asserting that the proper application of paternal authority is not in things already judged to be virtuous or vicious, but rather in the indeterminate matters between these extremes. "Things that are honorable and right in themselves, like loving virtue, defending the fatherland, and preserving friendship, must be done in any event, whether one's father commands them or not," and bad things must never be done, whatever one's father may order. "It is only with regard to the things in between, things that in and of themselves are neither honorable nor dishonorable, but which are approved or disapproved on the basis of how they are done, that one must obey one's father: such as when fathers tell their sons to go live at the country house, or enter into a useful marriage alliance, dress as he does, accompany him whenever he wants . . . and similar things. Not to do such things [when ordered by one's father] would be blameworthy and wicked." It is an extraordinary conclusion: the authority of fathers has its proper, and unquestioned, place in matters like residence, marriage, dress, and travel for which there are no moral absolutes, only family customs and interests (and paternal egos) to be protected. It was, if anything, an even more exaggerated notion of paternal authority than that limited to the duty to urge sons to do what is right and to punish them for doing what is wrong.

Pandolfini says that he and his companions were satisfied with their teacher's answer, which encouraged them to ask yet one more question: "if a son is in some public magistracy, and his father is a private citizen, which of them is to have precedence and to be more honored?" The question tantalizingly implies that a son in office whose father is a private citizen constitutes an inversion of the natural or expected order in which fathers rule both at home and in the republic. The boys' teacher speaks as a good civic humanist: "in public and political solemnities, meetings, and ceremonies, paternal rights and authority must yield and pay honor to the dignity of the son." But "in private gatherings for family occasions, the public honor of the son should be set aside, and the natural honor of the father must again be first and more worthy."[50] Fathers must rule in their own domestic spheres, and even the governors of the republic never emerge from the shadow of paternal authority and discipline.

[50]   Palmieri, *Vita civile*, pp. 55–7.

8

Family and State in the Age of Consensus

The Family Imaginary

Florentines seem to have reflected more on family life in the fifteenth century than at any other time, an impression that may derive from the survival in larger numbers from this period of that quintessentially Florentine genre, the memoir or book of *ricordanze*. But even within the genre there was heightened concern with the nature of family relations and their affective dimension. *Ricordanze* began in the fourteenth century chiefly as records of property accumulation and mercantile activity, and then expanded to include genealogies, records of marriages and births, and comments on emotional bonds, typically combining family history, civic chronicle, and personal memoirs with advice and admonition to children and heirs.[1] From roughly the mid-fourteenth to the mid-sixteenth century, scores, perhaps hundreds, of such books have survived from both the elite and upper ranks of the popolo, and, together with private letters, they constitute the most important sources for the history of upper-class families. But increasing attention to the family is also evident in government policies and legislation that addressed a variety of problems faced by Florentine families. Paradoxically, Florentines of this era both idealized the family and looked to government to resolve its deficiencies.

Perceptions, even the very meaning, of family varied enormously across the social spectrum. Within the elite, "family" could mean different things: the assemblage of all those bearing the same surname, including lateral branches,

---

[1] Jones, "Florentine Families and Florentine Diaries"; Bec, *Les marchands écrivains*; G. Ciappelli, "Family Memory: Functions, Evolution, Recurrences," in *Art, Memory, and Family*, ed. Ciappelli and Rubin, pp. 26–38.

often called, in a curious metonym, the "casa" (house), or "consorteria"; the agnatic lineage, or patriline, limited to the branches whose descent from a common known ancestor was recent and well established; and the household, the domestic residential unit of those who lived under one roof, but which also had a number of variations, including the nuclear family of parents with minor children, the patriarchal family of elderly parents and grown children (possibly already married), and the joint-fraternal family of brothers.[2] Despite their primary focus on agnates, Florentines were also intensely aware of cognatic kin (through their mothers) and affinal kin (acquired in marriage alliances). Donato Velluti reconstructed the precise relationships of all descendants, both men and women, of his great-grandfather Bonaccorso and also traced his cognatic and affinal kin, naming wherever he could the children (who belonged of course to other lineages) of Velluti women and extending his research to the marriages and children of the in-laws he acquired through his wife, Bice Covoni. Buonaccorso Pitti likewise emphasized the antiquity of his patriline, which he traced back eight generations, and like Velluti he too recorded the lineages with which Pitti men and women had formed marriage alliances. Even as his attention to cognates and affines was mostly limited to his and his father's generations, he still managed to name almost 400 persons as he surveyed ninety-four marriage alliances (*parentadi*) with seventy-four lineages (including several into which the Pitti married more than once), thus providing his children with a list of families on which he believed they could rely for help.[3] That quite distinct notions of family relations could coexist, for different purposes, in the consciousness of the same person emerges from the contrast between two lists compiled by Giovanni Rucellai: a reconstruction of "the descent of our family" over thirteen generations, embracing 197 persons, mostly men, with only occasional mention of the women who married into the Rucellai and produced all those men; and a record of the patriline's marriage alliances, beginning with the generation of his paternal grandfather, including not only the women who married the men of the patriline but also these women's siblings and the siblings' marriage alliances, altogether a list of 462 persons (345 men and 117 women) that highlights the extensive horizontal networks generated by marriage alliances.[4]

[2] F. W. Kent, *Household and Lineage in Renaissance Florence: The Family Life of the Capponi, Ginori, and Rucellai* (Princeton, 1977).

[3] A. Bloch, "Marriage Alliance and Political Survival in the Early Quattrocento: An Examination of the Memoir of Buonaccorso Pitti." My thanks to Professor Bloch for permission to report some of the conclusions of her unpublished paper.

[4] A. Molho, R. Barducci, G. Battista, and F. Donnini, "Genealogy and Marriage Alliance: Memories of Power in Late Medieval Florence," in *Portraits of Medieval and Renaissance Living: Essays in Memory of David Herlihy*, ed. S. K. Cohn Jr. and S. A. Epstein (Ann Arbor, 1996), pp. 39–70.

Such an expansive sense of family relations was possible only for large elite lineages with many marriage alliances. The popolo could try to emulate but could not match elite family histories and genealogies. Giovanni Morelli found among his family papers a notarial act redacted in 1170 in the name of an ancestor identified as Ruggieri son of Calandro son of Benamato son of Albertino. What he wrote about these distant ancestors was pure guesswork, but the precious document allowed him to extend the skeleton of the patriline back hundreds of years. Ruggieri was the father of Morelli's great-great-grandfather Giraldo, about whom he knew only that he was born in 1199, exercised the dyer's trade, and (unlikely as it seems) married a woman from the elite Barucci family. Of his great-grandfather Morello he says that he accumulated wealth and left a greater quantity of documents, joined the Wool guild, and became a consul in 1334. Even about his grandfather Bartolomeo, Giovanni could only say that he was a successful merchant who bought land and married Dea Cigliamochi and had seven children with her. Indeed, Morelli identified the families of the wives of his direct ancestors going back four generations. But information about ancestors down to and including his grandfather was limited in each generation to direct progenitors: except for occasionally acknowledging that there were siblings, he has nothing to say about them or any of their descendants. It is only with his father's generation that he suddenly gives a wealth of detail about uncles, aunts, cousins, and their spouses and children. Until this point, his historical family is a pure and thin patriline: an unbroken succession from one progenitor to the next.[5]

For most artisans and laborers, family "history" involved little more than grandparents and their descendants, especially among the majority who lacked a surname and whose patronymics provided a cumbersome way of establishing descent over at most a couple of generations. For these classes the living reality of the family was generally limited to the immediate household, which, as in all classes, could be more or less extended. But working-class households tended to be small. In the quarter of Santo Spirito in 1427, the 357 households with one or more workers in the woolen cloth industry averaged 3.9 persons, and 30% of these residential units consisted of one or two persons, in the latter case usually a childless couple.[6] The lack, or weakness, of extended family ties, by whatever definition, may have isolated artisans and workers as much as, or more than, their poverty did. The famous tale of *The Fat Wood-carver*, in which a group of friends (including the architect Filippo Brunelleschi) play a cruel practical joke in 1409 on a woodcarver called Grasso, persuading him that he is not himself and driving him in despair from the city, presupposes for the success of the prank that Grasso lacked family members to

[5] Morelli, *Ricordi*, pp. 81–200; *Mercanti scrittori*, ed. Branca, pp. 103–64.
[6] Franceschi, *Oltre il "Tumulto,"* pp. 266–7.

reassure and protect him. There was an actual Grasso, and although both his father and grandfather had served on the priorate (in 1380 and 1369), they were apparently dead by 1409. In the story, Grasso lives with his mother, during whose temporary absence from the city he is isolated and vulnerable to the scheming of his friends.[7] Where were the other members of his family? A similar absence of extensive family support networks is evident in the well known real-life story of Lusanna, an artisan's daughter, who in the 1450s took her claim that she had legally married Giovanni della Casa to the court of Archbishop Antoninus. Noteworthy is the meager presence of Lusanna's family in her emotional ordeal. Although she had four brothers, one of whom was very much engaged in the legal proceedings, and two half-brothers and a half-sister from her father's second marriage, the only family members present at the alleged marriage, and later among the witnesses testifying on her behalf, were her stepmother, the one brother and his wife, and some neighbors. Lusanna's father was an immigrant from Dalmatia, which suggests that recent non-Florentine origins, whether from the contado or elsewhere, contributed to weak or fragmented family ties among artisans and workers.[8]

In the age of consensus politics and civic humanism, official rhetoric surrounding the Florentine family was all idealization. The matrimonial bond was described in utopian terms. Bruni praised Dante's decision to marry, and marriage in general, by claiming that "nothing can be perfect where this is lacking, for only this love is natural, legitimate and permissible."[9] Palmieri similarly insisted that "of all the kinds of love of human pleasures, none is greater or more solidly joined by nature than love in the marriage bond," a "natural" love reinforced by reciprocal affection and by the practical benefits that the partners bestow on one another.[10] Similar praises of mutual affection between husbands and wives were expressed by the Venetian humanist Francesco Barbaro and the popular Franciscan preacher Bernardino da Siena. Filial and paternal love was even more lavishly lauded. Although Morelli was not yet three when his father Paolo died, he idealized him to the point of doubting that he could do justice to his father's "great deeds" and "virtues." Lamenting his loss, he remarked that among the great injuries suffered by orphans is that of having to exchange "the love and charity of the father toward the son, which is infinite, for that of outsiders, whether relatives or

---

[7]   Antonio Manetti, *Novella del Grasso legnaiuolo*, in *Novelle italiane: il Quattrocento*, ed. G. Chiarini (Milan, 1982), pp. 243–85; trans. M. Baca in L. Martines, *An Italian Renaissance Sextet: Six Tales in Historical Context* (New York, 1994), pp. 171–241.
[8]   G. Brucker, *Giovanni and Lusanna: Love and Marriage in Renaissance Florence* (Berkeley, 1986), pp. 4, 15, 19.
[9]   *Life of Dante*, in *Humanism of Leonardo Bruni*, ed. Griffiths et al., p. 87.
[10]   Palmieri, *Vita civile*, pp. 156–7.

friends." In remarkable pages of emotional self-examination over the death of his oldest son Alberto at the age of nine, Morelli acknowledged overwhelming love and grief, but especially guilt over never having adequately shown Alberto the extent of his love: "you loved him," he reproached himself, "and never did you let him be happy in your love."[11] In mid-century Giovanni Rucellai, who, like Morelli, lost his father before he could know him, wrote in his memoirs, the *Zibaldone*, that "it is said that the greatest love there is, is that of the father for his son."[12]

Elite Florentines cultivated idealized images of their lineages as well. A cult of genealogies emerged toward the end of the fourteenth century and blossomed in the fifteenth. Rucellai began the *Zibaldone* with a meticulous genealogical survey of all the family's branches and a history of the entire clan, emphasizing the family's political unity. Celebrations of lineage history, solidarity, and glory found expression in both paintings and buildings, and in what has been defined as not only a "cult of ancestors" but a cult of the transgenerational clan, including its past, present, and future members. Upper-class families typically clustered their separate residential units in the same quarter or neighborhood, maintaining ties, influencing local politics, and enhancing the image of the clan as a community bound by affection, loyalty, and common interest.[13] Even marriage alliances were idealized. In the *Vita civile* Palmieri theorizes the emergence from extended patriarchal families of independent lineages and entire *consorterie*: "At first the whole family [*casa*] consists in these [sons and grandsons]; then, when they have multiplied and can no longer be suitably gathered in one house, the lineages and large families [*le schiatte, le consorterie e copiose famiglie*] grow and spread out." These lineages, he adds, "give and receive in legitimate marriages, [and] through their marriage alliances and their love [toward each other] encompass a good part of the city, whence, being related by marriage, they charitably assist each other, conferring upon each other advice, favors, and assistance, which, in the course of life, result in benefits, advantage, and abundant fruits."[14] Palmieri, who did not come from a great lineage, here fashions a view of "a good part" of the city (even as it excludes most of the population) as an interlocking network of

---

[11] Morelli, *Ricordi*, pp. 143, 219, 501; *Mercanti scrittori*, ed. Branca, pp. 135, 173, 315; Trexler, *Public Life in Renaissance Florence*, pp. 159–86; and Trexler, "In Search of Father: The Experience of Abandonment in the Recollections of Giovanni di Pagolo Morelli," in Trexler, *Dependence in Context*, pp. 171–202. See also T. Kuehn, *Emancipation in Late Medieval Florence* (New Brunswick, N.J., 1982), pp. 55–71.

[12] Kent, *Household and Lineage*, pp. 45–62 (56).

[13] Ibid., chaps. 4 and 5, esp. pp. 274–7.

[14] Palmieri, *Vita civile*, p. 161; Herlihy and Klapisch, *Tuscans*, p. 353; Molho, *Marriage Alliance*, p. 344.

great families, idealizing the marriage alliance as the social institution holding "the city" together and as the source of the love that induces citizens to treat one another as members of one huge civic family.

Most famous among idealized views of the Florentine family is the ambivalent perspective of Leon Battista Alberti, the illegitimate son and grandson of exiles. The *Libri della famiglia*, written in the 1430s, contain some of the most lyrical and fulsome expressions of love, unity, and solidarity within a great family. Alberti was no doubt representing the ideology and rhetoric of the elite families, but just as surely he injected ironic contradictions and tensions into these representations. At the beginning of the dialogues, as [Leon] Battista's father Lorenzo is dying, his kinsman Adovardo says that he sees "clearly that you [Lorenzo] want all the others of our house to show the same love for each member of the family, the same concern and active care for the welfare and honor of the whole family, that you yourself have always shown." He then reassures Lorenzo of their intentions in this regard and begs him not to have doubts: "We want everyone to see that we are good and faithful kinsmen, in all that pertains to the needs and honor of the least member of this house no less than to your sons, who are not the last among those we love." The irony is that Alberti struggled unsuccessfully against the family for his father's inheritance; in the autobiographical *Vita anonyma*, he complains bitterly of his ill-treatment at the hands of relatives. Indeed, the fact that the Alberti spent a long generation in exile is itself ironic commentary on the many statements throughout the *Famiglia* about the honor that their performance of civic duty and devotion to the *patria* had earned them among their fellow citizens. Hundreds of similar statements throughout the dialogues have too often been read at face value, as if they were uncritical reflections of Florentine social attitudes and practices and of Alberti's approval of them. He was indeed reproducing the rhetoric and idealized images of the Florentine family, but also showing that family and civic life regularly contradicted and subverted those images, in which he was by no means a complacent believer.[15]

Idealized images were one thing, reality another. Florentine families were beset by problems that were not essentially new (a century earlier Dante had already complained, through the voice of Cacciaguida in *Paradiso* 15.103–8, of rising dowries and sexual practices that kept houses "empty of family") but

---

[15]   Alberti, *Della famiglia*, ed. Romano and Tenenti, p. 16; trans. Watkins, *The Family in Renaissance Florence*, p. 34; J. M. Najemy, "Giannozzo and his Elders: Alberti's Critique of Renaissance Patriarchy," in *Society and Individual in Renaissance Florence*, ed. W. J. Connell (Berkeley, 2002), pp. 51–78; T. Kuehn, "Reading Between the Patrilines: Leon Battista Alberti's *Della Famiglia* in the Light of his Illegitimacy," in Kuehn, *Law, Family, and Women: Toward a Legal Anthropology of Renaissance Italy* (Chicago, 1991), pp. 157–75.

that were exacerbated by demographic and marriage patterns after the Black Death. By 1400 Florence was a city of declining population, small households, and large numbers of widows, unmarried men, and illegitimate and abandoned children. As men postponed marriage, the perception at least that homosexual relations were more prevalent became a source of controversy and social anxiety. As political authority became self-consciously paternal, government intervened in a variety of ways to deal with the perceived dysfunctions of family and private life. The results were a combination of welfare legislation and policing of morality. Laws were passed and institutions created to protect orphans, shelter abandoned children, make it easier for fathers to provide dowries for daughters, and adjust inheritance law to help lineages preserve wealth and property. At the same time, government undertook initiatives to supervise prostitution, expand the prosecution of sodomy, monitor sexual misconduct in convents, and establish a firmer control over confraternities. Although these measures were aimed at different problems and were certainly not parts of a coordinated policy of reform, they emerged from widely held assumptions about the responsibility of the elite ruling class to act as collective and common fathers to the civic family. For the first time, most Florentines accepted that government's legitimate agenda went beyond war, justice, public order, and taxation to family issues and "private" matters that the political "fathers" of Florence saw as urgent public business. The humanist discourse of social and political virtue coincided once again with the aims of consensus politics, this time to produce an ideology of moral rectitude and conformity that it was government's duty to oversee and enforce.

Households, Marriage, Dowries

The most serious problem was that Florentine families were not producing enough children, especially because so many did not survive to adulthood. Fifteenth-century Florence was remarkably smaller than the pre-plague city. Its partial recovery from the catastrophe of 1348 raised the population to 55,000 in 1380, still half its pre-1348 numbers. Another wave of plagues struck, in 1400 (with an estimated 12,000 deaths) and again in 1417, 1422–4, and 1430, when 10 percent of the population died. Even before the last of these, the 1427 Catasto indicates a population just over 37,000, a third less than in the late fourteenth century. The ecclesiastical jurisdiction that included the immediately surrounding rural parishes within a radius of three miles had a population of 44,000, and the contado counted 125,000 inhabitants (but only 104,000 within the 1338 borders). Nor was there much recovery for most of the fifteenth century, as the city's population struggled to exceed 40,000. Except in upper-class families, small households were characteristic of the entire population: in 1427, 9,780 households averaged 3.8 persons. Recurrences of the plague, which rarely wiped away entire families, were no doubt one reason for this. But even in the second half of the century, when the plague subsided, the average Florentine household numbered fewer than five persons. In the sixteenth century, when the population began to grow again, it did so by first increasing average household size.

One-fifth of city households in 1427 consisted of only one person, the result of two aspects of Florentine marriage and inheritance practices: the many men who either married late or not at all, and the many widows who did not remarry. Among all classes, men in the city married in smaller numbers and later in life than did men in the countryside. And while there was less varia-tion in the ages at which women married, the city had many more widows than the contado. In all cities of Florentine Tuscany surveyed by the Catasto, the average age of marriage for women was just under 19, and for men just under 28. In the Florentine contado it was over 19 for women and just under 24 for men. But in Florence the average age of women marrying for the first time was between 17 and 18, and the vast majority of women who married did so by their early twenties; those who did not mostly entered convents. For men in the city, the average age at first marriage was around 30, but 12% of all men never married. The large age difference between husbands and wives (averaging 12 years, and in many cases much more) accounts for the startling number of urban widows: 25% of women over the age of 12 were widows in 1427. Many were widowed in their twenties, and few ever remarried. This combination of factors – the relatively small proportion of the population that married and the brief duration of marriages – kept the number of births low, even as some upper-class married couples had many children. Whatever plagues and other diseases were doing to limit the population, Florentine marriage patterns contributed significantly to the demographic crisis.[16]

Particularly crucial was the reluctance of men, especially from the upper classes, to marry early. Their motivation was in part economic: it took resources and capital to confront the prospect of marriage and children, and many preferred to wait until they accumulated sufficient wealth. In merchant and banking families young men were typically sent to learn, and then to oversee branches of, family businesses throughout Italy and Europe, and invariably they waited to marry until they returned home. Buonaccorso Pitti, born in 1354, postponed marriage until he returned from years of travel in northern Europe in 1391, when he was thirty-seven. Even men who did not leave the city, including those without financial reasons to delay marriage, generally married no earlier than thirty. This had clearly become a cultural

---

[16]   Herlihy and Klapisch-Zuber, *Tuscans*, chaps. 3 and 7; D. Herlihy, *Medieval House-holds* (Cambridge, Mass., 1985), chap. 6.

preference, one linked perhaps to assumptions about the stages in life at which men were prepared to assume domestic as well as political responsibilities. Alberti tells us that contemporaries were acutely aware of men's reluctance to marry early. In book one of the *Famiglia*, Adovardo counts twenty-two Alberti men between the ages of sixteen and thirty-six living alone and without a wife, and says: "it grieves me to see so many of you younger Alberti without an heir, not having done what you could to increase the family and make it numerous." In book two, Lionardo, a humanist and himself unmarried, sings the praises of marriage as having been instituted by nature and laments the hesitation of so many young men to take wives, which he attributes both to the attendant financial burdens and to an unwillingness to leave behind the "freedom" of bachelorhood: "Subjecting themselves to the yoke of marriage, perhaps, seems to them a loss of liberty and of the freedom to live as they wish." Therefore, "we must use every reason, method of persuasion, and reward, and every argument and all our planning and skill to induce our young men to take wives." He even suggests that fathers threaten to disinherit sons who refuse to marry by a certain age. Upper-class marriage was, it seems, so encumbered by social expectations and paternal pressures that many men tried to avoid it for as long as possible. One wonders if these marriage-shy young (and not so young) men were avoiding the inevitable re-subjection to their own fathers that marriage, children, and a role in their lineages' matrimonial strategies entailed.

While avoidance of marriage allowed some young men greater freedom to travel and pursue their own pleasures, many unmarried adult sons nonetheless remained in their fathers' households. Sons were subject to the legal authority of their fathers' *patria potestas*, which restricted the freedom to sign contracts or write wills. This generated a certain level of tension which occasionally erupted into conflict between fathers imbued with the culture's high sense of paternal dignity and power and sons who were enjoying, and from their fathers' point of view perhaps wasting, the years of freedom. In 1405, Lanfredino Lanfredini settled an old quarrel outside the family without consulting his wife or adult sons, thereby provoking the ire especially of his son Remigio, who was so incensed at his father's unilateral action that he severed all ties with the paternal household and left the city. Remigio assumed that, as an adult, he had a right to be consulted and to participate in the decision his father made, whereas the father's self-defense relied in turn on one of the central pieties of Florentine family culture: when accused of being a "traitor" against his son and the rest of the family, Lanfredino pleaded, "Remigio, you are my son and you should be content with my decisions; I did it for the best."[17]

[17]   Brucker, *Society*, pp. 64–6; T. Kuehn, "Honor and Conflict in a Fifteenth-Century Florentine Family," in his *Law, Family, and Women*, pp. 129–42.

Beneath idealizations of paternal authority and love (and in part because of inflated expectations surrounding the power of fathers), generational conflict was always latent, although it rarely exploded into the open as in this case.

For Florentine women, the major consequences of prevailing marriage patterns were pressure to marry early, expanding dowries and growing numbers of women unable to marry because of inflated dowries (and who thus entered religious life), and, among those who did marry, the dilemmas they faced, when their husbands died, over dowries, children, and pressures for and against remarriage. Pressure to marry early was motivated by urgency over marrying daughters before their virtue and purity were in any way compromised, even simply by loose talk, and by the many men who opted out of the marriage market or delayed marriage, thereby creating a situation in which marriageable young women outnumbered prospective husbands. Marriages in the upper class were negotiated in detail and at length, often through professional marriage brokers, because each marital union was also an alliance between two lineages entailing reciprocal obligations and long-lasting ties and the crucial matter of the dowry: its size, components, and schedule of payment.[18] Florentines from both elite and popolo described these negotiations in letters and *ricordanze*. When Buonaccorso Pitti decided to marry, he picked, not a bride, but the interrelated group of families into which he wished to marry. He let it be known that he was willing to leave the choice of a wife up to Guido di messer Tommaso del Palagio, "the most respected and influential man in the city," "provided he picked her among his own relatives." Pitti's motives were openly political: "I sent the marriage broker to him to tell him of my intentions, and I did so in order to acquire his good will and a marriage alliance with him, so that he would be obligated to work on my behalf for a reconciliation with the Corbizi," a family with which Buonaccorso had feuded in 1380. The broker came back a first time to say that Guido del Palagio would be pleased to have Buonaccorso "as his *parente*," and a few days later reported that Guido was able to offer in marriage Francesca, daughter of his cousin Dianora del Palagio and of Luca di Piero degli Albizzi. Pitti accepted immediately: marrying an Albizzi gave him an alliance with the family then emerging as the most influential within the ruling group.[19] In this case (or at least in Pitti's recollection of it) the dowry seems not to have played a major

---

[18]   Molho, *Marriage Alliance*; L. Fabbri, *Alleanza matrimoniale e patriziato nella Firenze del '400: studio sulla famiglia Strozzi* (Florence, 1991); H. Gregory, "Daughters, Dowries and the Family in Fifteenth-Century Florence," *Rinascimento* 27 (1987): 215–37; Foster [Baxendale], "The Ties That Bind"; and the translated essays of C. Klapisch-Zuber, *Women, Family, and Ritual in Renaissance Italy*, trans. L. G. Cochrane (Chicago, 1985).
[19]   Pitti, *Ricordi*, in *Mercanti scrittori*, ed. Branca, pp. 374–6, 392–3; cf. *Two Memoirs*, ed. Brucker, pp. 32–3, 45–6; Molho, *Marriage Alliance*, pp. 185–7.

role. It was the tie to the Albizzi that sealed the deal, and which Buonaccorso may have been after all along.

But for most Florentines dowries and their steady inflation were a central concern. Fourteenth-century upper-class dowries were normally between 400 and 1,000 florins. Even among the wealthy Alberti, 16 of 33 known dowries given to their women in the mid- to late fourteenth century were 800 florins or less; by the early fifteenth century (and despite their exile), 11 of 12 known Alberti dowries were 1,000 florins or larger.[20] By the late fourteenth century, some elite dowries reached between 1,000 and 1,500 florins.[21] In 1370 Michele di Vanni Castellani bequeathed a dowry of 1,000 florins to his daughter Antonia, having previously given the same amount to each of her two sisters. In 1381, after apparently difficult negotiations, Giovanni Del Bene agreed to pay a dowry of 900 florins for the marriage of his daughter Caterina to Andrea Quaratesi. He commented: "I could not reduce that sum, although I tried hard to persuade [the marriage broker] to adhere to the terms of our previous discussions. But [he] insisted upon it, alleging many reasons. So, to avoid the rupture of the negotiations, I surrendered on this point."[22] Average upper-class dowries moved steadily from about 1,000 florins in the second quarter of the fifteenth century, to 1,200 in the third quarter, over 1,400 in the last quarter, and 1,850 in the first quarter of the sixteenth century.[23] In one branch of the Strozzi, only 3 of 13 dowries up to 1445 exceeded 1,000 florins; between 1445 and 1486 only 2 of 13 were less than that; and from 1487 to 1510, 9 of 13 were over 2,000 florins and none less than 1,260.[24] These increases occurred in a period (until the sixteenth century at least) otherwise free of inflation, and in many cases represented real financial dilemmas for fathers, many of whom were faced with the unpleasant reality of not being able to provide adequate dowries for all their daughters. Dowries may have grown because of the imbalance between the supply of marriageable young women and the smaller pool of men willing to marry: girls' families were literally competing for husbands by offering larger dowries. Those who lost in this competition either married down the social hierarchy or sent daughters to convents. Whatever the cause of dowry inflation, contemporaries noticed and frequently decried the phenomenon.

To help families with this problem, in 1425 the government instituted an investment fund for dowries, the Monte delle doti.[25] Fathers could deposit a

---

[20]   Foster [Baxendale], "The Ties That Bind," p. 260, table 3.5.
[21]   Fabbri, *Alleanza matrimoniale*, p. 73.
[22]   Brucker, *Society*, pp. 52, 32–3.
[23]   Molho, *Marriage Alliance*, p. 310.
[24]   Fabbri, *Alleanza matrimoniale*, p. 213, appendix 2.
[25]   For what follows: Molho, *Marriage Alliance*, chap. 2.

sum of money at the birth of a daughter and be guaranteed a much larger sum for her dowry: after $7^1/2$ years 100 florins would mature to 250 florins, or after 15 years to 500 (with annual compounded interest rates of, respectively, 13 and 11%). The Dowry Fund was not an immediate success, and over the next few years the government introduced modifications (a third eleven-year option, the possibility of waiting until a girl had survived the earliest and most dangerous years of life before opening an account, lower initial deposits and thus higher interest rates) all designed to make it more attractive to invest, wait many years, and hope that their daughters survived to marry. Even so, in the first eight years of the fund, only fifty-six girls were enrolled. The chief flaw in the original plan was that, if a daughter died before marrying, both the deposit and its accrued earnings were forfeited, a defect finally corrected in 1433 when the government agreed to return deposits to fathers or brothers of girls who died without marrying. This is what families had apparently been waiting for, because over the next two months the fund attracted 879 deposits worth over 67,000 florins. By 1442, accounts amounted to almost 350,000 florins, and by the 1450s nearly three million.

Once it caught on, the Dowry Fund became central to the matrimonial strategies of Florentine families. In the fund's 150-year lifetime, accounts were opened for some 30,000 girls, slightly less than a fifth from the contado and district towns, the rest from city families. In 1480, just under a fifth of all city households (1,649 of 8,414) had girls with Dowry Fund accounts. Wealthy households, which were generally those of elite lineages, were more likely to invest in the fund than poorer ones. Whereas only 266 (9%) of the poorest third of Florentine households (with taxable wealth under 100 florins), and 14% of unmarried girls in those households, had accounts, 220 (46%) of the wealthiest 477 households (the 5.7% of households with taxable wealth in excess of 1,500 florins), and the same percentage of girls in these households, had accounts. In the middle, the 60% of households with taxable assets between 100 and 1,500 florins (which included much of the popolo and artisan community) were also prominently represented, but not in the same proportion to overall numbers as the wealthier elite: 1,163 of 5,090 households in this middle category (23%) had accounts in the names of 28% of their unmarried girls. Overall 27% of Florence's nubile women (2,684 of 9,964) had Dowry Fund accounts in 1480.[26]

Upper-class families took advantage of the fund in large numbers. Over its lifetime, accounts were opened for 113 Strozzi women, 104 Medici women, and 94 Rucellai women. These and other elite families not only had the resources to invest; they were also more in need of the service because of the steady inflation of dowries within their class and their generally larger

[26]   Ibid., chap. 3, table 3.1, p. 87.

numbers of children. Such families were more likely to open an account soon after the birth of a daughter and perhaps supplement it with a second deposit once the girl had survived the early years of life. A well known case is that of Caterina Strozzi, daughter of the exiled and (by the time of her marriage) deceased Matteo Strozzi and of Alessandra Macinghi (whose mother was an Alberti). In 1447 Alessandra, whose letters are a rich source of Florentine social history, wrote to her son Filippo, still in exile in Naples, to inform him that she had agreed to marry Caterina to Marco Parenti, son of a silk-manufacturer and grandson of a minor guildsman, and to provide her with a dowry of 1,000 florins. Daughters of Strozzi men and granddaughters of Alberti women did not normally marry men only two generations removed from the minor guilds, even ones that had become wealthy. But Strozzi political misfortunes and Alessandra's inability to provide a truly grand dowry made a marriage down the social hierarchy necessary. Caterina had two Dowry Fund accounts, both for 500 florins: a fifteen-year account that would mature in 1448, and an eleven-year account that would mature only in 1450. But Alessandra wanted to marry Caterina at the end of 1447, and, as she wrote to her son, since "whoever takes a wife wants money," she "could find no one willing to have part of the dowry in 1448 and the rest in 1450" and was forced to provide the second half as a "combination of cash and presents" which she would recover when the second account matured three years later. By the end of 1449, Caterina was pregnant and expecting her child in February of 1450. Alessandra was now worried that, if "God has other plans for Caterina before April" (which is to say, if she died in childbirth), the 500 florins from the eleven-year account, which had been opened on March 26, 1439, and would mature on that date in 1450, would be lost (except for the initial deposit). So she decided to purchase three months' worth of insurance on Caterina's life for the substantial sum of twelve florins. She did so against her son-in-law's opinion, who thought it money wasted in view of Caterina's good health. But Alessandra thought it the prudent thing to do and asked her son Filippo not to inform Marco of her decision so that he "wouldn't take it badly, and because it's our business." Such were the considerations forced on Florentine families by the dangers of childbirth and the rules of the Dowry Fund. As it happened, Marco's optimism was vindicated: Caterina gave birth to a son, Piero, and subsequently to seven daughters, for five of whom Marco opened fifteen-year accounts in the fund.[27]

---

[27]   *Lettere di una gentildonna fiorentina del secolo XV ai figliuoli esuli*, ed. C. Guasti (Florence, 1877; reprint edn. 1972); *Selected Letters of Alessandra Strozzi*, trans. H. Gregory (Berkeley, 1997), pp. 28–31, 50–1; A. Crabb, *The Strozzi of Florence: Widowhood and Family Solidarity in the Renaissance* (Ann Arbor, 1999); Fabbri, *Alleanza matrimoniale*; and Molho, *Marriage Alliance*, chap. 4.

Women, Property, Inheritance

A dowry was a woman's property, sometimes seen as her share of her father's estate, but more often as a bequest in lieu of it. Roman law prescribed that all children, female as well as male, share their father's inheritance, but prevailing legal opinion held that dowries justified the exclusion of daughters from inheritance.[28] Even as it was legally hers, the dowry was not a woman's to do with exactly as she pleased, and certainly not during the marriage. Shortly after marriage, the dowry was transferred directly from her father (or brothers) to her husband, who was required to acknowledge it in a notarized act that protected her right to recover it if he predeceased her. Dowries supported the marital household and sometimes provided husbands with investment capital. For those like Goro Dati, who did not have great family wealth, dowries were crucial to business activities. When, in 1393, he married his second wife Isabetta, whose deceased parents both came from modest families of the popolo, her cousins promised a substantial dowry of 900 florins, and, "apart from the dowry," Dati noted in his diary, the income from a farm in the contado. He also received his wife's trousseau, which the cousins valued at 100 florins, presumably as the final portion of the dowry, but which he thought was overestimated by 30 florins. The cash portion of 800 florins was duly paid within days of the marriage, and Dati then "invested it in the shop of Buonaccorso Berardi and his partners." Husbands were expected to declare the receipt of dowries, insure them, and pay the tax on the notarized documents. But Dati failed to declare Isabetta's dowry until nine years later, apparently out of pique against his wife's cousins for over-valuing the trousseau and thus not delivering the promised amount. But he knew he had to do so sooner or later in order to protect his wife's rights: "Yet I must do so, and if by God's will something were to happen before I do, I want her to be assured as can be of having her dowry, just as though it had been declared and insured. For the fault is not hers." Dati may also have been worried about Isabetta's health in her ninth (and last) pregnancy, and thus about the fate of the dowry if she died in childbirth. According to Florentine law, if a wife predeceased her husband, her children from this husband (but not those from previous marriages) inherited the dowry. If there were no children from this last marriage, the entire dowry went to the husband. As it happened, Dati finally

---

[28]   J. Kirshner, *Pursuing Honor While Avoiding Sin: The Monte delle doti of Florence* (Milan, 1978); T. Kuehn, "Women, Marriage, and *Patria Potestas* in Late Medieval Florence," in Kuehn, *Law, Family, and Women*, pp. 197–211; Fabbri, *Alleanza matrimoniale*, pp. 64–81; and Klapisch-Zuber, "The Griselda Complex: Dowry and Marriage Gifts in the Quattrocento," in her *Women, Family, and Ritual*, pp. 213–46.

declared the dowry and paid the tax just six days before Isabetta died, no doubt to ensure his and his children's right to inherit the dowry. Of the eight children (five sons and three daughters) he had with Isabetta, only one, a son, survived into adulthood, and he presumably inherited his mother's dowry. But until then it remained in Dati's hands.

The next year, as Dati was putting together capital for a new business venture, he listed his available resources and added: "The rest I expect to obtain if I marry again this year, when I hope to find a woman with a dowry as large as God may be pleased to grant me. If I do not marry, I will find the money some other way." He quickly found a new wife and the needed funds: in May 1403 he married a twenty-one-year-old widow, Ginevra Brancacci, and in July received from her kinsman Felice a dowry consisting of 700 florins (671 in cash with a trousseau worth 29 florins) and a farm at Campi in the contado. This time he declared and insured the dowry without delay. The marriage lasted seventeen years until Ginevra died in 1420. Dati then married Caterina Guicciardini, whose kinsmen provided a dowry of 615 florins.[29] Curiously, as each successive marriage took Dati to a socially more prestigious *parentado*, the dowries became smaller, a sign perhaps that he was marrying into households that, despite their lineages' notable names, were in some financial difficulty and had to settle for marriage alliances with a man they considered not their social equal.

Because of the magnitude of the sums involved and the uses to which they were put, husbands and their heirs, chiefly their sons, did all they could to avoid losing the dowry when the husband died. Struggles over dowries sometimes resulted in serious strains and conflicts between widows and their marital families. When a husband predeceased his wife, the dowry had to be returned to her unless she agreed to a different arrangement. It was here that the dilemmas imposed on women by the dotal system became particularly acute.[30] A widow could either remain in her husband's household and live with her children, in which case the dowry, although legally hers, would not be extracted from the husband's estate and paid back to her; or she could move out and remarry (sometimes under pressure from her natal family), taking the dowry with her but leaving her children behind because they belonged to their father's lineage. Husbands offered financial incentives in their wills to persuade wives not to leave. An example, from the mid-fourteenth

[29] *Two Memoirs*, ed. Brucker, pp. 114–15, 123–4, 132–4.
[30] Klapisch-Zuber, "The 'Cruel Mother': Maternity, Widowhood, and Dowry in Florence," in her *Women, Family, and Ritual*, pp. 117–31; I. Chabot, "Seconde nozze e identità materna nella Firenze del tardo medioevo," in *Tempi e spazi di vita femminile*, ed. S. Seidel Menchi et al. (Bologna, 1999), pp. 493–523.

century, is the testament of Fetto Ubertini, who bequeathed to his wife Pia, in addition to her dowry, the sum of 125 florins and an income "sufficient to maintain herself and a servant" on the condition that she "remain a widow and live with our children," adding that "if she withdraws her dowry, then I cancel the bequest of 125 florins, nor shall she receive living expenses . . . , but only if she leaves her dowry in my estate, and remains a widow, or becomes a tertiary [in one of the mendicant orders]."[31]

For widows still young enough to bear children, the pressure to remarry could be considerable, partly from assumptions about the moral and social dangers that sexually awakened young widows allegedly represented, and partly because their natal families were reluctant to lose the social capital of another *parentado*, another marriage alliance with the advantages deriving from the reciprocal obligations assumed by in-laws. By remaining with her children in her husband's household, a widow was less valuable to her natal family. But in order to reclaim the dowry and leave her husband's household, she had to accept separation from her children. Young widows were thus caught between the interests of their natal and marital families, between the incompatible desires to remarry and to be with their own children. Some Florentine men lamented their mothers' decision to remarry and remembered it as abandonment. Even when a mother's remarriage did not prevent continued contact with her children, it had damaging financial consequences for them, especially if, as often happened, assets had to be liquidated in order to restore to their mother the dowry that made her second marriage possible. Giovanni Morelli's mother, Telda Quaratesi, was among the Florentine women trapped in this dilemma. She was only twenty-four when her husband died in 1374, and she was quickly remarried to Simone Spini, "because she was very young," as Giovanni wrote. Giovanni and his siblings were brought up by their maternal grandparents, Matteo and Filippa Quaratesi, a relatively unusual arrangement made necessary by the deaths of Giovanni's father and all his paternal uncles in the plague of 1363, which left no close relatives in the Morelli patriline to assume care of them. Giovanni refers to his maternal grandfather as "our second father" and says that Matteo and Filippa "loved" him and his brother and sisters "like their own children." In these circumstances he probably had regular contact with his mother as a young boy, but he nonetheless experienced his mother's remarriage as betrayal and abandonment: "shortly after [our father's death] we lost our mother, who remarried." The bitter lament of having been "abandoned by his cruel mother" is twice linked in Morelli's recollections to the financial losses he suffered when their father's estate

[31]   Brucker, *Society*, p. 50.

was entrusted to guardians who in a short time diminished its value by 25 percent because of a variety of expenses, among them "our mother's dowry."[32]

Florentine inheritance law devoted considerable attention to the substantial sums of money and property that women took from their natal lineages, both dowries and non-dotal assets, and which they sometimes took with them again into a second marriage. All the parties involved (women, their children, husbands, and natal families) had an interest in controlling and ultimately possessing these assets. Out of deeply ingrained imperatives, Florentine men preserved and augmented property and assets within their lineages, ensuring that as much as possible came in and as little as possible went out. Limiting the inheritance rights of daughters through dowries was one way of preventing a lineage's patrimony from being dispersed, if, as was likely, daughters, become mothers, bequeathed their worldly goods to their children. But dowries themselves now represented in many cases significant portions of the paternal patrimony, which helps to explain the increasing pressure on young widows from their fathers and natal families to remarry, establish another *parentado*, and not let this considerable wealth slide into the hands of the daughters' marital kin. All Florentine families pursued the same combination of contradictory desires, pressuring their widowed daughters-in-law to leave their dowries in their husbands' (and children's) estates and encouraging their widowed daughters to reclaim their dowries and contract new marriages. This complicated an already contentious and frequently litigious inheritance system.

Florentine statutory law regulated inheritance in cases of intestacy, the absence of a valid will. Testamentary succession, on the other hand, was governed by a combination of custom, Roman law, and opinions of jurists in disputed cases. Florentine men generally left the bulk of their patrimonies in equal shares to all living and future sons, to grandsons if sons had died, or, if they had neither, to brothers, nephews, or other male agnates. In addition to giving dowries to daughters, and providing for the restitution of their own wives' dowries, they typically bequeathed income from, or use of, designated properties to wives, mothers, daughters, sisters, and other female relatives, and made any number of special bequests to relatives, male and female, as well as charitable bequests to confraternities, hospitals, and the poor. No laws limited or prescribed the bequests and legacies of testamentary succession,

---

[32] Morelli, *Ricordi*, in *Mercanti scrittori*, ed. Branca, pp. 141, 143, 165–7, 313; L. Pandimiglio, "Giovanni di Pagolo Morelli e le sue strutture familiari," *ASI* 136 (1978): 3–88; Pandimiglio, "Giovanni di Pagolo Morelli e la continuità familiare," *Studi medievali*, ser. 3, 22 (1981): 129–81; Trexler, *Public Life*, pp. 159–86; and Trexler, "In Search of Father," in *Dependence in Context*, pp. 171–202.

except for the generally accepted stipulation of Roman law that fathers could not irrationally disinherit children or refuse to dower daughters.[33] No laws prevented women from being named as heirs, even as it was customary in Florence to limit a daughter's share of the inheritance to the dowry if there were male heirs; where there were none, daughters could and often did inherit.

Communal legislative intervention was thus largely limited to cases in which there was no will, or the will was invalidated, and especially to the controversial area of women's inheritance rights in cases of intestacy. While most upper-class men wrote wills, it was much more common for women to die intestate. Most of this legislation limited women's rights to inherit from their own children, fathers, brothers, and mothers, or even to control their dowries. But it seems unlikely that such laws would have been needed unless it was perceived that too much property was passing into the hands of women amid confusion and disputes surrounding their rights to inherit and dispose of their dowries. As early as 1295 a law prohibited women from inheriting in intestate succession from their children (or grandchildren) if the deceased son or daughter had a living son, grandson, great-grandson, father, brother, sister, nephew (a brother's son), or cousin (the son of an uncle on his or her father's side). At most, in these circumstances women had a right to an allowance for living costs. Even in the absence of any of this long list of relations, a woman could inherit only one-fourth of her child's estate, and even then with a 500-lire limit (then about 250 florins) on real estate. This law was included in the 1325 redaction of communal statutes, where it is linked to a series of other restrictions on women's inheritance rights.[34] By this time women were barred from inheriting in intestate succession from a brother if he was survived by a son or daughter (or their children) or by another brother. In this case, a woman had the right, if and when she became a widow, to reside in her brother's house. Women and all others born "in the female line" (i.e., their daughters' and sisters' children, male or female) likewise could not inherit from their intestate fathers, grandfathers, or great-grandfathers if the deceased had a living son, grandson, or great-grandson, brother, nephew, or other descendant in the male line; they did, on the other hand, have a right to be dowered from such estates and to receive living expenses until they married. If a woman had

---

[33] J. Kirshner, "Disinheritance in Late Medieval and Renaissance Italy," *Ius commune: Zeitschrift für Europäische Rechtsgeschichte* 27 (2000): 119–214.
[34] *Statuti della Repubblica fiorentina*, 2 vols., ed. R. Caggese, vol. 2, *Statuto del Podestà dell'anno 1325* (Florence, 1921), book 2, rubrics 69–70, pp. 139–42; T. Kuehn, "Some Ambiguities of Female Inheritance Ideology in the Renaissance," in Kuehn, *Law, Family, and Women*, pp. 238–57.

no brothers, but only uncles or cousins, the law gave her the right of use (*usufructus*), but not inheritance, of her father's property, unless she had already been given a dowry. If she was widowed, she had the right to return to her father's home, or, if no male descendants remained, she again gained the use of the estate. To all of this, which was more or less standard practice among elite families, the law added that a woman could inherit from her own intestate mother only if the mother had no living sons. Since most women's estates consisted above all of their dowries, the law in essence prevented daughters (unless they had no brothers) from inheriting the dowries of their own mothers, thus channeling the assets that women brought to their marriages from their natal families into the hands of their sons and their husbands' patrilines.[35] With regard to her dowry, the statutes prescribed that when a woman died without children, the husband inherited the entire dowry; even if she left a will, her husband got one-third of her non-dotal goods.[36]

The limitations spelled out in 1325 were made even more restrictive in subsequent statutory redactions, especially that of 1415, in which the list of relations by whom a woman could be excluded from the paternal inheritance was expanded to include her deceased father's father and grandfather. Women's exclusion from their mothers' inheritance by their own brothers and brothers' children was extended to inheritance from their maternal grandmothers as well. If a woman had living sons (or grandsons from these sons), her maternal granddaughter was excluded by these uncles and cousins. Other changes in 1415 eliminated "usufruct" and replaced it with subsidies for living costs from the paternal estate both before marriage and in widowhood, and declared that no woman could dispose of her dowry, even in her will, in any way that damaged the rights of her husband, her sons, or their descendants.[37] Such at least were the intentions of Florentine legislators. Much less evident is the extent to which Florentines, both women and men, actually observed these laws. The very fact of intensifying restrictions suggests that, whatever the rules may have been (and it is worth emphasizing again that they applied largely to intestate succession), a good deal of property was being inherited and bequeathed by women, to the chagrin of many men.

---

[35] I. Chabot, "La loi du lignage: Notes sur le système successoral florentin (XIVᵉ/XVᵉ–XVIIᵉ siècles)," *Clio* 7 (1998): 51–72.

[36] J. Kirshner, "Materials for a Gilded Cage: Non-Dotal Assets in Florence, 1300–1500," in *The Family in Italy from Antiquity to the Present*, ed. D. I. Kertzer and R. P. Saller (New Haven, 1991), pp. 184–207.

[37] Chabot, "Loi du lignage," pp. 55, 58, 63; *Statuta populi et communis Florentiae publica auctoritate collecta castigata et praeposita anno salutis MCCCCXV*, 3 vols. (Freiburg [but actually Florence]: 1778–81), vol. 1, pp. 222–3.

Children, Hospitals, Charity

Florentine mothers and children faced dangers that were universal in pre-modern Europe, above all the high rate of mortality among infants and women in childbirth. It is difficult for us to imagine a world in which women had to go from one pregnancy to another merely to keep the population from declining. Within the wealthy upper classes that could afford large numbers of children, pregnancies were frequent. In what is surely an exceptional example, a Corsini wife gave birth to twenty children in twenty-four years between 1365 and 1389.[38] Dati recorded that his third wife Ginevra Brancacci, who entered their marriage in May 1403 with an eight-month-old son from her previous marriage, gave birth in April 1404, March 1405 (born prematurely at seven months), June 1406, June 1407, August 1408, July 1411, October 1412, May 1415, April 1416, June 1417, and July 1418. In 1427, children between the ages of 0 and 4 represented 15% of the overall population, and those between 0 and 14 fully 39%.[39] But huge numbers of them died in infancy or childhood. The *ricordanze* of Florentine fathers dutifully record the many births but also note with depressing frequency the deaths that were nearly as numerous. In 1422 Dati did some sad counting: of the twenty children born to him and his wives to that point, only five were still living. His fourth wife Caterina gave birth to seven more children, three of whom were still alive at the end of 1431.[40] Without knowing the fate of these three, we cannot be sure of how many of the twenty-six children born to Dati's four wives (plus the illegitimate son Maso born to his Tartar slave in Spain, where Dati was living between his first and second marriages) survived to adulthood. Despite all the pregnancies, and the deaths of several wives from complications of childbirth, the number of Dati's children who reached an age at which they might have had children of their own may have been no more than half a dozen; they outnumbered their mothers by only one. Between plagues and infant mortality, this was a society that struggled, at huge costs to women and children, simply to maintain its numbers.

Infanticide and abandonment (actual abandonment, not the separation of a mother from her children because of her remarriage) were problems of differing degrees of seriousness. Acts of intentional infanticide were extremely rare and considered heinous crimes meriting capital punishment. In 1407 a woman from the contado of Pistoia, already pregnant by one man, married another, who knew nothing of her condition, and gave birth to a boy whom she killed

[38]   Herlihy and Klapisch-Zuber, *Tuscans*, p. 81.
[39]   Ibid., pp. 238, 187; cf. Molho, *Marriage Alliance*, pp. 411–15.
[40]   *I libri di famiglia e il* Libro segreto *di Goro Dati*, ed. L. Pandimiglio (Alessandria, 2006), pp. 120–3, 131–2.

to hide her guilt. She was burned to death with the body of her dead child tied to her.[41] Although infanticide was perhaps marginally more common in rural areas than in cities, a survey of some 8,000 criminal prosecutions covering thirty-six years (1398–1434) in the courts of the Florentine vicars in the outlying districts yields only seven cases of infanticide, mostly linked to situations of adultery or incest.[42] More difficult to detect was virtual or presumptive infanticide resulting from neglect or smothering. At the end of the fifteenth century the bishop of Fiesole launched an investigation of suspected or confessed cases of suffocation; he excommunicated a number of married couples (mostly wet nurses and their husbands) for having suffocated babies (presumably unintentionally), and prohibited parents and wet nurses from keeping infants in their own beds. Subsequent absolutions cover a total of some 280 suffocations, equally divided between infant boys and girls, over a period of thirty-five years in the early sixteenth century, an average of eight per year in the entire diocese.[43]

Abandonment of children was a major problem. Children of destitute parents in the countryside, of the poor, ill, or transient in the city, as well as children born to domestic slaves, were the most likely to be abandoned, and not all were infants. Admissions to the city's foundling hospital of the Innocenti, which opened its doors in 1445, suggest the dimensions of the phenomenon. In its first decade, 813 children were admitted, 44.5% of them boys and 55.5% girls. Over the next twelve years admissions grew (a total of 1,754, averaging 146 per year, an 80% increase, with a similar sex ratio: 43.2% boys and 56.8% girls), suggesting that the hospital's very existence may have prompted more frequent abandonment. Economic conditions in the contado may explain why abandonment was more frequent there, but many of the city's abandoned children were the issue of illicit sexual unions between upper-class men and slave mothers. The Innocenti knew the parents or origins of 41 of the first 100 children admitted: 27 from the contado and 14 from the city, the latter mostly children of upper-class men and domestic slaves.[44] Of all the dysfunctions of upper-class Florentine families, the acquisition, importation, and sexual exploitation of domestic slaves were no doubt the most difficult to reconcile with the period's idyllic images of family life. Domestic

---

[41] I. Walter, "Infanticidio a Ponte Bocci, 2 marzo 1406: elementi di un processo," *Studi storici* 27 (1986): 637–48; Brucker, *Society*, pp. 146–7.

[42] Cohn, *Women in the Streets*, pp. 100, 105; cf., for a later period, G. Hanlon, "L'infanticidio di coppie sposate in Toscana nella prima età moderna," *Quaderni storici* 113 (2003): 453–98.

[43] R. C. Trexler, "Infanticide in Florence: New Sources and First Results," in *Dependence in Context*, pp. 203–24, esp. 212–16.

[44] P. Gavitt, *Charity and Children in Renaissance Florence: The Ospedale degli Innocenti, 1410–1536* (Ann Arbor, 1990), pp. 206–12.

servitude was not unknown earlier, but reduced population and scarce labor made it more common after the Black Death. In 1364 the government legalized the purchase and importation of slaves, provided they were not Christian,[45] and for the next century modest but significant numbers of slaves, mainly from the regions around the Black Sea where Genoese and Venetians controlled trade in both goods and humans, were brought to Italian cities for sale as domestic servants. A register of slaves sold in the city between 1366 and 1397 records 357 sales (70% of them, however, in only the first few years); 76% were Tartars and 90% women.[46] In the second half of the fifteenth century, African slaves begin to appear in the commercial operations (including the sale of a small number in Tuscany) of Florentines doing business in Portugal.[47] Among domestic servants in Florence between 1300 and 1530, non-Tuscans have been estimated at 14% and slaves less than 10%. If that is so, there must have been a large population of non-slave domestics, because the 1427 Catasto records 360 women slaves throughout the dominion, 294 of them in Florence, employed by 261 families.[48] These are many fewer than Genoa's slaves (estimated at 2,000), but they are nearly 1% of Florence's population in 1427. Most slaves spent their lives in their owners' households, were usually well provided for, and in many cases eventually freed. But girls and younger women were not infrequently sexual targets of owners, their sons, or others, and children born of such liaisons were usually entrusted to one or another of the hospitals that took in children: 22% of children admitted to San Gallo in the 1430s were there because of their mothers' "servile status."[49] Admission to a foundling hospital automatically freed children from both illegitimacy and slave status, which was not typically inherited.

To make pregnancies more frequent, it was common practice among those who could afford it to send infants to wet nurses. Wet nursing was a major preoccupation of wealthy Florentine parents, and a major occupation of working-class women, especially in the contado. Fathers established agreements with wet nurses who met their requirements of health and character. Usually within days or weeks of birth, infants were sent, sometimes considerable distances, into the countryside to wet nurses for an average of 18 to 20 months or even 2 to 2½ years. Live-in wet nurses were the most expensive, and city

[45]   G. A. Brucker, *Firenze nel Rinascimento* (Florence, 1980), pp. 369–70.

[46]   I. Origo, "The Domestic Enemy: The Eastern Slaves in Tuscany in the Fourteenth and Fifteenth Centuries," *Speculum* 30 (1955): 321–66 (336).

[47]   S. Tognetti, "Note sul commercio di schiavi neri nella Firenze del Quattrocento," *Nuova rivista storica* 86 (2002): 361–74.

[48]   C. Klapisch-Zuber, "Le serve a Firenze nei secoli XIV e XV," in her *La famiglia e le donne nel Rinascimento a Firenze* (Bari, 1988), pp. 253–83.

[49]   Herlihy and Klapisch-Zuber, *Tuscans*, p. 145.

wet nurses cost more than their countryside counterparts, and, perhaps for this reason, about two-thirds of families employing wet nurses found them in the contado.[50] Although criticized by humanists and religious writers who thought mothers should nurse their own children, wet nursing made it easier for parents to resume sexual relations and increased the frequency of pregnancies. Because of its ubiquity and importance for upper-class families, the commune legislated, and incorporated into the statutes, pay rates for wet nurses. The practice had its problematic aspects, beginning with the class dimension: the upper classes bought the milk of poor women whose own infants had either to have died or were themselves put out to other wet nurses. How many rural mothers may have been tempted to abandon or neglect their own children in order to take in city infants and thus augment the family income can only be speculated, but the whole system was predicated on a supply of women with milk but somehow without their own infants. Still more a matter of speculation is the psychological effect on children of living their first two years with one family and mother and then being returned to what they were told to accept as their real families. Again it is Giovanni Morelli who provides the intriguing clues. His father Paolo used to say that he never knew his own father because he "sent him to a wetnurse in the Mugello and kept him there until [Paolo] was almost a big boy," in this unusual case apparently until he was ten or twelve. Giovanni supposes that this happened because Paolo's mother had died and his father wanted neither the responsibility nor the cost of raising his youngest son at home. Paolo developed a hatred for his wet nurse that he carried with him all his life: Paolo "told our mother that this wet nurse of his was the strangest and wildest woman who ever lived and that she hit him so many times that just thinking about her he was filled with such anger that if he had been able to get his hands on her he would have killed her."[51] Paolo's anger against his wet nurse was no doubt genuine, especially if she beat him, but one wonders how much of it was displaced anger against a father who had abandoned him.

An early instance of government's expanding role in family matters was the institution of the magistracy that administered state guardianships for orphaned minors, the Magistrato dei Pupilli. From the 1360s to the 1380s, the Signoria and councils occasionally accepted petitions, submitted on behalf of minors whose fathers had died intestate, requesting the appointment of estate guardians until the children achieved their legal majority. Sometimes the government appointed guardians and sometimes assumed the responsibility

---

[50]   C. Klapisch-Zuber, "Blood Parents and Milk Parents: Wet Nursing in Florence, 1300–1500," in her *Women, Family, and Ritual*, pp. 132–64 (136, table 7.1); Gavitt, *Charity and Children*, pp. 162–70, 226–43.

[51]   Morelli, *Ricordi*, p. 144; *Mercanti scrittori*, ed. Branca, pp. 135–6.

itself. In 1384 the transfer of minors' estates to communal administration by testamentary delegation was allowed, because, according to the law, "many citizens deprived of affines and agnates in the nearest degree," or who, not trusting them, refused to appoint them as guardians, preferred to accept the commune's help in safeguarding the interests of minors. In other cases guardians designated by testators either refused such duties or performed them badly. Over the next ten years, seventy-one estates came under communal supervision, thirty-one of them by testators' wishes, and most after 1388, when legislation mandated using the income to reduce the public debt and restoring these sums to the estates with 5% annual interest when minors reached their legal majority. By 1393 the growing number of estates under communal guardianship necessitated the institution of the new magistracy, which managed estates, paid their wards' living expenses from the proceeds, and promised them 5% annual return on the property; income in excess of this went to the communal treasury for debt reduction. Nearly 100 estates came under Pupilli administration in 1400–9, 150 in 1410–19, and 223 in 1420–9. This did not evolve from a preconceived plan to intervene in the private testamentary and economic affairs of Florentine families: many simply trusted the government over their relatives. For 77% of the estates that came under government supervision, the reasons are known; half of these came via testamentary election. Communal management of minors' estates was thus largely a matter of citizens' choice, apparently motivated by frequent lack of trust among relatives, by conflicts of interest between minors and guardians, and by the fragile nature of that much lauded solidarity among kinsmen found in contemporary idealizations of the Florentine family. Intervention by the Pupilli became necessary or desirable when fissures appeared within a patriline or between in-laws who found it difficult to dissolve their affinal bonds amicably.[52]

Florence's hospitals contributed substantially to the assistance of children and the poor. According to Giovanni Villani (12.94), in the 1330s the city already had thirty hospitals with a total of 1,000 beds for "the poor and the infirm." Among older hospitals, the largest were San Gallo, San Paolo, and Santa Maria Nuova, which took in both the ill and the destitute poor. In the second half of the century and continuing into the fifteenth, hospitals became more numerous and specialized in their services. In the 1370s Niccolò di Jacopo Alberti funded the construction of a hospice for poor and widowed women, called the Orbatello, subsequently administered by the Parte Guelfa after the exile of the Alberti. The Orbatello housed some 200 women, mostly

---

[52]   C. Fisher, "The State as Surrogate Father: State Guardianship in Renaissance Florence, 1368–1532," Ph.D. dissertation, Brandeis University, 2003. My thanks to Dr. Fisher for permission to report some of the findings of her dissertation.

from the artisan and lower classes, and allowed them to bring their children with them.[53] Two more hospitals were founded within the next fifteen years: Bonifazio, named after its patron, the military captain Bonifazio Lupi, who asked that it be supervised by the Calimala guild; and San Matteo, built by the merchant Lemmo Balducci, who entrusted its administration to the bankers' guild.[54]

Care of abandoned children was traditionally one among many functions of Florentine hospitals, especially San Gallo and Santa Maria della Scala. In the early fifteenth century, the wealthy merchant Francesco Datini founded a hospital specifically for abandoned children. His motivation no doubt emerged from his having entrusted his only child, Ginevra, born out of wedlock, to the care of Santa Maria Nuova. Although he relinquished responsibility for raising her, Datini provided Ginevra with a 1,000 florin dowry and later bequeathed to her another 1,000 florins of real estate. In 1410, in the final and deathbed version of a will over which he agonized for many years with the prodding of his friend and spiritual adviser, the Florentine notary Lapo Mazzei, Datini decided to use his immense fortune to create a charitable trust under the control of the commune of his native city of Prato. Among other bequests, in addition to the gift to Ginevra, and money, land, a house, and household goods for his "beloved wife, mona Margherita," Datini left 1,000 florins to Santa Maria Nuova for the construction of a new foundling hospital.[55] In 1419 the guild of Por Santa Maria took over the project and petitioned the commune of Prato for the transfer of the bequest to the guild's consuls to aid in the already initiated construction of the hospital, subsequently known as the Innocenti, in piazza Santissima Annunziata. Among the guild representatives who took possession of the gift was Goro Dati. Soon thereafter, the guild engaged Filippo Brunelleschi to design the new building whose portico, with its mix of classical and Tuscan Romanesque elements, heralded the beginning of a new architectural style. Construction went on for more than twenty years, and in 1445 the Innocenti finally opened its doors. Hospitals became magnets for pious bequests, as charitable confraternities had been a century earlier.[56] Many citizens transferred to hospitals ownership of land, houses, or

---

[53] R. C. Trexler, "A Widows' Asylum of the Renaissance: The Orbatello of Florence," in *Dependence in Context*, pp. 415–48.
[54] Gavitt, *Charity and Children*, p. 18; J. Henderson, *Piety and Charity*; L. Sandri, "Ospedali e utenti dell'assistenza nella Firenze del Quattrocento," in *La società del bisogno: povertà e assistenza nella Toscana medievale*, ed. G. Pinto (Florence, 1989), pp. 61–100.
[55] Ser Lapo Mazzei, *Lettere di un notaro a un mercante del secolo XIV*, ed. C. Guasti, 2 vols. (Florence, 1880), 2:273–300; Gavitt, *Charity and Children*, pp. 33–59; and Trexler, *Public Life*, pp. 131–58.
[56] Henderson, *Piety and Charity*, pp. 344–53, 373–81.

other assets, while retaining the right of use until they died. Such bequests before death (*inter vivos*) were not infrequently attempts to reduce taxable wealth; during fiscal crises pressures mounted to tap the accumulating assets of hospitals and other charitable foundations, and the commune investigated and punished what it considered fraudulent transfers. To protect the material foundation of their charitable activities, hospitals petitioned the commune for tax-exempt status. Such exemptions long remained a source of contention, but by and large hospitals succeeded in protecting their wealth from both the commune and, with the commune's help, from the church as well.[57] In the case of the Innocenti, the legislative councils granted tax-exemption in 1430 on the grounds that "from so laudable an undertaking it can reasonably be hoped that divine mercy will be more favorably inclined perpetually to safeguard the liberty of the Florentine people and the benefactors of this hospital."[58] This is a typical expression of the idea that charitable works would generate divine favor and protection for the institutions and persons supporting them.

Policing Sodomy

Pervading the commune's social and moral policies in these decades was concern for the city's sanctification and its standing before the Almighty. Care of widows and orphans, provision of dowries, and promotion of marriage were among its benign manifestations. But it also generated a need to purify the city, to cleanse it of those behaviors and persons that might cause a loss of divine favor. Purification needs scapegoats, who in fifteenth-century Florence included both sodomites and women. A law of 1433 thundered against "the barbarous and irrepressible bestiality of women" and their "reprobate and diabolical nature" that forces men to "submit to them." Blaming men's reluctance to marry on women's inordinate desire for "expensive ornaments," the law was another in a long series of attempts to regulate dress and its attendant expenditures: at least thirty-three sumptuary laws were passed in Florence in the fourteenth century, and twenty-five more in the fifteenth.[59] But the earlier emphasis on benefits to the treasury from fines levied for violations of prohibitions against excessive opulence was now subordinated to moral concerns. Dramatic moralizing and scapegoating also accompanied the commune's supervision of sexual misconduct in convents through a magistracy created in 1421. Adopting the same theology of an angry God punishing the whole

[57]   Gavitt, *Charity and Children*, pp. 61–105.
[58]   ASF, Provvisioni, Registri, 121, ff. 78v–79 (October 29, 1430).
[59]   C. Kovesi Killerby, *Sumptuary Law in Italy, 1200–1500* (Oxford, 2002), p. 28.

world for the sins of the depraved, a 1435 prohibition against relations with nuns and access to convents began by invoking the Day of Judgment and its "angry judge" when the "worthy" will be welcomed into paradise and the "unworthy, accursed ones" consigned to the "eternal fire . . . with an infinite number of demons." Remarkably, here too the purity of the family is declared to be at stake, because nuns, as "brides of God," were violating holy matrimony. "Natural law has ordained that the human species should multiply and that man and woman be joined together by holy matrimony, [which] is and should be of such gravity and dignity that it should be respected by everyone. Nothing is more pleasing to God than the preservation of matrimony; nothing is more displeasing to him than its violation." Because of the failings of nuns through "carnal desire," "divine providence is perturbed and has afflicted the world with the evils of wars, disorders, epidemics, and other calamities and troubles."[60] Widely (and wildly) promoted fears of the dangers threatening the purity of the republic were no doubt necessary to preserve the unity of the civic family and protect unquestioning acceptance of its patriarchal leadership.

In these same years, the government adopted novel policies toward homosexual relations and prostitution. A flourishing homosocial culture had developed in Florence in which men formed friendships and liaisons within only partly concealed networks of sociability in shops, taverns, and even churches. Long-term relationships were rare, occasional encounters the norm. Those who engaged in homosexual acts generally divided into two distinct age groups with different sexual roles. Young men between the ages of roughly eighteen and thirty took the dominant, or active, role in encounters in which they penetrated, but were not penetrated by, passive partners who were largely adolescents and teenaged boys. Among those accused of sodomy, 90% of passive partners were eighteen or younger and 83% of active partners nineteen or older. As boys passed the threshold of their eighteenth or nineteenth year, most gave up the passive role and became active partners with younger boys. And as young men went past the age of thirty, and especially if they married, most abandoned the homosexual practices of their youth. Homosexual relations between adult men were less common, but not exactly rare. Three-quarters of active partners were unmarried, which suggests that for the majority of men marriage deterred further involvement in homosexuality, but the one-quarter of active partners who were married shows that, for a substantial minority, homosexuality and marriage were not incompatible. Homosexual practices were not an alternative, and certainly not a permanent, sexual preference: the vast majority of those who engaged in them did not do so to the exclusion of sex with women or for their whole lives. But many did for some part of

[60] Brucker, *Society*, pp. 206–7.

their lives, and they came from all levels of society. In fact, more came from either the elite or the artisan-working classes than from the upper ranks of the popolo. Men and/or boys accused of sodomy could be found in half of the 400 wealthiest families in the last quarter of the fifteenth century, but over 90% of the 110 richest families among these 400 had one or more accused. Among artisans and shopkeepers, accused sodomites came from a wide variety of professions, but teachers and students, despite the reputation given them by literary sources, accounted for only one-half of 1% of the accused and less than 1% of those convicted.[61]

Whether homosocial and homosexual relations increased after 1400 is difficult to say, but they certainly received more attention than before, from public authorities and moralists both lay and ecclesiastical. Intensifying fears of sodomy around 1400 were grounded in the assumption that Florentine men were avoiding marriage in preference for the pleasures of homosexuality or turning to the latter in the absence of marital sex because of the late age at which they married. Despite early laws prescribing severe penalties, including death, for sodomy, prosecutions were relatively rare in the fourteenth century and mostly limited to cases of abuse or rape of children. Just after the turn of the century, heightened fears put pressure on the government to do something about sodomy. In 1403 the legislative councils approved a proposal from the Signoria for the "elimination and extirpation" of sodomy, but what the law actually did was to institute the magistracy of the Officials of Decency (*Ufficiali dell'Onestà*) charged, not with punishing sodomy, but with supervising a new communal brothel, to which two more were added in 1415: if heterosexual outlets were provided for the city's unmarried young men, so it was assumed, they would be lured away from sodomy. The Officials of Decency kept records of the women employed, protected them by prosecuting abusive clients, and occasionally fined the women for violating regulations concerning dress and prescribed locations. Most of the women were non-Florentines and even non-Italian. But if the purpose was to "save" Florentine men from homosexuality, the scheme didn't work: more than half the men punished, who presumably reflected the overall clientele, were themselves non-Tuscans and 75% non-Florentines.[62]

In 1415 the newly redacted communal statutes underscored the need to suppress sodomy but took the approach that less severe penalties would permit more prosecutions and convictions. Over the next several years, other

---

[61]   M. Rocke, *Forbidden Friendships: Homosexuality and Male Culture in Renaissance Florence* (Oxford, 1996), pp. 120, 96–7, 134–47, 243–51.
[62]   R. Trexler, "Florentine Prostitution in the Fifteenth Century: Patrons and Clients" in Trexler, *Dependence in Context*, pp. 373–414; M. S. Mazzi, *Prostitute e lenoni nella Firenze del Quattrocento* (Milan, 1991).

laws vested authority for the punishment of sodomites in a variety of courts. In 1418, "desiring to extirpate that vice of Sodom and Gomorrah, so contrary to nature that the anger of the omnipotent God is incited not only against the sons of men but also against the community and even inanimate objects," the Signoria appointed a committee "to ponder and search their souls for ways and methods by which [sodomy] might be eradicated" from the city.[63] But the anxious rhetoric produced only an ambivalent and halting record of legislation and enforcement, which suggests a city divided between zealots determined to repress sexual practices considered deviant and realists reluctant to see the government involved in the business of policing sexuality, no doubt in part because so many of their own sons were bound to be implicated in a more vigorous prosecution of sodomy.

It was in this tense situation that the Franciscan Bernardino of Siena came to Florence in 1424 and 1425 and devoted several long sermons of his Lenten cycles to the perils and evils of sodomy. As he had done and would later do elsewhere, Bernardino denounced sodomy, with captivating rhetoric and a whole panoply of biblical, patristic, moral, and social arguments, as the worst of all sins, as an offense against nature, indeed as more offensive to God than any other sin, and repulsive even to the devil himself. In many cities his sermons were influential in mobilizing fears and persuading governments to pass tougher anti-sodomy laws. Bernardino explicitly linked sodomy to the demographic crisis and blamed it on what he saw as the dysfunctional aspects of contemporary families. On the first point, he was sure of the cause-and-effect relationship but less so of whether others had grasped it: "You don't understand," he said in a 1424 sermon, "that this is the reason you have lost half your population over the last twenty-five years. Tuscany has the fewest people of any country in the world, solely on account of this vice." Sodomites who refused to father children were guilty of "filicide" and murder of the unborn. Most extraordinary, however, were Bernardino's denunciations of mothers and fathers as responsible for the homoerotic inclinations of their sons. Mothers, he insisted, dressed up young sons to make them look pretty and alluring, in the process rendering them effeminate and even more appealing to older sodomites and receptive to their attentions. They thus spoiled their sons and robbed them of their masculinity. Fathers were also to blame. Referring to the "coldness of paternal love," Bernardino criticized their frequent absence and indifference as major reasons why their young sons turned to sodomy. He painted a picture of permissiveness and indulgence on the part of mothers, and of inadequate parental, and especially paternal, supervision, such that by the age of eighteen these unruly sons were like "unbridled horses, with no fear

---

[63]   Rocke, *Forbidden Friendships*, pp. 20–36; Brucker, *Society*, pp. 202–3.

of God or of the saints or of mothers or parents."[64] How accurate Bernardino's diagnosis was is difficult to say, since he certainly exaggerated for rhetorical and hortatory effect. Wealthy Florentines did spend large sums on clothes, which functioned as conspicuous advertisements of wealth,[65] and fifteenth-century paintings offer many examples of sumptuously dressed and androgynously beautiful boys. If Bernardino's assumption that mothers were the chief influence over sons while fathers remained emotionally distant is accurate, the period's frequent praise of stern paternal guidance and love may actually have been prompted by the fear that mothers had too much power because of the aloofness of fathers. If Florentine children, even beyond infancy, knew their mothers far better than they did their fathers, one reason was certainly that many mothers were approximately equidistant in age between their eldest children and their husbands. While Bernardino's explanations for the prevalence of sodomy were probably not correct, in the process of finding someone to blame he may have put his finger on real pathologies and dysfunctions in Florentine families.

In April 1432 the Signoria proposed and the councils instituted (by substantial but not unopposed majorities of 189–39 and 199–25) the Officials of the Night, an annually elected magistracy of six citizens, who had to be married and at least forty-five years of age, charged with receiving anonymous accusations against sodomites and selecting those they deemed sufficiently serious and credible to warrant investigation, interrogation, and a judgment.[66] Convictions required a confession, or two eyewitnesses, or four people willing to certify that the alleged acts were a matter of public knowledge. The Night Officials almost never convicted minors, concentrating instead on the older, active partners; workers, artisans and minor guildsmen had a greater chance of being convicted than did persons from elite families. Between 1432 and 1502, when the office was abolished, the Officials received more than 15,000 accusations (over 200 per year) and handed down approximately 2,400 convictions. Most of those convicted were punished with fines (50 florins for initial convictions and 100, 200, and 500 florins for subsequent convictions), a few by public humiliation, prison, or exile, while only a handful received death sentences for assault or rape of children. Jurisdiction over violent crimes, including homosexual assault and rape, was shared by the courts of the podestà, Capitano, and Esecutore (the latter until its abolition in 1435), as well as the

---

[64]   F. Mormando, *The Preacher's Demons: Bernardino of Siena and the Social Underworld of Early Renaissance Italy* (Chicago, 1999), pp. 109–63 (129, 130–7); Rocke, *Forbidden Friendships*, pp. 36–40.

[65]   Frick, *Dressing Renaissance Florence*, pp. 95–114.

[66]   Brucker, *Society*, pp. 203–4.

magistracy of the Otto di Guardia (Eight of Ward), but even counting the death sentences decreed by these courts brings the total number of men executed for crimes associated with sodomy to about six in the eighty years between 1420 and 1500.[67]

Although the Night Officials neither eliminated sodomy nor punished it with particular severity, they had, and used, broad authority to investigate consensual homosexual acts brought to their attention by anonymous accusers. Their policing of sodomy displayed the paradox of a policy that implicated and embarrassed many citizens, collected sizeable sums from at least some of those convicted, but stopped short of applying the kinds of penalties that might have deterred men and boys from the practice of sodomy. Convictions rose from eight in their first year to thirty-seven in 1435 and then declined: an average of thirteen per year until the 1460s, when they increased significantly, reaching their highest levels in the first five years of Lorenzo de' Medici's leadership when 535 men were convicted.[68] The fact that convictions peaked in 1435, the first year of the Medici regime, again in Lorenzo's shaky early years beginning in 1469, in 1480 after the Pazzi conspiracy, and in the precarious first (and only full) year of leadership of Lorenzo's son Piero, strongly suggests that the prosecution of sodomy was used as a political weapon. But its larger significance lies in the acceptance of a regime of surveillance and of the government's right and duty to discipline, punish, and shame those who engaged in sexual practices it could neither ignore nor suppress. Thousands of anonymous accusations, investigations, and interrogations resulted in social opprobrium for the "guilty," a sense of vindicated indignation for citizens who accused them out of a combination of civic duty, fear, and moralistic fervor, and a useful way for the Medici regime to intimidate opponents. The strange story of the policing of sodomy in Florence shows a city divided between defenders of morality and advocates (obviously not limited to those who practiced the "abominable vice") of a laissez-faire attitude willing to leave such matters to private consciences.

[67] Rocke, *Forbidden Friendships*, pp. 47–54, 78–9; L. I. Stern, *The Criminal Law System of Medieval and Renaissance Florence* (Baltimore, 1994); A. Zorzi, *L'amministrazione della giustizia penale nella repubblica fiorentina* (Florence, 1988).
[68] Rocke, *Forbidden Friendships*, pp. 270, n. 18, 237–41, 54–9, 198–9.

9

Fateful Embrace: The Emergence of the Medici

The Medici are so inextricably linked to Florence, having dominated its history for three centuries from the 1430s to the 1730s and left their imprint everywhere, that to many it seems impossible to imagine that what preceded them was not merely prologue and that the republic was not somehow destined to come under the leadership of these merchant-bankers who became patrons, *patres patriae*, popes, and princes. This is indeed the myth they wanted the Florentines to accept: that an unstable republic, unsure of itself and in need of a guiding hand, was fortunate enough to find it within, rather than imposed from without, and that the grateful Florentines themselves, recognizing the political skills and benevolence of the Medici, willingly elevated them to power. It is another version of the myth of consensus first adopted by the ruling elite of the preceding half-century, since the Medici appropriated the notions of civic family and beneficent patriarchy first developed by the oligarchy to consolidate its collective rule. Beneath both versions of the myth was the reality of a divided society: understanding the Medici regime, no less than for the pre-Medici oligarchy, requires that we see the underlying conflicts, opposition, and internal contradictions that made both regimes weaker than their myths allow.

A New Style of Leadership

From the vantage point of 1400, the chances of a single family emerging to the prominence the Medici gained even by the 1440s, let alone under Lorenzo, must have seemed remote. Not that it was unthinkable; indeed most of the communes of northern Italy had long since evolved into some form of one-family regime. But the Florentines had experimented with one-man emergency regimes in the 1320s and 1340s and in each case became quickly disenchanted with the reality of what initially seemed appealing. Moreover, the fate of the Alberti demonstrated the oligarchy's fear of families of great size and wealth with international connections and prestige; their long exile, which eliminated them as a political force even after they returned, stood as a warning to other families that might have been tempted to become too great or visible. Florentine fear of the "signore" and the story of the Alberti made it at least unlikely that any family would succeed in doing what none had ever done in this republic in which all watched like hawks for signs of unacceptable ambition.

In retrospect, nonetheless, signs of change were not lacking and developments were preparing the way, if not for the Medici, then for someone like them. Increasingly cut off from the corporate solidarities that had defined their political role and collective interests for so long, guildsmen found it increasingly necessary to look to powerful men for patronage, favors, assistance, and protection. A few patrons emerged as leaders of more extensive networks of allies and clients that were the foundation of their political prominence. Patronage had always been a crucial source of elite power, but after 1400 it became politically more pervasive and decisive, as patrons expected "friends" and clients to support them in scrutinies, legislative councils, and executive offices. And because political power depended on the size, extent, and cohesiveness of these circles of friends and clients, men with political ambition competed as never before to form and keep large and dependable networks of *amici*. Politics came increasingly under the influence of these major figures who commanded the support of clients, who enjoyed influence beyond the offices they held, and whose opinions shaped political debate and policy. In a few cases they remained powerful and visibly prominent for decades, among other places in the pratiche, which became more frequent (from 21 in 1385 to 37 in 1410), and to which more citizens were invited (193 total participants in 1385, 464 in 1410, 153 of whom made recorded speeches). But certain individuals enjoyed a regular and dominating presence. Among the 153 speakers in 1410, six spoke fourteen or more times, and one spoke thirty times: four of these same six and one other spoke in over a hundred meetings between 1403 and 1414. As noted in chapter 6, this was the core of the leadership group in the century's first two decades: Maso degli Albizzi, Piero Baroncelli, Filippo Corsini, Cristofano Spini, Rinaldo Gianfigliazzi, and, just beneath them in frequency of participation, Niccolò da Uzzano, Gino Capponi, and Lorenzo Ridolfi.[1] In the next decade Rinaldo degli Albizzi, Palla Strozzi,

---

[1]   Brucker, *Civic World*, pp. 264–5, 284–5.

and Neri di Gino Capponi also assumed positions within the leadership. The emergence of these "big men" was not necessarily a function of the offices they held. Rinaldo degli Albizzi served often as a military commissioner, but only once on the priorate (1416) and twice on the advisory colleges. Palla Strozzi served three times on the advisory colleges, but never on the Signoria. Power was now exercised less through office-holding than through patronage and behind-the-scenes channels, and this established important precedents for the emergence in the 1420s and 1430s of Cosimo de' Medici, who, although he became bigger than the rest and put them all in his shadow (or in exile), was neither the only nor the first "big man" of his generation.

Two further signs of the emergence of a new kind of political leadership were "successions" of sons to the dignities of prominent fathers, and public acknowledgments, under the influence of these same leaders, of the merits and "virtues" of leading citizens and sometimes even of the "successions." Neri di Gino Capponi followed his father into the leadership; three of Rinaldo Gianfigliazzi's sons became prominent in the oligarchy in the early 1430s; and Cosimo de' Medici inherited and vastly expanded the influence bequeathed by his father Giovanni. But the Albizzi are the most revealing example: when Rinaldo "inherited" his father's leadership role in the regime, the commune bestowed its formal approval by first honoring Maso with a state funeral and then, a few months later, conferring an honorary knighthood on Rinaldo. The Signoria in office in 1417 when Maso died (which included Filippo Corsini as Standardbearer of Justice) asked the councils to approve expenditures for the funeral, describing Maso as "dear to the *patria*, faithful to the state, beloved by the citizens, and resplendent with all the virtues." Although the councils agreed, there was opposition: a total of 115 in the two councils voted against it. The Signoria of April 1418 proposed Rinaldo's knighthood, describing him as a man "made famous not only by the distinguished deeds of his ancestors but also by his own virtue" and as "most worthy of supreme honors," given him in order to "show in how much affection Rinaldo is held on account of his love for the *patria* and his loyalty to the state and all citizens." This too was approved, but again with over one hundred dissenting votes.[2] Rhetorical echoes of the first measure in the second clearly imply that Rinaldo's virtues reflected those of his father and made him worthy of an honor that Maso had also enjoyed. Equally clear is that many in the councils were uneasy with this unprecedented official blessing of unofficial succession within the leadership. But the precedent was now established. A similar recognition of succession occurred at the funeral in 1429 of Matteo Castellani, who died while serving on the advisory college of the Sixteen and who had been awarded a knighthood

[2]   ASF, Provvisioni, Registri, 107, ff. 256–256v; 108, ff. 3v–4.

by the king of Naples when he was an ambassador in 1415, an honor subsequently confirmed by the Florentine government. The commune paid for his funeral, during which it also bestowed an honorary knighthood on his 12-year-old son Francesco.[3] Giovanni de' Medici also died in 1429, and the commune likewise paid for public honors at his funeral.[4] But in this case there was no knighthood for the son.

Most of the political writing of this period comes from civic humanists who celebrated (much in the spirit of the legislative enactments honoring the Albizzi) the patriotic virtues of the leadership elite. But one observer, the enigmatic and choleric Giovanni Cavalcanti, saw dangers in the politics of big men and their factions. Born around 1380 into an old magnate family, Cavalcanti chronicled the tumultuous events of the 1420s and 1430s, with particular attention to the eruption of factional divisions between the ruling oligarchy and the Medici, and expressed his dismay at the way factions and patrons were removing power from the institutions of government and, as he saw things, bringing about the triumph of private interests over the public good. Later in the century, the Medici were similarly accused by their critics, but Cavalcanti already saw evidence of these trends in the pre-Medici oligarchy. He describes a pratica to which he was invited, together with many others, to give counsel to the Signoria on how to respond to provocations by the duke of Milan. "We do not ask your advice for our benefit or special interest," he recalled the priors saying, "but we seek it as men who speak in the name of your commune, since, if today it is we who hold this office, tomorrow you will be here." As many speakers then rose to give their different views, Cavalcanti noticed that Niccolò da Uzzano, the most eminent of the group, slept until all the speeches were finished, then rose and spoke decisively and at length in favor of a strong response to the Milanese threat. "Once Niccolò said these things," the entire pratica "indicated its agreement with what he proposed," which prompted Cavalcanti to conclude that Niccolò, "together with other powerful men, had decided, in some private and secret place, that . . . he would express the view that he did and that the others would confirm and support it." Cavalcanti feared that pratiche were becoming a forum, not for exchanging and debating ideas, but for the ratification of policies already worked out in private by a few. As Cavalcanti told friends, "it seems to me that from this way of doing things tyrannical rule would replace constitutional government in the republic and that its governance would be conducted outside the palace [of the priors]." His friends agreed, adding that the "commune was being governed more at dinners and in studies than in the palace." "From

[3]   G. Ciappelli, "Il cittadino fiorentino e il fisco," p. 848.
[4]   ASF, Provvisioni, Registri, 120, f. 18v.

such abominable audacity," he concluded, "would result the greatest evils for the republic."[5]

Despite Cavalcanti's misgivings, the oligarchy ruled successfully for a long generation between the 1380s and the early 1420s, expanding Florentine power in Tuscany, surviving serious threats from Milan and Naples, and presiding over what was later remembered with nostalgia as a decade of peace and prosperity between 1414 and 1424. Had they been able to avoid the wars that engulfed the regime, the Medici, despite their wealth, might never have become more powerful than other leading families. Giovanni de' Medici was not among those who dominated the pratiche in these years (although, when he did speak, his opinions on financial and fiscal matters were highly respected),[6] and it was not at all evident before 1425 or 1426 that the Medici were about to become leaders of a strong faction that would challenge the coalition of smaller factions led by Rinaldo degli Albizzi, Palla Strozzi, and other leading oligarchs. But by the mid-1420s, the two essential conditions of the oligarchy's continued hegemony, containment of military expenses and relative harmony within the ruling group, were disintegrating. And when Cosimo emerged as the one man able to provide the needed funds for the hugely expensive wars that began in the mid-1420s, and, partly for this reason, began to play a leading role in the increasingly bitter divisions of the ruling group, the scene was set for the clash that led to Cosimo's expulsion by his rivals in 1433 and his victorious recall by his friends in 1434.

Fiscal Crisis and the Catasto

With tensions reviving between Milan and Florence, rifts developed within the leadership over how to respond to the Milanese occupation of Genoa in 1421 and provocative actions toward Bologna and farther south in the Romagna. Rinaldo degli Albizzi, Palla Strozzi, and others in the inner circle supported a hard line, while Averardo de' Medici, Cosimo's cousin and political ally, together with Lorenzo Ridolfi and members of the Guicciardini, Pandolfini, and Altoviti families initially urged restraint, chiefly because, having reduced military expenditures during the decade of peace, Florence was not prepared for war. But by 1423 spreading Visconti power in the Romagna persuaded the

---

[5]   Giovanni Cavalcanti, *Istorie fiorentine*, ed. F. Polidori, 2 vols. (Florence, 1838–9), 1:27–30; D. Kent, "The Importance of Being Eccentric: Giovanni Cavalcanti's View of Cosimo de' Medici's Florence," *Journal of Medieval and Renaissance Studies* 9 (1979): 101–32; M. T. Grendler, *The "Trattato Politico-Morale" of Giovanni Cavalcanti* (Geneva, 1973).

[6]   Brucker, *Civic World*, pp. 264–5, 294.

councils to accede to the Signoria's request for a war balìa. Although Giovanni de' Medici was thought by some, including Cavalcanti, not to favor war, he agreed to serve on the balìa, which sent commissioners, including Rinaldo, across the Apennines into the Romagna to coordinate efforts by Florence's newly hired mercenary captain, Pandolfo Malatesta of Rimini, to dislodge Visconti forces from the occupied towns. In 1424 Milanese threats of an attack by sea from Genoa sparked a major war that lasted until 1428. The next year, Florence launched an ill-advised and controversial war against the neighboring republic of Lucca, a conflict in which Milan again became involved and which lasted until 1433. And shortly thereafter hostilities against Milan began yet again and lasted until the early 1440s. Such a long period of nearly non-stop warfare had immense consequences for Florentine political and fiscal institutions and for the distribution of power within its ruling class. The internal political divisions sparked by these wars and their huge costs brought the Medici to power.

Initially, the war was a dismal failure for the Florentines. Major defeats from the summer of 1424 through the autumn of 1425 sent morale plummeting and military expenses skyrocketing, and threw the leadership into feverish debate over how to meet both the costs of the war and the protests against it.[7] Most immediately pressing was the need for added revenue: expensive mercenary forces commanded by condottieri who were also shrewd businessmen required ever higher sums far beyond what was available to the commune from ordinary revenues.[8] In 1424, 1426, and 1427, military costs alone averaged 470,000 florins per year; they remained high through 1428 and, after a brief respite in 1429, returned to these levels for at least three more years until 1432. In certain years of the earlier conflicts with Milan and Naples, war costs had been even higher: over 700,000 florins per year in 1390–2; approximately 600,000 in 1397, 1402, and 1403; 460,000 florins in 1409; and 550,000 in 1414. But between these exceptional years military expenditures were generally between 100,000 and 300,000 florins. What were once unusual levels of military spending became nearly constant in the nine years from 1424 to 1432. Also straining the communal budget in these years were record levels of interest owed on the communal debt. From the conclusion of the first Visconti wars in 1402 until the mid-1420s, annual carrying charges on the debt fluctuated between 167,000 and 280,000 florins. Although the combined cost of military outlays and interest payments exceeded 780,000 florins in 1402 and again in 1403, and approached 700,000 in each of the peak years of the

---

[7] Ibid., pp. 433–71; C. C. Bayley, *War and Society in Renaissance Florence: The De Militia of Leonardo Bruni* (Toronto, 1961), pp. 82–110.

[8] For what follows: Molho, *Public Finances*; Molho, "Fisco ed economia a Firenze alla vigilia del Concilio," in *Firenze e il Concilio del 1439*, ed. P. Viti, 2 vols. (Florence, 1994), 1:59–94.

war against Naples, they settled back to between 300,000 and 400,000 in the decade without major wars from 1414 to 1423. But in the mid-1420s borrowing soared and debt payments rose to 343,000 florins in 1426 and 370,000 in 1427. Combined military and debt costs, already at 628,000 florins in 1424, reached unprecedented highs of 894,000 florins in 1426 and 817,000 in 1427. Regular communal income (indirect taxes and direct levies on the contado and dominion) could not begin to cover these sums. From 1402 to 1420 annual income from gabelles averaged just over 200,000 florins and then declined just as the war began: from 1424 to 1432 it never reached 200,000 florins and averaged just over 150,000. Taxes on the subject territories yielded less than 100,000 florins per year before 1405, increased to between 110,000 and 160,000 in most years until 1416, and then declined to about 80,000 in the war years. The yawning gap between income and expenditures created a string of huge deficits. Although the commune had faced annual deficits of 500,000 florins in 1402–3, thereafter they were kept under 250,000 florins (except during the Neapolitan conflict) and in some years of the decade of peace were as low as 58,000 florins (in 1416) and a mere 22,500 (in 1420). But the deficit soared to 385,000 florins in 1424, reached a record 682,000 in 1426, and stayed high at 535,000 in 1427. Although data are incomplete for subsequent years, the level of borrowing indicates similar deficits through 1432.

Deficits were covered by unprecedented increases in borrowing, which took two forms: the forced loans (prestanze), which became a direct tax in all but name for most citizens; and special short-term loans extended by wealthy citizens in moments of particular need. The overall burden of forced loans doubled between the 1390s and 1424–33. In the 1390s the commune collected an annual average of 270,000 florins from prestanze, and in the following decade an average of 240,000. This was already an onerous burden for most Florentine households. In one gonfalone in the quarter of San Giovanni, the number of households paying full prestanza assessments fell from 397 in 1381 to 127 in 1397 and to only 51 in 1402, before recovering slightly to 95 in 1406. Citizens had the option of paying a portion of their assessments and forfeiting the right to interest, and in this gonfalone a fairly steady number of between 300 and 400 households chose this option. Even households with some taxable wealth were evidently unable to pay their full assessments. But attempts to tax a larger number of obviously poorer households resulted in a huge increase of those making no payment at all: from 93 in 1381 to 342 in 1397 and 860 in 1402. Smaller deficits in the decade of peace meant lower prestanze (only 4,000 florins in 1416, 61,000 in 1419, and 36,000 in 1420), but from the mid-1420s onwards, Florentines found themselves assessed for amounts that, cumulatively and annually, exceeded all earlier levels of taxation. In the eight years for which data are complete between 1424 and 1432, the commune collected forced loans of almost 4,335,000 florins, an average of

542,000 florins per year.[9] These immense sums were imposed on a population considerably diminished by plague, and, if so many households found the prestanze of the 1390s unbearable, the effect of levies twice as large a generation later must have been devastating. In the ten years from 1424 through 1433, assessments amounted to over 6,700,000. But by the early 1430s the sums actually collected began to fall short of assessments: whereas in 1430 the yield (629,000 florins) exceeded assessments (624,000), in the next year it was only 73% of assessments (690,000 out of 946,000 florins), and in 1432 only 63% (527,000 out of 834,000 florins). More and more households were simply unable to meet their obligations.[10]

Two major fiscal innovations emerged from this crisis: the Dowry Fund and the Catasto. The fiscal rationale behind the Dowry Fund was that it would draw money into the communal treasury in the form of deposits, which were used to purchase regular Monte shares at market value that were then credited to accounts at nominal value. As we have seen, however, deposits were meager until after the commune finally agreed (in 1433) to return them if girls died before marrying. While the treasury was of course obligated to pay out dowries representing a substantial accumulation of interest, the deferral of interest payments helped reduce carrying charges on the debt in the late 1430s and 1440s.[11] More immediate help came from the Catasto. Florentines had long complained that assessments for forced loans by neighborhood committees estimating household wealth entailed gross inequities, made still worse by favoritisms, patronage ties, and bribes. Even before the onset of the crisis, fiscal reform was debated in a large pratica of 1422 in which many argued that prestanze assessments evaluated taxable wealth largely on the basis of real property and that equity required that movable wealth and especially commercial investments also be included in a calculation of fiscal obligations. This was the basic idea already known as the Catasto. The argument against reform was that taxing investments and liquid assets would tighten credit and make it more difficult to borrow money, forcing the wealthy to invest elsewhere and depriving the poor of jobs and livelihoods. Of the wealthiest thirty-six participants in the 1422 debate, only six spoke in favor of the Catasto, twelve openly opposed it, and the rest either ignored it or mentioned it as one of several possible solutions. This initial discussion led to no legislative action.

Three years later, as the war caused ballooning deficits and forced loans, the Catasto was again being debated. Some former opponents now supported it, and Rinaldo degli Albizzi, who had previously taken no position on the

---

[9]   Molho, *Public Finances*, pp. 61–3, 68; Molho, "Fisco ed economia," pp. 93–4.
[10]   E. Conti, *L'imposta diretta a Firenze nel Quattrocento (1427–1494)* (Rome, 1984), pp. 81, 365.
[11]   Molho, *Marriage Alliance*, pp. 27–51; Conti, *L'imposta diretta*, pp. 39–47.

matter, was among its ardent promoters: "The institution of the Catasto is indeed just," he proclaimed. Debates continued for two more years without agreement: committees were appointed to study proposals and make recommendations, but the councils rejected them all. Cavalcanti says that Giovanni de' Medici championed the institution of the Catasto and that this made him popular with the guild community and the lower classes.[12] In fact, however, as late as March 1427 Giovanni opposed the Catasto in the pratiche while Rinaldo supported it. In May, on the eve of the councils' approval of the Catasto, Giovanni and two Medici allies were the only speakers who expressed doubts. He cautiously said that "Many have exhorted [on behalf of the Catasto], and some have doubted that it would bring the benefits that others claim." Uncertain about whether it would "bring good results," he "listened to the other citizens" and "decided to follow their opinion." Thus, if anything, he followed popular sentiment on the question. Among the priors who approved the Catasto and sent it to the councils were two Medici friends, and it is possible that, once Giovanni saw enthusiasm growing for it, he had his men support it in the Signoria. The reputation that the Medici acquired for supporting the Catasto, although not actually supported by the facts, was of considerable political use to them. As it turned out, the Catasto needed every vote it could get. On May 22, 1427, the Council of the Popolo approved it by a vote of 144–70 (only one vote over the required two-thirds majority); the next day the Council of the Commune gave its assent by a vote of 117–58 (with not a single vote to spare).[13] Arguments on both sides had brought divergent class interests back into Florentine political debate. Expressions of relief and satisfaction came from the guild community, which assumed that the wealthy would now pay more and that justice had been introduced into the fiscal system. Cavalcanti claims that Niccolò da Uzzano had never been assessed more than 16 florins in the prestanza rolls and was now faced with a tax obligation of 250 florins under the Catasto.[14] He was close to the mark: Niccolò and his brother Agnolo were assessed jointly at 20 florins in the prestanza of 1403, and Niccolò alone owed 232 florins every time the government collected Catasto assessments.[15] It is possible that Da Uzzano wealth increased over the years, but the difference (and Cavalcanti's point) lies in the Catasto's method of assessment.

---

[12]   Cavalcanti, *Istorie*, vol. 1, pp. 197–8.

[13]   Conti, *L'imposta diretta*, pp. 119–37. The Catasto law (ASF, Provvisioni, Registri, 117, ff. 38v–43) is published by O. Karmin, *La legge del Catasto fiorentino del 1427 (testo, introduzione e note)* (Florence, 1906).

[14]   Cavalcanti, *Istorie*, vol. 1, p. 214.

[15]   Martines, *Social World*, appendix II (tables on wealth), pp. 363, 375.

Every household was required to submit a declaration containing the names and ages of its members; its assessment in the most recent prestanza of 1426; the location of its principal residence; descriptions of all property owned in the city or contado; the value of all business activities, including invested capital and current inventories; credits in the public debt; sums owed by debtors; and all liabilities, including debts and other obligations. A household's principal residence was not taxed. For other properties taxable value was calculated from rental income, assumed to be 7% of its worth (hence, a house rented for 7 florins was valued at 100 florins). From the sum of assets liabilities were subtracted, including a deduction of 200 florins for each dependent (the capitalized value of the assumed annual per-person living cost of 14 florins). If assets exceeded liabilities, the difference was the household's taxable wealth, and its assessment – the amount it owed each time the government decreed a collection, which could be many times a year – was one half of 1% of taxable wealth.[16] Assessments remained in force until revised declarations were called for in 1431, and new ones again in 1433, which remained in force for three years. Thereafter, although household declarations based on quite different rules, but still under the name of the Catasto, were required in 1458, 1469, and 1480, the Medici regime returned by and large to the system of assessments by appointed committees. As originally conceived, the Catasto was in force only until the mid-1430s.

According to the 1427 declarations, the aggregate wealth of the city's almost 10,000 households (not counting therefore the considerable wealth possessed by ecclesiastical institutions) amounted to 10,169,109 florins. Taxable wealth after deductions (but before the 200-florin deduction for family members) came to 7,665,068 florins. Largely exempt were the poor and much of the working class (who continued nonetheless to pay the onerous indirect taxes): one in seven households had no taxable assets, and one in six owed no tax because liabilities exceeded assets.[17] Thus nearly a third of households owed no tax, and for more than half of them this was a consequence of the ample 200-florin per-person deduction. The remaining two-thirds of households had taxable assets ranging from a fraction of a florin to the 101,422 florins of Palla Strozzi, who thus owed 507 florins at each collection. Giovanni de' Medici was (officially at least) the city's second wealthiest citizen, with over 79,000 florins of net assets and tax assessed at 397 florins. Niccolò da Uzzano was the wealthiest in Santo Spirito (and sixth overall) with over 46,000 florins of taxable assets. By contrast, Rinaldo degli Albizzi's taxable wealth

---

[16] Conti, *L'imposta diretta*, pp. 138–49; R. de Roover, *The Rise and Decline of the Medici Bank, 1397–1494* (New York, 1966), pp. 21–31; Herlihy and Klapisch-Zuber, *Tuscans*, pp. 1–27; Brucker, *Society*, pp. 6–13.
[17] Herlihy and Klapisch-Zuber, *Tuscans*, pp. 94, 100.

was far less, at just under 12,000 florins. Twenty-eight households had 20,000 florins or more in net taxable assets, and 202 households had at least 5,000.[18] The wealthiest one hundred households (1% of the total) controlled a quarter of the city's wealth.[19]

Because the Catasto was not a direct tax, it did nothing to slow the growth of the public debt. It provided a seemingly more equitable method of assessing levies that were still interest-bearing loans to the commune. Wealthier Florentines shouldered the greater share of the Catasto's burden, even as many were able to conceal the true amounts of capital investments. Collections began in the second half of 1428, during which, according to Matteo Palmieri's meticulous register of tax payments, the commune required $12^{3}/_{4}$ collections; he paid 0.005% of taxable assets of 3,200 florins $12^{3}/_{4}$ times, for a total of slightly over 200 florins in these six months, or 6% of his net worth. The total tax debt for all city households in a single collection amounted to 24,962 florins; hence $12^{3}/_{4}$ collections meant a city-wide tax bill of just over 318,000 florins for the second half of 1428. In 1429 reduced spending required only $7^{1}/_{2}$ collections.[20] But in 1430, as collections increased, the fiscal pressure mounted. In this first full year of the war against Lucca the government decreed 25 collections, hence a total tax of 624,050 florins for the city, and 400 for Palmieri. In the first half of 1431, 19 collections imposed an overall burden of almost 475,000 florins. In the second half of the year, new assessments from the 1431 declarations replaced those of 1427. Perhaps because citizens were becoming more skillful at concealing assets, but perhaps also because years of heavy taxation had eaten away at patrimonies, the aggregate tax owed from a single collection now came to 18,594 florins, a reduction of 25%. But collections began to be levied more frequently and in multiples. Four to six simultaneous collections became common, and even more in emergencies. In July–December 1431, 21 collections (including 12 on one day in July) resulted in a city-wide tax bill of 390,000 florins. Together with the collections of the first half of the year and a still different tax levied a dozen times for a total of 82,000 florins, in 1431 citizens owed a grand total of 947,000 florins, possibly the most onerous year of the crisis and of the republic's history. But the single blackest day came early in the next year, when, on February 6, 1432, the commune imposed an astonishing cluster of 36 simultaneous collections:

---

[18]   Martines, *Social World*, pp. 365–78. Martines' data represent taxable wealth after deductions and exemptions, whereas Molho (*Marriage Alliance*, pp. 375–410) reports the much larger sums of declared assets *before* the often substantial deductions. One rather extreme example is Niccolò Barbadori: 51,770 florins in gross assets (*Marriage Alliance*, p. 378) and taxable wealth of 24,438 florins (*Social World*, p. 375).

[19]   Herlihy and Klapisch-Zuber, *Tuscans*, p. 100.

[20]   Matteo Palmieri, *Ricordi fiscali (1427–1474)*, ed. E. Conti (Rome, 1983), pp. 19–24.

taxpayers were required to pay 18% of their net worth all at once. For the whole of that year the total tax, from $42^{1}/_{2}$ collections and a variety of other imposts, amounted to 834,000 florins. When peace came in 1433, the commune's needs declined, but 24 collections and various other levies still resulted in taxes of 500,000 florins. From 1428 through 1433, the commune imposed a grand total of 152 collections,[21] and since each took 0.005 of net taxable wealth, this amounted to 76% of net assets – *not of income, but of taxable patrimony* – over six years: an average of 12.7% per year, nearly twice the expected 7% return on real estate and more than normal returns on commercial investments. Taxes were, to put it simply, exceeding income.

By 1431 a breaking point was reached, and increasing numbers of citizens were unable to pay the sums demanded. It was in this and the next year that yields slipped to 73% and 63% of imposed levies. Entire patrimonies were being consumed, among both popolo and elite. In 1427 Matteo Palmieri and his father possessed gross assets worth 4,635 florins; between 1428 and 1433 they paid over 2,600 florins and received 500 in interest, with resulting net payments of 2,100 florins, which were 45% of their gross assets and 70% of net assets.[22] At the upper end of urban wealth, Palla Strozzi's massive contributions illuminate the dilemma of a citizen, however rich, whose wealth was almost exclusively in land and Monte credits and who thus could not conceal and under-report assets. In 1431 he petitioned the Signoria saying that, in order to raise cash to pay taxes, he first tried, unsuccessfully, to sell land and redeem Monte shares and was now seeking permission to sell Monte credits to foreigners. The Signoria and councils approved (despite 64 and 50 negative votes).[23] The next year he informed the Signoria that the sale of Monte credits yielded far less than he had anticipated and requested some reduction in his 1431 assessment of 329 florins. To underscore the magnitude of his payments and debts, he claimed that since 1423 he had paid a total of 120,000 florins in forced loans – more than his net assets in 1427 – and had had to borrow 38,000 florins to meet these obligations.[24] Although the Medici also paid enormous sums between 1425 and early 1433 (over 91,000 florins, and, calculating interest received, net payments of 75,000), it did not have the same disastrous effect on them that it had on Strozzi, because, as bankers with European-wide investments, they were able to hide much wealth, as is clear in comparing their Catasto declarations with the bank's secret account books,[25]

[21] Molho, *Public Finances*, p. 92; Conti, *L'imposta diretta*, p. 365.
[22] Molho, *Public Finances*, pp. 97–8; Molho, *Marriage Alliance*, p. 397; Martines, *Social World*, p. 371.
[23] ASF, Provvisioni, Registri, 122, ff. 16v–17 (April 14, 1431).
[24] Molho, *Public Finances*, pp. 157–60.
[25] De Roover, *Medici Bank*, pp. 73–4, 99.

and also because their lucrative banking operations continued to generate enough profits to compensate for the fiscal drain. Moreover, his immense wealth gave Cosimo a crucial role in the management of the commune's finances, a role that brought him profit and power, but also the fear and resentment of many within the elite who saw the inexorable political consequences of his wealth.

Cosimo's Money and Friends

In the fourteenth century few could have imagined that Florence and the Medici would find themselves in such a fateful embrace. Around 1300, the Medici were among the more unruly elite families and, although not magnates, had marriage connections with magnates, including the Donati. Their first prior was in 1291, and, with fifty-two more by 1400, they could boast a political presence exceeded only by the Strozzi, Altoviti, and Albizzi. But throughout the century many of them resembled the worst of the old magnates in their frequently violent behavior, not only against others but within the family. No Medici were major players in the world of commerce and banking in mid-century. In the 1360s and 1370s, the family split between the Albizzi and Ricci factions, but the only one to play a leading political role in these years was Salvestro, whose open opposition to the Parte Guelfa, support for the war against the papacy, and leadership in the popular movement of 1378 caused his exile in 1382 and dimmed the family's influence in the post-1382 oligarchy. In the 1390s, several Medici were accused of conspiring against the regime and banished; one was even executed. And in 1400 the discovery of another plot involving family members led to the disqualification from public office of the entire *consorteria*, except Giovanni di Bicci, his brother Francesco, and the descendants of Vieri di Cambio.[26] This was hardly a position from which a rise to unprecedented power in the commune, in the space of only thirty-five years, could have seemed possible.

Vieri di Cambio, a distant cousin of Giovanni di Bicci but first cousin to Salvestro, ironically provided the opportunity for Giovanni to establish the financial foundations of his descendants' political rise. In the years of revolution and counterrevolution, Vieri had sided with the Parte Guelfa and Albizzi, ensuring himself a place on the balìa of 1382. He was also the only Medici in the second half of the fourteenth century to make a major fortune in trade and banking. Giovanni and Francesco began their careers as employees in the

---

[26]   G. Brucker, "The Medici in the Fourteenth Century," *Speculum* 32 (1957): 1–26; reprinted in Brucker's *Renaissance Florence: Society, Culture, and Religion* (Goldbach, 1994), pp. 3–28.

Rome branch of Vieri's far-flung operations. In the mid-1380s, Giovanni became branch manager and then partner, and in 1393 founded his own company in Rome which inherited much of the business and assets of the now retired Vieri. Four years later he relocated the company's main office to Florence, but kept a branch in Rome. He and his partners initiated the Florentine company with a capital investment of 10,000 florins; in 1402 they added a branch in Venice and the first of two wool manufacturing enterprises in Florence. But it was the Rome branch on which the great fortune, in both senses, of the Medici was built. Between 1390 and 1410 the dominant role in papal banking once enjoyed by the Alberti was shared by a number of Italian companies. Popes began the practice of appointing as Depositary of the Papal Chamber a single banker whose company received and kept on deposit church revenues from all over Europe, and paid out sums as ordered by the Curia, taking a percentage of the transactions as commission. This crucial and lucrative office was held by bankers from Lucca and Bologna until, sometime after 1403, the popes entrusted it to Florentines, first the Ricci and then the Spini.

During the Schism, with rival papacies in Rome and Avignon and endless discussions and plans for a council to settle the dispute and reunite the church, the Florentines maintained open working relations with both papacies, and in 1409 they hosted a gathering in Pisa of cardinals seeking to persuade both popes to resign in order to elect a new one.[27] The Council of Pisa elected a new pope, but the two existing claimants refused to abdicate, leaving western Christendom with a scandal of three popes that was finally resolved at the Council of Constance (1414–18). But the Pisan papacy was recognized by most of Europe as possessing the legitimate headship of the church and consequently controlled the lion's share of papal revenues. It was thus an event of the greatest significance for the Medici that in 1410, after the first pope of the Pisan obedience died, the conclave elected Giovanni's friend, the ambitious Neapolitan cardinal Baldassare Cossa, as John XXIII, until then papal legate to, and de facto ruler of, Bologna since his recovery of the city for the Roman papacy in 1403. Exactly where and why they became friends is not known. Cossa was later accused of buying his cardinalate with funds (10,000 florins) lent him by the Medici, and Giovanni had been Cossa's banker for at least a half dozen years before his election. In 1411 Cossa removed Doffo Spini as papal Depositary and installed two other Florentines who were in effect fronts for three Florentine banks, belonging to Giovanni de' Medici, his nephew Averardo, and the Carducci, which supplied the funds with which the nominal depositaries made initial loans to Cossa. Into the coffers of these banks, through

---

[27]   A. Landi, *Il papa deposto (Pisa, 1409): l'idea conciliare nel grande scisma* (Turin, 1985); A. W. Lewin, "*Cum Status Ecclesie Noster Sit*: Florence and the Council of Pisa," *Church History* 62 (1993): 178–89; Lewin, *Negotiating Survival*, pp. 136–67.

the hands of the depositaries, papal revenues began to flow. Large loans to the papal treasury in advance of the receipt of these revenues meant constant profits in the form of interest as well as commissions. Although Cossa happily took loans from a variety of Florentine companies as he was fighting alongside the Florentines against Ladislaus of Naples, Giovanni de' Medici emerged as his biggest supplier of quick cash. Between July 1411 and January 1412, he extended loans to Cossa totaling 23,000 florins. When the pope signed an agreement with Ladislaus involving a payment of 95,000 florins, Giovanni's bank collected the funds and transferred them to Naples. Apart from these very profitable loans, the volume of regular business was extensive: in a two-month period in 1413 the Medici bank received in its papal account almost 32,000 florins and disbursed 29,000, sums that steadily generated profitable commissions. This was the origin of the long-term Medici role in papal finances. Giovanni temporarily lost his privileged position at the Curia when Cossa was deposed by the Council of Constance in 1415, but he helped Cossa find safe haven in Florence, and when the ex-pope died in 1419 Giovanni (or possibly Cosimo) commissioned from Donatello and Michelozzo the great tomb with the pope's effigy in the baptistery. Giovanni also assisted Cossa in reconciling with the pope elected at Constance, the Roman Martin V of the Colonna family, motivated no doubt by the aim of regaining a share in papal banking. Martin initially favored the Spini, but when the venerable company declared bankruptcy in 1420 he turned to the Medici and appointed their Roman branch manager, Bartolomeo de' Bardi, as depositary. From then until the 1440s the position was controlled exclusively by Medici agents.[28]

More than half the profits of the Medici banking and commercial empire came from the bank's Rome branch. Medici account books for the years 1397–1420 show astonishing overall profits of 151,820 florins (three-fourths to Giovanni and one-fourth to his one remaining partner), of which 79,195 came from the branch that followed the Curia wherever it resided. Giovanni retired in 1420, and a new partnership was formed by his sons Cosimo and Lorenzo and Giovanni's former partner Ilarione de' Bardi, with capital contributions of 16,000 from the brothers and 8,000 from their partner, to which their Florence, Rome, and Venice branch managers made additions that brought the total to 31,000 florins. This company remained operative until 1435, and thus through the years of the fiscal crisis and the political conflict of 1433–4, and produced total profits of 186,382 florins; average yearly profits of over 12,000 florins represented a 40% annual return on the original investments. Papal banking provided an even higher proportion of the profits – 63% – than before 1420. The two-thirds of the profits enjoyed by Cosimo and Lorenzo

[28]   G. Holmes, "How the Medici Became the Pope's Bankers," in *Florentine Studies*, ed. Rubinstein, pp. 357–80.

(124,255 florins) enabled them to expand Medici banking and trading activities between 1435 and 1450 with new branches in Ancona, Avignon, Basel, Bruges, London, Geneva, and Pisa, to supplement the two wool shops with a silk manufacturing operation, and, of course, to make the large cash loans to the government during the fiscal crisis that were the foundation of Medici political power. Profits in 1435–50 amounted to an astronomical 290,791 florins, 70% of which (203,702 florins) went to Cosimo. Lorenzo's death in 1440 eliminated the prospect of a division of this huge patrimony. By the 1440s, the Rome branch no longer generated the same proportion of profits, but it still made more money than any other branch in the system: 88,511 florins in 1435–50, slightly more than 30% of the total.[29]

Underlying both the oligarchy's acquiescence in Cosimo's burgeoning influence in the early 1430s and its desperate attempt to rid itself of him in 1433 was the republic's growing dependence on his wealth to pay its bills. In order to raise quickly the cash needed to pay mercenaries, war balìe had often taken short-term loans from wealthy citizens with secure promises of prompt repayment and high interest. In 1425 the authority to contract such loans was transferred to the Officials of the Bank, who had broad discretionary powers to arrange loans, determine interest rates, and guarantee both repayment and interest with whatever communal revenues they chose. Bank Officials were themselves among the biggest lenders, deciding the terms of their own loans as of others; indeed, *only* lenders to the commune could serve as Bank Officials, perhaps because it was thought that only with control over their own loans (in effect, institutionalized and mandatory conflict of interest) would wealthy citizens be persuaded to put their money at risk. Loans were repaid usually within a few months when allocated revenues became available, with monthly interest rates between $2^{1}/_{2}$ and 4%, which translate to annualized rates of 30 to almost 50%. Bank Officials clearly wielded enormous power; their wealth allowed the government to meet military costs without waiting for the communal treasury to collect sufficient funds from forced loans and indirect taxes. Inevitably, the power to determine and shape foreign and fiscal policy fell into the hands of the wealthy men who served on these committees. Their names are known for the year from November 1427 through 1428 and for the two years and some months from December 1430 to early 1433: eighty-one citizens sat as Bank Officials in these two periods, of whom at least sixteen were either Medici or known allies, friends, and partisans of Cosimo and collectively held a quarter of the ninety-nine seats. Cosimo himself served three times, his cousin Averardo and more distant kinsman Bernardo d'Antonio each once. Four Medici friends appear more than once: Andrea de' Pazzi four times, Antonio Serristori three times, Niccolò Valori and Puccio Pucci twice.

[29] De Roover, *Medici Bank*, pp. 35–70.

Other Medici friends from the Corbinelli, Carducci, Tornabuoni, Bardi, Benci, Capponi, Bartolini-Scodellari, and Davanzati families also served as Officials. By contrast, among the many exiled or otherwise punished by the victorious Medici in 1434, only two had been Bank Officials, including Palla Strozzi, and two others had relatives among them. The Medici and their friends dominated the committees of Bank Officials.[30]

In thirty-four non-consecutive months for which records survive, sixty-eight individuals, companies, or pairs of brothers from fifty-three lineages made loans to the commune through the Officials of the Bank totaling just over 561,000 florins. If these fragmentary data are typical of the entire period of crisis, the Bank Officials borrowed approximately 200,000 florins, and thus a hefty percentage of the communal budget, every twelve months. Forty-six percent came from ten persons who were either Medici family members or allies. Cosimo's and Lorenzo's loans amounted to 155,887 florins (in just these thirty-four months), or 28% of the total. Other "Medicean" lenders included Andrea de' Pazzi (58,000), Antonio Serristori (26,000), and Cosimo's cousin Averardo (5,500). Still other lenders friendly to the Medici, or whose families became solidly pro-Medici after 1434, were Donato Bonsi (26,000 florins); Antonio Pitti (26,000); the brothers Giannozzo and Filippo Manetti (15,000); three Alberti (a total of 9,300); Niccolò Cambini (3,000); and Bernardo da Uzzano (14,000), a Medici partisan in 1434 despite the prominence of his kinsman Niccolò among the anti-Mediceans. These bring the share of loans by the Medici, their allies, and friends to 353,000 florins, or 63% of the total. Opponents of the Medici were not absent from the lists of creditors, but their share was far smaller. Only three lenders to the Bank Officials were exiled by the Medici in 1434, and their loans were modest by comparison: Niccolò Barbadori (1,120 florins), Piero Panciatichi (1,721), and Ridolfo Peruzzi (2,831). Two close relatives of prominent exiles were also among the biggest lenders: Bernardo Lamberteschi (35,000 florins), and Lorenzo di Palla Strozzi (with loans of almost 34,000 florins). But it was Cosimo and his friends who dominated the business of short-term loans to the government.

In addition to influence over foreign and fiscal policy, Cosimo's wealth also provided the means for building a patronage network, in the city and beyond, that was larger, more extensive, and more cohesive than other Florentine patrons could manage. He helped people directly with debts, dowries, and business dealings; and with his influence he secured political offices, assisted in court cases, and mediated disputes. These were traditional things that Florentine patrons had always done for their "friends" and clients. But Cosimo was able to do it on a much broader scale that crossed neighborhood boundaries and

---

[30]   Molho, *Public Finances*, pp. 218–21; D. Kent, *The Rise of the Medici: Faction in Florence, 1426–1434* (Oxford, 1978), pp. 352–7.

spread to every corner of the city. Again like most patrons, Cosimo cultivated ties outside the city as well; but whereas patrons of more limited means and ambitions confined their extra-urban networks to some portion of the contado, perhaps that from which their ancestors had emigrated or perhaps a town with which they had political ties, Cosimo spread his influence and sought friends and allies throughout the Florentine dominion. One dramatic example of this was the appeal to Cosimo by the entire city of Volterra, which rebelled against the imposition of the Catasto in 1429. One Volterran remarked: "We applied to Cosimo for aid and sympathy and advice, as our refuge and protector in every hour of need."[31]

What made Cosimo unlike all other Florentine patrons was his unusual influence at the papal court, or Curia, the center of the vast legal, financial, administrative, and diplomatic machinery of church government. From all over Italy and Europe people looked to the Curia for favorable legal judgments in its courts, to its various offices and departments for assistance with matters ranging from marriage, wills, and the legitimization of children to disputes with local ecclesiastical institutions over property or patronage rights, and to this or that powerful cardinal or even to the pope himself for titles and privileges. Giovanni de' Medici's close ties to John XXIII and Martin V had been essential to the bank's early success in Rome, and Cosimo continued that policy by cultivating even closer ties with Eugenius IV (1431–47), Nicholas V (1447–55) and Pius II (1458–64).[32] His influence with the papacy made Cosimo the gatekeeper to papal favor: many who sought a pope's ear or attention appealed first to Cosimo, knowing that a good word from the pope's powerful banker could open many doors. A study of more than 1,200 extant letters written to Cosimo reveals that 70% were requests for favors of one sort or another: 20% of these asked for Cosimo's intercession with Florentine committees or courts and 15% begged his intercession with the pope. As one petitioner put it in asking Cosimo to persuade Eugenius to consider a relative of his for an archbishopric, "you count for much with our Lord the Holy Father."[33] Cosimo's patronage and influence were unprecedented in their scope. Indeed, his connections abroad, and especially in Rome, made him seem, in some eyes, more like a prince than a republican citizen.

At home the faction Cosimo assembled was unlike the loosely bound clusters of families and friends that had been typical within the elite. It was tighter and larger, had well-defined leadership and a chain of command from the top to

---

[31] Kent, *Rise*, p. 235.
[32] G. Holmes, "Cosimo and the Popes," in *Cosimo "il Vecchio" de' Medici, 1389–1464*, ed. F. Ames-Lewis (Oxford, 1992), pp. 21–31.
[33] A. Molho, "Cosimo de' Medici: *Pater Patriae* or *Padrino?*" *Stanford Italian Review* 1 (1979): 5–33 (28–9).

an inner circle of advisers and lieutenants, and enjoyed the loyalty of rank-and-file who could be counted on to rally in moments of crisis.[34] Its center was the family, where cousins and selected members of other branches played pivotal roles. Perhaps reacting to the spectacle of Medici disarray and disunity in the fourteenth century, Cosimo and his closest advisers maintained friendly contacts among the branches. He and his cousin Averardo, his chief lieutenant in the early days, corresponded with members of five of the six main branches of the Medici *consorteria* and won their recognition of Cosimo's leadership. Beyond their kin, carefully considered marriage alliances cemented existing friendships and gained new allies. Two dozen Medici marriages between 1400 and 1434 were with families of their partisans. Three key lieutenants, Alamanno Salviati, Antonio Serristori, and Giannozzo Gianfigliazzi, married Averardo's daughters. Several marriages, including Cosimo's to Contessina, linked the Medici and the Bardi, thereby splitting the Bardi *consorteria* (some of whom sided with the Albizzi) and giving the Medici a foothold in the Oltrarno district. They pursued a similar policy of multiple marriages with the Tornaquinci and their non-magnate cousins, the Tornabuoni, culminating in the marriage of Cosimo's son Piero to Lucrezia Tornabuoni. And similarly useful marriages linked the Medici to important allies like the Acciaiuoli and Pitti. The Medici always married into the families of allies from their own elite class. Their many supporters from lower down the social hierarchy were never invited to become in-laws. About half the Medici partisans were from the quarter of San Giovanni, slightly less than half of these from the Medici gonfalone of Lion d'oro. Most of these neighborhood allies did not belong to the elite, and it was on the traditional patronage turf of the neighborhood that the Medici established the vertical links to guildsmen and new families, whereas their elite allies came mostly from other quarters of the city.

The Medici faction was not the "popular" party described in some older accounts. Because the essence of political patronage resided in the elite's cultivation of non-elite clients, and because the Medici offered such formidable inducements to clients seeking protection and favors, their patronage network gathered a visibly large number of non-elite families under its umbrella. Medici partisans were about evenly split between elite and non-elite. Within the elite they found allies among the recently repatriated Alberti, the Ricci (who were old foes of the Albizzi), and among magnate (or former magnate) families such as the Bardi, Pazzi, Gianfigliazzi, and Tornaquinci/Tornabuoni. Most of their lieutenants came from elite families: Alamanno Salviati, Luca di Buonaccorso Pitti, Agnolo Acciaiuoli, Nerone Dietisalvi-Neroni, Piero Guicciardini, and Luca degli Albizzi, who broke with his brother Rinaldo, married the granddaughter of Vieri de' Medici, and became a com-

---

[34]   For what follows: Kent, *Rise*, pp. 33–135.

mitted Medici partisan. In the non-elite wing of the party were some new families, several from Lion d'oro who were in the process of establishing themselves politically and economically, like the Della Casa, Martelli, Ginori, Masi, and Cambini;[35] families of, or descended from, notaries, like the Serristori; and the Pucci, minor guildsmen, one of whom, Puccio Pucci, achieved such prominence and notoriety that Mediceans were sometimes called the "Puccini." Resentment among anti-Mediceans over the influence that Pucci and a few others of the artisan class achieved in the party, and thus in communal politics, may be the origin of the old myth that the Medici party represented "popular" interests against the oligarchy. In fact, the great majority of leading Mediceans were from the elite: half of their partisans belonged to the group of citizens who spoke most frequently in the pratiche between 1429 and 1434, and at least twenty of them belonged to the ruling group's inner circle.[36] Although the Medici did not represent popular interests, they did cultivate the support of selected guildsmen, notaries, and new families to enhance their power in the struggle against their opponents.

Showdown

As soon as the war against Milan ended in 1428, internal tensions erupted. In January 1429 a large pratica discussed the dangers of factions and the need for unity; that same month 700 citizens signed an oath "to divest ourselves completely of partisanship and loyalty to factions, to consider only the welfare and honor and greatness of the Republic, and to forget every injury received up to this day on account of partisan or factional passions." In February a new magistracy, the Conservators of the Laws, was instituted (despite many dissenting votes in both councils) to review the suitability of officeholders and to determine if any belonged to illegal associations or societies seeking to influence elections. Citizens were invited to convey their suspicions to the ten Conservators, and over the next few years hundreds of accusations, implicating both Mediceans and their opponents, exacerbated partisan divisions. In December 1429, just as the government was deciding once again to go to war, this time against Lucca, the councils passed another law against factions (again over strong opposition) that aimed to "restrain the pride of the great which must be subdued and checked, so that no one, trusting in wealth or kinship or marriage alliances or patronage [*clientelis*] or factions, will dare do anything to disturb the peace and tranquility of the city." Concisely identifying the

---

[35] S. Tognetti, *Il banco Cambini: affari e mercati di una compagnia mercantile-bancaria nella Firenze del XV secolo* (Florence, 1999).
[36] Kent, *Rise*, pp. 104–35 (110–11).

nature of the bonds within factions, this "law against sowers of scandal" required the Signoria, together with eighty citizens drawn by lot, to meet twice a year to identify persons suspected of belonging to illegal associations, put to a vote anyone named at least six times, and punish anyone convicted by a two-thirds vote with banishment or loss of office-holding rights.[37] Secret accusations and public humiliations became favorite weapons of partisan antagonists. In 1432 Rinaldo degli Albizzi used such methods to banish the respected Neri di Gino Capponi, a war commissioner and frequent envoy whose initiatives in foreign policy Rinaldo resented. Two months later Neri's many friends had him recalled, and it was Rinaldo's turn to feel the sting of humiliation: a dress rehearsal of sorts for the drama that was to be played out in 1433 and 1434.

Such were the tensions and levels of mistrust within the ruling group as the disastrous war with Lucca drew Milan into the hostilities and intensified the commune's fiscal crisis to the point of dependence on Medici money to pay for a war to which Rinaldo was strongly committed. Before 1430 the configuration of the parties and the shape of looming confrontation between a Medici-led faction and the coalition around Rinaldo were still murky. Voices for and against the war were heard among Miceleans and anti-Miceleans alike. Palla Strozzi, who later joined the anti-Miceleans, opposed the war, whereas Neri Capponi, subsequently a Medici ally, favored it. Rinaldo initially supported the war with much conviction and served as civilian commissioner in the field. Cosimo's letters reveal no great enthusiasm for the war, although he remarked to his cousin Averardo that those responsible for the disaster it turned into ("and may God forgive them," he added) were the ones who opposed it when it was still possible to win quickly.[38] Early in 1430 he wrote to Averardo that "whether or not we approve of this undertaking, things have come to the point where the honor of the commune is involved, so that everyone must give it all the support they can." By October, when he realized it was to be a long and divisive affair, he suggested, again to Averardo, that they ought to steer clear of direct involvement. But two months later, in early December, the Florentine army suffered a disastrous defeat that prompted the appointment of a new balìa that included Cosimo and three of his closest allies. From that point on, the Medici and their friends held an increasing number of important positions in the prosecution of the war. Thus, although Cosimo was cautious at the outset, one year into the conflict he and his friends assumed a large share of the responsibility for bringing it to a successful conclusion, without any apparent protest from those who, at war's end, tried to destroy them.

---

[37]   *Commissioni di Rinaldo degli Albizzi*, vol. 3, pp. 170–2; Kent, *Rise*, p. 248; Brucker, *Civic World*, pp. 489–90.

[38]   Kent, *Rise*, pp. 253–88 (260).

By 1433, the magnitude of Medici influence over communal finances and military and foreign policy was starkly apparent, and their opponents panicked. Rinaldo reached back to the example of his father Maso, who had overcome the threat of the Alberti in the early 1390s, by accusing the Medici of a series of political crimes as a pretext for driving them from the city. Emulating the paternal model may have come naturally to this man who once wrote, in a postscript to an official letter from a diplomatic mission, that "before dawn, my father appeared to me in a dream and instructed me concerning the peace that must be concluded." Or, as one critical observer put it, "Messer Rinaldo wanted to do as his father had done in 1393, and carry out all his own vendettas."[39] But he would not have been able to persuade so much of the elite to take the drastic and risky step of exiling the Medici without serious allegations and evidence against them. In September 1433, just after Cosimo's and Averardo's arrest, the Signoria and the Otto di Guardia gathered testimony concerning alleged Medici misdeeds. Among other witnesses, ser Niccolò Tinucci, who had served as notary for the war balìe, presented a long and detailed case against Cosimo.[40] Although Tinucci had been friendly with Niccolò da Uzzano and his faction, he subsequently joined the Medici because of a personal dispute with a Da Uzzano ally, the chancellor ser Paolo Fortini, whom the Medici succeeded in having removed in 1427 (thus opening the way for the election of Leonardo Bruni). But in September 1433 Tinucci turned informant against the Medici and revealed details of conversations and things overheard or witnessed in their company. He may have been pressured to provide damning testimony against them, and, given his fluctuating loyalties, there are certainly grounds for doubting the veracity, or at least accuracy, of his claims. But "the activities which he attributes to the Medici and their friends," as the leading study of these years concludes, are "supported, in numerous precise details, from the letters identifying partisans and revealing their political preoccupations in this period."[41]

Tinucci's most damaging allegations were that the Medici bribed and pressured communal officials to do their bidding, illegally interfered in scrutinies and elections, and, worst of all, used their influence, money, and access to and frequent service on the balìe to prolong the war against Lucca because of the profits they made from loans to the commune. The first two accusations ring true, in part because they allege traditional forms of corruption in Florentine politics, and because after 1434 the Medici became regular and skillful manipulators of both elections and elected officials. Tinucci's example of bribery went back to 1427, when, he claimed, Giovanni de' Medici sought chancellor

[39] *Commissioni di Rinaldo degli Albizzi*, vol. 3, p. 76; Kent, *Rise*, pp. 245, 268–9.
[40] Tinucci's "Examina" in Cavalcanti, *Istorie*, ed. Polidori, vol. 2, pp. 399–421.
[41] Kent, *Rise*, pp. 222–33.

Fortini's removal and saw his opportunity in the election to the priorate of a Medici partisan, Luigi Vecchietti. In return for cooperation in sacking Fortini, Giovanni promised Vecchietti a loan of 800 florins for his daughter's dowry; to another prior, Francesco Nardi, he offered cash and an Alberti wife with a dowry of 2,000 florins; and to the Standardbearer of Justice Sandro Biliotti (another Medici *amico*) he likewise offered cash. According to Tinucci, Giovanni even wanted this priorate to exile Niccolò da Uzzano, but Vecchietti balked. Tinucci's allegations concerning electoral corruption were that in 1428 Giovanni conspired with another *amico* to penetrate official electoral secrets in order to influence a planned transfer of name tickets from the most recent scrutiny into the pouches of earlier ones. Such transfers allowed selected candidates to be drawn much sooner, and if a faction knew whose, and how many, name tickets remained in earlier pouches, it would know when to appoint cooperative accoppiatori who would select its preferred candidates for transfer, thus influencing the election of upcoming priorates. Officially, the identities of those approved in scrutinies and the composition of the pouches were secret, known only to the accoppiatori and the notaries who oversaw the voting. According to Tinucci, Giovanni persuaded his friend ser Martino di ser Luca, who had served as an elections notary in 1421 and 1426, to reveal the contents of the scrutinies of those years. When the Medici realized that Da Uzzano "and his friends" were more heavily represented in the pouches than they themselves were, they conspired to get Cosimo and Nerone di Nigi Dietisalvi-Neroni appointed among the accoppiatori. Consequently, Tinucci wrote, "Giovanni de' Medici, Averardo, Cosimo, Nerone di Nigi, ser Martino, and Puccio [Pucci] were able to regulate the scrutiny" and the transfer of name-tickets and "to control the office of Standardbearer of Justice as they wished, so that whenever necessary they would have enough votes to accomplish whatever they wanted." Tinucci possibly exaggerated the extent to which the Medici group controlled elections after 1428, but both episodes turned on the ways patronage ties could be used to subvert institutions for partisan benefit.

Most serious among Tinucci's charges against the Medici was that they conspired to prolong the war for their own profit. Given the length of the conflict and the fact that the Medici were among the few Florentines whose political (and financial) fortunes were raised by a war that was a disaster for the commune and the majority of its taxpayers, it is easy to see how, after the fact, their enemies concluded that Cosimo, Averardo, and their friends had indeed deliberately manipulated Florentine military and fiscal policy in order to keep the war going. The most blatant statement reported by Tinucci of Medici acknowledgment of complicity in prolonging the war could be interpreted as a projection of their enemies' suspicions: "Many times I heard Cosimo and Averardo say that the way to keep oneself powerful is to keep [the commune] in a state of war and to serve the needs of the war economy with ready cash, and then make loans to the commune that are secure and highly profitable. The people will have the impression of being helped by the very persons who reap [from such actions] profit, honor, greatness and power."[42] This seems too much of an open admission actually to have been spoken by the chronically cautious Cosimo. But Tinucci surrounds the allegation with a whole series of recollections of specific moments in which he claims they influenced the course of the war, sometimes from their position on the balìe, and sometimes by going around them, in order to prevent a quick conclusion. He alleges that Cosimo and Averardo worried that Rinaldo's capture of Collodi, near Pescia, would redound to his political benefit and tried to have him replaced as commissioner; that they got the balìa to send Alamanno Salviati and Neri di Gino Capponi as co-commissioners with Rinaldo but that when Capponi had some military success Averardo wanted to remove him as well. So he got ser Martino, now a member of the war commission, to write such angry letters to Capponi that the latter returned to Florence and left Salviati alone in the field with the troops. Salviati did nothing for two and a half months, "in order to prolong the war, as Averardo and Cosimo desired." Meanwhile, Rinaldo was capturing another town and would have taken Lucca itself if Salviati had mounted an offensive from his direction. To frustrate Rinaldo's efforts, they again used their influence with ser Martino to have the balìa recall and replace him with another Medici *amico*, Fruosino da Verrazzano, "for the sole purpose," says Tinucci, "of preventing Rinaldo from increasing his reputation and becoming too powerful." Tinucci may have exaggerated both the negative consequences of Medici actions in the war and their narrowly partisan political motives. But the story he tells is too detailed to have been completely invented, and it is supported by the testimony of Piero Guicciardini, a Medici friend, who reacted with disgust at the open display of elation by Averardo's son Giuliano upon learning of the defeat of Florentine forces in 1430: the event that ensured a longer war and opened the way for Cosimo and the Mediceans to assume control of it.[43] And even if they were exaggerated for partisan purposes, Tinucci's charges reflect the way the enemies of the Medici saw their growing influence and abuse of power.

Peace came in April 1433 with a treaty jointly negotiated, ironically, by Cosimo and Palla Strozzi. Apparently sensing that they might soon be the targets of a purge, the Medici began transferring cash to safe places and selling shares in the Monte,[44] and Cosimo spent the summer at a family estate in the Mugello. The storm broke when the priorate drawn for September–October turned up a majority of anti-Mediceans, and on September 5, at Rinaldo's

[42] Tinucci, "Examina," pp. 401, 418.
[43] Kent, *Rise*, pp. 276, 278.
[44] De Roover, *Medici Bank*, p. 54.

instigation (so says Cavalcanti), the Signoria summoned Cosimo to Florence and had him arrested. Four days later it summoned a parlamento and asked it to approve a grant of balìa powers to the Signoria and two hundred citizens, only about a quarter of whom were known enemies of the Medici. The balìa immediately voted to exile Cosimo to Padua, Averardo to Naples, and Cosimo's brother Lorenzo to Venice. But the Signoria kept Cosimo imprisoned in the palace for almost a month, for two reasons, as he would later write in his "Ricordi": to use the implicit threat of killing him as a way of pressuring his "friends and relatives" on the balìa to agree to measures against Medici interests; and to force him into bankruptcy by preventing him from using his financial resources or selling property or Monte shares. The first tactic seems to have worked, but Cosimo noted with evident pride that his financial empire did not collapse and that "many foreign merchants and lords offered us money and sent us large sums." Cash bribes to two members of the Signoria finally resulted in Cosimo's release and exile on October 3.[45]

Less than a year later he was back in Florence to begin thirty years of unofficial but unmistakable control of Florentine government and foreign policy. His remarkable reversal of fortune has several explanations. First is the curious reluctance of Rinaldo and other anti-Mediceans to do much damage to the Medici party. Evidently believing that to break Medici power it was sufficient to remove Cosimo and a few family members and allies, the anti-Mediceans left their patronage network largely intact. Most of Cosimo's friends remained loyal, even if quietly so, helping to protect Medici assets and agitating for his recall. Although the balìa conducted a new scrutiny, it did not nullify the older ones: the more than 2,000 citizens approved in the 1433 scrutiny were added to the existing pouches. Thus, while the Medici (excepting only the line of Vieri di Cambio) were barred from communal office, their friends and allies remained eligible. Although the Signoria and accoppiatori handpicked the next priorate of November–December 1433 – the first time since 1393 that name tickets were not drawn by lot – for some reason Rinaldo and his allies decided not to continue to handpick subsequent priorates, and the resumption of sortition soon proved fatal to the anti-Mediceans. The luck of the draw produced a pro-Medici Signoria for September–October 1434 that promptly set in motion the events that led to Cosimo's triumphant return.

Also crucial to Cosimo's survival in 1433–4 was the support he enjoyed from many Italian governments and ruling houses, no doubt because of the bank's central role in their finances. He received condolences and offers of

---

[45] Cosimo's "Ricordi" in W. Roscoe, *The Life of Lorenzo de' Medici* (London, 1862), pp. 408–13; and A. Fabroni, *Magni Cosmi Medicei vita* (Pisa, 1789); partly translated, partly paraphrased in C. S. Gutkind, *Cosimo de' Medici, Pater Patriae, 1389–1464* (Oxford, 1938), pp. 77–8.

assistance from rulers of several cities in the Romagna, from the Baglioni of Perugia, the Bentivoglio of Bologna, and from the condottiere Micheletto Attendoli whose 1431 contract to fight for the Florentines had been negoti- ated by Averardo.[46] Attendoli was the cousin of Francesco Sforza, who later, as duke of Milan, played a decisive role in the preservation of Medici power. But most important among Medici allies during the exile were the Venetians. Cosimo requested and received permission to move from Padua to Venice where he was treated like a visiting head of state, in part because of loans he extended to the Venetian government and also because of old ties of friend- ship through the bank's Venetian branch. In the "Ricordi" he recalled how "I was received, not as an exile, but as an ambassador . . . and with such honor and good will that it would be impossible to describe. [The Venetians] expressed sorrow over my misfortune and offered the power of their govern- ment and city and resources to provide for my every comfort." Venice even sent envoys to Florence to urge the revocation of Cosimo's banishment. No government in Italy could have been unaware of the fact that Medici financial and political clout was largely unaffected by their expulsion from Florence, and many were betting that the exile would be brief.

   Not least among the sources of support for the Medici during their crisis were the small communities and hill towns north of Florence. Cosimo noted that on his way out of Florentine territory in October 1433 the "men of the mountains" received him as an honored ambassador and provided him with an escort of twenty men as he moved into Ferrarese territory. And from farther east, north of their home territories in the Mugello and extending into the Romagna on the other side of the mountains, came offers of willing help. The Medici had long cultivated ties to these communities, both in formal political contexts as representatives of the commune to the district territories, and in their "private" but no less imposing capacity as landowners and local notables to whom (again, no doubt, because of favors, loans, and various forms of intercession) deference and assistance were due. This quasi-feudal dimension of Medici strength was to play a crucial role (for the first of several times) in the crisis that brought them home in September of 1434.

   With these resources Cosimo bided his time, refusing to take risks that would have made a return impossible, remaining in regular touch with the *amici*, and waiting for the right moment. It came at the end of August 1434, when the extraction of the new Signoria included four prominent Mediceans: Luca di Buonaccorso Pitti (who would go on to be one of the regime's chief lieutenants), Giovanni Capponi (a Bank Official in 1432), Neri Bartolini- Scodellari (also a Bank Official), and, as Standardbearer of Justice, Niccolò

[46]   M. Mallett, *Mercenaries and Their Masters: Warfare in Renaissance Italy* (Totowa, N.J., 1974), pp. 76–9.

Cocco-Donati, from a new family heavily dependent on Medici patronage. And not one of the other five was a known anti-Medicean. For several weeks everyone waited to see who would make the first move. At the end of September, the Signoria issued a summons to Rinaldo and his allies and announced a parlamento for the 29th at which, as everyone knew, the crowd would be asked to agree to the return of the Medici. Realizing that the moment of truth had arrived, Rinaldo refused the summons and, together with other leading anti-Mediceans, opted for a showdown in the streets and a risky all-or-nothing revolt against the pro-Medici Signoria. Between 500 and 1,000 armed retainers and supporters, including members of prominent anti-Medici families, gathered under Rinaldo's leadership behind the palace, as the Signoria assembled its own force of 500 men inside. Years of factional rivalry were about to be resolved with arms. But two men prevented an actual battle and guaranteed the defeat of the anti-Mediceans. The first was Palla Strozzi. Rinaldo hesitated to take the drastic step of attacking the palace without Strozzi's full support and the participation of his large private army, which might have tipped the balance in favor of the anti-Mediceans. Rinaldo begged Palla to join the fight, but Strozzi, who commanded more moral authority than any other Florentine and who had never opposed the Medici until the year of their exile, refused. According to Cavalcanti, he appeared without his troops, listened to Rinaldo's anguished dismay, mumbled something that Cavalcanti claims not to have heard, and went home.[47] Decades later, in his admiring biography of Strozzi, Vespasiano da Bisticci invented, or perhaps reported from sources unknown to Cavalcanti, the dignified and stoically fatalistic response that Strozzi allegedly made to Rinaldo's emissaries: that he did not wish to destroy what he had not made, namely the city, and that what Rinaldo and the others were doing would surely have led to its ruin.[48]

The other man who intervened that day to stop the insurrection was Pope Eugenius, who had come to Florence that summer at Rinaldo's invitation to escape the violence and instability that Rome's nobility inflicted on the papal city. Rinaldo's army was losing strength in the aftermath of Strozzi's great refusal, as many now saw the folly of an attack on the Signoria and the palace that was sure to fail. Eugenius offered to arbitrate and promised that no harm would come to Rinaldo if he agreed to lay down his arms. Medici financial power surely influenced Eugenius's advice. Despite his close ties to Rinaldo, whom he had made a Roman senator two years earlier and whose hospitality in Florence he had just accepted, the pope knew that the church's interests were better served by good relations with the Medici, who were still his

---

[47]   Cavalcanti, *Istorie*, vol. 1, pp. 572–3.
[48]   Vespasiano da Bisticci, *Le vite*, ed. A. Greco, 2 vols. (Florence, 1976), 2:153–4.

bankers and the key to the papal–Florentine–Venetian alliance that was trying to keep Milan out of Tuscany and the papal states. Did Eugenius lure Rinaldo into a trap? Or did he simply see the hopelessness of a revolt against both the government and the well organized Medici faction? Whatever Eugenius's motives may have been, Rinaldo could not compete with Medici power.

When Rinaldo agreed to papal arbitration, the game was up. The Signoria summoned a parlamento and, to ensure its docile cooperation, summoned, or perhaps agreed to the arrival of, huge numbers of armed peasants from the contado. Cosimo himself noted that more than 3,000 of them came from the Mugello, from the mountains farther north, and even from the Romagna, and that, as he added rather matter-of-factly, they came "to our house." These irregulars were in effect the Medici private army, the inhabitants of the areas into which the family had slowly extended its network of rural patronage and from which it now called in debts that were years in the making. Cavalcanti called them "a huge multitude of wild and fierce peasants" and said that they were under the command of Papi de' Medici, Cosimo's distant cousin who also lived and owned property in the Mugello. Under the menacing gaze of some 6,000 armed peasants at the direct orders of a family that dominated a whole area of the Apennines, the parlamento approved the balìa that recalled the Medici and banished Rinaldo degli Albizzi, Ridolfo Peruzzi, Niccolò Barbadori, Felice Brancacci, and all the anti-Medici leaders, including, to the surprise and dismay of many, Palla Strozzi: altogether seventy-three exiles and, counting their households, 500 persons. It was the largest group of exiles from Florence in over a century. Among the Albizzi, only Rinaldo and his son Ormanno were banished, probably because Rinaldo's brother Luca had become a Medici ally. Of the fifty-eight families with at least one exile, those hit particularly hard were the Bardi, Brancacci, Castellani, Gianfigliazzi, Guadagni, Guasconi, Peruzzi, and Strozzi, whose four exiles included, in addition to Palla, Matteo di Simone, the husband of Alessandra Macinghi. Cavalcanti wrote that the balìa gave Florence a "nuovo reggimento," but then thought better of it and added that, "although I say new *reggimento*, one didn't hear new voices, and neither the kind nor number of men changed; rather there was an addition of some men who had had no place in the previous *reggimento*."[49] While there was no wholesale replacement of the wider political class and changes were largely confined to the leadership, in this case Cavalcanti underestimated the full significance of what was about to change, not immediately, but over the course of many years, as a consequence of the events of '34.

[49] Cavalcanti, *Istorie*, vol. 1, pp. 587–8; Kent, *Rise*, pp. 289–351.

10

The Medici and the Ottimati: A Partnership of Conflict
Part 1: Cosimo and Piero

The significance of 1434 changed over time. Decades later, Cosimo's return from exile acquired the status of an historic turning point. But for the first ten, even twenty, years of the regime, many Florentines (although probably not Cosimo himself) thought, as Cavalcanti did, that little had changed: that a typical conflict between upper-class factions had been resolved (as in 1393) with the victory of one group and the exile of the other. Illusions of continuity were sustained by the absence of major institutional reforms. Through the mid-1430s, Bruni and Palmieri continued to laud the republic's liberty and ideals of participatory citizenship, with no suggestion that anything fundamental was different. Bruni could not have been happy about the exile of his friends Rinaldo degli Albizzi (to whom he had dedicated his *De militia* in 1421) and Palla Strozzi, but he remained as chancellor and gave no public signs of displeasure with the new regime. Although not as thick as those he had with the exiled anti-Mediceans, Bruni had ties to the Medici as well that went back many years.[1] In 1420 he had dedicated a translation of the *Economics* (then attributed to Aristotle) to Cosimo himself. In the regime's early years, Poggio Bracciolini, Ambrogio Traversari, and other humanists praised Cosimo as a model citizen in the mold of virtuous ancient Roman statesmen

---

[1] P. Viti, "Gli avvenimenti del 1433–1434," in Viti, *Leonardo Bruni e Firenze: studi sulle lettere pubbliche e private* (Rome, 1992), pp. 113–36; A. Field, "Leonardo Bruni, Florentine Traitor? Bruni, the Medici, and an Aretine Conspiracy of 1437," *Renaissance Quarterly* 51 (1998): 1109–50.

and as the embodiment of civic and republican virtues.[2] By 1439, in an analysis of the Florentine constitution written in Greek for the visitors to the ecumenical church council then meeting in Florence, Bruni did acknowledge that the character of Florence's polity had been transformed by reliance on great private wealth in wartime.[3] But no humanist or chronicler of the regime's first years either praised or damned the return of the Medici as a watershed event.

In fact, much did change, and from the very beginning. Cosimo and his lieutenants modified Florentine politics and the relationship between governors and governed in ways that aimed to ensure that he would succeed where the Albizzi had failed.[4] Whereas Rinaldo had evidently not understood that the methods of 1393 would not work in 1433, Cosimo drew useful lessons both from the near disaster he and his family had suffered and from his enemies' failure to consolidate their temporary victory. A major reason for Cosimo's success over the next three decades was that he never forgot how close he came to losing everything. For him and his family the memory of 1433 nourished the constant obsession with never losing control of politics and government, or with regaining it by any and all means whenever it was weakened. The most urgent imperative of Cosimo's political practice was not to repeat his own mistakes of 1433 or those of his foes in 1434.

First among the differences between the oligarchic and Medici regimes were the banishments, not only the far greater number sent into exile in 1434 in a clear attempt to break rival factions rather than simply removing their leaders, but also the controversial exile of Palla Strozzi, whose refusal to join the insurrection of September 1434 facilitated the peaceful return of the Medici, and for which messer Palla might have expected a measure of gratitude from Cosimo. Even Medici friends protested this decision, albeit to no avail. Unlike Rinaldo, who joined Milanese military campaigns against Medicean Florence, Strozzi suffered his exile decorously and, so says Vespasiano, without wishing even to hear harsh words spoken against his city. Despite this unimpeachable conduct, Cosimo repeatedly renewed Palla's banishment and let him die in exile in 1462. Yet the harsh (according to many, indefensible) treatment of Strozzi

---

[2] A. Brown, "The Humanist Portrait of Cosimo de' Medici, Pater Patriae," *Journal of the Warburg and Courtauld Institutes* 24 (1961): 186–221, reprinted in Brown, *The Medici in Florence: The Exercise and Language of Power* (Florence and Perth, 1992), pp. 3–52 (6–10); M. Jurdjevic, "Civic Humanism and the Rise of the Medici," *Renaissance Quarterly* 52 (1999): 994–1020.

[3] "Peri tes ton Florentinon Politeias (Constitution of Florence)," ed. A. Moulakis, *Rinascimento* 26 (1986): 141–90; trans. in Griffiths et al., *Humanism of Leonardo Bruni*, pp. 171–4.

[4] R. Fubini, "Problemi di politica fiorentina all'epoca del Concilio," in *Firenze e il Concilio del 1439*, ed. Viti, vol. 1, pp. 27–57 (37–8).

had a purpose: it loudly announced, at the regime's inception and periodically thereafter, that it was not only enemies who would not be tolerated, but also anyone who could compete with Cosimo in wealth or prestige,[5] and that the collegial and collective rule by an oligarchy of families of more or less equal authority and stature was finished. Now one family claimed a primacy not to be rivaled by others.

Institutional Controls

Unlike the balìa of 1433, which left the results of earlier scrutinies in place, the Medici balìa of 1434 destroyed the pouches of the 1433 scrutiny. Nullification of scrutinies was not unprecedented: it happened three times in the fourteenth century (1343, 1378, and 1382), all moments of a more or less violent overthrow of government and radical redefinition of the political class. But it had not happened since the elite returned to power in 1382 and made the continuity of its electoral institutions a cardinal feature of the regime's legitimacy. That, no doubt, was a major reason why Rinaldo and his allies did not cancel the existing lists of eligible citizens. Although the Medici scrutiny of 1434 and those that followed at more or less five-year intervals did not substantially change the social composition of the office-holding class, eliminating the old lists and starting afresh allowed the regime to keep specific families and individuals out of the way and were meant to spare the Medici unpleasant surprises in the bimonthly extraction of name-tickets of the sort that had scuttled their opponents. They nonetheless protected their friends by having the accoppiatori select certain citizens approved in pre-1433 scrutinies for inclusion in the new pouches.

Like that of 1433, Medicean scrutinies continued to nominate and approve large numbers of citizens for high office. The results of the 1434 scrutiny have not survived, and for none of the next four, held in 1440, 1444, 1448, and 1453, have lists of approved candidates survived for all four quarters. Partial lists suggest city-wide totals of about 2,000 in 1440 and 1444, approximately 2,800 in 1448, and perhaps 2,500 in 1453. But a large proportion of approved candidates came from a fairly restricted group of some 100 to 120 families. For example, of 508 candidates approved in San Giovanni in 1440, 81% came from the major guilds, and 58% of these came from the 25 families in the quarter with five or more successful candidates. In the same year in Santa Croce, 78% of those approved were major guildsmen, and 69% of these came from only 32 families. Candidates approved for the first time were generally

---

[5]   Vespasiano, *Vite*, vol. 2, pp. 155–62; D. Kent, *Rise*, p. 343.

between a fifth and a fourth of each year's total; but 85 to 90% of the newly approved were sons or brothers of already approved citizens.[6] Thus the Medici continued the policy, begun by the oligarchic regime, of making eligible for high office both the whole of the elite including many of its children (excepting of course marked political enemies) and a large majority of non-elite major guildsmen as well.

Elite families would have preferred to see eligibility restricted to members of their class and worried about the approval of too many non-elite citizens, although the latter of course were not actually placed in office in anything like the same proportion. Throughout the sixty years of Medici hegemony, elite Florentines frequently deplored the expansion of eligibility. Francesco Giovanni confided to his diary that the scrutiny of 1448 had qualified "many *gente nuova* who had no experience of government, to the great infamy of the leadership and displeasure of the good *popolani* accustomed to rule." Four decades later Piero Guicciardini (father of the historian Francesco) commented more calmly, but with evident disapproval, that the scrutiny of 1484 confirmed that "continuously new men make the grade, and in order to give them a place in the governing class, it is necessary to eliminate from it long-established citizens."[7] In fact, however, "new men" were rather infrequent. Families entering the Signoria for the first time were almost as rare under the Medici as they had been before 1434. In the 25 years from 1409 to 1433, a total of only 69 new families (2.76 per year) had their first priors; in the first five years of the Medici regime, the annual totals of new families were a little higher (5, 9, 10, 7, and 11), but in the 25 years from 1440 to 1464, only 72 new families entered the Signoria (2.88 per year).[8] In any case, in the eyes of most citizens Medici control of the extraction of name-tickets through their trusted accoppiatori negated any practical significance to the huge numbers of approved candidates and for the most part ensured that Medici favorites controlled the lion's share of offices. Since the Medici were so careful to exclude those whom they did not trust, from whatever class, and to include non-elite clients and favorites, for the first time the office-holding class was defined more by the interests and needs of a ruling faction, or regime, than by class or family solidarities.

Actual elections were entrusted to the accoppiatori: the Medici did not repeat the mistake of their enemies in restoring sortition. They handpicked the regime's first Signoria (of November–December 1434) and maintained close controls over the selection of priors uninterruptedly for the next five years

---

[6] N. Rubinstein, *The Government of Florence Under the Medici (1434 to 1494)*, 2nd edn. (Oxford, 1997), pp. 70–2.
[7] Rubinstein, *Government*, pp. 69, 247, 369.
[8] Najemy, *Corporatism*, pp. 321–2.

through a committee of accoppiatori that remained unchanged.[9] Never had the power to elect the Signoria remained in so few hands for so long. Eight of the nine accoppiatori of 1434–9 were from the inner circle of Medici partisans: Luca Pitti, Piero Guicciardini, Niccolò Cocco-Donati, Antonio Serristori, Giuliano Davanzati, Neri Bartolini-Scodellari, Nerone Dietisalvi-Neroni, and the minor guildsman Nero di Filippo Del Nero, whose son Bernardo later became a fixture of the regime under Lorenzo; the ninth, Simone Guiducci, had been on the priorate that approved Cosimo's return. After their term expired, new committees of accoppiatori went on selecting the priors according to the wishes of the Medici high command for many years, with only brief (albeit important) interruptions. Unprecedented power and terms of office for accoppiatori whose domination of elections undermined sortition and emptied the scrutinies of any real significance were the cornerstone of the regime's transformation of both the electoral system and the republic's political culture. Accoppiatori had the authority to choose, from among the long lists of those approved in the scrutinies, a small numbers of names to be placed in purses for each bimonthly extraction of name-tickets: these were called "a mano" elections. No longer were the names of all approved candidates included in the purses. For the election of a Standardbearer of Justice, the accoppiatori put three or four names in a purse; for the priorate they selected a minimum of ten, and by 1438 only five, for each of two pouches, the regular purse and the borsellino, for each quarter of the city. Communal law still called for two minor guildsmen in each priorate, and for these as well the accoppiatori picked a small number of candidates for each election. A different selection of names occurred for each bimonthly election, and extraction by lot proceeded only from these very restricted pools of handpicked candidates: it was used merely to determine which two among the five or ten handpicked favorites for each quarter would hold the office. And by carefully mixing in the names of candidates temporarily disqualified by *divieti* or for other reasons, the accoppiatori could easily guarantee the election of specific candidates for any given term.

Where the regime encountered difficulties was in securing authorization for appointing or reappointing accoppiatori, which had to come from a constituted source. In 1434 the balìa had done this with its extensive but temporary powers. Thereafter, proposals for extending the accoppiatori's mandate had to be submitted to the legislative councils, which approved them by only narrow majorities as early as 1435, and later sometimes rejected them. Reluctance by the councils, especially that of the Popolo with its heavy representation of non-elite guildsmen, to authorize the accoppiatori was the regime's most serious weakness in its first thirty years: a resistance that clearly shows that the regime was not perceived by the guild community as in any sense

---

[9]   Rubinstein, *Government*, p. 273.

"popular." Continuation of *a mano* elections was justified with arguments about security: as necessary in times of crisis and especially war. In fact, the councils terminated them in 1440 after the Florentine victory over the Milanese at Anghiari finally eliminated the threat posed by Rinaldo degli Albizzi and the exiles. In 1443 the councils approved a partial restoration of the accoppiatori for three years, and the balìa of 1444 created new ones who remained in office until 1449, a group that again included Luca Pitti and four members of the Medici inner circle: Tommaso Soderini, Alamanno Salviati, Manno Temperani, and Dietisalvi, the son of Nerone Dietisalvi-Neroni. Giovanni Cavalcanti, who had once considered the Medici faction, or at least Cosimo's father, as a preferable alternative to the pre-1434 regime, regarded the resumption of electoral controls in 1444 as a sign of the regime's "tyrannical method of rule." "Even before the public extraction of name-tickets took place, these ten tyrants selected those who were to sit in high offices; and the result was that everything that the people and the balìa had done was subordinated to the will of the ten tyrants. . . . They selected those whom they wanted, not those for whom the people had voted, and there was no need to hold a new scrutiny if they wanted to give so much authority to such a tyrannical way of governing."[10]

Even within the regime's inner circle, opinion was divided. In a 1446 pratica, termination of *a mano* elections was favored by eleven of twenty-nine speakers, including two pillars of the regime, Agnolo Acciaiuoli and Nerone Dietisalvi-Neroni; seven wanted a continuation of controls; and the remaining eleven either had no opinion or believed that, although it might be better to continue them, public clamor for a return to traditional elections was too strong to ignore. Cosimo, who participated in this debate, espoused this cautious view, and in a follow-up discussion a few days later most speakers agreed with him. How and when to end electoral controls was left to an ad hoc committee that included Cosimo, but a week later the committee's report abruptly reversed the view he had expressed in the pratica and decided to retain *a mano* elections "for the preservation and security of the present *status* of the republic . . . and for avoiding dangers and discord." In 1449, another pratica debated the question: again there were significant differences of opinion among the regime's leaders, and again they decided for a continuation of controls. Matteo Palmieri, of all people, addressed and peremptorily resolved the issue of how to reconcile their decision with public opposition: "Although it seems more popular that the purses be closed [i.e., that the powers of the accoppiatori be terminated], in the end security is to be preferred to popularity."[11] Nonetheless, later that

---

[10] Giovanni Cavalcanti, *Nuova Opera (Chronique florentine inédite du XVe siècle)*, ed. A. Monti (Paris, 1989), pp. 92–3; also in Cavalcanti, *Istorie*, vol. 2, p. 193.

[11] Rubinstein, *Government*, pp. 27–30.

same year *a mano* elections were terminated and sortition restored, but with a new war in 1452 a new balìa and the legislative councils reinstated controls. A year after peace finally came in 1454, the councils put both the balìa and the accoppiatori out of business once again and did so with emphatic majorities of 218–22 and 169–7. Remarkably, fully twenty years after the regime's inception, solid majorities in the councils, and no doubt within the city at large, still regarded *a mano* elections as an emergency measure and looked forward eagerly, indeed insistently, to the resumption of traditional elections.

To resolve the problem of popular opposition to electoral controls, the regime attempted to bypass the legislative councils by entrusting the authorization of accoppiatori either to the Signoria or to balìe. Undermining the authority of the statutory councils did not begin with the Medici. The pre-1434 regime had moved in this direction by creating new assemblies, staffed with friends of the regime or limited in some way to those approved for the chief executive offices, and by giving these new bodies primary jurisdiction in key areas of war and finances. First was the council of 81 instituted by the balìa of 1393 and authorized to approve forced loans and create future balìe.[12] New councils of 200 and 131 were created in 1411 with primary responsibility for military affairs. And beginning in the early 1420s and continuing beyond 1434, a council of 145, consisting of the Signoria, advisory colleges, various ex officio bodies and appointed members, was periodically convened to approve tax bills and elect the Bank Officials and war balìe.[13] It was in some respects a council (because it remained in force for many years) and in others a balìa (because its authority had to be periodically renewed by the statutory councils). But apart from this hybrid body, after 1393 and until 1433 the oligarchic regime made no use of balìe in the strict sense of plenipotentiary assemblies appointed for short periods with far-reaching powers to enact reforms. Both the anti-Medici balìa of 1433 and the first Medici balìa of 1434 were of this kind.

While the Medici did not invent the institution of the balìa, the regime's use of it was radically different from earlier practice: Medici balìe were often of long duration and permanently weakened the authority of the statutory councils, especially concerning elections and taxes. In the regime's first twenty years, there were three balìe. The first was the "great council" of 1438, so-called because it consisted of 348 members, two-thirds of them appointed by the other one-third of ex-officio members. This too was a cross between a council and a balìa: although created for an unprecedented period of three years, during which the appointed members were not replaced, it was

[12]   A. Molho, "The Florentine Oligarchy and the Balìe of the Late Trecento," *Speculum* 43 (1968): 23–51.
[13]   ASF, Provvisioni, Registri, 113, ff. 33–4; and 115, ff. 283–8. Cf. Rubinstein, *Government*, pp. 77, 80.

not a permanent addition to the commune's legislative assemblies. In fact, the Council of the Popolo approved the new body by only seven votes. All proposals regarding fiscal and military matters had first to come to this balìa, and, if approved, were then sent to the statutory councils. The 1438 balìa was also authorized to hold the next general scrutiny and approve *a mano* elections of the Signoria for the following three years. It did both, but once the scrutiny of 1440 was completed, the statutory councils voted for the restoration of traditional elections by lot; and when the balìa's term ended in 1441, it duly dissolved itself and reinstated sortition.

Clearly this was not the result the regime had hoped for. So in 1444 it tried again with the creation of another long-term balìa, this one for five years; again the statutory councils approved it only by tiny majorities. It consisted of 238 members, two-thirds ex officio and only one-third appointed (who remained as permanent members for the entire period); two-thirds of its members had been in the balìe of either 1434 or 1438 or both. Its powers were like those of its predecessor of 1438: authority over the next scrutiny and elections *a mano*, and first say on all fiscal legislation. Over the next couple of years the balìa even regularly bypassed the statutory councils in approving tax bills, until the latter reacted sharply in 1446 by limiting the balìa's powers and reasserting their own constitutional prerogatives; in fact, in 1447 they tried to dissolve the balìa before the conclusion of its five-year term. This balìa carried out two general scrutinies, in 1444 and 1448, but the regime's attempts to prolong its existence for another two years were repeatedly rebuffed in the Council of the Popolo, and the balìa of 1444, like that of 1438, was dissolved on schedule the next year. The third attempt came in 1452, when a new balìa was again narrowly approved in the statutory councils. Although initially instituted only for the duration of the war, in 1453 its projected term was expanded to five years. But with peace in 1454, the statutory councils quickly cancelled this latest Medicean effort to reform the conciliar branch of Florentine government. Francesco Giovanni commented that "to everyone who wanted the right way of life [*il ben vivere*] and a republican government [*populare governo*], the present *balìa* was in every respect hateful."[14] The abolition of *a mano* elections followed the next year.

Twenty years of trying to persuade or cajole Florentines of middle social status, the guildsmen who filled the seats of the statutory councils, to accept a structural, if still de facto, modification of both electoral and legislative institutions thus met, at best, with mixed results. Balìe did in fact conduct all the general scrutinies of these years, and the Signoria was elected by accoppiatori in all but six of the twenty-one years from 1435 to 1455. But the statutory councils regularly repudiated the attempts to extend or make permanent the

---

[14]   Rubinstein, *Government*, pp. 77–98 (89).

powers of the balìe, and by 1455 the regime faced an uncertain future. Having routinely supported extra-constitutional authority and electoral controls on the grounds that external dangers required tighter security at home, now that the wars were at an end the regime would need to find other and, as it happened, harsher means of persuasion in reimposing controls that were even more essential to its survival in peace than in war.

External Supports: Papacy and Sforza Milan

Cosimo's connection to the papacy and his influence in foreign and military affairs compensated for the regime's limited success in bringing domestic politics under secure control. Their role as papal bankers was the beginning of the Medici link to the church that lasted, despite some rocky moments, for over a century and allowed the family to survive political opposition in Florence and even exile. Giovanni de' Medici's good relations with John XXIII and Martin V carried over to Cosimo's dealings with Eugenius IV, at least until the early 1440s. Although Eugenius had been invited to Florence by Cosimo's enemies, he already had Medici connections, having for example acceded to a Medici request, in negotiations conducted by Medici partisan Nerone Dietisalvi-Neroni, to raise the status of the canons of the Medici parish church of San Lorenzo to equality with the cathedral canons, a decision the Signoria strongly protested and succeeded in having revoked.[15] Rinaldo might have been trying to lure the pope away from Medici sympathies by offering him safe haven in Florence in June 1434. But Eugenius was widely seen as having been influential in securing Cosimo's recall and political ascendancy, after which the pope remained for nine more years and ruled the church from Medici-dominated Florence. For the first seven or eight of these years, Eugenius supported the Florentine–Venetian alliance against Milan and was dependent on the military strength of the two republics, on the Medici bank for the smooth operations of papal finance, and on Medici loans. And his dependence on the interest from 100,000 florins of shares in Florence's public debt gave Cosimo added leverage over the pope.[16]

His alliance with Eugenius offered Cosimo the opportunity to stage, and finance, the event that, perhaps more than any other in the regime's early years, consolidated Cosimo's image as a head of state and almost an uncrowned prince. The Council of Constance had mandated the convocation of

[15]   R. Bizzocchi, *Chiesa e potere nella Toscana del Quattrocento* (Bologna, 1987), p. 93.
[16]   J. Kirshner, "Papa Eugenio IV e il Monte Comune: documenti su investimento e speculazione nel debito pubblico di Firenze," *ASI* 127 (1969): 339–82.

further councils at regular intervals. A council assembled at Basel in 1431 was quickly dominated by conciliarists and assumed an anti-papal stance with political support from Milan and Aragon. To undermine its legitimacy, Eugenius sponsored a council of union with the various Christian communities of the East, especially the Orthodox Greeks whose Byzantine (and still nominally Roman) Empire had gradually been reduced to a few pockets of territory surrounded by the Ottoman Turks, who were then preparing the final assault, which came in 1453, on the imperial capital of Constantinople. For decades the Greeks had been appealing to the West for help, and when the council at Basel welcomed and signed agreements with a Greek delegation, Eugenius responded by convening his own council at Ferrara in 1438 to which he invited the Byzantine emperor and a large contingent of 200 churchmen and theologians, altogether no fewer than 700 dignitaries. An historic council for the reunification of the two main branches of Christendom, so Eugenius hoped, would split the gathering at Basel and bring many of its participants to Ferrara. Loans from the Medici bank paid the expenses of the Ferrara council, including those of the impecunious Greeks: one loan for 10,000 florins was secured with half of Eugenius's 100,000 florins of Florentine Monte shares, and the collateral for a second and larger loan was nothing less than the papal town of Sansepolcro, east of Arezzo, which did indeed become part of the Florentine dominion.[17] But Eugenius could not make ends meet and was constantly short of money. Moreover, hostile Visconti armies were coming uncomfortably close to Ferrara, and, with the danger of plague in the area, the pope decided at the end of 1438 to accept an invitation to move the council to Florence. Negotiations for the transfer were conducted by Cosimo's brother Lorenzo.

Thus, early in 1439 the entire council packed up and moved to Florence, officially as guests of the commune, but, given the source of the funding that kept the council alive, in effect as guests of the Medici. Only five years earlier, Cosimo had faced the potential ruin of his family in exile; now he welcomed not only his friend the pope but also the Byzantine emperor John VIII Palaeologus, the Patriarch of Constantinople Joseph II, and a huge gathering of eminent cardinals, bishops, patriarchs, and theologians from east and west. Cosimo saw to it (he could so arrange these things through his accoppiatori) that he was Standardbearer of Justice when the council arrived and thus at the head of two delegations that welcomed Eugenius on January 27, 1439, and the Greek emperor and his retinue on February 15 – later memorialized in the sumptuous frescoes of Benozzo Gozzoli in the chapel of the new Palazzo Medici. Cosimo provided living quarters for the emperor in the empty palaces

---

[17] P. Partner, "Florence and the Papacy in the Earlier Fifteenth Century," in *Florentine Studies*, ed. Rubinstein, pp. 396–7.

of the banished Ridolfo Peruzzi in Santa Croce.[18] Putting his imperial guest in the homes of exiles made it clear that Cosimo could use for his own purposes the property of enemies whose cause was now hopeless; it was almost the action of a sovereign with the implication that the city was now his. Despite doctrinal divergences and cultural differences accumulated through centuries of estrangement, on July 6, 1439, the assembled prelates announced the declaration of union solemnly proclaimed in the cathedral of Santa Maria del Fiore, whose magnificent dome, designed by Brunelleschi, had been completed just a few years before. Although the union was widely rejected by both Catholic and Orthodox Christians, and certainly did not save Constantinople, many Florentines saw the remarkable event as a consecration of the leadership and international prestige of Cosimo and his family.[19]

Eugenius was Cosimo's link to another opportunity of ultimately even greater significance: the alliance with the condottiere Francesco Sforza, future duke of Milan. Before he was driven from Rome in 1434, Eugenius snatched Sforza away from the service of Filippo Maria Visconti and signed him to a contract to fight for the church. In fact, however, Sforza used his new employment mainly to continue dismembering the papal states and bringing the region of the Marche, on the Adriatic, under his control. Eugenius's alliance with Florence and Venice meant that Sforza also became the chief captain of the allied republics. In the fall of 1434 the balìa that recalled Cosimo committed the Florentine government to pay Sforza 50,000 florins on Eugenius's behalf.[20] Sforza soon signed a treaty with Florence that was the beginning of a long association sustained by a personal alliance with Cosimo, which eventually shaped Florentine foreign policy and relations among the states of Italy. Sforza came from a Romagnol family of mercenary captains, but when he allied with Cosimo he was already acting (and being treated) as if he were one of Italy's princes. He inherited from his father huge tracts of land in the South and used the territories he seized from the church in the Marche as his temporary base. But his ultimate objective was Milan, where his former employer, Duke Filippo Maria Visconti, had no heirs. At the center of speculation and intrigue in Italian politics in these years was the fate of Milan after Visconti's death. By the 1440s, the fear was growing in many quarters, including the Medici, that the looming disintegration of the Visconti state might result in the conquest of

---

[18]   Bartolomeo del Corazza, *Diario fiorentino (1405–1439)*, ed. R. Gentile (Anzio, 1991), pp. 79–81.
[19]   J. Gill, S. J., *The Council of Florence* (Cambridge, 1959); and *Firenze e il concilio del 1439*, ed. Viti.
[20]   R. Fubini, "Diplomazia e governo in Firenze all'avvento dei reggimenti oligarchici," in Fubini, *Quattrocento fiorentino: politica, diplomazia, cultura* (Pisa, 1996), p. 78; Partner, "Florence and the Papacy," in *Florentine Studies*, ed. Rubinstein, p. 394.

the whole of Italy north of the Apennines by the ever more powerful Venetian republic. To what extent Cosimo may have foreseen such an eventuality in the 1430s, when he established his alliance with Sforza, is difficult to say, but by the next decade he considered the territorial integrity and strength of Milan as the key to both preventing Venetian hegemony in northern Italy and protecting his regime in Florence. And the key to preserving Milan was Francesco Sforza.

Already by 1438 fears of Venetian expansion led to a truce between Milan and Florence. But when Filippo Maria's chief captain, Niccolò Piccinino, took advantage of the agreement to renew the assault on papal dominions by taking Bologna, which as always for the Florentines meant that the Milanese were too close for comfort, another war pitted Florence, Venice, Eugenius, the Angevin contenders in Naples, and Francesco Sforza against the alliance of Milan and Alfonso of Aragon, who was struggling to bring the southern kingdom into the Aragonese empire. In 1440 Piccinino, with Rinaldo degli Albizzi and other exiles in his entourage, took his troops into the papal state very close to Florentine territory in the Casentino, where he suffered a decisive defeat at Anghiari at the hands of forces directed by the Florentine commissioners Neri Capponi and Bernardo de' Medici, Cosimo's distant cousin.[21] It was the last gasp of the exiles. Rinaldo gave up the fight and died two years later, and a peace signed the next year recognized Florentine possession of the Casentino. In the aftermath of the council of 1439, the victory at Anghiari in 1440, and the peace of 1441 that further enlarged the Florentine dominions, the Medici regime seemed stronger than ever.

Cosimo was now ready to lead the Florentines into new, and by no means universally accepted, diplomatic and strategic positions. In 1442 Alfonso defeated his Angevin rivals and took control of the kingdom. For Eugenius, who had supported the Angevins, this was yet another setback after the loss of the territories he had been forced to cede to both Sforza and Florence. Nor had the peace of 1441 restored Bologna to papal control. The pope broke his pacts with Sforza and ended his old alliance with Cosimo, who had provided much of the money for Sforza's campaigns. With barely concealed hostility between Eugenius and Cosimo, the pope's presence in Florence was now awkward for all concerned. Thus, early in 1443, after living for nine years at Santa Maria Novella just a few hundred meters from the Medici palace, Eugenius finally returned to Rome, where he promptly removed the manager of the Medici bank's Rome branch, Roberto Martelli, from the office of papal depositary. Relations between the former allies remained frosty for the remainder of Eugenius's pontificate. In 1445 Florence's archbishop died and the regime recommended a number of possible successors, including Cosimo's cousin, the

---

[21] Bayley, *War and Society*, pp. 164–74.

bishop of Pistoia Donato de' Medici (son of the humanist Nicola di Vieri) and Giovanni di Nerone Dietisalvi-Neroni, a canon of Florence cathedral and brother of Dietisalvi in Cosimo's inner circle. Cosimo wanted a Florentine in the post and blatantly requested the appointment of someone "most faithful to this regime [*fidissimus huic statui*]," if not his cousin the bishop, then Dietisalvi's brother. But Eugenius was no longer willing to cooperate with the Medici, and early in 1446 he announced the appointment of Antonino Pierozzi as archbishop, a Florentine, but not from the Medicean circle or even the elite. This son of a notary was an Observant Dominican, one of the leading theologians of the century, and a determined church reformer at the local level. His tough-minded independence kept him from becoming a pawn of the regime and gave Cosimo, as we shall see, a major headache in the political crisis of 1458.[22]

By 1446 Cosimo openly supported both Sforza's ambitions, including an unsuccessful attempt to occupy Rome itself, and the efforts of the Bentivoglio in Bologna to keep that city free of papal rule and friendly to Florence. Eugenius died early in 1447 and was succeeded by the humanist Tommaso Parentucelli, a Tuscan and old friend of the Florentines, who, as Nicholas V, made peace with Sforza, brought the schismatic council of Basel to an end, and improved relations with Florence and Cosimo in a variety of ways, including the reinstatement of the Medici branch manager as papal depositary. In August 1447 Filippo Maria Visconti died. The struggle for Milan opened when the Milanese popolo proclaimed the Ambrosian republic the very next day. As the Venetians took advantage of the turmoil to gobble up cities and territories ever closer to Milan, Sforza at first fought with the Milanese republic to keep the Venetians at bay, but in October 1448 suddenly reversed himself, signed an agreement with Venice, and marched on Milan to make himself the new duke. Cosimo used all his considerable influence in Florence to support Sforza, especially when the Venetians, worried by Sforza's burgeoning power, terminated their alliance in 1449 and supported the Ambrosian republic against him.

Cosimo's alliance with Sforza and the latter's demands for more and more money caused controversy and acrimonious debate in Florence. Even within the balìa voices were raised against further subsidies to Sforza, and in the pratiche speakers troubled by Cosimo's abandonment of Venice and embrace of Sforza openly lamented that "an alliance between a *signore* and a republic is akin to an alliance of partridges and falcons." Cosimo's foreign policy was threatening to split the ruling group, and some of his most important domestic allies, including Neri Capponi, Alamanno Salviati, and Luca degli Albizzi,

[22] D. S. Peterson, "An Episcopal Election in Quattrocento Florence," in *Popes, Teachers, and Canon Law in the Middle Ages*, ed. J. R. Sweeney and S. Chodorow (Ithaca, 1989), pp. 300–25.

were so distressed by this reversal of the republic's traditional alliances that they became reluctant to support the new policy on diplomatic missions. Tightening control over foreign policy, Cosimo removed his critics from the inner circle, including Capponi, and limited the conduct of diplomacy to a small group of his most trusted lieutenants, in particular Agnolo Acciaiuoli and Dietisalvi Neroni.[23] Thus began the practice of semi-private diplomacy and foreign policy, increasingly under the thumb of the Medici group and removed from regular constitutional channels, a practice that was to culminate in the princely pretensions of Cosimo's grandson Lorenzo in the 1470s and 1480s.

Sforza took Milan, became its duke, and went to war against Venice with Florentine support. In 1451 Florence and Sforza agreed to a military alliance, and the Dieci di balìa who oversaw the war included Cosimo. When, in April 1454, Sforza and Venice ended hostilities and signed the Peace of Lodi, some Florentines believed that Cosimo was opposed to the peace, either because, as Marco Parenti speculated, he preferred the war to continue until Sforza had taken more territory from Venice,[24] or because he knew that his hold on domestic politics would again weaken without war. But most Florentines were relieved to see the long years of war come to an end. In March 1455 the five principal states of Italy (Sforza's Milan, Venice, Cosimo's Florence, the church under Nicholas V, and Naples under Alfonso of Aragon) signed a 25-year peace treaty with promises of mutual defense and preservation of the status quo throughout the peninsula. Cosimo's daring gamble proved in the end successful: at the core of the pacification of Italy was the new Florentine–Milanese alliance. Venice was contained, and Sforza's Milan was now ready and willing to protect the Medici regime against its internal enemies.

Cosimo's Coup

The Medici sought to build their regime with the collaboration of the city's leading families. Despite the frequent presence in offices of non-elite partisans, it was still primarily with the support of the ottimati, as the elite now liked to call themselves, that the Medici controlled electoral politics, fiscal policy, and foreign affairs. An early indication of the intention to anchor the regime in alliance with elite families was the quiet setting aside of the Catasto and the return to forced loans assessed by neighborhood committees that the wealthy families had always preferred.[25] When cooperation from wealthy

---

[23] Fubini, "Diplomazia e governo," in *Quattrocento fiorentino*, pp. 79–82.
[24] M. Phillips, *The Memoir of Marco Parenti: A Life in Medici Florence* (Princeton, 1987), p. 65.
[25] Conti, *L'imposta diretta*, pp. 181–3.

and prestigious families was extensive, to some the regime seemed headed toward the kind of broad upper-class consensus that undergirded Venice's legendary stability (at least in the perception of its Florentine admirers). In 1438 Niccolò Soderini, a Medici partisan in those early days, wrote to a friend that "at Florence there is an extremely strong regime which will prove permanent," adding that "we will eventually end up in the Venetian style, but it's happening very slowly."[26]

Dependence on the ottimati was also, paradoxically, the regime's weakness, because the elite was not easily reconciled to the hegemony of one family, much less of one man, a power everyone recognized but few, among both Medici partisans and ottimati supporters, were willing to acknowledge openly. Unlike Venice, where the doge was largely a constitutional figurehead and real power rested in the Senate, Florence's leading "private citizen" acted more like a reigning prince and was increasingly described by fawning humanists and propagandists as the "ruler of all things," as a model Platonic philosopher-ruler, and even as a latter-day Augustus.[27] While insisting that he was just another citizen, Cosimo did nothing to discourage such flattery. But many ottimati were clearly uncomfortable with it, preferring to see themselves as equal partners of the Medici and Cosimo as the first among equals, an ambiguous notion that contradictorily encompassed the equality of all and the preeminence of one. Lodged at the center of the elite's confused perception of Cosimo, this ambiguity obfuscated, even denied, an unpleasant truth, and it took the ottimati a long time to admit what foreigners could see more clearly, namely, that they were all gradually being reduced to the status of clients in a hegemonic patronage system: an entire class made dependent on the Medici for offices and voices in the regime, for financial favors and fiscal relief, advantageous marriages, beneficial positions in trade and banking, preferred treatment in Rome, lucrative ecclesiastical appointments, places of honor in civic rituals, and, not least, for protection of their social prestige and wealth from the popolo and the Catasto. Ottimati alternated between collective denial of this reality and resistance to it. War and the patriotic impulses it generated, together with the indispensability of Medici money for the republic's military and foreign policy, allowed the ottimati to tell themselves that their declining power as a ruling class was the temporary result of circumstances and that their former equality and collective hegemony would return once the emergencies had passed. That illusion no doubt sustained Niccolò Soderini's belief that the republic was evolving toward stable upper-class dominance on the Venetian model.

[26] P. C. Clarke, *The Soderini and the Medici: Power and Patronage in Fifteenth-Century Florence* (Oxford, 1991), p. 27.
[27] Brown, "The Humanist Portrait," in *The Medici*, pp. 15–22.

The mix of cooperation, denial, and resistance in ottimati reactions to Medici control was rooted in their own conflicted self-image: on the one hand, traditional defenders of the privileges and right to rule of the well-born, patrons in their own right, and enemies of popular governments; on the other, statesmen who had absorbed the languages of republican politics and humanism. In their attempts to rein in the Medici, the rhetoric of republican liberty served their purposes rather better than did old ideas (which they had never abandoned) about the privileges of their class. Although ottimati republicanism was obviously very different from that of the popolo, republican liberty could usefully be juxtaposed to Medici "tyranny." Appropriating the language of civic humanism signaled yet another step in the elite's evolution, as some now styled themselves aristocratic defenders of republican liberty and virtue. But in the equally important, and longer, moments of recognition that they were no longer masters of what they always considered their own house, and thus of acquiescence in Medici leadership, the ottimati also gave early signs of what was to be their final metamorphosis into a domesticated court aristocracy.

Three major crises punctuated the twenty years between 1458 and 1478, and all had at their core the problematic relationship between the Medici and the ottimati. The first, in 1458, was precipitated by the Medici party itself, desperate to regain the power lost in the restoration a few years earlier of traditional electoral and legislative institutions. Unlike the inception of the regime in 1434 which occurred under the legal authority of a duly drawn Signoria, what happened in 1458 was in essence a Medici coup d'état openly supported by threats of force from private armies and Milanese troops. In its aftermath, no illusions remained concerning the extensive extra-constitutional power on which the regime rested.

Among the final actions of the accoppiatori whose mandate ended in June 1455 was an evident act of political reprisal: the removal from the lists of eligible citizens of nineteen citizens, among them Giovanni Rucellai, already marginalized because of his marriage to Palla Strozzi's daughter; Mariotto Lippi, who had dared to say in a 1449 pratica that "the people desire the recovery of the old ways and their pristine liberty" and that the continued authority of the accoppiatori was earning them the "greatest enmity"; and Marco Parenti, the chronicler and son-in-law of Alessandra Strozzi.[28] Parenti's punishment probably had less to do with his connections to the Strozzi than with his actions as a member of the priorate of March–April 1454, when, persuaded that Cosimo opposed peace, he quickly proclaimed the ratification of the Peace of Lodi before a new war tax and another term for the war balìa could go into effect. Even though he apparently antagonized the Medici and provoked them to retaliate, in his chronicle he recalled the restoration of

[28]   Rubinstein, *Government*, pp. 30n, 34, 51n.

traditional electoral procedures in 1455 as a return to liberty: "It seemed to the citizens a recovery of some measure of liberty, being freed from the servitude of the accoppiatori," for once the latter lost their authority "other citizens lost their fear and dared from time to time to do something worthwhile on their own, without first asking those whom they were accustomed to regard as the chief citizens."[29]

Punishing the likes of Marco Parenti cost the Medici little. More serious was the defection of elite members of the regime and, worse still, of the inner circle. Standardbearer of Justice in the priorate of May–June 1454, which approved the balìa's dissolution, was the Medici insider Dietisalvi Neroni. Pushing aside such a man could have split the regime, and Cosimo preferred to send another of his inner circle, Tommaso Soderini, to reason privately with Neroni. Soderini could not save the balìa, but he did prevent Neroni's priorate from terminating *a mano* elections (which happened the next year). Cosimo's son Piero was so impressed with Soderini's loyalty that he arranged for him to become Standardbearer of Justice for July–August. But Soderini's own brother Niccolò, who had so confidently praised the direction of the regime some years earlier, now emerged as a critic of Medici methods and a supporter of reforms.[30] Within the inner circle some were no longer toeing the Medici line, choosing instead to support popular sentiment (of the sort that came from Mariotto Lippi and Marco Parenti) in favor of a restoration of traditional government and elections. Cosimo could do little unless and until the elite realized that its own class interests were threatened by the reviving influence of the popolo.

That realization came early in 1458 when the Signoria and legislative councils reinstated the Catasto, again threatening the wealthy with heavier taxes. Apprehension was fed by the prospect that the upcoming scrutiny would be the first in a quarter century not to be conducted by a balìa.[31] Suddenly rumors swirled about plans from within the Medici circle to "seize" or retake the government with another balìa, and Medici opponents responded with a law in April making it more difficult to create balìe and prohibiting any balìa from conducting an electoral scrutiny. With sortition having been restored, once again the chance selection of the draw for a new Signoria created the opportunity for action: Luca Pitti, one of Cosimo's most powerful lieutenants, became Standardbearer of Justice for July–August. Pitti's priorate proposed to the councils the creation of a new legislative body of carefully selected citizens, in effect a permanent balìa, and recommended that the scrutiny scheduled for the end of the year be held during Pitti's term of office. When the councils

---

[29]   Phillips, *Marco Parenti*, pp. 64–8.
[30]   Clarke, *Soderini and Medici*, pp. 51–9.
[31]   For what follows: Rubinstein, *Government*, pp. 99–153; and Clarke, *Soderini and Medici*, pp. 58–64.

firmly rejected both ideas, the Signoria, in an obvious attempt to intimidate council members with implied threats of reprisal for votes openly cast against these proposals, suggested that secret balloting be set aside in the stubbornly anti-Medici Council of the Popolo. But Archbishop Antoninus intervened and harshly denounced open balloting as a violation of council members' oaths and thus a matter of conscience that came under ecclesiastical jurisdiction; thirty-one members of an advisory pratica that the Signoria was trying to influence welcomed his condemnation of Medici tactics.[32]

Among Medici partisans, some saw matters in class terms: at stake was whether the ottimati were going to keep or lose control of government: "There are two alternatives," said Franco Sacchetti in the crucial pratica of August 1: "should we allow the *prestantes cives* [pre-eminent citizens] to be ruled by others, or should the others be ruled by them, as is right and just?" His views were seconded by Mediceans Tommaso Soderini and Otto Niccolini. Alessandro Alessandri escalated the sense of imminent crisis by asserting that the opposition was well organized and that the only solution was a parlamento. Mediceans were appealing to ottimati fears of an assault on traditional class privileges in order to push opinion toward the acceptance of an extra-constitutional resolution. Once the idea of a parlamento had surfaced, speaker after speaker declared the necessity of seeking Cosimo's opinion, and the pratica agreed to summon a parlamento if the idea had Cosimo's approval.[33] Cosimo knew it was a risky step, in part perhaps because large crowds could be unpredictable, but also because circumventing normal institutional channels might establish a precedent that could be used against the Medici. If it was to work, it needed to be orchestrated perfectly, and the indispensable element was again, as in 1434, the presence of an armed force. On the same day that the pratica was debating the conditions for calling a parlamento, Cosimo met with the resident Milanese ambassador, Nicodemo Tranchedini, to discuss military intervention from Milan and other allies. Tranchedini immediately wrote to Sforza, and the duke responded on August 10 that he was sending the lord of Faenza and his troops. Such reassurance was all that Cosimo needed: opposition leaders were arrested, a few tortured, and some 150 persons placed under house arrest. The next day, Cosimo remained at home with his armed retinue (and the Milanese ambassador) as mercenary troops surrounded piazza Signoria and the citizens filed in for the parlamento. According to one observer, only a few people actually heard the notary of the Signoria read aloud the proposals, and correspondingly few gave their approval. Knowingly or not, they "agreed" to the resumption of *a mano* elections for the next five years, the suspension of the law against balìe, the immediate institution of a balìa to hold a scrutiny,

---

[32]   D. Peterson, "State-Building, Church Reform, and the Politics of Legitimacy in Florence, 1375–1460," in *Florentine Tuscany*, ed. Connell and Zorzi, pp. 142–3.
[33]   Rubinstein, *Government*, pp. 113–15.

and the creation of a new council, the Cento (Hundred), that was meant to resolve the regime's institutional weakness. In a veritable purge, 1,500 citizens were removed from the lists of eligible officeholders. The police magistracy of the Otto di Guardia, which was given expanded powers to adjudicate political offenses and summarily punish the guilty, added to the ranks of the exiles many outspoken critics of Medici rule, including Girolamo Machiavelli, who was later arrested and executed for conspiring against the regime.

Selecting the members of the Cento was entrusted to the Signoria and all those who had served as Standardbearers of Justice since 1434 or whose name-tickets had been drawn for the office without holding it (the so-called "veduti"). This body put to a vote all former members of the Signoria and colleges (or "veduti" for the same) since 1434. Thus a select group of Medicean insiders (Standardbearers of Justice had all been carefully chosen by the accoppiatori) screened themselves and the office-holding elite of the previous twenty-four years (also mostly selected by the accoppiatori) to produce a still narrower group of trusted friends of the regime. Among the Cento's powers were to elect key magistracies (the Monte and Catasto officials and the Otto di Guardia) and to screen all legislation before it was sent to the older councils, which still, however, had to give final approval to laws and to any extension of the accoppiatori beyond the five years established by the parlamento. Finally, the balìa replaced the old title of the "priors of the guilds" with the "priors of liberty," an ironic exaltation of a liberty that had never seemed more threatened than in 1458. Sixty-five years later, in his *Florentine Histories* (7.4) Machiavelli commented wryly that the change was made "in order to have at least the name of the possession they had lost." Benedetto Dei, a woolen-cloth manufacturer and son of a goldsmith, wrote that the 1458 parlamento had been engineered by Cosimo and Luca Pitti, "who wanted to secure for themselves the *stato* and *reggimento* and make it completely stable." But they tried "in vain" to get the city back to work and normal life, "because of the pent-up feelings of the citizens who saw themselves deprived and stripped of all honor and office, so much so that many of the leading citizens left the city out of desperation and irritation at always having to see their enemies enjoying a free field with all the offices and honors and with their heads always in the trough. . . . And the city of Florence suffered such a blow and shock that it remained stunned and bewildered for more than eight years from 1458 to 1466."[34]

In the last six years of his life, Cosimo withdrew from any public or visible role, no longer holding offices or even speaking in the pratiche. But no one doubted that his power, exercised largely from his grand new family palace (see Plate 5) on the via Larga (where the accoppiatori also met), was greater

---

[34]   Benedetto Dei, *La Cronica*, ed. R. Barducci (Florence, 1984), p. 66.

Plate 5   Palazzo Medici (now known as Palazzo Medici-Riccardi), built 1445–60, designed by Michelozzo (Scala/Art Resource, NY)

than ever. In the spring of 1459 he welcomed the new pope, Pius II, the Sienese humanist Aeneas Sylvius Piccolomini, who stopped in Florence on his way to Mantua to preside over a council he had summoned to declare a crusade against the Ottomans, and Francesco Sforza sent his fifteen-year-old son, Galeazzo Maria, to escort the pope from Florence to Mantua. Private citizen Cosimo never seemed more like a reigning monarch than during these two "state visits." In his memoirs Pius said of him that he "was considered the arbiter of war and peace, the regulator of law; less a citizen than master of his city. Political councils were held in his home; the magistrates he chose were elected; he was king in all but name and legal status. . . . Some asserted that his tyranny was intolerable."[35] Machiavelli, noting the fate of his kinsman Girolamo, described the regime that emerged in 1458 as an "unbearable and violent" kind of rule in which "a few citizens plundered the city" and used "terror" and "fear" in order periodically to "retake power."[36]

The Ottimati Challenge Piero

Cosimo's death on August 1, 1464, brought the Medici, their inner circle, and the ottimati to a moment of truth over a question that had been looming for years: was Cosimo's leadership a family legacy to be inherited by his son Piero, or a personal achievement to be followed by a restoration of collective rule by either the Medici lieutenants or a wider group of ottimati? Assuming that they were Cosimo's political heirs, the chief lieutenants began exercising the collective leadership that they believed was legitimately theirs. Piero's reaction provoked a confrontation in which Medici "succession" was nearly thwarted but in the end imposed, again largely by armed force and the threat of military intervention from Milan. Although many historians persist in referring to the refusal of Cosimo's former allies to accept a Medici succession as a "plot" or "conspiracy," it was in fact no such thing. Their challenge to Piero was an open and legal attempt to restore constitutional government. Perception of conspiracy in these events reflects Medici propaganda: that they were Florence's destined and therefore legitimate rulers and that any attempt to limit their power could only have been an extra-legal act.[37] In fact, it was the Medici who invented and promoted the story that "conspirators"

---

[35]   Pius II, *Commentarii*, ed. L. Totaro (Milan, 1984), pp. 352–4. Cf. M. Meserve and M. Simonetta (trans.), *Commentaries* (Cambridge, Mass., 2003), vol. 1, pp. 316–19. Rubinstein, *Government*, p. 145; R. Hatfield, "Cosimo de' Medici and the Chapel of His Palace," in *Cosimo "il Vecchio*," ed. Ames-Lewis, pp. 221–44.

[36]   *Florentine Histories*, 7.4; *Discourses on Livy* 3.1.

[37]   On the legend of the "conspiracy": Phillips, *Marco Parenti*, pp. 241–59.

had sought to kill Piero at the height of the confrontation in the summer of 1466.

Cosimo's relations with his chief lieutenants soured in his last years. Agnolo Acciaiuoli, who openly criticized Cosimo and Piero in a letter to Francesco Sforza, was rumored to be trying to replace the Medici as Florence's chief link to Milan.[38] After Cosimo died, Dietisalvi Neroni wrote to the duke that "while Cosimo was alive, decisions were left to him; now those who remain at the head of the regime [are] Piero and a number of citizens supporting him, who were brothers to Cosimo and who will now be fathers to Piero."[39] Over the next year, Acciaiuoli went his own way, and even in the Cento voices were heard in favor of a return to traditional elections and government. Beyond the ruling elite was a sense that the air was freer with Cosimo gone and expectations that political controls would loosen. Although Parenti acknowledged that Florence was prosperous and at peace, for which he gave Cosimo some credit, he asserted that "nevertheless on his death everyone rejoiced, such is the love of and desire for liberty. It appeared to the Florentines that from his way of governing they had experienced a certain subjection and servitude, from which they believed his death would liberate them. This they desired and in this they delighted, putting off thought of any other good which they enjoyed."[40] Taking note of this mood, in September 1465 Dietisalvi Neroni told Sforza that "the citizenry would like a more broadly based and freer government, as is appropriate in *città popolari* like ours." Manno Temperani told a pratica that the people disliked the very word "balìa" and were unhappy with the fact that "all power had been entrusted to the will of a few and that all things were being governed according to their wishes." That same month the statutory councils terminated *a mano* elections and ordered a resumption of sortition and the restoration of eligibility to the many disqualified in 1458. "The whole city liked it," wrote Acciaiuoli, except Piero.[41] Some weeks later, Alessandra Strozzi told her exiled sons in Naples not to be surprised if their brother-in-law Marco was for the moment less than usually attentive to family business: "everyone's mind is on what is happening in the palace, to put the government back on track [*dirizzare lo Stato*] and decide how we are going to live. They're discussing it all day and those whose names were taken out of the pouches in 1458 are expecting to have them put back in. Marco is working hard on this, as are the others, to get it put to a vote." Once that is done, she

---

[38] M. A. Ganz, "Perceived Insults and Their Consequences: Acciaiuoli, Neroni, and Medici Relationships in the 1460s," in *Society and Individual*, ed. Connell, pp. 155–72.
[39] Rubinstein, *Government*, p. 156.
[40] Phillips, *Marco Parenti*, p. 14.
[41] Rubinstein, *Government*, pp. 160–2.

added, they'll take up the question of allowing "innocent exiles" to return: a
hope that, for the Strozzi, soon materialized, but not in the way Alessandra
expected.[42]

The luck of the electoral draw made Niccolò Soderini Standardbearer of
Justice for November–December 1465. A former Medici friend who fell out
of favor in the early 1450s as he watched his brother Tommaso grow ever
closer to the regime, Niccolò came into office with a reform agenda that
gave Medici opponents great encouragement. On just the second day of this
Signoria, Parenti wrote to his brothers-in-law in Naples that Niccolò's
election put the city "in an uproar," to the dismay of the Mediceans and
delight of their opponents: "it could not please me more to see where Florence
is going. . . . I cannot tell you what a great spirit he shows, and he has the
favor of all Florence. Everyone visits him at his house." "Never," he later
wrote, "had there been a Standardbearer who took office with such a spirited
welcome from the people and with such expectation of good."[43] The next day
Soderini delivered a long dramatic speech in a pratica, lamenting the decline
of political virtue and good government in Florence, corruption in the courts
and distribution of offices, and excessive taxation that was impoverishing
city and countryside.[44] He urged a new scrutiny: the first since 1458 and the
first in more than three decades not controlled by a balìa.

Unhappiness with Soderini and fissures within the ranks of the anti-
Mediceans quickly surfaced when the details of his recommendations for
both the scrutiny and eligibility to major offices became known. He succeeded
in attaching to the law authorizing the scrutiny, which was several times
rejected by the Council of the Popolo until both councils narrowly approved
it, the automatic admission to the scrutiny committee of all former
Standardbearers of Justice since 1434, including the "veduti," or, if they were
deceased, their sons or other relatives. It was controversial enough to desig-
nate such a small inner circle (selected over the years by Medici accoppiatori
no less) as a privileged elite with superior influence. But Soderini also wanted
to guarantee permanent eligibility for all citizens, and their descendants, who
had qualified in any scrutiny since 1444. Automatic re-qualification on the

---

[42]   Strozzi, *Letters*, ed. Gregory, pp. 178–9.
[43]   Marco Parenti, *Lettere*, ed. M. Marrese (Florence, 1996), p. 136; Phillips, *Marco
Parenti*, pp. 172, 174–5.
[44]   Clarke, *Medici and Soderini*, pp. 81–2; G. Pampaloni, "Fermenti di riforme
democratiche nella Firenze medicea del Quattrocento," *ASI* 119 (1961): 11–62;
Pampaloni, "Fermenti di riforme democratiche nelle Consulte della Repubblica
fiorentina," ibid., pp. 241–81 (Soderini's speech on 242–4); Pampaloni, "Nuovi tentativi
di riforme alla costituzione fiorentina visti attraverso le Consulte," *ASI* 120 (1962):
521–81.

basis of an earlier scrutiny had been tried once (in the 1330s) and was rescinded within a decade because it would have permanently ensconced a hereditary ruling caste. Both ideas were rejected as too oligarchic, and Soderini quickly fell from favor, accused by former supporters of trying to create a rigidly demarcated Venetian-like ruling nobility. His proposals exposed the full implications of the hope he had expressed thirty years earlier that Florence would "eventually end up in the Venetian style." Soderini left office at the end of the year defeated and humiliated, and the controversy destroyed the prospects of a united front of anti-Mediceans. A disappointed and disenchanted Marco Parenti wrote that "if he has done anything good, which he has, it is lost because of the very great evil of the division of Florence, which is now openly revealed and, one might say, stamped and sealed, so that now it can never be undone."[45]

What Parenti called the "division of Florence" was the emergence of a triangular conflict among Mediceans, ottimati, and popolo. In the absence of Medici controls, the divergent agendas of popular and elite approaches to the restoration of what both groups considered "traditional" constitutional government became evident. To a certain extent, the contrast between the two republicanisms reprised old differences between popolo and elite. But the positions of both classes had been changed by thirty years of Medici dominance, and neither was identical to its fourteenth-century predecessor. Through decades of oligarchic and Medici hegemony the popolo lost contact with its guild origins and focused instead on the restoration of an electoral system of broad scrutinies and sortition, originally invented by the elite. Aristocratic republicanism now shared the rhetoric of republican liberty and the antipathy to what it too saw as tyranny, but it was moving toward Niccolò Soderini's "Venetian-style" assumption that liberty could best be protected by a hereditary aristocracy of merit, a class of experienced leaders more likely to emerge from elite families than from either the middle class or a regime of favorites and clients. Dormant during the decades of Medici power, the latent conflict between these republicanisms surfaced in the vacuum that developed after Cosimo was gone. It was the first of many recurrences of this "division" over the next sixty-five years, with each side intensely aware that prolonged rifts would allow the Medici to impose their own solution.

Divisions among their enemies seemed on the verge of saving the Mediceans from being swept aside, when news arrived from Milan in March 1466 that Francesco Sforza was dead. At a critical moment Piero de' Medici lost his most important ally, and the hopes of his enemies revived. Over the next few months, political tensions intensified and the Signoria issued repeated calls for unity. At the end of May the anti-Medici movement reached its apogee

[45] Phillips, *Marco Parenti*, pp. 176–88 (180).

when 400 citizens signed an oath in defense of liberty and the "government of many," promising that "the city would be governed, as is customary, by a just and popular government, that in the future the extraction [of name-tickets] of our magnificent Signori will take place by lot as is now being done, and in no other way . . . , and that no violence shall be committed against any citizen illegally, so that citizens may understand that they are free to give counsel and to express their judgments about public matters."[46] First among the signatories were Cosimo's former high command: Manno Temperani, Luca Pitti, Agnolo Acciaiuoli, Giovannozzo Pitti, and Dietisalvi Neroni. Niccolò Soderini is eighth on the list (and the only one of his family). Among the ottimati are at least eight Capponi, seven Pitti, four Corsini, Acciaiuoli, Dietisalvi-Neroni, and Alberti, and three Rucellai, Alessandri, and Albizzi. At least fifteen other elite families, and dozens of families from the second rank of the elite, are represented on the list, including five Machiavelli. There is even a Medici: Piero's cousin Pierfrancesco, the son of Cosimo's brother Lorenzo and founder of the rival branch of the family that was to go its own way politically.[47] Another noteworthy name is that of Amerigo di Giovanni Benci, manager of the Geneva–Lyons branch of the Medici bank from 1459 to 1461, whose father had been the bank's general manager for twenty years until 1455.[48] Among scores of mostly unknown non-elite, including a few minor guildsmen and several notaries, a few stand out: two sons of Giovanni Morelli; the sculptor Lorenzo Ghiberti's son Vittorio; and the humanist Giannozzo Manetti's son Bernardo. Curiously absent is Marco Parenti; perhaps he preferred not to jeopardize efforts to effect the repatriation of his brothers-in-law. The long list eloquently testifies to the strength and social breadth of the movement to dismantle the Medici regime, as many who had been with them for years apparently assumed that the family's season of power was over. On the strength of this wide support, the priors of May–June and July–August 1466 (including several who had signed the oath) initiated discussions about abolishing the Cento.

At the end of August the confrontation came to a head and was dramatically resolved in favor of the Medici when several things happened all within the space of a few days: threats of armed intervention on behalf of both sides; the election of a pro-Medici Signoria; and a stunning reconciliation between Piero and Luca Pitti that broke the ranks of the anti-Mediceans. Rumors

---

[46]   G. Pampaloni, "Il giuramento pubblico in Palazzo Vecchio a Firenze e un patto giurato degli antimedicei (maggio 1466)," *Bullettino senese di storia patria* 71 (1964): 212–38.

[47]   A. Brown, "Pierfrancesco de' Medici, 1430–1476," in Brown, *The Medici*, pp. 73–102.

[48]   De Roover, *Medici Bank*, pp. 377–8.

flew that Piero, so advised, according to Parenti, by Tommaso Soderini and the ever-present Milanese ambassador, was ready to summon Sforza troops. Milanese cavalry were waiting near Bologna, and on the 27th Piero gave the order for them to begin entering Florentine territory.[49] Offers of military support for the anti-Mediceans came from Borso d'Este of Ferrara. According to a pro-Medici account, Ferrarese troops moved into the area north of Pistoia on the 26th,[50] but Parenti says that the request from the anti-Mediceans for their intervention came only after Piero had summoned the Milanese troops. In any case, two armies were on the borders of the Florentine dominion and ready to approach the city. Although neither did, rumors of troop movements and fears of invasion prompted both sides to prepare for battle in the streets.

Piero also assembled his own forces from the contado, as Cosimo had done in 1434, barricaded the family palace, closed off the neighborhood, and stockpiled arms, wine, and bread. Pitti and his allies also armed, but too slowly and timidly, according to Parenti, who accused them of being unwilling to take the risks, or perhaps spend the money, needed to win the looming battle: "each kept his hand in his own pockets," he caustically says. Parenti provides an intriguing explanation of how and why the anti-Mediceans fatally hesitated. As people throughout the city waited to see which way the wind was blowing, Niccolò Soderini arrived on horseback at Luca Pitti's palace in the Oltrarno, which served as anti-Medici headquarters, and urged Pitti, Agnolo Acciaiuoli, Dietisalvi Neroni, and all the others present to stop talking and take action, pleading with them to ride through the city and gather supporters with cries of "Liberty" and to attack Piero in his palace. According to Parenti, they all thought it a plan "likely to succeed, but one doubt held them back. This was fear of the lower classes roused up in arms. After Piero was defeated and his house and goods put to sack, having once tasted the delights of this vandalism, they might be excited to such a fury that the desire would come over them to turn upon the rest of the well-to-do, thinking in this way to be able to throw off their misery. . . . And perhaps, with growing boldness, they might rise against the government and take it for themselves, as they did in 1378." In this eerie replay of 1434, when Palla Strozzi declined to heed Rinaldo degli Albizzi's call to arms against the Medici, it was the memory of 1378 that held the anti-Mediceans back. Almost ninety years after the fact, the trauma inflicted on the Florentine elite by the Ciompi and the ensuing radical popular government still conditioned its response, or lack of it, to the Medici. Here was the social triangulation of Florentine politics in its most naked form: faced with the choice between the tyranny they despised and an alliance with the middle

[49]   Phillips, *Marco Parenti*, pp. 191–209.
[50]   P. Clarke, "A Sienese Note on 1466," in *Florence and Italy: Renaissance Studies in Honour of Nicolai Rubinstein*, ed. P. Denley and C. Elam (London, 1988), p. 50.

and lower classes to defeat that tyranny, the ottimati, however reluctantly, chose to stay with the Medici. Parenti commented that, although it was a "highly prudent consideration . . . , in their need it was very cowardly since matters had come to such a state that they had no other possible way of providing for their safety."[51]

On the 28th, the free sortition so ardently desired by the anti-Mediceans boomeranged by producing a Signoria for September–October more favorable to the Mediceans than the preceding priorates had been. Its Standardbearer of Justice was Roberto Lioni, a Medici ally and several times an accoppiatore. Parenti says he was "a judicious man and a good *popolano*, who by his nature should have followed the common good and liberty. Nonetheless, ambition led him to uphold Piero," and to believe "that he would be advanced by Piero to a place amongst the first citizens and be rewarded with considerable honors and profit." What Parenti saw, in other words, is that the potential rewards of Medici patronage were undercutting "natural" class solidarities. The same day, the outgoing Signoria tried to defuse the tense standoff in the city by summoning both Piero and Luca Pitti to the palace and asking them to disband their growing private armies, which were then streaming toward the city, Pitti's from the south and Piero's mostly from the north and the family's home base in the Mugello. Piero declined to appear, offering the excuse of his infirmity, the severe case of gout for which he is known as Piero the Gouty.[52] Parenti reports that Pitti obeyed the order to disarm, whereas Piero's party "did not entirely."

Luca Pitti, seeing the impunity with which Piero refused to obey either the summons or the order to disarm, knowing that the new Signoria was heavily Medicean, and cognizant of the extent of Piero's private army, lost his nerve. On the 29th, he accepted Piero's offer of a secret deal. Piero sent Francesco Sassetti, general manager of the bank since 1463, to lure Pitti into an agreement to switch sides in return for three things: an appointment as accoppiatore, some office for his brother, and the marriage of his daughter into the Medici family. Parenti adds a touch of pathos to his account of Pitti's capitulation: when Piero agreed to the marriage of Pitti's daughter "to someone he [Piero] held most dear," Pitti assumed, without asking, that Piero meant his son Lorenzo, only to discover, when the rewards of betrayal were paid, that Piero meant, not Lorenzo, but his wife Lucrezia's brother Giovanni Tornabuoni. Parenti, who could see where the Medici were now heading, as Pitti evidently could not, remarked that "Piero wished to reserve Lorenzo for a marriage

---

[51]   Marco Parenti, *Ricordi storici, 1464–1467*, ed. M. Doni Garfagnini (Florence, 2001), pp. 126–7; Phillips, *Marco Parenti*, pp. 194–5.

[52]   A. Brown, "Piero's Infirmity and Political Power," in *Piero de' Medici "il Gottoso" (1416–1469)*, ed. A. Beyer and B. Boucher (Berlin, 1993), pp. 9–19.

with nobility since he already felt himself to be more than a mere citizen." Marrying titled nobility meant reaching outside the ottimati and beyond Florence altogether.

With Pitti neutralized and a sympathetic Signoria in place, Piero made his move. On September 1 he ordered his soldiers into the city: not the Milanese troops, but rather his own private army, which Parenti estimated at 6,000 and the Milanese ambassador at an astounding 8,000. Although most of these troops came from the ancestral lands of the Medici in the Mugello and farther north, Piero also used his patronage ties elsewhere in the dominion to augment this force. Having cultivated over the years a nucleus of clients and friends in Arezzo, he appealed to them for help, and the chiefs of his Aretine patronage group put together a small force of sixty men, while the commune of Arezzo sent two hundred.[53] Whether and to what extent Piero made similar appeals to other subject cities where he had built patronage networks is not known, but his search for support in the subject territories beyond the old contado is an early instance of what became a crucial new source of power for the Medici under his son Lorenzo. A Sienese observer of Medici military preparations in 1466 claimed that one of their captains told him that, if a settlement had not been reached quickly, he could have put 10,000 troops in the city in defense of the Medici, not counting the Milanese, many from the territories of the Bardi di Vernio, the family of Piero's mother.[54] Such overwhelming force left no doubt concerning the outcome. In a pratica held the next day (in Piero's own house!) Luca Pitti himself advised summoning a parlamento, and as he spoke some 3,000 of Piero's troops surrounded the piazza della Signoria. Another coup was in the making, and the well-rehearsed and dreary drill duly unfolded that same day. The crowd approved a balìa, which began meeting two days later on the 4th and wasted no time in restoring *a mano* elections of the Signoria for ten years, later extended another ten years, by accoppiatori to be appointed by the Cento. In fact, during the remaining twenty-eight years of the regime, the election of the Signoria never again occurred by lot. The balìa gave the Otto di Guardia the authority to round up and arrest enemies of the regime. Agnolo Acciaiuoli and Dietisalvi Neroni learned of this on the 6th and hastily left the city, as Niccolò Soderini had done several days earlier. A procession of thanksgiving for the city's "deliverance from bloodshed" was held on Sunday the 7th, according to Parenti "as much a net in which to

---

[53]   R. Black, "Piero de' Medici and Arezzo," in *Piero de' Medici*, ed. Beyer and Boucher, pp. 21–8.

[54]   Clarke, "Sienese Note," p. 50; O. Gori, "La crisi del regime mediceo del 1466 in alcune lettere inedite di Piero dei Medici," in *Studi in onore di Arnaldo d'Addario*, ed. L. Borgia, F. de Luca, P. Viti, and R. M. Zaccaria, 5 vols. (Lecce, 1995), vol. 3, pp. 809–25.

trap men as for devotion." Searches, seizures, and arrests were carried out by the all-powerful Otto even as the procession was giving its thanks. All the anti-Medicean leaders, except Luca Pitti of course, and many less important people who had signed the oath of the previous May were exiled. Although the regime had survived and was now stronger than ever militarily, because of the loss of so many former supporters it was weaker in its ties to the frightened ottimati. Thus Piero decided to repatriate a long list of exiles from the class of '34, including Alessandra Strozzi's sons, Filippo and Lorenzo.[55]

In September, after his victory, Piero repeated the accusation he had made in late August of an assassination plot and added to it the charge that his opponents had conspired with Borso d'Este to invade the city and "overturn the government" by violent means. This was the origin of the legend that the anti-Medici movement was a conspiracy, and the chief piece of evidence adduced in support of the accusations was a confession allegedly made by Dietisalvi Neroni's brother Francesco. In fact, the longer statement in Francesco's own hand says nothing about a plot to assassinate Piero or invite a foreign invasion. Medici interrogators introduced these items into their own doctored version of Francesco's confession.[56]

After 1466, no ambiguities remained about the regime. The myth of the Medici as "first among equals" was now recognized as the fiction it had always been. A scrutiny scheduled for the end of 1468 was indefinitely postponed, and in the same year the exiles, supported by Venice, were defeated on the battlefield. Piero had re-established his family's power and asserted a de facto right of succession that was not challenged when he died in December 1469 and his twenty-year old son Lorenzo assumed the leadership. Lorenzo's marriage earlier that year to a woman from a Roman branch of the noble Orsini confirmed that the Medici no longer wished to be seen as mere Florentine citizens and bankers. Henceforth, Medici men and many of their women married into the noble families of Italy and, ultimately, beyond Italy. Piero's brief period at the helm was decisive for Medici fortunes. To him both family and regime owed their survival in the greatest crisis they faced between 1434 and 1494. And the manner and means of his victory in 1466 go far in explaining the immense difference, over a bridge of merely five years, between the regime of "first citizen" Cosimo and that of the boy "prince" Lorenzo.

---

[55] H. Gregory, "The Return of the Native: Filippo Strozzi and Medicean Politics," *Renaissance Quarterly* 38 (1985): 1–21; Crabb, *The Strozzi of Florence*, pp. 162–79.
[56] N. Rubinstein, "La confessione di Francesco Neroni e la congiura antimedicea del 1466," *ASI* 126 (1968): 373–87.

11

The Luxury Economy
and Art Patronage

Poverty and Wealth

Florence's changing economy had demographic consequences. Its reduced fifteenth-century population was of course in large part the consequence of recurrent epidemics, but another cause of persistent demographic stagnation lies in the contraction of the woolen cloth industry. After the expansion of the 1360s and early 1370s, annual production slipped to 20,000 bolts in 1380, 12,000–14,000 in the 1390s, and under 10,000 in the 1420s. In 1380 the guild had 283 registered firms, but only 132 were reported in the 1427 Catasto. In 1379 a third of household heads with occupations specified in the estimo worked in some phase of woolen manufactures, and 31% still did in 1404; but by 1427 only 18% were so employed. Because total population also declined from 55,000 in 1379 to only 37,000 in 1427, the loss of jobs was even greater than these percentages suggest.[1] Among the causes of the decline were increasing competition and the difficulty of securing sufficient supplies of English wool, partly because of interruptions in trade, but also because cloth manufactures were expanding in England and elsewhere. After mid-century the industry recovered, as producers abandoned their former concentration on luxury cloths and converted to lower quality, cheaper cloths from Mediterranean wool, for which they found profitable markets especially in the Ottoman Empire.[2]

[1] Franceschi, *Oltre il "Tumulto,"* pp. 3–31, 94–104.
[2] H. Hoshino, *L'Arte della Lana in Firenze nel Basso Medioevo: il commercio della Lana e il mercato dei panni fiorentini nei secoli XIII–XV* (Florence, 1980), pp. 194–211, 227–9, 231–303.

Benedetto Dei counted 270 wool shops in 1472.[3] Investors continued to come from both the elite (e.g., Albizzi, Altoviti, Capponi, Corbinelli, Velluti, Rucellai) and the popolo, and woolens continued to be exported throughout the Mediterranean, but not in the same quantities as in the 1360s and far fewer than before 1340.

Although woolworkers still outnumbered silkworkers 4:1 in 1427, silk had begun its slow rise. An independent association of producers of silk cloth had existed in the thirteenth century before joining the cloth retailers of Por Santa Maria, but they were mainly artisans, not merchant entrepreneurs, and remained a small and weak minority in the guild until the early fifteenth century. In 1427, 33 firms were producing silk cloth for export, 50 in 1461, and 44 in 1480; total value of production went from 230,000 florins in the 1430s to 300,000 in the early 1460s and 400,000 in 1490.[4] Even with the tripling of raw silk produced in the Florentine dominions between 1440 and the mid-sixteenth century,[5] silk had to be imported to meet the needs of manufacturers, who were now increasingly merchant-entrepreneurs producing for export to foreign markets. Among the earliest were merchants from the popolo: Francesco Della Luna, Benedetto Ghini, Parente di Michele Parenti (Marco's father), and Andrea Banchi, who sold his silks all over Italy and beyond, in Geneva and Constantinople.[6] By mid-century elite families and merchant-bankers began investing in silk production and using their international connections to good advantage to market their products. In the 1430s the Medici formed a partnership in a silk company, and by the 1460s several Pitti and an Antinori also did so. But the industry remained mostly in the hands of new families, some of which, like the Serristori and Cambini, accumulated big fortunes in a combination of banking, trade, and silk exports. As with woolens, silk cloth was manufactured in a series of decentralized stages by artisans working in their homes or shops. But because the steps were fewer than for wool, and especially because initial cleaning and combing were not needed as with raw wool, manufacturing silk cloth did not require a large force of unskilled workers. Thus the rise of this new textile industry could not replenish the population loss caused by the decline of wool production. Because silk cloth

---

[3] *Cronica*, ed. Barducci, p. 82.
[4] B. Dini, "La ricchezza documentaria per l'arte della seta e l'economia fiorentina nel Quattrocento," in Dini, *Manifattura, commercio e banca nella Firenze medievale* (Florence, 2001), p. 29.
[5] S. Tognetti, *Un'industria di lusso al servizio del grande commercio: il mercato dei drappi serici e della seta nella Firenze del Quattrocento* (Florence, 2002), p. 32.
[6] F. Edler de Roover, "Andrea Banchi, Florentine Silk Manufacturer and Merchant in the Fifteenth Century," *Studies in Medieval and Renaissance History* 3 (1966): 224–85.

required fewer workers (and despite the fact that many were highly skilled and well paid artisans), the proportion in production costs of labor to materials was the inverse of that in woolen cloth production: in woolens, labor represented 60–65% of costs and raw wool and other materials 35–40%, whereas in the silk industry, despite higher remuneration per worker, labor accounted for 30–35% and the expensive raw silk and other materials 65–70%.[7] Silk was a luxury product in which success depended on quality, and in turn on the refined skills of dyers, loom warpers, weavers, and the goldbeaters who produced the gold thread woven into brocades.

With the relative decline of the labor-intensive wool industry and the rise of silk and other forms of skilled artisan labor, Florence's economy underwent a major shift. Unlike the fourteenth century, in which a huge amount of wealth was paid out in wages to a large working class, in the fifteenth century, although skilled artisans were in great demand and enjoyed rising incomes, the declining demand for unskilled labor meant stagnating wages for what was still the bulk of the working population. Despite the demographic contraction (which ought to have raised wages in a structurally unchanged economy, and initially did so after 1348), wages and piece-rates held steady or even declined in both the building and woolen cloth industries in the fifteenth century.[8] Fortunately for workers, long-term price trends also remained remarkably steady until the end of the century. But short-term price fluctuations or periods of unemployment could throw households into chronic indebtedness, which further depressed real wages. For unskilled workers to afford basic necessities they needed steady and low prices, modest indirect taxes, and a favorable ratio of household size to incomes. An unskilled worker employed full time earned enough to support himself and one other person, but families of three or four with a single income could not make ends meet even with stable prices. Living costs in families of four or more also exceeded the incomes of skilled workers with higher earnings. Of 909 household heads identified in the 1427 Catasto as workers in the wool industry, 53% were deemed *miserabiles*, too poor to pay any tax, and they included 57% of wage-earners, 64% of unskilled Ciompi, and 43% of artisans (but fully 78% of weavers and spinners who worked at home).[9] Stagnant wages in the building and woolen cloth industries almost certainly depressed other workers' incomes as well, and when prices began their slow steady rise toward the end of the century the erosion of real wages created endemic poverty within the working class.

---

[7]   Tognetti, *Un'industria di lusso*, pp. 19–21.
[8]   R. A. Goldthwaite, *The Building of Renaissance Florence: An Economic and Social History* (Baltimore, 1980), pp. 318–19; Franceschi, *Oltre il "Tumulto,"* pp. 235–59.
[9]   Franceschi, *Oltre il "Tumulto,"* pp. 273–4.

Serious impoverishment prevailed in the subject territories. Heavy direct taxation of the dominion was gradually transferring wealth from the contado and district communities to feed the city's public debt (whose interest-bearing shares were owned almost entirely by Florentine citizens). Except for a few cities like Prato, which continued to be a major center of woolen cloth manufactures, and Pescia, where the silk industry flourished, protectionist measures were destroying the ability of producers in the territories to compete with Florentine industries. Most of the smaller cities lost wealth and population in the fifteenth century, as the spread of sharecropping (or *mezzadria*) slowed demand and economic growth in rural areas. Wealthy Florentines bought land from former freeholders, whose incomes had shrunk because of low prices and high taxes, and entered into sharecropping arrangements that gave half of each farm's annual production to the owner and half to the sharecropper, leaving the latter little incentive to specialize and produce surpluses for sale. Weakened productivity kept sharecroppers in depressed economic conditions, when, here too, lower population ought to have had the reverse effect. All these factors reduced incomes and demand in rural areas.[10]

Weak consumer demand in the bulk of the city and dominion population also drove the development of luxury industries. With handsome profits more likely in luxury goods than in labor-intensive industries that produced for the lower classes, investors naturally turned toward the former. Growing investment in luxury products also shaped elite tastes and increased demand for these products. Here was the paradox of Florence's fifteenth-century economy: on the one hand, ever greater displays of opulence and conspicuous consumption among the wealthy; on the other, working and rural classes unable to spend much beyond subsistence. Renaissance Florence's brilliant material culture did not have deep economic foundations: it did not spread wealth significantly beyond the skilled artisans who produced for the elite and the merchant-bankers who sold these products throughout Europe and the Mediterranean. Hence the severely unbalanced distribution of wealth: the wealthiest 100 Florentine households, each with at least 8,600 florins of net taxable wealth (1% of the city's nearly 10,000 households and less than two-tenths of 1% of all households in the city and dominion), controlled 26.5% of the city's wealth and 17% of that of city and dominion combined. The 202 households with 5,000 or more florins owned 36% of the city's wealth, and the 339 households with 3,000 or more florins controlled 45%. More than half the city's wealth was in the hands of about 6% of households.[11] Because large elite

[10]   S. Epstein, "Cities, Regions and the Late Medieval Crisis: Sicily and Tuscany Compared," *Past and Present* 130 (1991): 3–50 (19–20, 37–41, 44).
[11]   Based on the data in Herlihy and Klapisch-Zuber, *Tuscans*, p. 94, and Martines, *Social World*, pp. 365–78.

lineages often had several among the richest households, wealth was concentrated in a considerably smaller number of lineages than households. In the Catasto of 1458 the highest assessment of tax owed, that of Cosimo de' Medici (and his nephew Pierfrancesco), was in a league of its own at 576 florins. Two other assessments exceeded 100 florins: 132 for the heirs of Giovanni de' Benci, the Medici bank's former general manager, and Giovanni Rucellai's 102. Eight more households were assessed between 50 and 98 florins (including Jacopo Pazzi and Gino Capponi). Of the remaining 7,625 households that owed any tax (excluding the *miserabiles*), 49% owed less than 5 soldi (when 1 florin was worth 108 soldi) and 64% owed 10 soldi or less. If an estimated 3,000 households of *miserabiles* are added to the total, 63% of city households owed from zero to 5 soldi and 74% from zero to 10.[12]

Despite its uneven distribution, this was still an economy that offered opportunities for new wealth. Some large new fortunes were made in the fifteenth century, mainly by merchant families who enjoyed Medici favor. Niccolò Cambini, son of a minor guildsman and linen-cloth dealer, began working in the Naples branch of the Medici bank and his brother Andrea apprenticed with Florentine merchants in Lisbon. In 1420 they formed a merchant-banking partnership with Adovardo Giachinotti and members of the elite Guadagni, who were allies of the Albizzi. Fortunately for the Cambini brothers, the Guadagni partnership ended some years later, and they astutely joined the ranks of the Medici party under whose protection their business flourished. They were also neighbors of the Medici, and in the early 1440s Niccolò acquired a family chapel in San Lorenzo, a sign both of his success and of Medici favor. Like other merchant-banks, the Cambini accepted deposits (on which they returned 7–8% interest) and used the capital to export Florentine woolen and silk cloths to Rome and elsewhere in Italy and throughout the western Mediterranean, in particular the Iberian peninsula where Lisbon became the center of their operations. They also imported raw materials, including silk, wool, dyes, leather, and furs for the Florentine textile and clothing industries. By 1458, after Niccolò's death, his sons jointly declared gross assets of almost 9,000 florins, thus ranking them among the 62 wealthiest households, and purchased a family palazzo for 3,600 florins. Cambini fortunes increased in the 1460s, as they expanded their silk business, extended trading operations to the eastern Mediterranean, accepted still more deposits, and began making profitable but risky loans. In 1467 Francesco di Niccolò Cambini was appointed one of eight Officials of the Bank and thus became a trusted creditor of the commune together with Giovanni Rucellai and Francesco Sassetti, general manager of the Medici banking empire. It was the pinnacle of Cambini success. But the risks finally caught up with them: bankruptcy struck

---

[12] De Roover, *Medici Bank*, pp. 29–31.

in 1482, and, after lengthy legal proceedings, they sold off property, including the palace acquired thirty years earlier, to satisfy creditors.[13] The Della Casa similarly rose from humble origins to wealth and status with a banking operation under Medici protection. Two sons of the notary Lodovico della Casa, Antonio and Ruggieri, also began with the Medici, the former as an employee, partner, and then director of the Rome branch in 1435–8, the latter as director of the Geneva branch for many years until 1447. In 1439 Antonio founded his own company with Jacopo Donati and entered the profitable business of papal banking. He soon created two more companies, including one in Geneva where he sold Florentine silks.[14] Another brother, Giovanni, now famous as the lover of Lusanna,[15] directed the family's Rome company after Antonio's death in 1454 and married the daughter of an elite Medici ally, Marietta di Piero Rucellai. In the 1458 Catasto he and a fourth brother, Jacopo, declared gross assets of almost 8,700 florins.[16] Although the Spinelli had been on the outer edges of the elite since the 1320s under the Alberti umbrella, in the fifteenth century Tommaso Spinelli took his branch of the family to new economic heights in papal banking and silks.[17] And the Riccardi rose from obscurity to make, lose, and regain notable wealth.[18]

Perhaps the greatest success story among fifteenth-century "new" families is that of the Serristori, who not only made a huge fortune but also used it and Medici connections to enter the city's social elite. They descended, as their name implies, from a notary, ser Ristoro di ser Jacopo, who emigrated to Florence in the mid-fourteenth century from Figline in the upper Valdarno. While practicing the notarial profession, ser Ristoro bought property (much of it in Figline), invested in a wool shop in which he set up two of his sons, and left a considerable fortune to a third son, Giovanni, whom he sent to law school in Bologna and who alone among the brothers survived the plague of 1400. Messer Giovanni went into the merchant-banking business, and when he died in 1414, without male heirs, his nephews divided the estate whose business investments alone were worth 37,000 florins. Relations with the Medici must already have been well established, because one of two mediators they appointed to arbitrate the settlement was Cosimo's cousin Averardo, whose

---

[13]   Tognetti, *Il Banco Cambini.*
[14]   F. Arcelli, *Il banchiere del papa: Antonio della Casa mercante e banchiere a Roma (1438–1440)* (Catanzaro, 2001); De Roover, *Medici Bank,* pp. 211, 216, 284–5.
[15]   Brucker, *Giovanni and Lusanna.*
[16]   Molho, *Marriage Alliance,* p. 387.
[17]   P. Jacks and W. Caferro, *The Spinelli of Florence: Fortunes of a Renaissance Merchant Family* (University Park, Penn., 2001).
[18]   P. Malanima, *I Riccardi di Firenze. Una famiglia e un patrimonio nella Toscana dei Medici* (Florence, 1977).

daughter Costanza was already the wife of one of the nephews, Antonio di Salvestro di ser Ristoro (the patronymic had still not been definitively converted to a surname). Under Antonio the family business prospered. In 1427 he declared gross assets of almost 35,000 florins and net taxable wealth of over 28,000 (second highest in Santa Croce and fourteenth overall). Almost half his fortune was in Monte shares, a quarter in a merchant-banking operation, and a quarter in real estate, mostly in Figline. In 1430–2 Antonio served three times among the Officials of the Bank and made loans to the commune totaling over 26,000 florins. In 1433 Cosimo, anticipating the political storm that was about to break, deposited the assets of the local branch of his bank into Antonio's company for protection during the exile. Having gained Cosimo's trust, Antonio went on to serve on many balìe and as an accoppiatore. Although he declared significantly reduced taxable assets in 1431 and 1433, the company accumulated ever larger working capital from deposits with which it exported textiles and imported wool, dyes, silver, and everything from soap to sugar to alum. Antonio's sons married into the elite Capponi, Pazzi, and Strozzi families. In the 1450s they divided his estate but went into the silk business together and built a huge company whose capital investments rose from 6,400 florins in 1470 to 24,000 *fiorini larghi* (the new florin that was worth 20% more than the old, hence 29,000 old florins). Between 1471 and 1492 the Serristori manufactured and sold 40,000 kilos of silk cloth with sales of 355,000 *fiorini larghi* and total net profits over twenty-one years of 57,688 florins. They went on to be one of the pillars of the nobility under the principate.[19]

Despite these examples of new wealth, the old elite still controlled the lion's share. Of twenty-eight households with 20,000 or more florins of taxable wealth in 1427, half came from very old elite families (including the Alberti, Barbadori, Bardi, Medici, Panciatichi, Pazzi, Peruzzi, Strozzi, and Tornabuoni), and only six from really new families (including the Serristori).[20] In 1458 the old elite was even more prominently represented among the very wealthy, with seventeen of the twenty-four households declaring 10,000 or more florins of assets (e.g., Alessandri, Baroncelli, Canigiani, Capponi, Medici, Pazzi, Pitti, Rucellai, and Salviati), and two others that had joined the elite on Medici coattails (Benci and Dietisalvi-Neroni).[21] The indefatigable list-maker Benedetto Dei begins his roster of richest Florentines in 1472 with three Medici, two Rucellai, three Pitti, four Pazzi, and nine Capponi before including six members of the "new" Martelli. Besides the many new families, the

---

[19]   S. Tognetti, *Da Figline a Firenze. Ascesa economica e politica della famiglia Serristori (secoli XIV–XVI)* (Figline, 2003).
[20]   Using Martines's tables in *Social World*.
[21]   Using Molho's tables in *Marriage Alliance*.

rest of the list includes (in this order) one or more Canigiani, Tornabuoni, Soderini, Gianfigliazzi, Nerli, Guicciardini, Salviati, Portinari, Ridolfi, Antinori, Velluti, Frescobaldi, Albizzi, Vettori, Adimari, Cavalcanti, Corsini, Corbinelli, Peruzzi, Castellani, and Alessandri.[22] Giovanni Rucellai famously advised his sons to continue his merchant-banking business only if they attended to it personally, to keep up the appearance of "merchants" while in fact conducting themselves as "shopkeepers," and to avoid the risks of deposit banking and investing other people's money.[23] While this no doubt reflected his cautious awareness of the precariousness of wealth after setbacks toward the end of his life, he had nonetheless accumulated one of the city's great fortunes with the usual combination of economic ventures (and without any help from the Medici). As he reminisced in 1473, "In the trading and banking business I have been very fortunate, through God's grace, and careful and diligent. I began in this profession as a boy, indeed as an infant, and I have acquired great credit and trust. I founded several banking companies with various partners and had operations in many places outside Florence, including Venice, Genoa, Naples, and Pisa. I was a partner in seven woolshops in Florence at different times and with different partners. And in these businesses I made a lot of money."[24] Even political disaster did not dampen the entrepreneurial spirit of elite families. The Alberti commercial and banking empire prospered in exile. And Filippo Strozzi (1428–91) began the process of converting his father Matteo's modest estate into the greatest fortune of the age while he was still an exile in Naples. Introduced by relatives to international commerce and banking, and financed in part by his mother Alessandra's dowry and the sale of family property, he began businesses in Palermo and Naples. After he returned to Florence, the Strozzi bank, still based in Naples, made fabulous profits that increased Filippo's fortune from 32,000 *fiorini larghi* in 1471 to 112,000 in 1483 and 116,000 by his death in 1491 (and this does not include Monte holdings): 86 percent of his income of 90,000 florins between 1471 and 1483 came from the Naples company. So vast was Strozzi's wealth that, even with the huge expenditures on the palazzo he began building in 1489, he hardly knew what to do with it all: after his death, over 52,000 florins in cash was found in sacks stored in his house![25]

[22] *Cronica*, ed. Barducci, pp. 85–6.
[23] *Giovanni Rucellai ed il suo Zibaldone*, vol. 1, *"Il Zibaldone Quaresimale"*, ed. A. Perosa (London, 1960), p. 19.
[24] Ibid., pp. 120–1; F. W. Kent, "The Making of a Renaissance Patron of the Arts," in *Giovanni Rucellai ed il suo Zibaldone*, vol. 2, *A Florentine Patrician and His Palace* (London, 1981), pp. 18–20, 32–6, 79–80, 88–91.
[25] R. A. Goldthwaite, *Private Wealth in Renaissance Florence: A Study of Four Families* (Princeton, 1968), pp. 52–73.

Public and Private Patronage

Florence's vibrant artistic culture was shaped by its luxury economy. Artistic production reflected the social, economic, and contractual contexts of interactions between producers and consumers, who came from different classes, as well as the religious and aesthetic dimensions of consumer demand. Artists were mostly artisans formed by the guild traditions in which highly specialized skills were learned, perfected, practiced, and transmitted through training and apprenticeships. Like other cities with strong guild and artisan traditions, Florence had long been noted for the quality of its dyed cloth, furs, clothes, jewelry, furniture, woodworking, sculpting, and myriad products whose value lay in both high-quality materials and the talents of artisan-artists who crafted prized and admired objects from those materials. Skilled sculptors, painters, and master builders that we call artists and architects worked in shops they owned or rented, hired assistants, trained apprentices, signed contracts that stipulated, usually in meticulous detail, what they were to do, how much they were to be paid, what materials to use and who paid for them, and by when the work was to be completed. Surviving contracts show that artists were, and needed to be, good businessmen and negotiators who knew how to keep careful accounts, calculate costs, and make ends meet. Most of their paintings and sculptures were produced on commission; works produced without specific commissions and offered to the market were generally popular and less expensive products, such as terracotta reliefs, birth trays, and small devotional paintings. But big, expensive, and artistically innovative works were always the result of commissions, whether from institutions or individual patrons who paid for works produced in conformity with their wishes. This had long been the legal and economic framework of artistic production, and it did not substantially change after 1400.[26]

New factors nonetheless emerged from Florence's luxury economy and changing class relations to affect the production of art in the fifteenth century. The same socio-economic context that turned the silk industry into a showcase for the talents of skilled weavers and goldbeaters and the clothing industry into the same for tailors,[27] and made them both arenas of conspicuous consumption, also shaped the demand for art and thus the status of artists.[28] Growing

[26]   B. Cole, *The Renaissance Artist at Work* (New York, 1983); E. Welch, *Art and Society in Italy 1350–1500* (Oxford, 1997), pp. 103–29; H. McNeal Caplow, "Sculptors' Partnerships in Michelozzo's Florence," *Studies in the Renaissance* 21 (1974): 145–75.

[27]   Frick, *Dressing Renaissance Florence*, pp. 57–74.

[28]   An overview: R. A. Goldthwaite, *Wealth and the Demand for Art in Italy, 1300–1600* (Baltimore, 1993), pp. 176–255.

demand for luxury goods that enhanced the prestige of consumers was a crucial factor behind perhaps the biggest difference between fourteenth- and fifteenth-century art patronage: a gradual shift from a balance between public (or institutional) and private (or individual) patrons to a preponderance of private patronage. After about 1400 the transformation of class relations heightened individual patrons' desire to display their (and their families') status, honor, and "social identity."[29] With the elite having assimilated the civic and economic ethos of the popolo and, after 1434, lost political power to the Medici, and with families from the popolo continuing to make new fortunes in trade and banking, many in the elite felt the need for new cultural spaces in which to exhibit their superior social status. Conspicuous consumption of artworks, luxury clothing, great private palaces, but also of literary culture and humanism, met this need. Families of new wealth emulated the elite and also invested in culture to advertise their social rise and aspirations, making cultural patronage an arena of competition and mimetic rivalry both among elite families and between the classes. Although this patronage was private in the sense that wealthy individuals hired and paid artists and builders, the fact that so much of it was placed conspicuously on display to promote the patrons' "greatness" made it at the same time very public.

Contrasts between the fourteenth and fifteenth centuries should not however be overdrawn. Fourteenth-century private individuals and families also paid for a good deal of art, chiefly in churches, where citizens vied to establish their families' rights in chapels and sacristies in which they buried their dead and preserved family memory with artworks that included vestments, chalices, altarpieces, frescoes, tomb sculptures, and sculpted coats of arms. But fourteenth-century chapel patronage was conditioned less by the patrons' aesthetic and religious preferences than by the devotional and theological traditions of churches and religious orders. Here too, of course, "private" chapels were quite public in that they were meant to be seen by neighbors and visitors and thus to publicize family piety and wealth. Everyone knew that this or that splendidly decorated chapel belonged to a notable family, but, except for the occasional coat of arms (often not allowed) or tomb, there was little or nothing that identified the family, much less the individual, who endowed a fourteenth-century chapel or paid for its wall paintings. But by the fifteenth century, family patronage in ecclesiastical settings increasingly reflected the devotional and/or aesthetic choices of individuals who paid for this art, hired the artists of their choice, and, while putting the honor of their lineages on display, now also increasingly left their own distinctive imprint on what they commissioned.

[29]   J. Burke, *Changing Patrons: Social Identity and the Visual Arts in Renaissance Florence* (University Park, Penn., 2004).

Civic and public art flourished in the fourteenth century and into the first third of the fifteenth and then declined, in part because the biggest projects were by then completed. It continued thereafter in less monumental manifestations, such as the artistic commissions of confraternities. Like "private" patronage, the concept of "public" patronage requires care. Supervision of civic and ecclesiastical building projects was typically entrusted to citizen works committees, called "opere," vested with responsibility for spending funds assigned to them, keeping accounts, and selecting, hiring, and paying builders, sculptors, woodworkers, painters, and others artisans. They decided on specific building plans and sculptural programs and were thus involved in aesthetic and engineering decisions as well as administrative matters. Opere typically consisted of four, six, or eight "operai" appointed, or elected by scrutiny and sortition, for four- or six-month terms, and then replaced by new committees. With so many projects and short terms of office, scores of citizens served on opere at any given time, and hundreds, perhaps thousands, over the course of decades and generations. Although laymen without specialized training in the techniques of sculpture or the complex engineering of large-scale building, many developed recognized expertise and were regularly reappointed or elected to different opere.[30] They also served as judges in competitions for commissions. Public projects were not supervised by faceless government bureaucracies. Citizens assumed myriad responsibilities in a system of collective participatory patronage in which they significantly contributed, alongside builders and sculptors, to the creation of works of art.

The construction, decoration, and renovation of the palace of the priors always remained under communal supervision. Because the original structure was complete by 1315, operai were subsequently appointed by the Signoria only as needed until around 1470 when the Medici regime made the "palace operai" a permanent office.[31] For other projects the government assigned responsibility to the guilds or Parte Guelfa, which in turn elected the operai. At the cathedral, construction began under joint communal–ecclesiastical supervision, then briefly rotated among the five major commercial guilds, and in 1331 was definitively entrusted to the Wool guild. From as early as the twelfth century, the Calimala supervised the baptistery works and the church of San Miniato al Monte; it also acquired responsibility for two hospitals, and later the Franciscan basilica of Santa Croce. Por Santa Maria administered works projects at the hospital of Santa Maria Nuova from the thirteenth century and subsequently had responsibility for the convent of San Marco and

---

[30] D. F. Zervas, "Orsanmichele and its Operai, 1336–1436," in *Opera: carattere e ruolo delle fabbriche cittadine fino all'inizio dell'età moderna*, ed. M. Haines and L. Riccetti (Florence, 1996), pp. 315–43.

[31] Rubinstein, *Palazzo Vecchio*, pp. 118–21.

the construction of the Innocenti Hospital. In the 1330s it was also assigned the rebuilding of Orsanmichele, the communal granary that became a site of popular devotion to a miracle-working image of the Virgin. After Orsanmichele became an oratory, the image and the great tabernacle built by Orcagna to house it came under the care of the captains of the confraternity of Orsanmichele. The popular government of 1378–82 authorized the minor guilds to have images of their patron saints painted on the interior piers of the oratory. In the fifteenth century the bankers' guild administered two hospitals, and the Medici, Speziali, e Merciai had responsibility for a hospital, a church, and a convent.[32] Many confraternities controlled chapels or oratories in which they commissioned works of art.[33] Duccio's *Rucellai Madonna*, so called because it was for a long time in the Rucellai family chapel at Santa Maria Novella, was actually commissioned by a laudesi confraternity, the Compagnia di Santa Maria. Corporate supervision and patronage pervaded every corner of Florence's ecclesiastical and civic architecture and sculpture.

Particularly intriguing is the history of citizen participation in the well documented administration of the cathedral project by the Wool guild's operai.[34] For a generation after the guild's assumption of responsibility, attention shifted from the cathedral to the bell tower under the supervision of Giotto, who was appointed "magister et gubernator" of the combined works in 1334. In the mid-1350s, with the bell tower nearly finished, the operai oversaw crucial debates regarding the cathedral. An original plan, which had guided the early construction, was challenged by the proponents of a different design calling for three huge bays in the nave instead of five smaller ones and requiring major readjustments in what had already gone up; the operai presented both proposals to a meeting of a hundred citizens and held thirty-eight other meetings with experts and advisers. A decade later yet another plan was put forward, and the operai requested advice from a large committee of goldsmiths, painters,

---

[32] M. Haines, "L'Arte della Lana e l'Opera del Duomo a Firenze con un accenno a Ghiberti tra due istituzioni," in *Opera*, ed. Haines and Riccetti, pp. 267–94 (267–71).

[33] M. Wackernagel, *The World of the Florentine Renaissance Artist: Projects and Patrons, Workshop and Art Market*, trans. A. Luchs (Princeton, 1981; original German edition, 1938); D. C. Ahl, "'In corpo di compagnia': Art and Devotion in the Compagnia della Purificazione e di San Zanobi of Florence," in *Confraternities and the Visual Arts in Renaissance Italy: Ritual, Spectacle, Image*, ed. B. Wisch and D. C. Ahl (Cambridge, 2000), pp. 46–73.

[34] For what follows, chiefly M. Haines, "Brunelleschi and Bureaucracy: The Tradition of Public Patronage at the Florentine Cathedral," *I Tatti Studies* 3 (1989): 89–125; also H. Saalman, "Santa Maria del Fiore: 1294–1418," *Art Bulletin* 46 (1964): 471–500; L. Fabbri, "L'Opera di Santa Maria del Fiore nel quindicesimo secolo: tra Repubblica fiorentina e Arte della Lana," in *La cattedrale e la città; saggi sul Duomo di Firenze*, 3 vols., ed. T. Verdon and A. Innocenti (Florence, 2001), vol. 1, pp. 319–39.

and masons, led by the builder Neri di Fioravante. Their proposal (known as the plan of the "maestri e dipintori") was for a dramatic enlargement of the church with the addition of a fourth nave bay, a huge increase in the size of the crossing and thus of the space eventually to be covered by a dome, and the addition of a drum to elevate the dome to what seemed to many an impossible height. A large meeting of eighty citizens (including Salvestro de' Medici and Uguccione de' Ricci), together with the operai, guild consuls, master builders, and various experts, discussed the audacious plan and recommended that another committee of eight be appointed to evaluate its feasibility and safety. These eight, all laymen, included a Salviati, a Peruzzi, a Rucellai, a Bardi, an Albizzi, and Uguccione de' Ricci. Discussions continued throughout the next year concerning the drum and the projected cupola, and the construction site was kept open on Sundays to allow any and all citizens to inspect two large models of the rival plans. Although the operai and guild consuls had already decided for the plan of the "maestri e dipintori," they went to great lengths to mold public opinion in support of an idea that was risky and in a sense incomplete, because no one had any idea how to build a dome large enough to cover the immense space created by the plan, or whether the walls and piers could even bear its weight. On October 26–27, 1367, more than four hundred citizens filed in to have a look: elite, popolo, minor guildsmen, and artisans. Whether there really was near unanimity (only one person, Jacopo Alberti, is recorded as expressing doubts about the new plan), or whether the notary ignored a few more dissenting voices, the operai succeeded in winning widespread approval for an enlarged cathedral. Only after still more meetings of experts and prominent citizens did they definitively commit the opera, and communal funds, to the astonishingly bold plan.[35]

Early fifteenth-century public patronage displays both continuity and change in the relationship between artist-artisans and corporate patrons. As in the deliberations over the cathedral design in the 1360s, so also (if Lorenzo Ghiberti's later account in the autobiographical section of his *Commentarii* is accurate) in the famous competition announced in 1401 by the Calimala for the baptistery's second set of bronze doors, in which contenders were required to cast panels depicting the Sacrifice of Isaac, the decision-making process involved large numbers of citizens: Ghiberti claims he was declared the winner by a jury of thirty-four, whose judgment was confirmed by the baptistery operai, Calimala consuls, and then the entire guild.[36] But Antonio Manetti's

---

[35] C. Guasti, *Santa Maria del Fiore: la costruzione della chiesa e del campanile* (Florence, 1887; reprint edn. 1974), pp. 171–2, 199–205, 206–7, 218–20.

[36] Lorenzo Ghiberti, *I commentarii*, ed. L. Bartoli (Florence, 1998), p. 93; R. Krautheimer, with T. Krautheimer-Hess, *Lorenzo Ghiberti* (Princeton, 1956; third printing 1982), pp. 31–43.

Plate 6   Orsanmichele, rebuilt from 1330s (Brogi/Art Resource, NY)

(still later) *Life of Brunelleschi* asserts that the decision was actually for a joint commission, which, although unlikely, is not altogether implausible in view of what happened when Ghiberti and Brunelleschi faced off again over how to build the cupola. In 1418 the Cathedral Opera announced an open competition for design-models, with a 200-florin prize for the winner, and created a separate committee of overseers for the project. Brunelleschi astonished everyone by proposing that a dome could be built without centering or supporting scaffolding, a plan favored by some but derided by others as the height of folly (see Plate 2). Again meetings and extensive consultations followed, and the public was invited to view the Brunelleschi model. In the end, the consuls, operai, and cupola officials approved his bold plan, but they nonetheless appointed Brunelleschi and Ghiberti as co-supervisors of the project in a gesture of compromise perhaps intended to co-opt potential opposition.[37]

    The third great locus of civic patronage of these years was Orsanmichele (see Plate 6), where responsibility was shared among the confraternity, the

---

[37]   Antonio di Tuccio Manetti, *The Life of Brunelleschi*, ed. H. Saalman, trans. C. Enggass (University Park, Penn., 1970), pp. 78–83.

guilds, and the Parte Guelfa. In 1339 Por Santa Maria petitioned the Signoria to require each of the twelve major guilds to commission paintings or statues of their patron saints in the external piers of the granary whose reconstruction the guild was then overseeing. At the time only the Wool guild complied with a statue of St. Stephen by Andrea Pisano, and subsequently a few other guilds did so as well. But for a long time little happened until, in 1399, the Medici, Speziali, e Merciai commissioned a statue of the Virgin and Child; two years later the guild of Jurists and Notaries initiated discussions for the replacement (completed in 1406) of its old statue of St. Luke. Perhaps encouraged by these signs of reviving interest, in the same year the Signoria required all the other guilds with assigned niches in the external piers to commission statues of their saints and have them in place within ten years or risk having the niche reassigned. Over the next twenty years a dozen monumental sculptures were erected at Orsanmichele, including three each by Nanni di Banco, Ghiberti, and Donatello. Nanni di Banco, who had been producing large sculptures for the cathedral, sculpted St. Philip for the guild of shoemakers, the *Four Crowned Saints* for the stonemasons and carpenters; and St. Eligius for the blacksmiths, all in marble.[38] The Calimala turned of course to Ghiberti and commissioned a bronze St. John the Baptist, and the Cambio and Lana also engaged him to cast bronze statues of, respectively, St. Matthew and (a new) St. Stephen. And Donatello, who had also worked on the sculptural program for the cathedral façade, did the St. George for the guild of armorers and the St. Mark for the guild of linen manufacturers and used-cloth dealers, both in marble. The Parte Guelfa had the most prominent niche at Orsanmichele, at the center of the east side of the building overlooking the ceremonial route of via Calzaiuoli that connected the cathedral complex to the north and the palace and piazza of the priors to the south. For that prestigious location they commissioned Donatello to do a bronze statue of St. Louis of Toulouse, brother of Robert of Naples and a Franciscan Spiritual revered in the Guelf tradition. Orsanmichele's sculptures were the result of a remarkable collaboration of guilds, government, confraternity, and Parte Guelfa, and every work emerged from discussion and debate among the members of these civic bodies.[39] A register of deliberations kept by the Arte del Cambio detailing every decision involved in the commission of the St. Matthew from Ghiberti, and listing the names of guild members who served as operai and on the various sub-committees related to

---

[38]   M. Bergstein, *The Sculpture of Nanni di Banco* (Princeton, 2000), pp. 47–57, 114–31, 136–47.
[39]   D. F. Zervas, *The Parte Guelfa, Brunelleschi and Donatello* (Locust Valley, N.Y., 1987); Zervas, *Orsanmichele Documents/Documenti 1336–1452* (Ferrara, 1996); *Orsanmichele a Firenze/Orsanmichele, Florence*, ed. Zervas (Ferrara, 1996), pp. 181–207.

the project, is eloquent testimony to the participatory dimension of corporate patronage.[40]

But in these same decades traditions of corporate patronage were being challenged by both artists and patrons. Neither Ghiberti nor Brunelleschi was in the mold of the relatively self-effacing supervisors of building projects of the fourteenth century. Legends grew up around the competition for the baptistery door project, as memory of the event was shaped by Ghiberti's own recollections and by Manetti's partisan biography of Brunelleschi. This alone tells us that artisan-artists were redefining their relationship to patrons and the public (or having it redefined for them). Their own self-fashioning and the "thirst" for artist-heroes – a demand, even among corporate patrons, for the "best" artists – raised Ghiberti, Brunelleschi, and Donatello from artisan status and gave them greater autonomy. Ghiberti worked almost exclusively for corporate patrons: the Calimala (for the two sets of baptistery doors); the Lana, through their cathedral operai (among other things, for the St. Zenobius shrine in the east tribune of the cathedral); and both these guilds and the Cambio at Orsanmichele. While working on the second set of baptistery doors, he signed a contract in 1432 with the cathedral operai for the Zenobius shrine but did so little on it for the next five years that they terminated the agreement. Instead of turning to someone else, however, two years later they again asked Ghiberti to undertake the project, and this time he completed it. Brunelleschi's reputation as a rebel against convention may have been exaggerated by Manetti, but it was not completely invented. Manetti says that he simply walked away from the joint commission awarded for the baptistery doors and that years later his outbursts in heated meetings about the cupola caused him to be carried out of the room more than once. In 1420 he was unhappy about the co-supervisory collaboration with Ghiberti for the cupola but was not about to turn his back on that project. Manetti recounts that he pretended to be ill, forced Ghiberti to carry out on his own a technical procedure that he allegedly mishandled, and gradually forced his rival to retreat from the role of equal supervisor. True or not (as with the elaborate trick Brunelleschi allegedly played on the woodworker Grasso to rob him of his identity, as recounted in the *Novella del Grasso Legnaiuolo*, also written by Manetti), this was the kind of reputation Brunelleschi not only acquired but apparently encouraged about himself.

Competition for prized artists was beginning to undercut the traditions of collective supervision, consensus, and corporate control of both projects and artisan-artists. Even artists whose careers unfolded primarily within the framework of corporate and civic patronage began to be drawn in different directions by private patrons. The always busy Ghiberti found time to make

[40]   ASF, Arte del Cambio, 18; A. Doren, *Das Aktenbuch für Ghibertis Matthäusstatue an Or. S. Michele zu Florenz* (Berlin, 1906).

a bronze reliquary for the Medici. In the case of Brunelleschi, 1419–20 was a particularly significant moment in this transition. Within the space of two years, in addition to the cupola, he also accepted the commission from Por Santa Maria to design the Innocenti Hospital and commissions for three private chapels: one from Giovanni de' Medici to redesign the sacristy at San Lorenzo (where Giovanni and his wife are buried), and two others from elite members of the Wool guild, Tommaso Barbadori, who served on the Opera del Duomo in 1418, and Schiatta Ridolfi, a consul of the guild in the same year. According to Manetti, Brunelleschi was trying to convince the operai and consuls that he could build a dome without centering, and knowing that Ridolfi wanted to rebuild a family chapel with a dome in the church of San Jacopo sopr'Arno he offered to demonstrate on a smaller scale that it was possible. The Barbadori chapel in Santa Felicita and the sacristy in San Lorenzo also have domes,[41] and the three projects demonstrate that the fame Brunelleschi already enjoyed as the ingenious designer of the controversial project for the cupola was stimulating the private demand for art that was becoming a symbol of status for elite families.

Family Commemoration and Self-Fashioning

Endowments of family chapels, often as burial sites, went back to the end of the thirteenth century.[42] Evidence from testamentary bequests suggests that they became more numerous after the Black Death, and particularly after the 1363 plague, and by the early fifteenth century sometimes involved sizeable investments: compared with the average 200-florin bequest for fourteenth-century chapels throughout central Italy, after 1400 some Florentines were leaving as much as 500 or 1,000 florins for chapels in which they sought long-term patronage rights. Spending for chapel decorations also increased. Some fourteenth-century bequests for large narrative cycles reached 250–300 florins, but more common and smaller devotional paintings, usually for chapels but sometimes for domestic use, were much less expensive. Following the plagues, more testators wanted images of themselves included in the paintings they commissioned. After about 1400, bequests for art became larger, if not necessarily more numerous, than those of a generation earlier: the average bequest for all artworks (including paintings) increased fourfold, from 70 to 270 florins, as commissions became more imposing and more conspicuously linked to family commemoration.[43]

[41] R. King, *Brunelleschi's Dome* (London, 2000), pp. 45–6; Manetti, *Life of Brunelleschi*, ed. Saalman, pp. 68–9, 82–9, 98–9.
[42] Dameron, *Florence and Its Church*, pp. 184–9.
[43] S. K. Cohn, Jr., *The Cult of Remembrance and the Black Death: Six Renaissance Cities in Central Italy* (Baltimore, 1992), pp. 214–22, 245, 254–70.

Plate 7   Strozzi Chapel, Santa Maria Novella, altarpiece by Orcagna (Andrea di Cione) and frescoes by Nardo di Cione, mid-1350s (Studio Fotografico Quattrone, Florence)

Neighborhood churches were a focus of competition to enhance family prestige by endowing and decorating chapels. By the mid-fourteenth century, the Dominican basilica of Santa Maria Novella had chapels endowed by the Rucellai, Bardi, Guidalotti, and Strozzi, while patronage rights in the choir behind the main altar were claimed by the Ricci and Tornaquinci.[44] In the 1350s Tommaso Strozzi commissioned for the elevated chapel in the left transept (see Plate 7) the magnificent altarpiece by Orcagna in which Christ gives the keys to Peter and the laws to Thomas Aquinas. On the surrounding walls Orcagna's brother Nardo di Cione painted images of the Last Judgment, Hell, and Paradise, in which a man and a woman, possibly (but not clearly identified as) the donor and his wife, are twice depicted being welcomed among the blessed. Strozzi probably intended to honor Aquinas, the Dominican theologian (d. 1274) canonized in 1323 whose name he shared, but any representation of Aquinas certainly required the approval of the Dominicans. Sums were also left for the decoration of sacristies, chapter-houses (meeting rooms), and cloisters in which it was not possible to establish patronage rights as in chapels. In 1355 Buonamico di Lapo Guidalotti left money to the Dominican friars for "ornamenting and painting" the chapter house (now called the Spanish chapel), which Andrea Bonaiuti decorated a decade later with monumental frescoes including the *Triumph of St. Thomas Aquinas*, an elaborate representation of the history of philosophy and theology and Aquinas's doctrinal victories over heresiarchs like Arius and Averroes. Even more obviously than the Strozzi altarpiece, this was the result of an iconographical program devised by one or more Dominican theologians and motivated by pride in their new saint. In 1348 Turino Baldesi left over 300 florins to Santa Maria Novella for the depiction (executed by Paolo Uccello almost a century later in the Chiostro Verde) of the "entire" Old Testament "from beginning to end," with program and precise location left up to the Dominican preacher and theologian Jacopo Passavanti.[45] In all these examples, the works brought the patrons glory as well as greater assurance of salvation, but it was the Dominicans who decided what got painted where.

Santa Croce, the Franciscan basilica on the other side of town, was perhaps the city's most crowded site of family commemoration. The Peruzzi, Baroncelli, Cavalcanti, Tolosini, Cerchi, Velluti, Castellani, Rinuccini, Ricasoli, Alberti, Machiavelli, and several other families all had chapels here, and at least two branches of the Bardi had a total of four. An entire chapter in the early history

[44] E. Borsook, *The Companion Guide to Florence*, 5th edn. (London, 1988), pp. 129–49.
[45] D. Norman, "The Art of Knowledge: Two Artistic Schemes in Florence," in *Siena, Florence and Padua: Art, Society and Religion 1280–1400, Vol. II: Case Studies*, ed. D. Norman (London, 1995), pp. 176–87, 217–41; Cohn, *Cult of Remembrance*, p. 245.

of Florentine wall painting took place in these chapels between 1310 and 1330. Giotto or his assistants painted the (now largely lost) scenes from the life of the Virgin in the Tolosini chapel to the left of the choir, and Giotto himself painted most of the scenes of the life of Francis in the chapel founded by the banker Ridolfo de' Bardi to the right of the choir and the lives of John the Evangelist and the Baptist in the Peruzzi chapel next to the Bardi chapel. In the 1330s Taddeo Gaddi decorated the sumptuous Baroncelli chapel at the southern end of the transept with stories of the life of the Virgin, while at its northern end Maso di Banco painted the life of St. Sylvester in the Bardi di Vernio chapel. Around 1380–90 Agnolo Gaddi painted the legend of the True Cross (for which Santa Croce was named) in the choir, where the Alberti had patronage rights. Whatever influence patrons had in the production of these works was contained within the doctrinal requirements of the order. As with the Orcagna altarpiece and the chapter-house frescoes at Santa Maria Novella, the history, theology, and representational traditions of the order dominated the choice, placement, and interpretation of themes and protagonists. The Franciscan order was deeply divided between the Spirituals, with their insistence on the literal observance of the rule of poverty, and the Conventuals, who accepted a nominal poverty by which they used, but did not legally own, buildings, books, and other goods. Francis's memory and image were contested terrain, and the disputes culminated, in the very years in which Giotto was painting the Bardi chapel, in papal condemnation of the Spirituals' doctrine of apostolic poverty. A great merchant family like the Bardi would not in any event have wished to promote the uncompromising views of the Spirituals, for whom salvation depended on renunciation of all wealth and material goods, and the Francis of the Bardi chapel is indeed the obedient son of the church described in Bonaventure's official biography.[46] Fourteenth-century painters were no doubt selected for their skills and styles, but these in turn were shaped by the nature of the commissions and the religious ideologies behind them. Powerful families spent considerable sums to build and decorate chapels, but in the fourteenth century the paintings they commissioned said more about the religious orders than about the families.

Salvation and family commemoration remained the overriding motives, but fifteenth-century patrons were more involved in, and exerted more influence over, what they paid for. Among the first of these new patrons was the immensely wealthy Palla Strozzi. From at least the last quarter of the fourteenth

---

[46] R. Goffen, *Spirituality in Conflict: Saint Francis and Giotto's Bardi Chapel* (University Park, Penn., 1988), pp. 9–10, 51–77; C. Harrison, "Giotto and the 'Rise of Painting'," in *Siena, Florence and Padua, Volume I: Interpretative Essays*, ed. Norman, pp. 73–95; Norman, "Those Who Pay, Those Who Pray and Those Who Paint: Two Funerary Chapels," ibid., vol. 2, pp. 169–93.

century, the Strozzi held patronage rights in a chapel in the church of Santa Trinita, as did the Gianfigliazzi, Davizzi, Bartolini-Salimbeni, Ardinghelli, Scali, Spini, Davanzati, and, among so many elite names, the Compagni, in whose chapel Dino is buried. But one chapel was evidently not enough for the Strozzi. Fulfilling the terms of a bequest made decades earlier by his father Nofri for a new sacristy with adjoining chapel, Palla assumed direct control of the project after Nofri's death in 1418, hired his own builders, and introduced significant modifications. He is a good example of a private patron who already had considerable experience in artistic matters from his participation in civic and corporate projects. He had served on the Calimala committee that supervised Ghiberti's first set of baptistery doors and later sought the sculptor's advice on various projects (paying him for "several designs and services"), possibly including the Santa Trinita sacristy. Strozzi was also on the committee that decided the placement in the baptistery of Donatello's and Michelozzo's tomb for Pope Cossa, John XXIII. As a private patron his most notable commission was to the painter Gentile da Fabriano in 1423 for the *Adoration of the Magi* (now in the Uffizi) for the Santa Trinita sacristy. Palla, who was the first of the really big fifteenth-century spenders, included the "building and decoration" of the chapel and sacristy among the expenses, together with his father's funeral, various dowries, and business losses, that cost him the huge sum of 30,000 florins between 1418 and 1422.[47]

Across the river, in the Carmelite church of Santa Maria del Carmine, some chapels were endowed by the district's popular confraternities, others by elite families (Soderini, Brancacci, Serragli), by the emerging Lanfredini, and by families of the popolo (Ferrucci, Tinghi).[48] In 1465 the Del Pugliese, a family of new wealth and rising status, took over a transept chapel.[49] Most famous among the Carmine's chapels is the one partially decorated by Masaccio and endowed by the Brancacci. In 1367 Piero Brancacci left money for a family chapel whose construction was begun by his son Antonio in the 1380s. In 1389 another family member bequeathed funds for its decoration, but only

---

[47]   R. Jones, "Palla Strozzi e la sagrestia di Santa Trinita," *Rivista d'arte* 37 (1984): 9–106 (91); H. Gregory, "Palla Strozzi's Patronage and Pre-Medicean Florence," in *Patronage, Art, and Society in Renaissance Italy*, ed. F. W. Kent and P. Simons with J. C. Eade (Oxford, 1987), pp. 201–20; J. R. Sale, "Palla Strozzi and Lorenzo Ghiberti: New Documents," *Mitteilungen des Kunsthistorischen Institutes in Florenz* 22 (1978): 355–8; D. Davisson, "The Iconology of the S. Trinita Sacristy, 1418–1435: A Study of the Private and Public Functions of Religious Art in the Early Quattrocento," *Art Bulletin* 58 (1975): 315–33.
[48]   N. Eckstein, *The District of the Green Dragon: Neighbourhood Life and Social Change in Renaissance Florence* (Florence, 1995), p. 155.
[49]   Burke, *Changing Patrons*, p. 29.

in the 1420s did Masaccio and Masolino begin painting scenes from the life of the apostle Peter, patron saint of the chapel's founder. By this time Felice Brancacci, from a different branch of the family, had inherited the chapel rights, but it is unknown whether he or others chose the painters. In his 1430 testament Felice stipulated that, if his son died without an heir, all members of the Brancacci clan would inherit the chapel, and in a revised testament of 1432 he obligated his heirs to complete its decoration should he die before doing so. As it happened, Felice, exiled after the Medici victory of 1434, never had the chance, and the chapel was completed only in the 1480s when Filippino Lippi painted the sections left unfinished by Masaccio and Masolino.[50]

The main site of chapel patronage for the Oltrarno's elite families was Santo Spirito, whose new church was designed by Brunelleschi and built between the 1430s and 1490s. Control of building and chapel allocation was shared by the Augustinian friars, the citizen overseers of the opera, and the commune, which actually owned the church and provided much of the financing. Chapel assignment reflected the Oltrarno political and social hierarchy. Traditionally powerful Santo Spirito families that had had chapels in the old church received the prestigious new ones behind the main altar and in the transept: the Frescobaldi got three, the Corbinelli four, the Biliotti, Capponi, and newly prominent Nasi at least one each. Luca Pitti was made an operaio and given a chapel in 1458 without having to pay for its rights (presumably because of his central role in rescuing the regime that year). Families of lower status received nave chapels. More than in other Florentine churches, chapel decoration in Santo Spirito adhered to a general plan, which required altarpieces and stained-glass windows rather than wall paintings.[51]

San Lorenzo is in a category all its own because it was the Medici parish church and the first major site of their patronage. In the old church, torn down beginning in the 1420s and replaced according to a design by Brunelleschi, chaplaincies had been founded by moderately prominent families (Anchioni, Marignolli, later the Rondinelli and Ginori) and by artisans, notaries, and priests. Chaplaincies usually involved not the building of actual chapels but the appointment of a priest-chaplain to say masses for the soul of the testator. In 1336–7, for example, Chele di Aldobrandino bequeathed property outside the walls whose revenue was to pay for daily masses for the souls of Chele and his family at some altar in San Lorenzo that the prior and chapter were to

---

[50]   A. Molho, "The Brancacci Chapel: Studies in its Iconography and History," *Journal of the Warburg and Courtauld Institutes* 40 (1977): 50–98. D. C. Ahl, "Masaccio in the Brancacci Chapel," in *The Cambridge Companion to Masaccio*, ed. Ahl (Cambridge, 2002), pp. 138–57.

[51]   Burke, *Changing Patrons*, pp. 63–83.

make available.[52] Given the relatively small size of the old church and the existence by 1422 of nineteen chaplaincies, it is likely that some altars were sites of two or more.[53] Most were suppressed with the founding of the new and larger church, whose more numerous chapels were reallocated to the district's elite families. Operai appointed for three years in 1416 included members of the Rondinelli, Della Stufa, Guasconi, Dietisalvi-Neroni, and Giovanni di Bicci de' Medici, who served again in 1423 and 1426, as did his sons Lorenzo and Cosimo in 1432 and 1433. Giovanni asserted patronage rights in the new church in both a transept chapel and the old sacristy and quickly completed their construction. Work on San Lorenzo slowed in the 1430s, no doubt because of political turbulence and perhaps a lack of funds, and when it resumed around 1440 a meeting of leading members of the gonfalone and parish decided to transfer patronage rights over the choir to Cosimo in return for his assumption of the costs of the church's construction. It was unprecedented for an individual to assume financial responsibility for the building of an entire, and very large, church. Patronage on such a colossal scale brought with it great influence, and Cosimo was behind major changes in the roster of chapel patrons, as some families were pushed out and Medici allies (like the Dietisalvi-Neroni) and political clients (like the Cambini) invited in. Cosimo also determined that he himself would be buried in a floor tomb at the center of the crossing before the main altar. Patronage, piety, and political self-aggrandizement could not have been more completely fused.

The range of Cosimo's patronage was unlike anything even the wealthiest patrons had hitherto attempted, or dared attempt.[54] He (and his brother Lorenzo, since they commissioned jointly) extended their patronage to nearly every famous artist in the city, to artistic media and types of projects previously supported only by institutional patrons, to a long list of churches far beyond their neighborhood in and outside the city, and to several religious orders, plastering the Medici *palle* and images of their growing gaggle of patron saints anywhere and everywhere they could and associating the family with important sites in the city's processional, religious, and civic life. For example, ancient patronage rights over their former parish church of San Tommaso gave them a special interest in St. Thomas. Cosimo rebuilt the church and influenced the government to institute an officially supported ritual observance in the saint's honor. A generation later Piero was instrumental

---

[52]   W. M. Bowsky, *La chiesa di San Lorenzo a Firenze nel Medioevo* (Florence, 1999), pp. 139–42.

[53]   For what follows: C. Elam, "Cosimo de' Medici and San Lorenzo," in *Cosimo "il Vecchio,"* ed. Ames-Lewis, pp. 157–80.

[54]   For splendid illustrations, see D. Kent, *Cosimo de' Medici and the Florentine Renaissance.*

in having Donatello's *St. Louis of Toulouse* removed from the niche at Orsanmichele that faced onto the processional route of via Calzaiuoli to make room for Andrea del Verrocchio's bronze *Doubting Thomas and Christ*, thus identifying the prestigious site with the family's political power and patronage.[55] Bronze had been restricted to civic projects because of its immense cost, and Medici use of it conveyed their political pretensions and advertised their great wealth. Cosimo and Lorenzo had already commissioned the bronze reliquary chest from Ghiberti for the church of Santa Maria degli Angeli (a private commission for a public place). More grandiose were the bronze doors they asked Donatello to design for the San Lorenzo sacristy in which their parents' quasi-regal tomb of marble, porphyry, and bronze was placed. Beyond San Lorenzo, Cosimo's architectural projects included the rebuilding or renovation of several ecclesiastical institutions: San Marco, where he installed the Observant Dominicans and built the library that housed the great collection of manuscripts donated by Niccolò Niccoli; the Observant Franciscan convent of Bosco ai Frati in the Mugello near the family's country estates; the Badia in Fiesole; and a novitiate chapel at Santa Croce. Along the way he commissioned tabernacles by Michelozzo at San Miniato and Santissima Annunziata, large altarpieces and frescoes by Fra Angelico, paintings by Filippo Lippi, and a long list of other works that only seem "lesser" by comparison with the magnitude of the larger projects.[56]

Political messages in Medici-commissioned art became bolder. In the 1450s Cosimo had Benozzo Gozzoli paint the *Procession of the Magi* in the chapel of the family palace, with portraits of himself, his son Piero, and a representation (not an actual portrait) of the young Lorenzo di Piero, all with the Magi on their way to adore the child Christ. Although patrons had previously included images of themselves as participants in, or witnesses to, sacred dramas, never before had an entire family integrated itself so explicitly into sacred history. Dynastic implications are evident in the parallel between the three generations of kings and three generations of Medici, and in the presence of the Medici symbols on the caparison of the horse of the youngest king, Caspar, whose feast day coincides with Lorenzo's birthday (January 1).[57] Whether Cosimo

[55] K. J. P. Lowe, "A Matter of Piety or of Family Tradition and Custom: The Religious Patronage of Piero de' Medici and Lucrezia Tornabuoni," in *Piero de' Medici*, ed. Beyer and Boucher, pp. 55–69; J. Paoletti, " '. . . ha fatto Piero con voluntà del padre . . .': Piero de' Medici and Corporate Commissions of Art," ibid., pp. 221–50.
[56] J. Paoletti, "Fraternal Piety and Family Power: The Artistic Patronage of Cosimo and Lorenzo de' Medici," and C. Robinson, "Cosimo de' Medici and the Franciscan Observants at Bosco ai Frati," both in *Cosimo "Il Vecchio*," ed. Ames-Lewis, pp. 181–219.
[57] R. Hatfield, "Cosimo de' Medici and the Chapel of His Palace," in *Cosimo "il Vecchio*," ed. Ames-Lewis, pp. 221–44 (238).

commissioned or acquired Donatello's bronze *David*, he placed it prominently in the private/public courtyard of his palace. David had already begun the transition from prophet and precursor of Christ to a symbol of fortitude in defense of the *patria*. Years earlier Donatello had carved a marble *David* to go atop one of the buttresses of the north tribune of the cathedral, and the commune purchased it from the Cathedral Opera in 1416 and moved it to the palace of the priors. Cosimo's appropriation of David was an audacious statement of his and his family's self-identification with the civic virtues with which the biblical hero was associated; and the placement in Palazzo Medici established in effect a rival site of these virtues. But David was also a king, and the unprecedented youth of the Medici *David* also alludes, under the guise of civic virtue, to Lorenzo and the family's dynastic ambitions.[58]

Medici patronage, continued by Lorenzo with the same ubiquity if not magnitude,[59] set a standard that could never be matched by other families, and their political dominance may have dissuaded potential competitors from even trying. Compared to the fourteenth and early fifteenth centuries, there was a dearth of chapel decoration for several decades after the consolidation of the Medici regime. Other families may have been cautious about advertising their prestige too loudly, perhaps fearing that it might be seen as an attempt to rival the Medici. Certainly families not in good Medici graces shied away from patronage that conveyed public self-fashioning. But families or individuals seeking such favor used art to flatter the Medici. In the early 1470s, the exchange broker Guasparre Dal Lama, a (perhaps would-be) Medici client of modest social status, built a chapel in Santa Maria Novella and commissioned Botticelli to paint the *Adoration of the Magi* (now in the Uffizi) as its altarpiece. He used the painting to show off his ties to the Medici by having himself and several of them included in the picture, once again, if not in actual portraits, as types reflecting traditional Medici identification with the Magi.[60] Dal Lama had no family behind him, and the painting was a gesture of homage with no overtones of competition. Similarly, Francesco Sassetti, general manager of the Medici bank, commissioned a fresco cycle at Santa Trinita, whose ostensible content is the life of St. Francis, but which is also a commemoration of his dependence on the Medici. In 1479 Sassetti negotiated the transfer of rights in the chapel at the north end of the transept from the

---

[58]   A. W. B. Randolph, *Engaging Symbols: Gender, Politics, and Public Art in Fifteenth-Century Florence* (New Haven, 2002), pp. 139–92; S. B. McHam, "Donatello's Bronze *David* and *Judith* as Metaphors of Medici Rule in Florence," *Art Bulletin* 83 (2001): 32–47.

[59]   F. W. Kent, *Lorenzo de' Medici and the Art of Magnificence* (Baltimore, 2004).

[60]   R. Hatfield, *Botticelli's Uffizi "Adoration": A Study in Pictorial Content* (Princeton, 1976).

Plate 8   Sassetti Chapel, Santa Trinita, frescoes by Domenico Ghirlandaio, early 1480s (Scala/Art Resource, NY)

Petriboni-Fastelli family to his own and engaged Domenico Ghirlandaio to paint frescoes that were finished by 1485 (see Plate 8). The patron, his family, his Medici boss, and several in-laws are all prominently represented, especially on the altar wall, which first commands the visitor's attention. On the lowest level, surrounding the altarpiece, are portraits of the kneeling donors, Francesco and his wife Nera Corsi. No doubt because the death of their eldest son some years earlier had been followed by the birth of another who was given, in good Florentine tradition, the same name, Sassetti replaced Ghirlandaio's suggested depiction in the middle register of a story normally included in Francis cycles with the less common episode of *St. Francis Resuscitating the Roman Notary's Son*, set, not in Rome, but in the piazza outside Santa Trinita, where the miracle is witnessed by Sassetti's daughters and his prominent neighbors, including Neri Capponi, whose grandson married one of the daughters. Above it is depicted the *Confirmation of the Rule by Pope Honorius III*, set, once again, not in Rome but in Florence in the piazza of the priors, with the loggia and palace in the background and, in the foreground on the right, portraits of Sassetti, his son Federigo, Lorenzo de' Medici, and Antonio Pucci, whose son married another of Sassetti's daughters, and on the left Sassetti's other sons, all welcoming the arrival of Lorenzo's children with their teachers (including the poet Poliziano) from a lower level.[61] Sassetti was a "new man" who had risen with the fortunes of the Medici bank (ironically precarious at the very moment he had the chapel decorated) to become its general manager for thirty years. The first Sassetti prior, and the only one before 1500, was his brother Bartolomeo in 1453. Francesco's only major office was a term on the Sixteen in 1483. A creature of the Medici and utterly dependent on them, he never lost their trust and favor. The frescoes celebrate his ties to the Medici, implicitly expressing the hope, through the depiction of his and Lorenzo's children, that the link would persist into future generations. The family represented is limited to Francesco's wife, sons, daughters, and, through the latter, his powerful in-laws.

Equally Medicean, but far more prestigious and ancient than the Sassetti, the Tornabuoni had patronage rights to the choir at Santa Maria Novella that went back to a thirteenth-century Tornaquinci who donated the land on which the original Dominican church was built. Giovanni Tornabuoni was manager of the Medici bank's Rome branch, but his link to the family was not limited to business; his sister Lucrezia was Piero's wife and Lorenzo's mother. After some uncertainty owing to an old Sassetti claim to the high altar, in 1486 the Dominicans gave Tornabuoni and his entire *consorteria* full rights over both the choir and the altar. Indeed, he had already signed a contract with

[61] E. Borsook and J. Offerhaus, *Francesco Sassetti and Ghirlandaio at Santa Trinita, Florence: History and Legend in a Renaissance Chapel* (Doornspijk, 1981).

Ghirlandaio for the depiction of scenes from the life of the Virgin (to whom Santa Maria Novella is dedicated) and that of John the Baptist (his patron saint) "as an act of piety and love of God, to the exaltation of his house and family and the enhancement of the said church and chapel." In addition to specifying scenes and stories and their location, the contract also stipulated that Ghirlandaio "shall begin to paint one or other of the above-mentioned stories and paintings only after first doing a drawing of the said story which he must show to Giovanni; and the [painter] may afterwards start this story, but painting and embellishing it with any additions and in whatever form and manner the said Giovanni may have declared."[62] Quite unlike fourteenth-century fresco cycles that reflect the founders, saints, and ideals of the religious orders that approved them more than the patrons who paid for them, the paintings in the Tornabuoni chapel had their patron's approval in every detail. But they are also different from those in the Sassetti chapel at Santa Trinita. Whereas the latter showcase the ties of a parvenu to the city's most powerful family, the Tornabuoni frescoes are a lavish representation and commemoration of an extended kin-group without overt reference to the Medici. The *Annunciation to Zacharias*, in which the angel foretells the birth of the Baptist, is set in a space at once classical, civic, and sacred and is witnessed by many identifiable family members, including Giovanni himself and the elders of the *consorteria*'s other three branches (Tornaquinci, Popoleschi, and Giachinotti).[63] Even if the Medici are not directly present, however, such family commemoration would not have been possible without Giovanni Tornabuoni's many links to them.

Wealthy patrons who had the favor of the Medici could indulge some self-fashioning as long as competition was not overt. No doubt because of his family's long association with Santa Maria Novella, where many Strozzi were buried, in 1486 Filippo Strozzi bought from the Boni family the rights to the chapel to the right of the choir and made it his private burial place, in which he commissioned a sculpted tomb from Benedetto da Maiano and frescoes by Filippino Lippi of the lives of St. Philip and John the Evangelist, in which the *Raising of Drusiana* may have been intended as an allegory of his own return from the metaphorical death of exile. The contrast with the first Strozzi chapel, even across the obvious continuity of family burial traditions and chapel patronage, is illuminating. Although in the earlier one the donor and his family are apparently honored, it is Orcagna's severe, lawgiving Christ and the intimidating density of souls in the realms of the afterlife that dominate. In

---

[62]   *Patrons and Artists in the Italian Renaissance*, ed. D. S. Chambers (Columbia, S.C., 1971), pp. 173–5.
[63]   P. Simons, "Patronage in the Tornaquinci Chapel, Santa Maria Novella, Florence," in *Patronage, Art, and Society*, ed. Kent and Simons, pp. 221–50.

Filippo's chapel he himself is the center of attention in a visual fusion of the liturgical and the funereal surrounded by paintings whose subject matter he chose and stipulated in a contract with the painter.[64] Such self-glorification was not possible without Lorenzo's at least tacit permission.

Palace building was the ultimate in conspicuous consumption and advertisement of a patron's status and means, an immensely expensive and highly visible item of material culture. Older palaces, like Palazzo Spini in piazza Santa Trinita or the Mozzi palace at the Oltrarno end of the Rubaconte bridge (today's Ponte alle Grazie), were imposing urban fortresses intended as much for defense as prestige. Some, like the Peruzzi palaces near Santa Croce, faced inward around ancient family enclaves. Beginning in the fourteenth century, palaces were increasingly built facing major streets with more attention to decorative and structural features that set one apart from another, but they were still part of the continuous urban fabric, often with rented ground-floor commercial spaces. Fifteenth-century private palaces transformed entire neighborhoods. They were larger and occupied more ground area, and, wherever possible, their owners bought and cleared surrounding spaces to allow them to be seen from a greater distance and thus to dominate a piazza or street. Ground-floor shops disappeared, and now the lower levels sported imposing rustication, consisting of large rough-hewn blocks of stone, and often included stone benches for the many clients that every great builder and political patron hoped to see conspicuously congregating and waiting for a chance to see him.[65]

The new trend was inaugurated around 1410–20 by Niccolò da Uzzano who built a large palace with a rusticated façade in via de' Bardi. But it was Cosimo de' Medici who set the standard for all subsequent palace-building with a grand family townhouse that marked an epoch in elite domestic architecture (see Plate 5). According to a perhaps apocryphal story reported by Giorgio Vasari, Cosimo expressed a desire for a new palace to Brunelleschi, who produced a model for a freestanding structure that would have faced, and perhaps overwhelmed, the piazza of San Lorenzo. Vasari claims that, when Cosimo decided against it "because it seemed too sumptuous and grand, and to avoid envy more than expense," an angry Brunelleschi smashed his model and Cosimo later regretted that he did not accept it. Traditionally attributed to Michelozzo, the palace that Cosimo had built between the mid-1440s and mid-1450s combines Tuscan Romanesque elements with antique

[64]   D. Friedman, "The Burial Chapel of Filippo Strozzi in Santa Maria Novella in Florence," *L'arte* 3 (1970): 109–31; Goldthwaite, *Private Wealth*, pp. 69–72; Welch, *Art and Society*, pp. 11–15.
[65]   Y. Elet, "Seats of Power: The Outdoor Benches of Early Modern Florence," *Journal of the Society of Architectural Historians* 61 (2002): 444–69.

Plate 9   Palazzo Rucellai, facade by Leon Battista Alberti, 1450s (Scala/Art Resouce, NY)

features. But its rusticated façade and biforate windows certainly alluded to the palace of the priors and to an appropriation or sharing of the public authority that inhered in that quasi-sacred civic building (as the bronze *David* also did). Located at the point where the via Larga bends slightly to the right, Palazzo Medici presents itself in oblique and elongated view from the piazza of the baptistery and cathedral, thus creating a visual and symbolic link between the city's spiritual center and the home of its most powerful citizen and family.[66]

In palace-building Medici grandeur generated emulation, if not in specific architectural and design features, certainly in proclaiming the "magnificence," or virtuous liberality, of their builders and the pride of families within their ancestral neighborhoods.[67] Benedetto Dei listed twenty palace projects in his lifetime (among thirty-three major building projects),[68] and between the mid-1440s, when Cosimo began building, and the mid-1460s, at least ten palaces were constructed. It was almost as if others had been waiting for Cosimo to take the lead and not risk upstaging him. Giovanni Rucellai assembled several properties in the family's traditional site and built a palace on the Vigna Nuova, with its exquisite façade designed by Alberti (see Plate 9) and a loggia across the street.[69] Members of both elite families, including the Pazzi, Dietisalvi-Neroni, and Gianfigliazzi, and relatively newer families like the Spinelli,[70] Boni (today Palazzo Antinori), Gondi, Nasi (today Palazzo Torrigiani), and Del Pugliese[71] joined the fashionable ranks of palace-builders. Most palaces were more modest than Palazzo Medici, but Luca Pitti's palace across the river rivaled it (although the original structure was not nearly the size of the building subsequently enlarged as the residence of the grand dukes of Tuscany and the king of Italy). By far the largest and most ambitious of the palaces, "more grandiose than that of [the Medici]," as one foreign observer suggested, was the Strozzi palace begun by Filippo in 1489 (see Plate 10). Whereas the "average" upper-class palazzo cost between 1,500 and 2,500 florins, Filippo and his heirs spent an astounding 40,000 florins on a palace that lacked ground floor shops or any commercial space. Although equivalent in height to a modern

---

[66] B. Preyer, "L'archittetura del palazzo mediceo," in *Palazzo Medici Riccardi di Firenze*, ed. G. Cherubini and G. Fanelli (Florence, 1990), pp. 58–75.

[67] F. W. Kent, "Palaces, Politics and Society in Fifteenth-Century Florence," *I Tatti Studies* 2 (1987): 41–70.

[68] *Cronica*, ed. Barducci, p. 86.

[69] B. Preyer, "The Rucellai Palace," in *Giovanni Rucellai e il suo Zibaldone*, vol. 2, pp. 155–225; B. Preyer, "The Rucellai Loggia," *Mitteilungen des Kunsthistorischen Institutes in Florenz* 21 (1977): 183–98.

[70] Jacks and Caferro, *The Spinelli of Florence*, pp. 91–142.

[71] Burke, *Changing Patrons*, pp. 35–61.

Plate 10   Palazzo Strozzi, begun 1489 (Alinari/Art Resource, NY)

ten-storey building, it consists of only three floors and a dozen (albeit large) rooms intended for just the immediate families of two brothers.[72]

Palaces represented investment in family immortality and personal fame. Filippo Strozzi died in 1491 before his great palace was completed and thus never had the opportunity to express the sentiments he would no doubt have felt over this immense monument to his and his family's memory. But other great Florentine builders did express such feelings. Giovanni Rucellai was not the only Florentine to write in his *ricordanze* that "there are two principal things men do in this world: the first is to procreate, the second to build." Yet some conservative impulse in Rucellai toward modesty in spending, signaled by his reminder to himself in the very next sentence that "St. Bernard says one must build more out of necessity than desire, because building makes desire grow stronger rather than weaker," needed to be overcome for him to praise his own building without reservation. Perhaps he was reflecting some of the

[72]   R. Goldthwaite, "The Florentine Palace as Domestic Architecture," *American Historical Review* 77 (1972): 977–1012.

Plate 11   Santa Maria Novella, facade by Leon Battista Alberti, completed by 1470 (Erich Lessing/Art Resource, NY)

old moralistic condemnation of conspicuous building, expressed a century earlier by Giovanni Villani (12.94) who remarked that, although the innumerable country villas surrounding the city were a magnificent sight, their builders committed a serious error and sin in spending so uncontrollably and were considered insane for doing so. In one such mood Rucellai advised his sons to be "wise about spending," to avoid excess, and to practice thrift and prudent management. Big spenders, he warned, are ultimately avaricious because they can never acquire enough wealth by means fair or foul to satisfy their desires. Underscoring the distinction between "necessary" and "voluntary" expenditures, he advised waiting and reflecting before indulging in the latter to see if the "desire would pass in the meantime." But in other moods Rucellai overcame such scruples. As he reviewed his extensive building, "done for the honor of God, the honor of the city, and the memory of me," he said he agreed with the "common saying, which is true," that "making and spending money are among the great pleasures men take in this world," adding that it would be difficult to say "which is greater." "For fifty years I have done nothing but make and spend money; I have taken the greatest and sweetest pleasure in doing so, and I think the greater sweetness has been in spending than in earning." Much of that spending was for artworks and buildings, and in him we see, for the first time, the self-conscious collector of works known by the names and reputations of those who made them. Rucellai notes with satisfaction in the *Zibaldone* that "we have in our house many works of sculpture, painting, and intarsia by the best masters that have existed for a long time, not only in Florence but in Italy," and he gives their names: Domenico Veneziano, Filippo Lippi, Giuliano da Maiano, Antonio del Pollaiuolo, Maso Finiguerra, Verrocchio, Vittorio Ghiberti, Andrea del Castagno, Paolo Uccello, and Desiderio da Settignano. It is a remarkable list, and indicative of his awareness of the leading artists of the age. But when it came to building, Rucellai made himself the author, perhaps not surprisingly given his comparison of building and procreation. Besides the family palace, his main projects included the family burial chapel in the nearby parish church of San Pancrazio, with the marble replica of the Holy Sepulchre in Jerusalem, and the glorious façade of Santa Maria Novella. Although both were designed by Leon Battista Alberti, the great architect's name is absent, not only on the works themselves, but even in Rucellai's voluminous *Zibaldone*. Instead, both the sepulchre and the façade prominently feature the Rucellai arms and the name of Giovanni himself. The façade's inscription of his name and the year 1470 proclaims that he, not Alberti, not the friars, not the church, was its maker[73] (Plate 11).

---

[73]   *Giovanni Rucellai ed il suo Zibaldone*, vol. 1, ed. Perosa, pp. 15–17, 121, 20–7; F. W. Kent, "The Making of a Renaissance Patron," ibid., vol. 2, pp. 13, 52.

12

The Medici and the Ottimati: A Partnership of Conflict
Part 2: Lorenzo

Lorenzo de' Medici long ago became a figure of legend. Easily the most famous member of a family that later produced popes and grand dukes, he personifies the so-called golden age of Florence and Italy before 1494. In his *History of Italy* Guicciardini made him the indispensable guardian of the concord, happiness, and balance of power among the Italian states, whose death opened the door to the invasions and wars that engulfed Italy. Even in his own time, court poets and humanists extravagantly lauded him as the "savior of his country," "born to reach all the heights," dear to the Muses, a new Maecenas, and much more. Mythmaking around Lorenzo abandoned the model of the ideal republican citizen, as the vogue of neoplatonism elevated him to the rank of philosopher-king. Sixteenth-century architects of another phase of Medici rule and dynastic legend crafted in retrospect an image of Lorenzo as the figure on whose sacral presence and salvific power Florence and even all Italy depended.[1] In later centuries Lorenzo came to symbolize the entire age. Voltaire identified fifteenth-century Italy as one of Europe's four great cultural

---

[1] M. M. Bullard, *Lorenzo il Magnifico: Image and Anxiety, Politics and Finance* (Florence, 1994), chap. 1, "*Il Magnifico* Between Myth and History," pp. 3–41; N. Rubinstein, "The Formation of the Posthumous Image of Lorenzo de' Medici," in *Oxford, China, and Italy: Writings in Honour of Sir Harold Acton on His Eightieth Birthday*, ed. E. Chaney and N. Ritchie (London, 1984), pp. 94–106; F. W. Kent, *Lorenzo de' Medici*, pp. 1–9.

epochs (together with Periclean Athens, Augustan Rome, and the France of Louis XIV) and made Lorenzo its defining personality.[2]

Indeed, he was unlike any Florentine before him. Of the members of his family, and among all Florentine political leaders, only Lorenzo was a writer and poet of genuine merit, with an established place in the history of Italian literature. He was also the most innovative political leader in the republic's history. Whereas Cosimo remained in the role of a behind-the-scenes boss who, although no one doubted his power, represented himself as one of many leading citizens with whom he collaborated in governing, Lorenzo affected a far more visible, personal, and exclusive style of leadership and, moreover, did so from the very beginning, acting like a prince even before his father died in 1469. His unprecedented political style no doubt aimed at avoiding a repetition of the events of 1465–6. Seeing everything his family had built over decades nearly collapse must have been a frightening experience for the seventeen-year-old heir apparent. From it he drew political lessons that shaped a style of governance whose central feature was to make himself the indispensable point of reference for every public decision, election, and policy, for every officeholder and bureaucrat, for all aspects of Florence's dealings with its subject territories and other states, and for its religious and ritual life. Despite some reversals, he succeeded in making no one feel safe about doing anything in politics (and elsewhere) without his tacit or explicit approval. He thus placed himself, visibly, indeed ostentatiously, at the center of everything from elections and patronage to ritual and culture, seeking to disabuse the Florentines of the illusion fostered by his father and grandfather that the Medici were citizens like others, only with greater responsibilities. In attempting to make himself the charismatic center that Florentines had tenaciously resisted for two centuries, he opened up an abyss between his methods and those of Cosimo and Piero.

There was of course resistance, albeit unsuccessful. Lorenzo's reputation among those not beholden to the regime was never as brilliant as that fashioned by poets, humanists, and some modern historians; it was, in fact, often unfavorable. Despite Poliziano's claim that Lorenzo and his family enjoyed the "willing support of all good men" and that the "whole city rejoiced" in his safety when it became known he had survived the Pazzi conspiracy,[3] Lorenzo was in many respects a distant and unpopular figure for many Florentines. In

---

[2]   N. Rubinstein, "Lorenzo's Image in Europe," in *Lorenzo the Magnificent: Culture and Politics*, ed. M. Mallett and N. Mann (London, 1996), pp. 297–312 (302–3).

[3]   Angelo Poliziano, *Coniurationis commentarium*, ed. A. Perosa (Padua, 1958); Poliziano, *The Pazzi Conspiracy*, trans. R. Watkins and D. Marsh, in *Humanism and Liberty: Writings on Freedom from Fifteenth-Century Florence*, ed. R. Watkins (Columbia, S.C., 1978), pp. 171–83, (171, 180).

their private diaries some denounced his arbitrary and highhanded abuses of power. He was accused of preventing or forcing marriages against the wishes of families, of confiscating inheritances and manipulating the law courts to favor his friends and punish his enemies. Ottimati ambassadors sometimes complained about Lorenzo's private diplomacy and his insistence that they report to him first and only then say what he wanted them to say to the magistracies under whose authority they held their posts. Many grumbled about the lavishly expensive celebrations and state visits that more than once turned the city into a gigantic Medici theater. And those who knew of his interference in communal finances accused him of profiting at the public's expense. Giovanni Cambi recounted the injustice done to his father Neri, whom Lorenzo dismissed as Standardbearer of Justice because he had (quite legally) fined friends of Lorenzo whose absence had prevented the needed quorum for the election of a new Signoria. Cambi denounced Lorenzo, after his death, as "a greater tyrant than if he had been a ruler with formal authority [*signore a bacchetta*]." An offended member of the (Medicean) Martelli family also branded him a "tyrant." Alamanno Rinuccini called him "the malignant tyrant, who tried to become lord of the republic like Julius Caesar." Piero Parenti, son of Marco, recorded that at Lorenzo's death in 1492 "the lower classes were happy," and "the *popolo* and elite [*gentilotti*] not especially sad. The leading citizens were divided in opinion: those who were close to Lorenzo and held power with him were extremely sad, thinking they would lose their position and perhaps lose power altogether; others who weren't so close and were not involved in government instead rejoiced, thinking that the republic would recover its liberty and they would escape from servitude and enjoy a larger share in government. The people secretly accepted his death, especially because of their having been oppressed, since under his control the city was nothing other than enslaved."[4]

The myths of Lorenzo's magnificence and sacral presence may have been fashioned to cover this underlying dissatisfaction with his abuses of power and to mask the ever more brittle nature of his support with a mystification of that power. A golden age it may have seemed in retrospect, but Lorenzo's more than two decades of leadership were in fact filled with crises whose root cause was the precariousness of the support behind him. Although by the 1480s he seemingly achieved uncontested power and complete control of government, elections, and institutions, the other side of the coin was that, by turning himself into a prince in all but name, yet without legal authority, he

---

[4] A. Brown, "Lorenzo and Public Opinion: The Problem of Opposition," in *Lorenzo il Magnifico e il suo mondo*, ed. G. Garfagnini (Florence, 1994), pp. 61–85 (translations of Parenti, pp. 60, 70, 73–5); Piero di Marco Parenti, *Storia fiorentina*, ed. A. Matucci (Florence, 1994), p. 23.

weakened the consensus that his grandfather had tried to build among the ottimati and gradually lost the cooperation of their class. Worsening relations with the ottimati made tighter political controls necessary, and the apex of Lorenzo's power thus reflected the regime's growing weakness as each crisis further narrowed the circle of those whom he could trust. His progressive isolation from the ottimati led to revolutionary transformations in the exercise of power, both in his generation and beyond.

Lorenzo's Elders

That Lorenzo was only twenty years old and already married to a non-Florentine when he "succeeded" his father already signaled the beginning of a new era, a cultural as well as a political turning point for a city in which, by long custom, leadership in both politics and family belonged to men of experience and maturity to whom younger men were expected to defer. Communal statutes prescribed minimum age requirements for offices, and, while there were of course no age requirements for marriage, it was assumed that men undertaking its responsibilities had left behind the impetuosity and wanderlust of youth. Lorenzo broke all these social rules in a matter of months and, with a good deal of impetuosity still about him, was being treated by both Florence's leading citizens and the governments of Italy as the city's de facto prince. He was the first of his family to be born after the regime's inception, and thus the first to grow up with the expectation from birth that he would one day assume the reins of leadership. He was, in a sense, prisoner of a destiny for which he had been carefully trained by his father and teachers.[5] While still a boy, he participated in ceremonies welcoming distinguished visitors and in diplomatic missions to Milan and Naples. In 1465 he held office in the Parte Guelfa and was appointed to the scrutiny committee. Some sources report that he was sent to speak for his father to the Signoria and to negotiate with Luca Pitti in the decisive days of the confrontation, after which he was appointed to the Cento. He joined several confraternities and was already playing a role in the Medici patronage network as the recipient of letters from clients and favor-seekers. In 1469, as his father's health deteriorated, Lorenzo's quasi-anointed status was confirmed in two great public events that captured the attention of social and courtly elites all over Italy: a festive joust in February to celebrate the defeat of the exiles, but also to proclaim, by means of Lorenzo's staged triumph, his imminent assumption of leadership; and his lavish wedding in

---

[5]   F. W. Kent, "The Young Lorenzo, 1449–69," in *Lorenzo the Magnificent: Culture and Politics*, ed. Mallett and Mann, pp. 1–22.

June to Clarice Orsini.[6] When Piero died in December and the moment of Lorenzo's "ascension" was at hand, the Ferrarese ambassador reported that some citizens were calling the Medici regime a "principato" and recognizing the necessity of a "signore e superiore" with control over all political matters.[7]

In fact, however, reluctance persisted among ottimati at the prospect of a Medici dynasty, and the origins of Lorenzo's problems with them were not unlike those that pitted Piero against Cosimo's former lieutenants. Chief among those of Piero's high command who chafed at the prospect of recognizing his twenty-year-old son as their "superior" was Tommaso Soderini, who had remained loyal to Piero in the crisis of 1465–6 but now hoped to control the young Lorenzo to his own purposes. Yet, no doubt recalling the fate of his brother Niccolò and of the others who had challenged Piero, Tommaso was not about to risk an open break or attempt any restoration of "traditional" republican government. His strategy was more personal, and at the same time linked to foreign policy. Initially, he soothed Medici fears with a display of loyalty by organizing, on December 2, 1469, the same day Piero died, an unofficial but very public meeting in which 700 citizens proclaimed their support and confirmed Lorenzo in the "reputation and greatness" enjoyed by his father and grandfather. In Milan there was concern that Soderini and other leading citizens might try to alienate Florence from the Sforza to diminish Lorenzo's prestige. Just before Piero died, Lorenzo wrote to Duke Galeazzo Maria acknowledging that, just as his father and grandfather owed "everything they had" to the duke and his father, he, Lorenzo, similarly knew the duke to be the "author of his every honor and benefit." Since the house of Sforza has been the "upholder of our *stato* and *grandezza*," Lorenzo now asked Galeazzo Maria to "undertake my protection and support," not to alter traditional Sforza benevolence toward his "house," and to "extend to me the same affection" previously shown to his forebears.[8] Within five days the duke responded that his troops were ready to intervene to ensure the smooth transfer of power to Lorenzo.

Within a matter of months, however, Tommaso Soderini, Luigi Guicciardini, and Antonio Ridolfi were competing for influence over Lorenzo. Soderini in particular began to chart an independent course in foreign affairs with the aim of detaching Florence from the Milanese connection and allying it with either Naples or Venice or both. Otto Niccolini, a Soderini ally and Florentine ambassador to Naples in early 1470, sent detailed reports directly to Soderini

---

[6] N. Carew-Reid, *Les fêtes florentines au temps de Lorenzo il Magnifico* (Florence, 1995), pp. 24–6, 31–5.

[7] Rubinstein, *Government*, p. 200n.

[8] Lorenzo de' Medici, *Lettere*, vol. 1 (1460–1474), ed. R. Fubini (Florence, 1977), pp. 48–51.

rather than to the Signoria, much as Lorenzo wanted envoys linked to the Medici to send them to him. Lorenzo was apparently slow to realize the danger of those favoring a closer alliance with Naples, and he had to be warned by the Milanese ambassador Sacramoro Mengozzi that at stake in the debate over foreign policy was his own preeminence in the regime. In April an attempted revolt in nearby Prato by exiled anti-Mediceans resulted in the execution of fifteen conspirators and heightened the anxiety of those first few months.[9] In June an awakened Lorenzo rallied his supporters in a pratica convened to protect the Milanese alliance, but opposition among the ottimati had become evident.[10] In reports to Galeazzo Maria, the Milanese ambassador discussed this opposition and the apprehensiveness it aroused among both Mediceans and Milanese. Sacramoro urged Lorenzo to proceed more forcefully against his enemies and repeatedly invited Lorenzo, Soderini, and others to dinners during which he harangued Soderini, trying to persuade him to abandon policies or views that deviated from the Medici–Milan alliance. His frequent attempts to instruct Lorenzo in the art of recognizing ottimati machinations suggest that an uncertain and inexperienced Lorenzo was being guided by the duke's representatives. Galeazzo Maria put on a lavish public display of his unwavering support for Lorenzo when he and hundreds of members of his court made a ten-day state visit to Florence in March 1471, an event criticized by many Florentines because of the expense but also because the Medici–Milan alliance was becoming unpopular.[11]

Lorenzo tried to neutralize the opposition by reforming the Cento, the council entrusted in 1466 with electing the accoppiatori who in turn elected the Signoria. No longer trusting it to protect Medici interests, in July 1470 Lorenzo proposed removing the appointment of accoppiatori from the Cento and drawing future accoppiatori from among the forty or so persons who had held the office since 1434. The Cento rejected the idea, and, more surprisingly, the Medicean chancellor Bartolomeo Scala also criticized it. In January 1471 Lorenzo succeeded, this time with Soderini's support, in persuading the Cento to allow accoppiatori to be elected by their predecessors and the incumbent Signoria. Even so, Sacramoro and his duke were not happy with the occasional anti-Mediceans in the Signoria, and they urged Lorenzo to undertake a bolder reform of the regime's institutions. Sacramoro advised that "the security of the regime should outweigh the desire to appear too honourable."[12]

[9]   Ibid., p. 155.
[10]   P. Clarke, *Soderini and Medici*, pp. 180–96; Clarke, "Lorenzo de' Medici and Tommaso Soderini," in *Lorenzo de' Medici: studi*, ed. G. Garfagnini (Florence, 1992), pp. 67–101.
[11]   R. Fubini, "In margine all'edizione delle *Lettere* di Lorenzo de' Medici," in *Lorenzo de' Medici: studi*, pp. 168–77.
[12]   Clarke, *Soderini and Medici*, p. 204.

Lorenzo acted quickly. In July 1471 a strongly pro-Medici Signoria won the councils' approval, but over substantial opposition, for a balìa charged with making the Cento a more docile instrument of Medici (and Milanese) policy. Officially, the Signoria and accoppiatori selected the first forty members of the balìa, with whom they then appointed the remaining 200 members. According to Sacramoro, however, who probably had his say in the matter as well, Lorenzo picked the forty, including himself, Tommaso Soderini, and Mediceans from Luca Pitti to Matteo Palmieri: "from first to last," according to Sacramoro, "well chosen men," who, once they appointed the rest of the balìa, were made permanent members of the Cento, which thus became the malleable instrument that Lorenzo and his Milanese mentors desired. Now firmly under Medici control, the Cento received from the balìa exclusive authority to approve legislation on taxes, military matters, and elections. Two revolutionary changes occurred here: Lorenzo's forty handpicked permanent members of the Cento were in effect an unelected senate with life tenure; and the Cento's exclusive competence to approve crucial laws deprived the old communal Councils of the Popolo and the Commune of the last vestiges of their former legislative sovereignty. The balìa also held a general scrutiny, but the actual selection of officeholders was of course tightly controlled by accoppiatori, who mostly came from the handpicked forty and included Lorenzo himself. Although Lorenzo would find it necessary a decade later to perfect these reforms by instituting an entirely handpicked Council of Seventy, by 1471 the republican constitution was already an empty shell.

These reforms, however, could not prevent the rivalries and struggles for power that precipitated the worst moments of Lorenzo's period of leadership, the 1472 Volterra massacre and the 1478 Pazzi conspiracy and its violent aftermath. As shifting factions sought to detach Lorenzo from his Milanese protectors and undermine his influence, Lorenzo increasingly perceived any disagreement as a threat to his supremacy, causing him to react harshly and, in these two cases, with calamitous results. Both episodes show the underlying weakness and fundamental contradiction of the Medici system of governance. Because most Florentines were not ready to accept a principate and it was thus necessary to maintain the regime's republican trappings, Lorenzo had somehow to foster among the ottimati the illusion of a meaningful role in government. But what Lorenzo intended as window-dressing sustained among some ottimati a desire for a real share of power, something that Lorenzo (and his nervous Milanese backers) could never tolerate. Attempts to appease the ottimati regularly generated conflicts whose suppression only weakened their support for the regime. Moreover, the patronage system on which Medici power was built contained the seeds of instability in two senses. First, Lorenzo, even more than his grandfather, brooked no rivals as he sought to absorb the entire mechanism of patronage under his umbrella and become, in the suggestive expression of Benedetto Dei, "master of the shop [*maestro della bottega*]."[13] Accustomed to wielding influence as patrons in their own right, leaders of elite families found themselves reduced to the status of clients, or at best go-betweens, whose social prestige and political capital were undermined by humiliating dependence on a would-be prince young enough to be their son or grandson. Resentments of this sort motivated men like Tommaso Soderini and Jacopo Pazzi.[14] The second weakness of the Medici patronage network was that it necessarily discriminated between "ins" and "outs," putting some individuals and families closer to Lorenzo and his good graces than others, because he could not distribute favors equally to all. The effectiveness of patronage networks depended on that discrimination as a way of demonstrating and enacting their power in separating the inner circle from those at the edges and beyond. Visible distinctions between who did and did not enjoy the regime's favor inevitably produced disaffected outsiders. Aiming at a monopoly of power, the Medici denied political influence to anyone not in their favor and prohibited alternative patronage networks. Far from consolidating support for the regime, by marginalizing those who were not among Lorenzo's "friends" the patronage system forced them to look elsewhere, sometimes outside the city, for allies and friends. Once patronage became concentrated in one family, and indeed in a single "master of the shop" whose own major source of support lay outside the city, it began exporting internal rivalries and antagonisms, involving them in the riskier stakes of regional and Italian politics. Both the Volterra massacre and the Pazzi conspiracy had their origin in these dysfunctional aspects of the way the Medici used patronage as a means of holding power and trying to govern.

Lorenzo's Volterra Massacre

Although formally an autonomous commune, Volterra had long been under Florentine influence. A 1361 agreement gave Florence taxation rights and military control, including the office of captain, thereafter generally held by Florentine ottimati, who, as happened elsewhere in the dominion, developed patronage ties with prominent Volterrans, protected the city against infringements of rights or excessive taxes, and extended loans for tax debts. As these ties expanded, Florentine factional divisions were soon replicated in Volterran politics. When Volterra resisted the imposition of the Catasto in 1429, the

---

[13]   *Cronica*, ed. Barducci, p. 114.

[14]   F. W. Kent, "Patron–Client Networks in Renaissance Florence and the Emergence of Lorenzo as 'Maestro della Bottega'," in *Lorenzo de' Medici: New Perspectives*, ed. B. Toscani (New York, 1993), pp. 279–313.

Medici became its chief patrons and defenders, and after Cosimo achieved power the Florentine government cancelled all back taxes owed by the Volterrans. Volterra subsequently became a fertile field of patronage for several members of the family but also a site of rivalries that later developed within the regime.[15]

In 1470 alum was discovered on land owned by the commune of Volterra.[16] Alum was used in a variety of manufacturing processes, in particular for the dyeing of woolen cloth. A group of investors petitioned the Volterran priors for a lease to mine and sell alum; it was granted, but then contested by a subsequent committee of priors who claimed that the vote to approve it had been tainted by corruption and that a resource on public land ought to be exploited for the general benefit, not the profit of a private company. Some years earlier, when alum was discovered in papal territory, the Medici bank secured exclusive rights to purchase papal alum and sell it throughout Europe at prices kept high by their monopoly. Opponents of the Volterran lease contended that Lorenzo had organized the company in his clients' hands in order to control the new source and prevent increased supply from driving down prices. Opposition to the lease drew increasing support, especially when it became known that among the company's partners were two prominent Volterran allies of the Medici and a Florentine Medicean, Antonio Giugni. Since it was widely believed that the company represented Lorenzo's, and the Medici bank's, interest in controlling the alum market, the dispute became a test of strength between Mediceans and anti-Mediceans in both Florence and Volterra.

In June 1471 the Volterran government, now controlled by opponents of the lease, seized the mine and expelled its partners and workers. Florence's captain in Volterra, Ristoro Serristori, a Medici ally with two brothers in that year's balìa, wrote letters to Lorenzo and the Signoria (the latter sent first to Lorenzo for his approval) vociferously defending the company and denouncing the Volterrans, calling them "donkeys to be thrashed [*asini da bastonate*]" who needed a stern lesson for their insolence. He alerted Lorenzo to the political implications of the dispute, warning him that, just after the seizure and Volterra's appointment of envoys charged with defending its actions before the Florentine Signoria, in Volterra it was being "publicly said that what [its government] did was done with the advice and encouragement of leading citizens [in Florence], from whom they will always enjoy every favor. I write

---

[15] L. Fabbri, "Patronage and Its Role in Government: The Florentine Patriciate and Volterra," in *Florentine Tuscany*, ed. Connell and Zorzi, pp. 225–41.

[16] For what follows: E. Fiumi, *L'impresa di Lorenzo de' Medici contro Volterra (1472)* (Florence, 1948); R. Fubini, "Lorenzo de' Medici e Volterra," in Fubini, *Quattrocento fiorentino: politica, diplomazia, cultura* (Pisa, 1996), pp. 123–39.

this to you so that you will know how to proceed. They say that everyone is on their side except you and some crazy people." Several weeks later he commended Lorenzo for having finally "opened his eyes" to the danger and urged him to "recognize friends as friends and enemies as enemies."[17] These warnings got Lorenzo's attention and convinced him that prominent Florentines were using the issue to undermine him. In fact, the seizure of the mine occurred when the Florentine Standardbearer of Justice was Bardo Corsi, an ally and client of Jacopo Pazzi and an outspoken critic of the Milanese alliance.[18] Lorenzo saw these simultaneous challenges in Florence and Volterra as no coincidence, and this no doubt confirmed in him the necessity for a balìa, which came in July. After Lorenzo reinforced his control of key political institutions in Florence, Serristori punished four Volterrans for taking the alum mine.

Succeeding Serristori in October as captain in Volterra was Bernardo Corbinelli, who adopted a much more conciliatory approach. In fact, he was rebuked by the Signoria for failing to carry out its instructions and suspected of looking the other way when, in February 1472, angry Volterrans attacked and killed the two leading Volterran Mediceans among the company's partners. Their murder set in motion the recourse to a solution by force. The Volterrans introduced a militia into the city and appointed a committee for defense, which Corbinelli allowed and approved while also exiling several leaders of the local pro-Medici faction. Antonio Ridolfi, sent by the Florentine Signoria to restore order, sent back a reassuring picture of the situation denying that there was a crisis. Fearful of reprisals, the Volterran government dispatched emissaries to Florence to announce its willingness to restore the mine to the company. But Lorenzo had made up his mind, not only to recover the mine for his friends, but also to punish those who were using the dispute to weaken him politically. He rejected all appeals for compromise, both from the Volterrans, who even asked him to arbitrate the dispute, and from the Florentine bishop of Volterra, who wrote him several letters urging a peaceful settlement. What Lorenzo found intolerable was that leading Florentines were pursuing their own independent courses and policies in relations with the Volterrans, and he thus opted for a military strategy, both to punish the Volterrans and to convey a warning to uncooperative Florentine ottimati.

On April 30, 1472, Lorenzo's revamped Cento authorized the appointment of a war balìa. In order to mute criticism, Lorenzo carefully included among its twenty members, in addition of course to himself, Antonio Ridolfi, Bernardo Corbinelli, his occasional rivals Tommaso Soderini and Jacopo Pazzi (who had also advocated a peaceful solution), and other loyal allies and members of leading families (Pitti, Guicciardini, Serristori, Canigiani, and Gianfigliazzi).

[17]   Fiumi, *L'impresa*, pp. 88–95.
[18]   Fubini, "Lorenzo de' Medici e Volterra," pp. 132–3.

rans looked for allies beyond Tuscany, and he of
failed. Lorenzo engaged the services of the duke
e, Federico da Montefeltro, who led a combina-
Florentine and Milanese troops against Volterra
d possible sack, Volterra agreed on June 16 to a
licitly assured the town's safety with guarantees
tine government. But two days later, Federico's
ssacred an unrecorded number of citizens, and
vn.

rs the Milanese soldiers, still others the Volterran
k, but the Volterrans themselves blamed Lorenzo.
ar balìa had urged Federico and the Florentine
r at all costs, "with less regard for the safety of
in whatever way it takes. . . . Be determined to
ay, demonstrating with actions that, since they
have been unwilling to have compassion for their *patria*, they do not deserve
greater compassion from anyone else. . . . Make them understand their error
in not having had greater fear of a sack."[19] Lorenzo wanted an unconditional
surrender, with the safety of the town entirely at the discretion of Federico
and the commissioners, and after the event many Volterrans were convinced
they had been deliberately misled and betrayed, that the agreements had been
merely a ruse to get Federico's forces into the city for the town's castigation.
Federico claimed he was unable to control the soldiers, not all of whom were
his, but the Volterrans found that difficult to believe given that he limited the
sack to twelve hours and removed the army by the end of the awful day.
When he heard the news, Lorenzo claimed to be saddened and disturbed, and,
with the horror accomplished, he urged restraint. He decided that "we won't
say anything more about the sack, in order to forget it as quickly as possible.
Perhaps [the Volterrans] merited this because of some sin of theirs. We must
be content with our own conscience and the actions that we and this illustrious lord [Federico] took to prevent this evil from happening."[20] Chancellor
Scala delivered an oration of praise and congratulation for Federico in front
of the palace, but for decades thereafter chroniclers and poets wrote of the
massacre in anything but a celebratory mode. Francesco Guicciardini later
defended the commissioners, because his grandfather Jacopo was among them,
claiming that they tried to stop the violence and that the Florentines were
as distressed by the sack as they could possibly be.[21] Still later, Machiavelli

---

[19] Fiumi, *L'impresa*, p. 133.
[20] Ibid., p. 142.
[21] Francesco Guicciardini, *Storie fiorentine*, ed. A. Montevecchi (Milan, 1998), III,
p. 112; *The History of Florence*, trans. M. Domandi (New York, 1970), p. 26.

(*Florentine Histories* 7.30) wrote that the "news of this victory was received with great happiness by the Florentines; and because it had been entirely Lorenzo's undertaking [*tutta impresa di Lorenzo*], it greatly increased his reputation."

Pazzi Conspiracy and War

Between 1472 and 1478 Lorenzo and his regime were on a collision course with the papacy of Sixtus IV and with enemies both in and beyond Florence, a conflict that produced the most traumatic event in the fifteenth-century history of the Medici. Tensions grew between Lorenzo and a variety of antagonists, but with no single source.[22] Traditional frictions between Florence and the papacy over spheres of influence on their common border and ecclesiastical benefices were complicated by fissures within the regime, resentments over Lorenzo's tightening control of politics, patronage, and the local church, and increasing volatility in his relationship with the ottimati. At the same time the family banking empire entered into decline. Already in the mid-1460s Piero's foreclosure on a number of loans gave evidence of shrinking assets and inaugurated a policy of retrenchment that even reduced loans to the Sforza. General manager Sassetti decentralized the bank and allowed branches to pursue ventures more independently. But falling profits caused branches to close in Venice (for two years from 1469 to 1471 and again in 1481), Milan (1478), Avignon (1479), Bruges (1480), and London (1480). Only the Florence, Rome, Naples, and Geneva–Lyons branches remained after 1480. Whether because of poor management by Sassetti or neglect by Lorenzo, who was said to have little interest in its operations, the bank no longer provided the family with the financial resources it produced in Cosimo's time. Its supremacy even among Florentine banks was challenged by, among others, Filippo Strozzi and the Pazzi. The latter, whose resentment toward Lorenzo went back to 1471 when he had them punished in the scrutiny after Bardo Corsi criticized the Milanese alliance,[23] vied with the Medici for influence at the papal court and sought to replace them as the pope's bankers. Lorenzo's need for cash, even to keep the bank going, forced him to sell land in the Mugello, to borrow money from, of all people, the former exile Strozzi, and, in the 1480s, to divert public monies for his private use.[24]

[22] The best overall treatment is L. Martines, *April Blood: Florence and the Plot Against the Medici* (Oxford, 2003); see also J. Hook, *Lorenzo de' Medici: An Historical Biography* (London, 1984), pp. 73–117.
[23] R. Fubini, "La congiura dei Pazzi: radici politico-sociali e ragioni di un fallimento," in *Lorenzo de' Medici: New Perspectives*, ed. Toscani, pp. 219–47.
[24] De Roover, *Medici Bank*, pp. 358–75.

Meanwhile, relations worsened with Sixtus IV (Francesco della Rovere), his nephew Giuliano della Rovere (later Pope Julius II), and Sixtus's nephews in the Riario family, to which the pope was related through his sister. Sixtus sought more effective papal control over the semi-autonomous towns and principalities of the papal states, many of which had agreements with Florence that kept them within a Florentine sphere of influence. When Florence assisted the ruler of Città di Castello in Umbria in resisting papal forces, Sixtus pointedly blamed Lorenzo. The pope was also determined to wrest control of Imola, northeast of Florence in the Romagna, from Milan, but when Galeazzo Maria offered to sell Imola to Florence, and Lorenzo agreed, Sixtus loudly protested that the city was within the papal states and threatened a series of spiritual and temporal penalties that persuaded Galeazzo Maria to yield Imola to the papacy for 40,000 ducats. Sixtus put Lorenzo, still the pope's banker, in an impossible position by asking him to lend funds for the purchase. Knowing he would be severely criticized if he financed a papal acquisition against Florentine territorial interests, Lorenzo replied that he lacked such funds (which, given the weakness of the bank, could have been true) and also asked the Pazzi not to give Sixtus the money. Not only did the Pazzi do so, they also revealed to Sixtus what Lorenzo had requested of them, and the pope retaliated by depriving the Medici of the office of Depositary of the Apostolic Camera, thus removing the papal account from their bank. As the Medici and their domestic rivals increasingly looked to foreign powers in their search for allies and friends in the larger world of Italian politics, local antagonisms became potentially explosive.

Disputes over church offices, another important arena of patronage, were also a source of tension. Florentine governments had always wanted men of proven loyalty in the dominion's seven bishoprics, Fiesole, Pistoia, Volterra, Arezzo, Cortona, Pisa, and above all Florence. Popular governments had earlier tried to prevent the elite from exploiting the powerful office by prohibiting the election of Florentines to the Florentine diocese, but by the fifteenth century the ban had been relaxed and popes appointed a mix of Florentines and foreigners. Giovanni Dietisalvi-Neroni, whose candidacy Eugenius rejected in 1445, finally became archbishop of Florence in 1462,[25] just in time to become an embarrassment to the regime when his brother emerged as a leader of the anti-Medici movement. Giovanni was hustled off to Rome and, although Pope Paul II refused to replace him, he never again set foot in his diocese. This awkward situation no doubt underscored for Lorenzo the importance of selecting bishops carefully. Moreover, to protect his influence at the papal court and access to the favors crucial to Medici patronage, Lorenzo wanted

---

[25] Peterson, "An Episcopal Election," in *Popes, Teachers, and Canon Law*, ed. Sweeney and Chodorow, pp. 300–25.

a Florentine cardinal of his own choosing to safeguard his interests. He expressed this wish shortly after Sixtus IV's accession in 1471, but the pope politely brushed aside the suggested candidacy of Lorenzo's brother Giuliano. When Archbishop Neroni died in 1473, Sixtus appointed his nephew Pietro Riario to the Florentine see, but Riario died a year later. By then the rift between Lorenzo and Sixtus had become irreparable over Imola, where the pope installed as ruler his other Riario nephew Girolamo, who loathed Lorenzo for his attempt to thwart papal acquisition of the city. Sixtus then selected for the vacant Florentine archbishopric Francesco Salviati, a Florentine but a close curial ally of the Riario and first cousin to Jacopo Pazzi. Lorenzo had the Signoria refuse Salviati's appointment and champion instead the candidacy of Rinaldo Orsini, brother of his wife Clarice. Sixtus yielded and appointed Orsini, but refused to make him a cardinal. If Lorenzo failed to get his cardinal, he at least got a brother-in-law archbishop. Orsini remained in the post for the next thirty years but hardly ever appeared in the city and left the administration of the see in the hands of Lorenzo and his inner circle.[26]

Although Lorenzo succeeded in the appointment of Orsini, the defeat of Salviati's candidacy was yet another of the seeds of the conspiracy. Soon thereafter, the Medici bishop of Pisa died, and Sixtus, now openly at odds with Lorenzo, poked him in the eye by naming Salviati to the second most important episcopal see in the Florentine dominion. There was even some speculation that he would make Salviati a cardinal and destroy Lorenzo's hopes for a cardinal protector in Rome. But Lorenzo, again with the docile cooperation of the Signoria, refused for three years to allow Salviati to take possession of the Pisan see. When Lorenzo explained to the duke of Milan that the reason for this refusal was that Salviati had influential supporters in Florence, he acknowledged that at the heart of the dispute were divisions within the city and regime. Writing to Galeazzo Maria in December 1474 to ask for his support in the controversy, Lorenzo protested the "injustice and wrong" done to him by the pope, "who is offended, as far as I understand, for no other reason than that Francesco Salviati has been denied possession of the archbishopric of Pisa; and for this offence, if it is an offence, and which has been done by the entire city, [the pope] wants to take revenge against me alone." Lorenzo admitted that, if he had so wished, he could have pulled strings and put Salviati in office, "but I'm not inclined to permit such public humiliation for my own personal interest, for this city does not deserve such a thing from me." Lorenzo thus neatly reversed the relationship of public and private interests in the affair, for the government had in fact been acting on *his* determination to keep Salviati out of Pisa. "What makes this even more

[26] Fubini, "La congiura dei Pazzi," in *Lorenzo de' Medici: New Perspectives*, ed. Toscani, pp. 226–31.

difficult," he continued, "is that the pope loves a citizen of ours, as messer Francesco Salviati certainly is, who has deceived the city and acted against the wishes of our Signoria, more than he loves the honor of the whole city." He then came to the core of the matter: "what is especially important to me and to our entire regime [*stato*] is that there are some citizens here" (presumably Salviati's Pazzi in-laws) "who claim that this [campaign in Rome to secure Salviati in the Pisan see] is their own undertaking, and they've let the pope know that they'll keep on working, whether I like it or not," to bring about a resolution in Salviati's favor.

What troubled Lorenzo was less the prospect of Salviati as archbishop of Pisa than the fear that influential rivals within Florence might bring this about over and above his wishes. As he put it, again to the duke of Milan a few days later, the fact that the pope "received letters from many [Florentines] on Salviati's behalf seems to me the reason why, more than any other, he should be denied the possession [of the see]. For, since the Signoria and the men of the regime have determined that they do not want this, those who do want it and have written [to the pope] about it must be men who do not see eye-to-eye with those who govern, and it would seem strange indeed in a city as untrustworthy as Pisa to have [a bishop] agreeable to the latter and not to [the men of] the government." How, he asked rhetorically, could he possibly "support Salviati, so powerfully protected by his friends and relatives, once the pope had been told, in order to get him to confer the benefice on Salviati, that he would get possession of the diocese whether other citizens [i.e., Lorenzo and the regime] liked it or not?" A year later he explained (still to Galeazzo Maria) his continuing resistance to pressures from Rome by observing that Salviati was "bound to the Pazzi by marriage ties and obligations of friendship" and was "very much their thing," and that, if he (Lorenzo) relented, "what seems most important to me is that this would enhance the prestige of the Pazzi and do the opposite for me."[27] It was thus another test of Lorenzo's strength: at stake in essence was his ability to impose his will on his domestic rivals. Lorenzo could not tolerate a prelate in Pisa whose Florentine supporters were challenging his own power and whose protectors in Rome were his ever more declared enemies.

In the end, Lorenzo relented and agreed to Salviati's appointment in return for promises, later disputed, that no bishops would be appointed within the Florentine dominions without the consent of the Signoria and that a Florentine cardinal would be forthcoming. Although Sixtus and Girolamo Riario got Imola, and Salviati got his bishopric, the coalescing resentments generated by

[27]   Lorenzo de' Medici, *Lettere*, vol. II, ed. R. Fubini (Florence, 1977), pp. 58–9, 69–71, 124; N. Rubinstein, "Lorenzo de' Medici: The Formation of His Statecraft," in *Lorenzo de' Medici: studi*, pp. 54–6.

Lorenzo's resistance to both produced the plot, apparently hatched in Rome as early as 1475, to kill Lorenzo and Giuliano and terminate the Medici regime. Galeazzo Maria sent Lorenzo a number of warnings that something was afoot (and then, ironically, himself fell victim to an entirely separate assassination plot in 1476). Initially, the Pazzi, or at least Jacopo, the family's leader, were reluctant to take part, but they may have been goaded into doing so by an inexplicable provocation from Lorenzo. One of the Pazzi was married to a Borromei woman whose father died without sons or a will; the Pazzi assumed that his estate would be inherited by his daughter and thus come under the control of her Pazzi husband. But in 1476 Lorenzo had a law passed, retroactively valid, affirming that, in the absence of male children and in cases of intestacy, other male relatives (in this case the father's nephews) would have priority over daughters as heirs. The enraged Pazzi joined the conspiracy, together with Francesco Salviati, Girolamo Riario, Riario's military captain Giovanbattista da Montesecco, Jacopo Bracciolini (son of former chancellor Poggio), Pope Sixtus (who insisted, however, that he wanted no bloodshed), and Duke Federico of Urbino,[28] who just a few years earlier had done Lorenzo's dirty work for him in Volterra. Lurking in the shadows of the plot was also King Ferrante of Naples. After rejecting several plans, they decided to assassinate Lorenzo and Giuliano at the family palace on Sunday April 26, 1478, but at the last moment, realizing that Giuliano would not be present, the assault was relocated to the cathedral. And when Giovanbattista da Montesecco, designated as Lorenzo's assassin, changed his mind and refused to kill in church, he was replaced by two priests, one from Volterra, who, according to Poliziano, was motivated by the hatred that all Volterrans felt for Lorenzo.[29] Giuliano was killed; Lorenzo, slightly wounded, took refuge in the north sacristy and then fled back up via Larga to the family palace to rally his supporters.

In an uproar of confusion, the city was "bewildered with terror," according to the diarist Luca Landucci, a non-elite apothecary with no connection to the regime.[30] Salviati tried to seize the palace of the priors, but the Signoria, informed just in time, fended him off and retained control. Jacopo Pazzi, realizing that a popular uprising was the only hope of saving the day, rode into the piazza to rally the crowd with cries of "popolo e libertà," but the

---

[28]   R. Fubini, *Federico da Montefeltro e la congiura dei Pazzi: politica e propaganda alla luce di nuovi documenti* (Rome, 1986); M. Simonetta, "Federico da Montefeltro contro Firenze: retroscena inediti della congiura dei Pazzi," *ASI* 161 (2003): 261–84.

[29]   Poliziano, *Coniurationis commentarium*, ed. Perosa; trans. Watkins and Marsh, in Watkins, *Humanism and Liberty*, pp. 171–83 (173).

[30]   Luca Landucci, *Diario fiorentino dal 1450 al 1516*, ed. I. Del Badia (Florence, 1883; repr. Florence, 1969), p. 20; trans. A. De Rosen Jervis, *A Florentine Diary from 1450 to 1516* (London, 1927), p. 17.

ground had not been prepared for such an appeal, and when the city learned that Lorenzo was alive and that the conspirators had attempted to assault the government palace as well as the Medici brothers, no one dared side with failed conspirators who were already being mercilessly hunted down. Medici armed guards and pro-Medici mobs seized the plotters and began executing them on the spot. Guicciardini estimated that fifty people were killed that day, many hanged from the windows of the palace. "I do not believe," he commented, "that Florence had ever seen a day of such torment." The search for, and punishment of, the conspirators and anyone with any connection to them went on for weeks. Lorenzo even had one of those who escaped tracked down and returned from Constantinople to be hanged. Altogether more than eighty people were executed, many innocent of any involvement, some only because they were members of a family now damned in perpetuity. The Pazzi were destroyed, their property confiscated, the survivors forced to change their name, and daughters and sisters of the executed and exiled forbidden to marry for many years.

Writing thirty years later and after the fall of the regime, Guicciardini cheekily pointed to the irony in the conspiracy's outcome: although it nearly cost Lorenzo both his life and "lo stato," it nonetheless "gave him such a reputation and such advantages that one could say it was a most happy day for him. His brother Giuliano, with whom he would have had to share his wealth and compete for power in the regime, was dead. His enemies were gloriously removed through the power of the state, as were the shadows of doubt and suspicion that had previously followed him. The people took up arms on his behalf, and on that day they finally recognized him as *padrone* of the city and gave him, at public expense, the privilege of going about with as many armed guards as he wished for his personal security. And in effect he so thoroughly took control of the regime [*stato*] that he thereafter emerged, freely and completely, as arbiter and almost as lord [*signore*] of the city. The great but insecure power that he had had until that day now became very great and secure." Guicciardini finished his account with some thoughts about "civil discords": they end with the elimination of one faction, the victor becomes lord of the city, "his supporters and companions become his subjects, and the people and the multitude become enslaved. The *stato* is handed on as an inheritance and often passes from a wise man to a madman who pushes the city over the edge."[31]

Sixtus and Ferrante immediately declared war. On June 1 Sixtus excommunicated Lorenzo for the execution of Archbishop Salviati, a crime against Holy Church, said the pope, and ordered the Signoria to deliver him to Rome.

---

[31] Guicciardini, *Storie fiorentine*, IV, pp. 117–27 (124, 126–7); *History of Florence*, trans. Domandi, pp. 29–36 (34–6).

When it refused, he placed the city under an interdict on June 22. Ferrante sent troops into Florentine territory, commanded by his son Alfonso, duke of Calabria, and by Federico of Urbino, who quickly seized several towns. Lasting a year and a half, the war was fought both on the battlefield and on the turf of public opinion. In a letter of July 7 to the priors and people of Florence, Sixtus affirmed his love for the "Florentine community" and asserted that his only purpose was to punish Lorenzo and liberate Florence from his tyranny: since it was the "iniquity of Lorenzo and his accomplices" that disturbed the peace of Italy and made it impossible to unite against the common enemy (the Turks), Sixtus urged the Florentines to join him in restoring their liberty and ending the "tyranny of one man."[32] In other pronouncements Sixtus fulminated against the execution of Salviati as a crime that merited both the excommunication and the interdict. Among the Florentine government's responses were public letters written by chancellor Scala[33] and at least ten legal opinions (*consilia*) commissioned from Italy's most famous professors of law, who argued that it was the Signoria, not Lorenzo, that put Salviati to death, that the punishment was fully justified as an act of self-defense because Salviati was not dressed in ecclesiastical robes when he assaulted the palace, and that the pope's condemnations were invalid because he had acted arbitrarily and in violation of due process. In one of the earliest political uses of print technology, several of these texts, and at least one of Scala's letters, were printed and disseminated in a propaganda war for public opinion all over Italy.[34]

Military operations came closer to Florence than any since the Milanese incursions into Tuscany in the 1390s. A war committee (the Dieci) was instituted, with Lorenzo as one of its members (his first executive office). Initial setbacks were followed by some successes, but by November 1479 enemy troops had occupied a good part of the southern portion of the dominion, including the important towns of Castellina in Chianti, Poggibonsi, Certaldo, and Colle Valdelsa. Florence sought help from Venice and Milan, but Venice was occupied with the Turks and Milan was in the throes of political crisis following Galeazzo Maria's assassination and no longer a stable ally. Even after Lodovico il Moro, the murdered duke's brother, seized power from Galeazzo Maria's widow and her chief minister Cicco Simonetta in the summer of 1479 and declared his support for the Florentines, Milanese military help was still meager. Florence was largely alone in its war against Naples and the papacy, and, with territory being lost and treasure consumed, some in Florence began to accept Sixtus's argument that the republic was fighting only

---

[32] F. Di Benedetto, "Un breve di Sisto IV contro Lorenzo," *ASI* 150 (1992): 371–84.

[33] Bartolomeo Scala, *Humanistic and Political Writings*, ed. A. Brown (Tempe, Ariz., 1997), pp. 195–202; Di Benedetto, "Un breve di Sisto IV," pp. 376–81.

[34] K. Pennington, *The Prince and the Law, 1200–1600* (Berkeley, 1993), pp. 238–68.

to protect Lorenzo from papal wrath. Desire for peace was growing, and Lorenzo feared, as Guicciardini later put it, that "the citizens might deprive him of *lo stato*" in order to end the war. With Sixtus's enmity undiminished and Florence's allies unable or unwilling to help, the only solution was a separate deal with Naples. Lorenzo opened unofficial and secret negotiations with the dukes of Calabria and Urbino through personal emissaries, chiefly Giuliano Gondi and later Filippo Strozzi, whose ties in Naples forged over decades now helped to save the very regime that had kept him in exile there. By November, just when the military situation reached a low point for Florence, the outline of a settlement was reached.

Lorenzo then made the dramatic decision to go to Naples, with assurances of course that he would be welcomed and his personal safety guaranteed. On December 5 he had the Signoria and Dieci convene a pratica of forty leading citizens to inform them (without asking their opinion) that he was leaving the next morning for Naples. In Guicciardini's version of the speech, Lorenzo says that this was the only way to find out if the king and the pope were sincere in claiming that they were fighting him and not Florence: if it were so, they would have him, and the war would end; if not, he would find out what they really wanted and negotiate a settlement. He knew it would be dangerous, he said, but he was willing to take the risk because he placed the public welfare before any private good and because he recognized that the obligation that all citizens have to their *patria* was even greater in his case because of the greater benefits and status he enjoyed. He hoped that those assembled would not fail to "protect the *stato* and his position" in his absence and he "commended himself, his house, and his family" to them.[35] Lorenzo was confessing his vulnerability and acknowledging his dependence on the ottimati's willingness to remain loyal to him even as opposition to the war was beginning to erode his power. The real risk he faced was less whatever danger might lurk in Naples than the possibility that in his absence sentiment, even within the regime, might turn against him.[36] Once outside Florence he wrote to the dukes of Calabria and Urbino to inform them of his movements, to Florence's allies, the duke of Ferrara and Marquis of Mantua, to the Venetian, Ferrarese, and Milanese ambassadors in Florence to explain what he knew would be cause for anger in Venice and Milan, and to the Florentine Signoria repeating what he had said to the pratica before his departure.[37] The Dieci wanted to confer

---

[35] Guicciardini, *Storie fiorentine*, VI, pp. 142–3.
[36] N. Rubinstein, "Le origini della missione di Lorenzo a Napoli," in Lorenzo de' Medici, *Lettere*, vol. 4, ed. N. Rubinstein (Florence, 1981), pp. 391–400; Rubinstein, "Lorenzo and the Formation of His Statecraft," in *Lorenzo de' Medici: studi*, pp. 56–66.
[37] *Lettere*, vol. 4, pp. 249–69; English translation in C. M. Ady, *Lorenzo dei Medici and Renaissance Italy* (New York, 1962), pp. 74–5.

upon him a formal mandate to go to Naples and negotiate peace as their legal representative and that of the "whole people and commune of Florence." Another version of the mandate, drafted by chancellor Scala, said that he "should give much greater preference to the public interest [than to his own private interest]" and indeed "forget his own in order to consult the public interest."[38] Although Scala urged him to accept the mandate as the "honorable" thing to do, Lorenzo declined and preferred to act in a private capacity, perhaps in order to maintain a freer hand in the negotiations, perhaps also because he feared that the Cento, which ratified such mandates, might not approve this one in the face of growing opposition to him and "his" war.[39]

While he was in Naples, members of the inner circle warned Lorenzo that there was talk of political change. "Many different thoughts and words," wrote Scala in January 1480, "are being expressed both by your friends and by all manner of people." In February Scala told him there was discussion of a change of regime and offered the advice that "it is essential for you to be here, so that in procuring peace down there you don't find yourself with a worse war on your hands here." Antonio Pucci similarly judged that "your departure has upset everything and made our situation here worse."[40] According to Guicciardini, what many saw as Lorenzo's rash act of "throwing himself into Ferrante's arms" and the possibility that he might not even return encouraged some to speak ill of the governing inner circle and to complain that political offices and taxes should not be controlled by such a small number. Even more ominously, "many members of families of the regime" were contemplating "new arrangements," even promoting Girolamo Morelli as an alternative to Lorenzo. Morelli, the grandson of a brother of Giovanni Morelli, is mentioned by Guicciardini among the men from outside the elite raised to prominence by Lorenzo. He was Florentine ambassador to Milan for much of 1479, lauded by the Milanese to Lorenzo as a "sincere, beloved, and cordial friend" whom they were very sorry to see leave his post,[41] and indeed, so says Guicciardini, "so powerful that Lorenzo feared him."[42] These tantalizing suggestions of gathering opposition to Lorenzo point to disaffection among both elite families and regime members of lower social status often resented by the elite. In early 1480 "friends of the regime" judged it difficult merely to keep it going without a revolution and did all they could to have loyal priorates placed in office until Lorenzo's return.

[38] *Lettere*, vol. 4, pp. 367–8; Scala, *Humanistic and Political Writings*, ed. Brown, pp. 203–4.
[39] A. Brown, *Bartolomeo Scala, 1430–1497, Chancellor of Florence: The Humanist as Bureaucrat* (Princeton, N.J., 1979), pp. 90–3.
[40] Ibid., pp. 95–6.
[41] *Lettere*, vol. 4, p. 245, n. 9.
[42] Guicciardini, *Storie fiorentine*, VI, p. 145; IX, pp. 179–80.

In Naples Lorenzo discovered that the settlement tentatively agreed to by his emissaries was not definitive for Ferrante, who dragged out the negotiations and kept his guest in Naples for longer than Lorenzo expected.[43] Ferrante had the problem of placating Sixtus, who wanted no peace that kept Lorenzo in power, and, according to Guicciardini, the king delayed a settlement in order to allow time for a change of regime in Florence. For this reason Lorenzo's friends urged him to conclude matters if possible but in any case to return without delay. Lorenzo pressed for three things: complete restoration of Florentine territories; protection from papal aggression for Florentine allies in the Romagna (even though their cities were formally papal territory); and cancellation of Sixtus's demand that Lorenzo go to Rome and humble himself before the pope. Worried that matters in Florence were slipping from his control, Lorenzo came away with no guarantees on any of these points. But by February, Ferrante, now worried about a possible Angevin expedition from France to reclaim Naples, was suddenly eager to wrap up negotiations by giving unofficial assurances that Florence would regain its territories and that the Romagna lords would be shielded. The peace treaty still required that Lorenzo beg the pope's forgiveness in person,[44] but when the Ottomans attacked and occupied the port of Otranto in Puglia in the summer of 1480, Ferrante withdrew his forces from Tuscany, allowing the Florentines to reoccupy most of their territory, and Sixtus, anxious for the support of all the Italian states against the Ottomans, agreed to receive a delegation of Florentines without Lorenzo and allowed them to ask forgiveness on behalf of the Florentine people.

The (Insecure) Prince in All but Name

Although, as Guicciardini observed, the terms of peace more nearly resembled conditions usually imposed on those who lose wars, Lorenzo nonetheless returned in triumph in March 1480 to a city hungry for peace and a regime desperately glad to have him back. There had been no revolution, perhaps not even the beginnings of organized opposition during his absence. But Lorenzo was aware of the murmurings, and without delay he and his inner circle decided on yet another series of reforms to narrow the regime to the ever smaller group of those he trusted. In early April the priorate asked the councils for a balìa which passed by only one vote in the Cento and narrow margins in the other councils. Instead of carrying out its assigned tasks in the areas of

---

[43] L. De Angelis, "Lorenzo a Napoli: progetti di pace e conflitti politici dopo la congiura dei Pazzi," *ASI* 150 (1992): 385–421.
[44] *Lettere*, vol. 4, pp. 377–89 (381).

fiscal reform and elections (it never even held the promised general scrutiny), the balìa strengthened the regime by creating a new council, the Seventy, to which it entrusted an unprecedented combination of executive, legislative, and electoral powers. The Seventy were given final say on proposals to be submitted to the councils, thus replacing the Signoria in this crucial executive function. From its own membership it elected two new executive committees, the Otto di Pratica, which replaced the Dieci in foreign policy, and the Dodici Procuratori, who oversaw finances and the Monte. Their deliberations required approval from the Seventy, which thus superseded the Cento as the most important legislative body. Also entrusted to the Seventy were *a mano* elections of the Signoria and the appointment of the security and police magistracy of the Otto di Guardia. The Seventy thus became the "supreme agency of control" and "the principal organ for all important decisions." Never before had the different functions of government been so exclusively concentrated in one body. Moreover, the Seventy were to remain in office for five years: Guicciardini called it a "consiglio a vita," a senate with life tenure. In 1484 the three older councils of the Popolo, Commune, and Cento renewed the Seventy and its powers for another five years by comfortable but not overwhelming margins. Subsequent renewals occurred in 1489 and 1493, but this last, after Lorenzo's death, encountered serious opposition and gained two-thirds majorities with only three votes to spare in the Popolo, eleven in the Commune, and one in the Cento: clear evidence of the anti-Medici sentiment that was to erupt in the next year. But while Lorenzo was alive the Seventy governed with little opposition.[45]

The Seventy consisted of the balìa's first thirty members, selected by the Signoria, and forty others, all *veduti* Standardbearers of Justice, selected by the thirty. Sixty-five of the first Seventy had at one time or another served on a Medici balìa. Lorenzo was of course among the first thirty, who also included Tommaso Soderini, members of elite families (Capponi, Guicciardini, Ridolfi, Davanzati, Gianfigliazzi, Tornabuoni) and several non-elite characterized by Guicciardini as those who "would have had no influence without [Lorenzo's] support": Bernardo Buongirolami, Antonio Pucci, Girolamo Morelli, and two powerful insiders from lower-class backgrounds, Bernardo del Nero and Antonio di Bernardo di Miniato Dini, the minor guildsman who administered the Monte. Among the forty they appointed were members of elite families (Capponi, Corsini, Vettori, Pitti, Salviati, Rucellai, Albizzi, Valori) and more non-elite Medici clients: Giovanni Bonsi, Pierfilippo Pandolfini, and relatives of influential Medici insiders Giovanni Lanfredini, Agnolo Niccolini, and Cosimo Bartoli. In 1489 the roster of Seventy shows a similar mix. Official sources do not of course reveal the extent of Lorenzo's influence in these

---

[45]   Rubinstein, *Government*, pp. 228–30, 238–41.

selections. But because it was said (by the Milanese ambassador) that Lorenzo himself named the first forty members of the balìa of 1471, and because, according to Piero Guicciardini, Lorenzo also handpicked the members of the regime's last scrutiny council in 1484, it seems probable that he, perhaps with his inner circle of advisers, also chose the Seventy.[46]

Lorenzo's power in the 1480s was unprecedented in Florence and perhaps unmatched even by some of Italy's princes. No one held or even became eligible for important offices without his approval. No action or communication was undertaken by the foreign policy magistracy without his instructions. Lorenzo controlled fiscal policy through his "minister" of the Monte and placed himself on the powerful committee of the Seventeen Reformers both times it was appointed, in 1481–2 and 1490–1, with wide-ranging powers over finances and economic policy. With his influence on this committee, he took substantial public funds (by one calculation, over 50,000 florins) for his personal needs and got his hands on still more from various communal accounts, while his Monte officials withheld interest payments from citizens.[47] Elite families did not contract marriage alliances of which he did not approve. Intervening in the administration of justice, he compelled magistracies to carry out punishments on his orders. In 1488, for example, when a large crowd pleaded for mercy on behalf of a man sentenced to death by the Otto di Guardia for killing one of their staff, Lorenzo intervened on the spot and ordered that the execution take place immediately. He also ordered the seizure, torture, and exile of four people from the crowd who had encouraged the condemned man to escape.[48] These were the powers of a prince above the law.

But he was also an insecure prince who trusted fewer and fewer people and needed ever more arbitrary and personal power to compensate for the increasing fragility of his support. In the early 1480s several members of elite families were accused of conspiring against the regime or trying to kill Lorenzo. In 1481 members of the Frescobaldi, Baldovinetti, and Balducci confessed to a plan to murder him and were hanged. In 1484 a young Tornabuoni (Lorenzo's mother's family) was exiled to Sicily "because," as Landucci reported, "it was said that he had designs against Lorenzo. . . . Perhaps it wasn't so; I'm saying what people said in the city."[49] Frequent rumors, accusations, and confessions of plots against him no doubt gave Lorenzo good reason to seek security in greater controls at every level: within his inner circle; within the regime as

[46]   Ibid., pp. 227–8, 233, 244, 255, 359–63.
[47]   A. Brown, "Lorenzo, The Monte and the Seventeen Reformers: Public and Private Interest," in Brown, *The Medici in Florence*, pp. 151–211.
[48]   Brown, "Lorenzo and Public Opinion," in *Lorenzo il Magnifico e il suo mondo*, ed. Garfagnini, pp. 76–7.
[49]   Landucci, *Diario*, pp. 36, 38, 40, 48.

embodied by the Council of Seventy; in the scrutinies and elections of the Signoria; in the dominion; and in all the magistracies, courts, and councils of government. He sought such power because, among both old ottimati families and the popolo, acquiescence in Lorenzo's veiled principate was becoming more reluctant. Lorenzo knew that Alamanno Rinuccini, whose dialogue *On Liberty*, written after the Pazzi conspiracy and its bloody suppression, openly denounced him as a tyrant and detailed his abuses of power and corruption of communal institutions, was not the only member of the elite who thought he had gone too far.[50] He had fewer opportunities to hear or read the views of the popolo but was aware that the priorate of July 1482, whose proposal that the councils prohibit tax concessions to "private persons" was an obvious rebuke of Lorenzo's manipulation of the Monte, included Piero Parenti,[51] son of Marco. Piero was subsequently excluded from major offices for the remaining twelve years of the regime,[52] presumably for his part in this slap at Lorenzo. Growing resentment among ottimati and popolo toward Lorenzo's princely pretensions caused him to turn elsewhere and to ground his, his family's, and the regime's security in new foundations: in secretaries and bureaucrats from outside the elite, men beholden to him alone; in patronage networks in the cities and towns of the dominion; in a new politics of ritual and charisma directed at the lower classes; in marriage alliances with aristocratic families throughout Italy; and, not least, in the church. The most innovative dimensions of Lorenzo's style of governance lay in his cultivation of these new sources of power.

Guicciardini says Lorenzo favored "those from whom he believed he had nothing to fear because they lacked family connections and prestige," that he worried that men with great reputations and extensive family connections (his example is Tommaso Soderini) might become too powerful and prevent him from being "arbitro" of the city, and that he used to say that if his father had adopted a similar policy he would not have come so dangerously close to losing everything in 1466. Guicciardini, who belonged to the elite that Lorenzo increasingly mistrusted, thought that the most "oppressive and harmful" aspect of Lorenzo's character was suspicion and mistrust, which he attributed to his awareness of the need to "keep down a free city in which it was necessary to conduct public business through the magistrates, according to the statutes, and with the appearance and form of liberty." For Guicciardini, ottimati were the natural guardians of this liberty, and he equated "keeping down a free city" with Lorenzo's attempts to "keep down as much as he could all those

[50]   Ed. F. Adorno in *Atti e memorie dell'Accademia Toscana di Scienze e Lettere "La Colombaria"* 22 (1957): 270–303; trans. Watkins, *Humanism and Liberty*, pp. 193–224.
[51]   Brown, "Seventeen Reformers," pp. 177–81.
[52]   See Matucci's introduction to Parenti's *Storia fiorentina*, p. xiii.

citizens who he knew were esteemed because of their nobility, wealth, power, or reputation." Although Lorenzo gave these men, provided they were loyal to the regime, offices, ambassadorships, and similar honors, he "nonetheless did not trust them." Thus it was to men who owed their reputation to him, and "who would have had no standing without his support, that he entrusted control of scrutinies and taxes and to whom he confided his innermost secrets." Guicciardini lists ten such men: Bernardo Buongirolami (who made his family's first appearance in the priorate in 1467); Antonio Pucci (whose family had hitched its wagon to Cosimo's star before 1434, when they were minor guildsmen and neighbors); Agnolo Niccolini; Bernardo del Nero (a minor guildsman, but powerful member of the inner circle, member of the Seventy in 1489, and Guicciardini's later choice as spokesman and defender of the Medici in his *Dialogue on the Government of Florence*); Pierfilippo Pandolfini (on the Seventy in both 1480 and 1489); Giovanni Lanfredini (director of the bank's Venice branch in 1471–80, among Lorenzo's most important emissaries, and on the Seventy in 1489); Girolamo Morelli, Piero Alamanni, Giovanni Bonsi (on the Seventy in 1480); and Cosimo Bartoli. Guicciardini saw them all as social parvenus, but he was even more irritated by the prominence of three others: Antonio di Miniato Dini, whose authority over the Monte was such that "one could say he governed two-thirds of the city," and who sat on the Seventy in 1489; the notary Giovanni Guidi ("son of a notary from Pratovecchio who enjoyed so much of Lorenzo's favor that, having held all the other offices . . . he might have become Standardbearer of Justice"), who headed the chancery office that drafted legislation and was said to have selected the scrutiny committee of 1484 together with Lorenzo; and Bartolomeo Scala, "the son of a miller from Colle [Valdelsa]," who was made Standardbearer of Justice because he was chancellor, to the outrage and indignation of all "men of worth [*uomini da bene*]." Thus, Guicciardini concluded, although "men of worth" had some role in politics, there were so many "middling men [*uomini mezzani*]" in the councils and key offices that oversaw electoral and fiscal matters (and with whom Lorenzo had established secret understandings) that one could say that they, and not the old elite, were "lords of the game [*signori del giuoco*]."[53]

Behind even these newcomers there emerged under Lorenzo a new species of secretary, mostly notaries, who served as personal chancellors or secretaries to Lorenzo, occasionally accompanied ambassadors and even wrote their letters, engaged in unofficial, secret negotiations on Lorenzo's behalf (sometimes without the knowledge of the appointed ambassador), became secretaries to powerful committees like the Otto di Pratica, and were entirely and always

---

[53] Guicciardini, *Storie fiorentine*, III, pp. 110–11; IX, 179–81; *History of Florence*, trans. Domandi, pp. 25, 74–5.

Lorenzo's men. Niccolò Michelozzi, a humanist and son of Cosimo's favorite architect, became Lorenzo's personal chancellor and adviser to his son Piero and remained a loyal Medicean through the years of their exile, eventually replacing Machiavelli in the chancery when the Medici were restored in 1512. Most came from the subject territories, the best known being Piero Dovizi da Bibbiena and his brother Bernardo, the future cardinal and playwright. Piero Dovizi served as tutor to Lorenzo's children, and later became Piero de' Medici's chief secretary. Bernardo also began as secretary to Lorenzo and tutor to his son Giovanni, in whose service he remained as secretary and adviser when Giovanni became a cardinal. Lacking much connection to Florentine political traditions, loyal only to the masters they served, and perceived by the ottimati as ambitious, arrogant, and irreverent, these secretaries were among the earliest voices of an emerging view of politics in which fulfillment of their masters' personal ambitions was the highest goal. Lorenzo's confidence in them angered the ottimati, and several were reviled and exiled in the anti-Medici fervor of 1494.[54]

Like other elite families, the Medici cultivated patronage ties with the provincial elites, ecclesiastical and philanthropic institutions, and governments of the dominion cities. Such ties developed when elite Florentines served as podestà or captains in the subject towns, presiding over courts, police, and defense. If several family members formed good relations over time with particular cities, its citizens came to regard them as protectors and patrons, typically appealing to them for tax relief, settlement of disputes, or appointment of officials to administrative posts. The Capponi, for example, were linked to Pistoia through Neri di Gino, who, between 1421 and 1456, served once as podestà, twice as captain, and four times on committees overseeing everything from taxes to revision of statutes, providing support and favors that earned him a loyal following and, at his death, the honorary title of "protector and father of the city."[55] Likewise prominent in Pistoia were the Medici, of whom seven held offices by mid-century. Giovanni di Bicci was podestà in 1407, and when he died Pistoia honored him (and sought favor with Cosimo) by bestowing its insignia and arms on the family. Donato de' Medici was bishop of Pistoia for almost forty years. And Pistoia honored Piero as "father of the city" in 1464 and the Medici family as its "protector" in 1476.[56]

---

[54]   A. Brown, "Lorenzo de' Medici's New Men and Their Mores: The Changing Life-style of Quattrocento Florence," *Renaissance Studies* 16 (2002): 113–42.

[55]   W. J. Connell, *La città dei crucci: fazioni e clientele in uno stato repubblicano del '400* (Florence, 2000), pp. 83–7.

[56]   S. J. Milner, "Rubrics and Requests: Statutory Division and Supra-Communal Clientage in Fifteenth-Century Pistoia," in *Florentine Tuscany*, ed. Connell and Zorzi, pp. 312–32 (321–4).

Until mid-century the Medici and Pitti exceeded other families in the range of their patronage connections, but after Luca Pitti's humiliation in 1466 the Medici and, after 1470, Lorenzo became the undisputed masters of dominion patronage, as shown by the voluminous correspondence from governments, institutions, and individuals seeking favors and help. Letters came to many family members, including Lorenzo's mother Lucrezia who typically passed on to her son the requests she received.[57] From just Pistoia and its district, more than a thousand letters sent to the Medici between 1400 and 1494 have survived, over 900 of them after 1460, and over 660 to Lorenzo alone (even with the loss of most of the letters of the 1480s). Extant letters to Lorenzo from Pistoia are at least three times as numerous as the combined total of letters to Cosimo, Piero, and Lorenzo's uncle Giovanni, who until his death in 1463 was the chief Medici contact for Pistoia.[58] A similar story emerges from Arezzo, where Piero de' Medici displaced Luca Pitti as the most influential Florentine in local affairs, built a group of friends and clients (who offered military help in 1466), and introduced the young Lorenzo into Aretine patronage by letting him nominate Medici clients to offices. Lorenzo later strengthened the Medici presence in Arezzo by having his former tutor Gentile Becchi appointed bishop in 1473 and dominating more and more of the patronage channels to the point of excluding all rivals and becoming sole intermediary between Arezzo and Florence for fiscal matters, tax-exemptions for local markets and fairs, and appointments. Even if unable to fulfill all requests for tax reductions, he never failed when it came to recommendations for Medici clients, even when statutory regulations had to be ignored.[59] Lorenzo's involvement in Pisa was similarly extensive. In 1472 he pushed through the legislative councils a proposal defeated earlier in the year for the transfer of most of Florence's university (the Studio) to Pisa. By late 1473 the faculties of law and medicine were operating there (while the *studia humanitatis* remained in Florence). Lorenzo was among the Studio's governors who administered funding, much of it, ironically, from the income of Volterra's alum mines.[60]

Lorenzo's influence and power were everywhere in the dominion, especially within local governments. Even with a major lacuna in the documents for the 1480s, over 1,300 pre-1494 letters addressed to the Medici by local governments have survived, 915 of them sent to Lorenzo from Pistoia (which leads the list), Arezzo, Prato, Volterra, Pisa, San Gimignano, Cortona, and altogether

[57] See Lucrezia Tornabuoni, *Lettere*, ed. P. Salvadori (Florence, 1993).
[58] Milner, "Rubrics and Requests," pp. 324–7.
[59] R. Black, "Lorenzo and Arezzo," in *Lorenzo the Magnificent: Culture and Politics*, ed. Mallett and Mann, pp. 217–34.
[60] J. Davies, *Florence and Its University During the Early Renaissance* (Leiden, 1998), pp. 125–42.

no fewer than 125 communities large and small. Some were generic declarations of loyalty occasionally accompanied by gifts, but the letters Lorenzo sent in return reveal that the majority of requests asked him to appoint persons of his choosing, often for as long as he wished, to administrative offices (chancellors, schoolteachers, notaries, administrators of hospitals) and ecclesiastical positions. Lorenzo's patronage was larger in volume, more extensive in reaching all corners of the dominion, and more exclusive and personal than that of any other Florentine: he permitted no one to exercise anything like the same degree of influence and was unwilling to delegate contacts even to members of his family, as his father and grandfather had done.[61] His patronage nonetheless occurred in the context of already complex relations between the Florentine government and the dominion communities, which often appealed to him for protection *against* Florentine fiscal demands. Lorenzo's intervention on behalf of clients was sometimes perceived by these same communities as interference and was occasionally resented and even resisted. Letting him pick their chancellors or hospital administrators gained them his good will and such appointments added to his network of clients. But promoting his friends and favorites, his "creatures" as they were regarded, meant disappointing other candidates and embarrassing their local patrons or the governments in which they had served. In order to get or keep a client in office, Lorenzo did not hesitate to pressure the communities to overlook or annul their statutory prohibitions against re-election or extension of terms of office. A slow but steady erosion of local autonomies caused some grumbling and occasional anger but was generally accepted as the necessary cost of the benefits of being numbered among Lorenzo's friends and clients.[62]

Lorenzo's intervention in the dominion also extended to the Florentine podestà, captains and vicars, the frequency of whose correspondence with him, despite their official status as officers of Florentine government, is extraordinary. Nearly 1,700 such letters have survived, and, since here too there is a lacuna for the 1480s, the original total was much greater. Officials sometimes wrote to defend the sentences of their district courts, in response to Lorenzo's requests (which local governments had asked him to make) for leniency or pardons. Although Lorenzo could not arbitrarily overturn convictions or reduce penalties, these officials would have thought twice about simply rejecting his wishes. Lorenzo mediated between local governments and Florentine administrators

[61] W. J. Connell, "Changing Patterns of Medicean Patronage: The Florentine Dominion During the Fifteenth Century," in *Lorenzo il Magnifico e il suo mondo*, ed. Garfagnini, pp. 87–107; Connell, *Città dei crucci*, pp. 125–47.

[62] P. Salvadori, "Florentines and the Communities of the Territorial State," in *Florentine Tuscany*, ed. Connell and Zorzi, pp. 207–24; and Salvadori, *Dominio e patronato: Lorenzo dei Medici e la Toscana nel Quattrocento* (Rome, 2000).

and judges, just as he did between the communities and Florentine tax officials. Thus the administration of justice in the subject territories became ever more dependent on his discretion and influence, as he applied more or less pressure or leaned in one direction or another, for reasons that could be political or personal but which did not necessarily reflect the merits of the case. Most dominion officials belonged to elite Florentine families and wanted of course to avoid giving the impression of being bullied or intimidated by Lorenzo and thus losing face vis-à-vis the towns they governed. But they sometimes agreed to reduce jail sentences, cancel a death sentence, or forego the use of torture. Dominion governance and the prospects for impartial justice or standardized administration were seriously compromised by these interventions and the always tense relations between Lorenzo and the ottimati. Dominion localities quickly became accustomed to the notion that parallel to, and often more powerful than, official justice was Lorenzo's "private" and politically motivated justice.[63]

Building a Dynasty

Lorenzo may never have seriously contemplated the transformation of the republic into a principate, but he did seek new kinds of personal power that he tried to bequeath to his children. Building a dynasty and protecting his family's future, both in and out of Florence, became the overriding objectives of his last years. Patronage and favors were the daily nuts and bolts of a system of unofficial governance that put Lorenzo and his wishes in the anxious expectations of every officeholder in and out of the city and of clients and notables throughout the dominion. But it was ritual, ceremony, and the appropriation of religion by which he sought to make himself the always visible, indispensable, and yet mysterious and charismatic center of Florentine life: to place himself, in effect, in the consciousness and emotions of thousands who would never meet him, speak with him, or write him a letter. It has been argued that Lorenzo was the author, or promoter, of a "ritual revolution" in Florence.[64] In the early 1470s he suppressed, or showed deadly indifference to, a variety of traditional Florentine rituals, as the government cut funding for the annual celebrations on the feast day of the Baptist, and the religious spectacles organized by confraternities for the feasts of the Annunciation,

---

[63] Salvadori, *Dominio e patronato*, pp. 97–132; Salvadori, "Gli ufficiali estrinseci fiorentini e Lorenzo dei Medici," in *Gli officiali degli Stati italiani del Quattrocento,* ed. F. Leverotti, *Annali della Scuola Normale Superiore di Pisa*, Quaderni I (1997): 213–24.

[64] Trexler, *Public Life*, pp. 428–62.

Ascension, and Pentecost all either lapsed or suffered from inadequate support.[65] Even the festivals surrounding the cult of the Magi, so important to Cosimo, were terminated.

In the place of these now neglected traditional celebrations, Lorenzo himself became the organizing principle of new ritual spaces and forms. Observers noted precisely at what time, by what route, and in what company Lorenzo made his way around the city or into the countryside. His visits to churches, monasteries, and convents were eagerly awaited and well remembered events whose every detail was recorded by the flattered and entranced religious who believed (or gave to believe) they had been visited by a sacred person. Lorenzo continued his family's long-standing effort to claim patronage rights throughout the local church and to fuse the city's sacred spaces with the family's history and power. Although he lacked the funds that permitted Cosimo to rebuild churches and monasteries on a grand scale, he extended Medici patronage ties to a long list of ecclesiastical institutions in almost every religious order. He made gifts of relics and had ex-voto images of himself placed near the altars of churches that benefited from his attention or largesse.[66] He joined lay confraternities, several of which entrusted him with authority to settle disputes or rewrite their statutes, tasks that he delegated to others but which were remembered as the bestowal of his benevolence and wisdom. In the confraternity of San Paolo, whose membership included politically prominent citizens, Lorenzo played an active role over many years. His other confraternity memberships were usually honorary, although the honor was more often felt as Lorenzo's gift to them than theirs to him.[67] Even as he limited his appearances to particularly significant occasions, he could have a powerful effect on these lay religious associations. Originally a popular neighborhood confraternity, Sant'Agnese in Drago Verde in the Oltrarno was radically transformed by what has been described as a "Medicean infiltration." Lorenzo joined in the early 1470s, and in the 1480s a long list of his closest associates, including his secretary Niccolò Michelozzi and the chancellor Scala,

[65]   Newbigin, *Feste d'Oltrarno: Plays in Churches in Fifteenth-Century Florence*, 2 vols. (Florence, 1996); see also N. Eckstein, *The District of the Green Dragon*, pp. 55–60.
[66]   K. Lowe, "Lorenzo's 'Presence' at Churches, Convents, and Shrines in and outside Florence," in *Lorenzo the Magnificent: Culture and Politics*, ed. Mallett and Mann, pp. 23–36.
[67]   L. Sebregondi, "Lorenzo de' Medici confratello illustre," *ASI* 150 (1992): 319–41; K. Eisenbichler, "Lorenzo de' Medici e la Congregazione dei Neri nella Compagnia della Croce al Tempio," ibid., pp. 343–70; R. F. E. Weissman, *Ritual Brotherhood in Renaissance Florence* (New York, 1982), pp. 169–73; Weissman, "Lorenzo de' Medici and the Confraternity of San Paolo," in *Lorenzo de' Medici: New Perspectives*, ed. Toscani, pp. 315–29.

also joined and began monopolizing confraternal offices. Lorenzo dominated the association's charitable work, especially the annual distribution of bread to the poor, which henceforth became known as his own philanthropic gesture. In 1488 the company ignored its age requirements and elected Lorenzo's seventeen-year-old son Piero among its captains; the next year it bowed to Piero's wish to perform a Pentecost play in the church of the Carmine, where Sant'Agnese met, declaring that, since his family was the confraternity's "bene-factor," its captains "wished to provide him with every assistance," granting him "complete authority and power" to "make use of the said company and all its possessions" for the festival.[68] In such ways, Lorenzo co-opted and controlled confraternities, once viewed with suspicion as potential sources of political intrigue but now docilely dependent on him for honor, subsidies, and favor.

Lorenzo's attention to youth confraternities and working-class festive associations marks a significant innovation in Medici strategy. Youth associations appeared in Florence early in the fifteenth century, and their increasing popularity induced Pope Eugenius to impose regulations and ecclesiastical supervision. Boys' confraternities, soon affiliated with church schools, engaged in prayer and laud singing, attended orations, and performed plays.[69] Increasing emphasis on youthful innocence in the community's self-representation merged with the cult of Lorenzo's own youthful persona. He participated in these associations, enrolled his sons, and even wrote a religious play, the *Rappresentazione di San Giovanni e Paolo*, performed by the company of San Giovanni Evangelista which included his youngest son, Giuliano.[70] Partly as a result of Lorenzo's support, boys' groups became perhaps the most prominent actors in Florentine processional life: a development that links Lorenzo's Florence with Savonarola's across the political boundary of 1494. Lorenzo also supported festive associations of workers, called *potenze*, some based in neighborhoods, others in occupational groups, and consisting mostly of textile laborers who had been driven from the political stage a century earlier and now reappeared in festive garb. In the early 1470s, Lorenzo permitted the *potenze* to emerge more openly and display their fanciful division of the city into festive "kingdoms" ruled by "emperors," "kings" and "nobles," such as

[68] Eckstein, *District of the Green Dragon*, pp. 205–24 (213); Newbigin, *Feste d'Oltrarno*, vol. 1, pp. 206–8.
[69] I. Taddei, *Fanciulli e giovani: crescere a Firenze nel Rinascimento* (Florence, 2001); K. Eisenbichler, *The Boys of the Archangel Raphael: A Youth Confraternity in Florence, 1411–1785* (Toronto, 1998); L. Polizzotto, *Children of the Promise: The Confraternity of the Purification and the Socialization of Youths in Florence, 1427–1785* (Oxford, 2004).
[70] N. Newbigin, "Politics in the *Sacre rappresentazioni* of Lorenzo's Florence," in *Lorenzo the Magnificent: Culture and Politics*, ed. Mallett and Mann, pp. 117–30.

the "Kingdom of the Millstone" and the "Grand Monarchy of the Red City." *Potenze* exchanged elaborate ritualized visits and organized pageants that sometimes parodied the solemn representation of the social order enshrined in older communal rituals. The government authorized associations of both silk weavers (1481) and wool beaters (1488), who formed a company that was part confraternity, with a hospital for their poorer members, and part festive *potenza*. Lorenzo broke with two centuries of official repression of workers' associations in extending his patronage to these groups and allowing them a place on Florence's ritual stage. In 1489, for example, he made a loan of plates and table service (on which the Medici arms were of course prominently displayed) to the king of the *potenza* of Camaldoli in the Oltrarno for the group's May Day festivities.[71] As he restricted ritual for the political classes, Lorenzo cultivated previously marginalized groups of youths and workers: another tacit admission of the precariousness of his hold on the upper classes.

For a decade after the Pazzi catastrophe, Lorenzo suppressed most civic festivals, and when he cautiously permitted their resumption in the late 1480s their character had changed. In 1491 the San Giovanni festival featured a re-creation, with fifteen wagons drawn by fifty pairs of oxen, of the triumph of the Roman general and consul Lucius Aemilius Paulus, the conqueror of Macedonia who returned to Rome with immense booty. Although Vasari attributes the design of the triumphal wagons to the artist Francesco Granacci, a contemporary chronicler recorded that the whole pageant was Lorenzo's conception and that it was meant to highlight, through his identification with the Roman hero, Lorenzo's beneficence, popularity, and valor in protecting the republic against its enemies. It was, to say the least, a remarkably incongruous addition to the celebration of the feast day of the Baptist.[72] In place of the old community-based religious pageants, he promoted spectacles that marked the transition from festival to theater and sponsored scripted plays (including his own), saints' lives and Latin comedies, performed by youth companies instead of the adult confraternities that once staged traditional pageants. Lorenzo's direct involvement (reminiscent of his determination to control every aspect of patronage and politics) reveals an obsessive insistence on defining and controlling the city's festivals according to his tastes and interests, and probably also some apprehension about allowing people to manage them themselves.

Lorenzo's aim of elevating the Medici above all other Florentines required the one further crucial step of finally getting a cardinal who would give the family a power base independent of the vicissitudes of Florentine politics. To this end, and also to revive the bank's fortunes, he needed to re-establish

---

[71] Trexler, *Public Life*, pp. 368–87, 399–418 (411–13).
[72] Ibid., p. 451; Carew-Reid, *Les fêtes florentines*, pp. 91–2; P. Ventrone, "Lorenzo's 'politica festiva'," in *Lorenzo the Magnificent: Culture and Politics*, ed. Mallett and Mann, pp. 114–15.

good relations with the papacy, and the opportunity came with the election of Innocent VIII in 1484. After 1487, when Lorenzo married his daughter Maddalena to Innocent's son, Franceschetto Cybo, he regained some of the old Medici influence in Rome. Papal accounts and contracts were either restored or given anew to the Medici bank, which gave Lorenzo access to funds that he used in part to finance his new son-in-law's territorial ambitions.[73] That same year Lorenzo arranged Piero's marriage to Alfonsina of a Neapolitan branch of the Orsini. Since Lorenzo's wife was a Roman Orsini, and her brother was still Florence's archbishop, Piero's marriage solidified ties to a noble family with influence in both major states to the south.

But the greatest benefit of the alliance with Innocent was the pope's acquiescence in Lorenzo's ambition for his middle son Giovanni, who, in 1487, was only twelve years old. Even in an age in which the church was widely accepted as an arena for powerful families to pursue wealth and political aggrandizement, Lorenzo's zeal on behalf of so young a child raised eyebrows. Whether he believed that his family's ambition for princely status could only be realized through the church, or whether he thought, more modestly, that control in Florence would be strengthened by a family cardinal able to protect the bank and keep the friendship of successive popes, is a matter for speculation. In the early 1480s he tried to get Giovanni's foot in some ecclesiastical door: a benefice that might be the first rung of a ladder leading to a cardinalate. In 1484 Lorenzo even had troops seize the abbey of Passignano in order to install Giovanni as abbot.[74] He got both his Neapolitan and Milanese allies to press Innocent to grant Giovanni possession of prestigious monasteries in their territories. By 1487 negotiations were underway for a cardinalate, linked to those for the marriage of Lorenzo's daughter to Innocent's son, and in 1489 Innocent finally consented to make the thirteen-year-old Giovanni a cardinal. Because of the boy's age, the pope wanted the appointment kept secret and insisted that he wait three years before being consecrated in the office. Lorenzo, craving the political benefit of immediate publicity, could not wait, much to Innocent's annoyance. When Giovanni went to Rome, his father wrote him a letter impressing upon him that this was "the greatest honor ever bestowed on our house," urging him "to become a good churchman" and "to love the honor and estate of the Holy Church and Apostolic See more than anything in the world," and adding: "But even with this reservation, you will not lack opportunity to help the city of Florence and our family."[75]

---

[73] Bullard, *Lorenzo*, pp. 133–53.
[74] G. B. Picotti, *La giovinezza di Leone X* (Milan, 1927); E. H. Gombrich, "The Sassetti Chapel Revisited: Santa Trinita and Lorenzo de' Medici," *I Tatti Studies* 7 (1997): 11–35.
[75] Bullard, *Lorenzo*, p. 33; W. Roscoe, *The Life of Lorenzo de' Medici*, 10th edn. (London, 1862), pp. 467–70.

In lavish celebrations the Florentines indulged Lorenzo's need to hear expressions of joy and reverence for the holy youth who now represented and protected Florence in Rome, despite the huge sums the deal with Innocent had cost and the well-founded suspicion that much of the money had come from the public treasury. No one knew exactly how much: according to Piero Parenti, after the Medici were exiled a review of communal accounts showed that Lorenzo had taken 100,000 florins for Giovanni's cardinalate;[76] Giovanni Cambi thought it was 50,000, and Alamanno Rinuccini 200,000.[77] Widespread anger after the expulsion over Lorenzo's misappropriation of communal funds suggests that not everyone was as deliriously happy as Lorenzo wanted to believe when he himself wrote about the 1489 celebrations that there had never been "a truer and more universal happiness" in Florence. But it was not a moment to spoil the party. After all, a Florentine cardinal could indeed do good things for his city. Three years later, when the still adolescent but now consecrated cardinal returned home six weeks after his father's death, he was given a triumphal entry of the sort usually reserved for noble foreigners.[78] No one knew, of course, that just two years later the Medici would be in exile, or that, when they returned in 1512, cardinal Giovanni would be just months away from becoming Pope Leo X. Whether he ever fulfilled Lorenzo's admonition to "help the city of Florence" was later much debated, but he certainly helped his family.

In the almost quarter-century of Lorenzo's leadership, relations between the regime and the ottimati lurched from crisis to crisis, in large part because Lorenzo sought a kind of power alien to their notions of aristocratic rule. Although the regime seemed to emerge stronger after each crisis, in the sense that controls became tighter and opposition voices weaker, its hold on the ottimati became more fragile. This underlying instability left the city deeply divided and ill-prepared to face the suddenly more dangerous world that began in 1494. Beneath the apparent pacification of the 1480s, many ottimati feared that things had gone too far, and two years after Lorenzo died they brought down the regime. What had taken sixty years to build, defend, and consolidate collapsed in a matter of days. Decades later, the pre-1494 generation came to be seen as a time of enlightened rule, domestic tranquility, and cultural splendor. The culture was indeed splendid, but behind the facade of tranquility was a brittle regime that did not trust its own citizens, and least of all the ottimati.

[76] Parenti, *Storia*, p. 198.
[77] Brown, *Medici in Florence*, p. 177n.
[78] Trexler, *Public Life*, pp. 456–7; Carew-Reid, *Les fêtes florentines*, pp. 171–2.

13

Reinventing the Republic

French Invasion and Expulsion of the Medici

Lorenzo died on April 8, 1492. Within a week the councils confirmed twenty-year-old Piero in his father's offices, including the Seventy, in the absence of any movement to restore constitutional government (as in 1465–6) or organized demonstrations of support (as in 1469). But the apparent smoothness of the succession was deceptive, and discontents muffled in the 1480s soon emerged. When Piero began to "give audiences in his home, as his father had done, surrounded by armed" retainers, Piero Parenti wrote, "the city secretly lamented" his expanding power, "fearing once again that it might slide into servitude, and of yet a worse kind." Taking prophetic note of the growth of apocalyptic preaching, Parenti added that people "placed their hopes in the promises of preachers" who predicted that "from God would come a scourge such that men would be forced back to the right way of living. Entrusting themselves to God, they waited for events to unfold, unable to believe that the violence and intimidation employed by the Medici over fifty-eight years and through three successions should become permanent." It was not, or not yet, Savonarola to whom Parenti alluded, but rather a fiery Franciscan, Fra Domenico da Ponzo. Waiting for the "principali" to take the lead, the "*popolo* and the majority of citizens remained in suspense, not knowing what road events would take or to what conclusion they would lead. They desired true liberty, and waited for the opportunity; they were in truth unhappy with the present regime, and everyone lived in great anticipation." Some said that the purpose of Giovanni's triumphal entry in May 1492 was to win popular support for the crumbling regime. Parenti thought that Piero, desiring "complete governance of our city," searched ever more desperately for support, cultivating the loyalty of "young men and youthful gentlemen" by making them dependent on his good graces against the wishes of men of "mature age" from leading families, and trying to weaken the "authority of the *grandi*" to create more stable foundations for his own power.[1]

Parenti, Guicciardini, and the historian Bartolomeo Cerretani all located the cause of Piero's troubles in the resentment of ottimati excluded from the inner circle. Guicciardini says that Bernardo Rucellai (married to Lorenzo's sister Nannina) and Paolantonio Soderini (eldest son of the recently deceased Tommaso) tried to persuade Piero to "use his authority moderately" and to "come closer to a *vita civile*" (a phrase suggesting both the customs of citizens and constitutional, or republican, government) "rather than continue in those ways that gave a whiff of tyranny and for which many citizens had felt ugly toward Lorenzo." But when Rucellai and Soderini arranged the marriages of, respectively, a daughter and a son to children of Filippo Strozzi, the insecure Piero, fearing that the great families were uniting against him, spurned them even more openly. In this fatal behavior he was urged on by those secretaries and chancellors who "decided all things and arrogated to themselves immense power, as they had maliciously designed and sought to do from the beginning, to Piero's great harm; for anyone who thinks about it will realize that persuading Piero not to trust the wise citizens and friends of the regime was the beginning of his downfall."[2] According to Parenti, "the whole weight of the regime" was now reduced to ten persons: Piero, his secretaries, Bernardo del Nero, and only two men from elite families, Francesco Valori and Niccolò Ridolfi. "Piero let himself be led by them, and they used him as *capo* for their own preservation."[3]

Dangers from abroad soon overwhelmed and exacerbated these internal tensions. By 1493 Italy was abuzz with rumors and fears of an invasion by France's Charles VIII in pursuit of his claim, as heir to the Angevins, to the Neapolitan kingdom. The road to Naples went through Lombardy and Tuscany, and the French tried to persuade the Florentines to facilitate their descent through Tuscany. But Piero, his mother a Roman Orsini and his wife a Neapolitan Orsini, held to the Neapolitan alliance until the arrival of the French army in Tuscany. Parenti says that those who wanted to rid Florence of the Medici actually "awaited the French, wanted them to come, and called

[1] Parenti, *Storia*, pp. 27, 29, 32.
[2] Guicciardini, *Storie fiorentine*, X, pp. 186–8; *History of Florence*, trans. Domandi, pp. 80–2. Also Parenti, *Storia*, p. 43; Bartolomeo Cerretani, *Storia fiorentina*, ed. G. Berti (Florence, 1994), p. 190; Fabbri, *Alleanza matrimoniale*, pp. 213, 217; and Crabb, *The Strozzi*, p. 260, table A.3.
[3] Parenti, *Storia*, p. 47.

for them, albeit secretly, if their coming could bring the liberation of their city and the restoration of liberty." Even the Medici were split over whether to support Naples or France. In April 1494, a French ambassador departing the city was accompanied by Piero's brother Giuliano and their second cousins Lorenzo and Giovanni, sons of Pierfrancesco and grandsons of Cosimo's brother Lorenzo, who offered the ambassador hospitality at their villa at Cafaggiuolo in the Mugello, ignoring official plans for him to stay at an inn. Piero was furious that members of his own family displayed such warmth to France and feared that something more lay behind their gesture. Piero investigated, and the cousins admitted they had secretly become "men of the [French] king," retainers in effect, with a hefty annual fee, and that they were thus obliged to honor anyone representing Charles. A scandal erupted, with suggestions of a wider conspiracy involving Lodovico Sforza, Bernardo Rucellai's son Cosimo, and Paolantonio Soderini's brother Francesco, bishop of Volterra, and the episode revealed the presence of a pro-French party in the city. Although the Seventy wanted life imprisonment for the cousins, Piero agreed to a symbolic punishment of exile beyond the city limits (allowing them to live in their country villa) in order not to risk reprisals against Florentine merchants in France, including the Medici operation in Lyons, and also because his cousins had a following that might be provoked if they were treated harshly. Despite a show of reconciliation, the split in the family came fully into the open when the French arrived eighteen months later; Piero was exiled, and his cousins returned in triumph and changed their name from Medici to Popolani.[4]

As the French came closer, Piero kept putting them off while trying not to offend them. Parenti reports that he wanted to resist the French and stay with Naples because more and more citizens thought the arrival of the French would mean liberation from the regime. Parenti's dislike of Piero may have led him to exaggerate the number and fervor of those who saw the French as potential liberators, but he claims that, on the eve of their arrival, "so heavy was the yoke of the house of Medici" that this was the view of "the majority of citizens." Their "normal hatred" for the Medici was intensified, he adds, by Cardinal Giovanni's grasping for every vacant benefice: "thus, this family, having usurped both the ecclesiastical and the civic [spheres], was now intolerable." Growing numbers of people were speaking openly against the regime, he says, and the city was strewn with leaflets calling on the king of France to free them from the "tyrant." Facing the regime's intransigence, Charles increased the pressure by expelling Florentine merchants from France and threatening to

---

[4] Ibid., pp. 67–72; Brown, "Pierfrancesco de' Medici, 1420–1476," in Brown, *The Medici in Florence*, pp. 73–102; Brown, "The Revolution of 1494 in Florence and its Aftermath: A Reassessment," in *Italy in Crisis, 1494*, ed. J. Everson and D. Zancani (Oxford, 2000), pp. 13–40.

"liberate" the city. At the end of October, with French forces marching from Milan into Tuscany, criticism of official policy was voiced in the councils, and Piero lost his nerve. On the 26th, imitating his father's already legendary trip to Naples, he left the city with a few companions, went to Charles, placed himself at the king's mercy, and ordered Florentine commanders to surrender the fortresses of Pisa, Livorno, Pietrasanta, and Sarzana, and control of the entire western half of the Florentine dominion: "so great was the authority that Piero de' Medici arrogated to himself."[5]

When the news reached Florence, Parenti reports, people asked by "what authority he had" surrendered the fortresses. Piero tried, after the fact, to get a mandate for this action, but failed. Protests multiplied: some blamed him and his youth; others focused on the hated secretaries and advisers. Florence now faced two crises: the collapse of Piero's authority and with it the regime; and Charles's intention to enter Florence with an army that had already brutally sacked the town of Fivizzano in the northwest. On November 4 the Signoria called an emergency pratica of the regime's leadership. "Although they were his partisans," Parenti says, "they had already become extremely unhappy with Piero's actions, and, seeing themselves being led to disaster, began to turn their cloaks." The core of the regime was about to abandon Piero. To deal with the French threat, they decided first to ask the Dominican preacher Savonarola, "who had predicted this calamity," to lead a delegation to Charles to persuade him not to enter the city or, if he insisted, to limit the size of the arriving force and restrict its movements.

On November 8 Piero returned to the city, went to the family palace, and asked the military captain Paolo Orsini to approach the city with his forces, while the Medici began rounding up troops from the Mugello and the territory of Pistoia, apparently preparing for another resolution by force along the lines of 1458 and 1466. Rumors of a coup abounded, even of a plan to set various neighborhoods ablaze and "retake *lo stato per forza.*" Piero went to the government palace the next day with his retinue, but the Signoria, aware of his military preparations, refused him entry. An armed confrontation nearly ensued between the palace guards and Piero's men, but when cries of "popolo! popolo!" summoned the population to the defense of the palace, Piero backed off and went home. Not only the Signoria turned its back on Piero: Francesco Valori, until then a regime stalwart, and Piero Vettori, another loyal Medicean, rode into the piazza and led the crowd to police headquarters at the Bargello to seize arms in anticipation of a pitched battle. Piero's friends and relatives were also in danger: at least two were attacked, and Girolamo Tornabuoni, of the Otto, was killed. Cerretani says that Cardinal Giovanni narrowly escaped an angry crowd and had to disguise himself as a Franciscan friar to make it

---

[5]   Parenti, *Storia*, pp. 103, 110–14.

safely out of the city.[6] When the Signoria put a bounty on the heads of both Piero and Giovanni, all three brothers quickly left through the San Gallo gate, went to the family villa at Careggi and from there to Bologna. One of the Bibbiena brothers took Piero's infant son Lorenzo and his wet nurse to Urbino and then to Venice, while Piero's wife Alfonsina was sent for her safety to a nearby monastery. Thus did sixty years of Medici rule come to an inglorious end. Piero never set foot in Florence again, whereas Giovanni and Giuliano returned on the backs of Spanish troops eighteen years later.

Medici secretaries and advisers went into hiding. Some were arrested, and the Monte officer Antonio di Miniato Dini was executed for embezzlement of public funds (perhaps standing in for his bosses). Medici possessions were confiscated from the family palace, including works of art. Advised by a large pratica, the Signoria abolished the Seventy and the Cento and recalled a long list of exiles, including the Pazzi. There were disagreements over what to do with the former regime's inner circle: some advocated leniency and were supported by Savonarola, while others wanted justice. Differences over political reforms also surfaced: the priors were evenly divided between those who "leaned toward the *popolo*" and, as Parenti put it, those who "were in favor of tyranny and against popular liberty." But with the French demanding entry, politics had to wait. On the 12th Charles agreed to postpone his arrival for five days. Meanwhile the Signoria sent for troops from the contado and quietly placed them in strategic locations near and in the city. Charles arrived on the 17th, officially an ally and protector but also a potential enemy who had angered the Florentines by recognizing Pisa's independence and supporting Piero. Everyone feared that the French army might be unleashed against the city; young women were sent to convents for protection. Cerretani's estimate that 18,000 (of 40,000 French soldiers) entered the city is almost certainly too high, but Charles himself said he brought 10,000.[7] His mixed army of large and (to the Florentines) strange-looking soldiers from different parts of Europe, from Switzerland to Scotland, impressed and frightened the citizens. His representatives had already gone through the city marking with chalk homes suitable for French courtiers, noblemen, and soldiers (a detail Machiavelli later made famous when he remarked in chapter 12 of *The Prince* that Charles took Italy "with chalk"). Charles himself stayed in the Medici palace, where he began acting more like Florence's conqueror than its honored guest. When he demanded that the Signoria allow Piero to return, the Florentines responded angrily with near unanimity that, as Parenti put it, "they would rather die valiantly with arms in their hands in defense of their

[6] Cerretani, *Storia*, p. 206.
[7] Ibid., pp. 212–13; G. Guidi, *Ciò che accadde al tempo della Signoria di novembre dicembre in Firenze l'anno 1494* (Florence, 1988), p. 59.

liberty than agree to the return of the tyrant." Both Parenti and Cerretani report that the most eloquent spokesman for this view was Francesco Soderini, who made a long speech in a pratica in which he recalled Florence's centuries of armed resistance to would-be foreign conquerors. Another delegation went to Charles, again including Savonarola, to persuade him to relinquish the demand for Piero's return.

Charles and the Florentines were also at loggerheads over a formal agreement defining their alliance. He demanded recognition as the republic's overlord, by right of conquest according to the laws of France, with the authority to install a presiding representative once he departed. When the Florentines rejected the idea out of hand, tensions escalated with rumors and fears of a sack. Florentine negotiators, including Francesco Valori and Piero Capponi, presented a draft of an agreement, which Charles and his councilors dismissed with menacing words. In a moment that remains legendary, Piero Capponi allegedly tore up the document and said, in Cerretani's version: "Most Christian prince, we shall sound the bells if you sound your trumpets, and we shall show you this people in arms." Guicciardini tells a similar story. It is missing in Parenti, who does however say that Florentine attitudes toward the king were quickly transformed from good will to hatred, and that the government ordered contado infantry (he speaks of 30,000 men, a figure confirmed by Guicciardini, while Cerretani says 25,000) billeted in elite homes in the center so that they could quickly "run armed to the piazza [of the Signoria] at the sound of the bell."

Neither side wanted a catastrophic confrontation, and within a few days an agreement was reached that bound them "in friendship" and required Florence not to make other alliances without French approval, to pay Charles 120,000 ducats over seven months, at least to consider the repatriation of Piero, and to allow French control of the fortresses until Charles concluded the Neapolitan campaign. Charles recognized Florence's sovereignty over Pisa, but left the Florentines to figure out how to re-establish their rule. Both sides swore to observe the treaty in a ceremony in the cathedral on the 26th, and, after one more mediation by Savonarola, who told Charles that God had more important tasks for him than to remain idle in Florence, the French finally left on the 28th for Rome and Naples. Florence narrowly escaped what would have been the greatest disaster in its history. Parenti thanked God and Savonarola and lauded his fellow citizens, underscoring the contribution of women and children who impeded the movement of French troops and artillery by pelting them with stones from their windows. "I cannot sufficiently commend the greatness of spirit of our people, who, with the king of France in their city and surrounded by many thousands of his men, and still suspicious of the many and powerful citizens who were supporters of Piero, dared to oppose the king's will in order to preserve their liberty."

The Great Council

After sixty years of Medici dominance, the Florentines were suddenly faced with the task of reinventing their government and political order. Events had moved so quickly and unexpectedly that no one was prepared. An explosion of talk, debate, writing, and ultimately theorizing about politics began in those chaotic days at the end of 1494 and continued for two generations. During the Medici years, Florentines had largely stopped writing chronicles and reflecting publicly on politics; historiography was dominated by humanist chancellors who shied away from contemporary events, and with few exceptions political discourse had been limited to praise of the Medici. After about 1480, pratiche ceased even to be convened. At the end of 1494 all this changed with dramatic suddenness and amid profound uncertainty and widely divergent views about the future of the republic. There was to be no easy recovery of pre-Medici politics, no consensus about change, and the loss of moorings opened the way for significant departures from tradition.

Debates commenced as soon as the French departed, and initially the ottimati were in control. On November 30 a large pratica recommended calling a parlamento, which assembled on December 2 and confirmed the abolition of the Cento and Seventy, authorized the Signoria and colleges to appoint twenty accoppiatori, and entrusted the latter with electing the Signoria *a mano* for the next year, to avoid, so it was said, the possibility that sortition might put Mediceans in office as happened in 1434. A new scrutiny was scheduled for the following November, when it would be decided whether or not to destroy the existing pouches.[8] Among the Twenty were three ottimati who played a role in banishing Piero but who had also been central figures of the regime: Bernardo Rucellai, Francesco Valori, and Piero Capponi. At least ten were among the Seventy in 1489, and Cerretani remarked that most of them were among Lorenzo's "primi ministri." Five of the newly appointed Ten of Liberty and Peace on military and foreign affairs had similarly been on the Seventy, including Paolantonio Soderini and Piero Guicciardini.[9]

Protests erupted immediately over the preservation of such substantial continuity with the Medici regime. According to Parenti, a group went to the palace to complain that the parlamento had not been held "popularmente," since so much power had been given to just twenty men. Others insisted that the proposed list of accoppiatori should have been submitted to the "people"

---

[8]   G. Cadoni, *Provvisioni concernenti l'ordinamento della Repubblica fiorentina, 1494–1512* (Rome, 1994), vol. 1, pp. 1–32.

[9]   N. Rubinstein, "Politics and Constitution in Florence at the End of the Fifteenth Century," in *Italian Renaissance Studies*, ed. E. F. Jacob (London, 1960), pp. 148–83.

for approval. All "good citizens" felt aggrieved over having taken up arms for liberty only to see the "principali" intent on preserving the "*stato* of the same persons who had previously governed, except for the elimination of a few chiefs." They believed they had been tricked in particular by Guidantonio Vespucci, who promised to present to the people a draft of a new constitution that had not materialized. "Many came to the conclusion," says Parenti, "that the leading citizens did not want to subject themselves to the wishes of the people and that they intended to retain *lo stato*." So deep, according to Parenti, was the mistrust between the ottimati who engineered the parlamento and the "popolo" who expected a very different kind of political reform that there was danger of bloodshed and "civile guerra."[10] Even Cerretani, who did not share Parenti's "popular" perspective, said that because the Twenty assumed they could take possession of the *reggimento* of the city and "non vivere a popolo," the "whole city came to hate them in just a few days."[11] Precisely what was intended by those who wanted the city to "vivere a popolo" or be governed "popolarmente" was not yet clear. Also criticizing the election of the Twenty was a faction of ottimati "who wanted to live *popolarmente*," particularly Paolantonio Soderini who, supported by the "popolo," denounced the election's "dishonorable procedures." On the other side, Parenti identifies Piero Capponi and Francesco Valori as "enemies of the *popolo*." Yet Capponi and Valori were fierce rivals, each with a faction of followers and supporters, each eager to satisfy his own ambition and please his friends and relatives with offices. Parenti thus identifies factional antagonisms within the elite and an emerging conflict between elite and popolo, the latter initially led by ottimati who favored broader government.

Into these multiplying divisions Savonarola injected his charismatic preaching.[12] Until this point he had avoided overtly political themes, but his success in negotiations with Charles pulled him into the debate. On November 16, a week after Piero's departure, he alluded to the controversies, commenting rather ambiguously that "many would like to administer the government [*stato*] who cannot because they are not suited to it. Many are able and do not want to. . . . In the former regime many wanted to who were not able, and many were able and wanted to who should not have." On December 7, amidst protests over the Twenty, he reminded the Florentines of their narrow escape from danger and advised that if they wished to "renew" their city and bring about a "new government" they had to find new "ways of living" and pass a law preventing anyone from making himself "capo," an obvious reference to

[10] Parenti, *Storia*, pp. 147–51.
[11] Cerretani, *Storia*, pp. 221–2.
[12] D. Weinstein, *Savonarola and Florence: Prophecy and Patriotism in the Renaissance* (Princeton, 1970), pp. 144–58, 247–66.

the Medici, possibly also to the Twenty. If citizens prayed and attended (his) sermons, God would give them the grace to find a "good form for this new *reggimento* of yours, either as the Venetians do, or as God will best inspire you to do," since, he added, rejecting a famous comment by Cosimo de' Medici, "it is *not* true, as crazy and evil men say, that states cannot be ruled with 'paternostri,' which is a dictum of tyrants and not of true princes." Florentines should seek out good and humble men, those who usually shy away from government, and make them take their part in governing. They should reduce taxes, especially the gabelles, and eliminate the "feste" with which some foolish people say the popolo should be kept entertained, which is "true in tyrannies, not in free, republican cities [*città libere e civili*]." Over the next week Savonarola occasionally hinted at the swirling political controversies: "If you want to innovate beyond your old ways, it is necessary for you to think well about the modalities of your innovations and your new *reggimento*." He reached back to the political language of the old popolo when he reminded his listeners that "Florence is an *università*; and whenever a multitude or *università* of persons must direct themselves toward an end and a common good for all, there must be some *capo* who introduces and sets them on the right road." Evidently, there was one kind of *capo* to avoid and another to embrace. Addressing the "popolo," he urged them not to grumble or complain and to trust that he had taken and would continue to take "your side."[13]

Savonarola gave his most important political sermon on December 14.[14] According to Landucci, he wanted it attended by men, not women, and by the government. With "all the officials of Florence present," Savonarola proclaimed his view that Florence needed a well-regulated government of the many; otherwise, it would suffer constant dissension, factional divisions, and exiles. He urged moral and social reform: laws against all forms of immorality, including sodomy, poetry, gambling, taverns, and excessive luxury in women's dress; more equitable distribution of taxes; modest dowries; and repudiation of all would-be tyrants. On constitutional matters he stated boldly, referring to the parlamento, that the "form you have begun cannot stand unless you reorganize it. I believe there is no better form than that of the Venetians and that you should take them as your example, leaving out however certain things that are not appropriate and do not serve your needs, such as the doge." This was Savonarola's second reference to Venice, but he was still tantalizingly unclear about exactly what he meant, since Venice could be seen either as a broadly-based republic, given its large council, or as a tightly controlled oligarchy, given the concentration of power among several dozen families in the Senate.

[13]   Girolamo Savonarola, *Prediche sopra Aggeo*, ed. L. Firpo (Rome, 1965), pp. 81, 130–8, 198, 207.
[14]   Ibid., pp. 210–12, 220–4, 226–8.

He made two specific recommendations: first, "in order to encourage everyone to conduct himself virtuously, the guildsmen [*artefici*] should in some way be made eligible"; and second, major offices should be filled by election and minor ones by sortition. These recommendations gestured in different directions. Landucci expressed the popolo's preference for sortition in looking forward to the moment when the "pouches would be closed and extraction by lot resumed, just as we once lived *a comune*," adding that the city should "always be content with sortition."[15] Savonarola thus simultaneously embraced the popolo's desire for an expansion of the office-holding class and the ottimati's preference for controlled elections: an inconsistency that was at least consistent with his exhortations to reconciliation between supporters of the "old government" and the "new one."

Savonarola also proposed a controversial procedure for debating constitutional reform: "You have in your city sixteen standardbearers of the companies (as you call them), who embrace the whole city and all its citizens. Let all citizens meet, each one in his *gonfalone*, and let them discuss and examine what seems to them the best form to adopt for your government. Each *gonfalone* will submit the plan that its citizens will recommend, and thus there will be sixteen plans. Then let all the standardbearers assemble, and let them select those four among the plans that they judge to be the best and most stable and take them to the Signoria. . . . The Signoria will select one of the four plans. And you should believe without doubt that the reform selected in this way will be from God." A city-wide system of grass-roots consultation evidently frightened the elite. Parenti, who gives an accurate summary of the sermon of December 14, says that, although the "*popolo* liked" the plan, it was not in fact adopted. Instead, the Signoria proposed that five drafts for constitutional reform be solicited from existing governmental committees: the Signoria itself, their advisory colleges (acting jointly), the Twenty, the Ten, and the captains of the Guelf Party. All five plans were to be debated, presumably by these same bodies, "in the palace, with brother Girolamo present," until one was selected. Savonarola was apparently unhappy with the change: according to Parenti, he became "heated" on the subject and told a large crowd that God's will absolutely required that Florence be governed "*a popolo*, and not tyrannically" and that damnation, death, and loss of worldly goods awaited anyone who contradicted divine will. Savonarola's reaction frightened some people and caused a further change that was, if anything, still more removed from his original recommendation: two men were selected from each of the five committees to propose the specifics of the reform. Behind the controversy over procedure lay the question of whether executive offices would be filled by sortition or election. Parenti implies that reforms emerging from a

[15]   Landucci, *Diario*, pp. 92, 89.

broad consultation of citizens would have restored sortition, whereas a tightly controlled debate was more likely to approve election: "And in truth the matter was of the greatest importance, and much of the *popolo* resented this method of election, fearing that, if election were adopted, they would be left out. The friends of the former regime, who were numerous, were certain that they would be excluded from offices whenever a large multitude had the chance to vote on them."[16]

Savonarola's reiterated exhortation to imitate Venice made his intentions no clearer: "As I said before, I believe that the form of the Venetian government is a very good one, and you should not think it shameful to learn from others, because their form was given to them by God, and since they adopted it they have never had civil conflicts." But Parenti says the idea came, not from Savonarola himself, but from some ottimati who, seeing the popolo's unhappiness, wanted to offer something to soften their anger, and that Savonarola agreed to help placate the popolo by telling them he would always be on their side and their defender against the power of the "grandi." His promises that the Florentines would reap abundance and power if they obeyed God's commands, says Parenti, were "an excellent way of holding back the *popolo*, who realized that they had been duped by the *primati* [the ottimati] and were in no mood to be patient." He thus attributes to Savonarola the same wish to "brake" the popolo that he says motivated the ottimati who, "seeing the roaring of the people, and fearing that [their anger] might at some point be turned against them, thought about how they could strengthen and stabilize the government." Fearing that the popolo was "leaning toward revolution [*mutazione*]," some decided to favor an "almost Venetian-style reform" of election "carried out by all the citizens of the *reggimento*, at their pleasure." They judged this the best way "to put all citizens on an equal basis," which would remove the danger of revolution and prevent the ottimati from losing control of government. "But because there was disagreement among them, those who favored this solution came to an agreement with brother Girolamo and persuaded him that this was the best way. He had acquired great authority with the *popolo*, and whatever he said was bound to be approved by them. He thus spoke on this matter from the pulpit."[17] In Parenti's interpretation, the ottimati were willing to expand the number of those participating in elections provided that the old system of scrutinies and sortition was replaced by one in which smaller groups would nominate a limited number of candidates who would then be voted on in a larger assembly.

Despite this tactical alliance with the group around Paolantonio Soderini, Savonarola seems to have injected elements of his own, particularly concerning

[16]   Parenti, *Storia*, pp. 158–60.
[17]   Ibid., pp. 156–7.

the inclusion of "guildsmen" and grass-roots consultations in all gonfaloni. Many ottimati soon regretted having entrusted their political fortunes to the power of his sermons, seeing his independence and immense authority with the popolo as dangerous. "With brother Girolamo loudly proclaiming so many things from the pulpit, and apparently having taken upon himself the protection of our *popolo*," says Parenti, "those in authority were displeased. They lamented, although in secret, being subject to [his] power. It was one thing to govern a convent, they said, quite another to govern a city.... They considered it a great obstacle that the friar had acquired so much authority over the city, but they were in a situation where they could not contradict him."[18] Ottimati had approached him and sought his cooperation because of his influence with the popolo, but his political preaching only increased that influence. Whether he was following or leading an emerging popular view of political reform, Savonarola certainly had a major part in turning what began as a conservative replacement of the Medici regime with an oligarchy of former Mediceans into a revolutionary rearrangement that re-opened Florentine politics to the aspirations of a middle class reawakened from long dormancy.

Four of five drafts for constitutional reform commissioned by the Signoria have survived,[19] two from members of the Twenty (Domenico Bonsi, who became a loyal supporter of Savonarola, and Piero Capponi, who opposed him) and two from anonymous authors. All four assumed that a large council was to come into being, although Capponi insisted on the simultaneous institution of a smaller council that would conduct important elections and also serve as a permanent pratica to which the Signoria could regularly turn for advice. Landucci says that "many plans were devised and there was great controversy among the citizens, such that every day there was talk of summoning a *parlamento*," and, contrary to Parenti's information, he reports that the sixteen standardbearers did indeed submit reform drafts, all delivered to the palace on December 19 amidst still great disagreement. On Sunday December 21 Savonarola "preached again on politics, amidst much agitation because the citizens could not agree: some wanted it boiled and others roasted, some were with the friar, and others against him; and had it not been for this friar, it would have come to bloodshed."[20] Remarkably, the Signoria managed to sift through the drafts and disagreements and the next day presented a detailed proposal for the creation of the Great Council. Parenti commented that "it passed so easily that you would have said there had never been any controversy at all." Before submitting its proposal to the councils, the Signoria

---

[18]   Ibid., p. 159.
[19]   Guidi, *Ciò che accadde*, pp. 192–207; Weinstein, *Savonarola and Florence*, pp. 256–62.
[20]   Landucci, *Diario*, p. 93.

called a huge pratica of 200 citizens, to which many not invited also came, and had the proposal read aloud "in good order so that it was intelligible." Without asking for reactions, it dismissed the meeting so that "the matter could be understood and mulled over before it was put to the councils." It then reconvened the pratica and this time asked for opinions. Despite some opposition, most citizens spoke in favor.[21] After ratification by the advisory colleges, the Council of the Popolo passed it by a vote of 229–35, and the next day the Council of the Commune approved it by 195–16.

In the prologue to the law of December 22–23, 1494, the Signoria announced its intention "to attend with all its ability and strength to the preservation of the liberty that was for so long nearly suppressed and has recently been recovered," and to work for "the unity of citizens and all things that contribute to the public and general good, which consists in freely giving counsel, deliberating, and legislating in public and private matters, in the passage of excellent and well considered laws, and in that just distribution of honors and duties that characterizes a well-instituted republic."[22] Eligibility for the council extended to all citizens of legitimate birth whose names had ever been drawn for the Signoria or colleges, whether or not they assumed office (hence both those "seated" and those "seen"), or whose fathers, paternal grandfathers, or great-grandfathers had ever been "seated" or "seen." To these were added everyone approved in the scrutiny of 1484 and the members of the Councils of the Popolo and Commune, which ceased to exist once the Great Council came into being. Periodic additions of citizens could be made by the council itself. Its powers included final approval of all legislation and the election of the advisory colleges and other executive committees, except for the Signoria which was to be selected for the next year by the Twenty and thereafter "as the council will decide." Still undecided therefore was this most controversial question, and perhaps only for this reason was agreement possible for the law's passage. But the Twenty were so unpopular that they resigned in June 1495 and yielded the election of the Signoria to the council.[23] Also instituted was a Council of Eighty, selected every six months from candidates nominated by the advisory colleges and forty members drawn by lot from the Great Council, which voted on each nominee. Together with the Signoria, colleges, and Ten, the Eighty shared the authority to elect ambassadors and military commissioners and hire military forces. Legislation proposed by the Signoria had first to be approved by the Eighty and then by the Great Council. And, as Piero Capponi had recommended, the smaller council did indeed function as a permanent pratica, convened weekly by the Signoria.

[21]   Parenti, *Storia*, p. 161.
[22]   Cadoni, *Provvisioni*, pp. 33–60 (40).
[23]   Ibid., pp. 150–60.

Pre-1494 electoral practices made it inevitable that the regulations governing eligibility for the Great Council, which could be inherited from as far back
as one's great-grandfather, would produce a very large membership. Before
1434, all name-tickets had to have been drawn from one scrutiny's pouches
before extractions moved on to those of the next scrutiny. Therefore, nearly
every citizen approved in pre-1434 scrutinies was at least "seen" (*veduto*), if
not "seated" (*seduto*). After 1434, accoppiatori limited the number of name-
tickets in the pouches, and in the regime's first six years the *veduti* for the
Signoria were sharply reduced. But because political advantages and a degree
of prestige attached to having one's name at least drawn for major offices, the
Medici found it useful to increase the numbers of *veduti* whose names were
carefully recorded by the election secretaries.[24] Evidently the authors of the
law instituting the council did not count the names beforehand, for they stipulated only that, if membership exceeded 1,500, the council would be divided
into three sections for successive six-month terms and into halves if it did not
reach that number. Domenico Bonsi assumed that a division in two would
suffice, but Piero Capponi correctly guessed that the full membership would
be larger: "It seems to me," he wrote in his draft, "that messer Domenico
deceives himself considerably concerning the size of the council; they will be
such a multitude that I believe it will be necessary to divide them into four
councils."[25] When the lists were completed on January 14, 1495, the results
were an unpleasant surprise for the elite. Parenti estimates that 3,600 Florentines
qualified for the Great Council. Even after citizens in tax arrears were
eliminated, nearly 3,000 still qualified and each third of the council had almost
1,000 members. Many ottimati, "recognizing that [the council] was not to
their advantage, tried to block it; they delayed the building of the council's
hall, denounced the regulations, and, with the Signoria almost unanimously
on their side, tried almost everything to abolish the reform." But they were
unable to "resist the will of the *popolo*," says Parenti, and the preaching of
"brother Girolamo was in large part the reason for this."[26] Guicciardini too
emphasizes elite resistance to the council, chiefly by Bernardo Rucellai and
Piero Capponi who remained hostile to Savonarola and the new constitution,
but initially also by Francesco Valori (who later became Savonarola's chief
supporter). Until their resignation in June 1495, the Twenty were "hated by
the *popolo*" because they elected priors hostile to the council.[27] Fear of an
aristocratic coup pervaded these early months.

[24] Rubinstein, *Government*, pp. 41–4, 242–50.
[25] Guidi, *Ciò che accadde*, p. 198.
[26] Parenti, *Storia*, pp. 168–9.
[27] Guicciardini, *Storie fiorentine*, XII, pp. 218–21; XIII, pp. 225–7; *History of Florence*,
trans. Domandi, pp. 104–6, 109–10.

How much changed with the new constitution? Because at first election rather than sortition was used to select government committees in the council, Parenti's first reaction was that this system "was devised for no other reason than to return the government to the nobility," which "seemed finally determined to reassert its strength after a long hiatus." Even after the termination of the Twenty, the Signoria continued to be selected by election until 1499. Because the council consisted of descendents of the many *veduti* from the previous century, it could be seen as not having substantially changed the composition of the ruling class.[28] To be sure, council membership did not extend to the working classes previously excluded from the pouches. But what happened was revolutionary enough. Under the Medici regime, select committees handpicked officeholders from this large pool of eligible citizens, whereas under the 1494 reform 3,000 citizens simultaneously constituted a governing body endowed with real power over finances, taxes, and elections. And once the council's division into thirds was abolished (legislated in August 1495 and effective the following January),[29] every eligible citizen had the right to attend every meeting and vote on every piece of legislation and in every election. Never before had even a remotely similar number of citizens shared in real powers of government. Although the council's initial roster has not survived (hence the various estimates of its numbers), complete lists exist for 1496, when the council had 3,452 members,[30] and 1508, when its total of 3,575 included 3,005 major guildsmen (from 516 families) and 570 minor guildsmen.[31] The quorum for the unified council was at first 1,000, later reduced to 600 because of many absences, both voluntary and owing to tax arrears.[32] But it was not unusual for meetings to be attended by 800 or 1,000 members. And between 1495 and 1499 the council became larger, more open, and less amenable to elite interests and manipulation.

Because no hall in the palace of the priors could accommodate such numbers, in May 1495 the council appointed building commissioners (operai) to find a suitable meeting place. They quickly decided (encouraged by Savonarola, says Landucci) to build a new hall (the "sala grande") as an addition to the palace on its east (or back) side. Landucci followed the rapid progress of its construction: foundations in place by the end of July; roof vaulting by mid-August;

[28] R. Pesman Cooper, "The Florentine Ruling Group Under the 'Governo Popolare,' 1494–1512," *Studies in Medieval and Renaissance History* 7 (1985): 69–181.
[29] Cadoni, *Provvisioni*, pp. 185–91.
[30] G. Guidi, "La corrente savonaroliana e la petizione al Papa del 1497," *ASI* 142 (1984): 31–46 (40).
[31] Pesman Cooper, "Florentine Ruling Group," pp. 80, 113–14.
[32] N. Rubinstein, "I primi anni del Consiglio Maggiore a Firenze," *ASI* 112 (1954): 151–94, 321–47.

and roof beams in December. By February 1496, although finished flooring
and benches were still lacking, the council held its first meeting in the new
room, and, according to Parenti, 1,753 members attended. Two inscriptions
were placed in the hall. One, in Latin, solemnly announced that "This council
is from God, and woe to him who tries to undo it."[33] The other, in Tuscan,
warned, with reference to the now banned *parlamenti* so often used by the
Medici, that "he who wants to convene a *parlamento* wants to take control of
government away from the *popolo*." Contemporaries from the aristocratic
Guicciardini to citizens of the popolo like Landucci and Parenti had no
hesitation in referring to the council and the governments that emerged from
it as "popolare," which, in the lexicon of Florentine politics, still referred to
the popolo.

Savonarola's Holy Republic

More revolutionary than the size and powers of the Great Council was the
religious ideology that sustained it. Mixing religion and politics in Florence
was not new. The republic had always and increasingly wrapped itself in the
sacrality associated with saints, relics, images, processions, and the patronage of ecclesiastical communities and churches. No compilation of statutes,
whether of guilds or commune, ever lacked a dedication to the "honor and
reverence" of the Virgin and the saints. Religious ceremonies accompanied
scrutinies and the installation of each new Signoria. Electoral pouches were
stored at Santa Croce, and Franciscan friars oversaw and protected the integrity and honor of the sortition process. Natural disasters and political crises
prompted religious processions and heightened devotion to sacred objects and
images.[34] The Medici were assiduous patrons of monasteries, convents, and
churches, and perhaps nowhere more than at the Dominican convent of San
Marco was Medici power inscribed in religious and ecclesiastical frames.
Cosimo brought the Observant Dominicans from Fiesole to San Marco and
rebuilt the entire convent. Lorenzo revived its fortunes and made it a prestigious center of Dominican learning.[35]

---

[33] Landucci, *Diario*, pp. 112, 114, 121, 126; Parenti, *Storia*, p. 314; Rubinstein,
Palazzo Vecchio, pp. 40–2.
[34] Trexler, *Public Life*; Trexler, "Florentine Religious Experience: The Sacred Image,"
Studies in the Renaissance 19 (1972): 7–41.
[35] L. Polizzotto, "Lorenzo il Magnifico, Savonarola and Medicean Dynasticism," in
Lorenzo de' Medici: New Perspectives, ed. Toscani, pp. 331–55; Polizzotto, "Savonarola
and the Florentine Oligarchy," in *The World of Savonarola: Italian Elites and Perceptions of Crisis*, ed. S. Fletcher and C. Shaw (Aldershot, 2000), pp. 55–64.

Savonarola, a native of Ferrara, was originally assigned to San Marco by his order in 1482. His early sermons attracted little attention and he was soon transferred elsewhere, but he gained the admiration and friendship of the philosopher Giovanni Pico della Mirandola, who later urged Lorenzo to bring Savonarola back to oversee San Marco's reform. In the meantime Savonarola had found his prophetic voice and vocation, and when he returned to Florence in 1490 his public sermons were filled with polemics against a culture he saw as excessively profane and only superficially Christian. But he did not overtly criticize the regime or Lorenzo, who actually protected him.[36] The famous story according to which he withheld absolution from the dying Lorenzo for denying the Florentines their liberty is certainly apocryphal. Despite his criticism of Florentine culture and conspicuous wealth, Savonarola's learning and administrative skills earned him Lorenzo's favor. Savonarola also knew what happened in 1488 to the Franciscan demagogue, Bernardino da Feltre, whose inflammatory denunciations in Lenten sermons of usury and Jewish moneylenders provoked a crowd of hotheaded youths to attack a Jew and destroy his shop. The Otto di Guardia stopped the violence by threatening the boys' fathers with banishment and prohibited Bernardino from preaching in Florence.[37] The episode revealed the regime's nervousness over, and readiness to silence, dangerous preachers. Purveyors of prophecy found eager audiences in these years, both in sermons and increasingly in the new print medium. As early as 1479 a prominent Florentine print shop run by Dominican nuns was publishing traditional prophetic texts for booksellers and public singers, and "until the end of the fifteenth century, Florence was undoubtedly the most important center for the distribution of popular print publications on prophecy."[38] Parenti's description of Domenico da Ponzo's preaching in April 1492, just after Lorenzo's death, emphasizes its prophetic tenor: if people did not correct their ways, "horrible scandals" would afflict the city and "blood would run in the streets." Warnings from a worried regime persuaded him to soften his predictions. A year later, when he and the infamous Bernardino da Feltre returned for a meeting of the Chapter General of the Observant Franciscans and asked the government's permission to preach, the Otto authorized Domenico and were about to give permission to Bernardino as well, but,

---

[36] Weinstein, *Savonarola and Florence*, pp. 67–111; R. Ridolfi, *Vita di Girolamo Savonarola*, 5th edn. (Florence, 1974).

[37] Landucci, *Diario*, pp. 53–4, regretted the action of the Otto. Tribaldo de' Rossi, *Ricordanze*, in *Delizie degli eruditi toscani*, ed. I. di San Luigi, vol. 23, pp. 238–40 (partially translated by Brucker, *Society*, pp. 248–9); C. Bresnahan Menning, *Charity and State in Late Renaissance Italy: The Monte di Pietà of Florence* (Ithaca, N.Y., 1993), pp. 32–5.

[38] O. Niccoli, *Prophecy and People in Renaissance Italy*, trans. L. G. Cochrane (Princeton, 1990), p. 8.

"fearing the great numbers of people" who might attend his sermons and the unpredictable consequences, they changed their minds and denied him the pulpit. An already assembled crowd went away with "sorrow and displeasure," grumbling and denouncing the government. Domenico went to Piero de' Medici to get the decision reversed, and Bernardino, agreeing to say nothing about pawnshops or Jews, did finally preach before a crowd of ten thousand, says Parenti, who considered it "a most evident sign of the government's weakness."[39]

Savonarola returned to this explosive religious environment in 1490 and hammered away at what he saw as a widening abyss between the superficial observance of religious ceremonies and the true evangelical Christianity of the gospels, lamenting the incompatibility of genuine Christian faith with great wealth and the unjustifiable gap between rich and poor and thus gaining a reputation as the "preacher of the hopeless." This social critique, especially in the thunderous Lenten sermons of 1491 later characterized as the *terrifica praedicatio*, was directed not at the Medici but at the entire elite's arrogance, wealth, exploitation of the poor, and abuse of the church for careers and advancement. But when he denounced "tyrants" who listened to flatterers, imposed unfair taxes, exploited the poor, bought votes, and elected corrupt officials, it is inconceivable that the regime's leaders, perhaps even his patron Lorenzo, would not have suspected that such condemnations implicated them. What could Lorenzo think when Savonarola excoriated those who made their young sons prelates of the church out of family pride and ambition? In 1492, a delegation consisting of Domenico Bonsi, Guidantonio Vespucci, Francesco Valori, Paolantonio Soderini, and Bernardo Rucellai cautioned Savonarola not to go too far with his denunciations and dire warnings of imminent punishments. Savonarola later said he was sure, despite their denials, that they had been sent by Lorenzo. This too may be an invention of his early and adoring biographers, but that Savonarola thought reprisals from the regime at least a possibility is suggested by a 1491 letter to a friend in which he reports that "many have feared and still fear that what happened to Fra Bernardino might happen to me."[40]

The regime's fall unleashed the energy of Florence's volatile religious culture and catapulted Savonarola into the role of mediating between political and religious spheres both in search of new moorings and destined to find them in each other. Church reform and renewal of Christendom were the unifying themes of his evangelical and prophetic message. But whereas before

[39]   Parenti, *Storia*, pp. 27–8, 48–9; Weinstein, *Savonarola*, pp. 125–8.
[40]   Ridolfi, *Vita*, chaps. 4–6 (p. 60); Polizzotto, "Savonarola and the Florentine Oligarchy," pp. 56–7; A. F. Verde, "Girolamo Savonarola: ideologo e profeta, il quaresimale del 1491," in *Savonarola: democrazia, tirannide, profezia*, ed. G. C. Garfagnini (Florence, 1998), pp. 127–47.

1494 he framed the renewal as a turning away from the world and its temptations and thus as a traditional message of repentance and renunciation of wealth and worldly ambition, at the end of 1494 Savonarola began identifying Florence as the specific vessel of this renewal, as the chosen city and new Jerusalem in which the reform of Christian society would begin. In order to fulfill this divinely appointed task, Florence had to purify itself by expelling the tyrants, recovering liberty, and protecting the new republic whose heart was the Great Council. Thus the revived republic became a moral cause, a central chapter of sacred history and of the Almighty's plan for His people. Politics and religion became indistinguishable as Savonarola persuaded large numbers of Florentines that God was unfolding a design for salvation through their republic: a momentous conjunction through which his followers infused both their politics and their religion with exhilarating new meanings and goals. Amorphous religious yearnings, the hunger for something new underlying the fascination with prophecy, speculation about the last days and the establishment of a different order of things all found their calling. Republican traditions debilitated by sixty years of Medici rule were now revived by the conviction that the moral life or death of Christian society depended on them.

In this new and specifically Florentine version of his prophetic message, Savonarola told the Florentines what was both expected of them as God's elect and promised to them if they successfully carried out this work. On December 21, the day before the council was created, he urged them to take to heart five overriding principles and goals: fear of God; the common good and a limited desire for personal wealth; universal peace among themselves (including amnesty for supporters of the defunct Medici regime); political reform to institute a "new and holy government," based, he says again, on the Venetian constitution, and whose "seed" is the new council; and the conviction that "God's will is that Florence change its way of living." Repeatedly exhorting them to this combination of moral, political, and social reforms, he said that God's reward to Florence would be (and this was another new element in his preaching) wealth, glory, and power in measures they had never before enjoyed: "If you do this, your city will be glorious, because in this way it will be reformed with regard to both the spiritual and the temporal. And Florence will become richer and more powerful than ever and will extend its power [*imperio*] in many places."[41] Early in 1498, as he defended himself against

---

[41] *Prediche sopra Aggeo*, pp. 330–45, 213; Weinstein, *Savonarola and Florence*; also G. C. Garfagnini, "La predicazione sopra *Aggeo* e i *Salmi*"; P. Prodi, "Gli affanni della democrazia: La predicazione del Savonarola durante l'esperienza del governo popolare," and C. Leonardi, "Savonarola e la politica nelle prediche sopra l'*Esodo* e nel *Trattato circa el reggimento e governo della città di Firenze*," all in *Savonarola e la politica*, ed. G. C. Garfagnini (Florence, 1997), pp. 3–25, 27–74, 75–89.

multiplying enemies, Savonarola summed up this optimistic vision of Florence's destiny in his *Treatise on the Government of Florence*. Four "virtues" were needed to sustain the perfection of the new government: fear of God, love of the common good, love of one another, and justice, which "purges the city of bad men." Divine rewards awaited the purified city: "God, for justice also, will increase the city's empire, as he did that of the Romans." A government of men illuminated by these virtues will be "given by God" and "they will create on earth a government like that of heaven. They will be blessed with many spiritual and temporal blessings" and will enjoy true liberty and three kinds of happiness: earthly, spiritual, and eternal. Liberty, equated with freedom from tyrants, will allow the Florentines to be "safe in their city, caring with joy and peace of mind for their own households and for making an honest profit in business. When God increases their property or their status, they will not be afraid of someone taking these away." Under the promise of spiritual happiness, in which "everyone will be able to dedicate himself to the good Christian life," no one "will be forced by poverty to enter into bad contracts, because, since there is good government in the city, it will abound with riches and there will be work for everyone and the poor will earn a living." The city "in a short time will be restored to such religion that it will be like a paradise on earth," in which children will be given a healthy upbringing, good laws will protect the honor of women and boys, and the clergy will be reformed. The greatest rewards in heaven await those who "govern their cities well." Good government brings about so many beneficial consequences that it cannot fail to please God. Moreover, "since he who governs is more similar to God than he who is governed, it is obvious that, if he governs with justice, he is more loved and rewarded by God than he is for his private actions when he is not governing."[42] While the constitution of 1494 was not Savonarola's invention, its identification with sacred history and with divine will was indeed his, and of momentous consequence.

Over the next few years Florence was riven by factions and parties defined, for the first time, chiefly neither by patronage ties nor by class interests. Although class and faction continued to divide Florentines, ideology, religion, and Savonarola himself now did so at least as much, as the city was passionately divided between believers and enemies of his theological and millenarian defense of republican liberty and social reform. A large and vocal Savonarolan party, the *frateschi*, or, as their enemies derisively called them, the weepers (*piagnoni*), emerged in the council across class lines. Its leadership included prominent ottimati (Paolantonio Soderini, Giovanbattista Ridolfi, Francesco Valori, Jacopo Salviati, and Francesco Gualterotti) and many from the boundary

---

[42]   The *Treatise* is in *Prediche sopra Aggeo*, pp. 435–87 (476–84); trans. R. N. Watkins in *Humanism and Liberty*, pp. 231–60 (254–8).

between the elite and popolo (like Domenico Bonsi). Guicciardini gives a long list of prominent *frateschi*, and, ever cautious, says that his father Piero, although counted among them, conducted himself so "moderately" that he was not "completely ranked with them." With these leaders was the "*universale del popolo*, many of whom were drawn to these things." So deep were the "great conflicts and mortal hatred among citizens over the matter of the friar" that dissension separated brother from brother and fathers from their sons."[43] A list of 500 signatories to a petition sent on Savonarola's behalf to Pope Alexander VI in 1497 indicates the depth of his support (despite the many enemies, among them the pope, he had by then) from members of elite families (including the Albizzi, Aldobrandini, Corsini, Guasconi, Orlandini, Pitti, Ridolfi, Rucellai, Salviati, Strozzi, and Tosinghi), successful families of the popolo (like the Cambini, Gondi, and Pucci), and many more, both major and minor guildsmen.[44] Much of the cultural elite was also on his side. Marsilio Ficino was an early supporter who, however, quickly changed his mind. But many of the younger intellectuals who had once moved in Ficino's orbit gravitated toward the friar: Giovanni Pico (who died in November 1494); his nephew Gianfrancesco Pico, who wrote an influential biography of Savonarola; Giovanni Nesi, who defended his prophecies; and Girolamo Benivieni, who embraced Savonarola's vision of Florence's mission to preserve holy liberty. Even poets, despite the severe limitations Savonarola imposed on "Christian" poetry, came under his sway, particularly Ugolino Verino.[45]

For three years the Savonarolans pushed forward an agenda of moral and social reform to purify the republic and prepare it for the momentous political and sacred role the friar had assigned it. His powerful preaching became a political program through a large party of devoted followers who threatened sinners and a sinful city with dire punishments. And, perhaps for this reason, their moral reforms, while significant in the short term, failed to produce deep or durable changes in Florentine society. Their first objective was renewed severity against sodomy. In December 1494, Savonarola called for the stoning and burning of sodomites, and the councils quickly replaced fines with corporal punishments for convicted sodomites and the death penalty for a

---

[43] Guicciardini, *Storie fiorentine*, XIII, pp. 236–7.
[44] L. Polizzotto, *The Elect Nation: The Savonarolan Movement in Florence, 1494–1545* (Oxford, 1994), pp. 14–20, 446–60; Guidi, "La corrente savonaroliana"; G. Pampaloni, "Il movimento piagnone secondo la lista del 1497," in *Studies on Machiavelli*, ed. M. P. Gilmore (Florence, 1972), pp. 337–47.
[45] Weinstein, *Savonarola and Florence*, pp. 185–226; Polizzotto, *Elect Nation*, chaps. 2–4; *Studi savonaroliani: verso il quinto centenario*, ed. G. C. Garfagnini (Florence, 1996). On Benivieni: S. Roush, "Dante as Piagnone Prophet: Girolamo Benivieni's 'Cantico in laude di Dante' (1506)," *Renaissance Quarterly* 55 (2002): 49–80.

third conviction. In 1496 self-accusers were deprived of the immunity from prosecution they had previously enjoyed. Brigades of boys who renounced the vice and actively hunted down and intimidated sodomites produced a predictable backlash of opposing youth gangs that taunted the pious Savonarolans. Despite an increase in anonymous accusations (over 700 between late 1495 and 1497), the Night Officials prosecuted relatively few of the accused, and, although they convicted almost half of those they prosecuted, they and the Eight issued only three death sentences and commuted two of these to monetary penalties. Savonarola had to admit failure: "If you don't want to kill them," he conceded in a sermon of March 1496, "at least drive them out of your territory."[46]

Savonarola's attempt to organize Florentine children was similarly contested. Besides enlisting boys to police morals, in 1496 he instituted the first Florentine religious processions consisting entirely of boys, an innovation that provoked astonishment in some and fear in others. The *frateschi* tried repeatedly to pass laws that would have formally authorized youth groups to search out and denounce sodomites, gamblers, and other offenders. But the council regularly rejected them and in the end gave Savonarola nothing more than a sumptuary law regulating children's dress.[47] His remarkable proposal for women's self-governance was likewise a controversial failure. In the first known suggestion that political representation be applied to Florence's women, he urged that women's committees representing the quarters meet to discuss and decide their own collective reform. Protests erupted and Savonarola had to rescind the idea, even as one woman scolded him for yielding to those who feared putting women's issues in women's hands.[48] A third policy that stirred tensions was the call for expelling Jews and instituting a state lending institution, or Monte di Pietà, to replace Jewish moneylenders. Preaching against usury, Savonarola exhorted charity to the poor and recommended that public banks make loans against pawns for nominal fees. But there were more virulent anti-Jewish voices, especially that of Marco di Matteo Strozzi, a cleric who in August 1495 harangued crowds in piazza Signoria with arguments about why "these enemies of the cross of Christ," with "their old synagogue, their rites and their usury," should be removed from the city. In December 1495 the council approved the Monte di Pietà, which began operations the next year, and the expulsion of Jews. Although some Jews left the city, the order of expulsion was not enforced and was actually rescinded in November 1496,

---

[46] Rocke, *Forbidden Friendships*, pp. 204–23 (207).

[47] Polizzotto, *Elect Nation*, pp. 38–40; Trexler, *Public Life*, pp. 474–82.

[48] F. W. Kent, "A Proposal by Savonarola for the Self-Reform of Florentine Women (March 1496)," *Memorie domenicane* 14 (1983): 334–41; Polizzotto, *Elect Nation*, pp. 40–2.

apparently at the urging of Savonarola himself.[49] Some of his own supporters reproached him.

Savonarola's enemies were as passionate as his followers: indeed, anti-Savonarolans were called the *arrabbiati* (the enraged). Among their elite leaders Guicciardini mentions Piero Capponi, Tanai de' Nerli, Lorenzo di Pierfrancesco de' Medici, Guidantonio Vespucci, Bernardo Rucellai, Piero Alberti, and the Pazzi. Some less prestigious families (Martelli, Giugni, Canacci, Da Diacceto "and many others like them") joined them, but the anti-Savonarolans never had the same popular following that the *frateschi* enjoyed. According to Guicciardini, no single motive unified the *arrabbiati* in their antipathy to the friar: some were alienated by his religious ideology, others by the popular government he supported, still others by the campaigns against sodomy and gambling, or by the *frateschi*'s stubbornly pro-French foreign policy. Savonarola had no more dangerous enemy than Pope Alexander VI, whom he repeatedly denounced as the embodiment of a corrupt and fallen church. Constant criticism of the hierarchy and papacy brought the inevitable reaction. A first papal order to cease preaching came in October 1495, but a sympathetic Signoria urged Savonarola to resume during the Lenten season of 1496. In June 1497 Alexander excommunicated and silenced Savonarola for the rest of the year. Growing pressure from Rome, and the threat of interdicts and reprisals against Florentine banking interests, caused many Florentines, not his loyal followers but those in the middle who had given him the benefit of their doubts, to waver and then abandon him.

Complicating divisions between Savonarola's supporters and opponents was the Medici question. Since, at least nominally, everyone had been Medicean until the regime's collapse, former Mediceans were found among both *frateschi* and *arrabbiati*. But both parties also contained anti-Mediceans and were thus divided over the question of whether to prosecute key figures of the defunct regime. Savonarola initially won the favor of many former Mediceans with insistent pleas for amnesty and promotion of a law of March 1495 granting amnesty, except to those guilty of homicide or embezzlement, and allowing anyone sentenced to death to appeal to the council.[50] But in 1497 his reaction to a conspiracy to reinstate the Medici eroded Savonarola's standing with both Mediceans and others. In April, while the former Medicean Bernardo del Nero was Standardbearer of Justice, Piero de' Medici appeared with troops at the city gates awaiting word from allies within to launch an assault. The government reacted quickly and Piero departed. In May opposition to the *frateschi* emerged as anti-Savonarolan youth gangs, the *compagnacci*, violently

---

[49]   Polizzotto, *Elect Nation*, pp. 35–7; Bresnahan Menning, *Charity and State*, pp. 37–63; U. Cassuto, *Gli ebrei a Firenze nell'età del Rinascimento* (Florence, 1918).

[50]   Cadoni, *Provvisioni*, pp. 108–18.

disrupted his Ascension Day sermon. To calm the city, twelve "peacemakers" were appointed representing all factions.[51] The papal excommunication came in June, followed by another committee of "peacemakers" in July and a swelling dispute in August over elections in the council. In this tense situation Lamberto dell'Antella, who had been exiled for illegal contacts with Piero de' Medici, revealed that Piero's arrival in April had been part of a larger conspiracy whose alleged leaders were Bernardo del Nero, Niccolò Ridolfi (both among the July "peacemakers"), Lorenzo Tornabuoni, Giannozzo Pucci, and Giovanni Cambi. Also suspected of complicity was Lucrezia de' Medici, Lorenzo's daughter and wife of Jacopo Salviati. She fled the city but was later exonerated. A large pratica of two hundred found the five guilty and recommended the death penalty. But a huge debate erupted when they claimed their right of appeal to the Great Council. Although inclined to allow the appeal, the Signoria yielded to threats from its advisory colleges and reconvened the pratica,[52] where an overwhelming majority insisted that the dangers of a popular uprising, of possible involvement by foreign powers in the conspiracy, and of worsening disunity should the council reverse the death sentences were all too great to allow the appeal.[53] When the Signoria announced that it intended to reject the pratica's recommendation and proceed with the appeal, Francesco Valori made a fiery speech full of threats and intimidation against those priors (including Guicciardini's father Piero) favoring the appeal. That very day the five conspirators were executed. Savonarola, who had supported the law guaranteeing the right of appeal, did nothing to prevent his allies from denying it in this case. Cerretani even reports that "some said that brother Girolamo sent two friars to the Standardbearer of Justice to tell him that God wanted justice done."[54] Savonarola was severely criticized for the inconsistency and of course lost the support of the Mediceans. Now both Mediceans and non-Medicean *arrabbiati* saw him as more of a risk than he was worth and Francesco Valori as an outright danger.

At the end of 1497 Savonarola emerged from his silence and defied the pope's orders. At Christmas, with his ally Paolantonio Soderini as Standardbearer of Justice, he celebrated Mass again, and, with another supporter, Giuliano Salviati, in the same office in February 1498, he resumed preaching at the

[51]   A. Brown, "Partiti, correnti, o coalizioni: un contributo al dibattito," in *Savonarole: Enjeux, débats, questions* (Paris, 1997), pp. 59–79 (67–70); and Brown's "Ideology and Faction in Savonarolan Florence," in *World of Savonarola*, ed. Fletcher and Shaw, pp. 22–41 (28–9).
[52]   Jacopo Nardi, *Istorie della città di Firenze*, 2 vols. (Florence, 1858), 1:109.
[53]   *Consulte e pratiche della Repubblica fiorentina, 1495–1497*, ed. D. Fachard (Geneva, 2002), pp. 509–14; Guicciardini, *Storie fiorentine*, XV, pp. 258–60.
[54]   Cerretani, *Storia*, p. 238.

beginning of Lent to huge crowds of men and women in the cathedral. The archbishop's vicar, who was Alexander's representative and also a distant Medici cousin, tried unsuccessfully to prohibit the clergy from attending. Alexander was furious and again threatened Florentine merchants with reprisals and the city with an interdict. Led by a prominent anti-Savonarolan, Piero Popoleschi, the Signoria of March–April held several pratiche on the question of whether to enforce Alexander's new order prohibiting Savonarola from preaching. On March 14, at least thirty-two citizens spoke, many at great length in the friar's defense, even in the face of papal anger.[55] In the end the Signoria obeyed the papal demand, and Savonarola withdrew to San Marco with his followers. In the increasingly heated atmosphere that demanded a resolution, faith took a turn toward the hopelessly irrational. A Franciscan critic challenged Savonarola to prove the authenticity of his prophecies by means of a trial by fire, and, quite likely to Savonarola's surprise and dismay, his loyal but naïve lieutenant Fra Domenico da Pescia accepted and offered to undergo the ordeal in his superior's place. Even some of Savonarola's normally savvy political allies welcomed the test: emotional fatigue after almost four years of constant controversy was taking its toll. Guicciardini commented that "many citizens on both sides liked it because they were eager to see these divisions extinguished and an end to all these ambiguities."[56] The trial was scheduled for April 7, and, with the apparatus in place in piazza Signoria, the principals assembled in front of a large crowd. Last-minute squabbling over the "rules" and a sudden storm, and perhaps reluctance to go through with it, cancelled the ordeal. But Savonarola's enemies would not be denied. The next day, Palm Sunday, a furious crowd, with many *compagnacci*, attacked San Marco and then shifted their anger toward the nearby home of Francesco Valori, where he and his wife were both murdered. Valori was killed by a Ridolfi and a Tornabuoni to avenge the executions of their relatives the previous August. As the mob was readying to do the same to *frateschi* leaders Paolantonio Soderini and Giovanbattista Ridolfi, the Signoria sent soldiers to stop the mayhem. Savonarola and his two closest associates were arrested and escorted to the palace of the priors. More pratiche discussed whether and how to examine the three, but the outcome was now foreordained. Savonarola was examined by a committee of citizens and tortured to elicit a confession that he had lied and was a false prophet. Papal emissaries interrogated and then condemned him as a heretic and schismatic, and on May 23, in piazza Signoria, he and his associates, Domenico da Pescia and Silvestro Maruffi, were hanged,

[55] *Consulte e pratiche della Repubblica fiorentina, 1498–1505*, 2 vols., ed. D. Fachard (Geneva, 1993), 1:45–60.
[56] Guicciardini, *Storie fiorentine*, XVI, p. 268.

their bodies burned and their ashes thrown into the Arno.[57] For another half-century Florentines debated the meaning of Savonarola's life and the way they ended it.

Domestic Discord and Dominion Crises

Guicciardini says that the organizers of the anti-Savonarolan attacks, including Bernardo Rucellai, assumed that "with the friar gone, the Great Council would be finished; this is why they so vigorously opposed him, but in this they were deceived."[58] Former ottimati supporters and opponents of Savonarola now sought to present a united front against the council. In July 1498 a group met to discuss instituting a council of 150–200 elite citizens and putting the government "in the hands of men of worth and nobles."[59] Thus began four years of proposals and schemes by ottimati determined to modify the constitution of 1494. At the root of their error in believing they could now overturn the council was a failure to recognize the popolo's growing strength in the body. Initially, Savonarola mediated between his party's elite leaders and popular base, but in 1497 he came to depend more on Valori and the ottimati and in 1498 the alienation of much of the base turned violent. The chronicler Piero Vaglienti, a shopkeeper, blamed the proliferation of factions on "that devil of a friar Girolamo."[60] A strong popular party not only survived the weakening of its ties to Savonarola, and his and Valori's spectacular elimination from the scene, but actually grew stronger over the next few years. By 1499, the popolo had more political clout in the council than ever before, which made the ottimati still more determined to abolish or at least weaken it.

In the council the ottimati favored the election of candidates receiving the most votes among those with at least a majority.[61] This may seem counterintuitive, given that ottimati were a minority in the council. But the alternative was sortition, which left matters to chance, whereas voting allowed for the exercise of influence, favors, intimidation, and all the more or less subtle ways in which wealthy and powerful patrons and families could encourage votes for ottimati candidates. Under this system, in 1495–6 ottimati

[57] Ibid., XVI, pp. 267–80; Nardi, *Istorie*, 1:110–37; Cerretani, *Storia fiorentina*, pp. 240–55; and Weinstein, *Savonarola and Florence*, pp. 283–8.
[58] Guicciardini, *Storie fiorentine*, XVI, p. 276.
[59] S. Bertelli, "Embrioni di partiti politici alle soglie dell'età moderna," in *Per Federico Chabod (1901–1960)*, ed. S. Bertelli (Perugia, 1980–1), vol. 1, pp. 17–35.
[60] Piero Vaglienti, *Storia dei suoi tempi, 1492–1514*, ed. G. Berti, M. Luzzati, and E. Tongiorgi (Pisa, 1982), p. 74.
[61] For what follows: G. Cadoni, *Lotte politiche e riforme istituzionali a Firenze tra il 1494 e il 1502* (Rome, 1999), pp. 19–84.

elected to offices were proportionally more numerous than their share of the council. Guicciardini estimated that 200 men monopolized the key offices.[62] Apparently lacking confidence in their ability to translate numerical superiority into consistent victories in elections, the popolo preferred sortition and succeeded in restoring it, beginning in May 1497, for minor offices. Savonarola and his ottimati allies argued against it. Valori made his opposition clear in a pratica: "In important offices, like the Dieci, we need prudent and wise men, with greater dignity than others have. With regard to other offices, everything has been done to broaden participation, more to unite the citizens than for any other reason. . . . For my part, I will say that anyone who wants sortition seeks his own ruin."[63] For the moment they compromised: for minor offices only, after the council voted on the nominees, the names of all those approved by a majority of the council's voting members were placed in pouches from which officeholders were selected by lot. But in May 1499, under a priorate that included only two men from elite families, sortition was extended to all major political offices, including the Signoria and the Dieci. Until the return of the Medici in 1512, elections for the priorate, colleges, the Council of Eighty, and other offices, including the Otto di Guardia, were conducted in this way. For most offices, excluding the Signoria, even the selection of candidates was entrusted to sortition rather than nomination. Guicciardini said about the 1499 law that "the desires of the *popolo* were harmful to the city."[64] Ottimati hostility to institutions they had hoped just a few years earlier to control now became intense. Although they continued to dominate the foreign policy magistracy of the Dieci and the ambassadorships,[65] the popolo often controlled the Signoria and especially the advisory colleges (as Guicciardini complained) where it frustrated ottimati objectives. Unable to control the Great Council, the ottimati turned to the idea of a smaller and powerful senate to replace it.

Another source of conflict between the council and the ottimati was public finance,[66] which still depended on a combination of indirect taxes and loans, the latter still divided between forced loans paying modest interest and voluntary loans from the wealthy secured with higher and guaranteed interest. Early in 1495 the new government also authorized a direct tax of one-tenth (thus called the *decima*) on income from land, but it took nearly four years to complete the assessment of real estate values, and even then it yielded modest

---

[62] Guicciardini, *Storie fiorentine*, XV, p. 254.
[63] *Consulte e pratiche, 1495–1497*, p. 468; Cadoni, *Lotte politiche*, p. 52.
[64] Guicciardini, *Storie fiorentine*, XVIII, p. 303.
[65] Pesman Cooper, "Florentine Ruling Group," pp. 91–107.
[66] For what follows: L. F. Marks, "La crisi finanziaria a Firenze dal 1494 al 1502," *ASI* 112 (1954): 40–72; H. C. Butters, *Governors and Government in Early Sixteenth-Century Florence, 1502–1519* (Oxford, 1985), pp. 37–42.

sums. An increasingly costly war to recover Pisa and generally lower receipts from indirect taxes (compared to twenty years earlier) created a familiar fiscal crisis. Protecting the interests of its own middle-class creditors whose investments in the regular Monte and the Dowry Fund had frequently been neglected in favor of higher interest for wealthier creditors, the council was reluctant to approve new taxes whose receipts would have gone to such wealthy creditors. By 1499, after a failed campaign against Pisa with large financial losses, the council refused outright to approve new tax bills and instituted an audit of the Dieci's finances going back to 1494. Monte officials, charged with raising the needed loans, paying interest, and providing the Dieci with the sums they needed, found it increasingly difficult to persuade the wealthy to lend money. In early 1500 the council authorized a graduated version of the *decima* in which a progressive "ladder" (or *scala*, hence the *decima scalata*) imposed higher rates on higher incomes: 10% at lower income levels, 17% for incomes of 250–400 florins, and 27.5% for those over 400 florins. Guicciardini denounced the progressive tax rate, pointing out that, with three or four collections per year, those at the higher end would pay 100% or more of annual income from land. He also reported with disgust the speech made in favor of the *decima scalata* by one of the Twelve, Luigi Scarlatti, who openly taunted the wealthy, telling them that "if they complain that this tax will impoverish them, let them reduce their expenses; and if they can't keep their horses and servants, let them do as he does and walk to their country houses and serve themselves."[67] Although it is unclear how often the new tax was actually collected, fiscal policy, no less than electoral issues, was obviously exacerbating class tensions.

A third source of conflict was dominion and foreign policy. Between 1499 and 1502 the republic suffered military and regional crises with severe repercussions on domestic politics. In 1499 the government accused its chief captain, Paolo Vitelli, a controversial figure supported by many ottimati but suspect to much of the popolo, of having collaborated with foreign powers and sabotaged that summer's campaign. Vitelli was interrogated, tortured, and, although he never confessed, executed. Suspicions were rampant within the popolo that ottimati among the Dieci had conspired with Vitelli to prolong the war and prevent a Florentine victory in order to impoverish the popolo with taxes and provoke a political crisis that would bring down the council and reinstate the Medici.[68] Popular hostility against the Dieci mounted, and for over a year the popolo prevented their election by refusing to give the necessary majorities to candidates.[69] To the ottimati this obstructionism was

---

[67] Guicciardini, *Storie fiorentine*, XIX, pp. 321–2.
[68] Vaglienti, *Storia*, pp. 63, 66, 73, 76; Cadoni, *Lotte*, pp. 114–16.
[69] Guicciardini, *Storie fiorentine*, XVIII, pp. 301–2.

intolerable, and some called for solutions by force or radical constitutional changes. In September 1500 a compromise permitted the election of new Dieci, but with limited powers: they were forbidden to begin wars, make peace, enter into alliances, hire soldiers, or appoint civilian military commissioners without the approval of the Signoria and colleges. That same summer, an explosion of factional warfare in the subject city of Pistoia between the factions of the Panciatichi and Cancellieri families deepened the crisis of the Florentine territorial state beyond the already intractable problem of Pisa. Civil war in Pistoia had repercussions in Florence,[70] as ottimati supported their clients and friends and exacerbated the conflict. According to Guicciardini, the principal "friends" of the Panciatichi were his father Piero, Alamanno and Jacopo Salviati, and Piero Soderini, whereas the Cancellieri party included Bernardo Rucellai, Giovanbattista Ridolfi, and Guidantonio Vespucci. Pistoiese factions also looked beyond Tuscany for help, the Cancellieri appealing to the Bentivoglio of Bologna and the Panciatichi (old favorites of the Medici) seeking protection from the Vitelli and Orsini. Again the popolo suspected that ottimati were manipulating a crisis to provoke foreign intervention and impose constitutional reforms.

Renewed French intervention in Italy generated a new danger that intensified domestic antagonisms. In 1498 Charles VIII was succeeded by Louis XII, who invaded the peninsula the following year, drove Lodovico il Moro from Milan, and established alliances with Venice and the papacy in order to march on Naples. Florence signed an agreement with Louis obligating him to provide military help against Pisa in return for large amounts of cash. Delays in payments to the French troops caused their abrupt departure in the summer of 1500 and strained relations between Florence and Louis. Papal cooperation in French designs on Naples also obligated Louis to support the burgeoning ambitions of Pope Alexander's son Cesare Borgia, who from the end of 1499 had been swallowing up the petty principalities of the Romagna to install himself as the strongest power in central Italy. Florence watched all this with increasing nervousness, and in May 1501 Borgia suddenly invaded Florentine territory. Rumors of conspiracy and collaboration abounded: his arrival, says Guicciardini, caused "much anger in the city, because the *popolo* concluded that he had come by agreement with certain leading citizens who aimed in this way to overturn the government. . . . With poisonous feelings running high and people speaking angrily, especially against Bernardo Rucellai, Lorenzo di Pierfrancesco [de' Medici], the Nerli, and Alfonso Strozzi, there was great danger that crowds might run to the houses of leading citizens and set them on fire."[71] Guicciardini did not believe such a conspiracy actually existed, but

---

[70] Connell, *Città dei crucci*; Guicciardini, *Storie fiorentine*, XX, pp. 330–4.
[71] Guicciardini, *Storie fiorentine*, XXI, pp. 342–3.

others did and insisted that Borgia could not have come unmolested to within a few miles of the city without the complicity of powerful people. Vaglienti says it was clear that he "had come to overturn the government, since one morning, before [Borgia] departed, they [the citizens in league with him] convened the advisory colleges and gave the order to call a *parlamento* to remove the council and reorganize the government according to their wishes. And because they found the colleges unwilling to go along with them, and because according to a law passed in 1494 it was forbidden even to discuss the summoning of a *parlamento* . . . , they decided to leave well enough alone. . . . With the help of [Borgia's] troops, which these *grandi* had brought in for their own purposes, their aim was to abolish this council which they so hated because it prevented them from attaining their wishes."[72] To a group of ambassadors that included Piero Soderini (brother of Paolantonio and Francesco), Borgia claimed he wanted an alliance and contract (*condotta*) as the city's military captain. It seemed more a threat than an offer of friendship, especially because it was accompanied by demands that Florence reinstate the Medici, diminish the council's powers, and institute an oligarchic government.[73] The demands were rejected and he was persuaded to depart, but he then seized Piombino (on the coast, south of Pisa) and threw yet another scare into the Florentines, who saw his expanding power in whatever direction they looked.

May 1501 was but the prelude of worse to come from Borgia. In June 1502 Vitellozzo Vitelli, brother of the executed Paolo and one of Borgia's military commanders, seized Arezzo in the southeastern corner of the Florentine dominion and fomented rebellion throughout the Valdichiana to the south. When it became known that Piero de' Medici had accompanied Vitelli into Arezzo, the Florentines realized the magnitude of the danger. Although Borgia denied all complicity, most Florentines assumed that he was behind Vitelli and that behind him was his father the pope and a thus a wide conspiracy to overturn the republic and restore the Medici. Vitelli took Cortona, Sansepolcro, Anghiari, and many other towns whose inhabitants, seeing no reaction from Florence, surrendered to the name of Medici. Guicciardini was convinced that if Vitelli had sent his soldiers at that moment to Florence, the unprotected city would have yielded and the government fallen. The Signoria persuaded Louis that the attack on their dominion was part of an effort to push him out of Italy. Louis sent angry letters to Vitelli and promised the Florentines help. The newly elected Dieci, who included Piero Soderini, Piero Guicciardini, and Antonio Giacomini, sent Soderini to Lombardy to organize an expedition of French troops into Tuscany. Meanwhile the new Signoria for July–August, including Alamanno Salviati, came into office. Guicciardini's panegyric of the

[72]   Vaglienti, *Storia*, p. 131; Connell, *Città dei crucci*, pp. 207–14.
[73]   S. Bertelli, "Machiavelli and Soderini," *Renaissance Quarterly* 28 (1975): 1–16 (6).

deeds in this crisis of the man whose daughter Maria he had already married when he wrote the *Storie fiorentine* extravagantly lauds the decisiveness with which Salviati raised the funds needed to confront the rebellion. Salviati recalled the colleges into session, threatening to replace anyone who failed to appear, and insisted that they remain until they approved his financial measures. He also levied a special forced loan on the wealthy and threatened them with prosecution if they refused to pay. According to Guicciardini, it was the city's good luck to have, "one might say, as its *capo*, a person like Alamanno," a man "without fear who liked the vigorous and strong solutions" needed at that moment.[74] Guicciardini's praise of Salviati as the savior of the republic might be suspect in view of the marriage alliance, but Machiavelli too lavishly praises Salviati in the *First Decennale*, his narration in verse of Italian history from 1494 to 1504, as the one who "healed" three of Florence's "four mortal wounds" (Arezzo, the Valdichiana, and Pistoia, but not Pisa).[75] In fact, Florence owed its salvation at least as much to Louis, whose troops arrived in Tuscany at the beginning of July, causing Vitelli to flee and the conspiracy to collapse. Although Guicciardini briefly mentions that Piero Soderini was sent by the Dieci to Arezzo to retake possession for Florence, he obscures the major role played by Soderini, three times ambassador to the French court and much esteemed by Louis, in winning the king's sympathy and support. Guicciardini's slighting of Soderini reflects the hostility that he and other ottimati conceived for him after Soderini became lifetime Standardbearer in 1502.

At the height of the crisis over Arezzo, the Dieci sent as ambassador to Borgia Piero's brother Francesco Soderini, accompanied by their secretary, Niccolò Machiavelli. As Machiavelli reported in a dispatch, the duke repeated his insistence that Florence change its government: "I don't like this government, and I can't trust it. You [Florentines] must change it and offer guarantees of the observance of what you promise me. . . . If you don't want me as a friend, you'll find out what it's like to have me as an enemy." Machiavelli fired back that "the city had the best government it was able to devise and that, since it was itself quite satisfied with its government, its friends could also be satisfied."[76] Actually, not everyone was satisfied with it. Demands for constitutional reform continued to come from the ottimati. In January 1501 twelve ottimati devised a plan to deprive the council of legislative authority in crucial areas and institute a new council composed of the Eighty and another 120 citizens with life tenure.[77] The twelve included former supporters of

---

[74]   Guicciardini, *Storie fiorentine*, XXII, pp. 364–6.
[75]   Niccolò Machiavelli, *Tutte le opere*, ed. M. Martelli (Florence, 1971), p. 946.
[76]   Niccolò Machiavelli, *Legazioni, Commissarie, Scritti di governo*, ed. F. Chiappelli (Bari, 1973), pp. 120–1.
[77]   Cadoni, *Lotte*, pp. 141–2.

Savonarola (Giovanbattista Ridolfi, Antonio Canigiani, Piero Guicciardini, Bernardo Nasi, Alamanno Salviati, Lorenzo Lenzi, and Luca degli Albizzi) and enemies (Benedetto de' Nerli, Guidantonio Vespucci, Bernardo Rucellai, and Lorenzo di Pierfrancesco de' Medici); the twelfth was Piero Soderini, who had not taken sides in the Savonarola controversy. A pratica of forty leading citizens was unable to agree on the appointment of a balìa to reform the government; Guicciardini lamented their failure: "What a disgusting thing it is that among the city's leading citizens, who have the same interests and should reasonably have the same judgments about things, there is so little loyalty, so little unity, and so little courage in matters that one might say concern their very existence."[78] When in 1502 Borgia echoed ottimati calls for constitutional changes, many again believed they were conspiring with him to manipulate the popolo into political concessions.

During the Signoria of Alamanno Salviati, discussions on constitutional reform resumed.[79] Pratiche were convened in early July, and the Signoria asked for proposals from committees of ten appointed in each quarter. Despite some differences, all four committees recommended the institution of a smaller council of between 180 and 300 members, with authority independent of the Great Council in fiscal affairs and with tenure of 3–5 years. The Signoria submitted a proposal for a council of 192 members to the Eighty, which twice rejected it before giving its approval. But it went no further, because it had little support in the Great Council. In early August proponents of a smaller council changed tactics and focused efforts on extending the tenure of the Standardbearer of Justice, an idea that had been advanced in July by the Sixteen and the Dieci, who, alluding to Venice's system of lifetime tenure for its head-of-state, recommended "a magistrate for a long period, or a doge." After the Eighty rejected proposals for five- and six-year tenure for the Standardbearer, lifetime tenure was at first rejected and then, on August 22, accepted. The Great Council rejected it once but approved it on August 26 by a vote of 818 to 372. No doubt against the wishes of the ottimati, the law entrusted the election to the council and allowed each member to nominate one candidate, at least fifty years of age, from its membership. The quorum was raised to 1,500 and all nominees were voted on; those approved by a majority were put to a second scrutiny; all gaining majorities in the second scrutiny were put to a third vote. On September 22, an astonishing total of 2,000 council members gathered to carry out the election. They nominated 236 candidates: either not everyone made a nomination or groups had settled on candidates before the meeting, as the Savonarolans did the night before, when, according to Parenti, three or four hundred gathered in San Marco and decided to support Giovacchino

---

[78]   Guicciardini, *Storie fiorentine*, XX, pp. 337–8.
[79]   Cadoni, *Lotte*, pp. 155–70.

Guasconi. Three candidates gained majorities in the first balloting: Guasconi; Antonio Malegonnelle, also a Savonarolan and, according to some, the favorite of the Mediceans; and Piero Soderini. Only Soderini gained a majority in the second scrutiny, and his election became official when he did so again in the third ballot.[80]

Soderini won because few wanted government in the hands of either *frateschi* or Mediceans. But whose candidate was he? According to Guicciardini, the ottimati assumed that a lifetime Standardbearer from their own ranks would be "the true means for realizing their design." Alamanno and Jacopo Salviati thus "made every effort" to get Soderini elected. With the benefit of hindsight and the frustration of knowing that Soderini disappointed them in this as in so much else, Guicciardini criticized the ottimati for failing to create the senate before electing an "ambitious" man who would not want to share power. But in 1502 it was not necessarily unreasonable to suppose that Soderini might have cooperated with his fellow ottimati, especially given his participation in the 1501 meeting on constitutional reform. Moreover, Soderini's political career to this point had been chiefly in diplomacy; no Florentine in fact had been entrusted with more or more significant missions. In 1500 he reminded the Signoria that he had been away from Florence on diplomatic assignments for four of the preceding six years.[81] Given the crucial importance of good relations with France, his frequent missions to and familiarity with the French court no doubt made him appealing to many. Finally, Parenti considered him the neutral candidate who had the support of citizens least affected by strong ideological convictions (by "passione"). Soderini probably owed his election to a lack of close ties with any faction.

Soderini, Machiavelli's Militia, and Pisa

Piero Soderini assumed his office in November 1502 and held it for almost ten years. His decade of leadership was unprecedented: permanent tenure exposed him to a kind of visibility and scrutiny experienced by no other Florentine leader. Excepting only Savonarola, he was (and still is) the most controversial political figure in the republic's history. Cosimo and Lorenzo exercised great power but held relatively few official positions; neither regularly assumed institutional responsibilities. By contrast, Soderini was in the thick of daily negotiation, argument, and policy-making, going from meetings of the Signoria to pratiche to the Great Council, regularly seen and heard on every issue.

---

[80] R. Pesman Cooper, "L'elezione di Pier Soderini a gonfaloniere a vita," *ASI* 125 (1967): 145–85 (165).
[81] Ibid., p. 174.

Although, like the priors and all earlier two-month Standardbearers, he had only one vote in the Signoria, his permanent public role closely identified him with controversial policies. Both supporters and opponents held strong opinions about him, and he became a lightning rod for discontent, especially among the ottimati.[82] Having supported the idea of a lifetime Standardbearer on the assumption that he would protect their interests, many ottimati turned against Soderini when he failed to do so. Some cooperated with him, but others, particularly Bernardo Rucellai, opposed him strenuously, refusing even to hold offices. Rucellai's group wanted major constitutional overhaul: the council's abolition if possible, or at least the creation of an aristocratic senate. A group led by the Salviati participated in government but gradually became alienated from Soderini, some because of his preference for large pratiche, which often involved hundreds of citizens and weakened ottimati voices, or his loyalty to France, his Pisan policy, choice of military captains, or the militia. But the most serious charge against Soderini was that he sought excessive power for himself and his family. Accusations that he harbored tyrannical ambitions surfaced particularly in connection with the militia; critics feared he would use it to strike at his enemies and increase his power, perhaps even make himself "signore" of Florence. Guicciardini complained that his relatives were too prominent in government, intimating that the family aimed at Medici-style dominance. In 1507, the Pisan ambassador to Emperor Maximilian, Francesco Del Lante, reported to his government that Soderini was trying to purchase an imperial vicariate, which could have been a stepping-stone to princely power.[83] But it never materialized, and Guicciardini's characterization of Del Lante in another context as a "perfidious enemy of ours whose purpose was to trick us" raises doubts about his trustworthiness.[84] Whatever the truth of that rumor, there is no evidence that Soderini sought to augment the authority given him in 1502 or that he used the militia to protect himself or punish his enemies, not even in 1512 when domestic opponents collaborated with the Medici and foreign forces to bring him and the republic down.

Another cause of dissatisfaction with Soderini in certain circles was his support for religious and social policies inspired by Savonarola's reform program. Although Soderini's brother Paolantonio was a Savonarolan, Piero had steered clear of association with the *frateschi*. But as Standardbearer he successfully promoted a law allowing the Monte di Pietà to open more branches, attract endowments, and enjoy "an unprecedented period of prosperity."[85] He gave support in 1504 to new sumptuary legislation and in 1511 to a law

82   Butters, *Governors*, pp. 51–2.
83   S. Bertelli, "Petrus Soderinus Patriae Parens," *Bibliothèque d'Humanisme et Renaissance* 31 (1969): 93–114 (114). Cf. Butters, *Governors*, pp. 124–6.
84   Guicciardini, *Storie fiorentine*, XXIX, p. 456.
85   Polizzotto, *Elect Nation*, p. 224; Bresnahan Menning, *Charity and State*, pp. 91–2.

instituting a 1,600-florin ceiling on dowries. None of this makes Soderini a *fratesco*; but he clearly shared some of their views and/or courted their support while cultivating a reputation as "religious, pious, and without vices."[86] Here perhaps was one reason behind his and his government's appropriation of Michelangelo's *David* to project an image of political and military strength confident of the Almighty's favor. *David* was originally commissioned by the Cathedral Operai for the north tribune of the Duomo, but in 1504 its location became an issue of public debate. In a meeting, convened by the operai, of artists and architects (including Botticelli, Giuliano da Sangallo, Filippino Lippi, and Piero di Cosimo) to discuss the placement of the statue Florentines called "the giant," a majority favored placing it in the loggia on the south side of the piazza of the priors.[87] But an undocumented order, which could only have come from the Signoria and in all likelihood from Soderini himself, shifted the destination to the *ringhiera* (the platform from which the Signoria and chancellors addressed the public) in front of the palace.[88] *David* dramatically combined Savonarola's vision of Florence as the new Jerusalem with an image of muscular military preparedness, an ideal combination for a republic whose founding myth was divine approval of its popular constitution and whose most pressing objective was now the reconquest of Pisa.

Soderini survived in office for ten years owing to his considerable political skills, sound fiscal management, successes in foreign policy, and "concern to work within the law."[89] Some good fortune at the outset helped too. In 1503 the Borgia menace disappeared when Pope Alexander died and was replaced (after the one-month pontificate of Pius III) by Giuliano della Rovere, who, as Pope Julius II, made the ruin of Cesare Borgia his first objective: a task to which Soderini's government happily contributed by having Borgia's lieutenant and henchman, Don Miguel de Corella, known as don Michele, arrested and handed over to the pope. With Borgia removed, and Julius not yet the threat he later became, Soderini put the republic's finances in order. In 1504 the council accepted his plan for a combination of direct taxes acceptable to both elite and popolo. Government expenditures were contained, receipts from indirect taxes grew (to almost 200,000 florins a year by 1508, a third more than before 1502), and the Monte resumed interest payments. Guicciardini

---

[86] Cerretani, *Storia*, p. 311; Pesman Cooper, "L'elezione di Soderini," p. 172.

[87] Published in G. Gaye, *Carteggio inedito d'artisti dei secoli XIV, XV, XVI* (Florence, 1840), pp. 455–62.

[88] S. Levine, "The Location of Michelangelo's *David*: The Meeting of January 25, 1504," *Art Bulletin* 56 (1974): 31–49; N. R. Parks, "The Placement of Michelangelo's *David*: A Review of the Documents," *Art Bulletin* 57 (1975): 560–70; and the unpublished paper (kindly made available to me) by A. R. Bloch, "*Per la insegna del palazzo*: The Political Contexts of Michelangelo's *David*."

[89] Butters, *Governors*, p. 81.

grudgingly acknowledged that this was "in large part the result of [Soderini's] diligence" and his close monitoring of public finances.[90]

Soderini's major objective was the recapture of Pisa. So important was it that in 1503–4 the Signoria had the west wall of the council's new "sala grande" decorated with paintings of Florentine military triumphs that were meant to inspire the republic in the war for Pisa. It commissioned Leonardo da Vinci to paint the *Battle of Anghiari* (the 1440 victory over Milan) and Michelangelo to depict the *Battle of Cascina* (a 1364 victory over Pisa).[91] (Unfortunately, Leonardo left his scene incomplete, Michelangelo only got as far as doing the cartoon, and both artists left Florence in 1506.) But for several years the war was a dismal failure for Florence. Part of the problem was a complex command structure involving professional soldiers and Florentine civilians. Battlefield tactics were entrusted to a hired, generally non-Florentine, captain with overall responsibility and several condottieri more or less at his orders. Their selection, moreover, could be a matter of contention among political factions. Early in 1504, when Soderini wanted as captain Fabrizio Colonna (immortalized fifteen years later as the chief speaker in Machiavelli's *Arte della guerra*) and others preferred Giampaolo Baglioni, lord of Perugia, a compromise made Baglioni captain while Soderini got condottieri more to his liking. Strategy and coordination among the professional soldiers were in the hands of civilian commissioners selected by the Eighty. A frequent commissioner in these years was Antonio Giacomini, a Soderini ally, close to Machiavelli (who lauds him in the *Discourses*), and later the subject of admiring biographies by Jacopo Nardi and Jacopo Pitti. Policy was decided by the government, here too with complex and overlapping roles for the Standardbearer, Signoria, Dieci, Eighty, and the frequent pratiche. Every proposal received ample discussion, and military operations could be held hostage to quarrels between Soderini and his opponents, to rivalries among commanders in the field, and to the Great Council's reluctance to approve needed taxes. The biggest problem, as the events of 1505 were to demonstrate, was the unreliability of captains and condottieri who could, and often did, pick up and leave when it suited them. Machiavelli, observing all this as second chancellor for dominion affairs and secretary to the Dieci, began to ponder the possibilities of a different kind of army and command structure.[92]

[90] Ibid., pp. 39, 86, 90–2, 138; Guicciardini, *Storie fiorentine*, XXV, p. 412.

[91] Rubinstein, *Palazzo Vecchio*, pp. 73–5.

[92] For what follows: M. Hörnqvist, "Perché non si usa allegare i romani: Machiavelli and the Florentine Militia of 1506," *Renaissance Quarterly* 55 (2002): 148–91; J. M. Najemy, " 'Occupare la tirannide': Machiavelli, the Militia, and Guicciardini's Accusation of Tyranny," in *Della tirannia: Machiavelli con Bartolo*, ed. Jérémie Barthas (Florence, 2007), pp. 75–108; G. Sasso, "Machiavelli, Cesare Borgia, Don Micheletto e la questione della milizia," in Sasso, *Machiavelli e gli antichi*, vol. 2 (Milan and Naples, 1988, pp. 57–117); Butters, *Governors*, pp. 104–6, 112–13.

Under Giacomini's supervision operations resumed in 1503 and 1504 with some successes. But a direct attack on Pisa was postponed and time and treasure lost in a failed attempt to divert the Arno from Pisa and cut off its supply route from the sea. The year 1505 began badly with a defeat, followed by Baglioni's sudden decision not to continue as captain. In May a pratica met to discuss the military crisis, and as some speakers recommended candidates for the vacant captainship, others urged that the government rely more on its own infantry and increase their numbers. Machiavelli's views on the need for a homegrown militia were presumably well known, at least in government circles, and it is possible that some speakers were echoing his opinions. But the idea of a citizen militia went back at least to the Savonarola years when the *fratesco* Domenico Cecchi proposed it in his *Riforma sancta et pretiosa* as the best way of defending the republic and bringing unity to the city and order to the contado.[93] The idea was clearly in the air again, but it took another and disastrous defeat to persuade Soderini to promote it in the face of ottimati opposition. In August 1505 Giacomini and the new captain Ercole Bentivoglio of Bologna achieved a victory that seemed to open the door to a final assault on Pisa, but two defeats in early September crushed Florentine hopes and led to bitter scapegoating of Giacomini, Bentivoglio, and, not least, "our infantry," accused by Guicciardini of cowardice. Once again a pratica debated military reform and heard more proposals for strengthening the republic's forces. In December Soderini decided to test the waters and authorized Machiavelli to begin recruiting troops in the Mugello and Casentino. When, on February 15, 1506, Machiavelli mustered 400 of his new recruits in piazza Signoria, Luca Landucci wrote that "it was thought to be the finest thing ever organized by the city of Florence."[94]

In fact, however, not everyone was pleased. Guicciardini says many ottimati recoiled at the idea of arming peasants who might turn their anger and weapons against the city and its ruling class. They also feared that Soderini might use the militia as his private army to establish a "tyranny," and they became especially suspicious when Borgia's former enforcer don Michele was hired to lead a contado police force. Guicciardini confused the militia and contado police and asserted that Soderini wanted don Michele in charge of the militia as part of the same "evil plan." Don Michele did help train and discipline the militia, but he never commanded it. Cerretani speculated that ottimati objections to the militia were merely pretexts for attempts to undermine Soderini and his government: "some rejected the militia because they liked nothing Soderini did and feared he might make himself *signore*; others opposed it because they wanted to sow confusion to bring about the return of the Medici."

---

[93] Ed. U. Mazzone in *"El buon governo": un progetto di riforma generale nella Firenze savonaroliana* (Florence, 1978), pp. 181–206.
[94] Landucci, *Diario*, p. 273.

Cerretani believed that those who wanted a "change of government," whether to reinstate the Medici or install an aristocratic republic, tried to sabotage Soderini by denying him victory over Pisa and the means to achieve it and accusing him of using the militia to make himself "tyrant" of Florence.[95]

Over the protests, the militia was officially instituted in December 1506 with a law (written by Machiavelli) that placed it under a new civilian board, the Nine, in peacetime and under the Dieci in time of war. Machiavelli became the Nine's chancellor and held the post (with his other two) until 1512. The militia was a permanent, but not a professional, force: soldiers trained in peacetime were called into action as needed and otherwise remained civilians. Battalions consisted of at least 300 men, and their commanders ("conestabili") could not be from the same district; nor could they serve for more than a year with the same battalion, after which they were rotated to new commands.[96] Machiavelli here applied a principle he later elaborated at great length in the *Discourses*, namely, that the loyalty of armies should not be to their commanders. When that happens, he argued, armies belong more to commanders than to the republic, thus becoming "private" and a threat to the state. His goal was 10,000 armed men; by May 1507, 3,000 were enlisted and by the end of the year 5,000, with some battalions already at Pisa. Cerretani commented that "the whole of Italy was keeping an eye on it," especially the Venetians who sent observers.[97]

Pisa surrendered in 1509 after a siege that brought the population to the brink of starvation. Although it won no battles, Machiavelli's militia played its part in tightening the stranglehold. Early in the year he directed operations himself until the Eighty sent commissioners, including Alamanno Salviati, to negotiate the surrender. Machiavelli was among the signatories to the submission on June 4 and entered Pisa with the commissioners four days later. From Florence his chancery colleague Agostino Vespucci wrote that "it is not possible to say with how much delight and jubilation and joy this entire people has received the news of the recapture of Pisa. Everyone is going mad with happiness." Congratulating him for being "not the least part" of this "glory," Vespucci compared Machiavelli to the legendary Roman hero Fabius Maximus the Temporizer: "if I didn't think you might take excessive pride in it, I would dare to say that you conducted such a good operation with your battalions that, not by delaying but by hastening, you have restored the Florentine state." Another colleague told him: "one can truly say that you are the reason for this

[95]   Cerretani, *Storia*, p. 343.
[96]   The law is published in Niccolò Machiavelli, *Arte della guerra e scritti politici minori* (Milan, 1961), pp. 101–15.
[97]   Hörnqvist, "Machiavelli and the Florentine Militia," pp. 159–60; Cerretani, *Storia*, p. 347.

victory."[98] Outside the chancery Soderini was the man of the hour. According to Cerretani, the whole city went to the palace to congratulate him and the Signoria. Addressing the council, Soderini enthused that, after fifteen years and three million ducats spent on the war, it was certainly a glorious moment. With some exaggeration he boasted that there was now no more powerful state in Italy than Florence (Venice had just lost its territorial dominions in a crushing defeat by Julius II's League of Cambrai at the end of May). But he also issued a warning. "It is in your hands," he admonished the council, "to make this republic and its territorial empire great, which can only be done through the observance of justice. We have many complaints that these territorial governors of yours and indeed the magistrates here in the city render no justice at all. This is a great error, and you must be very careful about electing and conferring these dignities on good and prudent persons who deserve them. If you do this, your liberty and dominion will be very great indeed."[99] If Cerretani's account is accurate, here we have a glimpse of Soderini's tendency to moralize and preach political virtue, even in a moment of triumph, to his fellow citizens, another reason perhaps why the ottimati resented him.

The republic's prospects seemed promising. With the fourth wound now healed, the territorial integrity of its dominion was restored, and ottimati critics had one less thing to bemoan. Louis XII was still Florence's protector, ruling Milan and apparently on good terms with his ally Julius II. Despite the costs of war, public finances and the economy had improved. But Soderini and the republic still had one enemy about whom they could do little: Cardinal Giovanni de' Medici and his friends in Florence who waited for the opportunity to use his influence in Rome to topple the popular republic and its Standardbearer.

---

[98] Machiavelli, *Opere*, ed. Martelli, pp. 1107b, 1108b; *Machiavelli and His Friends: Their Personal Correspondence*, trans. and ed. J. B. Atkinson and D. Sices (DeKalb, Ill., 1996), pp. 180–2.
[99] Cerretani, *Storia*, pp. 380–1.

14

Papal Overlords

Between 1494 and 1512 the triangular conflict among ottimati, popolo, and Medici seemed to have narrowed to a contest between the rival aristocratic and popular republicanisms of ottimati and popolo. Resenting their humiliating subjection to the Medici, most ottimati welcomed the regime's collapse in 1494 and anticipated the foundation of an aristocratic republic modeled on Venice. Their expectations were trampled by the political energies unleashed in 1494, as the revived popolo made the Great Council the centerpiece of its broadly based republic. Once Piero Soderini made it clear that he would not countenance a dilution of the council's powers, his ottimati enemies began searching for whatever combination of allies could bring him and his government down. With Pope Julius and a Spanish army, a group of radical ottimati pulled the Medici back into power in 1512, in what initially looked like a restoration of the old regime but then increasingly came to be seen as something different, more autocratic, less bound to Florentine political tradition. With more trappings and overt power, but less support than its predecessor of 1434–94, the new Medici regime soon alienated almost everyone. As Medici interests and the family's power base shifted to Rome under two popes, Leo X and Clement VII, they never found a family member suited to governing Florence and eventually entrusted the task to a series of functionaries detested by nearly all Florentines. This was probably the most despised of all Florentine governments, and it lasted only fifteen years, until 1527, when Clement's catastrophic mishandling of foreign policy resulted in the horrific sack of Rome, the regime's disintegration, and the third expulsion and exile of the Medici. Another republic, the city's last, began, like that of 1494, under the ottimati, but it too quickly slipped from their grasp and became the most radically anti-aristocratic of all Florentine popular governments. It took a year-long siege by Emperor Charles V's armies to bring down this republic and restore the Medici, this time to a principate.

Although they were loath to acknowledge it, even before 1527 it was clear that the ottimati lacked the strength and unity to establish their Venice on the Arno and that Florence's future was now in fact a contest between Medici rule and popular republicanism. After 1434, all Florentine governments were species of one or the other. But, although unable to implement the constitution they preferred, the ottimati did have the power to determine which of these alternatives would prevail. When the Medici became intolerable, before 1494 and again before 1527, the ottimati threw them off and instituted an aristocratic republic, only to see it slide on each occasion into the very different republicanism of the popolo. And when the popular republic became in its turn intolerable to the ottimati, before 1512 and again during the last republic, they went back to the Medici. By 1530, the ottimati were finally determined not to re-open republican doors no matter how unappetizing a Medici principate seemed. Neither alternative was much to their liking, but in the end they detested the popular republic more than the oppressive Medici.

The Cardinal and a Controversial Marriage

That the Medici were even a contender for Florence's future was obscured during the early years of the exile. Piero's attempts to return by force discredited the Mediceans and diminished his brothers' chances for reconciliation with the republic. His death in 1503 (he drowned in the Garigliano river while fleeing with the French army from the defeat that sealed Spanish control of the South) relieved them of the burden of his unpopularity, and Cardinal Giovanni, still only twenty-eight, assumed political leadership of the family from his fashionable Roman court. Despite a 1497 prohibition that outlawed anyone even associating with the Medici, certain young ottimati visited him frequently, no doubt because of his influence with the new pope, Giuliano della Rovere, Julius II, thus keeping their options open in the event of a Medici restoration, and perhaps also to display their antipathy for Soderini. Giovanni's political coming-out-party was a banquet in September 1504 attended by some forty Florentines resident in Rome, an event whose scandalous implications necessitated a full report to the government by the Florentine ambassador.

Over the next few years Giovanni made his and his family's presence felt in a variety of ways, trivial and serious, to which Soderini's government responded with varying degrees of effectiveness. When Giovanni's sisters had a wax-model of Giuliano placed in Santissima Annunziata, where there had been wax ex-voto likenesses of their father Lorenzo before 1494,[1] Soderini promptly had it removed. More ominously, Giampaolo Baglioni's resignation in 1505 as Florentine captain turned out to be part of a (failed) plot involving the Orsini, Sforza, and Medici to restore the latter to power. And in the winter of 1507–8 Giovanni intervened in the selection of an archbishop to replace his uncle Rinaldo Orsini. After first promoting Guglielmo Capponi, whose appointment Soderini blocked by getting the Signoria to protest to the pope, Giovanni pushed another candidate, Cosimo de' Pazzi, who proved acceptable to both the Signoria and Julius. Guicciardini says that Giovanni's real aim, and success in the matter, was preventing Soderini's brother Francesco, bishop of Volterra, from gaining the Florentine see. With his greater resources and more extensive network of contacts (inherited from a century of Medici patronage) Giovanni thus showed he could prevail in a contest between the two Florentine cardinals.[2]

Giovanni's most serious challenge to Soderini and the republic was the controversial marriage in 1509 of his niece Clarice, Piero's daughter, to Filippo Strozzi the younger. A prestigious Florentine marriage would demonstrate that the Medici still had friends and influence "at home" and that their name had enough of the old magic to induce prominent ottimati to risk marriage with the exiled "tyrants." In particular, it would open the door to Florentine contacts and influence for Clarice's brother Lorenzo. For Filippo Strozzi, only nineteen years old at the time of the marriage negotiations in 1508, it was a huge gamble that nearly proved disastrous but eventually brought him immense wealth and political influence. He was the son of Filippo di Matteo, who returned to Florence after half a lifetime in Medici-imposed exile and augmented an already great banking fortune with which he began building the Strozzi palace. Filippo the younger was only two when his father died in 1491, and he and his brother Lorenzo were raised by their mother Selvaggia Gianfigliazzi, who depended for advice and support in matters both financial and political on Bernardo Rucellai, Piero Soderini's archenemy. Strozzi–Rucellai ties went back at least to the 1428 marriage of messer Palla's daughter Jacopa to Giovanni Rucellai, and in 1503 Filippo's brother Lorenzo married Bernardo's daughter Lucrezia.[3] As much for his own political purposes as for the possible advantages to Filippo, Bernardo encouraged Selvaggia to consider marrying

[1]   Lowe, "Lorenzo's 'Presence' at Churches," in *Lorenzo the Magnificent*, ed. Mallett and Mann, pp. 23–36 (29–33).
[2]   Butters, *Governors*, pp. 74–7, 90, 93, 127–9; Guicciardini, *Storie fiorentine*, XXIX, pp. 468–70; K. J. P. Lowe, *Church and Politics in Renaissance Italy: The Life and Career of Cardinal Francesco Soderini, 1453–1524* (Cambridge, 1993), pp. 67–72.
[3]   Goldthwaite, *Private Wealth in Renaissance Florence*, pp. 52–73, 77–103. See also Fabbri, *Alleanza matrimoniale*.

her son into the Medici family.[4] Because of the potentially explosive reactions, negotiations were conducted in secret and the marriage contract quietly signed in July 1508. Filippo was to marry Clarice within eight months, and the Medici promised an astronomical dowry of 6,000 florins. To camouflage the alliance's political implications, Filippo went to Rome to stage a romantic encounter with his bride-to-be.

Rumors leaked and the storm broke at the end of the year. Florentines talked of little else that December and January. The first reaction was angry denunciation from Soderini's allies, including Filippo's own half-brother Alfonso. Embarrassed and frightened by the general uproar, the Strozzi met to discuss their predicament and sent a delegation to the Signoria to plead that Filippo had acted rashly, on his own and without their knowledge, that the marriage had no political significance, and that they would do their utmost to quash it if this were still possible. With their long experience of exile, the Strozzi were aghast at the possibility that an ill-conceived marriage alliance by one of their young men might jeopardize the family's rehabilitation. For those who knew the city's early chronicles, it must have seemed an ominous echo of the legendary Buondelmonti marriage fiasco. Strozzi distress was exacerbated by the irony that Filippo proposed to marry into the very family that had imposed their exile. From family members in Florence and descendants of Strozzi exiles all over Italy came expressions of anguish and protestations of the family's innocence. Both his brothers wrote to Filippo, and his reply to Lorenzo reveals a shaken young man: "Now what can I or should I do? If I sever my ties with the Medici, which seems impossible, aside from the penalty to pay [as stipulated by the contract], we would bring down their whole-hearted hostility and I would be dishonored. However, if I go through with it, you say that I and all of us will be ruined, and you depict an inferno so black that it scares me. . . . I do not want you to lose on account of me anything that I cannot restore to you."[5] His response to Alfonso, who was much angrier than Lorenzo and who must have told him of the furious reaction from the popolo, is summarized by Guicciardini: Filippo "acknowledged the marriage alliance, saying he had entered into it because of the scarcity of [socially acceptable] alliances, and that he cared not at all about the opinions of the *foggiettini*" – an insulting metonym for the laboring classes that identified them with their small caps.[6] These remarks brought down still more anger on

[4] M. M. Bullard, "Marriage Politics and the Family in Florence: The Strozzi-Medici Alliance of 1508," *American Historical Review* 84 (1979): 668–87; Bullard, *Filippo Strozzi and the Medici: Favor and Finance in Sixteenth-Century Florence and Rome* (Cambridge, 1980), pp. 45–60; Guicciardini, *Storie fiorentine*, XXX, pp. 476–84.
[5] Bullard, *Filippo Strozzi*, p. 51.
[6] Frick, *Dressing Renaissance Florence*, p. 308.

Filippo's head, both for implying that Florence lacked sufficiently noble families into which he could consider marrying, and for mocking the popular government with the characterization of the council's members as poor and poorly dressed workers.[7] This comment evidently made the rounds, since Cerretani also reports Strozzi saying that he wasn't surprised at the outrage, "especially since the city was being governed by *foggettini*."[8]

At Soderini's urging, the Signoria unanimously summoned Filippo and ordered him to appear by December 25. Formal accusations were filed with the Otto di Guardia against a dozen people, including Filippo, Bernardo Rucellai and his sons, Lucrezia (Medici) Salviati and her husband Jacopo, Antonfrancesco degli Albizzi, the new archbishop Cosimo de' Pazzi, and Giovanbattista Ridolfi, all charged with crimes against the "stato" and conspiracy with intent to bring down the government. Filippo's brother Lorenzo reports that the harshest of the denunciations was written by Machiavelli on behalf of Soderini, who also made an impassioned speech before the Great Council. Feelings intensified on all sides. Alfonso Strozzi remarked that it might be necessary, in order to restore calm, for Bernardo Rucellai, Cosimo de' Pazzi and a few others to lose their heads. Rucellai, who was in Venice, prudently stayed there and wrote a long letter justifying himself to the Signoria. In January 1509 the Otto subjected Filippo to rather light punishment (a 500-ducat fine and three-year banishment to Naples, of which he served less than a year) on the grounds that he was not actually marrying a rebel, since daughters of rebels were exempted from that status. Soderini recommended that Strozzi be confined to Florentine territory, which would have prevented him from traveling to Rome to marry Clarice, but the Signoria refused to comply and the wedding took place in February 1509.

Political winds had shifted. Soderini failed to persuade the Signoria and the Otto of the marriage's dangerous political implications, and critics accused him of abusing his power and bullying government officials. Seeing the inevitable, he dropped his objections to the marriage and even supported a measure allowing Strozzi to return to Florence by the end of 1509. The episode revealed that the Medici had a growing number of friends in the city who could and would stand up to Soderini. But Soderini had also made his point. Filippo stayed quietly away from politics for the next four years and declined to take part in either a 1510 assassination plot against Soderini or the events that brought down the republic in 1512, from which, however, no one (apart from the Medici themselves) benefited more than he.

---

[7] Guicciardini, *Storie fiorentine*, XXX, pp. 478–9.
[8] Cerretani, *Storia*, p. 359.

Fall of the Republic and Return of the Medici

Pope Julius created the circumstances that allowed Soderini's domestic enemies to translate their longstanding antagonism into action. Having wreaked his anger against Venice in 1509, Julius turned it against France and assembled the league of states (now including chastened Venice) that would drive the French from Italy in 1512. Soderini's Florence, dependent for its survival on good relations with both the papacy and France, was in the impossible and ultimately fatal position of having to choose between them. Julius's hostility grew as Soderini's government made clear its intention to stay with France. In August 1510 rumors flew that the pope might invade Florence and bring the Medici back with him; in December a young Florentine ottimate, Prinzivalle della Stufa, arrived from Bologna (where Cardinal Giovanni was papal legate) and tried to persuade Filippo Strozzi to join a conspiracy against Soderini. Strozzi refused and revealed to the authorities that, according to Della Stufa, Julius himself was behind the plot. The pope was so furious that again there were fears he might launch an assault against Florence. In 1511 King Louis put the Florentines in a terrible predicament by convening a church council to depose Julius and insisting it be held in, of all places, Pisa. The Florentines stalled, tried to talk Louis out of the idea, but ultimately conceded. Julius was enraged, placed the republic under an interdict, and talked openly of his desire to do away with Soderini and restore the Medici as rulers of Florence.

In October 1511 Julius proclaimed the Holy League, which bound the papacy, Ferdinand of Spain, Venice, and the Swiss federation to the goal of expelling the French from Italy, while Spain and England signed a separate agreement against France. Commanding the League's army in Italy was Ferdinand's viceroy in Naples, Ramón de Cardona, while Julius's representative as cardinal legate was Giovanni de' Medici. Both sides wanted Florentine cooperation, but Soderini's government resolutely refused, promising the pope and Spain only that it would not declare war on them and guaranteeing Louis that it would not abandon their alliance. In February 1512 the French repulsed attacks in Lombardy by the Swiss and Venice and inflicted a horrible sack on Brescia for having welcomed the return of its former Venetian governors. On April 11, near Ravenna in the Romagna, one of the bloodiest battles of the age was fought in which a numerically superior French army consisting of 18,000 infantry and almost 5,000 cavalry defeated the League's army of 13,000 infantry and 3,200 cavalry, with losses in the thousands on both sides. Cardinal Giovanni and several of the League's captains, including Fabrizio Colonna, were taken prisoner, and the entire northern portion of the papal state, from Bologna to Rimini, fell to the French. Two days later, a Florentine pratica took notice of Cardinal Giovanni's imprisonment and urged the Signoria to congratulate Louis for the victory and keep him well disposed toward the republic.[9] The threat of a return of the Medici seemed to have dissipated on the battlefield at Ravenna.

But the League had too many tentacles, and the congratulations were premature. The emperor Maximilian, the king of England, and the Swiss attacked French positions on several fronts, and by the end of May a Swiss–Venetian army was retaking Lombard cities that had rebelled against the French. In Florence on June 16 a pratica worriedly contemplated the stunning reversal of fortune in which the "army of the pope and the Swiss" now had the French retreating to defensive strongholds and "in continuous decline." At the end of June the Swiss took Milan; Genoa rose in rebellion and restored its republic; and papal forces took Bologna, Parma, Piacenza, Modena and Reggio. In the face of this deteriorating situation, Louis decided to salvage what he could of his army and recalled it over the Alps, and as suddenly as that, less than three months after Ravenna, the French were gone and Julius and Spain were masters of the peninsula. Soderini's republic was bereft of allies and at the mercy of the vengeful pope. On June 30 a pratica discussed a papal brief in which Julius boasted of having "liberated Italy and the Church from the French" and ordered Florence to "organize processions and other manifestations of joy" as had happened "in many other places in Italy." Most speakers counseled the Signoria to tell the pope that he ruled over priests, "not over your illustrious Lordships," that, if he wished, he could discuss with the city's archbishop any celebrations they might want the local clergy to hold, but that no demonstrations would be organized by the government, especially because, as Veri de' Medici observed (mindful perhaps of the potential danger to himself of his very name) "it isn't true that the pope has expelled the barbarians and liberated Italy. There are more of them around than ever."[10]

Behind the bravado lay a fearful and divided city. Whereas Soderini and a majority of the council stayed with France (however much they regretted the embarrassment of the Pisan council), many ottimati wanted reconciliation with Julius, who demanded Soderini's removal. Everyone knew that pacifying the pope meant opening the doors to the Medici. Representatives of the League met in Mantua to discuss Italy's political reorganization, and above all the Florentine question. Julius sent to Florence an envoy, a Florentine and Medici partisan, Lorenzo Pucci, to demand that the republic join the League and contribute militarily and financially to its mopping-up operations in Lombardy. According to Cerretani, private visitors to Pucci told him that many were prepared to act on behalf of the Medici. Meanwhile Cardona's army moved south to Bologna and began crossing the Apennines. Although Ferdinand

---

[9]   *Consulte e pratiche, 1505–1512*, ed. D. Fachard (Geneva, 1988), p. 289.
[10]   Ibid., p. 310.

favored accommodation with Florence, his viceroy, the emperor, and the Medici all agreed to overthrow Soderini. By this point, even if Soderini had been willing to accede to the pope's demands or to ally with Ferdinand, matters were being decided by the viceroy, Cardinal Giovanni, and a group of radical ottimati determined to oust Soderini. On August 27 the Eighty and the Great Council ("with infinite praise") gave Soderini a ringing endorsement, insisting that he remain in office, that the Medici not be allowed to return, and that no money be paid to the viceroy. But behind this show of support, many ottimati were taking their distance from Soderini, refusing appointments as envoys to the viceroy even as they secretly negotiated with him and Giovanni. Machiavelli, who spent the summer mobilizing troops and reinforcing defenses throughout the dominion, was north of the city near Scarperia and Firenzuola when he received a short letter that day from his chancery colleague Biagio Buonaccorsi informing him that Soderini "does not at all like and is amazed by" the arrival of the viceroy's troops in the Arno valley south of Prato. "Do what good you can," Buonaccorsi wrote, "because we're not wasting time in discussions."[11]

Cerretani says Florence had 350 heavily armed knights, 500 light cavalry, and 14,000 infantry, but there was disagreement about where to concentrate them. Some wanted them at Prato, but the decision was to have them protect Florence, and, according to Cerretani, Medici sympathizers in the Dieci and pratiche conspired to leave Prato undefended. On Sunday August 29 Cardona's troops assaulted and sacked Prato, killing at least hundreds, although Cerretani says 4,500. The murderous attack stunned the Florentines and, amidst recriminations and accusations against Soderini for not properly defending Prato, the Eighty reversed themselves and agreed to readmit the Medici and pay the viceroy the money he wanted.[12] A day or two later four young ottimati – Paolo Vettori, Bartolomeo Valori, Gino Capponi, and Antonfrancesco degli Albizzi – entered the palace, demanded the release of thirty Medici friends who had been arrested as a precaution, and threatened Soderini with bodily harm if he did not resign. Soderini sent Machiavelli to Paolo Vettori's brother Francesco, who had been appointed commissioner of the city's internal defense force, to ask him to come to the palace to mediate the dangerous standoff. Finding Soderini "alone and frightened," Vettori negotiated his safe departure from the palace, accompanied the ex-Standardbearer to Vettori's house across the river, and spirited him out of the city to Siena and into exile, eventually in Ragusa.[13] On Wednesday, September 1, Giuliano de' Medici entered the city, as Cerretani puts it, "as a private citizen," and, "having shaved his beard and donned civilian clothes," went walking through the city with his friends.

[11] Niccolò Machiavelli, *Opere*, vol. 3, *Lettere*, ed. F. Gaeta (Turin, 1984), p. 353.
[12] Cerretani, *Storia*, pp. 438–42.
[13] Francesco Vettori, *Scritti storici e politici*, ed. E. Niccolini (Bari, 1972), pp. 143–4.

Over the next few weeks a complex struggle unfolded in which divisions among the ottimati opened the door for the Medici to return as rulers rather than private citizens. A particularly fascinating source for these decisive weeks is Cerretani's *Dialogo della mutatione di Firenze*, composed between 1520, the fictional date of the discussions it claims to record, and his death in 1524. The principal speaker, Giovanni Rucellai, was the son of Bernardo, Soderini's and the popular government's most intractable enemy. In the *Dialogo*, Giovanni is traveling to France as papal ambassador and near Modena meets two Florentine followers of Savonarola, Lorenzo and Girolamo, who had left the city in June 1512 fearing the impending disaster. Still devoted to the friar's memory and political program, they are on their way to Germany to meet another famous friar and champion of the purity of the "primitive" church, Martin Luther. Rucellai says he is stopping for the night at the home of Modena's papal governor, Francesco Guicciardini, and invites them to join him. When the discussion that evening at Guicciardini's house turns to Savonarola, the appropriately named Girolamo vigorously asserts that Savonarola was a "true prophet" who gave Florence the foundation of a "vivere publico" and that "he taught us how to live *civilmente* in a republic." Rucellai dismisses Savonarola's alleged prophecies, reminding Girolamo that the popular republic had collapsed despite the friar's promise of divine protection and without any of the dire punishments he predicted would befall those attempting to harm it. "It was all done with weapons held high," Rucellai boasts, "and I was among the ringleaders who intervened to destroy the council and call the *parlamento* and the *balìa* and send the Standardbearer packing. And we would have done it sooner had my companions and I not feared a multitude that [as things turned out] could be held bound by a thread."[14]

Girolamo and Lorenzo invite Rucellai to recount in detail the "mutatione" of 1512 and his own role in it. His account emphasizes two overriding themes: that the reinstatement of the Medici as rulers of the republic was desired and realized more by the radical ottimati than by the sometimes hesitant Medici themselves; and that what motivated these ottimati was fear of the "parte fratesca," the followers of Savonarola. Rucellai explains that "much of the nobility became [Soderini's] enemies" because he refused to give them a privileged voice and ignored the "counsel of the wise." They "began to ask how they could be free of him and saw no more convenient way than secretly giving favor to the house of Medici." All those who hated Soderini, he says, waited for the right occasion: "Many times in secret meetings we discussed how the Medici could be reinstated or how some night we could bring Giuliano into the city, then slowly bring in troops, seize the city and the palace, and kill

---

[14]   Bartolomeo Cerretani, *Dialogo della mutatione di Firenze*, ed. G. Berti (Florence, 1993), pp. 6–7, 11–12, 21–3.

Soderini." When Girolamo asks whether they ever feared the consequences of such plotting, Giovanni admits that "we feared the *parte fratesca*, because it had men from the nobility, numbers, money, and brains, and with these advantages defeated its enemies three times" (in executing the conspirators in 1497, recovering political strength after Savonarola's execution, and bringing Soderini under its influence).[15] After the sack of Prato and Soderini's removal, "we leaders of the *mutatione* were divided: some wanted only the expulsion of Soderini, while others, including myself, wanted to institute a new government [*fare nuovo stato*] with the Medici in charge, because we saw that, when the Spaniards left, things would go badly for us given the strength of the *parte fratesca*." According to Rucellai, "six of us thus went to Prato and spoke with the legate [Cardinal Giovanni], Giuliano, and messer Giulio. . . . And there we decided what had to be done for their safety." On September 7 a new council was instituted, composed of former officeholders and fifty others selected by them, and Giovanbattista Ridolfi was elected as Standardbearer for one year. Here at last was the senate the ottimati had long desired. But Rucellai and his companions considered the paucity of Medici "friends" in this council and the election of Ridolfi, a longtime leader of the *frateschi*, "the ambassadors of our ruin." Once again they went out to meet Cardinal Giovanni and persuaded him that Giuliano was "by his nature unsuited to the tasks of governing," that he had been tricked into accepting inadequate political changes, and that enemies of the Medici had "installed their leader in the palace."

Rucellai's group also took the initiative to alert the Medici to the risks inherent in the advice they were getting from the moderates. Even as the viceroy's troops were ravaging the countryside, stealing, taking hostages, and killing, in support of a Medici restoration, moderates like Lanfredino Lanfredini and Giovanni's brother-in-law Jacopo Salviati urged the Medici not to dismantle the Great Council: "they said the government had been in the hands of the entire citizenry [*l'universale civiltà*] for 18 years . . . and could not be taken away from them without a great uproar and the risk of destroying the city. . . . If he succeeded in seizing the government, [the cardinal] needed to decide with whom he would control it, because after a pause of 18 years the family's friends were reduced in numbers, impecunious, and not particularly valorous men." Thus, they concluded, to hold on to the government the Medici "would have to become ministers of violence." Rucellai's group countered the moderates telling the cardinal that "it was no obstacle that the Mediceans were not numerous, because at all times and in all places it is the few who carry out a *mutatione*, and that, once it is done, ambition and avarice persuade the majority to become friends of the regime in power. . . . For we are the sons of those fathers who, together with your father Lorenzo, made this city great

[15] Ibid., pp. 26–7.

and esteemed." The radicals thus persuaded Giovanni that Medici security depended on a "mutatione" and that to this end a parlamento was indispensable. Rucellai says the radicals asked the Spanish soldiers to frighten the city by riding menacingly around the walls as if they were looking for weak points for a possible assault. When the Spaniards assured the Florentine emissaries that Ferdinand had no intention of overthrowing the republic, "this reassured everyone, but made us [the radicals] fearful." Giovanni and Giuliano sent a similar message to the Signoria, "and we," says Rucellai, "seeing this timidity and lack of courage, and the reluctance of the Spaniards to support the Medici, went back" yet again to urge the Medici to undertake bolder moves.[16]

On Tuesday September 14 Giovanni finally entered the city, accompanied by 200 cavalry and 100 friendly citizens. Cerretani has Rucellai recall that the pro-Medici cries of "palle" lacked conviction and that the cardinal's return did not at all please the popolo. This, he says, "served our purposes," presumably because it helped convince the cardinal that more drastic measures were needed. "All the next day and night," says Rucellai, "we used all our best arguments to explain to the legate the danger he faced and that the only solution was a *parlamento*." Leading citizens came separately to confer with the cardinal, including Rucellai's father Bernardo, and by Wednesday evening, says Rucellai, Giovanni was inclined to follow their advice. Cardona told the Medici that his army was needed in Lombardy and "if they had need of his services they should not delay." The next day, September 16, they carried out the coup, as the viceroy's lieutenants seized the piazza, and Giuliano, accompanied by thirty-three ottimati, among them six Rucellai (including Giovanni di Bernardo), three Tornabuoni, and Prinzivalle della Stufa,[17] stormed into the meeting hall of the Signoria and occupied the building. Popular resistance to the coup was averted by a distribution of bread and the rumor that 6,000 Spanish infantry were already at Sesto Fiorentino and on their way to the city. "That," as Cerretani's Rucellai smugly recalls, "extinguished any spark" of rebellion. The swift transfer of power was signaled by the arrival at Palazzo Medici of a delegation from the Signoria to inquire as to the cardinal's wishes and by the announcement of a parlamento. Cardinal Giovanni was already selecting the members of the balìa that the parlamento would of course approve. But even now, according to Rucellai, "the Medici began to get it all wrong," because they assembled a balìa according to the wishes of the leading citizens, including moderates, and not "according to their own needs and those of their trusted friends." With the piazza still occupied by Spanish soldiers, the parlamento did what it was told. On Saturday the 18th the viceroy came to Florence and stayed in Palazzo Medici where he received the Signoria (another

[16]   Ibid., pp. 31–7.
[17]   Butters, *Governors*, p. 184.

symbolic confirmation of the transfer of power), and on Sunday the cardinal reciprocated by going to Prato to see off the viceroy as he took his troops north out of Tuscany.[18]

Giovanni then turned his attention to the balìa. Compared to those of the fifteenth century, it was a small group: forty-six citizens, who, with the Signoria, granted themselves, for one year, or longer if they judged it necessary, in what was still the only legitimate definition of sovereignty, "all the authority enjoyed by the *popolo* of Florence" to which, for good measure, they added the authority of all previous balìe. But Giovanni did not appoint a balìa entirely pleasing to the radical ottimati: it not only included moderates and even *frateschi* like Lanfredino Lanfredini, Piero Alamanni, Jacopo Salviati, Piero Guicciardini,[19] and a number of others prominent in Soderini's government; it also excluded Giovanni Rucellai, Prinzivalle della Stufa, and the men who had threatened Soderini at the end of August. Although some of these were represented by family members such as Bernardo Rucellai, Paolo Vettori's more moderate brother Francesco, and Della Stufa's father Luigi, Cardinal Giovanni clearly intended to proceed cautiously and not alienate prominent citizens who had had leading roles in government under Soderini. Indeed, apart from Soderini, no one was exiled, and Giovanni prevented reprisals against San Marco and supporters of the former government. His aim was evidently to win the acquiescence, however grudging, and wherever possible the active support of as many ottimati as could be persuaded not to oppose the new order. Many ottimati who had cooperated with the popular government and adopted moderate positions in September 1512 soon became Mediceans, a *trasformismo* exemplified by Jacopo Salviati, who, having once professed loyalty to the Great Council, now told the Medici that everything he did after 1494 was motivated by the goal of seeing them restored.[20]

Yet the break with the popular government was sharp and unequivocal. The balìa first dismantled Machiavelli's militia and the magistracy of the Nine, then the Great Council and the Eighty. In an act of unambiguous hostility, the regime treated the quasi-sacred Hall of the Great Council with spectacular contempt, turning it into a barracks, complete with tavern, gambling, and brothel, and held a great feast there. As Cerretani's Rucellai puts it, they "pushed it in the face of the *piagnoni*."[21] The balìa also eliminated the senate created on September 7, and Giovanbattista Ridolfi, too much a Savonarolan even for the Medici, was forced to resign in October. In November Machiavelli

---

[18]   Cerretani, *Dialogo*, pp. 38–42.

[19]   Polizzotto, *Elect Nation*, p. 246. Full list in G. Silvano, *"Vivere civile" e "governo misto" a Firenze nel primo Cinquecento* (Bologna, 1985), pp. 175–6.

[20]   Butters, *Governors*, p. 193.

[21]   Cerretani, *Dialogo*, pp. 45–6; Polizzotto, *Elect Nation*, p. 241.

was dismissed from his posts, no doubt because of his association with Soderini. Old Medici committees and electoral institutions were restored, including the accoppiatori, Cento, and Seventy. Despite the appearance of continuity with the pre-1494 past, it soon became clear that the Medici were groping their way toward a different kind of regime. But it proved to be an unstable halfway house between that earlier time and the principate that was only two decades away.

A Regime Adrift

Between 1512 and 1527 the Medici never satisfactorily resolved the question of who should manage the regime, or how. As head of the family, Giovanni would have been the logical choice, but even before he was elected pope his duties as cardinal and papal legate kept him in Rome and Bologna. Some advised that the regime needed a strong leader with power no longer camouflaged in the old myth of the Medici as citizens with a little more authority than others had. Despite the relatively few reprisals and exiles in the fall of 1512, the radical ottimati recognized that the Medici had enemies and would have to govern, as Paolo Vettori told the cardinal, "more with force than skill. . . . The city has lived well for ten years, and the memory of that time will always be your enemy." He boldly warned that Giuliano "does not yet understand the affairs of the city" and would be unable to assess properly the views of citizens motivated more by self-interest than devotion to the Medici. Giuliano's weaknesses and lack of sufficient interest in governing were widely perceived among the ottimati and confirmed by his frequent absences. Vettori recommended that he would thus need an inner cabinet of ten or twelve men and even within this group would ultimately have to rely on one or two to resolve disagreements and make decisions.[22]

In February 1513 a conspiracy to assassinate Giuliano (and possibly other Medici) was disclosed, and within days its leaders, Pietropaolo Boscoli and Agostino Capponi, were executed. A list of potential sympathizers was found that included, besides members of prominent families, Machiavelli and his friend Giovanni Folchi, whose confession to the authorities included a report of Machiavelli's percipient skepticism concerning the regime's leadership: "it appeared to him that this regime would not be governed without difficulty,

---

[22] *Ricordi . . . al cardinale de' Medici sopra le cose di Firenze*, in R. von Albertini, *Firenze dalla repubblica al principato*, trans. C. Cristofolini (Turin, 1970), pp. 357–9; Paolo Vettori, "Memorandum to Cardinal de' Medici about the Affairs of Florence," trans. R. Price, in *Cambridge Translations of Renaissance Philosophical Texts*, ed. J. Kraye, 2 vols. (Cambridge, 1997), vol. 2, p. 239.

because it lacked someone to stand at the tiller, as [the elder] Lorenzo de' Medici had properly done."[23] Although he had no part in the conspiracy, Machiavelli was arrested, tortured, and jailed for a month in the Bargello. Niccolò Valori, nephew of Francesco, a strong Soderini ally, and friend of Machiavelli, was similarly tortured and incarcerated; he claimed he tried only to dissuade Boscoli when he divulged the plot to him.[24] The complicity, suspected or real, of several ottimati undercut Medici trust in the leading families, and the regime's brutal reaction to this and other conspiracies and critics from Savonarolan circles in 1513 ended the hopes for moderation in Medici rule.[25]

Medici fortunes rose spectacularly when Cardinal Giovanni became Pope Leo X on March 11, 1513. Suddenly, the attention he could devote to Florentine affairs was very restricted and it became even more necessary to delegate power in Florence to family members. He first entrusted the task to his nephew Lorenzo. If Giuliano had difficulty understanding Florentine politics, Lorenzo was even less capable of doing so. Whereas Giovanni and Giuliano had grown up in Florence and were, respectively, nineteen and sixteen years of age when exiled in 1494, Lorenzo, born in 1492, was literally and culturally of another generation and had no experience of life in a republican polity. Among his grandparents, only his namesake was a Florentine, and the chief influence on him was his Neapolitan mother, Alfonsina Orsini. Lorenzo grew up in Rome amid courtly rituals, noble titles, and military trappings alien to Florence's civilian and republican customs. When he arrived in August 1513 to assume the reins of leadership (or rule, as he no doubt preferred to see it), his uncle gave him, through Giuliano, a set of guidelines (the so-called *Instructione*) counseling the careful placement in crucial magistracies of trusted friends to serve as informers, cooperation with leading ottimati, respect for older and prestigious families, and impartial administration of justice.[26] That Lorenzo even needed such advice was proof of his dangerous lack of familiarity with Florence's political culture and elite families. He was warned in particular "not to offend the families . . . accustomed to having *lo stato*," and, if he suspected someone's loyalty, to extend favor to other members of the same family. Despite the advice, Lorenzo and Alfonsina, who had a voice in many

---

[23] J. N. Stephens and H. C. Butters, "New Light on Machiavelli," *English Historical Review* 97 (1982): 58–9, 67.

[24] R. Pesman Cooper, "Political Survival in Early Sixteenth-Century Florence: The Case of Niccolò Valori," in *Florence and Italy*, ed. Denley and Elam, pp. 73–90.

[25] Polizzotto, *Elect Nation*, pp. 259ff.

[26] Published in *ASI* 1 Appendice (1842–4): 299–306. Albertini, *Firenze dalla repubblica al principato*, pp. 25–6; Butters, *Governors*, p. 205; and Silvano, "*Vivere civile*," pp. 35–41.

decisions, managed routinely to offend the ottimati with highhanded interventions in elections, magistracies, and the courts on behalf of favorites.[27]

According to Cerretani, Lorenzo and eight advisers "ran everything." Nerli identifies them: Piero Alamanni, Lorenzo Morelli, Jacopo Salviati, Pandolfo Corbinelli, Piero Ridolfi, Lanfredino Lanfredini, Filippo Strozzi, and Francesco Vettori.[28] Particularly important were Strozzi and Vettori. Strozzi was closer to Lorenzo than anyone except Alfonsina and was with him at every important event down to his illness and death in 1519. Lorenzo (and his mother) prevailed upon Leo in 1514 to put the Depository General of the Apostolic Chamber under Strozzi's control, making him in effect the pope's banker, and in 1515 Lorenzo appointed Strozzi to the equivalent office in Florence, the Depository of the Signoria. With government revenues deposited into, and disbursed from, his bank, Strozzi was able to divert public funds, disguised as private loans, to Lorenzo. Even more ominously, with significant portions of both papal and Florentine revenues flowing into the same bank, Strozzi ultimately enabled two Medici popes to appropriate huge sums from the Florentine treasury to pay for papal wars and family ambitions. Under Clement the looting of Florence through Strozzi's hands for the aggrandizement of the Medici reached staggering proportions.[29]

After two years as the republic's ambassador to the papal court, the period of his life best known for the memorable correspondence with Machiavelli,[30] Francesco Vettori returned to Florence in 1515 in Lorenzo's company and as his most important political adviser. Over the next four years, he supported Lorenzo's ambitions, accompanied him into war as civilian commissioner of the army under Lorenzo's command, and functioned as his personal agent in marriage negotiations in France.[31] Vettori continued to serve Lorenzo's reputation after his death in the brief and flattering biography he dedicated to Lorenzo's sister (and Strozzi's wife) Clarice. Describing himself as Lorenzo's "intimo servitore," Vettori rather improbably praised Lorenzo for humanity and modesty and for instilling obedience and order into a previously licentious and undisciplined army. Perhaps to soothe Clarice, who was reportedly incensed over the amorous escapades in which her husband and Lorenzo were

[27]   Stephens, *The Fall of the Florentine Republic, 1512–1530* (Oxford, 1983), pp. 73–95; Butters, *Governors*, pp. 226–75.
[28]   Butters, *Governors*, p. 231; Bartolomeo Cerretani, *Ricordi*, ed. G. Berti (Florence, 1993), p. 314.
[29]   Bullard, *Filippo Strozzi*, pp. 76–90.
[30]   J. M. Najemy, *Between Friends: Discourses of Power and Desire in the Machiavelli-Vettori Letters of 1513–1515* (Princeton, 1993).
[31]   R. Devonshire Jones, *Francesco Vettori: Florentine Citizen and Medici Servant* (London, 1972), pp. 109–42.

said routinely to engage, Vettori insisted that the "obscene lust" that infected so many young men did not touch Lorenzo (and by implication did not lead Filippo into temptation either).[32]

But Lorenzo was not well liked. One problem was the frequency of his long absences from the city. Although he had been advised to make himself available in regular audiences to citizens and to listen to their requests for help (but not actually to grant them all), he was away from Florence from September 1514 to May 1515, for much of the summer and autumn of 1515, from October 1516 to spring 1517, and again during the spring and summer of 1518 when he was in France for his wedding: cumulatively, for more than two of the fewer than five years in which he was meant to be governing Florence.[33] These absences did not make Florentine hearts grow fonder, especially because, not fully trusting even his friends among the ottimati, he assigned responsibilities of governance to a distant and young relation, Galcotto de' Medici, and later to his arrogant secretary Goro Gheri, notoriously more Medicean than the Medici, while his mother took control of the patronage network from the family palace.[34] Lorenzo's real objective was the acquisition of a territorial state, and Florence and its finances and institutions were merely a base from which to pursue more grandiose ends. In 1515 he told Galeotto that Florence was "my support and estate and, to put it better, *la poppa mia*," literally the breast, and thus the milk, nourishing his ambitions.[35]

A widening gap opened between the plan for "civil" governance outlined in the *Instructione* and Medici steps toward "princely" rule. In May 1513 the balìa granted Giuliano the power to act in the name of the commune as its "syndic and procurator," to make war and peace and to do anything the commune itself could do.[36] Although framed in the old language of corporate representation, such broad authority in the hands of one person was unprecedented. The mandate lasted only until September, by which time Lorenzo had replaced him. When Leo appointed Giuliano Captain-General of the Church in January 1515, Lorenzo, determined not to be outshone by his uncle, told his associates that he would soon be named Captain-General of Florence. He pressured the government to hire 500 troops and got himself appointed as their commander in June with a formal three-year *condotta*, a

[32] Vettori, *Scritti storici e politici*, pp. 261–72.

[33] R. Devonshire Jones, "Lorenzo de' Medici, Duca d'Urbino: 'Signore' of Florence?" in *Studies on Machiavelli*, ed. Gilmore, pp. 299–315 (305); Stephens, *Fall of the Florentine Republic*, pp. 93–5, 108.

[34] N. Tomas, *The Medici Women: Gender and Power in Renaissance Florence* (Aldershot, 2003), pp. 164–94.

[35] Butters, *Governors*, p. 264.

[36] Stephens, *Fall of the Florentine Republic*, pp. 72, 83.

stipend of 35,000 florins, and legal immunity for his soldiers and officers. Never before had a Florentine citizen been given command of what was in effect a private army (despite the purely formal, face-saving stipulation that he use it in conformity with government orders).[37] Lorenzo's captain-generalship was a controversial and dramatic step toward a very different relationship between the Medici and Florence.[38] Many opposed it (although not openly in the councils), and even some Medici friends feared the reaction it might provoke. Leo himself, who would have preferred a slower, more cautious approach to the assumption of such power, remarked: "I have named two captains who have no experience at all and hold offices [usually] held by trained and expert men. I don't know how they'll do if they have actually to exercise their offices."[39]

In foreign policy indecision and family disagreements also undermined support in Florence. Early in 1515 Louis XII died and was succeeded by his young son-in-law, Francis I, who immediately announced his intention to invade Italy and retake Milan. Opposing France were Spain, the emperor, and the Swiss, who had humiliated the French in 1512. Leo played a dangerous double game of secretly adhering to the anti-French league while negotiating with Francis and trying to win his support for papal sovereignty over Modena, Reggio, Parma, and Piacenza. It was rumored that Leo planned to give these territories to Lorenzo and, if the French expelled Spain from southern Italy, to install Giuliano on the Neapolitan throne. Family ambitions of the most naked sort now drove Medici policy into conflict with both church and Florentine interests. Two years earlier Vettori had lamented the contradiction between Leo's preoccupation with "giving states to his relatives" and his objective of protecting the church's prestige and power.[40] Now this contradiction and its potential dangers were magnified by the French invasion, Leo's wavering, the papacy's military weakness, and two other factors: Lorenzo's independent foreign policy, and reviving hopes among *frateschi* and anti-Mediceans that a French king was once again, as in 1494, coming to liberate Florence from tyranny.

Since Leo's election, preachers echoing Savonarola's critique of the church were seen as dangerously anti-Medici and subjected to repressive measures. Early in 1515 the regime arrested and forced the confession of one such preacher, Don Teodoro, and printed a pamphlet detailing his activities, the

---

[37]   Butters, *Governors*, pp. 264–5.
[38]   R. C. Trexler and M. E. Lewis, "Two Captains and Three Kings: New Light on the Medici Chapel," *Studies in Medieval and Renaissance History*, n.s. 4 (1981): 93–177.
[39]   A. Giorgetti, "Lorenzo de' Medici Capitano Generale della Repubblica fiorentina," *ASI*, ser. IV, 11–12 (1883): 194–215 (211).
[40]   Machiavelli, *Lettere* (1984), ed. Gaeta, pp. 392–3.

contents of his sermons, and the danger he represented. His large following prompted the Florentine archdiocese to tighten controls over preaching and religious meetings. Leo intervened with a brief that approved the silencing of Don Teodoro, praised the new controls, and instituted ecclesiastical and lay boards to suppress heresy. Medici nervousness over the continuing popularity of Savonarolan prophecy and political ideas was intensified by the excitement generated by Francis's intention to return French power to Italy. Leo and his cousin the archbishop, Cardinal Giulio, announced a synod of the Florentine church, which met in 1516–17, from which they expected an official condemnation of Savonarola and even tighter controls on preaching and religious publications. But pro-Savonarolan sentiment was still strong enough to block outright condemnation.[41]

There was in fact a good deal of pro-French sentiment in Florence, and even contacts with the French. Leo was urged by the foreign policy magistracy to reopen negotiations with Francis, and Lorenzo, aware of the implications for the Medici of growing pro-French sympathies, warned Leo that an uprising was possible if the pope openly sided with the anti-French league (as he did in July) and the French emerged victorious. To Leo's dismay, Lorenzo opened his own channel to Francis, perhaps trying to reach a separate agreement that would protect him however the war turned out. He had the Florentine ambassador Francesco Pandolfini deliver a letter to Francis assuring him of Lorenzo's loyalty and "servitù." When Francis pressed Pandolfini on what he thought Lorenzo would do if Leo joined the anti-French league, he replied that he did not think it would come to that. Francis insisted: "and what if it does?" To which Pandolfini, evidently so instructed, replied that Lorenzo "would not be lacking in the *servitù*" he had promised the king. This earned Pandolfini, and indirectly Lorenzo, a rebuke from Leo delivered by Giulio.[42] Leo even forbade the Florentine ambassadors appointed by Lorenzo, including Filippo Strozzi and Francesco Vettori, to go to the French court for fear that they were being sent to negotiate a separate agreement.[43] In the midst of the diplomatic wrangling, Leo and Alfonsina secretly introduced 1,000 troops into the city to prevent a revolt. On the eve of war, as confusion and indecision among the Medici themselves angered many Florentines and raised hopes of an imminent "liberation from tyranny," the Medici found it more urgent to deploy troops in defense of the regime than to contribute to the league's efforts to stop the French.

[41]   Polizzotto, *Elect Nation*, pp. 239–313.
[42]   Giorgetti, "Lorenzo de' Medici, Capitano Generale," pp. 212–13, n. 3.
[43]   Devonshire Jones, "Lorenzo de' Medici," pp. 302–3; Butters, *Governors*, pp. 268–71.

Leo wanted Giuliano to go to war and Lorenzo to stay home and mind the regime, but when Giuliano fell ill Lorenzo took the troops to Lombardy, formally in support of the anti-French league. He prudently never got near the fighting that erupted south of Milan in September between the French and the Swiss. With decisive help from Venice, the French routed the Swiss at Marignano, retook Milan, and snatched Parma and Piacenza from the papacy. But the expectations of anti-Mediceans in Florence were dashed when Francis quickly came to terms with Leo, agreed to meet him in Bologna, and assured him that he would not lay hands on the regime. Jacopo Pitti later commented that the papal–French accord "dulled the spirits that had been raised against the regime by the king's arrival, as they realized, to their intense sorrow, how much princes are by their nature more favorable to princes (as like to like) than they are to republics."[44] Leo traveled north for the meeting, but first stopped in Florence for a state visit complete with a triumphal entry on November 30 that was oddly discordant with the reality of his diplomatic humiliation and truncated territorial ambitions in Lombardy. Despite resentment over the huge expense and anti-Medici sentiments expressed in graffiti,[45] this most spectacular ceremonial event in Florence's history again turned the entire city into a ritual theater, adorned with triumphal arches representing the virtues allegedly embodied by the pope, through which he rode in a stately seven-hour procession from Porta Romana (see Map 2 and Plate 4), down via Maggio across the Santa Trinita bridge to piazza Signoria into via del Proconsolo, around the Duomo and finally to the papal apartments at Santa Maria Novella.[46] Music, poetry, and humanist oratory exalted the pope, but his sense of triumph must have been tempered by the realization that his family's political fortunes depended on the good graces of the French king waiting for him in Bologna.

Lorenzo came out of the near disaster better than his uncles did. Having promised Francis the constancy of his "servitù" and contributed nothing to the Swiss defense of Milan, he basked in the king's favor and joined his court in Pavia and Milan where, according to Vettori, in many "feste" he urged Francis to reconcile with Leo.[47] Francis apparently agreed to give Leo and Lorenzo a free hand in the papal states, for, just a few months later, Leo

---

[44]   Jacopo Pitti, *Istoria fiorentina*, ASI 1 (1842): 115.

[45]   Butters, *Governors*, p. 273.

[46]   J. Shearman, "The Florentine *Entrata* of Leo X, 1515," *Journal of the Warburg and Courtauld Institutes* 38 (1975): 136–54; J. Cox-Rearick, *Dynasty and Destiny in Medici Art* (Princeton, 1984), pp. 34–6; A. M. Cummings, *The Politicized Muse: Music for Medici Festivals, 1512–1537* (Princeton, 1992), pp. 67–82; I. Ciseri, *L'ingresso trionfale di Leone X in Firenze nel 1515* (Florence, 1990).

[47]   *Vita di Lorenzo de' Medici, duca d'Urbino*, in Vettori, *Scritti storici e politici*, p. 266.

deposed the duke of Urbino, Francesco Maria della Rovere, and installed Lorenzo in his place. In 1518 Lorenzo cashed in on his still vibrant French connection by marrying Francis's cousin, Madeleine de la Tour d'Auvergne, a marriage that brought him a huge income and a fief in the south of France, in return of course for serving the king's interests in Italy and Rome. It was the most prestigious marriage yet contracted by a Medici. As a cousin-in-law of the greatest king in Christendom, Lorenzo probably saw no limit to his ambition, and according to some, though denied by others, in the summer of 1518 he was determined to dissolve the republic and become Florence's prince. In October he went to Rome with Filippo Strozzi and Francesco Vettori and allegedly tried, and failed, to win Leo over to the plan.[48] True or not, many believed it and Lorenzo was as unpopular as ever when he suddenly became ill and died in the spring of 1519. Because Giuliano had died three years earlier, the Medici now had no legitimate heir to manage the regime.

As a stopgap Leo sent his cousin Giulio to Florence while they looked for a long-term solution. Giulio, born in 1478 (the year his father was murdered in the Pazzi revolt), was, like Leo, more inclined than Lorenzo to soothe ruffled ottimati feathers, and he initially gave the impression (which may have exaggerated actual Medici intentions) that he and Leo were contemplating a more broadly-based regime. He opened discussions with leading citizens, welcomed proposals for constitutional reform, restored sortition for some administrative offices, and slightly expanded the membership of the Seventy and Cento. He made gestures toward healing old wounds, reconciling with a number of Savonarolans, especially Girolamo Benivieni,[49] and allowing Machiavelli to return to the fringes of public life. Jacopo Salviati was sufficiently encouraged to resume involvement in politics and became a member of Giulio's inner circle. Expectations of a restoration of traditional republican government (which of course meant different things to different people) were high. Jacopo Nardi, the republican historian, had kind words for Giulio, comparing him to Piero Soderini and remarking that he "showed himself most humane in his actions toward the entire citizenry and very patient in his audiences." But there is a hint of the looming catastrophe (and very different political destiny that Giulio later inflicted on the city) in Nardi's comment that, of all the Medici regimes, none "concealed the principate" with a "greater appearance of *civiltà* and liberty" than Giulio's.[50]

Initial impressions were indeed deceiving. Giulio relinquished none of the regime's control, and when he returned to Rome late in 1519 he showed his

[48]   Devonshire Jones, "Lorenzo de' Medici"; Butters, *Governors*, pp. 301–6.
[49]   Polizzotto, *Elect Nation*, p. 248.
[50]   Nardi, *Istorie*, 2:61, 64; Stephens, *Fall of the Florentine Republic*, pp. 108–12; Silvano, "*Vivere civile*," pp. 82–6.

distrust of the ottimati by appointing Medici creatures as the executors of his decisions (as Lorenzo had done with Goro Gheri): at first Cardinal Silvio Passerini, then the notaries Jacopo Modesti and Agnolo Marzi, all three from the subject territories (respectively, Cortona, Prato, and San Gimignano), and, in 1524, after Giulio became Pope Clement VII, again Cardinal Passerini. In the 1480s the elder Lorenzo had begun the practice of entrusting key aspects of government to clients from outside the traditional political class, but now the Medici let such men act as their substitutes in positions of power.[51] As Medici creatures lacking any connection to the city's political life except as such, and totally dependent on Medici power for their own survival, these men were unswervingly loyal to their masters. For Florentines, who still thought of the inhabitants of the territories as *their* subjects, seeing the republic, or what was left of it, in the hands of Medici clients was intolerable, and their accumulating resentments now waited for an opportunity to erupt. But these functionaries and their assumptions about their relationship to the prince they served, although swept away in 1527, were actually harbingers of the state that lay beyond the republic.

Aristocratic and Popular Republicanisms

Between 1512 and 1527 the republic's uncertain future prompted an unprecedented outpouring of political ideas. Reflecting the underlying triangulation of Florentine politics were three main directions of thought: aristocratic and popular republicanisms and the nascent principate. Ottimati saw themselves caught between the Scylla of popular republicanism and the Charybdis of Medici autocracy. In the *Discorso di Logrogno*, written in 1512 as the Soderini republic was collapsing, Guicciardini worried that Florence could slide either into "tyranny" on the one side or "popular anarchy" on the other. Although he advised keeping both the Great Council and the lifetime head of state, he wanted power to legislate and direct foreign policy entrusted to a smaller council of "wise men," the "best of the city": all former Standardbearers of Justice, those who had served on the Ten at least twice, former ambassadors and commissioners-general, all appointed for life. "The entire weight of government ultimately rests on the shoulders of very few," as "has always been the case in every republic, ancient or modern."[52] By 1516 Guicciardini

---

[51] Stephens, *Fall of the Florentine Republic*, pp. 139–54.
[52] Francesco Guicciardini, *Opere*, ed. E. Lugnani Scarano, vol. 1 (Turin, 1970), pp. 249–96 (250, 276–8); trans. A. Moulakis, *Republican Realism in Renaissance Florence: Francesco Guicciardini's* Discorso di Logrogno (Lanham, Md., 1998), pp. 117–49 (117, 136–7).

saw the Medici as the chief obstacle to the realization of balanced aristocratic government. Prudently framing his protest against excessive Medici power as a "discourse on how to consolidate" their regime, he lamented their disinclination to share power with the ottimati. Those "young men" who support Lorenzo's ambitions (but this seems to refer to Lorenzo himself) "have been raised outside the city and are not accustomed to our ways. . . . Lacking knowledge of the things that pertain to the good governance of the city, they often make decisions and issue commands that bring harm and disorder." To let the regime rest on the family's power in Rome was a great error, because the pope would not live forever; without a solid alliance with the ottimati, the regime lacked internal support. Guicciardini acknowledged that the ottimati were politically weak, but without them the regime itself would be weak. There are "those who believe, and perhaps have made efforts to persuade" Lorenzo that the "greater security" of the Medici lay in "seizing absolute dominion of the city" both de facto and de jure, Guicciardini wrote, but although "I do not intend to discuss the issue, my judgment is that they could not make a decision more pernicious either for them or for us and that such a step would with time prove to be full of difficulties, suspicions, and ultimately cruelties."[53] This came from the man who, two decades later, would be the major voice for the continuity and permanence of the principate.

Guicciardini's nephew Niccolò was barely eighteen in 1519 when he composed a "discourse on the methods of the Medici" just before Lorenzo died, which echoed, in even stronger terms, Francesco's criticisms of 1516. After Giovanni's election to the papacy, he argued, the Medici had so much power and so little to fear that it was expected they would "govern the city more *civilmente* and with greater moderation. . . . But the exact opposite happened." Niccolò recalls the prediction of a "wise citizen" that Leo's election would bring more harm than honor or utility to the city, because with such power they would presume without fear to issue commands, appoint officeholders, help themselves to public funds, and generally govern the city in such a way as to be its unmasked "princes and lords." Lorenzo's appointment as Captain-General "deprived the city of all its remaining authority and power." Since it was now impossible to oppose the desires of one who controlled the armed forces, much of which consisted of mercenaries loyal to him rather than to the government, "there is nothing that can prevent it if this Captain hungers for the lordship" of Florence. "One can conclude that he is the author and

---

[53] Francesco Guicciardini, *Dialogo e Discorsi del reggimento di Firenze*, ed. R. Palmarocchi (Bari, 1932), pp. 267–81. See Silvano, "*Vivere civile*," pp. 59–67; J. G. A. Pocock, *The Machiavellian Moment: Florentine Political Thought and the Atlantic Republican Tradition* (Princeton, 1975), pp. 149–51; Albertini, *Firenze dalla repubblica al principato*, pp. 94–5.

prince of all things and could be called *aperto Signore*," a prince who no longer hides behind the old fictions. But Niccolò's recommendation is limited to naively encouraging Lorenzo to secure his control by inducing all to become his "friends" and treasure his rule as a "just prince," by maintaining a citizen militia rather than an army of foreigners, and by gaining the love of his subjects through virtue and humility: on all points, as Niccolò himself admits, the opposite of Lorenzo's actual behavior. The explanation for this timidity emerges in his fear that, once the protection afforded by papal power is no more, the people's anger against the regime would erupt in rage and produce a "government so popular that it would be worse than the current one."[54] This was the dilemma of the ottimati: much as they resented the Medici lording it over them, they needed these haughty lords with their military power and foreign connections to protect them against what would have been, and always had been in their eyes, the infinitely worse alternative of a radically popular government.

Once Lorenzo was dead, the ottimati were freer to contemplate constitutional change. Francesco Guicciardini wrote the *Dialogue on the Government of Florence* in the early 1520s but situated the fictional dialogue at the end of 1494, when the emergence of the Great Council scuttled ottimati hopes for an aristocratic republic. The speakers include Piero Capponi, a spokesman for the aristocratic republicans; Paolantonio Soderini, who defends the popular turn the revolution took; the author's father Piero, who remains cautiously neutral in the discussion of whether the Medici were tyrants or provided good government; and the principal speaker, Bernardo del Nero, the Medici client who rose to great power under the elder Lorenzo and was executed for his silence about the 1497 plot to reinstate Piero. In the preface, and thus in his own voice, Guicciardini acknowledges his discomfort in theorizing what might replace the Medici regime, given his "deep, indeed extraordinary, debt to the Medici family, having been employed and excessively honoured by two popes from that family. . . . In view of these obligations, to nourish thoughts against the position of their family seems unfitting." Most intriguing and curious is the selection of the non-ottimate Medicean Bernardo del Nero as the apparent voice of Guicciardini's own views. In the debate over the merits and abuses of the fallen Medici regime, Del Nero acknowledges that it was indeed a tyranny but argues that good government should be measured by its effects, not its constitutional legitimacy or the degree to which it protects a fictitious liberty, and that from this angle the Medici gave Florence the best government of which the city was capable. In book two, which turns to the future, Del Nero outlines a plan for a mixed constitution ultimately controlled by a senate with lifetime tenure, a solution not essentially different from that of the *Discorso di*

[54]   Text in Albertini, *Firenze dalla repubblica al principato*, pp. 365–75.

Logrogno. It is difficult to reconcile Del Nero's praise of the Medici with his advocacy of a mixed constitution controlled by the ottimati, and there is no evidence that the historical Del Nero ever entertained the ideas attributed to him in book two. Perhaps Guicciardini was dramatizing the contradictions of his class's relationship to the Medici: on the one hand regularly supporting Medici "tyranny" for protection against the popolo, on the other advancing their claims to a preponderant role in government in a classically mixed constitution.[55]

Imprudent as it was in these years to advocate openly republican solutions, such ideas generally adopted a historical frame of reference that camouflaged their implicit commentary on contemporary problems. In his *Discourses on Livy* (c.1515–18) Machiavelli explored the foundations of the Roman republic's greatness in its army, religion, and institutionalized political conflict of the plebs and the senatorial aristocracy. Praise of Roman republicanism, and especially the argument (I.4) that Rome's liberty was protected by the discord between the people and the *grandi*, constituted a sustained polemic against the ottimati's myth of peaceful Venice with its hegemonic aristocracy. Machiavelli's insistence that Rome's decline began when private wealth, patronage, and factions engulfed public authority and powerful citizens increasingly had recourse to "private methods" to advance their interests and punish their enemies (e.g., I.37) carried a not-so-veiled subtext of criticism of the Medici, who had perfected the "private" politics of patronage and factionalism. Machiavelli wrote the *Discourses* while still politically ostracized by the Medici, but after Lorenzo died Cardinal Giulio let the ice thaw and in late 1520 approved the commission from the Florentine Studio for the *Florentine Histories*, completed in 1525 and presented to Giulio, now Clement VII. Much of the second half of the book, from the political rise of Cosimo to the elder Lorenzo's death in 1492, highlights the corrosive effect of Medici wealth, patronage, and private power in conceptual terms borrowed from the *Discourses* but now elaborated with direct reference to them. It was Cosimo who first, and fatally, merged private methods and public institutions and who used his wealth to build a powerful faction that undermined the republic. Clement never reacted to Machiavelli's deconstruction of the old Medici regime; he either had no time for reading or was not a careful reader.[56]

But Machiavelli knew that Giulio, or those around him, would certainly read his contribution to the discussions on constitutional reform, the 1520

---

[55] Guicciardini, *Opere*, ed. Lugnani Scarano, pp. 299–483 (301–2); *Dialogue on the Government of Florence*, ed. and trans. A. Brown (Cambridge, 1994), pp. vii–xxviii, 4; Pocock, *Machiavellian Moment*, pp. 219–71; Silvano "*Vivere civile*," pp. 142–56.

[56] J. M. Najemy, "Machiavelli and the Medici: The Lessons of Florentine History," *Renaissance Quarterly* 35 (1982): 551–76.

Discourse on Florentine Affairs After the Death of Lorenzo, and this called for a more cautious approach. Reviewing the three "stati" that had governed Florence from 1393 (that of the ottimati until 1434, "lo stato di Cosimo" and his successors from 1434 to 1494, and the republic of 1494–1512), Machiavelli concluded that none had been a true republic, or in the case of the Medici regime a true princedom, because each served the interests of a faction or party or class rather than the common good, causing the excluded and discontented to become destabilizing enemies of these regimes. Machiavelli deemed it unwise and actually impossible to reinstate the old Medici system, as many were counseling, because such a regime would now face the hostility of the people, for whom the republic swept away in 1512 had been the most "civile" they had ever known. Moreover, whereas the elder Medici had governed within the bounds of "familiarity" and "citizen ways," the younger ones had become "grandi" and exceeded "all *civiltà*." The people and the Medici had thus moved in opposite directions, and the old hybrid solutions were no longer workable: a stable government in Florence must be either a true republic or a true princedom. Machiavelli dismisses the princedom because, with Lorenzo gone, there was no one around whom to build it and because Florence lacked the titled and feudal aristocracy that (as he had already theorized in *Discourses* I.55) was the indispensable foundation of a princely order. In fact, the city's history, customs, and social organization all required a republican form of government. "So I will leave aside further discussion of a princedom and speak of a republic, because Florence is a subject most suitable for assuming this form."

In the rest of the discourse Machiavelli outlines a constitution that he thinks can satisfy "the three kinds of men" found in all cities: the "primi" or leading citizens whose ambition must find some outlet, the "mezzani," or next tier of important citizens, and the "universalità dei cittadini," or rest of the citizenry. To the first group he conceded permanent status as a recognized governing elite and recommended that the Medici select sixty-five "amici e confidenti," one as Standardbearer of Justice for two or three years, and the others to be divided into groups of eight who would take turns staffing the Signoria. For the second group Machiavelli proposed a council of 200 members, appointed (again by the Medici) for life, to replace all the old legislative councils. Thus far his proposal aimed at "consolidating the authority" of the Medici and their friends. But the third group of citizens also had to be "satisfied," and this could never be achieved ("anyone who thinks otherwise is not wise") unless "their authority is restored" by reopening the Great Council with 1,000, or at least 600, members. Machiavelli acknowledged that it might have to be done slowly and in stages, but eventually the council should once again have the power to elect all officials, except the 65 and the 200, who would be appointed by Leo and Giulio for as long as they lived (the first hint that after their deaths matters should be handled differently). Machiavelli then lectured Leo and Giulio on the absolute necessity of the Great Council, advising them to reopen it themselves, on their own terms, before their enemies did so in opposition to them: "No stable republic was ever instituted that did not satisfy the whole body of citizens. And never will the whole body of Florentine citizens be satisfied without reopening the hall [of the Great Council]. Thus, to institute a republic in Florence, it is essential to reopen this hall and give back to the *universale* the power of assigning offices. And Your Holiness should know that anyone who plans to remove the government from your hands will plan first and foremost to reopen the council. And thus the better choice is for you to open it on your own secure terms and methods and thus to deprive your enemies of the chance to do so to your displeasure and to the destruction and ruin of your friends."

Until this point Machiavelli's plan looks like a version of the classical mixed constitution. These reforms would suffice, Machiavelli added, if Leo and Giulio "lived forever." But "since you will have to die," and because Machiavelli evidently discounted the possibility that other Medici would assume the reins of authority, maintaining a "perfect republic" required one more innovation: the intervention of the sixteen standardbearers of the companies of the popolo in the meetings and deliberations of both the Signoria and the council of 200. Neither body should be allowed to assemble without some of the Sixteen in attendance, who would have the power to veto the Signoria's decisions and appeal them to the council of 200, and similarly to block decisions of the 200 and appeal them to the Great Council. This unprecedented suggestion would have made the Sixteen the real arbiters of power by vesting them with the authority to give the council final say in any matter. The Sixteen "could be chosen either in the way they have heretofore been selected, either on the authority of Your Holiness or by the Great Council," and presumably by the council once pope and cardinal were no more. Machiavelli thus assigned to this popular magistracy the same veto power that the tribunes of the plebs (according to Polybius) had in the Roman republic. Behind the concessions to Medici power (about which he had little choice as long as Leo and Giulio were on the scene), Machiavelli tried to persuade them to acquiesce in restoring the popolo to political equality with the ottimati, reassuring them that this plan would not damage their position: "Considering this constitution as a republic, and without your authority, it lacks nothing; but considered while Your Holiness and Most Reverend Monsignore are still living, it is a monarchy." Their own security required the Medici to "organize the government in such a way that it will administer itself and Your Holiness will need keep but half an eye on it" and "to arrange things so that the institutions [*ordini*] can remain stable on their own. And they will always be stable when everyone has a hand in them, and when each person knows what he has to do and in what he can place his confidence, and when no class of citizen needs to have recourse to revolution out of either fear or ambition."[57] Needless to say, the Medici had no intention of implementing a plan so audacious and far-reaching, especially one whose ultimate purpose was to make them unnecessary.

Popular republican ideas flourished in the discussions in the Rucellai family gardens (the Orti Oricellari) hosted by Cosimo, grandson and nephew of the arch-ottimati Bernardo and Giovanni. Bernardo had hosted an earlier phase of the Orti's discussions characterized by opposition to Soderini,[58] but Cosimo reopened the Orti after Bernardo died and made it a center of literary, historical, and republican themes. Its participants included Machiavelli, Cosimo Rucellai and Zanobi Buondelmonti, the dedicatees of Machiavelli's *Discourses*, Luigi Alamanni, Battista della Palla, Antonio Brucioli, the historians Jacopo Nardi and Filippo Nerli, and the young Donato Giannotti, the most important republican theorist of the next generation and Machiavelli's chief intellectual heir. Nerli, one of the few Mediceans in the group, later recalled the powerful influence of Machiavelli and his reading of Roman history on the younger men in turning the historical and theoretical understanding of republicanism away from the ottimati's idealization of Venice and back to the ancient Roman republic. According to Machiavelli's Roman model healthy republics gave the people its due share and a free people was armed. These distinguishing features of Machiavelli's republicanism were subsequently echoed by Brucioli in his *Dialoghi della moral filosofia* of 1526[59] and elaborated by Giannotti in his *Della repubblica fiorentina* of the 1530s.

This was not an openly anti-Medici group, which would in any case not have been allowed, but in 1522 several former regulars of the Orti (Buondelmonti, Alamanni, Della Palla, Brucioli, together with Niccolò Martelli and several others, but not Machiavelli, on whom no suspicion fell) conspired with Cardinal Francesco Soderini in Rome to kill Giulio de' Medici and restore Piero Soderini to power. According to Martelli's confession, Francis I was ready to provide the necessary military muscle, but the conspiracy was revealed before they could act. Two conspirators were executed, others

---

[57] Machiavelli, *Opere*, ed. Martelli, pp. 24–31; Machiavelli, *Arte della Guerra e scritti politici minori*, ed. Bertelli, pp. 261–77; Silvano, "*Vivere civile*," pp. 91–109.

[58] F. Gilbert, "Bernardo Rucellai and the Orti Oricellari: A Study on the Origin of Modern Political Thought," *Journal of the Warburg and Courtauld Institutes* 12 (1949): 101–31; also in Gilbert, *History: Choice and Commitment* (Cambridge, Mass., 1977), pp. 215–46; Albertini, *Firenze dalla repubblica al principato*, pp. 67–85.

[59] Antonio Brucioli, *Dialogi*, ed. A. Landi (Naples, 1982), dialogues 6 ("Della republica") and 7 ("Delle leggi della republica"), pp. 95–205; Albertini, *Firenze dalla repubblica al principato*, pp. 73–8; C. Dionisotti, "La testimonianza del Brucioli," in Dionisotti's *Machiavellerie* (Turin, 1980), pp. 193–226.

fled, and Giulio punished the Soderini by confiscating their property, exiling several of them, and persuading Pope Adrian to imprison Francesco Soderini in Castel Sant'Angelo in Rome.[60] All discussion of constitutional reform was firmly squelched in the aftermath of the botched plot and lost opportunity to remove from the scene the member of the Medici family who was soon to inflict unimaginable catastrophes on both Florence and Rome.

The Nascent Principate

Two rather different approaches to constructing the principate came from Goro Gheri and Lodovico Alamanni. Gheri, from Pistoia, was a Medici client from his university days in Pisa where he studied law in the late 1480s. He preserved his ties to the family during the exile, and Leo sent him to Switzerland as papal nuncio, to Piacenza as papal governor, and between 1516 and 1519 put him in charge of the regime in Florence during Lorenzo's absences: a kind of prime minister who governed at Lorenzo's (and Leo's) pleasure and with the help of a cabinet of advisers. Choosing a non-Florentine to administer the regime reflected Medici distrust of the ottimati, who in turn resented such power in the hands of a *distrettuale* who strode in lordly fashion through the city accompanied by bodyguards. Gheri's reflections on the regime's future emerged from his long experience as a devoted Medici client and were grounded in the traditional euphemism for Florentine patronage, *amicizia*, which had come to mean docile and even servile loyalty. He insisted that the regime's security depended on a stark differentiation between its true friends and all others, with no tolerance for neutrality. Florentines, especially the ottimati, had to learn that the Medici expected complete commitment from their *amici*, whom they would reward handsomely, and considered all others enemies to be excluded from offices and even banished. Writing to Alfonsina in 1516, he urged punishment for an ottimate who had lamented the loss of liberty in 1512: "in a regime it is necessary to have friends and to base oneself upon them, but it is also required, when one can do so through judicial channels, to beat one's enemies and weaken them, and, in a similar way, warn one's allies, because [these allies] will see that the regime is being tended."[61]

---

[60] Stephens, *Fall of the Florentine Republic*, pp. 119–23; Silvano, *"Vivere civile,"* pp. 157–61; Lowe, *Church and Politics*, pp. 121–31.

[61] Stephens, *Fall of the Florentine Republic*, pp. 147–53 (150); Albertini, *Firenze dalla repubblica al principato*, pp. 27–31; Butters, *Governors*, pp. 278–93; Silvano, *"Vivere civile,"* pp. 86–91; K. J. P. Lowe, "Towards an Understanding of Goro Gheri's Views on *amicizia* in Early Sixteenth-Century Medicean Florence," in *Florence and Italy*, ed. Denley and Elam, pp. 91–105.

After Lorenzo's death, Gheri penned a memorandum to Leo, the *Istruzione per Roma*, in which he urged a Medici "succession" through Giuliano's illegitimate nine-year-old son Ippolito. But it was around the *amici* that Gheri believed the regime could be preserved. He favored a continuation of the old Medici practice of governing "civilmente" and with the cooperation of men selected for their willingness to "accept the station given them." Certain families and "powerful citizens" would have to be allowed a role in government, but they must not be permitted to take too much of the "stato." Gheri suggested that the way to apply a "brake" to the ambition of these ottimati would be to include with them certain "populari," but he qualified this with the insistence that any "widening" of the regime should not entail broader sharing of power: on the contrary, he favored narrowing the circle of those with "auctorità." Wider distribution of offices and honors would sharpen the distinction between "those who are the natural friends of the [Medici] and the others, for in this way the *amici* will be happier and better able whenever necessary to help the regime and preserve it, and all others who want such honors, seeing the difference separating an *amico* from one who is not, will undertake actions and gestures in order to be considered *amici*." And "with those disinclined to be domesticated [*che non si volessino domesticare*] or who do it insincerely, I would likewise be insincere with them," so that they will be unable to use whatever positions they have against the regime.[62] Gheri still accepted the assumptions of the old Medici patronage system; indeed, a long passage of the *Istruzione* praises the methods of the fifteenth-century Medici as a still valid model to be followed. He sought to construct a princely state with "friends" and natural allies, believing that exemplary rewards and punishments would serve as sufficient incentives to make those wavering in the middle join the "friends."

Lodovico Alamanni, born in 1488, was twenty years younger than Gheri and had more revolutionary ideas about how the Medici should build a principate. His father Piero was, according to Guicciardini, a Medici client who rose to favor under the elder Lorenzo, was later a close adviser to Piero de' Medici, briefly under house arrest in connection with the 1497 plot to restore the Medici, and among the moderate confidants of Cardinal Giovanni in the restoration of 1512. Lodovico's republican brother Luigi was among the anti-Medici conspirators in 1522. In his *Discourse on Securing the Regime in Florence in Devotion to the Medici*,[63] written in November 1516, Lodovico argued that a "well established regime" could never be taken from Lorenzo but could not be preserved after Leo's death either by ruling Urbino or by the regime in Florence as then constituted. He urged Lorenzo neither to underestimate his

[62]   Text in Albertini, *Firenze dalla repubblica al principato*, pp. 360–4.
[63]   Ibid., pp. 376–84.

enemies, since "most citizens are unhappy with the regime," nor to over-estimate the difficulty of consolidating his power despite this opposition. "If Augustus was able to secure his power in the city that produced all those Brutuses and Catos," and "if Cosimo succeeded in founding a regime so well that his successors maintained it for so long, and in a time when citizens were unaccustomed to being governed by one man," much more easily would Lorenzo be able to secure his power "now that the citizens have been trained not to know how to live without a chief [*capo*]," as demonstrated, Alamanni argues with some tendentious history, by the fact that, after expelling Piero de' Medici, they made first Francesco Valori and then Piero Soderini their "capo."

Lorenzo's power nonetheless required the citizens' acquiescence, and on the question of how to secure it Alamanni displayed startling originality. Gone were the days when the elder Lorenzo could walk the streets and converse with citizens, a "familiarity" now inappropriate for his younger namesake who neither could nor should "observe civic customs [*servare l'ordine civile*]." Florentines would have to be converted to the ways of the courts, and Alamanni contemptuously attributed their disinclination in this regard to their *asineria* (ignorance, foolishness, stubbornness) rather than to their professed notions of liberty: in refusing to show reverence or to remove their hoods for anyone, except the magistrates, they are as "alien to the ways of the courts as are few others." Although this "laziness" became custom and so much a part of their nature that older men could never be disabused of this "fantasia," there was nothing to fear from them because old men don't make trouble. But young men were another matter: "the youths could easily be stripped of these civic ways [*civiltà*] and become accustomed to courtly ways, if the prince so desires." By carefully selecting the young men he wishes to honor and bring into his service, by inviting them one by one into his company and confidence, and giving to each a role suited to his temperament, the duke will be able to remove their "civic habit," dissuade them from that "civiltà" that so alienates them from his customs, and draw them into "courtliness." For Alamanni this was to be a conversion, complete with a change of dress and a vow: "thus to those who, for his Excellency's sake, will take the [courtly] cape and leave aside the [civic] hood, it will be as if they had become friars, for they will renounce the republic and make a profession [of faith] to his order," and "never again will they be able to claim the status of citizens or the good will of the *popolo*." As each cohort of the young "is trained in [the duke's] school, it will come about that our city will not know how to live without a prince."

Alamanni's prescription was perceptive and prescient. Although it would not be as easy as he imagined, the conversion of the ottimati from a republican to a courtly order was indeed, in the long run, the resolution of Florence's identity crisis. The Medici had already been cultivating elite youth. Niccolò

Guicciardini commented that, when Lorenzo became Captain-General, "he turned many noble young Florentines who were soldiers or who aspired to this profession into his gentlemen . . . and thus there was formed in the city a nucleus of citizens who depended directly on him and were completely loyal to him." Florentines and foreigners who entered into such a relationship with Lorenzo, "paying court to him [*tenendogli corte*] wherever he might be, made such lavish gestures toward his authority and legitimacy that no one would have seen any difference between him and an actual, lawful *signore* of the city."[64] Francesco Vettori also noted that within a few months of his arrival in Florence in 1513 Lorenzo "drew to himself the good will of the majority of young Florentines." Young men (like the *compagnacci* who hounded Savonarola's followers) played an increasingly important and disruptive role in Florentine politics, and Lorenzo must have seen the potential of these irreverent youth, impatient with what they saw as the stodgy civic decorum of their elders. Shortly after the coup of 1512, he and Giuliano each founded a festive company, respectively the Broncone and the Diamante, whose armed young men participated in communal rituals as retainers of their lords and served as their bodyguards.[65] Growing awareness of this generational divide in Florentine politics led to Alamanni's speculations of 1516 and to those of Niccolò Martelli, ironically one of the conspirators of 1522, who from his jail cell also recommended that the Medici needed to win the loyalty of the city's youth.[66] But the revolution of 1527 showed that the republic and the Medici were still competing for the sons of the ottimati.

Do Machiavelli and his *Prince*, written in 1513 and dedicated to Lorenzo in 1516, belong among the theoretical contributions to the nascent principate? Some argue that *The Prince* inspired subsequent theorizing around the Medici state and that Alamanni was not only a reader of *The Prince* but its "disciple."[67] In its analysis of the different kinds of principalities and the ways princes can be successful, Machiavelli's famous pamphlet conceptualizes princely power in revolutionary ways. But *The Prince* says curiously little about Florence and its constitutional dilemma, focused as it is on the role that a bold and charismatic leader could play in the larger theater of Italy's struggle to liberate itself from foreign powers. And in the one chapter in which Machiavelli clearly does have Florence in mind (chapter 9 on the "civil princedom," where he theorizes the rise of a private citizen to the rank of prince with the support of

[64]   Ibid., p. 370.
[65]   Trexler, *Public Life*, pp. 515–21.
[66]   C. Guasti, "Documenti della congiura fatta contro il Cardinale Giulio de' Medici nel 1522," *Giornale storico degli archivi toscani* 3 (1859): 213–67; Trexler, *Public life*, p. 518.
[67]   Dionisotti, *Machiavellerie*, pp. 124–7.

his fellow citizens and asks whether it is safer to attempt this in alliance with the "grandi" or the "popolo") he advises the aspiring citizen-prince to befriend the people and build his state with their support. Nothing could be more distant from Alamanni's fundamental assumption that the principate would be built in alliance with the ottimati, albeit with their younger generation. Even in *The Prince*, Machiavelli's hostility to the ottimati is palpable in his contrast between the "grandi" who want to dominate and the "popolo" who seek only not to be dominated. Just before he was dismissed in November 1512, Machiavelli addressed a memorandum to the Medici ("ai Palleschi") in which he urged them to construct their new regime with the people, and not the ottimati whom he excoriated for "playing the whore between the people and the Medici."[68]

---

[68] Machiavelli, *Opere*, ed. Martelli, pp. 16–17.

15

The Last Republic and the Medici Duchy

In the twenty years between 1512 and 1532 Florentines incessantly debated the fate of their republic only to see it finally decided by external power. Three times, in 1433, 1494, and 1527, the Medici were exiled, and three times they returned: recalled in 1434 by friends in the city; restored in 1512 by both internal allies and a foreign army; but imposed in 1530 on an unwilling and defeated city after a year-long siege by the armies of Emperor Charles V, who two years later terminated Florence's long republican history and instituted the principate. This time the Medici returned to stay and to govern in relative stability until they died a natural death 200 years later. Behind so improbable a conclusion to the stormy relationship between Florence and its most famous family lay the events of 1527–30, which traumatized both ottimati and popolo: the radicalization of the republic during the siege terrified the ottimati, and the republic's isolation, abandonment, and crushing defeat devastated the popolo. In the aftermath of the siege and savage repression by emperor, Medici pope, and leading ottimati, even the kind of brief collaboration between elite and popolo that expelled the Medici in 1494 and 1527 was no longer possible. Brutalized by the ottimati, the popolo never again trusted them and refused to join the abortive revolts (in 1537, 1554, 1559, and 1575) of those few ottimati who rejected the inevitable. And now it was indeed inevitable because most ottimati, frightened by the popolo's radicalized republicanism, finally accepted the principate and, in the process, the final metamorphosis of their own class into a subservient courtly aristocracy.

Revolution

Clement's foreign policy wavered dangerously and irresponsibly between France and the empire. After allying with Francis in 1524, he reversed course after the massive French defeat at Pavia in February 1525 and accepted an agreement with Charles. But when Charles imposed Spanish rule on Milan, the pope did another about-face and in May 1526 formed the League of Cognac with France and Venice to limit imperial power in Italy to Naples. To protect its merchants from reprisals Florence did not officially join the league, but Clement insisted that it contribute financially and militarily. When Charles's Colonna allies attacked Rome in September 1526, Clement had to sign another agreement with the emperor, which he promptly repudiated. To frighten or punish the faithless pope, Charles sent into Italy an army of 12,000 German mercenaries, the famous, feared, mostly Lutheran *landsknechts* who joined forces with imperial Spanish troops under the Duke of Bourbon and began a disorderly march toward Rome that took them through Tuscany and perilously close to Florence. League forces were unable to stop this irregularly paid and unpredictable menace, and Charles himself was unable, or unwilling, to control it. As the imperialists descended into the Romagna and prepared to cross the Apennines in the late winter and spring of 1527, fear mounted in Florence, and many, including prominent ottimati like Niccolò Capponi, son of Piero who had defied the French in 1494, and Luigi Guicciardini, brother of Francesco who was now Lieutenant-General of the papal armies, demanded that the city be allowed arms for self-defense. In February Machiavelli was sent to papal military headquarters in the north to impress upon Guicciardini Florence's urgent need for defense, and he remained with Guicciardini through April as papal forces moved south from Parma to Bologna to Forlì. From this mission Machiavelli wrote his last letters, addressed to Francesco Vettori, assessing the immense danger that Florence faced. On April 16, reporting Guicciardini's decision to bring an army to Florence's defense if the imperialists threatened the city, he told Vettori: "we must not hobble about anymore, but rather fight with abandon; desperation often finds solutions that choice does not. . . . And I tell you from sixty years of experience that we have never faced such travails as these, where peace is necessary and war cannot be avoided, and yet we have on our hands a prince [Clement] who can provide neither for peace nor for war." Two days later, he ominously predicted that "whoever enjoys war, as these soldiers do, would be crazy to praise peace. But God will see to it that they have more war than we would like."[1]

---

[1]   Machiavelli, *Opere*, ed. Martelli, pp. 1250–2.

On April 1 Bourbon's army moved from Ferrara toward Forlì and began crossing the Apennines from Meldola to Santa Sofia, in Florentine territory, where it arrived on the 16th. A panicked Clement reopened negotiations with the imperial viceroy, who agreed to go to Florence and attempt a deal with Bourbon's envoys to spare Florence an attack in return for cash. After 80,000 florins were hastily collected, Bourbon raised the demand to an astronomical 300,000, making it evident that he and his hungry troops intended to sack the city. As a foretaste, they attacked towns in the Casentino and by the 26th were in San Giovanni Valdarno, only twenty miles southeast of Florence. But Guicciardini had already arrived with a Swiss–French force and Venetian troops and, although the contado suffered from the depredations of all three armies, the danger of a sack was averted.[2] Preferring easy slaughter to a battle in which they would have been outnumbered, Bourbon's troops moved on to Rome, where ten days later they inflicted the sack denied them in Florence.

On April 26, when the danger was most acute, seething anger against the pope and the regime erupted in what became known as the "Friday uprising." When Cardinal Passerini and Ippolito de' Medici left the city to meet the commanders of the league's armies, a group of young ottimati led by Piero Salviati and supported by Niccolò Capponi seized the palace demanding arms, the banishment of the Medici, and the restoration of the pre-1512 constitution. Luigi Guicciardini, Standardbearer of Justice, was willing to distribute arms but hesitant to concede the political demands. But with Capponi and the crowd crying "popolo e libertà" and insisting that the Medici be expelled, no less than Francesco Vettori, seeing the disintegration of the regime he had loyally supported since 1513, persuaded the Signoria to yield. Passerini and his troops returned and forcefully quelled the revolt, as an amnesty was negotiated, oddly enough, between Vettori on behalf of the "rebels" and Francesco Guicciardini for the regime. It was only a temporary reprieve for the regime, because the Medici were once again losing the ottimati. The revolution of 1527 began, like that of 1494, with men from leading families taking the initiative. But, also as in 1494, the ottimati were divided amongst themselves and unable to contain the revolt. Vettori was willing to accept a non-Medici government without severing ties to Clement and the church. Capponi wanted a complete break with the pope and even discussed with the imperial viceroy the possibility of support for the insurrection from the very imperial army threatening the city. But Guicciardini, still Lieutenant-General of the papal armies, remained committed to Clement. Rarely had the interests, aims, and convictions of leading ottimati pulled in so many incompatible directions.

---

[2]   Benedetto Varchi, *Storia fiorentina*, ed. L. Arbib, 3 vols. (1843; reprint edn. Rome, 2003), 1: 125–30.

On May 11 the news of the Sack of Rome arrived in Florence and sparked a second and successful revolt. Besides their horror over the destruction, pillaging, and loss of life, Florentines with businesses and banks in Rome saw "hundreds of thousands of florins," Vettori estimated, go up in smoke, and "everyone blamed the pope for these losses."[3] With Clement a prisoner in Castel Sant'Angelo and unable to protect either Rome or Florence, all but the smallest pockets of support for the regime now disappeared. Even Clement's banker Filippo Strozzi joined the revolt. Passerini and Ippolito were persuaded to leave the city, and on May 16 a balìa decreed that the Great Council would be reactivated in late June and that in the meantime smaller councils would govern. However, as in 1494, popular pressure quickly transformed the face of the revolution, demanding that the council reopen as soon as possible, with a minimum age limit of twenty-four (instead of twenty-nine), and that the council's hall, reduced to barracks for fifteen years, be quickly refurbished and re-consecrated. On May 21, 2,272 citizens attended the first session, and another 400 were turned away for lack of space. Eight days later the council decided by 1,298 to 134 that the Standardbearer of Justice should hold office for one year and be eligible for re-election, and on May 31 no fewer than 2,500 members carried out the election. Sixty members drawn by lot each nominated a candidate, and each nominee was put to a vote by the full council: the six with the most votes were the jurist Baldassare Carducci, Nero del Nero, Giovanbattista Bartolini (captain and military commissioner at Pisa), Alfonso Strozzi (Filippo's brother), Tommaso di Paolantonio Soderini (nephew of Piero), and Niccolò Capponi, who was elected in the second ballot.

Benedetto Varchi, a young revolutionary in 1527 who later made his peace with the principate and wrote a history of these years commissioned by Duke Cosimo, analyzed the strengths and weaknesses of these candidates in terms that reveal much about the party and class divisions that accompanied the birth of the last republic. Uncompromising anti-Mediceans favored either Carducci or Strozzi. But Carducci was absent from the city (in jail, in fact, in Venice for calling the pope a tyrant and a bastard[4]), and Strozzi, despite his loyalty to Soderini's republic, had been among the anti-Savonarolan *compagnacci*. Nero del Nero and Bartolini were supported by the "universale" for having enjoyed Soderini's favor and being ignored thereafter by the Medici, but they suffered from insufficient "grandezza." Tommaso Soderini had the advantage of being the son of Paolantonio, "who had, if not invented, greatly promoted the council in the time of the friar," and the nephew of Piero, "through whose incomparable prudence and integrity Florence had lived most

---

[3]   Francesco Vettori, *Sommario della istoria d'Italia (1511–1527)*, in Vettori, *Scritti storici e politici*, ed. Niccolini, p. 245.
[4]   Bernardo Segni, *Istorie fiorentine*, ed. G. Gargani (Florence, 1857), p. 42.

happily and peacefully." But it also worked against him, because many disliked the idea of Medici–Soderini alternation in power. "Only on Niccolò [Capponi] did all the factions concur," says Varchi: apart from the benefit of his father's reputation, "palleschi" liked him because he had been esteemed by the Medici; yet anti-Mediceans knew he never sought honors from the Medici; and "frateschi" considered him a man of integrity who had fought for liberty. What set him apart from Soderini was that he openly opposed the Medici even before the "Friday uprising" of April 26.[5] The political fault lines in 1527 still reflected deep divisions over the Medici, Savonarola, and the Soderini republic, as well as the class division that attributed "grandezza" to some and not to others. Interestingly, Guicciardini, Vettori, and Filippo Strozzi were not considered despite their support for the revolution in its initial phase. Strozzi, who had long collaborated with Clement, ruined his relationship with the new republic in a matter of days by bungling the assignment of recovering the citadels of Pisa and Livorno and letting Ippolito de' Medici escape from his control. Soon enough all three, faced with the stark choice between Clement and the republic, stayed with their Medici pope.

The republic of 1527–30 witnessed an explosion of popular political, religious, and military energies that only intensified once Clement's determination to retake Florence for his family produced the war and siege that became the gravest threats to the city's survival in its long history. At each stage of the conflict, ottimati voices grew weaker and more suspect to a radicalized popolo that refused compromise with Clement, revived the memory of Savonarola and his vision of the holy republic, and put a huge portion of the city's population under arms in a resurrected militia. Hatred of the Medici boiled over. Pierfilippo Pandolfini denounced their "tyranny" and accused them of inflicting "slavery" and "calamities" and shedding the "blood of so many innocent citizens." Cosimo's tomb at San Lorenzo, said one citizen, had named him *pater patriae* "unworthily and in dishonour of liberty." The Medici "have always been tyrants and have always slandered this city, decapitated citizens, and stolen the money of the commune. . . . Those who have always kept the city in slavery (I recall to Your Lordships the events at Prato [in 1512]) deserve to be burned in their palace and given to the dogs."[6] No Medici were executed, but a committee of five syndics investigated fraudulent financial accounts and the looting of Florentine wealth since 1512. Family members and associates were fined and had property confiscated for tax evasion, malfeasance, and fraud. Francesco del Nero, the Medici client who ran the

---

[5] Varchi, *Storia*, vol. 1, pp. 211–13; cf. C. Roth, *The Last Florentine Republic* (1925; reprint edn. New York, 1968), p. 54.
[6] Stephens, *Fall of the Florentine Republic*, pp. 221, 234; Roth, *Last Republic*, p. 111.

Depository for Filippo Strozzi, was accused of laundering payments of millions of florins from the Monte to the Medici, Strozzi banks, papal treasury, and papal armies. Official findings did not come close to such figures, but the syndics found him guilty of falsifying accounts to cover a variety of illegal transfers. Clement himself was declared the commune's debtor for over 200,000 florins, actually a fraction of what he had stolen from the city through various channels, including Strozzi's connivance. Accusations against Mediceans came fast and thick in the republic's first year. The criminal court of the Quarantia, created in 1502 and abolished in 1512, was revived to adjudicate crimes against the government; it convicted and imprisoned some, but the acquittal of many others suggests that public anger (measured by the number and virulence of anonymous denunciations received by the Otto di Guardia) was contained, if not muted, by the court's relative moderation. Death sentences recorded by the confraternity that offered consolation to the condemned were not markedly more numerous under the republic than during the preceding and subsequent years of Medici rule: 16 in 1527, 24 in 1528, 30 in 1529, and 23 in 1530 (and several in this last year were victims of Medici vengeance after the capitulation) compared to 18 persons executed in 1520, 22 in 1522–3, 14 in 1525, and 16 in 1526, 19 in 1531, 30 in 1533, 24 in 1534, 14 in 1535, 13 in 1536, 28 in 1537, and 23 in 1540.[7] Moreover, most death sentences under the republic were not imposed on the Medici and their elite friends. Two non-elite citizens, Carlo Cocchi and Ficino Ficini (nephew of Marsilio), were executed for praising the Medici and advocating their return: the only two mentioned by Giannotti in denouncing the severity of such punishments.[8] Jacopo Alamanni, an implacable *anti*-Medicean and intemperate critic of Capponi's moderation, was executed for inciting a riot, but also, as some suspected, because he knew of Capponi's secret negotiations with Clement.[9]

Intense feeling against the Medici and their allies was fueled partly by anger at Clement's criminally reckless foreign policy, which exposed the city to such danger, and partly by the systematic draining of Florentine wealth through his ottimati friends into the sinkhole of papal follies. And it was sustained by a millenarian religious ideology, which, as the astonished Guicciardini observed during the siege of 1529–30, but without really comprehending it, generated faith that "moves mountains" and the obstinacy and certainty needed to face impossible hardships.[10] Resurgent Savonarolan piety fueled the last republic.

[7]   S. Y. Edgerton, Jr., *Pictures and Punishment: Art and Criminal Prosecution During the Florentine Renaissance* (Ithaca, N.Y., 1985), p. 237.
[8]   Donato Giannotti, *Della repubblica fiorentina*, in *Opere politiche*, 2 vols., ed. F. Diaz (Milan, 1974), 1: 307.
[9]   Varchi, *Storia*, vol. 1, pp. 494–7.
[10]   Guicciardini, *Ricordi*, ed. R. Spongano (Florence, 1951), p. 3; *Maxims and Reflections of a Renaissance Statesman*, trans. M. Domandi (New York, 1965), p. 39.

San Marco recovered the prestige and political importance it enjoyed under Savonarola, prominent citizens again cultivated the support of the friars, public preaching received renewed government support, and the council passed new laws for the moral purification of the city. Prophecies were declared fulfilled, as *piagnoni* once again identified their cause with the republic's liberty and in opposition to the repulsed Medici tyranny. While no doubt a source of strength, especially during the traumatic siege, the republic's millenarian and puritanical strains also revived Savonarolan intolerance. Barely three weeks after the revolution, "in order to return the city and the republic to all the conditions and institutions" of "the popular government before 1512, and especially those that concern the health of the soul and the establishment of the good life," the restored Great Council ordered Jews to close their lending operations and leave the city, although once again the order was not rigorously enforced and some Jews remained as proposals for expulsion within six months were repeatedly rejected. New laws restricted dress, dowries, prostitutes, sodomy, and blasphemy; taverns were regulated and gambling forbidden. To publish books now required the Signoria's permission, and clerics were authorized to supervise discussions of religion.

In February 1528 Niccolò Capponi theatrically implored the council to declare Christ King of Florence. Only 18 of 1,100 had the courage to vote against it. In June 1529 the republic's submission to Christ was renewed in recognition of "the most precious gift of the most holy liberty granted to this most devoted people by work of God" and in dutiful acknowledgment of the promise "of the Holy Spirit, speaking through the mouth of Moses" when he said "If you will hear my voice and will observe my covenant and obey my commandments, you will be my chosen people above all others."[11] Not everyone, even among loyal republicans, was pleased with the religious fervor that suffused these years. After the fall of the republic in which he held Machiavelli's old post of secretary to the Ten, Donato Giannotti, in his treatise *On the Florentine Republic*, criticized those who "were so presumptuous under that cloak of religion that no one dared to say anything that contradicted their opinions." He accused the *piagnoni* of "giving the most false interpretations" of Savonarola's utterances and persuading citizens, even during the worst of the siege, that they should leave all to God's will. The friars could have put an end to such "hypocrisy" by staying out of politics and "remembering that discussion of government occurs in the palace [of the priors] and not at San Marco." Their lay followers who made "such a show of holiness" in the council but outside of it were no better than others "were the worst citizens of all."[12]

---

[11] Stephens, *Fall of the Florentine Republic*, pp. 214–15; Roth, *Last Republic*, pp. 63–79; Polizzotto, *Elect Nation*, pp. 351–2.

[12] Giannotti, *Della repubblica fiorentina*, 3.18, in *Opere*, vol. 1, pp. 325–7.

This may have seemed clear to intellectuals like Giannotti after the surrender, but that the city was able to endure the suffering of the siege was due in no small part to the conviction that the republic was under the special protection of a divine providence that had indeed chosen the Florentines.

Siege

For two years Clement demanded, and the republic refused, the reinstatement of his family.[13] To achieve his objective Clement needed the help of the very emperor whose army had raped Rome. In November 1527 they reached an agreement, and in December Clement was finally released. Capponi immediately realized the danger to Florence of their rapprochement: Charles wanted Clement to deny England's Henry VIII his divorce from Charles's aunt Catherine of Aragon, and the price would inevitably be military assistance for Clement's recapture of Florence, which thus needed either Charles's protection or an accommodation with Clement. Capponi might have preferred an alliance with Charles, but Florence had formally joined the French led League of Cognac in April and reaffirmed its commitment in June. Traditional Florentine pro-French sentiment, especially among anti-Mediceans, would have made an alliance with Charles difficult in any case, but the emperor himself closed that door by insisting that the Florentines satisfy the pope's demands first. Despite intense anti-Medici feeling in the city, Capponi opened secret negotiations with Clement, who took full advantage of Charles's refusal to strike a separate deal with Florence to insist on his family's complete restoration. Capponi fell under a cloud of suspicion as fear mounted that he might accept the pope's demands. Although re-elected in June 1528, he emerged from the first ballot with only fourteen more votes (out of 1,944) than Baldassare Carducci, the leader of the emerging opposition party that rejected compromise with Clement.

There was one other possible avenue of escape: a military victory for the league and expulsion of imperial power from Italy. In 1528 full-scale hostilities resumed, and that summer the French seemed on the verge of taking Naples and winning the war when an outbreak of plague among the league's troops and the defection of Andrea Doria, who took Genoa and its fleet over to the imperial side, suddenly reversed the outcome. As Capponi persisted in seeking an agreement with Clement, he was caught between former Medici friends, now inclined to compromise in order to forestall disaster, and an angry and intransigent opposition, mostly non-elite, that mistrusted him and tried to monitor his actions and prevent him from negotiating without the approval of his advisory committees. In April 1529 his negotiations with the

[13] For what follows: Roth, *Last Republic*.

pope in violation of laws against such "private" diplomacy were uncovered; he was tried by the Eighty and, although acquitted of treason, was removed from his office. In his place the council elected Francesco Carducci (kinsman of Baldassare, who had gone to France as ambassador). Just as military confrontation became unavoidable, power passed from moderate ottimati to men from non-elite families, supported by a few elite allies, resolutely determined to resist Clement's demands. In June 1529 Charles and Clement signed the Treaty of Barcelona in which the emperor pledged support for the restoration to the Medici of all property and privileges and sealed the deal by promising his illegitimate daughter, Margaret of Austria, in marriage to Alessandro de' Medici (officially the younger Lorenzo's illegitimate son, but more likely Clement's). In early August the crushing news that Francis had agreed in the Treaty of Cambrai not to intervene further in Italy made an imperial attack inevitable.

The Florentines set about strengthening their defenses. In January 1529 Michelangelo was elected to the revived Nine of the Militia and in April was made "Governor General and Procurator of the Fortifications," with responsibility for reinforcing the dominion fortresses of Livorno, Pisa, Empoli, Pistoia, and Prato and designing new fortifications for the city around the church of San Miniato, on a hill south of the Arno that oversaw the enemy camp and provided an ideal artillery emplacement. By the fall of 1529, as the siege neared, city residents replaced contado recruits in hauling building materials and provisions up the hill, day and night, to the worksite. As construction projects continued at the gates and bastions, the government ordered the systematic destruction of all buildings within one mile of the city, including the villas of the wealthy and the humble homes of villagers, in order to deprive the besiegers of anything useful, and welcomed and fed thousands of suddenly homeless people. When the siege began in October 1529, Florence was well fortified and nearly impregnable.

Defense was entrusted to two very different armies. One was a professional army of about 10,000 mostly Italian mercenaries, although the effective fighting force was perhaps two-thirds of that, under Governor-General, and later Captain-General, Malatesta Baglioni of Perugia, his second-in-command Stefano Colonna, six colonels, and eighty captains, most non-Florentines. The second army was the citizen militia voted into law[14] by the council in November 1528, which ultimately numbered 10,000 in a population of 60,000. Unlike Machiavelli's militia, this force consisted chiefly of city residents. "Knowing from long experience that cities and their liberty are defended more effectively and with more ready spirit by their own citizens against both external enemies and those who might wish to live in them as tyrants," the law organized the

---

[14]   Published in *ASI* 1 (1842): 397–409.

new Ordinanza on the basis of the ancient gonfaloni created by the Primo Popolo in 1250. All citizens on the tax rolls between the ages of 18 and 50, whether or not they sat in the council, were required to enroll in their gonfalone's company. Service was mandatory for men under, and voluntary for those over, 36 and was extended to 60 during the siege. Although primarily a defensive force, not suitable for offensive campaigns or open pitched battles, the militia fought effectively in occasional skirmishes just beyond the walls.

The militia was also a force for unity and cohesion during the desperate months of the siege, a source of pride, a constant marching manifestation of the republic's morale. On separate days in each quarter, all those enrolled were required to attend Mass and one by one "swear an oath not to wield arms except for the honor of God and the common good and in defense of liberty." Public orations inspired "obedience to their commanders, military discipline, defense of the fatherland, and the preservation of its liberty." In his "Discourse on Arming the City" of early 1529 Giannotti praised the oath and orations as "a beautiful ceremony and very useful to the republic, for through it their spirits will marvelously exert themselves toward *virtù* and the defense of the *patria*. And nothing moves tender spirits more than seeing that they are honored by public magistrates. And when religion is added, one cannot imagine how many marvelous effects will result."[15] In combining patriotism, exaltations of republican liberty, Savonarolan religious fervor, denunciations of wealth, exhortations to fraternity and charity, and appeals to Florence's communal past and popular traditions, the orations are the most revealing expressions of the republic's ideological temper. Initially four were required, one in each quarter, for the oath-taking ceremonies, but in 1529 they were expanded to biannual cycles culminating in orations to the entire city on February 9, the anniversary of the election in 1528 of Christ as King of Florence, and on May 15, the eve of the liberation in 1527. As major public events, they attracted judgments, praise, and sometimes criticism from observers for performance, style, and content. Luigi Alamanni's oration of January 1529 reproved the Florentines for their excessive love of wealth and linked moral virtue and political liberty to poverty and the willingness to take up arms for the public welfare, not for private gain or vengeance. Varchi commented that it "wasn't heard well because he has a weak voice and the church of Santa Croce is large. So his oration was immediately printed. It was dignified and full of piety, praising poverty as the source of all good things. Many, even among his friends, told him his oration was more suited to the sermons of friars than to orations for soldiers." In February 1530, Piero Vettori (Francesco's staunchly

---

[15] Donato Giannotti, "Discorso di armare la città di Firenze fatto dinanzi alli Mag.ci Signori e Gonfaloniere di Giustizia l'anno 1529," in *Opere*, vol. 1, p. 180. Cf. Trexler, *Public Life*, p. 537.

republican cousin) lauded military discipline and adduced the model of the ancient Etruscans: "We can thus hope, if we turn our spirit to this praiseworthy exercise, to bring back to life the empire and glory of those warlike Tuscans, since we were born under the same sky that begets glorious and noble souls. Nor should we think that [this region's] nature has changed, rather that the cause of our lazy sleep has been poor discipline." The militia, he exclaimed, echoing Petrarch's *Italia mia* (and Machiavelli's quotation of it at the end of *The Prince*) has "clearly shown that ancient valor in Italian hearts is not yet dead" and has "restored honor to an afflicted Italy."

Pierfilippo Pandolfini's oration of January 1529 was more political and historical than those of Alamanni and Vettori. Citing the Romans for their political organization and military traditions, and reinforcing his arguments with what "Aristotle teaches in his *Republica*," Pandolfini insisted that the health of popular government depends on legal equality between rich and poor. Of the three "parts" of the city, the wealthy, poor, and those in between, only those neither wealthy nor poor can be entrusted with responsibilities of governance, since the wealthy are unable to obey magistrates not of their class and letting the rich rule produces "a city of masters and slaves, not of free men," while the poor, "constrained by excessive necessity, do not know how to govern and are suited only to servile obedience." Only those in the middle who neither desire the possessions of others nor have possessions desired by others are suited to govern, as shown (so Pandolfini argued) by the large number of non-noble men who made Rome great. Attacks on the wealthy as unfit for leadership in republics echoed similar arguments by Machiavelli and may have been inspired by him. But they also point to traditions of popular government that go deeper into the Florentine past. Exhorting his listeners to "imitate their ancestors" and embrace the unity and concord that are possible only with justice, Pandolfini recalled Florence's long history of conflict between the popolo and the elite families:

> As is shown by all those who have written the history of Florence, the struggle between the *popolo* and the *grandi* in this city goes back very far and almost to the beginning, and no other solution was ever found except to arm the multitude under a popular government. Thus came about the institution of the Standard-bearer of Justice who [with his armed force] ensured that justice was done and the insolent conspiracies of the powerful were suppressed without consideration of persons. And this remedy was most beneficial for as long as the magistrates came from the middle sort of men of the *popolo*. When these brakes [on the insolence of the *grandi*] were abandoned through negligence, the *popolo* fell into slavery to the powerful, from which it was liberated by [divine] providence and by the *virtù* of Giano della Bella, whose fame, notwithstanding that he died in exile because of the envy and ill will that the powerful directed against him because of his favors to the *popolo* and the glory that this earned him, will live

for as long as these walls still stand and as long as the Florentine name endures. For he restored and strengthened our liberty with those holy bonds of the Ordinances of Justice, and by arming the people and organizing it into the sixteen companies [of the gonfaloni], he instituted the free and popular form of governing the republic that lasted 130 years.

Pandolfini's history was slightly faulty (Giano's government did not institute the military companies of the gonfaloni), but his comment that free government ended "130 years" later clearly alludes to the Medici. Pandolfini added that "after about 1400, as the city became weaker, arms fell into disuse and justice was corrupted, the power of certain families grew and their rivalries and conflicts caused the destruction of liberty." He concluded with a passionate appeal to the militias to prevent their restored liberty from ever again falling into the hands of those who would suppress it, as happened, he reminds them, in 1512, when the "leaders of that wicked conspiracy" became the authors of every kind of atrocity and evil. Even as it announced the birth of a new and purified Florence, the last republic reached back to the communal past for models and inspiration in what was still perceived as a struggle between a rapacious elite and a virtuous popolo. Although Pandolfini never mentions the Medici by name, the allusions to them and the message that the militia was designed above all to keep the city free of them are unmistakable. Varchi remembered that "Pandolfini's oration was considered by many very beautiful both for his language and for his style of delivery," but that not everyone liked it, for, as he added, perhaps in a gesture of prudence toward his Medici duke: "Many others, of better judgment in my view, thought it disjointed and boring. And in truth it was a long and rather immoderate invective against the Medici."[16]

Under the command of the Captain-General of the imperial forces, Philibert de Chalon, Prince of Orange, the approaching enemy army initially included some 11,000 German, Spanish, and Italian troops and at peak strength numbered perhaps 30,000. As Orange moved slowly but steadily north into the upper Arno valley in the late summer of 1529, Carducci's government decided to concentrate its defenses at Florence and not to engage the enemy at any of the cities on the route, particularly Perugia and Arezzo, where it might have been possible to inflict a decisive defeat on the still growing force. In October Orange moved from Figline to San Donato to Apparita (so named because it affords the first full view of the city from that direction) and into the Pian di

[16] *Documenti per servire alla storia della milizia italiana*, ed. G. Canestrini, *ASI* 15 (1851): Alamanni, pp. 342–9; Pandolfini, pp. 350–76 (358–9, 374–5). Albertini, *Firenze dalla repubblica al principato*: Vettori pp. 418–24 (419–20). Varchi, *Storia*, vol. 1, pp. 529–30; vol. 2, p. 278. Cf. Trexler, *Public Life*, pp. 533–5.

Ripoli. On October 12 artillery fire from the heavily fortified walls marked the beginning of the ten-month ordeal (see Plate 12). Orange's army encamped south of the river, but for many months communications and supply routes remained open to the north. An assault in early November failed, and the war at the walls settled into occasional artillery exchanges and skirmishes in the hills. Orange found it impossible to break through and soon gave up trying. On this front it became a war of attrition, with heavy casualties, whose outcome depended on food supplies to both the besieged Florentines and an irregularly paid and poorly disciplined imperial army always in danger of disintegration.

In the dominion the war was a contest for control of cities and fortresses in which the soon-to-be-legendary Francesco Ferrucci emerged as a brilliant strategist whose victories (until the last battle) sustained the morale of the besieged city. After displaying his skill in disciplining troops as an assistant commissioner, Ferrucci was appointed to protect the fortress at Empoli, the key to the lower Arno valley and, through it, contact with Pisa and the outside world. In November–December 1529 he conducted raids against imperial positions and brought San Miniato al Tedesco under Florentine control. In January 1530, at Orange's urging, Charles sent another army to surround Florence to the west and north and complete the encirclement. Conditions immediately worsened as fewer convoys made it through the blockade and food prices soared in mid-winter. By spring 1530 the government instituted rationing and punished hoarding, as disease spread and death rates soared. Civilian deaths are estimated at possibly a third of the approximately 90,000 people in the city at the beginning of the siege (including the many who took refuge from the devastated countryside). To pay its mercenaries and secure munitions and provisions, the government imposed higher taxes, including forced loans, taxes on ecclesiastical property, and the confiscation and sale of the property of "rebels" who had fled the city and joined the enemy, among them Francesco Guicciardini and Francesco Vettori, who were now in Clement's entourage advising him how to conquer their city. As leading ottimati made the only choice they could to save themselves, their property, and status in the city of their ancestors, the republic passed even more firmly into the hands of intransigent anti-Mediceans. Rafaello Girolami, elected Standardbearer in December 1529, was an unswerving republican who preserved continuity with Carducci's government. Even into the spring and summer of 1530, with the city isolated and food supplies dwindling, morale remained high: citizens paid the huge sums asked of them and auctioned off their valuables to provide the government with still more revenue. Processions and orations continued, and graffiti proclaimed that the city was "poor but free."

Meanwhile, negotiations both public and secret sought agreements with both pope and emperor, but Clement's demands were always unacceptable

Plate 12 Fresco of the Siege of Florence of 1529–30, painted in Palazzo Vecchio by Giorgio Vasari, 1561–2 (Alinari/Art Resource, NY)

and Charles routinely rebuffed Florentine envoys and told them to deal first with Clement. Appeals to France also came to nothing, and Venice would not challenge the emperor if France refused to intervene. Captain-General Baglioni was conducting negotiations of his own, not on behalf of his employers, but to position himself for a soft landing into Italian politics and control of Perugia (in papal territory, after all) once the war ended, as he now believed inevitable, with the republic's demise. The Florentines knew of Baglioni's early contacts with the pope and considered them potentially useful, but he persisted even after the government broke off all negotiations with Clement and ordered Baglioni to do likewise. As the military situation worsened for Florence, Baglioni was ever more inclined to make his own deal with the pope and Orange.

After most of the dominion had fallen to imperial forces, Ferrucci revived Florentine hopes in April with a surprise attack that recaptured Volterra, but in doing so he left Empoli vulnerable and it fell at the end of May. Communications with Pisa and the ports were now cut off, and Orange could simply wait for hunger to achieve what his armies could not. In late June Florentine forces stole out of the city, attacked an enemy camp north of the river, and inflicted many casualties. All remaining men up to the age of sixty, including an additional 6,000 artisans, were armed and readied to fight. But by July food supplies were nearly exhausted, and only a dramatic breakthrough could prevent surrender and possibly a sack. Ferrucci finally secured the government's permission to bring his forces toward Florence and attack the besiegers. From Volterra he went to Pisa and came east with a force of 3,000 infantry and 300 light cavalry. Orange took 3,000 infantry to engage him near Pistoia, which left only 5,000 enemy soldiers outside the walls. Within the city many pressed for an attack on the depleted imperial forces: in the last recorded speech of a pratica, Bono Boni urged the Signoria to inform Baglioni and Colonna "that the will of the people is that the enemy be assaulted, begging you that, besides confiding in God, you confide in yourselves, in whom victory is hoped, which will be moreover to your honor and to the good of the city."[17] Baglioni insisted that an attack was too risky and did nothing and, while he may have been correct, many suspected he had made a deal with Orange not to attack. Orange intercepted Ferrucci north of Pistoia at Gavinana, where the decisive battle was fought on August 3. Orange was wounded and died and at one point Ferrucci seemed about to win the day, but additional contingents of imperial troops overwhelmed and annihilated the Florentine force. Ferrucci himself was among an estimated 2,000 casualties that day. When the news of the defeat reached Florence the next day, the government still favored a breakout attack, but Baglioni refused. The inevitability of surrender began to

[17]   Roth, *Last Republic*, p. 311.

change some minds, as several hundred members of the Oltrarno militia declared their support for Baglioni. When the Signoria sent envoys to discharge him he attacked and killed one of them. Facing the possibility that their own Captain-General might allow the besiegers to inflict the calamity he had been hired to avert, the frightened government backed down and agreed to surrender to the imperial representatives. On August 12 ambassadors went to the enemy camp and signed the capitulation; the next day the Great Council met, for the last time, to approve a forced loan of 80,000 florins the city was required to pay for the siege to be lifted, although only in late September did the besiegers finally move away and remove the danger of a sack. Losses were staggering: according to Varchi, combat casualties amounted to 8,000 in the Florentine armies and 14,000 among the besieging forces, while civilian deaths in the city from plague, hunger, or enemy action are estimated at over 30,000.[18] Upon his return Guicciardini described the "miseries and ruin of the city and *contado*" as "much greater than we imagined: the people exhausted, their resources and houses destroyed for many miles around Florence and in many towns of the dominion; the peasants infinitely diminished in number; the lower classes practically gone."[19]

Imposition of a New Order

After the surrender Baglioni and the pope's representative Bartolomeo (Baccio) Valori controlled the city and held a pathetic parlamento (Varchi says three hundred attended) which, surrounded by Baglioni's troops, approved a balìa that disbanded the council and militia, deprived the Signoria of its authority, appointed the next one, removed the Dieci, and replaced the Otto. Restructuring Florentine government was the emperor's prerogative, not the pope's, and for the next two decades Florence, although never formally annexed to Charles's dominions, was in effect an imperial protectorate. On October 28 an imperial decree installed Alessandro de' Medici as "caput" of the government and dominion of the Florentine Republic.[20] Preserving the republic for the moment, at least on paper, and not making Alessandro its duke was Charles's way of keeping Clement in line by giving him only half of what he wanted. In February 1531, delicately balancing papal and imperial pretensions, the balìa elected Alessandro perpetual head of all Florentine magistracies as a gesture of obedience to Clement, "father and protector of his beloved *patria*." Over the next year, as the old republican magistracies lived their last days without

[18] Varchi, *Storia*, vol. 2, p. 521; Roth, *Last Republic*, p. 320.
[19] Albertini, *Firenze dalla repubblica al principato*, p. 181.
[20] D. Marrara, *Studi giuridici sulla Toscana medicea* (Milan, 1965), p. 6.

any power, Clement asked leading ottimati for their views on political and con-stitutional reform. Clement and Charles probably had no intention of being dissuaded from instituting a principate, even by those, like Guicciardini, who had remained loyal to Clement throughout the last republic, but they knew that any settlement would require concessions to ottimati sensibilities. Most ottimati, having seen their attempt to replace the Medici with an aristocratic republic overwhelmed by the popolo's deep hatred of the Medici and resentment against the ottimati themselves for collaboration in "tyranny," now accepted the necessity of acquiescing in a Medici lordship, even as they ineffectually quibbled over its constitutional form, as the safest guarantee of their own survival. Just as the Ciompi revolt and the popular government of 1378–82 persuaded the non-elite major guildsmen never again to ally with minor guilds-men and artisans against the elite, so the last republic convinced the ottimati never again to ally with the popolo against the Medici.

Revenge was the first desire of the ottimati that needed to be satisfied, and Clement cleverly let them assume responsibility for the harsh repression that ensued. Ottimati who had sided with Clement returned to find their property ruined by war and picked clean by the republican government. An angry Guicciardini arrived as the pope's enforcer and presided over a crackdown in which, despite initial promises that vengeance would not be exacted with violence, republican and *piagnoni* leaders were rounded up, jailed, tortured, and in many cases executed. He wrote in October that "we have made a good beginning, having detained all those rogues and begun to examine Carduccio [Francesco Carducci], and thus we shall continue, for indeed, if one wishes to put this state on a proper footing, mild measures are useless." After a phony confession extracted with torture, Carducci was beheaded, and Guicciardini actually objected when Rafaello Girolami was not given a death sentence (although he was found dead in his cell anyway, poisoned, as Varchi reports the rumor, by order of Clement). Vettori similarly complained that the repub-lic's leading *piagnone* cleric, Fra Benedetto da Foiano, was not being tortured in Rome, but Clement let him starve to death.[21] At least 200 persons, among them Donato Giannotti and Jacopo Nardi, were imprisoned or exiled. In inflicting these punishments Guicciardini "showed himself," wrote Varchi, "the cruelest and most enraged of all." Some even dubbed him "ser Cerretieri," Walter of Brienne's hated henchman and executioner. Class hatreds were now open and raw: Guicciardini wrote that "we [ottimati] have as our enemy an entire people,"[22] and Vettori expressed the fear and anger with which ottimati

---

[21]   Polizzotto, *Elect Nation*, p. 400, n. 47; Albertini, *Firenze dalla repubblica al principato*, p. 442.
[22]   Quoted by R. Ridolfi, *The Life of Francesco Guicciardini*, trans. C. Grayson (London, 1967), pp. 211–12, 221; Varchi, *Storia*, vol. 2, p. 578.

now viewed the popolo in enumerating "how many enemies we have": the militia, which "would do anything and risk any danger" to be armed again and rule the city; the members of the defunct council "who will always be intent upon our ruin"; and the lower guildsmen and artisans. That was indeed the entire popolo. With so many enemies, he concluded, "we must think about holding power by force" and "with fear." Late in 1532 Vettori could still refer to the republicans as "the most wicked, obstinate, and ignorant men in the world, who cared nothing about going without bread, wine and everything necessary to life to ruin themselves and destroy the villas and property [of others]. And we'd be fooling ourselves if we thought they wouldn't do it again"[23] (a remarkable echo of Leonardo Bruni's denunciation of the Ciompi in his *History of the Florentine People*). In venting such feelings and exacting retribution, the ottimati played right into Clement's hands by driving a permanent wedge between the classes and ensuring that they could never again ally against the Medici. Roberto Acciaiuoli warned that "the purge of suspect men" was going on too long and keeping the city "in terror" with punishments that would be deemed "cruelties" if dragged out.[24] By thus isolating themselves the ottimati weakened their dwindling chances of forestalling the end of their role as a governing class.

In 1531 the leading ottimati avoided endorsing the principate, arguing that the moment was not right and hoping to defer it for as long as possible. But early in 1532 Clement convened a group of ottimati, including Filippo Strozzi, who was again his banker and now eagerly supported dissolving the republic and establishing a principate. Only Jacopo Salviati, ironically the grandfather of the then thirteen-year-old boy who would become duke in 1537, was opposed. Strozzi consulted leading ottimati, including Vettori, who at first objected but acquiesced once he knew that Clement had made up his mind.[25] A second round of written opinions[26] from Francesco and Luigi Guicciardini, Vettori, and Acciaiuoli still opposed making Alessandro "principe assoluto," but they all accepted Medici lordship with the fig leaf of a pro forma consultative role for ottimati. Francesco Guicciardini expressed the desperation of his class in admitting that "we are forced to desire any solution which may ensure our power in the government, of whatever kind it may be."[27] His brother Luigi and Vettori submitted what were in effect drafts of the legislation that

---

[23] Vettori, *Scritti storici e politici*, pp. 305–9; Albertini, *Firenze dalla repubblica al principato*, p. 463; cf. Devonshire Jones, *Francesco Vettori*, pp. 245–6.

[24] "*Due pareri* di Ruberto Acciaiuoli – anno 1531–32," *ASI* 1 (1842): 446.

[25] Segni, *Istorie*, pp. 230–1.

[26] Felix Gilbert, "Alcuni discorsi di uomini politici fiorentini e la politica di Clemente VII per la restaurazione medicea," *ASI* 93, vol. 2 (1935): 3–24.

[27] Ridolfi, *Life of Guicciardini*, p. 221.

ended the republic. On April 4, 1532, the balìa created the committee of Twelve Reformers (including Vettori, Baccio Valori, Roberto Pucci, Roberto Acciaiuoli, and Francesco Guicciardini) who wrote the new constitution, which became law on April 27. On May 1 the last priorate handed over the insignia of sovereignty to Alessandro.

Although it changed much, the 1532 reform was not a complete break with the past. Alessandro became hereditary "duke of the Florentine Republic," and the priorate was abolished (two months short of its 250th birthday) and replaced by the Magistrato Supremo consisting of the duke (or his lieutenant) and four advisers. Two councils with life tenure were instituted, the 200 and the 48 (or Senate), the latter selected from the ranks of the former. But all other officials were still elected by a combination of scrutinies and sortition, and the duke's four advisers were chosen four times a year by rotating committees of accoppiatori within the Senate. On the surface at least, this government preserved the republican distinction between executive and legislative powers, and the ottimati who devised it believed they had instituted a Venetian-style mixed government with an important role for themselves in the Senate. The Twelve Reformers of April 1532 became the first members of the Senate, and the balìa constituted the nucleus of the 200. Thereafter Alessandro increasingly appointed members of both bodies, and Duke Cosimo steadily deprived the councils of power by arrogating decision-making functions to himself and his ministers. Alessandro's reign still had much in common with the old Medici system that depended on ottimati support in return for a semblance of prominence in councils and magistracies. His very title was indicative of the Janus-like aspect of this transitional period: he was duke, not of Florence, but of the Florentine Republic.[28]

The biggest new fact on the ground was the construction of the huge fortress now called the Fortezza da Basso. Here too the initiative apparently came from the ottimati: Filippo Strozzi, Francesco Vettori, and Luigi Guicciardini all urged that a fortress be built to protect the unpopular regime and for storage of arms confiscated after the siege. Charles wanted it as a potential refuge where his daughter Margaret could "be secure in case of any uprising" after her marriage to Alessandro, which Charles kept putting off. The architect Antonio da Sangallo the younger recommended the western gate of Porta a Faenza for a fortress straddling the old wall. On July 15, 1534, the foundation stone was laid, and work began immediately with thousands of forced and unpaid laborers recruited from the dominion. When Clement died on September 25, 1534, fear of a popular uprising intensified the pace of construction. By the end of 1535 the first section was finished, and Charles ordered the

---

[28]   A. Anzilotti, *La costituzione interna dello Stato fiorentino sotto il duca Cosimo I de' Medici* (Florence, 1910), pp. 25–39; Varchi, *Storia*, vol. 2, pp. 637–45.

installation of the already present garrison of imperial troops under the command of Alessandro Vitelli (son of Paolo, executed by the republican government in 1499). Duke Alessandro reaffirmed the clause of his marriage contract stipulating that, if he died without legitimate male heirs, the emperor would take possession not only of the Fortezza but of the fortresses of Pisa and Livorno as well. The Fortezza safeguarded Charles's power in Florence and Tuscany; for the first time, military fortifications at the walls of the city protected foreign occupiers against the people of Florence.[29]

Alessandro's many enemies included the exiles scattered around Italy and France, his cousin Ippolito who joined the exiles (but died suddenly, perhaps at Alessandro's order, in 1535), and potentially the French crown, which encouraged the exiles but never gave them adequate military support. Filippo Strozzi, who had already quarreled with Alessandro and then lost his patron and reason for being a Medicean when Clement died, also joined the exiles, as did Baccio Valori. When Charles came to Naples in 1535, leading exiles went to appeal for his support against the "tyrant" Alessandro. In a memorable oration before the emperor, Jacopo Nardi, the old Savonarolan, republican, and future historian, defended Florentine "liberty," accusing Alessandro of tyranny both in ruling arbitrarily and oppressively and lacking a legitimate title. Nardi argued that the emperor himself had promised in August 1530 to respect Florence's "liberty" and that the law of 1532 was therefore invalid. Alessandro also arrived in Naples in January 1536 accompanied by Guicciardini, Vettori, and two young Medici, twenty-one-year-old Lorenzo di Pierfrancesco and sixteen-year-old Cosimo, son of Maria Salviati, the elder Lorenzo's granddaughter, and of Giovanni de' Medici, called "delle Bande Nere," who had died fighting in the papal armies during the war of the League of Cognac. Guicciardini presented Alessandro's defense, insisting that the "liberty" promised by Charles referred not to any particular form of government but rather to Florence's status as an independent state free of foreign domination, and that, precisely because Charles had recognized its independence, the Florentine government had the authority to enact whatever reforms it chose. Confronting each other in Naples were different notions of liberty promoted by two factions of ottimati,[30] with the exiles ironically imploring the intervention, in defense of Florentine liberty, of the very imperial power that had crushed the republic, and Guicciardini, equally ironically, invoking Florentine independence to defend the legitimacy of a regime totally subservient to imperial power. Charles upheld the reforms of 1532 and supported

[29] J. R. Hale, "The End of Florentine Liberty: The Fortezza da Basso," in Rubinstein, *Florentine Studies*, pp. 501–32.

[30] Marrara, *Studi giuridici*, pp. 12–17; Nardi, *Istorie*, book 10, chaps. 19–36, vol. 2, pp. 255–79; Varchi, *Storia*, vol. 3, pp. 133–231.

Alessandro by allowing the marriage to Margaret to take place and then visiting Florence. On April 29, 1536, with Guicciardini at his side, he made his triumphal entry, received from Alessandro the symbolic keys to the gates of the city, and immediately handed them back, thus underscoring that ducal sovereignty was in the emperor's gift.[31]

What seemed settled and secure was undone in an instant when, on January 6, 1537, Alessandro was murdered by his cousin Lorenzo di Pierfrancesco, called Lorenzino, who styled himself a classical tyrannicide intent upon restoring liberty and a "vivere politico."[32] But Lorenzino led no movement and immediately fled the city. Alessandro's chief minister, Cardinal Cybo, kept the sensational event secret for two crucial days as he brought Alessandro Vitelli, then in Arezzo, back to Florence to take control of the Fortezza. When the news broke, according to Varchi, "everyone shared in the general happiness, but no one did anything," either because they lacked arms or didn't quite believe the report or, as Varchi speculated, because they lacked leaders. "Small groups and crowds formed in the streets, and everyone spoke his mind freely. . . . They talked about reopening the council and who would be suitable as Standardbearer and who should be rewarded or punished."[33] Yet the assassination sparked no uprising. Traumatized by the siege, surrender, and elite-led repression of 1530, the popolo no longer trusted the ottimati and would not follow even the few voices of resistance. Secret meetings of *piagnoni*, mainly from the working class, indulged in mystical prophecies of impending liberation from both the Medici and ottimati for about a year until they were revealed and suppressed.[34] But this time *piagnone* prophecy did not inspire the popolo to revolution.

Less easily controlled was the political situation. Cybo wanted to assume power himself by having the Senate of forty-eight name Alessandro's illegitimate five-year-old son as a figurehead successor, but Guicciardini and Vettori blocked this and also crushed the few and weak calls for a republican restoration which they knew would bring a ferocious reaction from Charles and probably imperial annexation. Facing one last time the dilemma they had been wrestling with for almost half a century, the leading ottimati attempted a compromise between their aspirations and the ever greater ineluctability of Medici lordship. Varchi says that among the forty-eight were forty-eight different opinions about what to do, except on one point, namely, that they all agreed not to resurrect the council. Not willing to risk that even a conser-

[31] Varchi, *Storia*, vol. 3, pp. 234–43.
[32] His self-defense is in the *Apologia*: Lorenzino de' Medici, *Scritti e documenti* (Milan, 1862; reprint edn. 1974), pp. 3–16.
[33] Varchi, *Storia*, vol. 3, pp. 266–7.
[34] Polizzotto, *Elect Nation*, pp. 420–32.

vative republican restoration might revive the popolo they now loathed, they declined to travel the road of 1494 and 1527 and decided instead to anoint the seventeen-year-old Cosimo, not as duke but as "capo e primario" of Florentine government. On January 15 Vettori wrote to his old friend Filippo Strozzi, now with the exiles, to explain that the quick decision was necessary because of their fear that "the popolo, *our enemy and yours*, might seize those few arms it still had to throw us out, rob us, and kill us." He impressed upon Strozzi that the fortresses were in imperial hands and thousands of imperial troops just beyond the borders of Tuscany were ready to intervene if necessary.[35]

Fearful of the popolo and now also that Florence might be invaded and swallowed up into Charles's empire, few ottimati hesitated in replacing Alessandro with another Medici. Cosimo seemed the perfect choice: young and (so they thought) likely to remain under their tutelage; and heir to both branches of the family. The Senate "elected" Cosimo on January 9 and the next day tried to circumscribe his authority by prohibiting him from making decisions or even opening public letters without his four advisers, by requiring his lieutenant to be selected from the Senate, and by buttressing the Senate's constitutional role. Cosimo and his handlers, confident of the imperial power behind them, ignored these restrictions and soon dismissed the venerable ottimati who had presumed to control him. Charles's ambassador in Rome, Count Cifuentes, sent to negotiate among Cosimo, the ottimati, and the exiles represented by Donato Giannotti, kept the fortresses under imperial control, confirmed Cosimo in the powers granted to Alessandro while still withholding the ducal title, and rejected the exiles' offer to end their opposition if Cosimo abided by the restrictions of January 10. That summer the exiles resorted to arms. Filippo Strozzi, his son Piero, Baccio Valori, and Antonfrancesco degli Albizzi (the latter two, ironically, among the ottimati who forced Piero Soderini out of office in 1512) brought several thousand troops to Montemurlo, between Prato and Pistoia, and were waiting for more when they were surprised and defeated by Vitelli's forces on August 2. Piero Strozzi escaped, but the others were taken to Florence, humiliated before Cosimo and his mother in Palazzo Medici, jailed, tortured, and some beheaded in full view of the populace in piazza Signoria. Filippo Strozzi was tortured in the Fortezza he had urged Alessandro to build and either took his own life a year later or, according to Segni, was murdered.[36] Cosimo's handling of the crisis won the confidence of the emperor, who gave him his ducal title two months later.

---

[35] F. Diaz, *Il granducato di Toscana – I Medici* (Turin, 1987), p. 67, n. 4; and Albertini, *Firenze dalla repubblica al principato*, p. 209, n. 1.

[36] Segni, *Istorie*, p. 370; *Cronaca fiorentina, 1537–1555*, ed. E. Coppi (Florence, 2000), p. 10.

Montemurlo became legendary as the republic's last stand, but what really died in 1537 was the last illusion of the ottimati, despite other, equally ineffectual, revolts in succeeding decades. The ferocious punishments meted out to the rebels stunned the ottimati in Florence. To Guicciardini, Vettori, and others who had had no qualms about the death sentences they inflicted on the leaders of the last republic, the summary execution of so many of their peers brutally conveyed the message that Cosimo and the emperor who protected him would no longer accord privileged status to their class. Gone was the century-old assumption that the Medici had to govern with the ottimati. Those who cooperated could enjoy the duke's favor; those who resisted ran enormous risks. But the young duke had no use for Guicciardini, who withdrew to write his fatalistic *History of Italy* and died in May 1540. Vettori never recovered from the tragedy of his old friend Filippo Strozzi and died even sooner, in March 1539. Their deaths and the execution and exile of other leading ottimati eliminated the elite's traditional leadership and cleared the political stage for Cosimo and his non-ottimati advisers to write new rules for Florentine politics and society.

Ducal Government

Cosimo's government survived under the patronage, protection, and implicit threat of imperial power.[37] Until 1543 Charles's garrisons held the Fortezza and the key fortresses of the dominion; his armies in Milan and Naples were ready to intervene at any sign of trouble; and he demanded heavy subventions for his wars elsewhere in Europe.[38] Papal hostility under Paul III (1534–49) and French support for Piero Strozzi and the exiles kept the duchy dependent on Charles, and nearly every aspect of Cosimo's government was conditioned by this dependence. Because his authority derived from imperial decrees of 1530, their reconfirmation at Naples in 1536, and Charles's grant of the ducal title in September 1537, Cosimo could claim that he was not bound by the laws of the republic, by the constitutional reform of 1532, or by the restrictions attached to his election. Nonetheless, especially in the early years, he ruled through magistracies and laws that, except for the suppression of the priorate, remained largely unchanged. Indeed, the statutes of 1415 remained

[37]   An overview: E. Cochrane, *Florence in the Forgotten Centuries, 1527–1800* (Chicago, 1973), pp. 13–92.

[38]   G. Spini, "Il principato dei Medici e il sistema degli stati europei del Cinquecento," in *Firenze e la Toscana dei Medici nell'Europa del Cinquecento*, vol. 1 (Florence, 1983), pp. 177–216; reprinted in Spini, *Michelangelo politico e altri studi sul Rinascimento fiorentino* (Milan, 1999), pp. 57–86.

in force into the eighteenth century. Cosimo brought profound changes to Florentine government and political culture, but they occurred piecemeal, tentatively, experimentally, and through existing institutions. He assumed de facto legislative sovereignty without any formal revision of constitutional principles, as laws began to be promulgated first with the pro-forma approval of the Magistrato Supremo and the councils and then simply in his own name. Cosimo eventually turned the Magistrato Supremo into an appeals court and an extension of his jurisdiction.[39] When he succinctly stated in 1558 about one of his edicts that the law "we ourselves have made . . . invalidates every [prior] statute and was made for the whole state,"[40] he declared both that his decrees overrode existing legislation and applied to all his dominions, not just to Florence. Individual edicts, called *bandi* (including those prohibiting the posses-sion of arms and unauthorized assembly and severely punishing contacts with exiles), claimed priority in both senses, but he neither abrogated the republican statutes in toto nor extended a uniform law code over all his territories.

Cosimo also modified the exercise of executive power. Chief among the innovations was the institution (or increased prominence) of "auditori" who oversaw various areas of governance as his personal representatives, convey-ing his wishes and orders to the magistracies, and reporting to him anything he needed to know. They included the auditore delle riformagioni, who presided over the 200 and Senate and superintended ducal rights within the dominion; the auditore fiscale, who supervised criminal courts from which the govern-ment collected monetary penalties (particularly the Otto di Guardia e Balìa), sometimes overturned their rulings, initiated new proceedings, and handed down decisions on his own; and the auditore della giurisdizione (instituted in 1532), who protected ducal jurisdiction, particularly against ecclesiastical claims. In practice, the assignments of the auditori were vaguely defined, overlapping, and always ad hoc, but this flexibility was also the key to their effectiveness. Cosimo used them whenever and wherever he needed to impose his will against councils, magistracies, or courts. When, in 1556, the auditore fiscale Alfonso Quistelli, authorized by Cosimo to intervene in "serious cases" before the Otto, asked him to clarify what he meant by "serious cases," Cosimo refused to be constrained by definitions: "We will order you [to intervene] from time to time whenever we learn that some injustice is about to occur."[41]

---

[39] G. Pansini, "Il Magistrato Supremo e l'amministrazione della giustizia civile durante il principato mediceo," *Studi senesi* 85 (1973): 283–315.

[40] E. Fasano Guarini, "The Prince, the Judges and the Law: Cosimo I and Sexual Violence, 1558," in *Crime, Society and the Law in Renaissance Italy*, ed. T. Dean and K. J. P. Lowe (Cambridge, 1994), pp. 121–41 (135).

[41] E. Fasano Guarini, "I giuristi e lo stato nella Toscana medicea cinque-seicentesca," in *Firenze e la Toscana*, pp. 229–47 (237).

But auditori could exercise considerable influence in the areas assigned to them. In 1549 the auditore fiscale Jacopo Polverini drafted the law, known as "la Polverina," punishing opposition to Cosimo as *laesa maiestas* and threatening capital punishment for any intention to harm the duke or even failure to report such intentions in others.

Unlike the traditional rotating civilian committees that served for short terms, the auditori were trained in law and held their posts for as long as Cosimo had confidence in them. And they were never Florentines. Polverini was from Prato and was followed as auditore fiscale by Alfonso Quistelli from Mirandola in 1556 and Aurelio Manni of Siena in 1565. Polverini was also auditore delle riformagioni and was followed by Francesco Vinta of Volterra in 1556 and Vinta's son Paolo in 1570. Lelio Torelli from Fano in the Marche was auditore della giurisdizione from 1546 to 1576. Cosimo also made use of secretaries whose roles evolved from those of similar functionaries employed by the Medici before 1527. Francesco Campana was Duke Alessandro's "primo segretario" and continued under Cosimo until he died in 1546. He was succeeded by Torelli, who, as both first secretary and an auditore, became in effect Cosimo's chief minister. Torelli presided over and expanded the staff of secretaries (there were ten by 1551), assigning them specific areas of responsibility such as state philanthropy, hospitals, ducal correspondence, and even diplomatic missions.[42] Like the auditori, the secretaries came from anywhere and everywhere within and beyond the dominion (e.g., San Miniato, Pescia, Volterra, Bibbiena), except Florence, and their origins and the powers they had over citizen councils and committees testify to Cosimo's reluctance to trust Florentines, especially the ottimati. Members of the old elite continued to fill the councils and the judicial, financial, and administrative committees but were steadily deprived of power by the authority of the auditori and the bureaucratic permanence of the secretaries. Particularly revealing of the diminished independence of the citizen committees is the Otto di Guardia,[43] whose jurisdiction was particularly crucial to maintaining public order, suppressing dissent, and criminalizing opposition to Cosimo's government and person: crucial tasks that could not be left to citizens whose patronage ties and marriage alliances might yield politically or socially inflected justice, whether toward leniency or severity. In 1558 Cosimo had his auditore Quistelli dismiss the entire board of the Otto in the middle of their term because of a decision

---

[42]   R. B. Litchfield, *Emergence of a Bureaucracy: The Florentine Patricians, 1530–1790* (Princeton, 1986), pp. 77–83; Diaz, *Il granducato*, pp. 89–101, 175–6; Fasano Guarini, "I giuristi e lo stato," pp. 235–40.

[43]   J. K. Brackett, *Criminal Justice and Crime in Late Renaissance Florence, 1537–1609* (Cambridge, 1992).

he did not like.[44] Auditori became instruments of Cosimo's personal intervention and oversight in all aspects of government and an extension of his sovereignty. In 1545 he created an inner cabinet, the Pratica Segreta, consisting of the auditori, the two chief financial officials, and two members of the magistracy that administered the dominion (all ducal appointees), and in 1550 instituted a supreme civil and criminal court, the Consulta, which also included the auditori and an unspecified number of other appointees. Here too a useful overlapping of responsibilities permitted Cosimo to use the Pratica and the Consulta flexibly, and it was with these bodies, not the Magistrato Supremo staffed by ottimati, that he discussed and decided government policy.

Like most Renaissance princedoms, the Medici duchy trumpeted an ideal of impartial, fair, and speedy justice: equal justice to all classes and standardization of norms, procedures, and penalties throughout the dominion. "An excellent prince," begins a 1545 law, "should strive for nothing with greater zeal or vigilance than for justice equitably administered among all his subjects according to their rights and their transgressions." A 1558 law establishing new penalties for sexual violence proclaimed that "justice requires that all those guilty of the same crime be punished in the same way" and that punishments be applied "equally against any person of whatsoever estate, rank, dignity, or condition."[45] Thus in 1543 the penalties specified in the Florentine statutes for violent crimes were extended to the entire dominion, and in 1549 all dominion magistrates inflicting capital or corporal punishments were required to submit their decisions for review to the magistracy of the Conservatori di Legge and in 1550 also to the Otto. Interventions by the auditori also pursued the same goal. Yet the duchy maintained the jurisdictional structures inherited from the republic, including the complex grid of judicial districts in the dominion (the *podesterie*, *capitanati*, and *vicariati*) with their varying mixes of civil, criminal, and appeals jurisdiction, and continued the practice of sending Florentine citizens (mostly from the elite) to serve in these districts for limited periods. And it kept the Ruota, the civil court of appeal created in 1502 and staffed by non-Florentine jurists, now appointed by Cosimo, with jurisdiction over the entire dominion. Compilations of statutory law negotiated with the separate localities under the republic also remained in force, as did a series of privileges and partial jurisdictional autonomies. A surprising number of fiefs, including five with limited autonomy created by Cosimo himself, and many more of imperial origin with varying degrees of immunity from Florentine

[44] Fasano Guarini, "The Prince, the Judges and the Law," pp. 130–1; Diaz, *Il granducato*, p. 173, note 2.
[45] E. Fasano Guarini, "Considerazioni su giustizia stato e società nel Ducato di Toscana del Cinquecento," in *Florence and Venice: Comparisons and Relations*, 2 vols. (Florence, 1979–80), 2:135–68 (135–6).

Map 3   Boundaries and principal cities and towns of the contado and district of Florence and the grand ducal state of Tuscany in 1574 (based on the map by E. Fasano Guarini, enclosed in *The Journal of Italian History* vol. 2, n. 2 [1979])

law and taxes dotted the ducal dominions. Apologists and admiring Venetian ambassadors extolled the "incomparable justice" administered by the duke's "expert, experienced, and intelligent men," but observers closer to the ground frequently complained of justice delayed and distorted. In 1546 a sharp reduction of the personnel of dominion magistrates aimed at cutting expenses and increasing magistrates' income. In the regions farthest from the capital, in the Maremma in the southwest and the mountains to the north and east, the lack of sufficient police and bureaucracy led to worsening banditry, which reached crisis proportions by the 1580s.

Nor did the duchy achieve the intention of subjecting city, contado, and district in equal degree to uniform jurisdiction. To the extent that there was an integrated territorial state (but actually two states, since the "stato vecchio" of Florence and the "stato nuovo" of Siena after 1555 remained legally and administratively distinct entities) (see Map 3) it was more the republic's legacy than Cosimo's creation.[46] Cosimo sought to bring law and administration under centralized supervision, but he did not standardize them, and even attempts at centralized control of still largely disparate systems sometimes met with resistance as localities guarded their traditional autonomies. A good example is the attempt to bring the dominion's hospitals (over a thousand, many of them tiny) all under the supervision of the magistracy of the Capitani del Bigallo, instituted in 1542 and staffed largely by the old elite. But the Capitani's demand for a full accounting of the hospitals' properties and finances, and for payment to the ducal treasury of surplus earnings, was largely ignored. Accepting the reality of this resistance, Cosimo decided not to waste resources and deprived the Bigallo captains of the bureaucratic staff they needed to enforce their reforms. Instead, in 1560 he created the Nine Conservatori of the Jurisdiction and Dominion to oversee appointed chancellors whose presence was required in each locality's councils. The Nine and their chancellors supervised local institutions, including hospitals, but did not intervene in their finances or collect revenue. They cast a wider but looser net than that of the Bigallo captains and allowed communities to continue running their own hospitals and much else, just as the republic had done.[47]

Finances and Economy

Ducal fiscal institutions were likewise inherited from the republic. The most important direct tax, the *decima*, which collected (actually slightly more than)

[46]   E. Fasano Guarini, *Lo stato mediceo di Cosimo I* (Florence, 1973).
[47]   N. Terpstra, "Competing Visions of the State and Social Welfare: The Medici Dukes, the Bigallo Magistrates, and Local Hospitals in Sixteenth-Century Tuscany," *Renaissance Quarterly* 54 (2001): 1319–55.

10 percent of annual income from city and contado property, had been instituted by the popular government in 1495. District communities continued to pay direct taxes based on the estimo, which in 1547 was extended to Pisa (previously exempt according to the terms of the 1509 surrender). And the ancient gabelles were still in place. Although Cosimo declared in a 1561 *bando* annulling the tax on commercial profits (the "arbitrio") that he was constantly searching for ways to alleviate the tax burden,[48] the historian Segni noted that a new indirect tax meant to be collected only in 1551 was never removed, "just like all taxes in our city, which are imposed to meet some particular need but continue in their voraciousness even when that need has passed."[49]

Particularly for the war against Siena, Cosimo borrowed heavily: at least 2½ million scudi. (The scudo was a new gold coin, originally worth 7 lire and later slightly more, first minted by the last republic in 1530 and then by Alessandro and Cosimo, who replaced the florin's lily and image of John the Baptist with likenesses of themselves.[50]) He broke with tradition in borrowing almost exclusively from foreigners and only rarely from Florentines,[51] perhaps fearing the influence such loans could generate and the sympathies some ottimati still harbored for France and the republic. Moreover, the biggest Florentine fortunes were those of bankers operating outside Tuscany (in Rome, Venice, Genoa, Lyons, and elsewhere) and would have been difficult to control. He borrowed from bankers who also financed the Habsburgs: the Genoese (over 300,000 scudi from Niccolò Grimaldi alone) and the Fugger of Augsburg (over 425,000 scudi, and perhaps much more since he borrowed another 410,000 from a consortium of "merchants of Antwerp," where the Fugger were also active). He even borrowed from his Habsburg overlords, including a 1555 loan of 100,000 scudi from Philip II. These were private loans contracted by Cosimo, sometimes jointly with his wife Eleonora, and the combination of their private status and foreign origin left Cosimo free to use the funds as he wished (subject of course to the approval of the kings of Spain) without having to consult Florentine councils or creditors. Yet at least a third of this indebtedness was repaid from direct and indirect taxes collected by the Florentine treasury.[52] Most Florentines may have been unaware of the siphoning

[48] Diaz, *Il granducato*, pp. 149–62 (153).
[49] Segni, *Istorie*, p. 507.
[50] C. M. Cipolla, *Money in Sixteenth-Century Florence* (Berkeley, 1989), pp. 13–18, 61–76.
[51] Bresnahan Menning, *Charity and State*, pp. 213–14.
[52] G. V. Parigino, *Il tesoro del principe* (Florence, 1999), pp. 56–74; A. Teicher, "Politics and Finance in the Age of Cosimo I: The Public and Private Face of Credit," in *Firenze e la Toscana*, pp. 343–62.

off of public funds to pay for their duke's territorial ambitions, his court, and even his private investments. For Cosimo was the ultimate merchant-prince: having become duke with very little personal wealth, he died with a total worth estimated at almost 1,200,000 scudi (not including jewels and other princely appurtenances). Indeed, he ran something of a family business from the ducal palace, regularly diverting public funds to personal investments in an artful blurring of the boundary between state finances and private and family interests.[53] Most of the increase in his personal patrimony took place following the Sienese war and took two forms: accumulations of real estate and lucrative lending. Having had to borrow money in order to finance the war, Cosimo emerged from it with enough wealth to makes loans of 200,000 scudi to Emperor Maximilian in 1565, 180,000 scudi to Charles IX of France in 1569, and 200,000 to Philip II in 1572.[54]

Cosimo transformed the Monte di Pietà, the lending institution created in 1496 to make small loans to the poor, into an instrument of ducal patronage and government finance. In the 1530s, to attract capital the Monte began accepting deposits on which it paid 5% interest, and by the 1540s considerable numbers of Florentines from all classes had opened accounts. Because the Dowry Fund was phased out in these same years, some fathers began using the Monte di Pietà as a safe, long-term vehicle for dowry growth, while husbands used it as a secure place to invest their wives' dowries. The Monte continued its original function of making small loans to the poor, secured against pawns, on which it charged 5% interest. Vastly increased capital from deposits made it possible to increase the scale of this lending, and there was apparently a huge demand for short-term loans among poorer Florentines. Between 1545 and 1548 an astonishing 163,000 pawns were accepted for loans, and in 1567–9 almost 171,000 pawns were accepted against loans totaling 370,000 florins. Approximately 90% of pawn-secured loans were repaid with interest, and the resulting profits expanded resources for both more loans to the poor and interest on deposit accounts. But the Monte di Pietà now became a source of cheap money for Cosimo's friends and clients, as he ordered it to extend its lending, in much larger amounts but at the same 5% interest rate, to anyone he approved, including himself, for purposes ranging from private favors to charity to military expenses and the immense costs of his son Francesco's wedding to Joanna of Austria in 1566. Between 1564 and 1574 the Monte made 249 such loans totaling over 427,000 scudi, of which 185,000 went to Cosimo and other Medici, and the rest to persons designated by Cosimo, who thereby brought them into his debt at no cost to himself with money that was not his. The many poor who paid the same rate of interest thus subsidized huge

---

low-interest loans to the duke and his favorites. Only in 1568, after years in which interest payments on deposits exceeded interest collected on loans (because 10% of small loans went uncollected) did Cosimo finally approve an increase in the rate on large loans to 6%. This was still a bargain, and cut-rate loans to the rich continued into the 1570s.[55]

Cosimo took considerable interest in economic matters, supporting the growth of new industries, such as mining and sugar production and, most significantly, favoring silk production, even as woolens were enjoying a last phase of prosperity before their definitive decline in the seventeenth century.[56] To promote sericulture gabelles were occasionally reduced or even eliminated, but such actions were inconsistent and lacked an overall plan. In 1545, for example, in order to increase revenue and bring the entire dominion under the same tax regulations the ducal government annulled for three years all exemptions from gabelles that the republic had negotiated with subject towns. For Pescia and the nearby Valdinievole (between Pistoia and Lucca), this overturned a two century-old agreement allowing free trade with Florence. Protests prompted the reinstatement of the exemptions in 1547, but Cosimo nonetheless insisted on his right to impose tariffs and regulate the import or export of goods. Over the next twenty years, Pescia's officials complained, many "prohibitions and innovations" and various "annoyances, orders, and exactions have been pursued by Your Excellency and the magistrates, with much expense and inconvenience."[57] It was symptomatic of the limits of ducal intervention in the economy and finances: chronic fiscal and provisioning needs regularly derailed any idea (if such there really was) of removing barriers to trade, opening up production and markets, and extending such policies to the entire dominion. In this case, he cancelled customary exemptions, then restored them, but made the restoration precarious by invoking ducal power to impose whatever taxes or restrictions he thought necessary to solve a local problem or raise revenue, thus causing "expense and inconvenience" and presumably confusion, since the Pescians never knew what was coming next and could not count on a stable fiscal or regulatory environment. A second example is Cosimo's policy toward the Jews. In an effort to revive commerce, between 1545 and 1551 Cosimo invited Portuguese Jews to Pisa and elsewhere in the

[55] Bresnahan Menning, *Charity and State*, pp. 133–207 (173, 176).
[56] P. Malanima, "L'industria fiorentina in declino fra Cinque e Seicento: linee per un'analisi comparata"; A. Rolova, "La manifattura nell'industria tessile di Firenze del Cinquecento"; and J. Goodman, "Tuscan Commercial Relations with Europe, 1550–1620: Florence and the European Textile Market," all in *Firenze e la Toscana*, pp. 295–341.
[57] J. C. Brown, *In the Shadow of Florence: Provincial Society in Renaissance Pescia* (Oxford, 1982), pp. 140–8 (146); Brown, "Concepts of Political Economy: Cosimo I de' Medici in a Comparative European Context," in *Firenze e la Toscana*, pp. 279–93.

dominion and granted them freedom to practice their religion and do business without official harassment. But in 1567 he reversed course and required Jews to wear a yellow badge, and in 1570, as part of the deal with Pope Pius V that brought Cosimo his grand ducal title, he forced them to live in specified areas in Florence and Siena. Twenty years later Duke Ferdinand reversed the policy again in a successful attempt to build Livorno into a major port, inviting Jews to settle there with full privileges of internal self-government, religious autonomy, and freedom to pursue commerce. Over the next two centuries Livorno's Jewish community prospered and grew to almost 5,000.[58]

Economic policy suffered from excessive and always changing regimentation and over-regulation, prohibitions against exporting raw silk or agricultural products and importing manufactured products, attempts at price and production controls, and much more, all motivated by short-term considerations and enforced by officials ready to track down and punish infractions, confiscate account books, search and seize. Partly this reflected Cosimo's temperament: minute attention to every detail, locality, document, problem, and complaint. He obviously worked longer days and devoted more effort to the business of governing than any Medici before him and perhaps more than most contemporary European rulers. But if the economic fortunes of the duke and his family were thriving, perhaps as they had not since the days of his great-great-great-grandfather Cosimo, the same cannot be said of the majority of his subjects. Evidence of worsening poverty in the mid-sixteenth century ranges from the Monte di Pietà's many loans to the poor to a dramatic increase in the numbers of abandoned children. Whereas the Innocenti took in an average of 200 children per year in the second half of the fifteenth century, in the 1530s the annual average jumped to 540. In the famine year of 1539 almost 1,000 children were admitted; and from 1547 to 1552 yearly totals were 417, 518, 654, 635, 884, and 607. In 1579 the Innocenti housed approximately 1,200 children (968 of them females), including many who spent their entire lives there. Demographic trends were partly behind this: after almost two centuries of contraction and stagnation, population was increasing. Censuses in 1552 and 1562 recorded 59,000 city inhabitants, a 40 percent increase since the fifteenth century; 500,000 people now lived within the boundaries of the subject territories of 1427 (when the population was 262,000), and nearly 600,000 in all the territories comprising the "stato vecchio" of Florence, excluding Siena and its territory. Prices rose with population, and, as wages failed to keep pace, famines became more frequent. In addition to the other reasons why parents gave up children, many now did so because they were unable to feed them. But the crisis of the Innocenti, constantly in debt and increasingly

[58] Diaz, *Il granducato*, pp. 141–2n; 301–2; R. G. Salvadori, *Breve storia degli ebrei toscani* (Florence, 1995), pp. 45–56.

unable to support the huge numbers entrusted to its care, was also exacerbated by ducal exploitation of the institution in a manner similar to that of the Monte di Pietà. Cosimo turned the Innocenti into a bank that accepted interest-bearing deposits, and the revenues from its considerable landed holdings had to feed this debt before it fed the children.[59] The Marucelli chronicle, regularly noting the high cost of grain and the suffering it entailed, says that in the winter of 1548–9 there was "a *grandissima carestia* of everything," "huge numbers of poor people and great cruelty among citizens, and not a single act of charity, so that in the streets nothing but the cries of the poor was heard." Many people and animals perished, "and it was said that throughout the *contado* many fathers, seeing their children dying of hunger, hanged themselves, threw themselves into wells or off steep cliffs, completely overcome by desperation."[60]

Courtly and Cultural Discipline

Under the Medici duchy Florence's ottimati were transformed from a civic elite into a disciplined courtly aristocracy. Although the process began with the elder Lorenzo and was not complete until the seventeenth century, Cosimo's reign was crucial. Backed by his imperial protectors, he finally deprived the ottimati of their traditional political role, even if they relinquished it quite as much as it was taken from them. Cosimo compensated them with protection from the popolo and with new forms of social prestige, including the court and its rituals, a military-religious order that defined aristocratic status, and the beginnings of what became a flood of "noble" titles that persist to this day. Alliances between monarchy and aristocracy were common in early modern Europe, since they needed each other, as Machiavelli said in the *Discourses*. But in Florence this alliance was new to a political culture that had known neither, and it finally made of the Florentine elite a "nobility" in a compact in which it yielded power in return for prestige and honors, just as the popolo had 150 years earlier.

Florence's republican traditions and urban physiognomy constrained the emergence of the Medici court. One problem was where to put it; another was whether and how to keep court, government, and ducal residence distinct. Symbolically rejecting old notions of the Medici as citizens among others, in 1540 Cosimo abandoned the family palace on the via Larga and moved

---

[59]   P. Gavitt, "Charity and State Building in Cinquecento Florence: Vincenzio Borghini as Administrator of the Ospedale degli Innocenti," *Journal of Modern History* 69 (1997): 230–70 (238–9, 241, 264).
[60]   *Cronaca fiorentina*, ed. Coppi, pp. 93–5.

with his new bride Eleonora da Toledo into the old palace of the priors, thus physically occupying and politically transforming the seat of former republican sovereignty. But the palace was still the locus of government, and the awkward cohabitation of ducal residence and government offices recalled the days when Piero Soderini also lived in the palace with his wife. Since this was not a comparison Cosimo wanted to encourage, in 1549 he and Eleonora bought and moved their growing family into Luca Pitti's palazzo across the river. But the "palazzo vecchio," as the "old" or former quarters of the ducal family was now referred to, remained the official residence and ceremonial site, with the former hall of the Great Council transformed into the "sala d'udienza."[61] But Cosimo lived regularly neither in the old palace nor at Pitti, preferring to move among his many residences in the city, countryside, and even Pisa. To the extent that the court followed him, it was thus mobile and had slow and small beginnings. Even by the 1560s it supported only 168 persons, less than half the average size of other Italian courts. Only in the early seventeenth century did the court count a "respectable" 457 persons with annual expenses of 130,000 scudi. Cosimo spent much less than that and took dwindling interest in defining protocol and ceremonial rituals; indeed, the earliest diaries of Florentine court etiquette date only from 1589. In 1561 the Venetian ambassador reported that, whereas Cosimo once had a lavish table to which any and all courtiers were invited, kept a "regal stable" of horses, and spent much on hunting, now "he keeps only what he needs" and "is quite withdrawn and solitary. At home he doesn't really live like a prince with the exquisite luxuries that other princes and dukes are accustomed to. He lives like a grand *padre di famiglia* and always eats with his wife and children at a moderately elaborate table." Cosimo apparently lost his taste for court life, but he initiated the acculturation of his elite subjects into a courtly discipline that took deeper root under his successors.[62]

Since Florence had never had a titled nobility, Cosimo had to create one, or at least a reasonable facsimile thereof. His chief instrument was the Order of the Knights of Santo Stefano, named in honor of the martyr pope and saint commemorated on August 2, the date of the victories over the rebel exiles in 1537 and 1554. Established in 1562 with its own endowment (hence, again, at no cost to the government) Santo Stefano was a military and pseudo-religious

[61] S. Bertelli, "Palazzo Pitti dai Medici ai Savoia," in *La corte di Toscana dai Medici ai Lorena*, ed. A. Bellinazzi and A. Contini (Rome, 2002), pp. 11–109 (11–15).

[62] M. Fantoni, *La corte del granduca: forme e simboli del potere mediceo fra Cinque e Seicento* (Rome, 1994), p. 38; Fantoni, "La formazione del sistema curiale mediceo tra Cinque e Seicento," in *Istituzioni e società in Toscana nell'età moderna*, 2 vols. (Rome, 1994), 1:165–78; and Fantoni, "Architettura, corte ed economia: alcune riflessioni sul caso mediceo," in *La corte di Toscana*, pp. 110–28.

order whose mission, formally at least, was to constitute a navy and make the duchy a Mediterranean power. Its ranks were filled by ducal decree, with Cosimo himself as Gran Maestro. In a memorandum in his own hand, Cosimo outlined the knights' obligation to give service at court each year in designated rotations, with lifetime annuities awarded to the "worthiest" among them who thus "become the prince's slaves." According to the statutes written by auditori Francesco Vinta and Lelio Torelli and court historian Benedetto Varchi, admission required application and "proofs of nobility" for both paternal and maternal grandparents. Implementing such notions in a society whose elites had eschewed titles, and whose intellectuals from as early as Dante had insisted that nobility was in deeds and not blood, took creativity, flexibility, and no doubt a sense of humor, as merchants, cloth manufacturers, doctors, and even some ducal secretaries made the case for their "nobility" while enhancing their chances of approval by providing their own endowments. Cosimo admitted whomever he wanted, and acceptance into the Order was more than anything a sign of the prince's favor. Florentines were actually a minority among the knights of Santo Stefano, as Cosimo and his successors admitted large numbers of non-Florentines from their Tuscan dominions, Italians beyond Tuscany, and some foreigners, including of course Spaniards. Of 392 applicants accepted in the first decade, half were Tuscan and only a hundred Florentine; by 1631 over 400 Florentines and 600 other Tuscans had been admitted, and by the end of the grand duchy in 1737 the 1,000 Florentines made knights of Santo Stefano since 1562 constituted little more than a third of all Tuscans given the honor. Having to wait in line with "upstarts" of humble origins from the city and the dominion to join the ranks of the knights constantly reminded the ottimati that their place in the new ducal order depended on the prince's pleasure.[63] Cosimo's improvised and socially heterogeneous "nobility" rendered increasingly obsolete the division between the old social elite and the popolo, as well as that between Florentine citizens and inhabitants of territories they once considered subject to them. As families from throughout the dominion became increasingly prominent both locally and in the ducal administration,[64] the city elite that for so long competed with the popolo and the Medici for supremacy in the republic now contented itself with its share of the new noble order and with its decidedly un-noble role as functionaries in the ducal bureaucracy.[65]

[63]   F. Angiolini, *I cavalieri e il principe: l'Ordine di Santo Stefano e la società toscana in età moderna* (Florence, 1996), pp. 1–45, 67–82; Angiolini, "Politica, società e organizzazione militare nel principato mediceo: a proposito di una 'Memoria' di Cosimo I," *Società e storia* 9 (1986): 47–51.
[64]   G. Benadusi, *A Provincial Elite in Early Modern Tuscany: Family and Power in the Creation of the State* (Baltimore, 1996).
[65]   Litchfield, *Emergence of a Bureaucracy.*

What the Order of Santo Stefano did for ottimati, the academies did for writers and artists. In 1540 a small group of literati began meeting informally and then organized themselves into the Accademia degli Umidi for the promotion of the Tuscan vernacular. Cosimo and his advisers were suspicious of unauthorized associations, and within weeks new members, mostly from his inner circle, joined the association, rewrote its statutes, changed its name to the Accademia Fiorentina, and prepared it for incorporation in 1542 into the ducal administrative apparatus. Among its officers were censors who monitored members' writings and public lectures. Cosimo and his secretaries controlled the membership and intervened with further reforms in 1547 and 1553 to contain disputes with tactical exclusions and readmissions.[66] To a few carefully selected writers and humanists among the exiles he offered the chance to return without abjuring their republican pasts. Piero Vettori, an orator of the last republic, returned to a university post in 1538; in 1543 Benedetto Varchi returned and accepted a stipend, a prominent role in the Accademia Fiorentina, and, shortly thereafter, the commission to write the history of the last republic.[67] In 1562 Cosimo created the Accademia del Disegno for painters, sculptors, and architects, and had its statutes drafted by six artists, including Bronzino and Giorgio Vasari, under the supervision of his first secretary Torelli and the humanist and ducal official Vincenzo Borghini, who presided over the academy as the duke's lieutenant. The statutes emphasized obedience to the duke as the "benevolent father of the men of the arts" and reminded the consuls that they were administrative officers who "must not presume to act on their own authority." When protests over exclusions followed the admission of the first seventy-five members, Borghini assured Cosimo that they were nothing more than the "outbursts of children." In providing aspiring artists with instruction in mathematics, geometry, anatomy, and other subjects, and also functioning as a confraternity for charity, devotional activities, and funerals, the Academy offered both social and professional benefits and impressed upon its members the "rewards of conformity."[68]

Religious policy was largely a function of the duchy's relations with the papacy. Because of his many disputes with Paul III (1534–49), Cosimo initially tolerated heterodox religious ideas, particularly the "evangelism" of Juan de Valdés and the mix of Lutheranism and Calvinism in the immensely

---

[66] M. Firpo, *Gli affreschi di Pontormo a San Lorenzo* (Turin, 1997), pp. 167–76; M. Plaisance, "Une première affirmation de la politique culturelle de Côme Ier: la transformation de l'Académie des 'Humidi' en Académie Florentine (1540–1542)," in *Les écrivains et le pouvoir en Italie à l'époque de la Renaissance*, 2 vols. (Paris, 1973–4), 1:361–438.

[67] Firpo, *Gli affreschi*, pp. 218–90 (260–74, 282–3).

[68] K.-e. Barzman, *The Florentine Academy and the Early Modern State: The Discipline of* Disegno (Cambridge, 2000), pp. 8–9, 23–59, 143–214.

popular *Benefit of Christ* of Benedetto Fontanini of Mantua. Only when the decrees of the Council of Trent and the necessity of better relations with subsequent popes mandated a tougher policy did Cosimo's government join the suppression of heresy, although never with the consistent severity practiced elsewhere. But with one group, the Dominicans at San Marco who continued to venerate the memory of Savonarola, albeit with no following in the laity, Cosimo had no patience whatsoever. When, in 1545, he was told that a friar was preaching Savonarolan doctrines, questioning the legitimacy of Cosimo's rule, and calling for a return to popular government, Cosimo accused them all of conspiring with France against him and tried to have the Dominicans removed from San Marco and replaced by Augustinians. Paul III blocked this, but two years later Cosimo persuaded the Dominican order to allow him to banish any friars he saw as threats.[69] By this time the old Savonarolan prophetic message had lost its appeal, and Cosimo probably overreacted. But in the mid-1540s a still insecure regime needed to deliver the message that, despite its tolerance for mild religious heterodoxy, there would be none at all for political dissent.

Victor and Vanquished

Cosimo and his advisers inherited a precarious and detested regime, stabilized it, consolidated ducal power, and founded a dynasty that lasted two hundred years. Draconian punishments, intimidation, spies, censorship, and imperial protection all played their roles, but, except for some exiles, in the end most Florentines, chastened and disciplined, accepted the new order. Some were never reconciled: Michelangelo refused to set foot in Cosimo's Florence. But dissent was marginalized and most intellectuals behaved. Despite unhappiness in some quarters and a few conspiracies, there were no revolts or widespread movements of opposition within Florence or the dominion. These were not insignificant achievements in a city that had three times expelled the Medici. While never fully escaping the need for foreign protection, Cosimo gradually asserted his state's independence in Italian politics. He did not create a modern professional bureaucracy or a unified regional state, but he managed to hold together the agglomeration of territories assembled by the republic, collect taxes, administer justice, and build roads and bridges.

Cosimo's greatest crisis came from without: the war for Siena that was also a war against the exiles and their French allies.[70] Occupied by imperial troops

---

[69] Polizzotto, *Elect Nation*, pp. 432–7; Firpo, *Gli affreschi*, pp. 317–25.

[70] A. D'Addario, *Il problema senese nella storia italiana della prima metà del Cinquecento (La guerra di Siena)* (Florence, 1958); R. Cantagalli, *La guerra di Siena (1552–1559)* (Siena, 1962); Diaz, *Il granducato*, pp. 109–27.

since 1541, Siena rebelled and expelled the Spanish garrison in July 1552. Cosimo faced the twin dangers of renewed French intervention in Italy at his doorstep, and at a moment when Charles V was at war with the Lutheran princes of Germany, and the prospect that exiles would use Siena as a base either for attacking the duchy or fomenting rebellion within Florence. Anti-Medici exiles in Rome, Venice, Lyons, and elsewhere had a military leader and source of funding in Piero Strozzi, who inherited his father's vast banking fortune and was now King Henry II's viceroy in Italy. Exiled bankers, and still others outside Florence who were not exiles but whose businesses depended more on good relations with France than with Spain, allowed themselves to be tempted by the prospect of removing Cosimo. Thus the conflict between France and the empire over Siena also became the last war for control of Florence.

By August 1552 Strozzi was in Siena to lead French and exile forces, and throughout 1553 hundreds of thousands of scudi came pouring in from anti-Medici Florentine bankers all over Europe, including the Strozzi, Guadagni, Salviati, and especially from Bindo Altoviti, the leading Florentine banker in Rome who, although no enemy of the Medici until now, provided huge sums and even organized a contingent of troops led by his son. In March 1554 Cosimo, having learned from his informers in Rome that this erstwhile Medici ally was plotting with the French and the exiles, wrote to the brother of Pope Julius III to urge the pope to expel Altoviti and other anti-Mediceans in the Florentine nation in Rome and to "take away their properties which, once confiscated, would reasonably come to me. And in this manner you will reveal their folly and insolence; for our part we will proceed according to the laws of justice, which cover the loss of their property and their life, including that of their criminal sons, who I hope will repent of their recklessness. I think no one will be the people's fool more than Bindo, who will throw away his fortune in order to be thought mad." In May Altoviti, summoned by the pope, confirmed that he and other Florentines in Rome "had secretly decided to pay for 3,000 infantrymen in the service of their city, and had secretly made twelve white flags with the inscription 'Libertas'." Altoviti acknowledged "that he was the leader" and was "determined to risk his life and that of his sons to liberate his homeland, and that he wanted to play the rest of the game; and that the other wealthy Florentines of Lyons, Venice, Ancona, and other places agreed with this honorable enterprise." A week later anti-Medici Florentines in Rome held a procession representing the return of the Israelites to the promised land.[71] Reaching back to the greatest of all Florentine exiles, Altoviti's

---

[71]   P. Simoncelli, "Florentine Fuorusciti at the Time of Bindo Altoviti," in *Raphael, Cellini and a Renaissance Banker: The Patronage of Bindo Altoviti*, ed. A. Chong, D. Pegazzano, and D. Zikos (Boston, 2003), pp. 285–328 (306, 309, 312–13); M. M. Bullard, "Bindo Altoviti, Renaissance Banker and Papal Financier," ibid., pp. 21–57.

troops placed on their standard the words with which, in *Purgatorio* 1.71–2, Dante's Virgil explains to Cato of Utica the pilgrim's goal (changing "he" to "I" and substituting political liberty for spiritual freedom): "I go seeking liberty, which is so precious, as they know who give up their life for it."[72] It was not perhaps the most hopeful of associations, for, while Dante's pilgrim found the spiritual freedom he sought, his author never returned home.

Nor did the exiles. With the emperor's military help and financial assistance from bankers in Antwerp and Genoa, Cosimo assembled an army of Spanish, German, and Italian (but no Florentine) troops, and hired an imperial captain (from, coincidentally, the Medici family of Milan). Despite Strozzi's daring forays into Florentine territory (reminiscent of Ferrucci's heroics in 1530), the promised French reinforcements never arrived (again as in 1530), and in August 1554 the exiles were crushed at Marciano near Siena with thousands of casualties. Cosimo exulted and organized processions in Florence, with the captured banners hanging upside down from Palazzo Vecchio. Prisoners from leading exile families were publicly executed (as in 1537). Segni says that most of the population celebrated the victory because they were tired of the war and blamed Strozzi for causing it. Another chronicler reports that, at the news of the victory, the "nobles" remained quiet, "since most of them were hostile to the duke, and, on the contrary, favorable to that freedom promised by Strozzi, which confirms the proverb that no amount of gold can buy freedom."[73] Siena continued to fight for its independence, and Cosimo's army laid siege to the city, which, at the edge of starvation, surrendered in April 1555. Even so, republican holdouts moved to Montalcino, and it took two more years, amid the ever-shifting interests of Spain, France, and the papacy, before Cosimo fully gained control of Siena. Yet Charles insisted on retaining sovereignty and granted the city to Cosimo as an imperial fief, with the usual obligations of vassalage.[74] Even in his greatest victory Cosimo was legally subordinate to his protector: as Segni put it, "like a good subject," Cosimo was "in the shadow of the emperor." This was certainly among the motivations behind his subsequent quest for a grander title.

Accomplished with foreign troops and loans, the conquest of Siena was largely a personal triumph for Cosimo that brought little or no benefit to the Florentines. Years later he almost acknowledged as much when he had Vasari commemorate the victory on the ceiling of the hall of the former Great Council by depicting the expansion of "all our territories together" as the result of

---

[72] D. Pegazzano, "Il gran Bindo huomo raro et singhulare: The Life of Bindo Altoviti," in *The Patronage of Bindo Altoviti*, pp. 11, 18–19; Segni, *Istorie*, p. 548.

[73] Simoncelli, "Florentine Fuorusciti," p. 315.

[74] D. Marrara, "I rapporti giuridici tra la Toscana e l'Impero (1530–1576)," in *Firenze e la Toscana*, pp. 217–27.

a war planned by Cosimo himself without advisers.[75] Cosimo's mistrust of the elite was sealed by the participation of the ottimati exiles in the 1554 war (and again by the Pucci conspiracy of 1559).[76] The Marucelli chronicler denounced the war, declared his sympathies for the besieged and betrayed Sienese, reviled the tyrannical Spaniards, and reported widespread dissatisfaction in Florence with Cosimo and his policies: "Such was the hostility generated within the *popolo* that almost every morning sonnets and placards were found posted in various places, and if I had possessed any copies Cosimo would have punished me." Evidently he got his hands on at least one of them, a "sonnet" (copied into the chronicle) that excoriates Cosimo for three pages as a tyrant who destroys his city and ruins his subjects.[77] But the acquisition of Siena consolidated the principate by ending the threat of the exiles, who lost an immense fortune in the ill-fated attempt at a fourth Medici expulsion, and, whatever the underlying mood, Cosimo came through the crisis without a revolt at home. However much some may have sympathized with Strozzi, the exiles, and the Sienese, there was no uprising of either ottimati or popolo. If, for Cosimo, that was the most significant outcome of the war, others saw matters differently. Segni worried that, because Cosimo "rules over people who suffer servitude only with extreme reluctance, [but] without knowing how to live free, he seems almost forced to maintain himself in power by giving himself up as prey to foreigners and the arms of barbarians."[78]

---

[75] R. Williams, "The Sala Grande in the Palazzo Vecchio and the Precedence Controversy between Florence and Ferrara," in *Vasari's Florence: Artists and Literati at the Medicean Court*, ed. P. Jacks (Cambridge, 1998), p. 170.
[76] Brackett, *Criminal Justice*, p. 128.
[77] *Cronaca fiorentina*, ed. Coppi, pp. 195–8.
[78] Segni, *Istorie*, p. 572.

Epilogue: Remembrance of Things Past

There is no place to draw a line and claim that there the story ends. Symbolic markers abound: Cosimo's "retirement" in 1564 from daily governance (ceded to his son Francesco); his acquisition of the grand ducal title in 1569 from Pius V (with subsequent imperial ratification); his triumphal coronation in Rome in 1570; and Francesco's smooth succession after Cosimo's death in 1574 – all signs of the acceptance of the new order in the city, dominion, and wider Italian and European world. There was one more (alleged) conspiracy, uncovered in 1575, involving Orazio Pucci (whose father was convicted and executed in the 1559 Pucci plot), several members of the Capponi family (including two grandsons and a grandnephew of Niccolò Capponi), Piero Ridolfi (Filippo Strozzi's grandson), and a descendant of Machiavelli. Beyond the government's accusations, executions, and tenacious pursuit of those who fled, the reality of this conspiracy is murky. It may have been real; but it also brought in more than 300,000 scudi in confiscated property and disposed of potential enemies from families with a history of opposition to the Medici: a timely reminder, at the beginning of Francesco's reign, that opposition would continue to be punished harshly and swiftly.[1] But those who once called themselves the "ottimati" had already absorbed the message. The ruling house put distance between itself and the "nobility" in a variety of ways, including its marriages. Cosimo originally sought marriage to Alessandro's widow, the emperor's natural daughter, and had to settle for the daughter of the Spanish viceroy in Naples. But in 1565 Francesco married the archduchess Joanna of

---

[1] J. Boutier, "Trois conjurations italiennes: Florence (1575), Parme (1611), Gênes (1628)," *Mélanges de l'École Française de Rome* 108 (1996): 319–75 (327–42).

Austria, daughter of Emperor Ferdinand I and sister of Emperor Maximilian II. And in 1600 Grand Duke Ferdinand married his brother's daughter Maria to King Henry IV of France. Royal and imperial marriages likewise symbolized a new era.

Perhaps more significant than boundaries between eras, however, was Cosimo's deliberate cultural policy of linking his new order to the republican past. Even as he buried the republic, he allowed its memory to be preserved. His historians presented the principate as the necessary consequence and pre-destined successor to the republic: not only in the anti-republican polemics of Filippo de' Nerli, but also in works more sympathetic to the republic by former republicans Bernardo Segni (Niccolò Capponi's nephew) and Benedetto Varchi, who made their peace with Cosimo and wrote histories of the last republic and the transition to the principate without renouncing their, or Florence's, republican past. Later Jacopo Pitti wrote his admiring life of the republican military hero Antonio Giacomini, dedicated to and perhaps commissioned by Cosimo, and a fiercely pro-republican history of the city up to the last republic.[2] Imagined continuity, or evolution, in political history had its counterpart in the Accademia Fiorentina's simultaneous cultivation of Florence's glorious literary past through public lectures on Dante and Petrarch and its defense of the modern vernacular as constitutive of the cultural identity and even the legitimate borders of the duchy.[3]

A more complex dialogue between republican past and ducal present occurred in what the principate did and did not do to Florence's urban fabric. The most significant additions were the Fortezza, which predated Cosimo, and Giorgio Vasari's two major architectural projects: the Uffizi, in which the ducal offices were concentrated (including the formerly independent guilds that once had their own meeting halls); and the above-ground corridor that connects the ducal residence at Pitti to the Uffizi and Palazzo Vecchio. Otherwise, Cosimo left the spatial and architectural configuration of the city largely as it had evolved under the republic. Some spaces were symbolically appropriated: the Loggia dei Lanzi and the piazza in front of Palazzo Vecchio were filled with new sculptures exalting Cosimo's virtues.[4] And the hall in Palazzo Vecchio built in 1495 for the Great Council and trashed by the Medici regime

---

[2]   Albertini, *Firenze dalla repubblica al principato*, pp. 306–50; A. Montevecchi, *Storici di Firenze: studi su Nardi, Nerli e Varchi* (Bologna, 1989); essays on Varchi, Pitti, Segni and others in *Storiografia repubblicana fiorentina (1494–1570)*, ed. J.-J. Marchand and J.-C. Zancarini (Florence, 2003).

[3]   M. Sherberg, "The Accademia Fiorentina and the Question of the Language: The Politics of Theory in Ducal Florence," *Renaissance Quarterly* 56 (2003): 26–55.

[4]   S. B. McHam, "Public Sculpture in Renaissance Florence," in *Looking at Italian Renaissance Sculpture*, ed. McHam (Cambridge, 1998), pp. 149–88.

of 1512–27 was redecorated by Vasari and his assistants with paintings that glorified Cosimo as a new Augustus bringing his city to its golden age.[5] But the piazza, the loggia, the old Palazzo, and even its huge hall, all creations and landmarks of the republic, were allowed to remain, transformed, but recognizably what they had always been.

A chief architect of the remembrance of the republican past was Vasari, who, in his *Lives* of the Florentine artists, invented the powerful framework in which the history of Florence's artistic production has for centuries been seen as a story of continuity and accumulating legacies punctuated by moments of revolutionary transformation that fulfilled, rather than repudiated, the past.[6] In another work, the *Ragionamenti*, Vasari dramatized the significance of the decision to let the monuments of the republican past survive the transition to the principate. The *Ragionamenti* are a long dialogue, written after the war against Siena, in which Vasari explains to Cosimo's son Francesco the rationale for his remodeling of the interior of Palazzo Vecchio and the meaning of the paintings with which he decorated its many rooms, especially the great hall. As they discuss the narrow passageways and irregularly shaped spaces of the old palace, Vasari has the young prince ask why he did not recommend tearing it down and replacing it with something "modern" that would have displayed the skills of Florence's builders. Vasari's answer makes of the palace and the decision not to destroy it a synecdoche of the larger policy of cultural and political continuity with the republican past. Cosimo's concern, says Vasari, was not to "alter the foundations and the maternal walls of this place, because in their old form they established the origin of his new government." The "maternal walls" of the old order were thus the womb from which Cosimo's government was born. Vasari makes the link to politics explicit: just as the duke "preserved the old laws of this republic and added to them new ones for the well-being of his citizens," he similarly preserved the palace while "imposing order and measure on its old, distorted, and irregular" spaces and walls, to show that he knew how to bring perfection to architecture as much as to government. For he who knows how to bring to new life something broken and near death "without destroying very much" merits more praise than one who simply razes the old and builds anew. Moreover, Vasari tells Francesco, many of his new paintings depict the "honorable actions of the republic," and "it seemed inappropriate" to paint them "on new walls and stones that had not been witnesses to the valor of the Florentines as these old [stones and

[5]   K. W. Forster, "Metaphors of Rule: Political Ideology and History in the Portraits of Cosimo I de' Medici," *Mitteilungen des Kunsthistorischen Institutes in Florenz* 15 (1971): 65–104.
[6]   P. L. Rubin, *Giorgio Vasari: Art and History* (New Haven, 1995).

walls] were, since, from the time they were built in 1298," the Florentines had honorably fought their enemies and subdued the surrounding territories.

Nor, Vasari continues, could Cosimo have ignored what he owed to his family and the greatness they acquired during the republic. The "fateful stones" of the old palace "acknowledged the wisdom, goodness, and love that the great Cosimo *vecchio* bestowed on them and on the *patria*, and they were thus always devoted to him, hoping that he who would one day share his name and surpass him in virtue would renovate them and make them more beautiful." Vasari even asserts that the many objects brought to Palazzo Vecchio from Palazzo Medici after the family's expulsion in 1494 have changed the "nature" of the building, which "used to be so volatile because of its old forms of government, and has now become secure and no longer unstable." Therefore Duke Cosimo did not want any architect to suggest altering its old form and preferred instead that "on these stones, honored by so many victories old and new, every sort of embellishment be carried out" to "bear witness to the faith of this place" with paintings in honor of the gods on the upper level and the "illustrious men of the Medici family" beneath "with an abundance of portraits of distinguished citizens and fathers of this republic."[7]

At the end of the dialogue Vasari tells Francesco that after "reading the histories old and new of this city" in order to depict the republic's conquest of its neighbors and the history of the Medici family, and considering the travails and difficulties of those times and the peace and concord "which we enjoy in this current state," it occurred to him that "the many exertions of the citizens of bygone days and of your ancestors were almost a ladder leading our lord Duke Cosimo to this present glory and happiness."[8] Vasari's image mirrored Cosimo's strategy of rooting himself and his principate in the republican past. Not the least of the duke's achievements was to have preserved so much of that past, even as he firmly put it in the past. He was perhaps less likely to acknowledge that the motivation behind this strategy was an unspoken recognition that his and his principate's legitimacy was grounded in the republic, in its independence, its legal and institutional framework, its laws and statutes, its territorial conquests, its cultural achievements, and all those "exertions of the citizens of bygone days." Indeed, in the controversy of the early 1560s

---

[7] Giorgio Vasari, *Ragionamenti sopra le invenzioni da lui dipinte*, ed. C. L. Ragghianti (Milan, 1949), pp. 14–17. See P. Tinagli, "Claiming a Place in History: Giorgio Vasari's *Ragionamenti* and the Primacy of the Medici," in *The Cultural Politics of Duke Cosimo I de' Medici*, ed. K. Eisenbichler (Aldershot, 2001), pp. 63–76.

[8] Vasari, *Ragionamenti*, p. 245. On the complex ways in which the art produced under Cosimo's influence elaborated his relationship to his ancestors, see Cox-Rearick, *Dynasty and Destiny in Medici Art*.

between Florence and Ferrara over whose ambassadors should have precedence in diplomatic ceremonies, against the argument that the Este had been dukes for much longer and that the Medici had come to power violently against a republic whose existence they terminated, the Florentines countered that Cosimo was in fact heir to a republic, changed only in externals, whose origins went back to the Romans.[9] Cosimo regarded the republican past ambivalently: on the one hand, he needed it to bolster a legitimacy weakened not only by his state's violent origins but also by his status as a creature, indeed a vassal, of the emperor; on the other, he was wary of it because he feared its resurrection. One wonders if Cosimo ever read what Machiavelli says in the *Florentine Histories* (2.34) about another duke, Walter of Brienne, who tried to make the Florentines accept his lordship. If so, he may have remembered the moment in which the priors go to Brienne to persuade him that he can never succeed in extinguishing the Florentines' desire for liberty "because one often sees liberty retaken by those who had never known it, only because of the memory of it left by fathers who loved it. . . . And if their fathers ever forget it, the public buildings, the offices of the magistrates, and the banners of free institutions will recall it."

[9] Williams, "The Sala Grande in the Palazzo Vecchio," in *Vasari's Florence*, ed. Jacks, pp. 163–81; R. Scorza, "Vasari's Painting of the Terzo Cerchio in the Palazzo Vecchio: A Reconstruction of Medieval Florence," ibid., pp. 182–205.

Index